THE
ISO 9000
HANDBOOK
2ND EDITION

Edited By
Robert W. Peach

Published by
CEEM Information Services ✦ Fairfax, Virginia

THE ISO 9000 HANDBOOK

Edited by: Robert W. Peach
Robert Peach and Associates, Inc.
200 W Cornwall Road 126
Cary, NC 27511-3802
Tel: 919-319-1982; Fax: 919-319-1984

Published by: CEEM Information Services
10521 Braddock Road
Fairfax, Virginia 22032
Tel: 800-745-5565, 703-250-5900; Fax: 703-250-4117

Second Edition, Third Printing

Printed in the United States of America

Director, CEEM Information Services: Mark Morrow
Senior Editor: Tom Tibor
Editor: Susan C. Hatch
Assistant Editors: Mary Kathryn Campbell, Leah Wilbur
Marketing Director: Kathy Watkins
Design & Production: James P. Gildersleeve

ISBN 1-883337-31-3

TABLE OF CONTENTS
Sections and Chapters

SECTION I: INTRODUCTION

    1   BACKGROUND AND DEVELOPMENT OF ISO 9000 1

SECTION II: THE ISO 9000 SERIES STANDARD

    2   OVERVIEW OF THE ISO 9000 SERIES STANDARD 15

    3   THE ISO 9001 STANDARD 39

SECTION III: THE REGISTRATION AND AUDIT PROCESS

    4   REGISTRATION AND SELECTING A REGISTRAR 131

    5   THE AUDIT PROCESS 149

SECTION IV: IMPLEMENTING ISO 9000

    6   A BASIC GUIDE TO IMPLEMENTING ISO 9000 169

    7   QUALITY SYSTEM DOCUMENTATION 209

    8   A QUALITY SYSTEM CHECKLIST 245

    9   QUALITY IN THE DEVELOPMENT AND USE OF SOFTWARE 259

    10   USING ISO 9000 IN SERVICE ORGANIZATIONS 277

SECTION V: THE ISO 9000 FAMILY AND RELATED STANDARDS

    11   REVIEW AND REVISION OF ISO STANDARDS 291

    12   THE LEGAL LIMITATIONS OF ISO 9000 REGISTRATION AND EU PRODUCT
       LIABILITY AND PRODUCT SAFETY 321

    13   EMERGING STANDARDS FOR ENVIRONMENTAL MANAGEMENT SYSTEMS 335

    14   COMPARING ISO 9000 QUALITY REQUIREMENTS, MALCOLM BALDRIGE NATIONAL
       QUALITY AWARD GUIDELINES AND DEMING/SPC-BASED TQM PRACTICE 345

SECTION VI: THE DEVELOPING CONFORMITY ASSESSMENT FRAMEWORK

    15   EUROPEAN UNION CONFORMITY ASSESSMENT 357

16   Registrar Accreditation 381

17   Credibility of Quality Systems Certification: How to Deal With Scopes of
     Certification, Conflicts of Interest and Codes of Conduct 403

SECTION VII: STATUS REPORT: ISO 9000 IN GOVERNMENT, INDUSTRY AND AROUND THE WORLD

18   ISO 9000 Around the World 419

19   ISO 9000 in US Government Agencies 429

20   ISO 9000 in Various Industry Sectors 439

SECTION VIII: APPENDICES

Appendix A: Contributors to This Book 499

Appendix B: Standards and Directives 507

Appendix C: ISO 9000 Consultants and Training Services 521

Appendix D: ISO 9000 Registrars 559

Appendix E: Additional Resources 563

Appendix F: Acronyms & Glossary 585

Appendix G: ANSI/ASQC Q9000 Series 593

Index 677

EXTENDED TABLE OF CONTENTS

How to Use This Handbook xiv
Editor's Preface to the Second Edition.. xvi
About the Editor xviii
About the Publisher xix

SECTION I: INTRODUCTION

   1 BACKGROUND AND DEVELOPMENT OF ISO 9000 1
      The European Union and Origins of EC 92 4
      European Union Conformity Assessment 5
      The Role of the ISO 9000 Series 9
      Concerns About ISO 9000 Registration 11
      The Move to ISO 9000 Is On 13

SECTION II: THE ISO 9000 SERIES STANDARD

   2 OVERVIEW OF THE ISO 9000 SERIES STANDARD 15
      Uses of the Standards 16
      Definition of Terms 17
      Types of Standards in the ISO 9000 Series 21
         Guidance Standards 22
         Conformance Standards 33
         Other Useful Standards in the ISO 9000 Family 35
            ISO 9000-2 35
            ISO 9000-3 35
            ISO 9000-4 35
            ISO 9004-2 35
            ISO 9004-3 35
            ISO 9004-4 36
            ISO 10011 36
            ISO 10012 36

   3 THE ISO 9001 STANDARD 39
      Clause 4: Quality System Requirements 42
         4.1 Management Responsibility 42
         4.2 Quality System 49
         4.3 Contract Review 53
         4.4 Design Control 55

4.5 Document and Data Control 65
4.6 Purchasing 73
4.7 Control of Customer-Supplied Product 80
4.8 Product Identification and Traceability 81
4.9 Process Control 82
4.10 Inspection and Testing 90
4.11 Control of Inspection, Measuring and Test Equipment 97
4.12 Inspection and Test Status 104
4.13 Control of Nonconforming Product 105
4.14 Corrective and Preventive Action 107
4.15 Handling, Storage, Packaging, Preservation and Delivery 110
4.16 Control of Quality Records 114
4.17 Internal Quality Audits 117
4.18 Training 121
4.19 Servicing 126
4.20 Statistical Techniques 128

SECTION III: THE REGISTRATION AND AUDIT PROCESS

4   REGISTRATION AND SELECTING A REGISTRAR **131**
    How to Select a Registrar: Benchmarks for the Screening Process 132
    Steps in the Registration Process 141

5   THE AUDIT PROCESS **149**
    Internal Quality Audits 150
        What Is An Audit? 150
        The Role of the Auditor 151
        Phases Of The Audit: PERC 154
    Interview or Inquisition: Successful Communication Techniques 164

SECTION IV: IMPLEMENTING ISO 9000

6   A BASIC GUIDE TO IMPLEMENTING ISO 9000 .... **169**
    Making the Quality System Visible 171
    Asking the Right Questions 176
    Getting Ready for ISO 9000 Registration 183
    How to Avoid Common ISO 9000 Pitfalls 190
        Five Quality Failures 191
    The Registration Audit Process 197
        Auditee's Responsibilities 199
7   QUALITY SYSTEM DOCUMENTATION **209**
    Quality System Documentation Development 210
        System Documentation and ISO 9000 211

The Structure of Documentation 215
Implementation 216
Review 217
The Quality Manual: Structure and Content 218
Creating Procedures 222
Procedure Planning and Development 222
Procedure Structure and Format 225
Procedure Format 227
Procedure Administration and Control 227

8   A QUALITY SYSTEM CHECKLIST 245
Management Responsibility (4.1) 246
Quality System (4.2) 247
Contract Review (4.3) 248
Design Control (4.4) 248
Document and Data Control (4.5) 249
Purchasing (4.6) 249
Control of Customer-Supplied Product (4.7) 250
Product Identification and Traceability (4.8) 250
Process Control (4.9) 251
Inspection and Testing (4.10) 251
Control of Inspection, Measuring and Test Equipment (4.11) 252
Inspection and Test Status (4.12) 252
Control of Nonconforming Product (4.13) 253
Corrective and Preventive Action (4.14) 253
Handling, Storage, Packaging, Preservation and Delivery (4.15) 255
Control of Quality Records (4.16) 255
Internal Quality Audits (4.17) 256
Training (4.18) 256
Servicing (4.19) 257

9   QUALITY IN THE DEVELOPMENT AND USE OF SOFTWARE 259
Software Quality Challenges 260
Use of ISO 9001 261
Mapping 9001 to 9000-3 261
The TickIT Scheme 264
An American Software-Specific Arrangement 265
Staffing Up with Software Auditors 266
Software Sensitivity 267
Other Software Standards and Models 268
IEEE Software Engineering Standards 268
SEI Capability Maturity Model 270
Australian Standard: Software Quality Management System 271
Emerging Trends 271

10   **Using ISO 9000 in Service Organizations** 277

Factors Affecting Use of the ISO 9000 Standards 278
Special Characteristics of Services 280
Managing Service Quality Through Process Control............................. 281
ISO 9004-2, Guidelines for Services.. 282
Use of ISO 9001 or ISO 9002 by Service Organizations 283

SECTION V: THE ISO 9000 FAMILY AND RELATED STANDARDS

11   **Review and Revision of ISO Standards** 291

Updating the ISO 9000 Quality Standards: Responding to Marketplace Needs 292
   Modifications Common to All Five Standards 293
   Impact of the Revisions 301
Vision 2000: The Strategy for the ISO 9000 Series Standards in the '90s 302
   1. The Stake 303
   2. Basic Concepts 306
   3. Analysis of the Marketplace for the ISO 9000 Series Standards 310
   4. Vision 2000 312
TC 176 Standards Issued and Being Developed 317

12   **The Legal Limitations of ISO 9000 Registration and EU Product Liability and Product Safety** 321

The Role of ISO 9004-1 322
Registration and Its Limitations 326
   Documentation as a Paper Trail 326
   All Registrars Are Not Equal 326
   The Potential Liability of Consultants and Registrars 327
   ISO 9000 Is Not a Complete Defense to a Claim 327
EU Liability and Safety Directives 328
   Product Liability Directive 329
   Product Safety Directive 330
   Council Regulation 339/93 on Product Safety Conformity 331
   Machinery Safety Directive 332
   Proposed Services Liability Directive 332
   Liability and Safety Directives: Implications for Companies............. 333
Product Liability Prevention 333
The Future 334

13   **Emerging Standards for Environmental Management Systems** 335

What Is Driving the EMS Movement?.. 336
The Need for a Single EMS Standard 337
EMS Initiatives Under Development 337
   BS 7750: Environmental Management Systems................................. 337
   Requirements of BS 7750 338
   Eco Management and Audit (Eco Audit) 339

E4, the Emerging US Standard 339
Responsible Care® 340
Eco-labeling 342
The Search for an International EMS Standard 343

**14 COMPARING ISO 9000 QUALITY REQUIREMENTS, MALCOLM BALDRIGE NATIONAL
QUALITY AWARD GUIDELINES AND DEMING/SPC-BASED TQM PRACTICE 345**
Overview of the Three Systems 346
ISO 9000 Compared to MBNQA 347
ISO 9000 Compared to Deming-based TQM 350
Deming-based TQM Compared to MBNQA 350
Three-Way Comparison of Documentation and Control 352
Three-Way Comparison of the Required Degree of Prescriptiveness 353
Three-Way Comparison of Theory/Application 354

SECTION VI: THE DEVELOPING CONFORMITY ASSESSMENT FRAMEWORK

15 EUROPEAN UNION CONFORMITY ASSESSMENT 357
What Is Conformity Assessment? 358
The EU's Single Internal Market 359
Technical Trade Barriers 359
Goals of the New System 359
1. EU-wide Directives 360
2. Harmonized Standards 366
3. Consistent Conformity Assessment Procedures 369
4. Competent Certification and Testing Bodies 374
The European Union and Other Countries 375

16 REGISTRAR ACCREDITATION 381
Registrar Accreditation 382
Accreditation Bodies in Europe 382
Accreditation in the United States 384
Accreditation Bodies in Canada 387
Criteria for Accrediting Certified Bodies 387
EN 45012: Criteria for Registrars 388
Recognition of Registration Certificates 391
ISO's Council Committee on Conformity Assessment (CASCO) 392
International Accreditation Forum (IAF) 392
European Network for Quality System Assessment and Certification (EQNET) 394
European Committee for Quality System Assessment and Certification (EQS) . 394
The European Accreditation of Certification (EAC) 395
The European Organization for Testing and Certification (EOTC) 395
Auditor Certification 396

17 CREDIBILITY OF QUALITY SYSTEMS CERTIFICATION: HOW TO DEAL WITH SCOPES OF
     CERTIFICATION, CONFLICTS OF INTEREST AND CODES OF CONDUCT **403**
        Scope of Certification/Registration of a Supplier's Quality System 405

SECTION VII: STATUS REPORT: ISO 9000 IN GOVERNMENT, INDUSTRY AND AROUND THE WORLD

18 ISO 9000 AROUND THE WORLD **419**
        ISO 9000 in Mexico and South America 420
        The Canadian ISO 9000 Registration System 422
        Pacific Rim Countries 425
19 ISO 9000 IN US GOVERNMENT AGENCIES **429**
        Department of Agriculture (USDA) 430
        Department of Commerce (DOC) 430
        Department of Defense (DoD) 432
        Department of Education (DOEd) 432
        Department of Energy (DOE) 432
        Department of Health and Human Services (DHHS) 433
        Department of Interior (DOI) 434
        Department of Labor (DOL) 434
        Department of State 435
        Federal Trade Commission (FTC) 435
        General Services Administration (GSA) 435
        International Trade Commission (USITC) 435
        National Aeronautics and Space Administration (NASA) 436
        Nuclear Regulatory Commission (NRC) 436
        Office of Management and Budget (OMB) 437
        US Postal Service 437
20 ISO 9000 IN VARIOUS INDUSTRY SECTORS **439**
        General Introduction and Overview of the QSU/Deloitte & Touche Survey 441
            Reasons to Pursue Registration 441
            Selecting Registrars and Consultants 442
            Overall Barriers 442
            Costs of Registration 443
            Benefits 443
            Savings 444
        QSU/Deloitte & Touche Survey of Companies by Industry 445
            Reasons to Register 445
            Barriers to Registration 446
            Costs 446
            Savings 447
        The Chemical Industry 448
            The Chemical Industry: Past and Present 448

ISO 9000: Problems Facing the Chemical Industry 452
Chemical Industry Case Study: Betz Laboratories, Inc. 463
Chemical Industry Case Study: Monsanto Chemical Company 467
The Computer Industry 470
Computer Industry Case Study: Unisys 470
The Auto Industry 474
The Automotive Industry Action Group and Joint Quality Initiatives 474
ISO 9000: What Every Supplier Must Know 477
Auto Industry Case Study: Ford of Europe 479
The Steel Industry 484
Quality Systems Assessments in the Steel Industry 484
Steel Industry Case Study: Taylor-Wharton Cylinders 486
Small Companies 489
QSU/Deloitte & Touche Survey of Companies by Size 489
Small Company Case Study: Techni-Test 495

SECTION VIII: APPENDICES

Appendix A: Contributors to This Book 499

Appendix B: Standards and Directives 507

Appendix C: ISO 9000 Consultants and Training Services 521

Appendix D: ISO 9000 Registrars 559

Appendix E: Additional Resources 563

Appendix F: Acronyms & Glossary 585

Appendix G: ANSI/ASQC Q9000 Series 593

Q9000-1: Quality Management and Quality Assurance Standards—
Guidelines for Selection and Use 593
Q9001: Quality Systems—Model for Quality Assurance in Design,
Development, Production, Installation and Servicing 615
Q9002: Quality Systems—Model for Quality Assurance in Production,
Installation, and Servicing 629
Q9003: Quality Systems—Model for Quality Assurance in Final
Inspection and Test 641
Q9004-1: Quality Management and Quality System Elements—Guidelines 651

Index 677

LISTING OF TABLES AND FIGURES

Figure 1-1:	Eighty Countries That Have Adopted the ISO 9000 Standards	2
Table 2-1:	Supplier-Chain Terminology	17
Figure 2-1:	Typical Life Cycle Phases of a Product	20
Figure 2-2:	Relationship of Concepts	21
Figure 2-3:	Structure of the ISO 9000 Standards	22
Table 2-2:	Contents of ISO 9000-1: 1994	24
Table 2-3:	Contents of ISO 9004-1: 1994	26
Table 2-4:	Cross Reference of ISO 9000 Quality Assurance Requirements	34
Table 2-5:	Cross Reference List of Clauses in ISO 9000 and ISO 9004-1	37
Table 3-1:	Relationships of Organizations in the Supply Chain	40
Figure 5-1:	Nonconformity Report	160
Table 6-1:	Making the Management of Quality Visible	171
Table 6-2:	Making Product and Service Requirements Visible	174
Table 6-3:	Making the Quality of Your Process Visible	176
Figure 6-1:	Certification Pressure Matrix	177
Figure 6-2:	The Design to Disposal Continuum	180
Figure 6-3:	High-Level Activity Flowchart	187
Table 6-4:	Schedule of Conformity	189
Table 6-5:	The Corrective Action Loop	197
Figure 7-1:	Documentation Hierarchy	215
Table 7-1:	Document List	226
Figure 7-2:	The Classic "White Space" Danger Zones	230
Table 9-1:	ISO 9001 Clauses That Are Applicable to Software	262
Table 9-2:	ISO 9001 and ISO 9000-3 Cross Reference	264
Table 9-3:	Mapping the ISO 9000-3 Guidelines Against ANSI/IEEE Standard 730, Software Quality Assurance	269
Table 9-4:	Five Levels of the Capability Maturity Model	270
Table 10-1:	Examples of Services	280
Figure 10-1:	All Work Is Accomplished by a Process	282
Figure 10-2:	Service Quality Loop	283
Table 10-2:	ISO 9004-2 and ISO 9004-1—Cross Reference of Quality System Elements and Causes	284
Table 10-3:	Phases of the Product Realization Cycle	287
Table 11-1:	Relationship of Organizations in the Supply Chain	293
Table 11-2:	Contents of ISO 9001, ISO 9002 and ISO 9003	298
Table 11-3:	Contents of ISO 9004-1	300
Table 11-4:	Generic Product Categories	306
Figure 11-1:	ISO 9000—Future Architecture	315
Figure 11-2:	ISO Standards Development Process	318

Table 14-1:   Extent to Which ISO 9000 Requirements Align with MBNQA Guidelines 348

Table 14-2:   Extent to Which ISO 9000 Requirements Align with Deming Principles 351

Figure 14-1:   Required Documentation/Control Comparison 352

Figure 14-2:   Required Degree of Prescriptiveness Comparison 353

Figure 14-3:   Theory/Application Comparison 354

Figure 15-1:   Information to Accompany CE Mark by Manufacturers in European Union 365

Figure 15-2:   Overview—EC 92 Conformity Assessment Procedures—The Modules 370

Figure 15-3:   Conformity Assessment Process 371

Figure 15-4:   Conformity Assessment Procedure Modules 372

Figure 16-1:   Accreditation in the United Kingdom 383

Figure 16-2:   Accreditation in the United States 385

Figure 16-3:   Accreditation Pyramid 388

Table 18-1:   Canadian Quality Standard Equivalents 422

Table 20-1:   Reasons to Attain ISO 9000 Registration 441

Table 20-2:   Factors in Selecting a Registrar 441

Table 20-3:   Satisfaction with Registrars 442

Table 20-4:   Barriers to Registration 442

Table 20-5:   External Benefits of Registration 443

Table 20-6:   Internal Benefits of Registration 443

Table 20-7:   Two Primary Reasons for Registering by SIC Code 445

Table 20-8:   Main Barriers to Registration by SIC Code 446

Table 20-9:   Average Internal, External, Registrar and Total Costs Associated with
               Implementing ISO 9000 by SIC Codes 446

Table 20-10:   Average Annual Domestic Savings by SIC Codes 447

Table 20-11:   Average Number of Years to Recover Costs by SIC Codes 447

Table 20-12:   SISAP Audit Criteria 484

Figure 20-1:   The Most Important Reason for Attaining ISO 9000 Registration, by
               Company Sales Volume 489

Table 20-13:   Factors in Selecting a Registrar 490

Figure 20-2:   The Greatest Barrier to Preparing for Successful ISO 9000 Registration Effort,
               by Company Sales Volume 491

Table 20-14:   Average Internal, External and Registrar Costs by Company Sales Volume 492

Figure 20-3:   Average Domestic Annual Savings Associated with Implementing ISO 9000
               Compared with Average Domestic Costs Expended to Achieve Current
               Level of Registration, by Company Sales Volume 492

Table 20-15:   Average Total Annual Domestic Savings, by Company Sales Volume 493

Table 20-16:   Average Number of Years to Recover Costs, by Company Sales Volume 494

Table B-1:   Selected EU New-Approach Directives 509

Table B-2:   EU Product Directives 510

Table B-3:   EU Legal Requirements for Industrial Equipment and Consumer Goods 510

HOW TO USE THIS HANDBOOK

This second edition of *The ISO 9000 Handbook* is fully updated and expanded from the first edition, published in November 1992. Formerly 11 chapters, the book now contains 20 chapters—arranged in the order of a typical registration process. It discusses everything a company that wants to implement an ISO 9000-based quality system and/or desires to pursue registration should know—from exploring the history of the European Union (formerly European Community), to writing quality systems documentation, to understanding the larger conformity assessment framework.

The second edition also includes the 1994 ASQC Q9000 series standards, verbatim. We have reprinted each standard in the Q9000 series: Q9000-1, Q9001, Q9002, Q9003 and Q9000-4.

In addition, there is an expanded resource section that includes information on where to obtain standards and directives; profiles of consultants and training services; a list of ISO 9000 registrars; and other resources, including publications, companies offering software services, and information hotlines, networks and databases.

Revisions to ISO 9000

Directives of the International Organization for Standardization require that all standards be reviewed every five years. Based on inputs from member countries, ISO/Technical Committee 176 reviewed and revised the five standards in the ISO 9000 series and published them in the third quarter of 1994.

This Handbook references the new 1994 standards. It refers to the revised standards as ISO 9000 **with no reference to a date.** A reference to "ISO 9001," for example, always means the revised 1994 version.

For readers familiar with the 1987 version of the standards, there are comparisons throughout the Handbook between the language of the 1994 standard and the 1987 standard. In these comparisons, the 1987 standard, for example, is referred to as ISO 9001:1987 to distinguish it from the revised 1994 standard.

All clauses bear the revised 1994 names. For example, the guidance standards ISO 9000 and ISO 9004 have been renumbered as ISO 9000-1 and ISO 9004-1. And Clause 4.5, formerly "Document Control," has been changed to "Document and Data Control."

Although this Handbook does not use the US terminology, readers should know that the US numbering system for the series has changed. Once referred to as the ANSI/ASQC Q90 series, the name is now the ANSI/ASQC Q9000 series. This change also applies to the ISO 10000 series—all new issues of ISO standards will be preceded by ANSI/ASQC Q—."

European Union

According to the Office of Press and Public Affairs of the European Commission Delegation, there have been some changes in terminology regarding the European Union and some of its institutions.

A December 13, 1993 press release stated, "The **European Union** is now the umbrella term referring to a three "pillar" construction encompassing the European Community and the two new pillars—Common Foreign and Security Policy (including defense) and Justice and Home Affairs (notably cooperation between police and other authorities on crime, terrorism and immigration issues)."

"The **European Community** continues to exist as a legal entity within the broader framework of the Union. As before, it encompasses all policies derived from the founding Treaties, such as the single market. However, the European Union will always be the easiest term to use, in view of the difficulties of delineating what is strictly EU or Union business."

As a result, the editors have chosen to use the umbrella term, European Union, throughout the book, unless the European Community is mentioned in a historical context. For example, we still refer to EC 92 (not EU 92) because the term EC 92 originated prior to these changes and remains the historically accurate term.

User-Friendliness

Because the topic of international standards can be complex, we have tried to simplify it in a variety of ways. In Chapter 3, for example, CEEM Information Services' editors have tried to explain each clause of the standard in simple, practical language. The requirements in each clause are paraphrased and are noted with a corresponding icon. Guidance from other standards immediately follows each requirement and is distinguished by a different icon. In addition, interpretations written by various experts appear in boxes throughout the chapter.

We have also included chapter overviews at the beginning of each chapter that outline its structure and introduce its main topics. Appendix F includes a list of definitions and acronyms. We hope that using a consistent, easily identifiable format and user-friendly appendices will help you better understand the standards and this book.

EDITOR'S PREFACE TO THE SECOND EDITION

As the 21st century draws near, American business faces expanding international competition. The economic superpowers, the United States and the Far East, will soon be joined by the unified market of the European Union.

The key to economic success in this global marketplace will be higher-quality products and services. This emphasis on increased quality is demonstrated by the growing acceptance of international quality standards, such as the ISO 9000 series standard. Meeting and exceeding the requirements of ISO 9000 quality assurance and quality management standards is fast becoming essential to succeed in an ever more competitive marketplace.

The primary objective of the second edition of this Handbook is to fully update and expand the first edition of *The ISO 9000 Handbook*. In a single, comprehensive source, this second edition contains all the information that an organization needs to understand the ISO 9000 series and to initiate the process of implementing the standards. This book also describes recent developments in the European Union in the "bigger picture" of product standards, product certification and conformity assessment.

Whatever the motivation, whether to protect sales to the European Union, to respond to the requirements of large customers, or to adopt the standard on the basis of good quality practice, there is a need to understand not only the content and use of the standard, but also the marketplace factors that are influencing adoption of the ISO 9000 series standard worldwide.

The publishers of *Quality Systems Update (QSU)* are well-qualified to provide the material for such a handbook. (Subscribers to *QSU* will recognize that some material contained in the Handbook has appeared in previous *QSU* issues. This material has been fully updated.) My responsibility as editor has been to work with the CEEM Information Services staff to ensure that the contents of the Handbook are accurate and unbiased.

In carrying out this process, input has been solicited from a variety of knowledgeable contributors. While many of the conditions affecting registration to the standard are constantly changing, each contributor has made every effort to be as current and as accurate as possible in discussing the subject matter of this Handbook.

The contributors to this Handbook come from a variety of backgrounds and thus reflect different points of view regarding quality system standards issues. Most of these differences are not substantive and will, we believe, contribute positively to the reader's appreciation of the broad spectrum of factors that influence the application of ISO 9000.

In a few cases, however, the opinions of the contributors conflict, or may seem to conflict. As long as the facts used by the contributors are correct, no attempt has been made to resolve these differences. Rather, such differences reflect the diverse judgments and perspectives of people throughout American industry and should contribute to the comprehensiveness of the Handbook.

Underlying the increasing level of ISO 9000 registration activity is the fact that the ISO 9000 standards describe a technically sound quality system for use by manufacturing and service organizations. The standards are proving to be a valuable foundation for expanded quality practice to which principles of Total Quality Management (TQM) are applied. Many companies initially make use of the standards in response to external demands—customer requirements, regulatory compliance or market competition. They soon find that meeting all requirements of the standard results in significant internal benefits and that the rewards are well worth the necessary cost and effort.

I trust that this Handbook will provide the information readers need to apply the standard successfully in their own organizations and to achieve the benefits of an improved quality system, and that readers will discover that this is only the beginning of an era of continual improvement in the quality capability of all segments of commerce and industry.

— Robert Peach

ABOUT THE EDITOR

ROBERT W. PEACH

Robert W. Peach is principal of Robert Peach and Associates, Inc., Quality Management Consultants in Cary, North Carolina. He currently chairs the ASQC's Standards Council and Registrar Accreditation Board and is a delegate to TC 176's Committee on Quality Assurance, where he chaired the writing of ISO 9004-1. Prior to establishing his own company, Mr. Peach established and managed the quality assurance activity at Sears Roebuck and Company for more than 25 years. He is an ASQC Certified Quality Engineer and registered professional engineer in quality engineering.

Mr. Peach is a Fellow of the American Society for Quality Control (ASQC) and has received the Edwards Medal for leadership in the application of modern quality control methods. Past service in the ASQC includes vice president of Publications, technical editor of *Quality Progress* and chairman of the Awards Board. Through ASQC he aided in evaluating contractor quality programs for NASA's Excellence Award for Quality and Productivity.

Mr. Peach is a member of the Executive Committee of the American National Standards Institute (ANSI) Z-1 Accredited Standards Committee on Quality Assurance, and he chaired the writing of the ANSI/ASQC Z-1.15 Standard, *Generic Guidelines for Quality Systems.* He also served as a member of the ANSI International Standards Council and Certification Committee.

Mr. Peach has served as project manager of the Malcolm Baldrige National Quality Award Consortium, which administers the awards process managed by the National Institute of Standards and Technology, and has followed that as a technical advisor to the award administrator.

Mr. Peach is also a delegate to the International Laboratory Accreditation Conference (ILAC) and serves on the Electronics Components Certification Board (ECCB). He has also served as a member of the Board of the American Association for Laboratory Accreditation (A2LA).

Mr. Peach has spoken over 200 times to organizations on the subject of quality management, is author of the ASQC home study course "Successfully Managing the Quality Function." He also has been an instructor in quality control in the Graduate School of the Illinois Institute of Technology and has taught courses in quality engineering for the ASQC Professional and Technical Development Division. He has received degrees from the Massachusetts Institute of Technology and the University of Chicago.

ABOUT THE PUBLISHER

CEEM INFORMATION SERVICES, A DIVISION OF CEEM

In recent years, global competition has intensified, and US regulatory and legislative policy has become more pervasive, shattering many long-held business assumptions. Since 1979, CEEM has responded to this changing business climate by offering carefully tailored publications, seminars, workshops and conferences designed to provide middle and senior management with timely and accurate information. CEEM's staff has extensive experience and expertise in conference management, journalism, marketing, travel and training programs, and the company's products enjoy an international reputation.

CEEM Information Services, a division of CEEM, provides executives and managers with up-to-date information through its newsletters, guidebooks, handbooks, reports and videos. These products cover an array of topics, including critical ISO 9000 quality systems registration developments, environmental issues, international product standards and laboratory certification. A number of joint ventures have expanded CEEM Information Services' value to the business community. A pilot project with Dun & Bradstreet provides greater availability of CEEM's ISO 9000 registered company database, and market research on quality systems with Deloitte & Touche has resulted in the most extensive US/Canadian ISO 9000 survey available.

CEEM Training Services, another division of CEEM, offers courses on similar topics, and **Patriot Travel Group** handles both corporate and leisure travel arrangements.

A substantial percentage of CEEM's profits is returned to improving products and services. As a result, the company has gained an international reputation for excellence. CEEM now addresses global markets through an expanded international marketing effort. To further CEEM's mission to benefit others, at least ten percent of net profits is donated to charity. To protect its customers, CEEM offers a full money-back guarantee on all its courses, training materials and publications.

CEEM was first established as the Center for Energy and Environmental Management. Because its scope has broadened, its board of directors voted to adopt the acronym CEEM. A full mission statement is available upon request.

BACKGROUND AND DEVELOPMENT OF ISO 9000

BY DONALD W. MARQUARDT

This chapter provides an overview of the background and development of ISO 9000. Specifically, it discusses the following:

- The development of the European Union
- The EU conformity assessment system
- The ISO 9000 series
- Reasons for the ISO 9000's popularity
- Concerns about registration.

INTRODUCTION

In 1987, the International Organization for Standardization (ISO) published the ISO 9000 series international standards. The ISO 9000 series are generic standards for quality management and quality assurance. The standards apply to all types of companies; they can be adapted to fit both small and large corporations in all sectors of the economy, including manufacturing and service.

While ISO publishes thousands of standards, the five documents in the ISO 9000 series (ISO 9000-1, ISO 9001, ISO 9002, ISO 9003 and ISO 9004-1) are having a growing impact on international trade. The quality of products—both tangible products and services—is perceived as a key element in improving a company's competitiveness. Since the ISO 9000 series is becoming an internationally recognized common language for quality, the standards are viewed as facilitating global trade and helping to improve the economies of the world.

As of this writing, 80 countries have adopted the ISO 9000 series as a national standard, and thousands of companies worldwide have become registered to ISO 9001, ISO 9002 or ISO

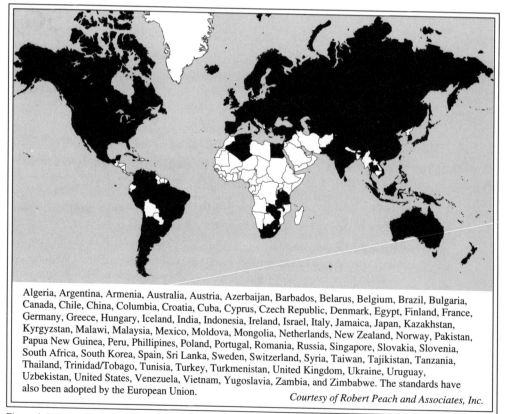

Algeria, Argentina, Armenia, Australia, Austria, Azerbaijan, Barbados, Belarus, Belgium, Brazil, Bulgaria, Canada, Chile, China, Columbia, Croatia, Cuba, Cyprus, Czech Republic, Denmark, Egypt, Finland, France, Germany, Greece, Hungary, Iceland, India, Indonesia, Ireland, Israel, Italy, Jamaica, Japan, Kazakhstan, Kyrgyzstan, Malawi, Malaysia, Mexico, Moldova, Mongolia, Netherlands, New Zealand, Norway, Pakistan, Papua New Guinea, Peru, Phillipines, Poland, Portugal, Romania, Russia, Singapore, Slovakia, Slovenia, South Africa, South Korea, Spain, Sri Lanka, Sweden, Switzerland, Syria, Taiwan, Tajikistan, Tanzania, Thailand, Trinidad/Tobago, Tunisia, Turkey, Turkmenistan, United Kingdom, Ukraine, Uruguay, Uzbekistan, United States, Venezuela, Vietnam, Yugoslavia, Zambia, and Zimbabwe. The standards have also been adopted by the European Union.   *Courtesy of Robert Peach and Associates, Inc.*

Figure 1-1: Eighty Countries That Have Adopted the ISO 9000 Standards.

9003. The standard has been adopted in the United States as the ANSI/ASQC Q9000 series. (Previously, the US version of the standard was known as the Q90 series.)

Government agencies worldwide are also beginning to use the ISO 9000 series. In the United States, the Department of Defense (DoD) and the National Aeronautics and Space Administration (NASA) have officially approved the use of the ISO 9000 standards in contracts. The US Food and Drug Administration (FDA) has incorporated the ISO 9001 standard into its Good Manufacturing Practices (GMP) regulations for medical devices. In Canada, the government's purchasing arm, Supply and Services Canada, will soon demand ISO 9000 registration of most of its suppliers.

A driving force for ISO 9000's popularity has been the development of regional economic groups of nations, particularly the European Union (EU), formerly called the European Community. To understand fully the developing role of the ISO 9000 standards, it is important briefly to explain the history of the European Union and of EC 92. (References to EC 92 refer to the drive to create a single internal market by the end of 1992, when the European Union was still known as the European Community.)

WHAT DOES ISO STAND FOR?

ISO refers to the International Organization for Standardization, founded in 1946 to develop a common set of manufacturing, trade and communication standards. Although it is commonly referred to as ISO, the ISO name technically does not stand for anything.

According to ISO officials, the organization's short name was borrowed from the Greek word, *isos*, meaning "equal." *Isos* also is the root of the prefix, "iso," which appears in "isometric" (of equal measure or dimensions) and "isonomy" (equality of laws or of people before the law). Its selection was based on the conceptual path taken from "equal" to "uniform" to "standard."

The Geneva, Switzerland-based organization is composed of 92 member countries. The American National Standards Institute (ANSI) is the United States member body to ISO.

All standards developed by the International Organization for Standardization are voluntary; no legal requirements force countries to adopt them. However, countries and industries often adopt and attach legal requirements to ISO standards, thereby making the standards mandatory. The International Organization for Standardization develops standards in all industries except those related to electrical and electronic engineering. Standards in these areas are made by the Geneva-based International Electrotechnical Commission (IEC), which has more than 40 member countries, including the United States.

ISO is structured into approximately 180 technical committees that draft standards. Member nations form technical advisory groups (TAGs) that provide input into the standards development process. ISO receives input from government, industry and other interested parties before promulgating a standard.

THE EUROPEAN UNION AND ORIGINS OF EC 92

Perhaps the single most visible factor driving the acceptance of the ISO 9000 series is the effort to unify the 13 major European nations that form the European Union into a single internal market. The full members are Austria, Belgium, Denmark, France, Germany, Greece, Ireland, Italy, Luxembourg, the Netherlands, Portugal, Spain and the United Kingdom.

The European Union originated with the 1957 Treaty of Rome, which was established to abolish tariffs and quotas among its six member states and to stimulate economic growth in Europe. (The original members were France, West Germany, Italy, Luxembourg, the Netherlands and Belgium.)

Economic growth slowed during the 1970s and early 1980s, and Europe began to fear that the US, Japanese and Pacific Rim economies would dominate the world economy of the 21st century. The European nations were concerned that they would fall behind partly due to the differences among their technical standards and requirements.

Differing national product certification requirements made selling products in multiple national markets in the European Union a costly undertaking, requiring duplication of tests and documentation, and separate approvals from national or local regulatory authorities.

In response, the European Union called for a greater push toward a unified market—a Single Internal Market—and for the removal of physical, technical and fiscal barriers to trade. In 1985 the EU Commission presented a program for establishing a single internal market. The goal was to create a single set of procedures for conformity assessment that is simpler and less costly for manufacturers.

The Single Internal Market program was based in part on the 1979 *Casis de Dijon* decision of the European Court of Justice, which established the principle of mutual recognition. This principle states that products that meet the requirements of one EU member state could freely circulate in other member states, a concept similar to the interstate commerce clause of the US Constitution.

The 1985 program, presented in a White Paper, drew upon the rationale of the *Casis de Dijon* decision. The move to a single internal market was further expedited by the Single European Act, adopted in February 1986. This Act amends the 1957 Treaty of Rome. The combined intent of the White Paper and the Single European Act was to abolish barriers to trade among the 12 member states and to complete an internal European market by the end of 1992.

The single market—known as EC 92—became effective at midnight on December 31, 1992. Its goal is to encourage trade and to increase confidence in the safety and reliability of products marketed in the European Union. To better understand this framework of standards and product certification—and ISO 9000's role in that framework—it is important to introduce the European Union's conformity assessment program.

EUROPEAN UNION CONFORMITY ASSESSMENT

In preparation for EC 92, the European Union began developing a comprehensive framework for conformity assessment activities. *Conformity assessment* refers to all processes—product testing and certification, quality system registration, standards and laboratory accreditation— that may be used to ensure that a product conforms to requirements. The conformity assessment system, when successfully completed, will give customers confidence that products conform to all requirements.

This system has the following three major components:

- EU-wide directives and harmonized standards
- Consistent conformity assessment procedures
- Competent certification and testing bodies.

EU-wide Directives and Harmonized Standards

In the European system, products are classified into two categories: *regulated* products and *non-regulated* products.

Most products sold in the European Union are non-regulated products. *Non-regulated* products are those not covered by EU legislation. The European Union's strategy for

---

THE EU REGULATORY HIERARCHY

The 12 nations that make up the European Union (formerly the European Community) are bound by its regulations. The regulatory process begins with the European Commission. A proposal is drafted by the Commission and is sent to the European Parliament. The Parliament, with its 518 members, votes on the proposal. However, this vote is not binding on the European Council.

The European Council comprises many working groups, each of which consists of civil servants from the member states. These groups examine the proposals and, if necessary, make changes. The proposal is then forwarded to the Committee of Permanent Representatives, made up of civil servants from the member states. When this Committee reaches agreement, the proposal is forwarded to the Council of Ministers. The makeup of the Council depends on the subject matter of the proposal. The Council of Ministers decides whether to adopt the legislative proposal. It acts by majority vote. As a result of the process, regulations and directives are created.

Regulations are directly binding on the member states; they do not require any action on the part of each state. Directives do not directly create new law but instruct member states to amend their national legislation within a prescribed period.

The European Court of Justice has judicial oversight. It interprets and applies European Union law.

ACCREDITATION, CERTIFICATION AND REGISTRATION

Terms such as *accreditation, certification* and *registration* are often used interchangeably, creating some confusion. To clarify the meanings, the Conformity Assessment Committee of the International Organization for Standardization, in its *ISO/IEC Guide 2: General terms and their definitions concerning standardization and certification* defines the terms as follows:

Accreditation: Procedure by which an authoritative body gives formal recognition that a body or person is competent to carry out specific tasks.

Certification: Procedure by which a third party gives written assurance that a product, process or service conforms to specific requirements.

Registration: Procedure by which a body indicates relevant characteristics of a product, process or service, or particulars of a body or person, and then includes or registers the product, process or service in an appropriate publicly available list.

Although certification and registration are slightly different steps in the same process, they are used interchangeably. In Europe *quality systems certification* is used more widely than *quality systems registration*, which is the preferred US terminology.

---

removing technical barriers to non-regulated products is to rely on the principle of mutual recognition and on product certification by a third party.

In effect, a US exporter of a non-regulated product can certify to a US standard for technical specifications, and if these standards are accepted in at least one EU country, they will be accepted in the European Union through the principle of mutual recognition.

Regulated products are those that have important health, safety, or environmental implications. Their requirements are spelled out in directives—official EU legislation—that are binding on all member states of the European Union.

Each directive deals with a class of regulated products and spells out the essential requirements for compliance. However, directives do not list specific technical requirements—they reference appropriate technical standards that are being developed by the major European or international standards organizations. (These organizations are developing "harmonized" standards to eliminate the jumble of standards of the individual twelve member states.)

Consistent Conformity Assessment Procedures

Depending upon the requirements of a particular directive, conformity assessment can require one or more of the following:

- Type-testing of the product
- Third-party audit of the quality system
- Testing of regular production

- Depending on the health, safety, and environmental risks of the product, a manufacturer's self-declaration of conformity.

This approach, known as the *modular approach* to conformity assessment, provides manufacturers with options from which to choose in order to demonstrate compliance with a directive. (Please refer to Chapter 15 for an in-depth discussion of conformity assessment procedures.)

The Quality Assurance Route to Conformity Assessment

As mentioned above, some EU directives require quality system registration. For other directives, quality system registration is not an absolute requirement. However, to ensure confidence in the quality of products circulating throughout Europe, the European Union has strongly emphasized quality assurance.

The European Union has adopted the ISO 9000 series as part of its conformity assessment plan to establish uniform systems for product certification and quality systems registration. *Registration* involves the audit and approval of a quality system against ISO 9001, ISO 9002 or ISO 9003 by an independent organization, also known as a third-party registrar.

For some businesses, achieving ISO 9000 series registration satisfies an immediate customer requirement. However, for many companies ISO 9000 series registration is only an important first step for doing business internationally. Additional regional, national or trading bloc requirements may exist with respect to product technical requirements which are outside the scope of the ISO 9000 standards.

Competent Certification and Testing Bodies

The European Union has recognized that confidence in the conformity assessment system and on the products sold throughout the European Union depends on confidence in the competence of certification and testing bodies. Thus, the European Union has encouraged the development of standards such as the EN 45000 series. The EN 45000 standards establish requirements for testing, certification, and accreditation bodies.

The European Union has also encouraged the formation of organizations such as the European Organization for Testing and Certification (EOTC) to promote consistent practices in testing and certification and to promote the mutual recognition of test results.

Implications for the United States

The economic implications of the European Union's efforts are far-reaching. The European Economic Area (EEA) Treaty became effective on January 1, 1994, extending the European Single Market to include four of the six EFTA countries. The EFTA countries included are Finland, Iceland, Norway and Sweden. (The two EFTA countries not included are Switzerland, who rejected membership in a referendum, and Liechtenstein, who is redefining its relationship with Switzerland to become part of the EEA.)

This expanded European Single Market is now the largest free trade zone in the world, comprising 372 million people and 17 countries. The treaty reinforces the free flow of goods, services, people and capital throughout the EEA.[1]

Interest in European integration has also extended to other countries with the signing of Association Agreements with Poland, Hungary and the Czech and Slovak Federal Republic. With the inclusion of other Eastern European countries and the former Soviet republics, the European Union could eventually develop into a multi-trillion dollar market of 500 to 800 million people.[2]

The United States is the European Union's biggest foreign supplier. In 1992, the United States exported about $100 billion in goods to the countries of the European Union. About half of all sales of US subsidiaries overseas are in Europe—about $600 billion annually.[3]

US companies are understandably eager to gain and maintain an economic foothold in this market. Manufacturers can foresee millions of new customers for products and services. The challenge is to meet both product and quality system standards and conformity assessment procedures necessary for unrestricted trade within this market.

DEVELOPMENT OF THE ISO 9000 SERIES

In the past two decades, "quality" has emerged as an important aspect of commerce and industry. Various national and multinational standards developed in the quality systems arena for commercial and industrial use, or for military or nuclear power industry needs. Some standards were guidance documents. Other standards were used in contracts between purchaser and supplier organizations.

In 1959, the US Department of Defense (DoD) established the MIL-Q-9858 quality management program. In 1968, the North Atlantic Treaty Organization (NATO) essentially adopted the tenets of the DoD program in the NATO AQAP1, AQAP4, AQAP9 series of standards. In 1979, the United Kingdom's British Standards Institution (BSI) developed the first commercial quality assurance system standards from its predecessors. These standards were designated the BS 5750 series, Parts 1, 2, and 3.

Despite the commonality among these predecessors to the ISO 9000 series standards, there was no real consistency until Technical Committee 176 (TC 176) of ISO issued the ISO 9000 series standards in 1987. ISO is a worldwide federation of national standards bodies (ISO member bodies). The American National Standards Institute (ANSI) is the US member body to ISO. Countries that have member bodies to ISO have national technical advisory groups representing them to ISO. In the United States, the American Society for Quality Control (ASQC) administers the technical advisory group (TAG) to TC 176 on behalf of ANSI.

THE ROLE OF THE ISO 9000 SERIES

The ISO 9000 series standards have two primary roles:

Quality Management The ISO 9000 series standards provide guidance for suppliers of all types of products who want to implement effective quality systems in their organizations or to improve their existing quality systems.

Quality Assurance The standards also provide generic requirements against which a customer can evaluate the adequacy of a supplier's quality system.

These two roles are complementary. In the context of programs for quality system registration, as in the European Union, the quality assurance role is more visible, but the business value of both roles is important.

ISO 9001, ISO 9002 and ISO 9003 were developed primarily for two-party contractual situations—to satisfy the customer's quality assurance requirements. The aim is to increase the confidence of customers in the quality systems of their suppliers. This is particularly important when the supplier and the customer are in different countries or when the distance between them is great. This benefit is accomplished by:

- Establishing consistent quality practices that cross international borders
- Providing a common language or set of terms
- Minimizing the need for on-site customer visits or audits.

Another aim of the ISO 9000 series is to harmonize international trade by supplying a set of standards with worldwide credibility and acceptance. The ISO 9000 series, however, has assumed a larger role in both the European Union and around the world.

In short, the series has become accepted as a *de facto* baseline requirement that is separate from its use within the EU-regulated industry structure. Manufacturers and service industries report that some standard contract forms now include quality system registration queries.

Why this expansion? The reasons are outlined below.

Legal Requirements

For some companies, registration to ISO 9001, ISO 9002 or ISO 9003 is a legal requirement to enter the regulated EU market. Registration might also help a company meet a domestic regulatory mandate.

Liability Concerns

Legal concerns are also driving registration. Some companies register a quality system, at least in part, for the role ISO 9000 registration may play in product liability defense. Companies that sell regulated products in Western Europe may be subject to increasingly stringent product liability and safety requirements that are moving toward the strict liability concepts prevalent in the United States.

An EU product liability directive, for example, holds a manufacturer liable, regardless of fault or negligence, if a person is harmed or if an object is damaged by a faulty product. In addition, an EU product safety directive requires manufacturers to monitor product safety. The possible consequence of these directives would require companies to document that they have adequate quality systems for their production processes. These procedures would demonstrate more thoroughly that products meet specified requirements, thus minimizing liability claims. (See Chapter 12 for a discussion of the product safety and product liability directives and other legal issues.)

Contractual Requirements

Companies are being asked by purchasers of their products and services to become registered to ISO 9001, ISO 9002, or ISO 9003 as a precondition to placing a contractual purchase order.

In many cases, suppliers have multiple sites making the same product. When only some of the sites are registered, the supplier may be required by the customer to ship only from the registered site(s).

Registration of Subcontractors

The ISO 9001 and ISO 9002 standards require the supplier to ensure that materials purchased from subcontractors conform to specified requirements. As a consequence, an increasing number of companies are requiring that their subcontractors become registered, even though the ISO 9001 and ISO 9002 standards do not specifically require quality system registration of subcontractors.

Reduction of Multiple Assessments

ISO 9000 registration reduces the need for multiple assessments. Customers often audit their suppliers' quality systems. Suppliers, in turn, must undergo multiple assessments in order to sell to different customers. ISO 9000 registration reduces the need for multiple assessments based on the confidence that a quality system is in place.

Internal Improvement

Although external market pressure has stimulated many companies to seek ISO 9000 registration, other companies have implemented ISO 9000 for its internal benefits. Companies that have implemented the standards have often discovered that internal improvements in facility performance and quality have lasting value at least equal to the market prestige of ISO 9000 approval. A well-established quality system can increase productivity and reduce costs associated with inefficiencies.

The ISO 9000 standards can also be used as a foundation or building block for implementing broader quality systems such as Total Quality Management (TQM) and for meeting more stringent quality goals such as the criteria of the Malcolm Baldrige National Quality Award in the United States.

The Marketplace

Market pressure is fast becoming the greatest impetus for ISO 9000 series implementation. Companies are implementing the ISO 9000 series to keep up with registered competitors and to distinguish themselves from nonregistered competitors.

Part of this drive stems from the global trend toward quality that emerged during the last decade. Prior to this trend, national quality systems standards originated in certain commercial, industrial and military sectors. As trade increased, so did the desire for a consistent set of international quality standards. The publication of the ISO 9000 series has improved international attempts at harmonization and has accelerated the trend toward quality as a key aspect of international trade.

CONCERNS ABOUT ISO 9000 REGISTRATION

Despite their worldwide acceptance, the ISO 9000 series standards and the issue of ISO 9000 registration have raised some concerns.

Are Standards and Product Certification Trade Barriers?

Standards facilitate a common international industrial language, provide consumer confidence and promote product safety. Standards can also facilitate and encourage trade. Used improperly, however, standards can hinder worldwide trade.

One argument is that standards generally lag behind the development of the latest technology and thus become nontariff barriers to trade. Although standards may fall behind technical innovations, periodic review and revision keeps them from lagging behind so much that they become a nontariff barrier to trade.

In addition, standards are reviewed and revised on a regular basis. ISO's policy mandates that all standards be reviewed every five years. Based on the suggestions of member bodies from many countries, ISO Technical Committee (TC) 176 has reviewed and revised the five standards. The revised ISO 9000 series incorporates changes that do not significantly alter the basic structure of the standards but instead improve their usability. Modifications reflect companies' experience with using the 1987 standards and progress in the quality field.

A related argument states that not only standards, but also product certification systems adopted to facilitate trade within an area can consequently act as a trade barrier.

In the early 1970s, for example, Europe developed a regional certification system for electronic components. This system, in effect, became a nontariff barrier to trade for American and Japanese manufacturers. The groups adversely affected petitioned the international electronics standards body, the IEC, to develop an international system to replace the regional one.

A major misunderstanding about the ISO 9000 series is revealed, however, when examples like this are cited. The ISO 9000 series deals only with quality systems, not with a product's technical or performance specifications. The above example deals with product certification to regional technical specifications. These can become nontariff trade barriers for suppliers in other countries that have different technical specification standards for the same class of products.

Time and Costs

Achieving registration to ISO 9001, ISO 9002 or ISO 9003 requires money and time. It takes companies an average of slightly more than a year to prepare for their first registration effort. The average cost for registrar fees alone was $21,000.[4] (Please refer to Chapter 20 for more information from the joint *Quality Systems Update*/Deloitte & Touche ISO 9000 survey.)

Some companies have established product quality baselines considered to be above the level provided for in the ISO 9000 series. In such instances, the ISO 9000 standards may appear to add cost without adding real value. Many companies that believed their quality system exceeded the requirements for ISO 9000 registration, however, subsequently discovered that this was not true for all elements of their systems.

A Level Playing Field

A related concern is whether a level playing field will hurt high-quality companies. According to this argument, all products manufactured by ISO 9000 registered companies initially may be viewed favorably. Such recognition may benefit the manufacturer that previously produced to lower-quality standards, for now its products are viewed on a par with all others. A universal quality standard may tend to level the playing field among international competitors, thereby benefiting European manufacturers more than their US counterparts.

This example reveals another misunderstanding of the ISO 9000 series standards. While the ISO 9000 series does represent a universal quality standard, there is no expectation that because two companies are both registered, the levels of each company's quality system and products are the same.

Registration means that both companies have quality systems that at least meet the scope of the stated standard (ISO 9001, ISO 9002 or ISO 9003), that each quality system element is adequate and that it is consistently deployed. Ample opportunity remains for suppliers to succeed in the marketplace if they offer products with better conformance to technical specifications and customer expectations than those of their competitors.

Uncertainty in the EU System

The EU product certification system has also created a good deal of uncertainty, making it difficult for some US companies to plan. The regulatory framework is still developing. The status of directives and which products they cover is unclear, as are the conformity assessment requirements for specific products. In addition, the timetable for deciding these questions keeps shifting. Other unresolved issues have surfaced as well, including the accreditation of registrars, the certification of auditors and inconsistent audit procedures.

These are genuine problems. They affect both European and non-European suppliers. However, these problems concern the procedures for implementing the testing, accreditation and certification systems. They are not related to the content or structure of the ISO 9000 standards themselves.

Some perceive the European Union to be exploiting the differences between the United States and European standard-setting systems and government-business relationships to its advantage. The European system is government-oriented with an emphasis on third-party verification, while the US system is driven by the private sector and has often relied on manufacturers' self-declaration of conformity.

US manufacturers are not as familiar as European companies with a government-driven standards system such as the one being implemented in the European Union. This unfamiliarity with the system, coupled with the many uncertainties about the developing EU system for conformity assessment, leaves US manufacturers in the dark about how to meet various requirements. Europeans who are more familiar with the system and who have an ability to influence it may have an advantage.

Ingenuity and flexibility have always been a cultural advantage for the United States, however. Many US firms have proven their ability to become registered and to compete effectively.

THE MOVE TO ISO 9000 IS ON

Despite the costs and the unsettled issues, the global drive toward quality system registration to the ISO 9000 standards is well under way. Nations, regional bodies such as the European Union, and customers worldwide are using registration to the ISO 9000 series standards as a means to differentiate quality companies from others in the field.

Companies deciding not to jump on the bandwagon may well find themselves running to catch up with international competition. John Hinds, president of International Organization for Standardization (ISO), says that US companies must understand and adopt international standards if they are to compete effectively in the world. According to quality expert Philip Crosby, "it's becoming very clear now that quality is not so much an asset *per se* as a price of getting into the game. If you don't have it, you can't play. And if you can't produce it, they won't be interested in you."

ENDNOTES

[1] "European Single Market Expands," *European Community Quarterly Review*, Vol. II, Issue 2 (Spring 1994): 2.

[2] Timothy J. Hauser, "The European Community Single Market and US Trade Relations," *Business America*, 8 March 1993.

[3] *ibid.*

[4] *Quality Systems Update*/Deloitte & Touche, "ISO 9000 Survey," July 1993.

OVERVIEW OF THE ISO 9000 SERIES STANDARD

This chapter is an overview of the ISO 9000 series standards. It discusses the 1994 version of the standards, with appropriate references to revisions made to the 1987 version. This chapter explains ISO 9000-1 and ISO 9004-1 in detail while introducing ISO 9001, 9002 and 9003. (Please refer to Chapter 3 for a detailed explanation of ISO 9001.) Chapter 2 covers the following topics:

- Uses of the Standards
- Definition of Terms
- The ISO 9000 Series
  - Guidance Standards
    - ISO 9000-1
    - ISO 9004-1
  - Conformance Standards
    - ISO 9001
    - ISO 9002
    - ISO 9003
- Other Useful Standards in the Quality Family.

INTRODUCTION

As mentioned in the first chapter, the ISO 9000 series is a set of generic standards that provide quality management guidance and identify generic quality system elements necessary to achieve quality assurance. ISO 9000 standards are independent of any specific industry or economic sector. An individual company determines how to implement these standards to meet its specific needs and the needs of its customers.

The ISO 9000 series covers a broad scope of quality system elements—they are basic and uncomplicated. A company that has achieved ISO 9000 registration can attest that it has a documented quality system that is fully deployed and consistently followed. This does not necessarily imply, however, that the company produces better quality products than those of its competitors.

Standards in the ISO 9000 series are **not** product standards. They do not include any technical requirements. According to Clause 4.3 of ISO 9000-1, the quality system requirements in the ISO 9000 series are complementary **to** but not substitutes **for** distinct product technical requirements.

Basically, the ISO 9001, ISO 9002 and ISO 9003 standards require a company to document what it does, do what it documents, review the process and change it when necessary. To illustrate the objective of ISO documentation: if a company suddenly replaced all its personnel, their replacements, properly trained, could use the documentation to continue making the product or providing the service as before.

ISO 9001, ISO 9002, and ISO 9003 requirements do not constitute a full-fledged total quality management system; rather, they provide many of the basic building blocks for such a system. The ISO 9000 standards tell companies what to do, but not how to do it. The choice of methods is left to the management of the organization.

USES OF THE STANDARDS

According to Section 6 of ISO 9000-1, there are four primary uses for the ISO 9000 standards. These include the following:

- Guidance for quality management
- Contractual agreements
- Second party approval or registration
- Third-party certification or registration.

In both *contractual* and *noncontractual* situations, an organization—referred to in the standard as the "supplier"—wants to install and maintain a quality system to strengthen its competitiveness and to achieve the needed product quality in a cost-effective way. Thus, the ISO 9000 standards offer valuable guidance for internal quality management.

Additionally, in a *contractual* situation, the customer wants to know whether its supplier can produce products or services that consistently meet necessary requirements. According to ISO 9000, in a contractual situation both supplier and customer must agree on what is acceptable.

In a *second-party* approval or registration situation, the customer assesses its supplier's quality system and grants formal recognition of conformance with the standard.

In a *third-party* situation—evaluation by a certification body—the supplier agrees to maintain its quality system for all customers unless otherwise specified in an individual contract.

A particular organization can be involved in one or more of the above situations. For example, a supplier may purchase some materials without contractual quality system requirements and purchase others with contractual requirements.

DEFINITION OF TERMS

Before discussing the ISO 9000 series further, it is necessary to define common terms that are used in the standard. One purpose of the ISO 9000 standard is to create a consistent international "language of quality." Most of the definitions quoted below are taken from *ISO 8402, Quality management and quality assurance—Vocabulary.* 2nd Edition 1994.

What Is an Organization?

An organization for the purposes of the standard is "a company, corporation, firm, enterprise or institution or part thereof, whether incorporated or not, public or private, that has its own functions and administration." This is a broad definition; the quality system elements in ISO 9000 apply to almost any type of organization.

Supplier-Chain Terminology

The terminology in the 1987 version of ISO 9000 was not consistent. ISO 9000-1, Clause 3.8 improves the terminology and presents the following table:

Table 2-1: Supplier-Chain Terminology			
Standard	**Relationships of Organizations in the Supplier-Chain**		
ISO 9000-1	Subsupplier	Supplier	Customer
ISO 9001	Subcontractor	Supplier	Customer
ISO 9004-1	Subcontractor	Organization	Customer

The requirements of ISO 9001, ISO 9002 and ISO 9003 are addressed to the supplier. The guidance in ISO 9004-1 addresses the organization.

The supplier provides products/services to its customer(s). In a contractual situation, the customer is referred to as the purchaser and the supplier as the contractor. The supplier receives goods and services, if necessary, from either subsuppliers or subcontractors. (Please refer to the beginning of Chapter 3 for a more detailed chart of the supply chain.)

What Is a Product?

A product is defined as the "result of activities or processes." A product can be tangible, such as assemblies or processed materials, or intangible, such as information, or a combination of both, such as a service. In Clause 4.4 of ISO 9000-1, the standard classifies products into four generic product categories: hardware, software, processed materials and services.

HARDWARE

Hardware refers to a "tangible, discrete product with distinctive form." Thus, hardware products normally consist of "manufactured, constructed or fabricated pieces, parts and/or assemblies." (ISO 9000-1, 3.1)

SOFTWARE

Software is an "intellectual creation consisting of information expressed through supporting medium." Software can be in the form of "concepts, transactions or procedures". Some examples are computer programs and the content of books and procedures. (ISO 9000-1, 3.2)

PROCESSED MATERIAL

A processed material is "a tangible product generated by transforming raw material into a desired state." This state can be "liquid, gas, particulate, material, ingot, filament or sheet." (ISO 9000-1, 3.3)

SERVICE

A service is a "result generated by activities at the interface between the supplier and the customer, and by supplier internal activities to meet the customer needs." (ISO 8402:1994) Note from this definition that there are services provided within an organization. Thus, an organization can have internal suppliers and customers.

According to the standard, many companies include more than one generic product category. Often, hardware, software and services will all be part of the organization's offering to its customers.

What Is Quality?

Quality has many meanings—many of which are subjective, such as the concept of "excellence." In the quality management field, however, the meaning is more specific. According to ISO 8402:1994, quality is "the totality of characteristics of an entity that bear on its ability to satisfy stated or implied needs."

In a contractual situation, stated needs are specified in contract requirements and translated into product features and characteristics with specified criteria. In other situations, implied needs are identified and defined by the company, based on knowledge of its marketplace. The needs of the customer, of course, change with time. Thus, companies should review quality requirements periodically.

Generally, quality in a product or service refers to "fitness for use" or "fitness for purpose." Most organizations produce products to meet specific criteria such as technical specifications. As ISO 9000-1 notes, however, "specifications may not in themselves guarantee that a customer's requirements will be met consistently..."

Clause 4.5 of ISO 9000-1 looks at the following four facets of quality:

- Quality due to definition of needs for the product
- Quality due to product design
- Quality due to conformance to product design
- Quality due to product support.

An effective quality system will address all four facets of quality.

What Is a Quality System?

A quality system is "the organizational structure, procedures, processes and resources needed to implement quality management." (ISO 8402:1994, Clause 3.6) It should "only be as comprehensive as needed to meet quality objectives."

Earlier in the industrial era, product quality was associated only with inspection after the fact. To improve quality control and prevent problems from occurring, manufacturers developed tools such as statistical process control and installed quality control departments. Quality standards such as ISO 9000 are based on the idea of building quality into every aspect of the enterprise, with an integrated quality management system.

Clause 5, Quality system elements of ISO 9004-1 states that the quality system involves all processes in the life cycle of a product that affect quality, from initial identification of market needs to final satisfaction of requirements. Figure 2-1 illustrates the typical life cycle phases of the product.

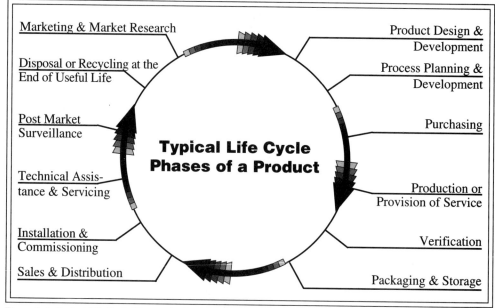

Figure 2-1: Typical Life Cycle Phases of a Product.

What Is Quality Management?

Quality management refers to "all activities of the overall management function that determine the quality policy, objectives and responsibilities and implement them by means such as quality planning, quality control, quality assurance and quality improvement within the quality system." (ISO 8402:1994) According to quality systems consultant Ian Durand, "Quality management is not separate from general management. When used effectively, quality management should be an integral part of an organization's overall management approach."

What Is Quality Assurance?

Quality assurance includes "all the planned and systematic activities implemented within the quality system and demonstrated as needed to provide adequate confidence that an entity will fulfill requirements for quality." (ISO 8402)

What is an entity? It is anything that can be "individually described and considered." For example, an entity can be a process, a product, an organization, a system, person or any combination of these.

The purpose of a quality assurance system is to prevent problems from occurring, detect them when they do, identify the cause, remedy the cause, and prevent reoccurrence. A more succinct summary is offered by Ian Durand. "The basis of a quality system," he says, "is to

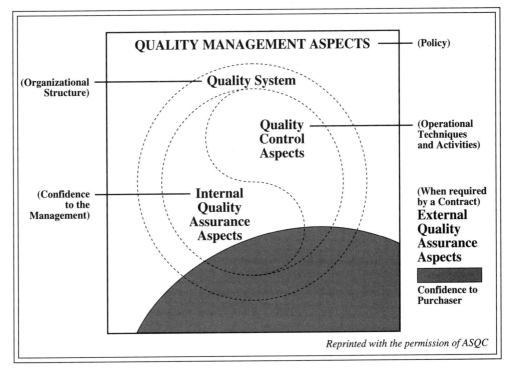

Figure 2-2: Relationship of Concepts.

say what you do, do what you say, record what you did, check the results, and act on the difference."

Figure 2-2 illustrates the relationship of these concepts.

TYPES OF STANDARDS IN THE ISO 9000 SERIES

The basic ISO 9000 series consists of five standards: ISO 9000-1, ISO 9001, ISO 9002, ISO 9003, and ISO 9004-1. The standards fall into two categories: guidance standards and conformance standards.

ISO 9001, ISO 9002 and ISO 9003 are *conformance standards*. They are used for *external quality assurance*—to provide confidence to the customer that the company's quality system will provide a satisfactory product or service. They will be discussed later in the chapter.

ISO 9000-1 and ISO 9004-1 are *guidance standards*. This means they are descriptive documents, not prescriptive requirements. ISO 9000-1 and ISO 9004-1 provide guidance to "all organizations for quality management purposes." These documents are used for internal quality assurance, which are "activities aimed at providing confidence to the management of an organization that the intended quality is being achieved."

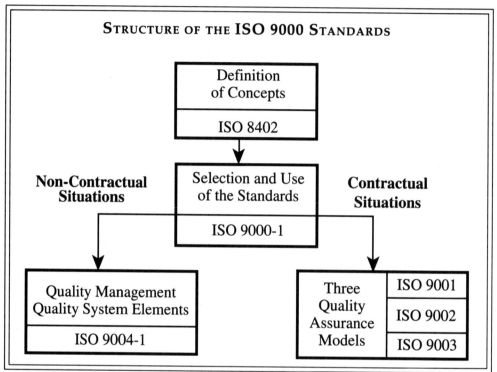

Figure 2-3: Structure of the ISO 9000 Standards.

Guidance Standards

ISO 9000-1

ISO 9000-1, Quality management and quality assurance standards—Guidelines for selection and use introduces the ISO 9000 series and explains fundamental quality concepts. It defines key terms and provides guidance on selecting, using, and tailoring ISO 9001, ISO 9002 and ISO 9003 for external quality assurance purposes. It also provides guidance on using ISO 9004-1 for internal quality management. It is the "road map" for use of the entire series.

Editor's Note: *The 1994 revisions of ISO 9000 and 9004 are designated ISO 9000-1 and ISO 9004-1, with titles unchanged; this permits use of "part numbers" such as ISO 9004-2 and ISO 9004-3 to accommodate additional guidance standards addressing individual subjects.*

Topics Covered in ISO 9000-1

The following are some of the key points discussed in ISO 9000-1.

The Quality Objectives of an Organization

In *Clause 4.0, Principal Concepts*, ISO 9000-1 describes an organization's basic quality objectives. Each organization should do the following:

- Achieve, maintain and continually improve the quality of its products
- Improve the quality of its own operations to meet the needs of its customers and stakeholders
- Provide confidence internally that quality is being fulfilled, maintained and improved
- Provide confidence to the customer and other stakeholders that requirements for quality will be achieved in the delivered product (ISO 9000-1)
- Provide confidence that quality system requirements are fulfilled.

The standard emphasizes that every organization has five groups of stakeholders: customers, employees, owners, subsuppliers and society. In addition, there may be government requirements, environmental regulations and other stakeholders. The quality expectations vary with each group. An effective quality system addresses the requirements of all groups of stakeholders. This concept of quality goes well beyond simply meeting customer specifications. It encourages companies to anticipate all stakeholder expectations and exceed them.

All Work as a Process

ISO 9000 emphasizes a process-based view of the organization. Clause 4.6 and Clause 4.7 of 9000-1 emphasize that all work is accomplished through processes. A process is any transformation that adds value. Outputs of processes can be either tangible or intangible. That is, they can be either product or information related.

The work of organizations is accomplished through a network of processes. To achieve quality, an organization needs to identify, organize and manage its network of processes and the interfaces between those processes. The final result should be an integrated quality system.

When evaluating a quality system, an organization should ask three key questions:

- Are the processes defined and are procedures appropriately documented?
- Are the processes fully deployed and implemented as documented?
- Are the processes effective in providing the expected results?

Management Review of the Quality System

Subclause 4.9.2 emphasizes the importance of systematic management review of the quality system. *Subclause 4.9.3, Quality System Audits* emphasizes the importance of audits, whether conducted by the organization itself, the customer or an independent body. The goal of management reviews and internal audits is a more effective and efficient quality system. (Chapter 5 describes the internal audit process.)

Table 2-2: Contents of ISO 9000-1: 1994

0   Introduction
1   Scope
2   Normative references
3   Definitions
4   Principal concepts
    4.1   Key objectives and responsibilities for quality
    4.2   Stakeholders and their expectations
    4.3   Distinguishing between quality system requirements and product requirements
    4.4   Generic product categories
    4.5   Facets of quality
    4.6   Concept of a process
    4.7   Network of processes in an organization
    4.8   Quality system in relation to the network of processes
    4.9   Evaluating quality systems
5   Roles of documentation
6   Quality system situations
7   Selection and use of international standards on quality
8   Selection and use of international standards for external quality assurance

Annexes

A   Terms and definitions taken from ISO 8402
B   Product and process factors
C   Proliferation of standards
D   Cross-reference list of clause numbers for corresponding topics
E   Bibliography

The Role of Documentation

Section 5 of 9000-1 discusses the role of documentation. The purpose of ISO 9000 documentation is not to create a bureaucracy nor to generate a paper factory but to help the organization:

● Achieve required (product) quality
● Evaluate quality systems
● Achieve quality improvement
● Maintain the improvements.

Documentation also plays a role in auditing by providing objective evidence that a process is defined, procedures are approved and changes to procedures are controlled. Documentation allows organizations to measure current performance and thus measure the effect of changes—both positive and negative.

Tailoring the Standard to a Contract

Clause 8.4, Additional considerations in contractual situations notes that in certain situations, the standards can be tailored to the contract; certain quality system elements or subelements called for in the standard may be deleted or other elements may be added, such as statistical process control. When tailoring is required, it should be specified in the contract.

Both parties should review the proposed contract to make sure they understand its requirements. In second-party situations, the customer assesses the quality system prior to awarding the contract and continually audits the quality system after awarding the contract.

ISO 9004-1

ISO 9004-1, Quality management and quality system elements—Guidelines provides guidance to all organizations for internal quality management purposes without regard to external contractual requirements. ISO 9004-1 examines most of the quality system elements contained in ISO 9001, ISO 9002 and ISO 9003 in greater detail. It can help organizations determine the extent that each quality system is applicable to them.

The Role of ISO 9004-1

Misunderstandings are common regarding ISO 9004-1's relationship to other standards in the ISO 9000 family, and its own potential value. Although ISO 9004-1 is clearly identified as a guideline standard and has no specific requirements, suppliers proceeding through the registration process will find the guidance standard to be helpful. For example, ISO 9004-1 clauses—such as those on design review, statistical methods and corrective action—contain elements that may lay the groundwork for fulfilling ISO 9001 requirements.

ISO 9004-1 also includes subjects not addressed explicitly in ISO 9001, such as quality economics (quality cost approaches) and continuous quality improvement. Perhaps it receives the most attention from the legal profession, since 9004-1 also addresses product safety and liability—a subject not appearing in ISO 9001, 9002 and 9003. (See Chapter 12 for further discussion regarding the legal aspects of ISO 9000 registration.)

ISO 9004-1 may also help suppliers that anticipate registering to ISO 9001 or ISO 9002 but are under no pressure to do so and have not yet set a registration timetable. Such a supplier may want to consider tailoring a quality management plan to its own present and future needs based on a combination of ISO 9004-1, Malcolm Baldrige National Quality Award Criteria, and relevant standards in its own industry. Later, if customers require evidence of an effective quality system, the organization can implement the requirements of ISO 9001, ISO 9002 or ISO 9003 to demonstrate the effectiveness of its quality system.

Another use of ISO 9004-1 is by suppliers already registered to ISO 9001 or ISO 9002. These suppliers recognize that the content of these standards are only a foundation and want to experience the benefits of improved quality management practice. In such cases, the discipline established by registration provides an excellent base to ensure that capabilities, once adopted, remain effective.

Topics Covered in ISO 9004-1

The following is a brief introduction to some of the topics covered in ISO 9004-1. (Guidance offered by 9004-1, cross-referenced to the corresponding clauses in ISO 9001, is also described in Chapter 3.)

The foreword to ISO 9004-1 stresses several points about the 1994 version:

- The revision integrates editorial changes to align the terminology with ISO 8402 and to better serve the process and service industries
- The revision introduces some general management concepts, such as that of a process
- More emphasis is placed on planning and preventive action
- New methods for the financial reporting of quality management effectiveness have been introduced.

Table 2-3: Contents of ISO 9004-1

  0 Introduction
  1 Scope
  2 Normative references
  3 Definitions
  4 Management responsibility
  5 Quality system elements
  6 Financial considerations of quality systems
  7 Quality in marketing
  8 Quality in specification and design
  9 Quality in purchasing
 10 Quality in processes
 11 Control of processes
 12 Product verification
 13 Control of inspection, measurement and test equipment
 14 Control of nonconforming product
 15 Corrective action
 16 Post production activities
 17 Quality records
 18 Personnel
 19 Product safety
 20 Use of statistical methods

Annex A: Bibliography

Organizational Goals 0.2

ISO 9004-1 recommends each company "should ensure that the technical, administrative and human factors affecting the quality of its products will be under control, whether hardware, software, processed material or services." The aim is to reduce, eliminate and prevent quality deficiencies.

To achieve its objectives, companies should develop a quality system that is appropriate to the type of activity and to the product being offered. The goal is to meet desired customer needs for quality at an optimum cost to the organization. The standard encourages companies to consider costs, benefits and risks inherent in most products.

The benefits for the customer lie in product or service satisfaction; for the company it is increased profitability and market share. A key issue is the cost of poor quality in marketing and design deficiencies, rework, repair, replacement, reprocessing and other costs. An effective quality system satisfies customer needs while protecting the company's interests. It also addresses the needs of both society and the environment.

Management Responsibility (4.0)

ISO 9004-1 emphasizes that the responsibility for a quality policy belongs to management, as does defining and documenting the organization's quality policy. A company's quality policy is "the overall intentions and direction of an organization with regard to quality, as formally expressed by top management." (ISO 8402, 3.1) It is one element of the corporate policy and is authorized by top management.

Management is ultimately responsible for establishing a quality policy and all decisions concerning the quality system. It is up to management to do the following:

- Define general and specific quality responsibilities
- Delegate appropriate responsibility and authority
- Clearly establish the organizational structure
- Identify quality problems and initiate preventive measures
- Provide sufficient and appropriate resources to achieve quality objectives
- Determine training needs
- Identify quality factors that affect new products, processes or services
- Exercise adequate and continuous control over all activities affecting quality
- Emphasize preventive actions to avoid problems
- Write procedures simply, unambiguously and understandably

Quality System Elements (5.0)

This lengthy section of ISO 9004-1 covers the key elements comprising the structure of a quality system. A quality system applies to all activities that affect quality and involves all phases in the life cycle of a product, from initial market research through post-market surveillance and disposal or recycling at the end of the product's useful life.

Configuration Management. ISO 9004-1 adds configuration management to the structure of the quality system. According to ISO 9004, Part 7, Clause 3.1, a configuration consists of the "functional and physical characteristics of a product as set forth in technical documentation and achieved in the product". Configuration management is defined in *ISO 9004, Part 7: Guidelines for configuration management* as the technical and organizational activities of configuration identification, control, status accounting and audit. ISO 9004-1 emphasizes that the quality system should include documented procedures for configuration management to the extent appropriate.

Documentation of the Quality System. The quality system of an organization should be documented in a systematic, orderly and understandable manner in the form of policies and procedures. Not everything must be documented, only procedures that affect the quality of the product or service.

Typically, the quality system is documented in a quality manual. The purpose of a quality manual is to outline the quality system and to serve as a reference. Supporting the quality manual are documented quality system procedures and work instructions.

Quality Plans. When there is a new product, process or significant change to an existing product or process, the organization should prepare and maintain a documented *quality plan*. A quality plan is "a document setting out the specific quality practices, resources and sequence of activities relevant to a particular product, project or contract." (ISO 8402, 3.13) The quality plan may be part of the overall quality system. A quality plan for a specific project usually references the applicable parts of the quality manual. (See Chapter 7 for a discussion of quality plans.)

Quality Records. Documentation also includes maintaining quality records such as design charts, inspection and testing records, audit results, etc. These provide evidence of conformance to specified requirements and the effective operation of the quality system.

Auditing the Quality System. An effective quality system includes provisions for regular auditing to determine if the system is achieving its objectives. Section 5.4 outlines the necessary elements for an effective internal auditing program. These include:

- Planning and scheduling the activities and areas to audit
- Gathering an audit team whose members are independent of those directly responsible for the specific activities being audited
- Documenting the audit procedures, including recording its results and agreeing on timely corrective actions
- Reporting the audit conclusions to management responsible for the area audited
- Assessing and documenting the effectiveness of corrective actions.

(See Chapter 5 for more information on internal audits.)

Review and Evaluation of the Quality System. ISO 9004-1 recommends that management regularly review and evaluate the quality system. The review should include results from internal audits, assessments of whether the objectives were fulfilled, and possible considerations for updating the quality system.

Quality Improvement. ISO 9004-1 adds a clause concerning quality improvement. The quality system should facilitate and promote continuous quality improvement. Management can create an environment for continuous improvement by doing the following:

- Encouraging and sustaining a supportive style of management
- Promoting values, attitudes and behavior that foster improvement
- Setting clear quality improvement goals
- Encouraging effective communication and teamwork
- Recognizing successes
- Providing training and education geared to improvement.

Financial Considerations. Clause 6 emphasizes the importance of measuring a quality system's effectiveness. The results can be used to identify inefficient activities and to initiate internal improvement. Clause 6 describes the following three methods, among others, for analyzing the financial data.

- The *quality-costing* approach. This approach addresses quality-related costs, arising both from internal operations and external activities. Using this approach, prevention and appraisal cost are considered investments, while failure costs, both internal and external, are considered losses.
- The *process-cost* approach. This approach analyzes the costs of conformity and the costs of nonconformity for any process. The costs of the former are incurred to fulfill customer expectations. The costs of the latter result when processes and products fail to meet requirements.
- The *quality loss* approach. This approach focuses on losses due to poor quality. Losses can be intangible, such as loss of future sales due to customer dissatisfaction or lower work efficiency or they can be tangible, such as internal and external failure costs.

ISO 9004-1 recommends that the financial reporting of quality activities—whatever method is used—should be related to other conventional business measures, such as sales, turnover or added value.

Quality in Marketing (7.0)

The standard notes that the marketing function should take the lead in establishing adequately defined and documented requirements for product or service quality. This involves determining the need for a product, defining the market demand, determining customer requirements, communicating these requirements and ensuring that all relevant parts of the organization are capable of meeting them. Clause 7.0 emphasizes the importance of defining product specifications thoroughly and establishing a method of obtaining and analyzing customer feedback.

Quality in Specification and Design (8.0)

Clause 8 discusses ways to translate customer needs into technical specifications for materials, products, and processes. This clause discusses in detail the following:

- Design planning and objectives
- Product testing and measurement

- Design review
- Design verification
- Design qualification and validation
- Final design review and production release
- Market readiness review
- Design change control
- Design requalification
- Configuration management in design.

Quality in Purchasing (9.0)

Since purchases become part of the organization's product, they directly affect quality. Clause 9.0 recommends that all purchasing be planned and controlled by documented procedures. This includes purchasing services such as testing, calibration and subcontracted processing. Clause 9.0 covers the following elements of quality in purchasing:

- Requirements for specifications, drawings and purchase documents
- Selection of qualified subcontractors
- Agreement on quality assurance
- Agreement on verification methods
- Provisions for settlement of disputes
- Procedures for receiving inspection, planning, and control
- Maintenance of quality records related to purchasing.

Quality of Processes (10.0)

Clause 10 discusses the quality of processes. Planning of processes should ensure that they proceed under controlled conditions in the specified manner and sequence. Clause 10 covers the following management elements:

- Planning for process control
- Verifying the capability of processes to produce in accordance with product specifications
- Controlling and verifying supplies, utilities and the environment insofar as these affect product quality characteristics
- Proper planning, control and documentation of product handling.

Control of Processes (11.0)

Clause 11 details the control of all processes in the life cycle of the product or service. Specifically, it covers the following:

- Material control, traceability and identification
- Equipment control and maintenance
- Process-control management
- Documentation

- Process-change control
- Control of verification status
- Control of nonconforming product.

Product Verification (12.0)

This clause looks at the process of verifying products, including incoming materials and parts, in-process verification, and finished product verification.

Control of Inspection, Measuring and Test Equipment (13.0)

Clause 13 emphasizes the importance of well-controlled measuring systems to provide confidence in decisions or actions that are taken based on measurement data. Topics discussed include the following:

- Elements of measurement control, including calibration and traceability to reference standards
- Subcontractor measurement controls
- Corrective action
- Outside testing.

Control of Nonconforming Product (14.0)

Clause 14 recommends establishing procedures for dealing with nonconforming product to prevent the customer from inadvertently receiving the nonconforming product and to avoid further processing of nonconforming product. The steps outlined in the clause include the following:

- Identification
- Segregation
- Review
- Disposition
- Action
- Avoiding recurrences.

Corrective Action (15.0)

Corrective action is necessary to eliminate quality problems or to minimize their occurrence. Clause 15 covers the following:

- Assigning responsibility for instituting corrective action
- Evaluating the significance of the problem
- Investigating possible causes
- Analyzing the problem
- Eliminating the causes
- Implementing process controls to avoid recurrence
- Recording permanent changes resulting from corrective action.

Post-Production Activities (16.0)

The responsibility for quality continues beyond the production phase. Clause 16 covers the following:

- Storage methods to increase shelf life and avoid deterioration
- Protection of product quality during delivery
- Installation procedures
- Servicing
- Post-marketing surveillance to establish a warning system for reporting product failures or shortcomings
- Market feedback regarding performance to monitor quality.

Quality Records (17.0)

Clause 17 focuses on establishing and maintaining documented procedures for quality records. Records can include inspection reports, test data, qualification reports, calibration data, etc. The clause discusses records that must be controlled, including drawings, specifications, inspection procedures and instructions, work instructions, quality plans, etc.

Personnel (18.0)

Clause 18 discusses the need for personnel training. Appropriate training should be provided to all levels of personnel that perform activities affecting quality. This includes executive and management personnel, technical personnel, process supervisors and operating personnel. The clause covers the following:

- Qualification requirements for personnel
- Motivating all personnel toward quality performance.

Product Safety (19.0)

This clause focuses on identifying safety aspects of the products and processes to enhance safety. Steps in the process include the following:

- Identifying relevant safety standards
- Evaluating and testing for safety
- Analyzing instructions and warnings for the user
- Developing a product recall method
- Developing an emergency plan in case recall becomes necessary.

Use of Statistical Methods (20.0)

The final clause in ISO 9004-1 recognizes the appropriate use of statistical methods. Documented procedures should be established and maintained for applying statistical methods to, among others, market analysis, product design, reliability specification, process control and process improvement. The clause lists specific statistical methods that can be used, including design of experiments, statistical sampling and other methods.

Conformance Standards

ISO 9001, ISO 9002 and ISO 9003, which are conformance standards, are used for *external quality assurance*—to provide confidence to the customer that the company's quality system will provide a satisfactory product or service.

The three conformance standards are not levels of quality; they differ only in comprehensiveness so that they can be adapted to different types of organizations. For example, ISO 9002 does not include design control as a quality system element.

ISO 9001

ISO 9001, Quality systems—Model for quality assurance in design/development, production, installation and servicing is the most comprehensive of the conformance standards. It includes all elements listed in ISO 9002 and ISO 9003. In addition, it addresses the design, development and servicing capabilities not addressed in the other models.

ISO 9001 is used when the supplier must ensure product conformance to specified needs throughout the entire product cycle. It is also used when the contract specifically requires a design effort. ISO 9001 commonly applies to manufacturing or processing industries, but it can also apply to services such as construction or to professional services, such as architecture and engineering. (The requirements of ISO 9001 are discussed in detail in Chapter 3.)

ISO 9002

ISO 9002, Quality systems—Model for quality assurance in production, installation and servicing addresses production and installation. In the 1994 revised standard, the only distinction between ISO 9001 and ISO 9002 is that ISO 9002 does not include the design function. (In the 1987 version of the standard, ISO 9002 also did not include the servicing element.)

ISO 9002 applies to a wide range of industries whose work is based on technical designs and specifications provided by their customers. It is relevant for products that do not involve a design aspect and is used when the specified product requirements are stated in terms of an already-established design or specification.

ISO 9003

ISO 9003, Quality systems—Model for quality assurance in final inspection and test is the least comprehensive standard. It addresses only the requirements for detection and control of problems during final inspection and testing. ISO 9003 applies to organizations whose products or services can be adequately assessed by testing and inspection. Generally, this refers to less complex products or services.

Other Useful Standards in the ISO 9000 Family

ISO 9000-1 includes references to other useful guidance standards in the ISO 9000 series. Some of these standards have already been published. Others are in draft form. They are briefly introduced below. Those that have been published are discussed in greater detail in other chapters of this Handbook.

Table 2-4: Cross Reference of ISO 9000 Quality Assurance Requirements

ISO 9000 Clause and Title	Quality Assurance Requirements		
	ISO 9001	ISO 9002	ISO 9003
4.1 Management Responsibility	◆	◆	●
4.2 Quality System	◆	◆	●
4.3 Contract Review	◆	◆	◆
4.4 Design Control	◆	○	○
4.5 Document and Data Control	◆	◆	◆
4.6 Purchasing	◆	◆	○
4.7 Control of Customer-Supplied Product	◆	◆	◆
4.8 Product Identification and Traceability	◆	◆	●
4.9 Process Control	◆	◆	○
4.10 Inspection and Testing	◆	◆	●
4.11 Control of Inspection, Measuring and Test Equipment	◆	◆	◆
4.12 Inspection and Test Status	◆	◆	◆
4.13 Control of Nonconforming Product	◆	◆	●
4.14 Corrective and Preventive Action	◆	◆	●
4.15 Handling, Storage, Packaging, Preservation and Delivery	◆	◆	◆
4.16 Control of Quality Records	◆	◆	●
4.17 Internal Quality Audits	◆	◆	●
4.18 Training	◆	◆	●
4.19 Servicing	◆	◆	○
4.20 Statistical Techniques	◆	◆	●

KEY:

◆ Comprehensive requirement
● Less comprehensive requirement than ISO 9001 and 9002
○ Element not present.

ISO 9000-2

ISO 9000-2, Quality management and quality assurance standards—Part 2: Generic guidelines for the application of ISO 9001, ISO 9002 and ISO 9003 offers application guidance in implementing the standards. Guidance from ISO 9000-2 that corresponds to each clause in ISO 9001 is described in Chapter 3.

ISO 9000-3

Software is discussed in *ISO 9000-3, Quality management and quality assurance standards— Part 3: Guidelines for the application of ISO 9001 to the development, supply and maintenance of software.* This standard provides guidance to supplier organizations that produce software or products that include a software element. The primary rationale for this standard is that software development, supply and maintenance—unlike other manufacturing processes—does not have a distinct manufacturing phase. The key process is the design phase. ISO 9000-3 offers suggestions regarding appropriate controls and methods that apply to the design phase. (ISO 9000-3 is discussed in detail in Chapter 9.)

ISO 9000-4

ISO 9000-4, Quality management and quality assurance standards—Part 4: Guide to dependability programme management provides guidance on dependability program management. It focuses on the reliability, maintainability and availability characteristics of products such as transportation, electricity, telecommunications and information services. It covers the essential features of a comprehensive dependability program. In Clause 1, *Scope*, the standard emphasizes that its requirements are "aimed primarily at controlling influences on dependability at all product life-cycle phases from product planning to operation."

ISO 9004-2

ISO 9004-2, Quality management and quality system elements—Part 2: Guidelines for services is geared to organizations that provide services or whose products include a service component. It takes into account factors that may differ from a product offering, such as customer interaction and customer assessment. (ISO 9004-2 is discussed in greater detail in Chapter 10.)

ISO 9004-3

ISO 9004-3, Quality management and quality system elements—Part 3: Guidelines for processed materials applies to organizations whose products consist of processed materials such as solids, liquids or gases that are delivered in pipelines, drums, tanks or cans. Clause 7.11 points out the importance of statistical sampling and evaluation procedures and their application to in-process controls and final product specifications. ISO 9004-3 includes guidelines on process control, process capability, equipment control, and maintenance and documentation. (ISO 9004-3 is discussed in greater detail in Chapter 20.)

ISO 9004-4

All companies should strive for continuous quality improvement. *ISO 9004-4, Quality management and quality system elements—Part 4: Guidelines for quality improvement* describes fundamental concepts and methods for quality improvement. In the Introduction, the standard notes that "the motivation for quality improvement comes from the need to provide increased value and satisfaction to customers." Everyone in the organization should be alert to how each process can be performed more effectively and more efficiently with less waste and resource consumption. A fundamental concept of quality improvement is that companies should "seek opportunities for improvement, rather than waiting for a problem to reveal opportunities." (Clause 3.1.4)

ISO 10011

ISO 10011, Guidelines for auditing quality systems focuses on auditing. It is designed for all auditing situations: first, second and third-party. ISO 10011-1 looks at the overall process of establishing, planning, performing and documenting quality system audits. 10011-2 provides guidance on the education, training and experience needed to carry out an audit. And 10011-3 examines the process of managing an audit—from the initial planning to the closing meeting. (See Chapter 5 for more information on the 10011 series.)

ISO 10012

In many products or processes, quality depends upon accurate measurements. *ISO 10012-1, Quality assurance requirements for measuring equipment—Part 1: Metrological confirmation system for measuring equipment* includes detailed guidance for a supplier's measurement system to ensure accurate and consistent measurement. (See Chapter 6 for more information on ISO 10012, Part 1.)

Table 2-5: Cross Reference List of Clauses in ISO 9000 and ISO 9004-1	
ISO 9001 Clause and Title	**Quality Management Guidance ISO 9004-1**
4.1 Management Responsibility	4
4.2 Quality System	5
4.3 Contract Review	Not Present
4.4 Design Control	8
4.5 Document and Data Control	5.3, 11.5
4.6 Purchasing	9
4.7 Control of Customer-Supplied Product	Not Present
4.8 Product Identification and Traceability	11.2
4.9 Process Control	10, 11
4.10 Inspection and Testing	12
4.11 Control of Inspection, Measuring and Test Equipment	13
4.12 Inspection and Test Status	11.7
4.13 Control of Nonconforming Product	14
4.14 Corrective and Preventive Action	15
4.15 Handling, Storage, Packaging, Preservation and Delivery	10.4, 16.1, 16.2
4.16 Control of Quality Records	5.3, 17.2, 17.3
4.17 Internal Quality Audits	5.4
4.18 Training	18.1
4.19 Servicing	16.4
4.20 Statistical Techniques	20
Quality Economics	6
Product Safety	19
Marketing	7

3

THE ISO 9001 STANDARD

ISO 9001 is the most comprehensive conformance model in the ISO 9000 series and includes all the clauses contained in ISO 9002 and ISO 9003. This chapter discusses the requirements of ISO 9001:1994 in detail. It also discusses the changes made to ISO 9001:1987, where appropriate.

The chapter includes guidelines taken from *ISO 9000-2, Quality management and quality assurance—Part 2: Generic guidelines for the application of ISO 9001, ISO 9002 and ISO 9003*. Like ISO 9000-1 and ISO 9004-1, ISO 9000-2 is a guidance document; companies do not seek to become registered to any of these documents but rather use them for assistance when implementing ISO 9001, ISO 9002 or ISO 9003.

Finally, this chapter includes some information from ISO 9004-1 and, where appropriate, interpretation of ISO 9001 elements by experts in the field. (See Appendix A for contributor biographies.) This interpretation takes two forms: comments by The Victoria Group, a management consulting company in the quality field; and question-and-answer interpretations which previously appeared in *Quality Systems Update* newsletter.

INTRODUCTION

As mentioned in the previous chapter, the 1994 version of the standards have clarified the three key terms, supplier, purchaser and subcontractor. Table 3-1 charts the various ways in which these terms are used, not only in the ISO 9000 series, but also in the US DoD's military standards, the US Food and Drug Administration's Good Manufacturing Practices (GMP) requirements, and in the Malcolm Baldrige National Quality Award Criteria.

Table 3-1: Relationships of Organizations in the Supply Chain			
	Companies Supplying Products to You	Your Organization	Companies to Whom You Provide Products
ISO 9001, 9002, 9003 (Contractual External)	Subcontractor	Supplier	Customer ~~Purchaser~~
ISO 9004 (Guidelines, Internal)	Subcontractor ~~Supplier~~	Organization ~~Company~~	Customer
Military Standards MIL-Q-9858A MIL-I-45208	Subcontractor	Contractor	Procurer
Medical Device Good Manufacturing Practices (GMPs)	Component Supplier	Manufacturer	User
Malcolm Baldrige National Quality Award Criteria	Supplier	Company	Customer

From chart developed by Dale Thanig, Dynatech Laboratories, Chantilly, VA.   (Revisions to 1987 Issue Noted.)

The introduction to ISO 9001 introduces the three standards that can be used for external quality assurance purposes. The 1987 reference to quality systems as "suitable for two-party contractual purposes" has been replaced by the broader statement, "quality system requirements suitable for the purpose of a supplier demonstrating its capability, and for the assessment of the capability of a supplier by external parties." This statement recognizes the growth and importance of the third-party registration system.

The 1994 revision also emphasizes the generic quality of the standards. The standards are independent of any specific industry or economic sector. The introduction notes that "it is not the purpose of these International Standards to enforce uniformity of quality systems."

The Scope section states that ISO 9001 contains quality system requirements for use where a supplier's capability to design and supply conforming product needs to be demonstrated. ISO 9001:1987 emphasized that the requirements specified are "aimed primarily *at preventing nonconformity* at all stages from design through to servicing." (Emphasis added.) Customer satisfaction was implied throughout the 1987 standard. ISO 9001: 1994, however, adds an explicit statement regarding customer satisfaction by stating that the requirements in the standards are "aimed primarily at achieving customer satisfaction by preventing nonconformity at all stages from design through to servicing."

Thus, the expanded wording of the standard identifies customer satisfaction as an ultimate purpose of nonconformity prevention. This is reinforced in *Subclause 4.1.1, Quality Policy*, where the standard notes that the "quality policy shall be relevant to the supplier's organizational goals and the expectations and needs of its customers."

ISO 9001: KEY POINTS

The introductory clause of ISO 9001 gives an overview of the structure of the ISO 9000 series, explains the applicability of each section and emphasizes significant aspects of the ISO 9001 standard. Several key points include the following:

Three Distinct Models
First, the *Introduction* states that "the alternative quality assurance models...represent three *distinct* forms of quality-system requirements..." In other words, ISO 9001, ISO 9002 and ISO 9003 do not represent three steps on a ladder of excellence but rather are separate, independent standards. Equally important is to ensure that the scope of registration applies to the goods or services which a company produces or wishes to procure. It is not uncommon for a company to hold registration for only part of its commercial operations.

Complementary Requirements
The introduction further explains that requirements specified in the standard are always *complementary (not alternative)* to the technical (product) specified requirements. There are many situations where compliance with a published standard specific to a particular product or range of products will require more of the supplier than does the ISO 9000 standard. The individual product specification requirements remain supreme.

ISO 9000 series registration does not solve all problems, nor is registration a substitute for complying with the government regulatory requirements such as the US Environmental Protection Agency (EPA).

Prevention of Nonconformity
Section 1.0 Scope states that "the requirements specified in this International Standard are aimed **primarily at achieving customer satisfaction by preventing nonconformity** at all stages from design through to servicing." (Emphasis added) The prevention of nonconformity is explicit and prominent in the 1994 version. The standard reminds the

(continued on next page)

ISO 9001: Key Points

(continued from previous page)

user that the ultimate purpose is to achieve customer satisfaction. A system of prevention, monitored through all stages of design, production and servicing, is used in quality management. The language of ISO 9001 thus mirrors the tenets of Total Quality Management (TQM).

Related Documents

Sections 2.0 and 3.0 stress the importance of ensuring that related documents or special definitions are made clear to all readers. The terminology in International Standard ISO 8402:1994 should be used to ensure wide reader understanding of the standard. In the 1994 version, ISO 8402:1994 now constitute provisions of the standard through reference in this text. Thus, ISO 8402:1994 is no longer a guidance- or reference-only document.

— The Victoria Group

CLAUSE 4: QUALITY SYSTEM REQUIREMENTS

The main body of ISO 9001 is contained in the quality system requirements of Section 4.0. There are 20 clauses in all. The first quality system requirement is management responsibility.

4.1 Management Responsibility

INTRODUCTION

This clause describes the responsibility of management for developing a quality system. The major responsibilities include the following:

- Establish a quality policy
- Organize personnel
- Verify quality
- Review the quality system.

ISO 9004-1 GUIDANCE

ISO 9004-1 adds a general introductory clause that defines quality management as encompassing "all activities of the overall management function that determine the quality policy, objectives and responsibilities, and implement them by means such as quality planning, quality control, quality assurance and quality improvement within the quality system." (Clause 4.1) The clause emphasizes that the responsibility for and commitment to a quality policy belongs to the highest level of management.

4.1.1 Quality Policy

ISO 8402, Quality Management and Quality Assurance—Vocabulary, defines a quality policy as "the overall intentions and direction of an organization with regard to quality, as formally expressed by top management... The quality policy forms one element of the corporate policy and is authorized by top management."

ISO 9001 REQUIREMENTS

According to ISO 9001, the requirements of the organization regarding the quality policy are the following:

- Define quality policy, quality objectives, quality commitment
- Document the quality policy
- Make sure everyone in the organization understands, implements and maintains the policy.

The 1994 version of this clause has added the following requirement to ISO 9001:1987: "The quality policy shall be relevant to the supplier's organizational goals and the expectations and needs of its customers." This enhances the role of the quality policy with respect to the customers' expectations and needs and to the supplier's internal policy needs.

The 1994 version also refers to "management *with executive responsibility* for quality" to define and document its policy. This change re-emphasizes the importance of high level management involvement in the quality system development process. The words "management with executive responsibility" is repeated throughout the standard.

Finally, the clause emphasizes not only taking action to prevent the occurrence of product nonconformity but "any nonconformities relating to product, process and quality system."

ISO 9000-2 GUIDANCE

ISO 9000-2 recommends that management ensure that the quality policy is:

- Easy to understand
- Relevant to the organization
- Ambitious, yet achievable.

Since commitment to a quality policy starts at the top of an organization, management should demonstrate its commitment visibly, actively and continually.

ISO 9004-1 GUIDANCE

In Clause 4.0, *Management Responsibility*, ISO 9004-1 counsels that management should do the following:

- Define objectives pertaining to key elements of quality, such as fitness for use, performance, safety and reliability
- Consider the costs associated with all quality elements to minimize quality losses
- Ensure that appropriate levels of management define specialized quality objectives

- Provide sufficient resources to achieve its objectives
- Determine the level of competence, experience and training necessary
- Control all activities affecting quality
- Emphasize preventive actions to avoid occurrence of problems
- State written procedures simply, unambiguously and clearly
- Indicate methods to be used and the criteria to be satisfied.

4.1.2 Organization

4.1.2.1 Responsibility and Authority

ISO 9001 REQUIREMENTS

The organization is required to define the responsibility, authority and the interrelation of all personnel affecting the quality of product and service to customers. This refers to personnel who must prevent the occurrence of product nonconformity, identify and record any product quality problems, recommend solutions, verify their implementation, and control further processing, delivery or installation of nonconforming products until the problem has been corrected.

ISO 9000-2 GUIDANCE

Individuals in the organization should do the following:

- Be aware of the scope, responsibility and authority of their functions
- Be aware of their impact on product and service quality
- Have adequate authority to carry out their responsibilities
- Understand clearly their defined authority
- Accept responsibility for achieving quality objectives.

4.1.2.2 Resources

ISO 9001 REQUIREMENTS

Management shall make sure the company has adequate resources and trained personnel to carry out any verification work. The following verification activities include:

- Inspection, testing, and monitoring
- Design reviews
- Internal quality system audits.

This clause has been renamed from the 1987 version—which was called "Verification Resources and Personnel"—and it expands the requirement to provide adequate resources and training personnel for management, work performance and verification activities.

ISO 9000-2 GUIDANCE

Effective verification requires objectivity and cooperation among those involved. Adequate verification resources and personnel can involve the following elements:

- Awareness of standards
- Adequate training
- Production schedules that allow time for inspection, testing and verification
- Appropriate equipment
- Documented procedures
- Access to quality records.

4.1.2.3 Management Representative

ISO 9001 REQUIREMENTS

The basic requirement is to appoint a management representative who has authority to implement and maintain the quality system.

This clause adds to the earlier 1987 version the requirement that the management representative report "on the performance of the quality system to the supplier's management for review and as a basis for improvement of the quality system." The clause also notes that the management representative's responsibility may also include liaison with external bodies on matters that relate to the supplier's quality system. This may include regulatory and product standards-setting bodies that set requirements affecting the supplier.

ISO 9000-2 GUIDANCE

If the management representative has other functions to perform, there should be no conflict of interest with those functions.

SUBCLAUSE 4.1.2.3: THE MANAGEMENT REPRESENTATIVE

By: **Elizabeth Potts**, President ABS Quality Evaluations, Inc.
     Stephen Gousie, Partner, Information Mapping, Inc.
     Robert Hammil, Senior Staff Consultant, Perry Johnson, Inc.
     John Cachat, President of IQS, Inc.

Question

ISO 9001 Subclause 4.1.2.3 states: "The supplier's management with executive responsibility for quality shall appoint a member of the supplier's own management who, irrespective of other responsibilities, shall have defined authority for ensuring that a quality system is established..." What does the term "irrespective of other responsibilities" mean? What background or qualifications should this person possess, and where should the position fall in an organizational structure?

(continued on next page)

The Management Representative

(continued from previous page)

Answer

The panel of experts disagreed on whether the management representative may oversee ISO 9000 series registration as a secondary responsibility. Elizabeth Potts maintained that the term "irrespective of other responsibilities" does not preclude the representative from having other duties and from those other duties taking precedence.

"This phrase allows companies the flexibility and opportunity to structure their organizations to meet their needs and not be forced to comply with an imposed requirement to have a person assigned only to the quality system," she said. "This further enhances a wider application of the standard to all types of organizations and organizational structures."

While agreeing that the management representative may have other responsibilities, the three other panelists said the quality system had to be the first priority.

As a Primary Responsibility

Steven Gousie said the term "irrespective of other responsibilities" means that the management representative must assign equal or higher priority to ISO 9000 than to other responsibilities. The management representative's primary responsibilities are to ensure that the requirements of the ISO 9000 series standard are implemented and maintained, Gousie said.

"This would include primary responsibility for ensuring that the organization is prepared for the initial registration audit, and for the periodic ongoing audits to maintain registration," he said. That person should be familiar with the requirements of ISO 9000 and the appropriate external quality assurance standard. He or she should also be familiar with the company and able to show how the organization meets each of the requirements of the standard, Gousie said.

"Most organizations have their management representative attend one of the lead assessor courses," he said. "While this will help the representative to better understand the registration audit process, it is not an absolute requirement. Knowledge of the requirements of the standard can be obtained by attending one of the many ISO 9000 overview seminars or working closely with an ISO 9000 consultant."

The position should be considered a management position and the person in it given direct access to the most senior person in the organization, Gousie said. In most cases, he added, the management representative is also the quality assurance manager.

"There is no specific requirement that the management representative be the quality assurance manager," Gousie said. "Where the quality function is closely meshed with production, the production manager might fill this responsibility."

Must Have Defined Authority and Responsibility

Robert Hammil said the management representative must have "defined authority

(continued on next page)

The Management Representative

(continued from previous page)

and responsibility" for ensuring that the requirements of the ISO 9000 series are implemented and maintained. "Ultimately, the management representative is the facility's quality system overseer, sponsor, and champion," Hammil said. "He or she is the person whom others, both within the facility and outside of it, consult on any matter pertaining to the quality management system."

Hammil said the management representative shoulders a heavy burden. "Though the management representative may have duties apart from the quality system, the person assuming this role must, in order to be effective, make a serious and long-term commitment to the activity." According to Hammil, candidates should posses a number of qualifications, including the following:

- Be knowledgeable about traditional quality assurance and about quality control technologies
- Have an understanding of the series standards and the strategic role ISO 9000 plays in the company
- Have a commitment to the importance of ISO 9000
- Be an authority figure, ideally with seniority and experience that cuts across departmental lines, though not necessarily from senior management
- Have superior communication skills
- Carry the backing of the chief executive officer or general manager.

"He or she must have the trust, confidence, and backing of the highest authority in the facility," Hammil said. "This could, and often does mean that the management representative reports directly to the chief executive officer, at least insofar as quality management system responsibilities are concerned."

Prioritizing Job Responsibilities

John Cachat agrees that "the highest priority for the individual's time will always be to ensure that ISO requirements are implemented and maintained," he said. "The larger the organization the more full-time the job becomes." Cachat said the management representative should have a broad understanding of the organization and products or services offered. That person should also have excellent communication, interpersonal and sales skills. "Knowledge of the ISO specs can be gained over time," he explained.

The position's standing within the company hierarchy may vary, according to Cachat. "If a positive, quality- and customer-oriented environment exists, the position in the structure is less important," he said. "If ISO, organization, structure, and discipline are lacking, the position should be a high—if not the highest—ranking member of management."

Selecting the Management Representative

Selecting the management representative is entirely up to the company, according to Potts. The background and qualifications of the person are up to the company. "For

(continued on next page)

The Management Representative

(continued from previous page)

organizations with a distinct quality department it is typically the quality manager, but management representatives have ranged from lab supervisors to presidents of corporations," she said.

The decision regarding where to place the position on the corporate hierarchy is also left to the company, Potts said. "What is most important is that the individual be able to demonstrate that he or she has the authority and responsibility for implementation and maintenance of the ISO 9000 quality system and has access to all appropriate personnel—including top management—to raise issues and ensure resolution relative to that implementation and maintenance."

4.1.3 Management Review

ISO 9001 REQUIREMENTS

Continual review of the quality system is necessary to maintain its effectiveness. Subclause 4.1.3 calls on management to do the following:

- Conduct regular management reviews of the system to make sure it remains suitable and effective
- Keep records of its reviews.

ISO 9000-2 GUIDANCE

The scope of management reviews should encompass the following elements:

- Organizational structure
- Implementation of the quality system
- The achieved quality of the product or service
- Information based on customer feedback, internal audits, process and product performance.

The frequency of reviews is not specified but depends on individual circumstances. In terms of follow-up, problems should be documented, analyzed and resolved. Required changes to the quality system should be implemented in a timely manner.

SUBCLAUSE 4.1.3: MANAGEMENT REVIEW

The management representative is an individual who, "**irrespective** of other responsibilities," has the duty and authority to review the quality system to "ensure its continuing suitability and effectiveness" in satisfying the requirements of the standard. The management representative must belong to the supplier's management team and not be an external person, i.e., a visiting consultant.

The management review requirement is often mishandled. It is now required to be performed by executive management. Management must be concerned with the overall process, not just with audit results. The following questions can serve as guidelines:

- Is the system working effectively?
- What are the quality metrics, both internal and external?
- Will changes be made within the operation of the company that will radically affect the system?
- Is technology changing in a way that necessitates rewriting documentation?
- Is the company achieving its stated quality policy and objectives?

— *The Victoria Group*

4.2 Quality System

 ISO 9001 REQUIREMENTS

Clause 4.2 requires companies to prepare a documented quality system. This involves preparing documented quality procedures and instructions and effectively implementing them.

The elements contained in Clause 4.2 were originally contained in a Note to ISO 9001:1987. Notes are advisory language, not requirements. Now the same material is in the body of the standard. This is a significant change, since what was advisory now becomes a requirement. Clause 4.2 is divided into three subclauses, as described below.

4.2.1 General

 ISO 9001 REQUIREMENTS

Subclause 4.2.1 requires a quality manual that defines the documentation structure of the quality system: "The supplier shall prepare a quality manual covering the requirements of this International Standard. The quality manual shall include or make reference to the quality-system procedures and outline the structure of the documentation used in the quality system." A quality manual was not specifically required in ISO 9001:1987.

The subclause also references guidance on quality manuals, contained in ISO 10013. Remember, this is only advisory. The guidance contained in ISO 10013 is not to be interpreted as part of the requirements of Subclause 4.2.1.

4.2.2 Quality System Procedures

 ISO 9001 REQUIREMENTS

Subclause 4.2.2 states the basic purpose of the clause—to establish and implement a documented quality system. It notes that the degree of documentation required for procedures depends on the methods used, the skills needed and the training acquired by the personnel responsible for carrying out the particular activities.

4.2.3 Quality Planning

 ISO 9001 REQUIREMENTS

Subclause 4.2.3 lists the elements that in ISO 9001:1987 were listed in a Note. These elements are now requirements and include the following:

- Preparing a quality plan and a quality manual
- Identifying controls, resources and skills necessary to achieve required quality
- Updating quality control, inspection and testing techniques as necessary
- Identifying extraordinary measurement requirements
- Clarifying standards of acceptability
- Ensuring the compatibility of the design, production, installation, inspection and test procedures
- Identifying suitable verification methods
- Identifying and preparing quality records.

In regard to quality plans, the 1994 version of the standard adds the statement, "the quality plans...may be in the form of a reference to the appropriate documented procedures that form an integral part of the supplier's quality system."

 ISO 9000-2 GUIDANCE

The quality manual can be structured as a tiered set of documents, with each tier becoming more detailed. Quality policy would be the top tier, while detailed procedures and work instructions and record-keeping forms would be in lower tiers. (See Chapter 7 for more information about structuring the quality manual.)

Quality plans define how quality system requirements will be met in a specific contract or for a specific class of products. An example might include a detailed sequence of inspections for a particular product, types of inspection equipment and quality record requirements.

 ISO 9004-1 GUIDANCE

In Subclause 4.4.4, ISO 9004-1 stresses that the goal of the quality system is to provide confidence that:

- The system is understood and effective

- Products and services actually satisfy requirements and customer expectations
- The needs of both society and the environment have been addressed
- Emphasis is on problem prevention rather than detection after occurrence.

The quality system applies to all activities related to the quality of a product or service. These activities range from initial market research and design through to installation, servicing and disposal after use. Marketing and design are especially important for determining and defining customer needs and product requirements.

SUBCLAUSE 4.2.3: QUALITY PLANNING IN THE REVISED ISO 9001

By: **Dennis Abarca**, Account Manager, P-E Handley-Walker Inc.
Tom Bair, Managing Director, Tom Bair & Associates
Ira J. Epstein, VP of Government Services, Managing Director, Stat-A-Matrix
Peter Melville, ISO 9000 Project Manager, Butler Quality Services

Question

Clause 4.2.3 Quality Planning of the recently approved revision to the ISO 9001 external quality assurance standard states: "The supplier shall give consideration to the following activities, as appropriate, in meeting the specified requirements for products, projects or contracts," and then lists eight activities. What is meant by "as appropriate" and how do you define "project?" Are the eight activities mandatory?

Answer

QSU's panel of experts agreed that the meaning of the term "as appropriate" may vary from company to company. Moderator Ira J. Epstein said that the meaning of the term depends on the relationship of the activity to the quality of the company's product or services.

"The beauty of ISO 9000 in general is that it is full of subjective words," said Epstein. "Many people look at these terms as a weakness but in actuality these subjective words are the basis for its strength. The subjective term 'as appropriate' and other subjective terms are intended to permit the supplier to design his [or her] own quality system to make it efficient and effective."

Epstein said that only the company can determine what is appropriate. "No outside experts can tell a supplier what is appropriate for him [or her] in these types of situations," he said. "It is the supplier's responsibility to interpret the term 'as appropriate' and to make it less subjective in the written quality plan. Subjective terms should not be used in the supplier's quality plan as he [or she] develops it.

Peter Melville said the term "as appropriate" is tied to contract review. "I would define 'as appropriate' as meaning quality plans are required to demonstrate conform-

(continued on next page)

Quality Planning in the Revised ISO 9001

(continued from previous page)

ance to a requirement for each characteristic that affects quality in the product, especially where these characteristics have been reviewed as part of contract review."

Tom Bair also agreed that the term "as appropriate" varies. "What is appropriate for one industry may not be appropriate for another," he said. "It really depends upon the application of what we're talking about with the first consideration being safety."

What Is a Project?

"Project," according to Epstein, refers to a specific program or activity as defined by the company. "Quality plans are usually written to be applicable to a specific project or program or contract whereas the quality manual is intended to apply across the entire supplier's organization or operation."

Quality manuals are now mandatory in the revised ISO 9001 series standard, he said. In those cases where a supplier provides a single product or single service, all of the quality system procedures may be included in the quality manual and the quality plan would be unnecessary, he said.

Quality plans, on the other hand, are not mandatory, he said. "It certainly takes on a stronger emphasis since it has been moved from a note to the normal text," he said. "However, the subjective terms 'timely consideration' and 'as appropriate' provide the leeway and flexibility for the suppliers."

The term "project," according to Peter Melville, refers to projects carried out under contract, such as installation and construction projects carried out on the customer's premises.

According to Dennis Abarca, "project" relates to the product or service being offered by the company. "It could be the development of a product," he said.

Bair said that the term "project" may refer to an internal project relating to the quality system. "It could very well mean a project for determining how a total cost- of-quality system would be implemented in every one of the standards of ISO or every one of the elements of a company's quality assurance manual."

Mandatory Planning Activities

Epstein said that the eight activities outlined by the clause only become requirements if they are applicable to the company. "If they are applicable then they are mandatory," Epstein said. "If they don't apply, obviously the supplier does not have to include that element in his [or her] quality plan."

Melville agreed with Epstein that the activities are mandatory if they apply to the company's product or service.

Abarca said that the elements are required if applicable to the product, project, or contract.

(continued on next page)

Quality Planning in the Revised ISO 9001

(continued from previous page)

"If it does not apply because of the nature of the company's product then it needn't be addressed," he said. "Where it's obvious that any of these elements do apply then it becomes a prescriptive requirement."

Abarca said that the eight activities are required if relevant to the product or service. He said that most companies complying with the ISO 9001 series standard probably already are complying with the provisions of the clause.

"However, they may not have been documenting how the requirements for quality have been met," he explained. "You literally have to document how any of these activities have been achieved or integrated into the development process."

Bair said that, in his opinion, the eight activities are not mandatory. "They are illustrative in nature, samples to basically get your thought train going," he said.

4.3 Contract Review

 ISO 9001 REQUIREMENTS

It is important for the supplier to thoroughly understand the customer's needs. Clause 4.3, in Subclause 4.3.1, requires that the supplier establish and maintain documented procedures for contract review and for the coordinating contract review activities.

Clause 4.3 is divided into the following three additional subclauses.

4.3.2 Review

 ISO 9001 REQUIREMENTS

ISO 9001:1987 referred only to a contract. ISO 9001:1994 also includes pre-contract tender arrangements, as well as contract and ordering requirements.

In Clause 3 Definitions, the standard defines the terms "tender" and "contract; accepted order." A tender is an "offer made by a supplier in response to an invitation to satisfy a contract award to provide product." A contract or accepted order are "agreed requirements between a supplier and customer transmitted by any means."

The subclause and the definition thus takes into account verbal orders. In these situations, the "supplier shall ensure that the order requirements are agreed before their acceptance."

The basic requirements of the review process are the following:

● Contract requirements are adequately defined and documented
● Any requirements that differ from those in the contract or tender are resolved
● The supplier is capable of meeting the contract requirements.

4.3.3 Amendment to contract

ISO 9001 REQUIREMENTS

Subclause 4.3.3 focuses specifically on contract amendments and calls on the supplier to identify how amendments to contracts are made and "correctly transferred to the functions concerned" within the organization.

4.3.4 Records

ISO 9001 REQUIREMENTS

Subclause 4.3.4 requires suppliers to maintain records of contract review.

ISO 9000-2 GUIDANCE

The contract review process steps are:

- Review the contract
- Achieve agreement
- Discuss results of contract review
- Discuss draft quality plan (if existing).

The contract review procedure should have the following features:

- An opportunity for all interested parties to review the contract
- A verification checklist
- A method for questioning the contract requirements and addressing the questions
- A draft quality plan
- Provision for changing the contract.

ISO 9004-1 GUIDANCE

ISO 9004-1, *Clause 7.0, Quality in Marketing*, discusses the role of the marketing function in establishing quality requirements for the product. Marketing should first determine the need for a product or service, define the market demand accurately, determine customer requirements, and communicate these requirements clearly within the company.

ISO 9004-1 emphasizes the importance of considering requirements for all elements of the total product, whether hardware, software, processed materials or services. The marketing function should also ensure that all relevant organizational functions be capable of meeting the requirements.

These product requirements can be detailed in a statement or outline of product requirements, which are translated into "a preliminary set of specifications as the basis for subsequent design work." This is also known as a product brief. A product brief may include the following elements:

- Performance characteristics (e.g., environmental and usage conditions and reliability)
- Sensory characteristics (e.g., style, color, taste, smell)
- Installation configuration or fit
- Applicable standards and statutory regulations
- Packaging
- Quality assurance/verification.

The marketing function should establish an "information monitoring and feedback system…" to analyze the quality of a product or service.

CLAUSE 4.3: CONTRACT REVIEW

Contract review is another area that is often poorly handled. The requirement is hardly onerous or unreasonable. The principal elements of contract review activity are the following:

- The scope of the contract is clearly defined
- The requirements are adequately documented
- Any variations are identified and resolved
- The capability to fulfill the contract exists:
- Technically: the skills exist in-house or can be acquired
- Financially: the work can be done for the price
- Delivery: the work can be delivered according to requirements
- Amendments to the contract are effectively handled.

A subclause that is new in the 1994 standard, Subclause 4.3.3, requires that there is either a new procedure addressing contract amendment or that the existing procedure is updated to provide for the appropriate distribution of change orders.

— The Victoria Group

4.4 Design Control

The essential quality aspects of a product—such as safety, performance and dependability—are established during the design and development phase. Thus, deficient design can be a major cause of quality problems. ISO 9001:1994 establishes separate requirements for design review and design verification. The 1994 version includes the following subclauses:

4.4.1 General

4.4.2 Design and Development Planning

4.4.3 Organizational and Technical Interfaces

4.4.4 Design Input

4.4.5 Design Output

4.4.6 Design Review

4.4.7 Design Verification

4.4.8 Design Validation

4.4.9 Design Changes

4.4.1 General

 ISO 9001 REQUIREMENTS

The general requirement is for suppliers to establish and maintain documented procedures to control and verify product design to ensure that it meets specified requirements.

4.4.2 Design and Development Planning

 ISO 9001 REQUIREMENTS

The supplier shall develop design plans for each design activity. The plans should define each activity and assign the responsibility to qualified personnel who have adequate resources. Design plans should be updated, as necessary.

 ISO 9000-2 GUIDANCE

Design activities should be sufficiently specific and detailed to permit effective verification. Planning procedures should take into account:

- Sequential and parallel work activities
- Design verification activities
- Evaluating the safety, performance and dependability incorporated in the product design
- Product measurement, test and acceptance criteria
- Assignment of responsibilities.

4.4.3 Organizational and Technical Interfaces

 ISO 9001 REQUIREMENTS

Design input can come from a variety of sources. The responsibilities and authorities of these sources must be defined, documented, coordinated and controlled. The basic requirements include the following:

- Identify the interfaces between different groups
- Document, transmit and regularly review the necessary information.

 ISO 9000-2 GUIDANCE

To function effectively, the information procedure should establish the following:

- What information should be received and transmitted
- Identification of senders and receivers

- Purpose of information
- Identification of the transmittal mechanism
- Document transmittal records to be maintained.

4.4.4 Design Input

 ISO 9001 REQUIREMENTS

Design inputs are usually in the form of product performance specifications or product descriptions with specifications. The requirements include the following:

- Identify all design input requirements pertinent to the product
- Review the selection for adequacy
- Resolve incomplete, ambiguous or conflicting requirements.

Input requirements also include applicable statutory and regulatory requirements. Also, design input "shall take into consideration the results of any contract review activities."

 ISO 9000-2 GUIDANCE

A *design description document* can serve as a definitive reference throughout the design process. It should quantify all requirements as much as possible, with details agreed to between the customer and supplier. The document should identify design aspects, materials, and processes that require development, including prototype testing.

4.4.5 Design Output

 ISO 9001 REQUIREMENTS

Design outputs are the final technical documents used throughout the process, from production through servicing. They can include drawings, specifications, instructions, software and servicing procedures.

The requirement is to document design output "in terms that can be verified and validated against design-input requirements." This wording is more generic and less restrictive than the wording in ISO 9001:1987, which reads "in terms of requirements, calculations and analyses." The design output must:

- Meet design input requirements
- Contain or reference acceptance criteria
- Identify design characteristics crucial to safety
- Include a review of design output documents before release

4.4.6 Design Review

ISO 9001 REQUIREMENTS

In ISO 9001:1994, design review is now a separate subclause. The standard requires formal documented reviews of design results. Participants at the design reviews shall include both representatives from all functions concerned with the design stage and any other specialized personnel, as required. As with most every clause, Subclause 4.4.5 requires the supplier to maintain records of the design reviews.

4.4.7 Design Verification

ISO 9001 REQUIREMENTS

The requirement of Subclause 4.4.7 is to establish a design verification plan to ensure that the design output meets design input requirements.

In a Note to Subclause 4.4.7, the standard lists various design verification activities, such as alternative calculations, comparisons with proven designs, tests and demonstrations, and reviewing the design stage documents before release.

ISO 9000-2 GUIDANCE

In most cases, two or more of these measures are used. Design reviews and/or type-testing may be a regulatory requirement. Design verification should involve personnel independent of those who did the work under review.

ISO 9000-2 includes many questions that the design review can address. Some of these include the following:

● Do design reviews satisfy all specified requirements?
● Are product design and processing capabilities compatible?
● Are safety considerations covered?
● Are the materials and/or facilities appropriate?
● Are components or service elements standardized?
● Are purchasing, production, installation, inspection and testing plans technically feasible?
● Has software been validated, authorized and verified?
● Where qualification tests have been performed, were the conditions representative of actual use?

4.4.8 Design Validation

ISO 9001 REQUIREMENTS

ISO 9001:1994 includes a separate subclause on design validation. Unlike design verification, which matches the design output to input requirements, design validation ensures that the product conforms to defined user needs and/or requirements.

In a Note, the subclause emphasizes that validation may take place not only on the final product but may be necessary at earlier stages, and multiple validations may be necessary if there are different intended uses of the product. Thus, in addition to the end product, there may be major product components that can be validated from the customer's point of view.

4.4.9 Design Changes

ISO 9001 REQUIREMENTS

Designs may be changed or modified for many reasons. The requirement is for authorized personnel to identify, document, review and approve all design changes and modifications before their implementation.

ISO 9000-2 GUIDANCE

Design changes in one component should be evaluated for their effect on the overall product. Sometimes, improving one characteristic may have an unforeseen adverse influence on another. The new design output should be communicated to all concerned and the changes documented.

ISO 9004-1 GUIDANCE

Clause 8.0, Quality in Specification and Design, discusses the specification and design function in detail. The overall design function should "result in a product that provides customer satisfaction at an acceptable price that gives a satisfactory financial return for the organization." The product must be "producible, verifiable, and controllable under the proposed production, installation, commissioning, or operational conditions."

The topics covered in Clause 8.0 include the following:

- Contribution of specification and design to quality
- Design planning and objectives (defining the project)
- Product testing and measurement
- Design review
- Design qualification and validation
- Final design review and production release
- Market readiness review
- Design change control
- Design requalification

● Configuration management in design.

These topics expand on subjects covered in ISO 9001. The results of the final design review should be "appropriately documented in specifications and drawings which then form the design baseline." The quality system should provide for a market readiness review to determine "whether the organization has the capability to deliver the new or redesigned product."

Regarding design change control, the quality system should provide a procedure for "controlling the release, change and use of documents that define the design input and the design baseline (output), and for authorizing the necessary work" to implement changes throughout the product cycle.

ISO 9004-1 stresses the need for "periodic re-evaluation" of the product to ensure that the design is still valid compared to all specified requirements.

A ROAD MAP FOR DESIGN CONTROL

"Design output meets design input," sums up the entire intent of the design requirements. Clause 4.4 can be met following this suggested road map:

1. Plan what is to be done.
2. Document that plan.
3. Assign someone to review the contract and document the designated person.
4. Create an input specification that includes "acceptance criteria."
5. Follow up as progress is made and make sure that the plan is still being followed.
6. Review how the system is working with the involved employees and document the progress. Perform design reviews at previously defined stages in the evolution of the design.
7. At the end of the task, make sure the output matches the input.
8. Conduct tests and keep records. Do these in accordance with the "acceptance criteria" in step (4) above.
9. Make sure that a good method of tracking changes is in place and that everyone understands the rationale for all changes made.

Design Validation

The 1994 version of the standard includes, in Subclause 4.4.8, a requirement for design validation. The standard makes a distinction between verification and validation. The software engineering profession, for example, has long made this distinction. There is a recognition that much in process design verification may well have little direct linkage to the defined requirements. Thus it is possible to have a design project that has been successful in every verification phase, but that fails to meet the user requirements in any way. The introduction of this new requirement is going to cause some design organizations to rethink some of their strategies. For most it will probably require some reorganization of test methodologies, even if there is no actual increase in the amount of testing being performed.

Design Changes

The 1994 version of Subclause 4.4.9 calls for approving changes and modifications "before their implementation." One important consideration for companies is to provide the necessary levels of authorization to allow for implementing essential changes or modifications quickly to meet production or customer needs.

— The Victoria Group

Does Design Control Apply to Process Design?

By: **Joseph A. Chiaramonte**, Senior Staff Engineer, Underwriters Laboratories, Inc.
Jeffrey P. Tuthill, President, EC Technical Compliance
William J. Deibler, II, Partner, Software Systems Quality Consulting
Serge E. Gaudry, Senior Consultant, FED-PRO, Inc.

Question

Do the requirements of ISO 9001 *Clause 4.4, Design Control*, apply strictly to product design or do they also apply to process design? If process design falls within the scope of Clause 4.4, can the requirements be used for service companies or companies that employ continuous processes and that typically seek registration to ISO 9002?

Answer

Three of four experts agreed that Clause 4.4 also applies to process design and that it may be applicable to the service industry and to companies that employ continuous processes such as those in the chemical industry.

Establishing Design Verification

Joseph A. Chiaramonte said Subclause 4.4.2 addresses "each ... activity" with respect to design and development planning. "Suppliers of hardware may use existing processes in the design of new products, or they may design new processes for existing products," he said. "In all cases, the supplier must determine the points at which verification functions must be established throughout design and development activities."

According to Chiaramonte, in certain contractual situations such as a government contract for military parts, the contract may specify which processes must be baselined and certified. Design verification functions, however, might still be established on the basis of partially manufactured product parameters at various points during critical processes. "Alternatively, process parameters may be used to form the basis for such verification points," he said.

The requirement clearly applies to hardware suppliers, he said, but it also applies to planning design and development activities that are used to produce services, software, or processed materials. "Unless contractual requirements prescribe specific verification points in the design process, the supplier must establish them on the basis of the relevant design input/output criteria, process/product complexity and other related factors or requirements," Chiaramonte explained.

Clause 4.4 as Guidance in Process Control

Jeffrey P. Tuthill said Clause 4.4 may be used as guidance in process control. He said that Subclause 4.4.1, *General*, specifically references the control and verification in the design of product. "A company is obligated to plan, document and control its processes in accordance to Clause 4.9 in an ISO 9001 quality system, but using Clause 4.4 as supplemental guidance is appropriate," he explained.

(continued on next page)

Does Design Control Apply to Process Design?

(continued from previous page)

Tuthill said it is unlikely that a registrar would rely on Clause 4.4 to assess process design in a company unless the operation is part of the design and development functions. "In this case the audit body may overlook the product design stipulation in *Design Control, General* and make use of Subclauses 4.4.1 through 4.4.6 in the assessment," he said. He said that all companies should implement the "best achievable" quality system. "Regardless of particular company organization, it is wise to consider all of Clause 4.4 in the structure and documentation of any design discipline—whether it be product or process," he said.

ISO 9004-3

William J. Deibler, II said that process design falls within the scope of Clause 4.4 to the extent that production engineering provides input to, or controls, product design, and that process is integral to the product offering. He said that Clause 4.2 suggests that "identification and acquisition of ... processes" are activities that should be addressed by the quality system, but it makes no mention of process design. "This ambiguity about the correct position of process design is addressed in *ISO 9004-3, Quality management and quality system elements—Part 3: Guidelines for processed materials* that consistently attempts to replace 'product' with 'product and process,'" he said.

Deibler said that ISO 9004-3 uses the term "design development" to include development of a process design that meets product requirements. "Other paragraphs in the standard emphasize the need for process as well as product reviews during the design development stages," he said.

Process Networking

Serge E. Gaudry said that Clause 4.4 applies strictly to product design and does not address process design issues. That, however, changes in the 1994 standard. "The key here is the insertion of the Design Review clause in ISO 9001:1994. This implies that documented reviews of the design results be planned and conducted," according to Gaudry. He said that ISO 9000-1 makes it clear that a quality system under ISO 9001 or 9002 must take process networking into consideration during the product design phase.

"Specifically, the organization must highlight the main processes associated with the product design issue," he said. "ISO 9000-1 further states that each process should have an owner in the organization with overall responsibilities and authority to handle interfacing within the organization. One can easily draw the conclusion that this process ownership and assignment of responsibilities applies to every aspect of the quality system."

He said that the ISO 9000 series standards are based on the premise that all work is ultimately accomplished by processes and that every process has inputs that generate results termed "outputs of the process." "The concept of a process as defined in ISO 9000-1 applies equally to 9001 and 9002," he explained. "Under the new revisions these concepts can be utilized by those seeking 9002 registration."

Subclause 4.4.8 Design Validation

By   **Harvey S. Berman**, Manager of Corporate Quality and Reliability, UL
     Michael P. Enders, Principal, American Quality Resources
     Jeffry J. Omelchuck, Principal, International Quality Associates
     Chuck Rhodes, Executive Director, Management Resource Group

Question

Clause 4.4.8 Design Validation of ISO 9001:1994 states: "Design validation shall be performed to ensure that product conforms to defined user needs and/or requirements." With the addition of this clause in the 1994 version of the standard, will it be necessary to make changes to the design, engineering, or the quality system?

Answer

QSU's panel of experts agreed that many companies already comply with the requirements of Clause 4.4.8. However, to be in compliance some companies will have to make changes to the way they bring new products to market.

Moderator Harvey S. Berman said that most companies should have no difficulty meeting the requirement because they already perform design validation.

"We were typically looking at validation as a last step in the verification process," he said. "I don't think [the change] is going to have much of an impact."

He defined validation as ensuring that the product conforms to a defined user need. "If you're not going to do that in your design then you're taking a shot on manufacturing something that no one needs," he said. Berman said that the biggest challenge for most companies will be revising their quality manuals to reflect the added requirement.

Michael P. Enders agreed that many companies already perform design validation in the course of bringing a new product to market, but they often bypass the validation step when improving on an existing design, he said.

This practice may result in a number of disputes between ISO 9000 registrars and clients. "I guess my experience is if a company had the option of comparing a new design to an old design against sending it out for testing," he said, "they'd opt for the first choice because it's far less expensive."

Enders said the disagreements most likely will revolve around whether a design has sufficiently changed to warrant additional testing.

The 1987 version of the standard not only gave companies the option of performing design validation, but gave them several options for performing it. The 1994 version mandates that validation take the form of physical testing. "It seems on the surface that some of the flexibility is removed from the new standard," he said. "It definitely sounds to me like they've broken it out from the theoretical design verification and put it into the empirical actual testing of product."

Jeffry J. Omelchuck agreed that the impact will vary from company to company. "In

(continued on next page)

Design Validation

(continued from previous page)

general, if the design process had a validation step in it, then there may not be any kind of addition or change required," he said. He said the revision focuses more attention on the need to subject prototypes to testing. The critical question that must be asked is: "Does it actually meet user requirements?" he said.

Chuck Rhodes said problems will arise for companies that have not clearly identified user needs in the past.

"Some companies have commercialization processes well in place. Other organizations have nothing but intuitive processes," he said. "They should not underestimate the complexity of this activity because it affects all departments in an organization."

Rhodes predicted that it will be necessary for many companies to formalize their procedures for validating designs, and that the validation will have to be carried out earlier in the design process for many companies that already include it as a step in bringing new products to market. "What it really means is that you cannot really validate a design until you understand the ultimate need that the product is going to satisfy," he said. "This will give reinforcement to the original identification of the need."

4.5 Document and Data Control

Clause 4.5 covers procedures to control documents. ISO 9001:1994 has added "data" to the title of the clause. A Note to Subclause 4.5.1 emphasizes that document and data can be in any type of media, such as hard copy or electronic media.

4.5.1 General

ISO 9001 REQUIREMENTS

The supplier shall establish and maintain procedures to control all documents and data. These can include external documents such as standards and customer drawings.

ISO 9000-2 GUIDANCE

Document control applies to all documents and/or computer records pertinent to design, purchasing, production, quality standards, inspection of materials and internal written procedures. Internal written procedures describe the following:

- How documentation for these functions should be controlled
- Who is responsible for document control
- What is to be controlled
- Where and when is it to be controlled.

ISO 9004-1 GUIDANCE

ISO 9004-1, Clause 17.0, *Quality Documentation and Records,* offers the following examples of the types of quality documents that require control:

- Drawings
- Specifications
- Inspection procedures and instructions
- Test procedures
- Work instructions
- Operation sheets
- Quality manual and quality plans
- Operational procedures
- Quality system procedures.

It also stresses that "sufficient records be maintained to demonstrate achievement of the required quality and verify effective operation of the quality management system."
ISO 9004-1 gives the following examples of the types of quality records that require control:

- Inspection reports
- Test data
- Qualification reports
- Validation reports
- Audit reports
- Material review reports
- Calibration data
- Quality cost reports.

4.5.2 Document and Data Approval and Issue

ISO 9001 REQUIREMENTS

Documents and data must be reviewed and approved for adequacy before they are issued. To avoid using invalid and/or obsolete documents, companies must establish and make available a master list or similar procedure that identifies the current revision status of the documents. Subclause 4.5.2 also requires that:

- The appropriate documents be available at all relevant locations
- Invalid or obsolete documents are removed or "otherwise assured against unintended use."

ISO 9001:1994 has added to the 1987 version the requirement that "any obsolete documents retained for legal and/or knowledge-preservation purposes are suitably identified."

4.5.3 Document and Data Changes

 ISO 9001 REQUIREMENTS

The basic requirement is to identify changes in documents and/or data and to review and approve the changes. The review and approval process should be performed by the functions/organizations that performed the original review "unless specifically designated otherwise."

Editor's Note: *The intention is to ensure that changes made in documents already issued follow the same approval process as conventional industry practice. This would be a system in which a document is issued by a designated originating activity (department), before it passes through one or more approval stages. These stages may be organizationally in the same department or another department. One situation where waiving the approval process might be acceptable is if a supplier had field-installation responsibilities, and its qualified personnel were empowered to modify a product or practice on the spot, an approval mechanism might not be available or practical.*

 ISO 9000-2 GUIDANCE

Supplier documentation is usually subject to revision. This requirement applies both to internal and external documentation, such as national standards. Organizations should consider the effect that changes in one area may have on other parts of the organization and the actions that should be taken to assess this effect. Other things to keep in mind include:

● Planning the circulation of a change proposal to avoid disruption

● Timing the change's implementation.

CLAUSE 4.5: DOCUMENT AND DATA CONTROL

Poor document control is something that frequently lets companies down, and it is very important. ISO 9001 requires that there be a master list of every document that forms part of the controlled system, so that it is clear as to which specific documents make up that system. The requirement covers all documentation—not merely manuals, procedures and work instructions that relate to the quality system itself. On the other hand, it doesn't include everything. For example, a manager's memo is not typically a "controlled document" within the meaning of the standard.

A master list of documents makes it possible for those using documents to make sure that they have the right one. It is appropriate that a master set of each document on the master list accompany that list. In addition, it is useful that copies of all documents be distributed where they are likely to be used.

Make sure that relevant paperwork and documents are where they are needed for people to do the job right. Put a system in place to ensure that when a document changes, all the old copies are removed to prevent accidental use. Also ensure that, when changes are made, either the original author makes them or someone else who has all the relevant information.

In the 1994 version of Clause 4.5, the requirement that "obsolete documents are promptly removed from all points of issue or use" has been modified to allow for other means of rendering such documents "otherwise assured against unintended use." It is safe to assume that documents can be readily accessible if they are in some way clearly marked as "not current."

For the first time, the standard specifically mentions that 'documents of external origin' must be included within the controlled system. This means customer specifications, national and international specifications, regulatory documents, etc.

— *The Victoria Group*

Document and Data Control Requirements of the ISO 9000 Series Standard

By: **Charles McRobert,** President, Quality Practitioners, Inc.
David Middleton, Vice-President, Excel Partnership, Inc.
Joseph Tiratto, President, Joseph Tiratto and Associates, Inc.

Question

Does ISO 9001, *Clause 4.5, Document and Data Control,* cover all documents in the company or only documents covering product technical information? What are some of the general requirements of this clause?

Answer

The experts agreed that the language used in the clause is drafted broadly. Charles McRobert stressed that "a document is any means of conveying technical information concerning the product or the quality system from the conceptual phase to installation and servicing."

Controlled Documents

The list of controlled documents includes product drawings and specifications, quality manuals, procedures, process sheet specifications, recipes, formulations, purchase orders, product labels, packaging instructions, product rosters, training records, contracts, and inspection and test criteria.

David Middleton noted that the "scope of the quality system should define the service provided within a company's scope of activities." For example, a customs clearance company should include customer notification under its controlled document plan if informing customers of delays is part of that company's scope of activities. In another example, a manufacturer of general engineered products would not need to control documents covering analysis of wage rates since those documents do not directly impact product quality.

Joseph Tiratto noted that guidance on this issue can be found in *ISO 9000-2, Generic guidelines for the application of ISO 9001, ISO 9002 and ISO 9003.* Tiratto said ISO 9000-2 states that document control should include "those documents and/or computer records pertinent to inspection of materials and the supplier's internal written procedures which describe the control of documentation for these functions."

Document Changes

Tiratto noted further that Clause 4.5 of ISO 9001 requires controls for the preparation, handling, issuance and recording of changes to documents. He pointed out that this requirement "applies not only to internal documentation, but also to externally updated documentation."

Middleton pointed out that document control is a common weak link found during third-party audits. He said this problem is usually remedied by identifying "relevant documents" (those that directly impact product or service quality) and by demonstrating document control by date, review status, approval, and master list. For further guidance on the issue, Middleton suggested reading Section 17 of ISO 9004-1.

CLAUSE 4.5.2: WHAT IS AN ACCEPTABLE MASTER LIST?

By: **James Highlands**, President, Management Systems Analysis
Foster Finley, Senior Consultant, Deloitte & Touche
Stephen Hedman, President, Hedman Consulting Services
William E. Cox, President, TQM Consulting

Question

ISO 9001 Subclause 4.5.2, *Document changes/modifications* states: "A master list or equivalent document control procedure identifying the current revision status of documents shall be established and be readily available to preclude the use of invalid and/or obsolete documents." What is an acceptable master list?

Answer

The panel of experts agreed that an acceptable master list can be as simple as a handwritten document or as sophisticated as a computerized database. It all depends on the size and dynamics of the company.

Master Lists versus Alternatives

According to James Highlands the contents of a master list of documents are always determined by the document control procedure used. "In some cases a master list is not required when alternative provisions are established in the document control procedure," he said. In reading the requirements, many companies overlook the option of using an equivalent procedure in place of a master list.

Suppliers use master lists as references or indexes to procedures manuals, he said. Such lists typically include: the identifier or number of the document, title, latest revision level, and occasionally the date of issue. It may also include the distribution of the document or the identification of the approving authority for the document. "The key here is [deciding] what alternative controls are applied by the document control procedure," Highlands said.

One example of an alternative control is the procedure for drawings that are controlled by most engineering departments, he said. "A master file of drawings is maintained, which identifies the revisions made or references an engineering change notice that describes the changes."

When the master drawing is revised, it is reviewed and approved by the project manager and is issued to holders of the controlled drawing as identified on a distribution list. Distribution is accompanied by a receipt that must be signed by the recipient and returned with the obsolete drawings. "The number of permutations here is endless," he said. "The true test is whether an individual who is not familiar with the system can read the document control procedure and determine the latest revisions of each document and who holds copies. Whatever data on the master list needed to perform this activity is required."

(continued on next page)

What Is an Acceptable Master List?

(continued from previous page)

Types of Lists

Foster Finley said the master list serves two purposes: It meets ISO 9000 series require-ments for document control, and it serves as a barometer of the breadth and penetra-tion of a company's quality management systems documentation. "It may be in the form of a comprehensive, real-time computer database," he said. "Or it may entail multiple, independent lists."

Finley said an acceptable master list can be any list that identifies documents and current revisions for the quality management system. The creation of such documents, however, is not always feasible.

"The scope, complexity, and sophistication of the company must be established," Finley said. "Along one end of the continuum might be a small company with a very limited product offering. Representative of the other extreme would be a large, vertically integrated manufacturer with an extensive product offering." Preferred vehicles for identifying revisions to first and second-tier documentation include a table of contents, cross reference or other matrix, according to Finley.

"The most robust approach to the creation of acceptable master lists is to catalog all quality management systems documentation but to allow segmentation of the lists in any logical manner that suits the company's needs," Finley said. "This alternative gives companies the flexibility to create sub lists that are easier to use and maintain."

Another approach is to create and maintain a documentation matrix or master list containing all company documents and their current revision levels. "While this would undoubtedly satisfy the standard, it is not a specific requirement," he said. "Endeavoring to accomplish this in a large, complex organization might undermine the intent of the standard. Such a list might become obsolete so quickly and prove so cumbersome to use that it loses its effectiveness as a source for control."

Where companies rely on computerized databases to catalog all quality management system documentation, Finley said, the focus may shift from preventing inadvertent use of documents to preventing misuse.

Formats for Master Lists

Stephen Hedman agreed that a master list must also be easy to understand and effective in preventing obsolete documents from being used when manufacturing a product. Hedman said one system for a small eight-person metal stamping shop assigns an issue letter to each section of a controlled document blueprint and index page.

When the documents are updated, he said, the revision is accompanied with an updated index page. The index page is maintained in a file labeled "current docu-ments." Such a system, he said, probably would not work in an organization with complex processes.

(continued on next page)

What Is an Acceptable Master List?

(continued from previous page)

Hedman said that he was most impressed by a network system that controlled all documents electronically. "Anyone could access the document library to check on document status, but only one or two could access to make changes," he explained.

William E. Cox suggests using the table of contents of a procedures manual to keep tabs on documents. "By adding columns for the latest document revision number and date, a user of the manual can readily tell what the most recent revision should be," he said. "A distribution list for the procedures in the manual can be added at the end of the table of contents." Cox said that the table of contents should also be considered as a controlled document and assigned a separate revision number and date. "Knowing what the latest version should be, this tells the user at a glance whether the contents of a manual are up-to-date," he said.

"On the other hand, if each document has a unique, different distribution list that can be incorporated into the procedure itself as a separate section, any procedure revision will then be distributed to the holders of controlled copies of the procedure," he explained. Cox added, however, that this practice should be avoided unless there is a "strong" business reason for each document to have a unique distribution list.

What the Master List Should Include

In general, Cox said, a master list should include the following: title of each controlled document, holders of each controlled document, and the current revision number and date. He said that controlled documents should include quality manuals, work procedures, detailed work instructions, product specifications, related software files, quality standards, quality plans, inspection instructions, and engineering, assembly and installation drawings.

Resolve Acceptability Before Audit

In any case, Foster Finley said companies should resolve any potential issues over the acceptability of the master list prior to an audit. "The decision of a competent registrar will be guided by the overall effectiveness of a document control procedure in preventing use of non-applicable documents," he said.

Use of a master list alone does not preclude the inadvertent use of non-applicable documents, Finley said. "It merely serves as a key element in a document control procedure. Therefore the acceptability of any master list must be judged relative to its ability to serve this purpose."

4.6 Purchasing

4.6.1 General

ISO 9001 REQUIREMENTS

The basic purchasing requirement is to establish and maintain documented procedures to ensure that the purchased product conforms to specified requirements.

ISO 9000-2 GUIDANCE

Planned and adequately controlled purchasing procedures ensure that purchased subcontracted products, including services, conform to specified requirements. Suppliers should establish effective working relationships and feedback systems with all subcontractors.

ISO 9004-1 GUIDANCE

Clause 9.0, Quality in Purchasing discusses procurement quality in detail. The section states that "purchases become part of the organization's product and directly affect the quality of its product." A procurement quality program should include the following elements:

- Requirements for specification, drawings, and purchase orders
- Selection of acceptable subcontractors
- Agreement on quality assurance
- Agreement on verification methods
- Provisions for settling disputes
- Receiving inspection planning and control
- Quality records related to purchasing.

4.6.2 Evaluation of Subcontractors

ISO 9001 REQUIREMENTS

The requirements for the evaluation of subcontractors include the following:

- Evaluate and select subcontractors on the basis of their ability to meet requirements
- Establish and maintain records of acceptable subcontractors
- Define the type and extent of control exercised over subcontractors.

ISO 9000-2 GUIDANCE

The supplier may employ several methods for choosing satisfactory subcontractors, including the following:

- Reviewing previous performance in supplying similar products (including services)
- Satisfactory assessment of an appropriate quality system standard by a competent body
- Assessment of the subcontractor by the supplier to an appropriate quality system standard.

The supplier's quality records should be sufficiently comprehensive to demonstrate the ability of subcontractors to meet requirements. Factors can include the following:

● Product compliance with specified requirements
● Total cost for the supplier
● Delivery arrangements
● Subcontractor's own quality systems
● Performance of subcontractors (should be reviewed at appropriate intervals).

4.6.3 Purchasing Data

 ### ISO 9001 REQUIREMENTS

The requirements for purchasing data include the following:

● Clearly and specifically describe the product ordered in the purchasing document, including where applicable:
● Type, class, style, grade, or other precise identification
● Title or other positive identification, and applicable issue of specifications, drawings, process requirements, inspection instructions, and other relevant data, including requirements for approval or qualification of product, procedures, process equipment and personnel
● Title, number, and issue of the quality system standard that applies to the product
● Review and approve purchasing documents for adequacy of specified requirements.

 ### ISO 9000-2 GUIDANCE

The purchasing data should define the technical product requirements to the subcontractor to ensure the quality of the purchased product. This can be done by reference to other applicable information such as national or international standards or test methods.

Companies should assign responsibility for reviewing and approving purchasing data to appropriate personnel.

4.6.4 Verification of Purchased Product

 ### ISO 9001 REQUIREMENTS

This requirement takes into account the following two situations for verifying that subcontracted product conforms to specifications:

● Where the supplier verifies purchased product at the subcontractor's premises
● Where the supplier's customer or representative, by contract, verifies at the subcontractor's premises and the supplier's premises.

In the first situation, the supplier "shall specify verification arrangements and the method of product release in the purchasing documents."

In the second situation, the standard adds two caveats:

- Verification can't be used by the supplier as evidence of effective quality control by the subcontractor;
- Verification by the customer doesn't absolve the supplier of responsibility for providing acceptable product nor any subsequent rejection by the customer.

ISO 9004-1 GUIDANCE

In Clause 9.0, ISO 9004-1 notes that agreements with the supplier "may also include the exchange of inspection and test data" to further quality improvements. A clear agreement on verification methods can "minimize difficulties in the interpretation of requirements as well as inspection, test, or sampling methods."

CLAUSE 4.6: PURCHASING

The 1987 standard's use of the words *purchaser, supplier* and *subcontractor* confused some readers. The wording has been changed in both ISO 9001:1994 and ISO 9004-1:1994. The *purchaser* was the person or organization buying the goods or services produced within the system under review. This person is now called the customer throughout the standard.

The *supplier* is the company or organization whose quality system is under discussion. The *subcontractor* is the vendor, supplier, or person from whom the company obtains materials, services, or personnel impacting the product or service the company sells.

The purchaser was the party **now** referred to as the customer. The supplier is **always** the company whose quality system is under review. The subcontractor is **always** the person from whom the supplier is buying product. (Refer to Table 3-1.)

On-site Verification

Where the supplier elects to carry out on-site verification at a subcontractor's premises, the standard requires that the verification arrangements and the method of release be specified in the purchasing documents. This does not require detailed descriptions. It could be a reference to a separate document that was independently supplied, or to a published product specification that was to be used, etc.

There remains the option for 'customer verification' which can take place either at the subcontractors' site or at the supplier's site, but as the standard makes crystal clear, acceptance by the customer at either location does not remove the supplier's liability to provide acceptable product, nor does it preclude the customer from subsequently rejecting that same product at a later date.

— The Victoria Group

SUBCLAUSE 4.6.2: ASSESSING SUBCONTRACTORS

By: **Ronald Muldoon**, Quality Consultant, Brown & Root, Inc.
Stephen Nicholas, President, Experts in ISO 9000, Ltd.
Ralph D. Schmidt, Director, Thornhill USA
Kevin Drayton, Principal, Senior Consultant, Kevin Drayton Associates
Ian Durand, President of Service Process Consulting, Inc.
Dennis Arter, Owner, Columbia Audit Resources

Question

ISO 9001 *Subclause 4.6.2, Evaluation of Subcontractors* states: "The supplier shall evaluate and select subcontractors on the basis of their ability to meet subcontract requirements including quality system and any specific quality assurance requirements." What does "evaluation" mean? How does a supplier set up an effective, documented evaluation system?

Note: In the 1987 version of the standard, the term used was "assessment." In this context, the terms evaluation and assessment are synonymous. ISO 8402, in Clause 4.6, uses the term "Quality evaluation." ISO 8402 states that "quality evaluation" may be used for qualification, approval, registration, certification or accreditation purposes.

Answer

Ian Durand noted that "in the context of ISO 9001, the evaluation has a scope that extends beyond quality requirements to include all requirements the supplier chooses to place on its selected subcontractor" list. He said that quality system and quality assurance requirements noted in the first sentence of Subclause 4.6.2 could include service aspects such as "on-time delivery performance in addition to technical quality history."

In addition, Durand said the supplier might consider other factors such as the financial security, market position, interpersonal skills, and customer satisfaction policies of the subcontractor.

Types of Subcontractors

Ronald Muldoon said the assessment of subcontractors depends on how critical the procured item and the nature of the relationship is between the supplier and subcontractor—that is, whether it is long-term or periodic. "For long-term relationships the records should concentrate on the performance and the effectiveness of corrective actions to prevent recurrence of nonconformances," he said.

"For periodic relationships, the assessment should concentrate on the capability to produce what is required to meet that particular purchase order." Muldoon said that, "in addition to assessing the subcontractor's ability to meet the quality requirements, [the supplier must assess] the subcontractor's ability to meet the technical, commercial, and schedule requirements of the contract."

Ralph D. Schmidt recommends that suppliers make a list of subcontractors and divide
(continued on next page)

Assessing Subcontractors

(continued from previous page)

the list in two—those critical to the quality of the supplier's services and those having minor or no impact on the supplier's quality. For example, he said, vehicles used as rental cars are critical to quality, but the products used to clean them are probably not.

Schmidt said subcontractors on the critical list should be given written quality requirements. "The ideal is a survey for them to fill out to determine their ability to conform," he said. "Critical subcontractors not complying with your needs should be replaced with ones that are capable. If the subcontractor is the only one of its kind, visits, discussion, and audits are in order to assure conformance. You may have to invest money and training in the subcontractor to assure your quality."

He said that a supplier-receiving system is "vital" to tracking subcontractor performance. The system should keep track of receipts, deviations, rejections, complaints, test reports, and certificates of compliance, which in turn become part of the subcontractor performance file. "Subcontractors may furnish suppliers their quality manual for review and may be certified or registered under a system," Schmidt said, adding that in such cases supplier audits may be waived if registration is pertinent and the manual covers critical subcontract aspects.

Developing a Supplier Validation and Verification System

To satisfy this clause of the standard economically, Kevin Drayton suggests companies should have a supplier validation and verification system in place. The system must ensure that the supplier has chosen a company that is capable of producing product to its requirements and that the company has an auditable, documented quality system as part of its overall business strategy.

Drayton said the validation and verification system typically includes surveys, on-site audits, capability studies performed by the subcontractor and verified by the supplier, and a review of products and processes via statistical techniques.

"It is quite obvious that when a system such as the one described here is implemented, the objective evidence of the subcontractor's ability to meet requirements is quite easy to gather and maintain," Drayton said.

Methods of Assessment

There are many ways to assess subcontractor capabilities. According to Stephen Nicholas, examples include the following:

- Completion of a quality assurance questionnaire
- Issuance of a certificate of compliance or analysis
- Past experience
- Testing and approval of a prototype or sample
- Provision and approval of a quality plan prior to contract award
- An audit of the subcontractor's quality system

(continued on next page)

Assessing Subcontractors

(continued from previous page)

● A requirement for ISO 9000 registration.

"The depth and sophistication of the assessment depends upon a value analysis of the goods or services being purchased and often results in the subcontractor's receiving a quality grading or rating from the supplier," Nicholas explained. "This grading may differ for different goods or services and will be subject to upgrading or downgrading throughout the supply contract." He said the type and extent of quality records that should be maintained should be proportional to the sophistication of the assessment and its frequency. The riskiest items contain the most comprehensive records, he said.

"Where subcontractor problems are encountered, the corrective action may be to downgrade the subcontractor assessment pending further investigation or audit, or to call in the subcontractor so the supplier and subcontractor may develop a joint corrective action to eliminate the nonconformance," Nicholas said. "This partnership approach may lead to the upgrading of the subcontractor on the database and a reduction in the need for the supplier to assess the subcontractor so vigorously or frequently."

Dennis Arter said other possible assessment methods could include a listing in a register for a particular product line or written responses to a questionnaire. He said the process of evaluating potential suppliers must be documented in an in-house procedure and the results recorded. He noted that this record usually takes the form of an "Approved Subcontractor List," but it may be as simple as a notation or signature in the vendor's file folder.

Arter said suppliers must have a program for keeping approved subcontractors on and off a list. Arter said subcontractor performance "needs to be evaluated on a periodic basis." He noted that some subcontractors need an annual evaluation, while others might be evaluated every three years.

Required Documentation to Demonstrate Subcontractor Assessments

The panel gave the following examples of documentation that should be maintained to demonstrate that an adequate assessment has been performed of subcontractors:

● Receiving reports, test reports, specifications, and certificates of compliance
● Copies of complaints, investigations and implemented changes that have been agreed to
● The subcontractor's quality manual, recognitions, audits, third-party registration and scope
● Periodic scheduled subcontractor reviews, internal and on-site.
● Documentation of completed corrective actions as referenced by the audit reports
● Statistical evidence of capability and control
● Periodic assessment of process output and effective implementation of quality plans as supported by the subcontractor ratings program.

(continued on next page)

Assessing Subcontractors

(continued from previous page)

Subcontractors Registered to ISO 9000?

Stephen Nicholas said the clause should not be interpreted to mean that suppliers should be selected purely on the basis of quality or on the basis of their achieving registration to the ISO 9000 series standards. "Suppliers commonly fall into the trap of believing that an ISO 9000 quality system guarantees or even enhances the quality of the product," he warned. The only guarantee of ISO 9000 series registration, he said, is that the subcontractor has a quality system capable of assuring that products consistently will meet specified requirements.

Nicholas said that it is up to the supplier to determine which records must be maintained on the subcontractors, and that decision should take into account whether it is important that the goods failed to meet specified requirements. He said there is no requirement that the supplier audit the subcontractor.

Muldoon agreed that when a company is registered to the ISO 9000 series standards, this does not guarantee that its products meet high quality standards. Rather it assures customers that a contract review has been performed as required by Clause 4.3 of ISO 9001 and 9002. "The review ensures that the subcontractor understands the requirements and has the capability to meet the contractual requirements," he explained. "The subcontractor with an ISO 9000 quality system is also more accustomed to doing front-end planning with the bid, providing documentation, and controlling its [own] subcontractors."

In assessing subcontractors holding ISO 9000 registration, a company should focus on those aspects of the purchase order that have not already been covered by the registration audit, according to Muldoon. This strategy is cost-effective for all parties.

Ralph Schmidt added that although ISO 9000 registration does not guarantee that the product will meet requirements, a list of subcontractors registered under ISO 9001 or ISO 9002 may satisfy a third-party audit.

Guidance for Specific Industries

Joseph Tiratto pointed out that guidance documents helpful in this area have also been prepared for specific industry sectors such as chemicals and software. For example, in *ANSI/ASQC Q90 ISO 9000: Guidelines for use by the chemical and process industries*, an assessment of the subcontractor's ability consistently to meet requirements may be based on the following evidence:

- On-site assessment of subcontractor's quality and/or performance data (current and historical)
- Trials or demonstration in the supplier's laboratories or plant. For example, the supplier may have to rely on inspection and testing when a subcontractor's appraisal is not feasible (i.e. spot purchases of bulk material)
- Documented evidence of successful use in similar processes
- Third-party assessment and registration of the subcontractors quality systems to an acceptable standard.

(continued on next page)

Assessing Subcontractors

(continued from previous page)

Developing a Teaming Relationship

Kevin Drayton said assessment and selection of subcontractors is good business practice, in addition to being a requirement of the ISO 9000 series standards. "Materials-driven businesses have long relied on quantity of subcontractors to make up for poor quality," he said. "Today's marketplace is rapidly changing that philosophy. Time and time again it is proven to be more cost-effective to slim down the number of subcontractors and form what are known as teaming relationships with them."

Drayton defined this relationship as one where both supplier and subcontractor understand and respect their interdependence and inter-reliance. "Rather than the adversarial relationships which characterized the old-style vendor-contractor relationship, businesses who team have quality as a focus and success as a mutual goal," he argued.

"As with all of the clauses, the ISO 9000 standards series is not requiring anything frivolous, expensive, or unnecessary," Kevin Drayton said. "It is simply setting forth a requirement needed to ensure that there is maintained a systematic and effective strategy for consistently meeting the requirements of your customers, both today and tomorrow."

4.7 Control of Customer-Supplied Product

ISO 9001 REQUIREMENTS

The requirement for control of customer-supplied product is to establish and maintain documented procedures for verification, storage and maintenance of customer-supplied products. Products that are lost, damaged or unsuitable must be recorded and reported to the customer. (In the 1987 version, the clause referred to "purchaser-supplied product.")

The standard emphasizes that "verification by the supplier does not absolve the customer of the responsibility to provide acceptable product."

ISO 9000-2 GUIDANCE

Customer-supplied product is any product owned by the customer and furnished to the supplier for use in meeting the requirements of the contract. The supplier accepts full responsibility for the product while in its possession.

Customer-supplied product could be a service, such as the use of a customer's transport for delivery. The supplier should make sure that the service is suitable and that its effectiveness can be documented.

CLAUSE 4.7: CONTROL OF CUSTOMER-SUPPLIED PRODUCT

Customer-supplied product, as referenced in Clause 4.7, refers to items the customer provides to the supplier which are to be incorporated into the product and then returned in final form to the customer. The scope of this clause should not be underestimated. The software house that is supplying a turn-key package to a client, but is incorporating some hardware, printers, modems and network systems that are already in place is in the situation of utilizing "customer supplier product" if any of those items or interfaces for them are delivered to the supplier's site for any purpose. The company that receives packaging from a customer, or even wooden pallets used to ship materials, is handling customer-supplied materials, as is the company whose customer leaves trailers in the supplier's parking lot for loading.

The standard clearly states that the company must ensure that the customer supplier product is up to par. It is the duty of the customer, however, to provide adequate materials, even though the supplier is going to check it out.

Responsibility for Ongoing Maintenance

One area that is often overlooked is the need to identify and define the responsibilities and needs for the support and maintenance of such items. The responsibility for ongoing maintenance activities should be clearly spelled out at the time that customer-supplied product is identified.

— The Victoria Group

4.8 Product Identification and Traceability

In some cases, contracts require the organization to trace specific materials or assemblies throughout the process of their development, through delivery and/or installation. Product (and service) traceability refers to the ability to trace the history, application or location of an item or activity by means of recorded identification.

ISO 9001 REQUIREMENTS

Where appropriate, the supplier shall establish and maintain documented procedures for identifying the product during all stages of production, delivery and installation. To the extent that traceability is a specified requirement, individual product, or batches thereof, must have a unique identification.

ISO 9000-2 GUIDANCE

There are many identification methods, including marking, tagging or documentation, in the case of a service. The identifier should be unique to the source of the operation. Separate identifiers could be required for changes in various aspects of the production process.

Traceability may require identifying specific personnel involved in phases of the operation. This can be accomplished through signatures on serially-numbered documents, for example.

CLAUSE 4.8: PRODUCT IDENTIFICATION AND TRACEABILITY

The key words in this clause are, *"Where, and to the extent that, traceability is a specified requirement..."* The level of required traceability is left to the discretion of the company unless specifically called for under contractual obligations, regulatory requirements or industry norms. Some companies, such as one that manufactures inexpensive pencils, could decide that there is no traceability requirement at all.

This also allows the company some latitude in determining the type of traceability, encompassing, for example, traceability of materials within the factory and finished product traceability to the customer.

Product-identification requirements can also vary widely. They range from identification by serial number and full test and inspection records to virtually no identification at all. Once again, the company must decide, document its decision, and then adhere to it. Companies should realize that if there is an industry norm for identification and traceability, auditors will expect to see that norm being followed. If there is a regulatory requirement, companies are required to follow it.

— The Victoria Group

4.9 Process Control

Preventing problems by controlling the production process is preferable to discovering them at the final inspection. Process control activities often include statistical process control methods, procedures for accepting materials into the process, and the proper maintenance of process equipment and essential materials.

ISO 9001 REQUIREMENTS

The clause requires the supplier to do the following:

- Identify and plan the processing steps needed to produce the product
- Ensure that the processes are carried out under controlled conditions
- Provide documented instructions for work that affects quality
- Monitor and approve necessary processes
- Observe and stipulate relevant criteria for workmanship, where practical
- Maintain equipment to ensure continuing process capability.

The last requirement was not included in the 1987 version. The implication is that where process instrumentation is establishing (controlling) quality, it must be calibrated in the same manner as inspection and test equipment.

ISO 9000-2 GUIDANCE

The adequacy of production process control should take into account the adequacy of the measurement processes. When effective process control depends upon consistent operation of process equipment and essential materials, the supplier should include within the scope of the quality system the proper maintenance of such process equipment and essential materials.

 ## ISO 9004-1 GUIDANCE

Clauses 10.0 and 11.0 in ISO 9004-1 discuss quality of processes and control of processes. This was changed from the 1987 version, which used the word "production." The change is designed to incorporate service businesses as well as manufacturing.

Clause 10.1 discusses planning for controlled production. Controlled conditions include "appropriate controls for materials, approved production, installation and servicing equipment, documented procedures or quality plans, computer software, reference standards/codes, suitable approval of processes, personnel, as well as associated supplies, utilities, and environments."

Clause 10.0 recommends that companies do the following:

- Conduct process capability studies to determine the potential effectiveness of a process
- Develop work instructions that "describe the criteria for determining satisfactory work completion and conformity to specification and standards of good workmanship"
- Verify the quality status of a product, process, software, material or environment
- Verify the capability of production processes to produce in accordance with specifications
- Control and verify auxiliary materials and utilities, "such as water, compressed air, electric power, and chemicals used for processing," where important to quality characteristics.

Clause 11.0 offers guidance in the areas of:

- Material control and traceability
- Equipment control and maintenance
- Special processes
- Documentation of work instructions, specifications and drawings
- Process change control
- Control of the verification status of material and assemblies (see ISO 9001, Clause 4.12)
- Control of nonconforming materials.

 ## ISO 9001 REQUIREMENTS

Special Processes

Unlike the 1994 version, the 1987 version of the standard discussed special processes in a separate subclause (4.9.2). The reference to special processes is now part of Clause 4.9. In a Note, the clause says that "Such processes requiring pre-qualification of their process capability are frequently referred to as special processes." The requirements regarding special processes are the following:

- Continuously monitor special processes by qualified personnel to ensure that requirements are met
- Maintain records for qualified processes, equipment and personnel.

ISO 9000-2 GUIDANCE

ISO 9000-2 emphasizes that all products are produced by processes. Special processes are those whose results cannot be fully verified by subsequent inspection and testing of the product and where processing deficiencies may become apparent only after the product is in use. Special processes are particularly common in producing processed materials. Critical product quality characteristics in this area include the following examples:

- Metal parts (strength, ductility, fatigue life, corrosion-resistance following welding, soldering, etc.)
- Polymerized plastic (dyeability, shrinkage, tensile properties)
- Bakery products (taste, texture, appearance)
- Correctness of financial or legal documents/software.

Special processes may require:

- Comprehensive measurement assurance and equipment calibration
- Statistical process control and special training.

Clause 11.4, Process-control management of ISO 9004-1 notes that process variables should be monitored, controlled and verified at appropriate frequencies to assure:

- Accuracy and variability of equipment used to make or measure the product
- Skill, capability and knowledge of workers
- Accuracy of measurement results and data used to control the process
- Special environments, time, temperature or other factors that affect quality
- Certification records that are maintained for personnel, processes and equipment.

For more information regarding special processes in the chemical industry, see the box on the next page.

CLAUSE 4.9: PROCESS CONTROL

Suitable Maintenance of Equipment

The 1994 standard includes a requirement for "suitable maintenance of equipment to ensure continuing process capability." Many companies already have formal planned maintenance programs and activities, but these have nearly always been left out of the management system. Now they will need to be incorporated. Such a program need not be complex or onerous. The planned maintenance will need to be laid out, the activities defined to a level appropriate to the skills and training of the maintenance staff, and records kept of the work performed.

Where the appropriate equipment is "run until it breaks and then is fixed", then that should be stated. It is, after all, the company's system—not the auditor's. Examples of "run until it breaks" equipment would include process control computers, some forms of automatic test equipment, hand tools and similar items. Where "routine maintenance" is basically operator-driven, such as lubricating and cleaning metal-working equipment, then this activity can now be referenced in work instructions.

The term "suitable" is open to interpretation. The supplier has the absolute right to determine suitability, but a process-knowledgeable auditor equally has the right to question the program that has been defined. The key to the success of this requirement will lie in auditors recognizing that they will have to prove "unsuitability" by providing evidence of adverse effects on deliverable product before a noncompliance can be written up.

Work Instructions

Work instructions, which are referred to in Clause 4.9: Process Control, can take the form of anything from a representative sample to a detailed written document. A work instruction can be a video tape. It could be a model of the work on display by the operator. This is quite common in high-volume electronic manual assembly and can work very well.

It is important to assess the training and skills of employees when evaluating where to make use of work instructions. In determining the use of work instructions, the standard cautions companies to consider "where the absence of such instructions would adversely affect quality." In assessing whether an employee is correctly performing his or her job, there are three possible responses:

- A work instruction exists that details these responsibilities
- Records exist proving the individual was hired with a particular skill; or
- The employee has received on-the-job training; records exist to document the training and to prove it has been performed.

The scope of Clause 4.9 has also been extended to cover servicing activity, so when such work lies within the registered scope of a company, all the requirements of this clause need to be applied to the activity.

— The Victoria Group

Subclause 4.9.2: Special Processes, and Chemical Producers

By: **Ian Durand,** President, Service Process Consulting, Inc.
   Robert W. Belfit, President / Chairman, Omni Tech International, Inc.
   Joseph Tiratto, President, Joseph Tiratto and Associates, Inc.
   Terry Heaps, Project Administrator, QA Services, Vincotte USA, Inc.

Question

Does the reference in Clause 4.9 to special processes encompass all production processes used by chemical producers? Some auditors have affirmed that it does, basing their decision on the interpretation that all processes are "one, large, special process."

Answer

All four experts referred to published industry guidelines in answering this question. The American Society for Quality Control (ASQC) book, *ANSI/ASQC Q90/ISO 9000 Guidelines for Use by the Chemical and Process Industries,* was referenced by three experts.* Two experts referenced European Chemical Industry Council (ECIC) guidelines.

The experts agreed that the reference to special processes in Clause 4.9 could cover all the production processes used by a chemical producer. Bob Belfit, however, said he interprets this clause differently. Belfit suggested that when proceeding through the registration process, a chemical producer should interview potential registrars to ascertain the possible interpretation.

Belfit cited the example of a product that is "manufactured under as much control and testing as possible, but requires the shipment be delayed until the customer has utilized the product in his process, and therefore releases the product for shipment."

Belfit said these special processes are not those generally run on a regular basis, and "therefore the processing parameters and testing parameters have not or cannot be defined precisely to ensure that the product will perform in the customer's application." He concluded that "special processes in the chemical industry imply that it is not possible through process control, in-process testing, or final testing to establish whether the product will perform in the customer's application."

On the other hand, Belfit pointed out, "the production of benzene, styrene, ethyl alcohol, polystyrene, or polyvinyladine chloride are processes that are run on a continuous basis. These are, in reality, commodity products." He said the performance of these products in the customer's application is predictable based on the process controls, the end-process analysis, and/or the product analysis of the final product. "These products are covered by Clause 4.9 in the general statement under process control," Belfit said.

Prevention versus "Find-and-Fix"

Ian Durand noted that examining the central theme of the ISO 9000 series is important

(continued on next page)

Special Processes and Chemical Producers

(continued from previous page)

in interpreting the reference to special processes. He said the overall emphasis of the ISO 9000 series is on "preventing quality problems before they occur, rather than relying on 'find-and-fix' approaches."

For this reason, Durand said, "it is not unusual for registrars to look for, and prefer to find, attention given to controlling all processes that affect the quality of the "total market offering," i.e., both the tangible goods and accompanying services."

Durand noted that "in the real world there are always trade-offs between process control and inspection and testing." He said Clause 4.9, *Process Control*, and 4.10, *Inspection and Testing*, should be considered complementary. In establishing the balance between the two approaches, Durand said such factors as the feasibility of subsequent inspection, the relative effectiveness and costs, and the specific processes and products being considered should be evaluated.

To illustrate, he noted that in some chemical industries, skilled operators assess color, granularity, texture and handling characteristics to complement process control. Durand concluded that assessing relevant factors and establishing a balance between process control and inspection requires working knowledge of the industry and the specific processes and products under consideration.

For example, Durand said that keeping levels of airborne contaminants below specified thresholds during production of solid-state devices is essential. "Complete reliance on inspection and testing is generally not a viable alternative to cleanliness and sanitation during food preparation either," Durand added. He said that both of these examples are types of chemical processes.

Chemical Processes as Special Processes

Terry Heaps also agreed that a case could be made for including special processes as part of all production processes. Heaps noted that "confusion may exist, if any does exist, in the manner with which auditors approach special processes, since there is little difference between the requirements for special processes and process control in the ISO 9001 and ISO 9002 standards."

Heaps said ECIC guidelines state that chemical processes may be considered special processes for a variety of reasons, including the following:

- A characteristic can be measured only during the process and not in the finished product
- A characteristic of the product changes (matures) after the product has been delivered
- The complete characteristics of a product are not known
- There is no satisfactory method of measuring a product characteristic.

"There may be a greater emphasis on the results of the in-process inspection and testing and calibration of the equipment used to make or test the product than may be

(continued on next page)

Special Processes and Chemical Producers

(continued from previous page)

required for a conventional process," Heaps said. Heaps cited other ECIC guidelines concerning customer requirements. For example:

- A specification is agreed for certain characteristics inspected or tested during the process
- Before accepting the contract, the product is evaluated after use in this product or process
- The process and/or the source of raw materials is not changed without the customer's agreement
- Specified statistical process control methods are used.

Special skills, capabilities, and training personnel may be needed to meet any additional quality requirements.

Joseph Tiratto said that "processes of the chemical process industry are generally considered special processes." He cited ECIC guidelines as a reference. In addition, Tiratto cites guidelines in *ANSI/ASQC Q90/ISO 9000: Guidelines for Use by the Chemical and Process Industries*. These guidelines include the following:

- Equipment used to make or measure product
- Operator skill, capability and knowledge
- Environmental factors affecting quality
- Records of qualifications.

* *ANSI/ASQC Q90/ISO 9000: Guidelines for Use by the Chemical and Process Industries* is available from ASQC Quality Press, 611 East Wisconsin Avenue, Milwaukee, Wisconsin 53202, 1-800-952-6587.

CLAUSE 4.9: PROCESS CONTROL - DOES SUITABLE MAINTENANCE OF EQUIPMENT INCLUDE CALIBRATION?

By: **Robert Kennedy**, US National Director of Operations, Quality Mgt. Institute
Larry Bissell, Vice-President of Management Standards International Ltd.
Graham Cartwright, Managing Consultant, MRA International
Ren Verasco, Assistant VP of Quality Management, Chubb Services Corporation

Question

Clause 4.9 Process Control of ISO 9001 states: "The supplier shall identify and plan the production, installation and servicing processes which directly affect quality and shall ensure that these processes are carried out under controlled conditions." A list of controlled conditions includes "suitable maintenance of equipment to ensure continuing process capability." Does this refer to calibration, and if so what type of equipment is affected?

Answer

QSU's panel of experts was split on whether calibration is included by the phrase: "suitable maintenance of equipment."

Moderator Robert Kennedy said that subparagraphs D and G of clause 4.9 both have to do with making certain that nonhuman assets are performing properly. Calibration, he said, is included in so far as it pertains to the truthfulness of measuring or test equipment in use.

"Calibration is done to perform a lie-detector test," he said. Process control is much more encompassing than that. "It really has to do with the equipment functioning properly in all respects, the availability of equipment as specified by whatever their production plan calls for, and the maintenance of that equipment."

Kennedy said that, although calibration is addressed in much greater detail in clause 4.11.2 (B), a company's failure to calibrate equipment properly or to use calibrated equipment may also violate subparagraphs D and G of clause 4.9.

Larry Bissell agreed that calibration is covered to some extent by clause 4.9. Process capability, he said, is the overall variation with the process of the measuring device compared with the acceptable range.

Bissell said that the primary purpose of clause 4.9 is to address the need for preventive maintenance on equipment that is used to produce the product. "An additional impact is on the calibration requirements," he said. "In order to ensure that the equipment continues to be capable ... that same equipment must be maintained in a calibrated state."

He said that clause 4.11.2 requires companies to identify all inspection, measuring and test equipment, including measurement devices that can affect product quality. The pertinent language in clause 4.9 is merely for clarification, he said.

"The primary purpose of [the clause] is to address the need for preventive mainte-

(continued on next page)

Process Control

(continued from previous page)

nance on all equipment, but as a subset of that primary need is the recognition and the need to include calibration of measurement devices on the equipment."

Most companies, he said, will not have to do anything different under the new standards with respect to clause 4.9. "If in fact organizations took the shortcut route or a minimum approach, then they may be impacted," he said.

Graham Cartwright said that calibration is not covered. "It does refer to process equipment," he said. "Definite evidence of the provision of control of maintenance of process plant and equipment is now required."

Cartwright said the evidence would take the form of maintenance procedures, schedules, and records relating to those items that affect process capability.

"Assessors will concentrate on the outputs of these maintenance systems rather than the details of the system itself," he said.

Ren Verasco also said that calibration is addressed primarily in clause 4.11.2.

"In 4.9 we're talking about suitable maintenance, which has to do with preventive maintenance," he said. "Calibration is simply a subset of preventive maintenance."

He said that equipment maintenance refers to all production equipment and that testing equipment, which is covered by clause 4.11.2, deals specifically with the calibration of test and inspection equipment. "While 4.11.2 deals specifically with the calibration of test and inspection equipment, 4.9 talks about the maintenance of production equipment in general," he said.

Kennedy added that it is also important to remember that a given piece of equipment may not be used solely for measurement and test or for production. It is now common for the same piece of equipment to serve both of these functions, according to Kennedy.

4.10 Inspection and Testing

This clause looks at the following three areas of inspection and testing:

- Receiving
- In-process
- Final inspection.

4.10.1 General

 ISO 9001 REQUIREMENTS

In contrast to the 1987 standard, which did not include an explicit requirement for inspection and testing, the 1994 version in Subclause 4.10.1, *General*, states that the "supplier shall establish and maintain documented procedures for inspection and testing activities" to ensure that product requirements are met. This includes documenting the inspection and testing procedures in the quality plan or documented procedures.

This placement in a separate "General" subclause reinforces the need for the procedure.

4.10.2 Receiving Inspection and Testing

 ISO 9001 REQUIREMENTS

Receiving inspection allows suppliers to verify that subcontractors are fulfilling their contractual obligations. The supplier is required to do the following:

- Ensure that incoming products are not used or processed until they have been inspected or otherwise verified
- Verify in accordance with the quality plan and the documented procedures.

 ISO 9000-2 GUIDANCE

This subclause does not imply that incoming items must be inspected and tested if the supplier can use other defined procedures that would fulfill this obligation. These defined procedures should include:

- Provisions for verifying that incoming items, materials or services are accompanied by supporting documentation
- Provision for appropriate action in the event of nonconformities.

 ISO 9004-1 GUIDANCE

Clause 9.7, Receiving Inspection Planning and Control, notes that the "extent to which receiving inspection will be performed should be carefully planned....The level of inspection should be selected so as to balance the costs of inspection against the consequences of inadequate inspection."

Clause 9.8, Receiving Quality Records, stresses that appropriate records should be kept to "ensure the availability of historical data to assess subcontractor performance and quality trends." Companies should also consider maintaining "records of lot identification for purposes of traceability."

4.10.2.3 Release for Urgent Production Purposes

 ISO 9001 REQUIREMENTS

The supplier is required to positively identify and record incoming product to permit recall and replacement, if necessary.

 ISO 9000-2 GUIDANCE

The release of incoming product subject to recall should generally be discouraged as a matter of good quality management practice. There are two exceptions:

- An objective evaluation of quality status and resolution of any nonconformities can still be implemented
- Correction of nonconformities cannot compromise the quality of adjacent, attached or incorporated items.

The supplier's procedures should accomplish the following:

- Define responsibilities and authority of people who may allow incoming product to be used without prior demonstration of conformance to specified requirements
- Explain how such product will be positively identified and controlled in the event that subsequent inspection finds nonconformities.

4.10.3 In-Process Inspection and Testing

ISO 9001 REQUIREMENTS

The supplier is required to do the following:

- Inspect and test product as required by the quality plan or by the documented procedures
- Hold the product until the required inspection and tests have been completed.

The exception is when the product is released under positive recall procedures. The release under positive recall procedures, however, would not preclude the inspection required above.

ISO 9000-2 GUIDANCE

In-process inspection and testing applies to all forms of products, including services. It allows for early recognition of nonconformities.

Statistical control techniques are commonly used to identify product and process trends and prevent nonconformities. Inspection and test results should be objective—including those carried out by production personnel.

ISO 9004-1 GUIDANCE

Clause 12.2, In-Process Verification, lists the following types of verification checks:

- Set-up and first-piece inspection
- Inspection or test by a machine operator
- Automatic inspection or test
- Fixed inspection stations at intervals through the process
- Patrol inspection by inspectors monitoring specified operations.

4.10.4 Final Inspection and Testing

ISO 9001 REQUIREMENTS

Regarding final inspection and testing, the supplier is required to carry out all specified final inspection and tests, including those specified either on receipt of product or in-process. No product shall leave the company until every activity specified in the quality plan or documented procedure has been satisfactorily completed.

ISO 9000-2 GUIDANCE

Final inspection involves the examination, inspection, measurement or testing upon which the final release of a product is based. Release specifications should include all designated release characteristics.

ISO 9004-1 GUIDANCE

Clause 12.3, Finished Product Verification, lists the following two types of final production verification:

- Acceptance inspections or tests
- Product quality auditing.

Acceptance inspections are used to ensure that the "finished product conforms to the specified requirements." Product quality auditing that is performed on representative sample units may be either continuous or periodic.

4.10.5 Inspection and Test Records

ISO 9001 REQUIREMENTS

The supplier is required to establish and maintain records that indicate whether the product has passed inspections and test procedures. The 1994 standard adds the point that when the product fails to pass an inspection and/or test, the procedures in Clause 4.13 for nonconforming product apply. The new standard also requires that records identify the inspection authority responsible for releasing product. It includes a reference to Clause 4.16.

ISO 9000-2 GUIDANCE

Inspection and test records facilitate assessment according to specifications and are useful for regulatory requirements and possible product liability problems.

ISO 9004-1 GUIDANCE

Clause 17.0, Quality records, discusses in detail procedures for establishing and maintaining quality records, including inspection and test records.

Clause 17.3, Quality records control notes that all documentation should be maintained in "facilities that provide a suitable environment to minimize deterioration or damage and to prevent loss."

CLAUSE 4.10: INSPECTION AND TESTING

ISO 9001 quite rightly places a good deal of emphasis on the importance of inspection and test as a means of demonstrating compliance with specifications. Contrary to a commonly held view, the standard does not emphasize inspection and test as a means of controlling quality but as a means of assessing compliance. In terms of evaluating the effectiveness of the system, this apparently philosophical point is of considerable importance.

The 1994 version, in Clause 4.10.1 includes a generic requirement to "establish and maintain documented procedures for inspection and testing activities." The objective of these procedures is to verify that "specified requirements" are met. The requirements shall be in either the generic procedures, or in some form of quality plan.

Controlling quality and meeting specified requirements are two quite different concepts. The standard also recognizes that there are distinctly differing requirements for this function at the receiving, the in-process, and the final inspection and testing stages of the operation.

The entire process of inspection and test is fundamental in demonstrating conformance—no amount of process control can actually demonstrate that the product is compliant—but the standard provides for the company to determine for itself what to do and how to do it. The common thread remains the same—decide what to do, write it down, do it and keep records to prove that it has been done.

— The Victoria Group

Must Product Shipment Await Testing?

By: **Elizabeth A. Potts**, President, ABS Quality Evaluations, Inc.
Bud Weightman, President, Qualified Specialists, Inc.
Dan Epstein, Independent Consultant
Stephen S. Keneally, President, Scott Technical Services, Inc.

Question

Based on statistical control of process and historical product test results or on performance, is it acceptable to release a product before all testing has been completed? For example, test results normally take up to one month and there is insufficient storage space for more than a week's production of bulk product. If so, must the customer be notified, and under what ISO 9001 clause should notification take place?

Answer

The panel of experts agreed that there are times when product may be shipped prior to completion of testing, but they disagreed as to the circumstances under which that shipment may take place.

Elizabeth A. Potts said there is little room for interpretation. "The standard means exactly what it says," she explained. "Specified inspections and tests need to be completed and documented prior to shipment. At the time of contract, certain inspections and tests are explicitly or implicitly agreed to by the parties to the contract."

The supplier would be deviating from the terms of the agreement by shipping before completion or documentation of all tests, according to Potts. "The supplier must get consent of the other party to the agreement, namely the customer, to do so," she said.

Potts said issues such as limited storage or lengthy reliability testing would have to be addressed by the customer and supplier well in advance of shipment. "These issues should be addressed in the supplier's quality system to meet the requirements of *Clause 4.3, Contract Review*," Potts said.

Shipping with Notification

Bud Weightman acknowledged that Subclause 4.10.4 prohibits a product from being dispatched until the required inspection and testing is completed. However, he said, the supplier may elect to ship before that with proper notification.

"If the supplier elects to do so he has the obligation to notify the customer under the requirements of ISO 9001, Clause 4.3," he said. The clause states: "The tender, contract or order shall be reviewed by the supplier to ensure that...the supplier has the capability to meet contract or accepted order requirements."

Weightman said "capability" refers to the supplier's ability to deliver the product with all of the test results at the time of the shipment to the customer. The customer should provide documented evidence that it will accept the product without complete test results at the time of shipment, he added.

(continued on next page)

Must Product Shipment Await Testing?

(continued from previous page)

"The supplier's decision to ship product with incomplete test results should be based upon historical product test results, product performance data, and documented evidence of statistical process control which could be submitted to the customer as an added assurance that the product test results will comply with stated requirements," Weightman explained.

Contract Requirements for Extended Testing

Dan Epstein said there are circumstances that would allow shipping the product prior to completing the testing, but the example of limited space is not one. "Contractual obligations may require extended testing in the form of endurance, reliability, or life testing," he said. "In addition, satisfactory completion of these tests may determine product acceptability."

Moreover, Percent Defect Allowable (PDA)—the customer-defined acceptable quality level—and Six Sigma requirements—a statistical quality level equating to approximately three defects per million—may be contractually imposed, Epstein said. These allow a supplier to compute an acceptance limit only after a period of time, possibly after many shipments. The customer, he said, may have specified a delivery schedule that is in conflict with the supplier's ability to determine acceptability. Potts notes that both partners should understand that this is an issue at the time of contract and should address it under contract review procedures.

If the original contract does not provide any of these conditions (i.e., purchase order, performance specification, etc.) and the customer is expecting products and services from an ISO 9000 registered facility, Epstein said, it is the obligation of the supplier to notify the customer of the system noncompliance under ISO 9001 Clauses 4.2 and 4.3. "Ideally, every attempt should be made to avoid these sorts of problems during the contract review process of Clause 4.3," Epstein said.

Shipping and Traceability

Stephen S. Keneally said the clause appears to require that all testing be completed prior to shipping. Nevertheless, many industries, such as aerospace, defense and integrated circuits, routinely ship and assemble while samples from the production lot continue to be tested, he said.

"Depending on the product and industry, elaborate systems of maintaining traceability are used in the unlikely event if 'life testing' or long-term reliability or environmental tests result in the product being rejected and the lot being recalled," Keneally explained.

In regulated industries such as defense electronics, medical devices and pharmaceuticals, the traceability and testing requirements are part of the product approval cycle, according to Keneally. He said any changes to the manufacturing, inspection and testing process would require re-approval by the appropriate regulatory agency or the customer.

(continued on next page)

Must Product Shipment Await Testing?

(continued from previous page)

In commercial industries, he said, the revised quality plan should reflect reduced inspection, skip-lot inspection, or periodic versus 100 percent lot-by-lot testing. It should also reflect an analysis of whether statistical process control data and historical product test results justify changes.

"The manufacturer develops the quality plan and test procedure and has the option to change them when warranted," Keneally said. "It is common sense and good business practice to reduce non-value-added activity when processes are under control and statistical or other data support reduction of inspection or testing activities. Obviously, sufficient history should be available before radical changes are made."

Keneally said customers need only be notified if their contract or specification indicates what tests are to be performed or if catalogs and other sales literature reflect specific tests with the implication being that suppliers conduct such tests in every case.

According to Keneally, *Clause 4.13, Control of nonconforming product* establishes the supplier's responsibility to notify customers when product is found to be nonconforming. "It is the supplier's responsibility to notify customers should a problem with the product come to their attention through other uses or applications," he said. "The supplier is responsible for notifying customers of the possibility of a problem so that inadvertent use or installation is prevented."

4.11 Control of Inspection, Measuring and Test Equipment

The 1994 version of the standard divides the clause into two subclauses: General and Control procedure.

4.11.1 General

 ISO 9001 REQUIREMENTS

The supplier is required to do the following:

- Establish and maintain documented procedures to control, calibrate and maintain the inspection, measuring and test equipment to demonstrate conformance of the product to requirements.
- Use equipment in a manner that ensures that measurement uncertainty is known and is consistent with the required measurement capability.
- Check and re-check the capability of any test software or test hardware used as forms of inspection
- Make technical data pertaining to measurement devices available when required by the customer.

4.11.2 Control Procedure

ISO 9001 REQUIREMENTS

Subclause 4.11.2 spells out in detail the requirements for testing accuracy, calibration of equipment, handling of equipment and documentation of the checking procedures. These include the following:

- Identify necessary measurements; the accuracy required; and the appropriate inspection, measuring and test equipment
- Identify, calibrate and adjust all equipment
- Establish, document and maintain calibration procedures
- Ensure that equipment is capable of required accuracy and precision
- Identify equipment to indicate calibration status
- Maintain calibration records
- Assess and document the validity of previous inspection and test results when equipment is out of calibration
- Ensure suitable environmental conditions for calibration, inspection, measurement and testing
- Ensure accuracy and fitness for use when handling, preserving and storing equipment
- Safeguard inspection, measuring and test facilities.

ISO 9000-2 GUIDANCE

Clause 4.11 addresses the suitability of the equipment used in monitoring quality. *ISO 10012-1, Quality assurance requirements for measuring equipment—Part 1: Management of measuring equipment,* offers guidance for the management of measuring equipment. However, the guidance in ISO 10012-1 does not add to or otherwise change the requirements in ISO 9001, except where conformance to ISO 10012-1 is required.

Measurements may include less tangible instruments, such as polling, questionnaires or subjective preferences.

The requirements of this clause also should be applied to measurements subsequent to producing and inspecting a product (e.g., handling, storage, packaging, delivery or servicing).

ISO 9004-1 GUIDANCE

In Clause 13.2, ISO 9004-1 notes that the control of measuring and test equipment and test methods should include the following factors, as appropriate:

- Suitable specification and acquisition
- Initial calibration prior to first use in order to validate required bias and precision
- Testing of software and procedures controlling automatic test equipment
- Periodic recall for adjustment, repair and recalibration to maintain required accuracy in use
- Documentary evidence that covers instrument identification, calibration status and procedures for all handling procedures
- Traceability to accurate and stable reference standards.

CLAUSE 4.11: CONTROL OF INSPECTION, MEASURING AND TEST EQUIPMENT

Clause 4.11 discusses control of inspection and test equipment and calibration. The standard requires that the supplier establish and maintain documented procedures to "control, calibrate and maintain inspection, measuring and test equipment (including test software) used by the supplier to demonstrate the conformance of product to the specified requirements. "

It is easy to misread the requirement laid down in this section. It does not require calibration of **all** equipment. It is only equipment used to "demonstrate the conformance of product to the specified requirements." Equipment that is used for in-process measurement need not be calibrated, provided that the measurements made are not the last opportunity to record some item that is a deliverable specification. The same measurement, repeated at final release test or inspection, must be made on calibrated equipment. Remember the words "demonstrate conformance." If any measurement taken in-process is part of demonstrating conformance, or in other words, measuring a specified deliverable, the equipment used must be controlled.

In one example, an audit team demanded that each of 35,000 gauges and meters at a certain refinery be calibrated in a manner traceable to national standards. The company correctly calibrated only those gauges which influenced the quality of the product and those that were used to demonstrate conformance to specified requirements.

Demonstrating conformance is not confined to a single site in the company. Test and inspection equipment must be under traceable calibration control at those locations or places in the process where conformance can be demonstrated.

Portable Transfer Standard

External calibration to recognized national standards by the National Institute for Standards and Technology (NIST) or a recognized accredited laboratory or test house is an expensive business. Normal practice, therefore, is to have a certain amount of the critical equipment calibrated externally, and then to use this equipment to calibrate the rest. This is known as using a "portable transfer standard."

It is an economical way of establishing calibration of **all** test and inspection equipment without breaking the bank. When adopting this approach, it pays to remember that the equipment providing the "portable transfer standard" should be an order greater in its measurement capability than the equipment being checked. This assures the accuracy of the secondary equipment measurement capability.

ISO 10012-1, Quality Assurance Requirements for Measuring Equipment—Part 1: Management of Measuring Equipment is now referenced as a guidance document for structuring calibration systems, but this will be excessive for most companies unless they operate a full calibration laboratory system.

— The Victoria Group

How Far Do You Take Calibration Programs?

By: **Robert W. Belfit, Jr.**, President, Chief Executive Officer, Omni Tech International Ltd.
     Bud Weightman, President, Qualified Specialists, Inc.
     Roderick Goult, Chief Executive, The Victoria Group
     Peter M. Malkovich, Director of ISO 9000 Consulting and Training Services,
         Process Management International

Question
Do the requirements of Clause 4.11 imply that all inspection, measuring and test equipment must be put on a calibration program or does it merely require the calibration of certain equipment?

Answer
In general, the panel of experts agreed that the standard does not require all inspection, measuring and test equipment to be put on a calibration program. One panelist, Robert W. Belfit Jr. however, disagreed, maintaining that no such equipment should escape periodic scrutiny. Nevertheless, he said, there are varying levels of calibration and not all equipment need be subjected to the same degree of scrutiny. "Why would one want to produce data and not know the accuracy and precision?" asked Belfit. "The question should be, how do we keep the measurement process under process control?"

Level of Calibration Required
Belfit said the level of calibration required varies with each piece of equipment. He said it is important to consider the following factors:

● What the measurement will be used for
● The required tolerance versus equipment capability
● The ruggedness of the equipment
● Working conditions
● Frequency of use
● Possible malfunctions
● Whether the measurements will be supported by other data
● Whether the measurements will be used to support a specification or claim.

Bud Weightman said it is not necessary to put all such equipment on a calibration program provided "objective evidence exists" to substantiate that the supplier made a "conscientious" decision. "It is the supplier's responsibility to identify those characteristics of the design and processes which could have a direct effect on quality," he said. "Characteristics could include specific product dimensions and process-related elements that require an inspection, test or measurement to verify conformance to the stated requirements of the design output."

Calibration to Demonstrate Conformity
Roderick Goult said the standard is confusing with respect to calibration. "Handle

(continued on next page)

How Far Do You Take Calibration Programs?

(continued from previous page)

with care. Formal, traceable calibration is very expensive," he said. "Only do what you absolutely have to. The rest can be validated [as against being calibrated] by checking it against formally calibrated equipment; in other words, by using a portable transfer of the standard." Goult said there are two apparently confusing statements contained in ISO 9001, Clause 4.11. The first requires the calibration of equipment used to demonstrate product conformance to specified requirements, and the second, in Clause 4.11.2 b), deals with the calibration of inspection, measuring and test equipment that "can" affect product quality.

In the first statement, he said, only measuring equipment used for conformance testing need be formally calibrated. However, the last opportunity to assure compliance is commonly interpreted to be very early in the process, possibly even at receiving inspection, he noted. The second statement implies something completely different, Goult said. "The escape from massive and pointless expense comes from the use of the word 'can,' he said. "Who is to define what can or cannot affect product quality? That is for the supplier to judge, and unless the decision is clearly flawed, the auditor is not in a position to argue."

Peter M. Malkovich agreed that use of the word "can" is significant. "In other words, if the equipment does not control and/or verify quality, it does not have to be included in the calibration program," he said. "Hence, there is equipment that may not affect quality and equipment that may be used as a work aid or indicator only. Such equipment can be excluded from the calibration program, and should be identified as 'Not Calibrated' with the reason why it is not included." For example, he said, it is not necessary to calibrate gauges and equipment used to monitor the condition of the plant or to indicate that something is operating. They still must be checked periodically to establish that they do work.

Malkovich said firms should calibrate all equipment that affects quality and other equipment used for important measurements. Nevertheless, he said, firms must be prepared to demonstrate why excluded equipment does not affect quality.

Labeling Uncalibrated Items

Weightman suggests that companies back up their decision not to calibrate certain pieces of equipment through documentation. Possible examples include affixing "calibration not required" stickers to them; stipulating which types of equipment will be used in design output documents; including an evaluation of the inspection, measuring and test equipment in process capability studies; and having procedures that document which types of equipment will be calibrated and which will not.

He also suggests that companies evaluate "all potential sources" where inspection, measuring and test equipment is in use to determine their potential effects on quality. Such sources include equipment owned by the firm, equipment owned by employees, equipment on loan, equipment provided by the customer and equipment used in vendor processes or operations.

PREVENTIVE MAINTENANCE REQUIREMENTS: YES OR NO?

By: **Bud Weightman**, President, Qualified Specialists, Inc.
   Joseph DeCarlo, Division Manager, TUV Rheinland of North America, Inc.
   Dr. James Lamprecht, Author and Consultant
   Chuck McRobert, President, Quality Practitioners Inc.
   Joseph Tiratto, Joseph Tiratto and Associates, Inc.

Question

ISO 9001, *Clause 4.11, Inspection, Measuring and Test Equipment*, has been interpreted to include requirements for "preventive maintenance" of equipment. However, the only clear requirement is for calibration. Does a requirement exist for preventive maintenance?

Consensus Answer

All four experts agree that ISO 9001 does not specifically require preventive maintenance of equipment. However, experts' commentary ranged from implied requirements to a requirement under special circumstances.

A Built-In Requirement?

"I believe that ISO 9001 has a 'built-in' requirement for preventive maintenance, although preventive maintenance is not specifically spelled out," commented Bud Weightman. He said ISO 9001, Clause 4.11.2 b), states that the supplier shall "identify all inspection, measuring and test equipment that can affect product quality, and calibrate and adjust them at prescribed intervals, or prior to use, against certified equipment..."

Joseph DeCarlo said that ISO 9001 Clause 4.11 only outlines requirements for calibration of equipment and not for preventive maintenance of equipment. "Therefore, while preventive maintenance is certainly part of any sound quality system, it is not an ISO 9001 requirement," DeCarlo said. "If, however, a manufacturer specifies preventive maintenance in their own procedures, i.e., quality system, then it does become a requirement that an ISO auditor will look for."

Joseph Tiratto agreed that ISO 9001, Clause 4.11 does not specifically require preventive maintenance. "However," Tiratto said, "the emphasis of ISO 9001 is to be proactive rather than reactive."

Calibration Interval

Weightman argues that the process of assigning the calibration interval is critical. He pointed out that a supplier should compare its inspection, measuring and test equipment to the measurements to be made and designate an appropriate calibration interval (assuming all other Clause 4.11 requirements have been met).

If adequate history of the equipment is available and all other Clause 4.11 requirements have been met, Weightman said, "this [calibration] interval should be based on the inspection, measuring and test equipment's stability, known degree of drift, degree of usage, and environment," where the inspection, measuring and test equipment is being used.

(continued on next page)

Preventive Maintenance Requirements: Yes or No
(continued from previous page)

More than Just Calibration

Dr. James Lamprecht emphasized that Clause 4.11 addresses more than just calibration. "The precision and accuracy of some measuring and test equipment is also required," but he asked that "in many cases it would be prohibitively expensive to conduct capability analysis on all instruments." Suppliers also may not know how a capability study or accuracy study could be conducted on a particular set of gauges or instruments.

"Common sense and experience is relied upon in most cases to determine if a [process] instrument as opposed to a lab instrument is misbehaving,'" Lamprecht said. "For new instruments you can always rely on the vendor's documentation. In many cases, if you subcontract your equipment calibration/maintenance program, your supplier will—should—provide you with the necessary data."

Lamprecht said determining how many instruments should be placed under "control" is hard. According to Lamprecht, nearly all laboratory instruments have to be under control, but process monitoring instruments are more difficult to manage.

He said the ISO 9001 standard requires a supplier to demonstrate the conformance of product to the specified requirements." Taken to the extreme, this requirement might include the office thermostats. However, temperature sensors, pressure values, flow meters, and pH meters used to verify specifications are important instruments that must measure to required accuracy, Lamprecht said.

"Remember that while an instrument does not specifically fall under the scope of the ISO 9000 series, it might well have to be controlled as per OSHA [Occupational Safety and Health Administration] or EPA [Environmental Protection Agency] requirements," Lamprecht concluded.

Case Study

Chuck McRobert noted how differing interpretations of the standard can significantly impact individual companies. According to McRobert, "the word 'maintain' in the standard refers to the calibration activity and not to a separate 'preventive maintenance' system."

He noted the case of one Canadian registrar that interpreted the term "control" in ISO 9001, Clause 4.8, to mean preventive maintenance for all processing equipment in the chemical processing industry. McRobert said that the interpretation caused the company significant additional costs not encountered with a "more realistic and practical registrar."

In addition to ISO 9004-1 Guidelines, Weightman said, ISO 8402 provides guidance, defining "preventive action" as "an action taken to eliminate the causes of a potential nonconformity, defect or other undesirable situation to prevent occurrence." He pointed out that further guidance is given in ISO *10012-1, Quality assurance requirements for measuring equipment—Part 1: Management of measuring equipment.*

4.12 Inspection and Test Status

ISO 9001 REQUIREMENTS

The supplier is required to do the following:

- Identify the inspection and test status of the product throughout production and installation to ensure that only acceptable product has been used
- Identify the inspection authority responsible for the release of the conforming product.

The test status must be indicated by suitable means.

ISO 9000-2 GUIDANCE

The status should indicate whether a product has the following:

- Not been inspected
- Been inspected and accepted
- Been inspected and is on hold awaiting decision
- Been inspected and rejected.

The most certain method of ensuring status and accurate disposition is physically to separate these product categories. In an automated environment, however, other methods can be used, such as a computer database.

ISO 9004-1 GUIDANCE

Clause 11.7 addresses control of verification status. Identification of verification status should be by suitable means "such as stamps, tags, notations, or inspection records that accompany the product, or by computer entries or physical location." Identification should be capable of indicating the following:

- Verified versus unverified material
- Acceptance at the point of verification
- Traceability to the unit responsible for operation.

CLAUSE 4.12: INSPECTION AND TEST STATUS

The main requirement in the context of this paragraph is to clarify the breadth of application. The identification of inspection and test status means more than the simple question—"has it passed this test or that inspection?" It would be lunacy to get into a position where no one knew what had been tested and inspected and what had not!

This is only part of the story—the full requirement is that it should be possible to identify any element at any stage of its progress through the process, within the framework of the way that the system is established. In other words, if the process is batch-oriented, then it is possible that a single item may get separated from a batch and if it is pre-inspection it may not be possible to tell which batch it is from. It will, however, be possible to replace it in the correct place in the production chain. Once the batch has been inspected, then it must be possible to tell that item has received such an inspection. This requirement continues throughout the process, from receiving to dispatch.

— The Victoria Group

4.13 Control of Nonconforming Product

4.13.1 General

ISO 9001 REQUIREMENTS

The supplier is required to establish and maintain a procedure to prevent the inadvertent use or installation of a nonconforming product. The nonconforming product should be segregated where practical.

ISO 9000-2 GUIDANCE

A nonconforming product—either an intermediate or final product or service—is one that fails to meet specifications. This applies to a nonconforming product that occurs in the supplier's own production as well as nonconforming products received by the supplier.

The procedures for controlling a nonconforming product should include the following:

- Determining which product units are involved in the nonconformity
- Identifying the nonconforming product units
- Documenting the nonconformity
- Evaluating the nonconformity
- Considering alternatives for disposing of the nonconforming product units
- Physically controlling the movement, storage and processing of the nonconforming product units
- Notifying all functions that may be affected by the nonconformity.

4.13.2 Review and Disposition of Nonconforming Product

 ISO 9001 REQUIREMENTS

The supplier is required to do the following:

- Define the responsibility for review and authority for the disposition of nonconforming product
- Document the disposition of the product.

Nonconforming products may be the following:

- Reworked
- Accepted without repair by concession of the customer
- Re-graded for alternative application
- Rejected or scrapped.

ISO 9000-2 GUIDANCE

Suppliers should consider the procedures in Clause 4.13 in relationship to the risk of failure to meet customer requirements. Actions (a) through (d) in Subclause 4.13.2 all carry degrees of risk. In the long term, action (d) may carry the lowest risk.

ISO 9004-1 GUIDANCE

ISO 9004-1, *Clause 14.0, Control of nonconforming product,* includes the following guidance:

- Procedures to deal with nonconforming product "should be taken as soon as indications occur that materials, components, or completed product, do not or may not meet the specified requirements."
- The persons who review nonconforming items "should be competent to evaluate the effects of the decision on interchangeability, further processing, performance, reliability, safety and aesthetics."
- "A decision to accept product should be documented, together with the reason for doing so, in authorized waivers, with appropriate precautions."

CLAUSE 4.13: CONTROL OF NONCONFORMING PRODUCT

ISO 9001, Clause 1.1, states "the requirements specified are aimed primarily at achieving customer satisfaction by **preventing** nonconformity at all stages, from design through servicing" (emphasis added). Fortunately, the authors of this standard were realists and, despite the stated intent of Clause 1.1, it has been recognized that even in the best of all possible worlds things still go wrong. Then there is a need to design the system so as to prevent the "unintended" ("inadvertent" in the 1987 version) use or installation of the nonconforming product or service. There must be a clear and unequivocal method of making sure that nonconforming product is properly identified and isolated until such time as the procedures that have been created to manage the review and disposition of this unacceptable product or service have been put into effect.

The procedure to be followed must be defined. Questions to guide the process include the following:

- Who has the authority to sentence nonconforming material?
- How is the review to be carried out?
- What are the options for disposition?
- Is the process and the authority the same across the entire company or are there different authorities and responsibilities in various areas of the operation—from design to after-sales service?

All of the above must be defined and documented.

— The Victoria Group

4.14 Corrective and Preventive Action

As the addition of the word "preventive" in the above title implies, the 1994 version of Clause 4.14 places more emphasis on prevention than the 1987 version. Thus, the required corrective and preventive actions are identified in separate subclauses, as described below. Corrective action is directed toward eliminating the causes of **actual** nonconformities. **Preventive** action is directed toward eliminating the causes of **potential** nonconformities.

4.14.1 General

 ISO 9001 REQUIREMENTS

The basic requirement is to establish and maintain documented procedures for implementing corrective and preventive action.

Actions taken should be appropriate to "the magnitude of problems and commensurate to the risks encountered."

The supplier must implement and records any changes in documented procedures that result from corrective and/or preventive actions.

4.14.2 Corrective Action

ISO 9001 REQUIREMENTS

The supplier's procedures for corrective action are required to include the following elements:

- Effectively handle customer complaints and nonconformity reports
- Investigate and analyze the problem and record the results
- Determine the effective corrective action
- Ensure that corrective actions are taken effectively.

4.14.3 Preventive Action

ISO 9001 REQUIREMENTS

Subclause 4.14.3 lists the following key steps for preventive action:

- Use all available information, such as work processes, audit results, quality records and customer complaints to detect, analyze and eliminate potential causes of nonconformities
- Determine a method for preventive action
- Initiate preventive action and ensure that it is effective
- Submit any relevant information on actions taken for management review.

ISO 9000-2 GUIDANCE

This clause explains what an organization must do when things go wrong. Analysis of nonconformities can be performed by using inspection and test records, process monitoring, audit observation and all other available feedback methods. Corrective action procedures should include the following:

- Establishing responsibility for taking corrective action
- Defining how the action will be carried out
- Verifying the effectiveness of the corrective action.

Procedures should also take into account nonconformities discovered in a product that has already been shipped and designated as satisfactory.

ISO 9004-1 GUIDANCE

According to ISO 9004-1, *Clause 15.2, Assignment of responsibility* for corrective action, the "coordination, recording, and monitoring of corrective action related to all aspects of the quality system should be assigned within the organization. The analysis and implementation may involve a variety of functions, such as design, purchasing, engineering, processing and quality control."

A problem affecting quality "should be evaluated in terms of its potential impact on such aspects as processing costs, quality-related costs, performance, reliability, safety, and customer satisfaction."

CLAUSE 4.14: CORRECTIVE AND PREVENTIVE ACTION

The clause pertaining to nonconforming products is followed, logically, by a clause on corrective action. Often the weakest part of quality systems, corrective action loops are frequently designed only to address the immediate problem while failing to act to avoid its recurrence. Another common problem is that they often deal only with matters of products or services while overlooking the system. ISO 9001, Clause 4.14 addresses both the product/service **and** the system. The standard requires a rigorous examination of all the quality data and records to detect and remove all potential as well as actual causes of nonconformance. This is proactive—not reactive—quality.

The division of the 1994 version of Clause 4.14 into corrective and preventive actions reinforces the primary intent of the standard, which is preventing nonconformity at all stages.

Product, Process and System Investigation

The 1994 version of Clause 4.14 clarifies that the investigation of nonconformance has to operate on three levels: on the product, on the process and on the system. Any one of the three can be the cause of a nonconformance and therefore require a corrective action. Companies with a system that reflects corrective action regarding only product issues must now extend that system to cover the other two sides of the conformance triangle.

Preventive Action

In *Subclause 4.14.3, Preventive action*, the 1994 standard includes enhanced requirements for prevention, with a new requirement to submit the relevant information regarding problems—including details of the actions taken—to management for review. Once again, the revised standard is seeking to ensure that management becomes fully engaged in operating the system.

A new procedure or procedures will be required by most companies to specifically address the requirements of Subclause 4.14.3. Companies should carefully consider the matter of the comprehensive analysis of all available data. It would be very easy to end up with a procedure that—while being very comprehensive in its coverage—would require too much time and effort to fulfill. The preamble statement in 4.14.1 must be the guiding action, that actions "shall be to a degree appropriate to the magnitude of problems and commensurate with the risks encountered."

— The Victoria Group

4.15 Handling, Storage, Packaging, Preservation and Delivery

 ## ISO 9001 REQUIREMENTS

The requirements in this clause include the following:

- Establish and maintain documented procedures for handling, storage, packaging, preservation and delivery
- Provide a method to prevent damage or deterioration
- Provide secure storage and stipulate appropriate receipt and dispatch methods
- Control packaging, packing and marking processes
- Provide appropriate methods for preserving and segregating products when they are under the supplier's control
- Protect product quality after final inspection and test, including delivery to destination.

 ## ISO 9000-2 GUIDANCE

The requirement applies to incoming materials, materials in process, and finished product. The procedures should provide proper planning, control and documentation.

The handling methods should include provision for the transportation unit such as pallets, containers, conveyors, etc., to prevent damage. Another factor to consider is the maintenance of the handling equipment.

Suitable storage procedures should take into account the following:

- Physical security
- Environmental control (temperature and humidity)
- Periodic checking to detect deterioration
- Legible, durable marking and labeling methods
- Expiration dates and stock rotation methods.

The packaging procedures should:

- Provide appropriate protection against damage, deterioration or contamination as long as the material remains the responsibility of the supplier
- Provide a clear description of the contents or ingredients, according to regulations or to the contract
- Provide for checking packaging effectiveness.

For some products, delivery time is a critical factor. Procedures should take into account various types of delivery and variations in potential environmental conditions.

ISO 9004-1 GUIDANCE

Clause 16, Post-production Activities, emphasizes the need for a documented system for incoming materials, materials in process and finished goods. Section 16 also refers to the need for proper and complete installation instructions.

CLAUSE 4.15: HANDLING, STORAGE, PACKAGING, PRESERVATION AND DELIVERY

Clause 4.15 is fairly straightforward. All the clause asks is that these operations be managed in a way that keeps the product secure from deterioration, loss or damage from the start of the process until the responsibility of the supplier passes to someone else. The usual problem here is that once again there is a tendency to forget that these activities take place throughout the entire process, not merely at the end.

There is also a requirement to ensure that items kept in storage for any period are regularly reviewed to ensure that deterioration is not occurring—control of shelf-life by the use of FIFO (First In, First Out) techniques being one example of how this is achieved. In other cases, it may mean that special provisions have to be made for long-term storage, such as the use of desiccants or other means of product protection. In the case of software, the nature of the storage medium is volatile, and this fact must be taken into consideration when storage facilities are arranged.

Secure versus Designated Storage Areas

The 1994 version of Clause 4.15 replaces the 1987 version's use of the words "secure storage areas" with the statement "The supplier shall use designated storage areas or stock rooms..." This change should prevent undue confusion over the word "secure." It is clear that the original intent was that "secure" meant that the product was safe from damage, but not every auditor fully understood that and expected to find an industrial equivalent of Fort Knox at every site visited!

— The Victoria Group

SUBCLAUSE 4.15.3: DO SECURE STORAGE AREAS OF STOCK ROOMS MEAN LOCKED?

By: **Ian Durand**, President, Service Process Consulting
Charles McRobert, President, Quality Practitioners, Inc.
Joseph Tiratto, Consultant, Joseph Tiratto and Associates, Inc.
Robert Bowen, President, r. bowen international, inc.

Editor's Note: *ISO 9001:1987 states in Subclause 4.15.3 that the supplier "shall provide secure storage areas or stock rooms..." The wording of ISO 9001:1994 has been changed to "The supplier shall use designated storage areas or stock rooms..." Nevertheless, the question regarding the need for a secure storage area has been a subject of discussion and various interpretation. As background concerning the need for this change, we are reprinting verbatim the discussion from the first edition of The ISO 9000 Handbook, which references the 1987 standard, concerning this issue.*

Question

ISO 9001 Subclause 4.15.3, *Storage*, requires suppliers to provide secure storage areas or stock rooms to prevent damage or deterioration of product pending use or delivery. Does secure mean a locked area, or does it merely refer to proper training and discipline for appropriate personnel?

Consensus Answer

All four experts agreed that use of the word "secure" does not necessarily connote a locked room. Ian Durand maintains this interpretation is also in keeping with proposed revisions to ISO 9001 and 9002 external quality assurance standards. Those revisions may ultimately reduce the range of interpretations.

Charles McRobert said there is no shortage of expert opinions on the topic. "There are as many interpretations of secure storage as auditors," he said. "Some look for walls, gates, padlocks and guardian staff to dispatch product."

Unfortunately, traditional interpretations lead to a clash of philosophies in auditing a facility where Just-In-Time is employed. "Efficiency in today's manufacturing world requires a more sophisticated approach to the locked stock room of yesterday," McRobert said.

Good Business Practices

"As an auditor, I accept both the traditional approach or the open concept. My approach to either case is to determine if the employees are following the concepts of material management as determined by their company and are exercising the self-discipline required to make any system successful," he said.

Durand supported this view and emphasized that the ultimate arbiter for interpreting the standards must be good business practice. If a proposed interpretation or response does not support prosperity of the company in the long term, it usually means the

(continued on next page)

Do Secure Storage Areas or Stock Rooms Mean Locked?

(continued from previous page)

standard's intent is being misconstrued, or viable alternatives have been overlooked. Durand said this basis for interpretation is clearly stated in Section 5 of ISO 9000: "In both [contractual and non-contractual] situations, the supplier's organization wants to install and maintain a quality system that will strengthen its own competitiveness and achieve the needed product quality in a cost-effective way."

Joseph Tiratto said the storage clause does not specifically require storage areas or stock rooms to be locked. However, regulatory requirements may specify that hazardous material be kept in locked areas.

Durand noted that the clause applies throughout the product realization process—starting with receipt of incoming material, parts or subassemblies—and continuing until the product is ready for delivery. Response to the requirements of 4.15.3 must be integrated with those of related clauses, such as inspection and test status and control of nonconforming product.

Tiratto said the storage clause merely requires storage areas or stock rooms to be so designated, and to be equipped and operated to prevent product damage or deterioration prior to use or delivery. "Control procedures shall stipulate the methods and authority for receipt and dispatch to and from these areas," Tiratto said. "Procedures are also to include the control and shipment of a product that has a shelf life, expiration date and any environmental condition. Storage employees are to be included in training procedures established in accordance with ISO 9001, Clause 4.18."

Robert Bowen agreed that a locked storage area is not required. He interpreted the essential features of secure storage to mean defined, controlled material flows and accurate inventories and work practices aimed at preventing damage or deterioration of inventory.

Advice to Companies

The intent of the clause is to ensure that appropriate items are available when needed, according to Bowen. In developing practices to prevent damage or deterioration, he said, many companies could take advantage of existing cycle count programs, which randomly sample inventory accuracy by requiring a clerk to count selected part numbers. This is one of many acceptable ways to fulfill the requirement to "assess the condition of product in stock at appropriate intervals."

"The duties of this clerk can easily be expanded to accommodate ISO 9000 requirements," Bowen said. "As the clerk counts inventory, he can physically examine stock for damage or deterioration. Upon completion, a simple notation on the cycle count record indicates the status of damage or deterioration. These cycle count records become the basis for corrective action of damaged goods and act as the quality record to demonstrate achievement of Subclause 4.15.3."

4.16 Control of Quality Records

ISO 9001 REQUIREMENTS

The supplier is required to do the following:

- Establish and maintain documented procedures for handling, maintaining and disposing of quality records (includes pertinent subcontractor quality records)
- Store records effectively and to prevent loss or damage
- Establish and record retention times of quality records
- Make quality records available for evaluation by the customer or its representative.

All quality records shall be legible and identifiable to the product involved. In a Note, the standard emphasizes that records can be hard copy, electronic or any other media.

ISO 9000-2 GUIDANCE

The purpose of quality records is to demonstrate required quality and the effectiveness of the quality system. Quality records are referred to throughout ISO 9001. Effective quality records contain direct and indirect evidence that demonstrates whether the product or service meets requirements.

The records should be readily accessible. They may be stored in any suitable form, either as hard copy or on electronic media.

Sometimes customers may be required to store and maintain selected quality records that attest to the quality of products (including services) for a specified part of the operating lifetime. The supplier should provide such documents to the customer.

International standards do not specify a minimum time period for retaining quality records. Suppliers should consider the following:

- Requirements of regulatory authorities
- Product liability and other legal issues related to record-keeping
- Expected lifetime of the product
- Requirements of the contract.

Aside from these considerations, retaining records five to seven years is common practice.

ISO 9004-1 GUIDANCE

Clause 17.2, Quality Records, in ISO 9004-1 gives the following examples of quality records that require control:

- Inspection reports
- Test data
- Qualification reports
- Validation reports
- Survey and audit reports

- Material review reports
- Calibration data
- Quality-related cost reports.

CLAUSE 4.16: CONTROL OF QUALITY RECORDS

The ISO 9001 standard continually refers to the need for records to demonstrate completed actions. Clause 4.16 does not call for the creation of additional records, but points out that records must be identified, sorted, stored and maintained in a manner that makes them easily accessible.

The difference between the quality records filing system and any other in a business is that a great deal of the information contained in these records should be decentralized to be instantly available when required. This means that the maintenance of the defined quality records will need to be monitored by the process of internal audit to ensure that everyone is doing what they should.

Often, however, too much importance is attached to fulfilling the requirements of this clause. Contrary to popular belief, the clause does not require fireproof safes, bank-vault storage, microfiche, or other similar methods of storage. Once again, the level of protection required for records depends upon the nature of the business, as well as any contractual or statutory requirements. The records connected with the construction of a nuclear power station need to be kept somewhat longer, and under more secure conditions, than the records for making a compact disc.

Some registrars have definite ideas about record-retention times. It is a good idea to establish whether the company's record-retention policy agrees with the registrar's demands during an initial meeting. The record-retention policy should be clarified and agreed upon before the audit team arrives on-site.

Procedures for Access
A minor change in the 1994 version of Clause 4.16 is the requirement to maintain procedures for "identification, collection, indexing, **access**, filing...", etc. A specific reference to access will be necessary in the control document.

— The Victoria Group

Clause 4.16: Electronic Control of Documents

By: **Joseph Tiratto,** President, Joseph Tiratto and Associates, Inc.
   Robert D. Bowen, President, r. bowen international, inc.
   Ian Durand, President, Service Process Consulting, Inc.
   Charles McRobert, President, Quality Practitioners, Inc.

Question
How can electronic documents be controlled to meet the requirements of ISO 9000 series standards?

Answer
All four experts agreed that generating and tracking documents electronically is allowed by the ISO 9000 series standard, according to the Note in Clause 4.16 that states "Records may be in the form of any type of media, such as hard copy or electronic media."

Advantages of Electronic Media
Bowen said that ISO 9000 series document control principles apply equally to all media; he also pointed out four distinct advantages of electronic media:

Accuracy: Immediate on-line review of proposed changes by all knowledgeable persons and a transaction history file showing the date and nature of changes.

Authenticity: Secure sign-on functions to ensure controlled access to *read and write* functions.

Completeness: On-line edit-checks that ensure all required information is complete before a document is released.

Currency: Instantaneous removal of all obsolete documents. Uniform start-up of all concerned persons when initiating procedures or changes.

Other strengths noted by Bowen include immediate update of suppliers' documents through electronic data interchange. In addition, "many organizations find it easier to establish a planned review system of quality-related documents if those documents are on-line." He noted that setting up a database reminder to review documents at specified agreed-upon intervals is easy to accomplish.

McRobert said that he had worked with "nearly paperless" companies whose document-control systems were excellent. He agreed with Bowen's contention that electronic control of documents makes review and approval of documents and highlighting of changes easier.

McRobert noted that "some auditors with misguided zeal have requested hard copies of all controlled documents with approval signatures." He suggested that any company whose auditor suggests this approach "immediately seek relief" from this requirement.

(continued on next page)

Electronic Control of Documents

(continued from previous page)

Document Control

Durand pointed out that controlled documents can include mechanical assembly drawings, circuit schematics, process flow charts, physical reference samples, pictures of reference samples, or video tapes illustrating proper work methods.

He agreed that using electronic media for document control has many distinct advantages. He said the complexity of such systems should not be a roadblock, pointing to the demanding access and control requirements of electronic fund transfer financial-control systems and security and administration systems.

Durand noted that a number of software programs are currently available to handle documentation and quality records of an ISO 9000-based quality system.

Tiratto agreed that documents can be generated electronically in accordance with *ISO 9000-2, Quality management and quality assurance standards—Part 2: Generic guidelines for the application of ISO 9001, ISO 9002 and ISO 9003.*

He noted, however, that in accordance with ISO 9001, *Clause 4.16, Control of quality records,* document control should include written procedures that describe the following:

- How documentation should be controlled
- Who is responsible for the control
- What is to be controlled
- Where and when the control is to take place.

Tiratto said the procedures should also include back-up provisions for electronically stored documents that are readily retrievable. He said back-up provision can also be electronically processed.

4.17 Internal Quality Audits

 ## ISO 9001 REQUIREMENTS

The supplier is required to do the following:

- Establish and maintain documented procedures for internal quality audits of the quality system
- Schedule audits according to the status and importance of the activity
- Carry out audits according to documented procedures
- Record audit results and communicate them to the appropriate personnel
- Perform timely corrective action.
- Record the effectiveness of the corrective action in follow-up audit activities.

The 1994 standard adds the general requirement that internal quality audits be carried out by personnel independent of those directly responsible for the activity being audited. In a Note, the clause reminds companies that the results of internal quality audits form an integral part of management review activities. The clause also refers companies to the guidance included in ISO 10011.

ISO 9000-2 GUIDANCE

The purpose of an audit is to make sure the system is working according to plan, to meet regulatory requirements, or to provide opportunities for improvement. Auditors should be selected and assigned according to the criteria contained in ISO 9001, Subclause 4.1.2.2.

Internal audits may also be initiated for other reasons, including the following:

● Initial evaluation of a system for contract reasons
● When nonconformities jeopardize the safety, performance or dependability of the products
● Verification of corrective actions
● Evaluation of a system against a quality system standard.

ISO 9004-1 GUIDANCE

Clause 5.4, Auditing the quality system in ISO 9004-1 suggests that companies formulate an appropriate audit plan that covers:

● Planning and scheduling the specific activities and areas to audit
● Assigning qualified personnel to conduct audits
● Documenting procedures for carrying out audit, reporting the results and agreeing on corrective action.

Companies should submit documented audit findings, conclusions and recommendations to management on reporting and follow-up matters. The items that should be covered include:

● All examples of nonconformities or deficiencies
● Appropriate and timely corrective action.

CLAUSE 4.17: INTERNAL QUALITY AUDITS

Internal quality audits are the mainstay of system conformance. The quality system audit is a powerful tool for continuous improvement. The standard requires a planned, systematic and on-going process of audits to ensure that the documented system is effectively implemented and that corrective actions are taken in a timely manner. The prevention concept ensures that the system is working as planned and that corrective action is taken when it is not.

It is normal to expect that every area shall be audited at least once a year, with areas that produce bad audit reports receiving more frequent scrutiny. The full audit plan should be properly documented—as should the audit reports—complete with details of the effective implementation of any corrective and preventive actions. The 1994 version of Clause 4.17 adds the additional requirement that "follow-up activities shall verify and record the implementation and effectiveness of the correction action taken." In a Note, the standard adds a reminder that "the results of internal audits form an integral part of management review activities." This reinforces the requirement of *Clause 4.14, Corrective and preventive action*, to refer system changes resulting from corrective and preventive actions to management review.

— The Victoria Group

FORMAL TRAINING REQUIREMENTS FOR AUDITORS?

By: **Ian Durand**, President, Service Process Consulting, Inc.
    Robert Bowen, President, r. bowen international, inc.
    Joseph Tiratto, Joseph Tiratto and Associates, Inc.

Question

ISO 9001, Clause 4.17, *Internal Quality Audits*, has been interpreted to mean formal audits by staff trained to ISO 10011 by outside trainers. Does an actual requirement for formal training exist?

Consensus Answer

No specific requirement for training exists, according to both Ian Durand and Robert Bowen. Durand points out that the only explicit requirement found in ISO 9001, 9002 or 9003 relating to auditors is found in Subclause 4.1.2.2 which states that the supplier shall "...assign trained personnel for management, performance of work and verification activities including internal quality audits."

Bowen cites Clause 4.18 in ISO 9001 and Clause 4.17 in ISO 9002. He said the qualification requirement indicates that the appropriate education, training, and/or experience is needed. He said the "specific definition of these categories must be determined by each organization."

Joseph Tiratto agrees that ISO 9001 does not specifically require that internal audit staff be trained by outside trainers. He points to Clause 4.18 and Subclause 4.1.2.2 of ISO 9001 to support his argument. Tiratto noted that several organizations have developed internal auditor training courses. He said the Institute of Quality Assurance in the United Kingdom is in the process of establishing requirements for certification of internal auditor training courses.

Basic Requirements

Bowen listed the basic requirements of most internal auditors. The list includes the following:

- Demonstrated understanding of the general structure of quality systems
- Demonstrated understanding of a company's proprietary quality system
- Professional understanding of auditing techniques such as audit planning and audit checklists
- Excellent communication skills.

He said that most organizations are unlikely to have sufficient in-house understanding of the ISO 9000 series standard, so formal outside training is usually required.

Additional Requirements

Durand emphasized that additional audit staff requirements could be a good decision for some companies. "A company might decide that auditing practices described in

(continued on next page)

> ### Formal Training Requirements for Auditors
>
> *(continued from previous page)*
>
> ISO 10011 might make business sense," he said. By the same token, Durand said that sending a few "well-chosen people to outside audit training makes good sense to assure that those performing internal audits have developed adequate auditing skills."
>
> Durand concluded that the "cardinal rule in designing a quality system based on the ISO 9000 series is to act in the best long-term interests of the business." He said going beyond the minimum requirements of the standard may be the best business decision.

4.18 Training

ISO 9001 REQUIREMENTS

The supplier is required to do the following:

- Establish, maintain, and document procedures to identify training needs
- Provide appropriate training for all personnel performing activities affecting quality
- Maintain records of training.

ISO 9000-2 GUIDANCE

Training is essential to achieving quality. Training should encompass the use of and underlying rationale for the quality management approach of the supplier. The training process should include the following:

- Evaluate the education and experience of personnel
- Identify individual training needs
- Provide appropriate training, either in-house or by external bodies
- Record training progress and update to identify training needs.

ISO 9004-1 GUIDANCE

Clause 18.0, Personnel of ISO 9004-1 discusses the training, qualification and motivation of personnel. Companies should consider training "all levels of personnel within the organization performing activities affecting quality." This includes "newly recruited personnel and personnel transferred to new assignments."

The various levels of personnel within a company require specialized training. Executives and management require training in the "understanding of the quality system together with the tools and techniques needed" to operate the system.

Training for technical personnel "should not be restricted to personnel with primary quality assignments, but should include assignments such as marketing, procurement, and process and product engineering."

Process supervisors and operating personnel should receive thorough training, including instruction in the following:

- Proper operation of instruments, tools and machinery
- Reading and understanding documentation
- Relationship of their duties to quality and safety in the workplace
- Certification or formal qualification in specialized skills (such as welding)
- Basic statistical techniques.

Clause 18.3, Motivation, looks at efforts to motivate all personnel in the organization. An effective motivation program focuses on elements such as the following:

- Communicating to all employees an understanding of their tasks and the advantages of proper job performance
- A continuous quality-awareness program
- A mechanism for publicizing quality achievements and recognizing satisfactory performance.

CLAUSE 4.18: TRAINING

The training requirements of ISO 9001/9002 are very general and take the global view of quality—that is, every person in any company performs "activities affecting quality." The choice of training required is made on the basis of appropriate education, training or experience. The company is left to decide what is appropriate, with the exception of certain regulated areas where there are statutory requirements for training.

The company is then asked to record its training decisions, follow them up and make sure that the training continues to be appropriate throughout the individual's career. Many companies do an extremely good job of providing extensive employee development training that is carefully and completely documented, but then forget about the need to support a person's current activities with appropriate training. The standard is specifically interested in the training that relates to those activities currently being performed by the employee. It is most important to capture and record the details of "on-the-job" training. The basic purpose is to ensure that the next person to be trained for that same task receives the same training, thereby ensuring consistency in performing the task.

— The Victoria Group

Documenting Personnel Qualifications

By: **Ira Epstein**, Vice-President of Government Services, STAT-A-MATRIX
   Dean Stamatis, Ph.D., President, Contemporary Consultants Co.
   Raymond P. Cooney, Ph.D., Consultant, R.P. Cooney & Associates
   Kirk Eggebrecht, Executive Manager, Geo. S. Olive & Co.

Question

Most quality systems (especially to ISO 9000) are adopted after a company has been in business for quite some time and where employees have been working at a job, possibly for years. How should personnel qualifications be documented as per Clause 4.18?

Answer

The panel of experts agreed that companies have a certain amount of discretion in documenting personnel qualifications.

Ira Epstein mentioned the following two aspects of documentation that must be considered:

- A requirement for written procedures that identifies training needs
- A requirement for records of training that has been accomplished.

Identifying Training Needs

Training needs may be dictated by external sources such as government or professional societies, Epstein said. Examples include training requirements for workers in the nuclear reactor industry or workers in the medical industry. Other training requirements may be established by the customer in a contractual situation.

"Contracts should be reviewed carefully to determine if training requirements are specified," he said. An example might be the requirement for training in nondestructive inspection cited in many Department of Defense contracts. "Many of the training requirements from these two sources often require certification and re-certification of personnel," he said. The most common source of training needs comes from internal management, which typically is most familiar with the job and with any necessary training, he noted.

Raymond P. Cooney said the supplier determines the appropriate mix of education, training, and experience needed for personnel to perform certain tasks and to ensure that personnel are properly qualified. He said that companies frequently upgrade or "tighten-up" training and qualification procedures when implementing ISO 9001 or 9002. "If employees' experience on the job qualified them without needing to go through the new system, a note to that effect in the employees' personnel files or other appropriate place would be adequate documentation."

Experience as a Substitute for Education and Training

Epstein noted that experience may be substituted for education and training at the

(continued on next page)

Documenting Personnel Qualifications

(continued from previous page)

discretion of management, provided this does not conflict with education and training requirements imposed by customers and other external sources. In cases where experience is accepted as a substitute, training records must be appropriately noted, possibly by a brief narrative of the person's experience.

"The subject of training must be considered in context with the rest of the quality system and not in isolation," Epstein said. "If an audit of the quality system is being accomplished, training should be one of the last elements of the system to be audited. It would be difficult if not impossible to make a valid judgment of the adequacy of training without making a judgment of the adequacy of the rest of the quality system."

Epstein added that training procedures, training, and related documentation may appear satisfactory, but will raise an auditor's suspicions if there are high levels of nonconformities in other system problems.

Training and Testing Criteria

Dean Stamatis said the intent of the clause is to establish requirements for training, certifying, and re-certifying employees involved in performing critical and specialized functions at a given organization. "It covers all employees performing routine, critical, and specialized functions related to deliverable items. This includes both the management and non-management personnel. In addition to this general impact the clause may also include requirements specified by the customer's contract."

"As part of the audit and the Clause 4.18 requirements it is also essential to look at the responsibility for developing training and testing criteria," Stamatis said. "Here, the auditor looks for consistency in operating the training sessions for normal/generic, special, certification, and re-certification sessions."

Stamatis said the criteria for such an evaluation probably is contained within the quality manual under the heading for the quality management and administration department. He said auditors may also be interested in addressing customer-imposed requirements while auditing this section.

Records of Training

"The format for both procedures and records are not specified in ISO 9001," Epstein said. "Format is determined by the supplier to satisfy his needs, his customers' needs, and the needs of society. The extent of documentation and the format should be as simple as possible and yet satisfy the above needs."

Dean Stamatis lists the following information as typical with respect to appropriate records:

- Employee's name and identification number
- Employee's department
- Date and duration of training
- A check mark for certification or re-certification

(continued on next page)

Documenting Personnel Qualifications

(continued from previous page)

- Location of training
- Type of training
- Name of the course
- Certification number
- Function of the certification
- Expiration date
- Name of the instructor.

Auditors may also be interested in viewing records and verification documents of training for employees who are unable to attend or be present at a scheduled session. "Although the concerns of Clause 4.18 may be very frightening to some companies, in reality they are nothing more than a substantiation of the quality system that the company itself has defined in its own quality manual," Stamatis said.

According to Raymond Cooney, "the system for keeping qualification records need not—should not—be rigid or onerous. The simplest, easiest, most flexible system that works is the best. Qualification records can take many forms."

Cooney said that qualification records must have credibility and utility. "This implies two things," he said. "Responsible people must sign off on the records. Oftentimes this means both the employee and appropriate management. Secondly, records need to be readily accessible to those who need to use them."

Good business practice, he said, dictates that a supplier be able to answer the question: How do we know that a person doing or being told to do a job is qualified to do it?

According to Stamatis, the following documentation or procedures are required before verification: a quality assurance certification or re-certification notice, a quality certification record, a quality certification card, and a list of attendees for training. He said those documents usually can be found in the trainee's department, the training department, or the quality department if the training is quality-related.

Job Descriptions

Kirk Eggebrecht said it is important to consider any single element of ISO 9001 in the context of the document as a whole. "The supplier's specific procedures for addressing training and work assignments will be a function of the approach used to address other ISO 9001 requirements, such as Design Control (4.4), Process Control (4.9), Internal Quality Audits (4.17), and many others," he said.

"In addressing these requirements, many suppliers conclude that job descriptions are needed for each unique position in the organization." Typically, he said, these job descriptions prescribe the specific skills, training, and experience required for that position. "The make-up of these job descriptions then determines the make-up of the information needed in each employee's personnel and training file," he said.

(continued on next page)

Documenting Personnel Qualifications

(continued from previous page)

"Naturally, the key to any quality system is that there is a match between the job requirements as documented, and the employee's qualifications as documented," Eggebrecht said. "If there is a mismatch, the supplier should have procedures implemented to provide the appropriate training and supervision until the prescribed qualifications are met."

In the case of employees who have been performing a job for years without any formal training, he said, registrars allow suppliers to "grandfather in" experienced workers, exempting them from prescribed training or educational requirements. However, to qualify for this treatment, the employee must have demonstrated a proven capability.

"Floaters" Raise Flags

Some companies designate certain employees as "floaters" meaning they perform more than one type of job as necessary. "These situations can be red flags in the eyes of a registrar and rightly so," he said. "Often, these super employees are not qualified to perform all the duties they are assigned." Companies that use employees for more than one job should have a separate job description for those positions.

This increases the number of positions that must be documented, but it narrows the job requirements for the individuals assigned to such special positions. If the person is not qualified for all the jobs he or she may be called on to perform, then the practice should be discontinued or modified, according to Eggebrecht.

New Employees

New employees should be trained by a designated instructor, and that training should be documented. There should be a sign-off procedure authorized by a designated person or position, who may or may not be the instructor, Eggebrecht said. When hiring skilled employees, companies must have specific procedures that address the employee's placement in the organization along with a transition period for them to become familiar with the position.

"The same amount of care, control, and effort should be taken in recruiting and transitioning new employees as is prescribed in training and transferring existing employees," he said.

4.19 Servicing

 ### ISO 9001 REQUIREMENTS

With the 1994 revisions to the ISO 9000 series standard, the clause on servicing is now also included in ISO 9002. The basic requirements calls on the supplier to do the following:

- Establish and maintain documented procedures for servicing (when required by contract)
- Verify and report that servicing meets specified requirements.

ISO 9000-2 GUIDANCE

In planning procedures for servicing, suppliers should:

● Clarify servicing responsibilities

● Plan service activities (supplier or externally provided)

● Validate design and function of necessary servicing tools and equipment

● Control measuring and test equipment

● Provide suitable documentation and instructions

● Provide backup technical advice, support, and spares or parts supply

● Provide competent, trained service personnel

● Gather useful feedback for product or servicing design.

ISO 9004-1 GUIDANCE

Clause 16.2, After-Sales Servicing, notes that instructions for products should be comprehensive and supplied in a timely manner. Instructions should cover assembly and installation, commissioning, operation, spares or parts lists, and servicing of products. In the area of logistical back-up, responsibility should be clearly assigned and agreed among suppliers, distributors and users.

CLAUSE 4.19: SERVICING

Quality applies to after-sales servicing just as much as to the prime supply of any goods or services. So the standard requires that procedures be established for ensuring that the specified requirements of the servicing operation are achieved. These may be specified by direct contract, by implied contract, or by statutory provisions. The complexity of the system created to control and monitor the service function will depend upon how significant a portion of a business it may be, and can range from a simple document to cover the occasional after-sales return, to a complete, independent quality system to cover the post-contract service and maintenance of a product through its entire life cycle.

The requirement is to have documented procedures for handling the activity, determining the requirements to be met by products before being returned and maintaining records of the activity. These records are also referenced in Clause 4.14 as a potential source of data for identifying possible preventive activities.

— *The Victoria Group*

4.20 Statistical Techniques

ISO 9001 REQUIREMENTS

The 1994 standard includes two subclauses: *4.20.1, Identification of need*, and *4.20.2, Procedures*. The requirements include the following:

- Identify the need for statistical techniques to establish, control and verify process capability and product characteristics
- Establish and maintain documented procedures for statistical techniques.

ISO 9000-2 GUIDANCE

Statistical techniques are useful in every aspect of an organization's operation. Useful statistical methods include:

- Graphical methods to help diagnose problems
- Statistical control charts to monitor and control production and measurement processes
- Experiments to identify and quantify variables that influence process and product performance
- Regression analysis to provide quantitative models for a process
- Analysis of variance methods.

The documentation resulting from these methods can be used to demonstrate conformance to quality requirements.

ISO 9004-1 GUIDANCE

In *Clause 20.0, Use of Statistical Methods*, ISO 9004-1 suggests that the application of statistical methods may include:

- Market analysis
- Product design
- Reliability specification, longevity/durability prediction
- Process control/process capability studies
- Determination of quality levels/inspection plans
- Data analysis/performance assessment/defect analysis
- Process improvement
- Safety evaluation and risk analysis.

CLAUSE 4.20: STATISTICAL TECHNIQUES

The thoughtful use of statistical processes can result in significant benefits. What is most often overlooked is that Clause 4.20 not only refers to the commonly recognized techniques of statistical process control (SPC) and inspection sampling but also to all other analysis techniques that are also statistically based—from the simple Pareto chart through to the most sophisticated design tools like finite element analysis and failure mode and effects analysis (FMEA).

The standard requires that whatever the methods used should be appropriate and valid. It is the latter requirement that is most often not met, particularly in the use of statistical sampling techniques. The auditor should establish that any sampling being performed is carried out against known risks.

There is no requirement for the use of statistical methods, but when they are used, it is essential that staff involved in their use understand what they are doing and why. This will often require training.

Remember that as statistical techniques will be used throughout the organization, it will be necessary to ensure that there is some formal identification process that has a global effect. In many cases, it may be sufficient to attach to certain jobs the responsibility for identifying a need for statistical techniques and then defining which techniques are to be used.

— The Victoria Group

4

REGISTRATION AND SELECTING A REGISTRAR

This chapter includes two articles. The first one, written by Bud Weightman, should help buyers assess the positives and negatives of each registrar they are considering. The information should also help buyers choose a registrar that knows their industries, that works with companies of various sizes, and that is competitively priced. The guidelines and questions cover the following issues:

- Deciding to register
- An overview of the consulting versus registration issue
- Registrar fees
- The registrar's financial stability
- Conducting background checks on registrars
- Auditor qualifications
- The audit team
- A registrar's list of clients
- Halting the registration process.

The second article, written by Elizabeth Potts, describes the registration process including the following topics:

- Completing your application
- Documentation review

- The pre-assessment
- The actual assessment
- Achieving registration
- Maintaining registration through surveillance
- The costs and time involved.

HOW TO SELECT A REGISTRAR: BENCHMARKS FOR THE SCREENING PROCESS

BY R. T. "BUD" WEIGHTMAN

Editor's Note: *The article that follows aims to assist in the critical registrar selection process. Since a version of it was first printed in the January 1992 issue of Quality Systems Update, it has gained nationwide attention, becoming a benchmark in the United States for buyers and registrars alike. Many companies have handed out reprints to their suppliers for use as a guideline for their registrar selection processes. Reprints are available by writing or calling Bud Weightman or CEEM Information Services.*

Introduction

As ISO 9000 series quality system registration services expand in the United States, companies interested in registration are becoming hard-pressed to separate the qualified from the ill-qualified registrars. One dilemma is selecting the best service for a particular industry or type of business.

ISO 9000 registration is driven primarily by manufacturers and suppliers and by specific industries scrambling to meet perceived and actual requirements for quality system registration. Part of these requirements are contained in EU (formerly EC) directives that are a key aspect of the European Union's Single Internal Market program and its adoption of the ISO 9000 series standard. In many cases, self-imposed market positioning or a customer-expressed requirement has fostered the move toward registration. (See Chapter 15 for a discussion of EU directives and their requirements for quality system registration.)

Types of Registrars

Over 50 companies offer ISO 9000 quality system registration in the United States. Some of these companies have direct ties to one of the twelve EU (European Union) or seven European Free Trade Association (EFTA) countries. Other companies offer ISO 9000 series quality system registration under a Memorandum of Understanding (MOU) with EU member state registrars (known as "certified bodies" in the EU). Still others are in the start-up process and are not yet accredited. Companies providing registration services in the United States include the following:

- Established or newly founded European certification bodies opening new offices in the United States
- European certification bodies that have formed an agreement with US registration companies
- US industry accreditation or product certification organizations that have expanded the scope of their services
- Quality-related service companies that have expanded their service base
- Newly formed registration companies.

Registrar Accreditation

A key issue for companies selecting registrars is whether the registrar is accredited. Accreditation is the initial evaluation and periodic monitoring of a registrar. It is performed by an accreditation body (known as an "authoritative body" in the European Union). Registrars can be accredited by more than one authoritative body. In this case, a supplier has the opportunity to choose the registration scheme under which it wishes to participate (i.e., the scheme of a specific country).

Regardless of the accreditation scheme under which a quality system registration company operates, all must be evaluated against the requirements of *EN 45012, General Criteria for Certification Bodies Operating Quality System Certification.* (See Chapter 16 for more information.) Further guidance is contained in the ISO/IEC (International Electrotechnical Commission) *Guide 40, General Requirements for the Acceptance of Certification Bodies*, and *ISO/IEC Guide 48, Guidelines for Third-Party Assessment and Registration of a Supplier's Quality System.*

Not all accreditation bodies have embraced EN 45012, but US and European accreditation bodies have adopted this and other schemes for use on a global basis. It would be prudent for manufacturers or suppliers operating in the international marketplace to ensure that their chosen quality system registrar meets internationally accepted requirements.

Why Register?

One of the first questions a company must ask itself is "Why must I register my quality system?" Here are some common and crucial reasons:

- An EU directive for a regulated product specifies quality system registration as a method of compliance
- A customer demand for quality system registration exists. Customer perception of a registrar's reputation may vary with the relative perceived status of a registrar and may be a part of the registrar decision process
- A customer is in an EU member country
- A domestic customer also sells its products to an EU member country
- A customer is located in a third country that has adopted ISO 9000 quality system standards
- The marketing potential of quality system registration is important
- Improving a basic quality system while working towards internal quality improvement is an important company goal—an ISO 9000 quality system is an excellent starting point for total quality.

MARKETPLACE

A particular company market may influence registrar choice. Some questions to ask include the following:

- Does a chosen quality system registrar specialize in registration of suppliers producing specific products?
- Is a specific registrar required by a customer?
- Is a specific registrar preferred by a customer?
- Is a notified body registrar required by an EU directive?

COMPETITOR REGISTRATION

Some companies minimize their registrar selection process activities by making a snap decision to choose the same registrar their competition did and to become registered to the same ISO 9000 quality system standard. Depending upon the competition's decision-making skills, this choice may be a good one, or it could be one the company may live to regret.

Some questions to consider in going this route include the following:

- Is your competitor registered under ISO 9001, 9002 or 9003?
- Is it appropriate for your company to choose ISO 9002 when you have specific product design responsibilities, just because your competitor did?
- Was the competitor's registrar willing to register it under ISO 9002 when product design responsibilities are evident?
- Is there another registrar that may be a better fit for your company's specific needs? For example, does your company need to consider a registrar that can service multiple locations or multiple scopes of registration?

Consulting Versus Registration

Some customers (or even your competition) may perceive that a conflict of interest exists if a registrar offers and performs consulting and assessment or registration services.

ISO/IEC *Guide 48, Guidelines for third-party assessment and registration of a supplier's quality system* states in part:

> *An organization that, directly or through the agency of subcontractors, advises a company how to set up its quality system, or writes its quality documentation, should not provide assessment services to that company, unless strict separation is achieved to ensure that there is no conflict of interest.*

Some action has been taken both internationally and in the European Union regarding standardization of the accreditation process. The two organizations driving the process are the International Accreditation Forum (IAF) and the European Accreditation of Certification (EAC) organization. The EAC represents 17 accreditation bodies in EU and EFTA countries.

Because of the potential for conflict of interest, one of the topics the EAC is examining is the clear-cut division of responsibility between registration and consulting services where both are offered by a registrar. Its goal is to draw a clear line between the two, with strict enforcement of the policy.

If a registrar offers these services directly or through an affiliate, it is incumbent upon the company to find out how the registrar keeps these activities separate. One document that may help companies make this decision is a guideline established by the EAC called *EAC Guidelines on the Application of the EN 45012 European Standard for Bodies Certificating Suppliers' Quality Systems*. (See Chapter 16 for more information.)

Some questions a company may want to ask are the following:

- Is there a clear division of responsibilities between registration and consulting?
- Are any of the registrar's following personnel involved in consultation:
  - Governing board member(s)?
  - Certification board member(s)?
  - Principal(s)?
  - Owner(s) or stockholder(s)?
- Does the registrar subscribe to its stated policies when it or its affiliate(s) jointly perform registration and consultation activities?

The registrar should have a policy that gives rise to the following:

- A statement specifying that the registrar has no involvement in consultation activities
- A statement specifying that individuals involved in the certification procedure—including those acting in a managerial capacity—have not been involved in any consultancy activities toward a specific supplier—or in any company related to that supplier—within the last two years
- A statement specifying that the company does not market consultancy and accredited certification together
- A statement specifying that marketing material, written or oral, does not give the impression that the two activities are linked
- A statement specifying that nothing is implied by the registrar that would suggest that

registration would be simpler, easier, or less expensive if any specific consultancy services were used

- A statement specifying that the registrar's assessors are not permitted to advise or give consultancy as part of an assessment

- A statement specifying that the registrar does not imply that the use of both of its services, registration and consultation, would bring any business advantages to the client. This would ensure that the certification remains and is seen to remain impartial.

Costs

Considerations that will affect cost include the size of an organization, the ISO 9000 series number selected (i.e., 9001, 9002, 9003), the scope of registration (i.e., one product, a product line, or an entire family), and the location of a facility.

Costs also could include the following:

- Application fee
- Preparation and initial visit
- Review of quality system manual
- Review of revisions to the quality system manual
- Initial visit and number of auditors sent
- Pre-assessment charge if a contract is signed
- Assessment charges
- The number of auditors sent by the registrar specifically for the assessment
- Certification charges or fees
- Report writing
- Surveillance fees
- Listing fees.

Questions to consider when weighing registration costs include these:

- Will the client be required to pay if the registrar performs a follow-up visit to verify the implementation of corrective action related to deficiencies identified during the assessment?

- Will the cost of surveillance be included in the registration fee, or will each surveillance be an additional charge? How many surveillances will be performed over the life of the registration? How many quality system elements are covered during each surveillance? How long will each surveillance (or periodic inspection) last?

- What is the cost of modifying the scope of a registration? What is the cost of reassessment after the expiration of the original registration? Will it be the same as the initial assessment? Will it take as long as the initial assessment?

- What are the cancellation charges?

- What is the billing rate? Is it regulated by the person-day or by the hour? Is overtime applicable? What is the billing rate for travel time? Are travel expenses and lodging billed at reasonable rates?

- Will the registrar's auditors be traveling from a location within the United States or from Europe?

Editor's Note: *Please refer to Chapter 20 for three articles on the Quality Systems Update/ Deloitte & Touche ISO 9000 Survey. The articles examine the internal and external costs of registration, among other issues.*

Financial Stability

It is unclear whether all authoritative bodies check the registrar's financial status or whether it is verified during the accreditation process. If your registrar goes into bankruptcy or ceases business, it is possible that your registration will become void. An exception to this outcome is if your registrar has MOUs with other registrars that call for a transfer of registration in this case. Considering the impact this could have on you, you will probably want to do your own checking on a registrar's financial security.

Questions to ask concerning a registrar's financial security include the following:

- Does the registrar publish information on its financial security?
- If the registrar goes out of business, is the supplier's registration secured?

Background Checks

A key element in choosing a registrar is checking on its background and company policies. Here are some questions to ask:

- How long has the company been in business?
- Is a list of previously registered companies available, including contact names and telephone numbers?
- Is a complete description of a quality system registration system available, including an application, the appeals process, and policy regarding registration suspension, withdrawal or cancellation?
- How will clients be notified of any rule changes? Are clients permitted to comment on any of the changes? How long do clients have to implement changes once notified?
- Does the registrar require notification of any applicable customer complaints?
- Will the registrar grant quality system registration to ISO 9001, 9002 or 9003? Some registrars will not grant certification or registration to ISO 9003.
- What is the source of a registrar's accreditation? Is the source an EU member state or one recognized by the European Union? If not, when will the accreditation entity be recognized? Has the accreditation entity adopted EN 45012? If not, does it have plans to do so?

Other questions to consider when selecting a registrar include the following:

- With which registrars (certifying bodies) does the registrar have memoranda of understanding?

- Which US state laws govern the agreement with a registrar? Where would any legal differences occur?

- Does the registrar subcontract any of its registration activities to another organization? If so, does the subcontracted service follow the registrar's policies and regulations? Is the use of a subcontracted service agreeable?

- Does the registrar have a confidentiality agreement with:
  ○ Employees?
  ○ Subcontracted organizations or personnel?
  ○ Members of its governing board?
  ○ Members of its certification committee?

- Does the registrar allow the use of its symbol or logo? What are the restrictions or requirements governing the logo's use?

Assessment and Registration

There are several questions to ask about the quality system assessment and registration process, including the following:

- How soon can the quality system assessment be performed?

- How long will the registration agreement last? (Generally, it lasts one to three years.)

- Will a controlled quality system manual be required for submission, and how long will it take to review the document?

- How are clients notified of quality system omissions or deficiencies? How long will they be allowed to make the necessary modifications?

- Must quality system manual amendments—based upon the registrar's review—be corrected and implemented prior to the assessment?

- Once accepted, will a client be required to submit a quality system manual for review and approval prior to making and implementing any revisions?

- Can a quality system be less than 100 percent implemented to receive registration, or will registration be withheld until a system is fully implemented?

- Will a client be notified of any deficiencies in a quality system before the assessment team leaves the site? If so, will the notification be verbal or in writing?

- How much time is given to correct identified deficiencies?

- Will a reassessment or partial assessment be performed to verify corrective action implementation of deficiencies identified during the initial assessment?

- Will changes or revisions in a quality system manual necessitate a reassessment?

- Will a reassessment be required if a modification to the registration scope is requested?

- What is the frequency of the periodic surveillances? How many quality system elements are covered during each surveillance?

Auditor Qualifications

The registrar's auditor qualification and certification program is important information to have before making a quality system registrar decision. A recognized auditor qualification or certification program assures that manufacturers and suppliers are repeatedly audited in the same manner and at the same level of intensity.

Be sure that the method the registrar uses provides the best assessment possible. Here are some points to consider when evaluating a registrar's auditor certification requirements:

- Does a registrar's internal training program or certification follow a specific scheme that may or may not be affiliated with a national scheme?
- Under what scheme does the registrar operate? Is it a national scheme such as the Institute of Quality Assurance (IQA) (e.g., provisional assessor, registered assessor, or registered lead assessor) or the American Society for Quality Control (ASQC) or the Registrar Accreditation Board (RAB) accreditation scheme (e.g., quality system provisional auditor, auditor, or lead auditor)? The IQA-administered scheme is backed by the governing board of the UK National Registration Scheme for Assessors of Quality Systems. This system has worldwide recognition. The RAB scheme has been introduced recently and should parallel the IQA scheme.
- Has the auditor participated in a 36- to 40-hour ISO 9000 lead auditor training course? The course may or may not be registered to a national scheme such as the UK's IQA or the US's RAB-administered registered course.
- Is a registrar's quality system auditor acceptance based upon the ASQC Certified Quality Auditor (CQA) program? If so, the CQA certification should be followed by an RAB-approved 16-hour ISO 9000 series course, followed by an approved test.

Auditing Team

A registrar should be questioned about its auditing team. Here are some questions to consider:

- What are auditor experience, training, and educational requirements? Are auditor backgrounds verified?
- Do auditors receive training in both ISO 9000 series standards and company procedures and policies prior to certification?
- What are the standards or criteria used to qualify auditors?
- Are the standards or criteria recognized and accepted by the European Union?
- What levels of auditor qualification exist (auditor-in-training, auditor, or lead auditor) and what responsibilities do these auditors have during the assessment process?
- During the assessment process, will at least one auditor be familiar with a client's product or technology?
- Does the client have the right to review auditor qualifications?
- Can the client object, with cause, to the audit team members?

Client List

If the registrar offers a list of suppliers or manufacturers it has registered, make sure the following questions are answered.

The list should include an outline of the "scope" of registration.

- What is the frequency of the list publication? (The list should be published at least annually.)
- What is the charge for the list?
- Will clients be placed on a mailing list to receive the list, or will a separate request be required?
- How does the registrar determine the technical competence of an assessor?

Halting the Process

Questions concerning quality system suspension, withdrawal and cancellation should include the following:

- What is the registrar's policy regarding the suspension, withdrawal or cancellation of the quality system registration?
- Will the registrar withdraw or cancel the quality system registration if a product, process or service is not supplied for an extended period of time? Ask the registrar to define the rules.
- How will a client be notified of quality system registration suspension, withdrawal or cancellation?
- Will the registrar publish the quality system registration suspension, withdrawal or cancellation?

Conclusion

The importance of selecting a registrar cannot be overemphasized. The agreement is a long-term commitment and dissolving it can be costly. The purchaser of such services could help eliminate future problems by doing some up-front work and making an informed decision by asking planned questions, comparing registrar responses, and choosing the registrar that is best suited to its needs.

STEPS IN THE REGISTRATION PROCESS

BY ELIZABETH POTTS

Introduction

The previous section discussed the process of selecting a registrar. Once this decision is made, what can and should be expected from that registrar? This section describes what to expect at each step in the process. Regardless of which registrar is selected, the registration process generally consists of the following six basic steps:

- Application
- Document Review
- Pre-Assessment
- Assessment
- Registration
- Surveillance.

This article also considers the time and costs of registration.

Application

To begin the registration process, most registrars require a completed application, sometimes called a contract. The application should contain the rights and obligations of both the registrar and the client. It should contain such registrar rights as access to facilities and necessary information, as well as liability issues. It should contain such client rights as confidentiality, the right to appeal and complain, and instructions for the use of the registration certificate and associated marks. In addition to the above client rights, clients should also check conditions for terminating the application, should it become necessary.

Prior to issuing an application, the organization should assure itself that the registrar fully understands the extent of the operation to be certified and that the certification is within the registrar's accredited scope. Different methodologies are used to set a registrar's accredited scope. In the United States for instance, the Standard Industrial Classification (SIC) Codes are used. In Europe, a similar system of codes, Nomenclature Generale des Activites Economiques Dan les Communautes Europeenes (NACE), is used to define scope. In all cases, the registrar should be willing to work with the organization to define the extent of certification and how it will be achieved.

For large companies with centralized functions such as purchasing or design that elect to use more than one registrar, it is crucial to determine each registrar's policy relative to acceptance of registration by another registrar. Whether or not the registration of centralized functions that form part of a specific site registration is accepted or not can greatly impact the overall time and cost of registration.

Document Review

Once the application is completed with basic information on the company's size, scope of operations, and desired time frame for registration, the registrar typically requests the company to submit documentation of its quality system.

This documentation is generally in the format of a *quality manual.* Most registrars do not wish to see every detailed procedure the company has created at this point in the registration process. What they are looking for is the overall document that describes the quality system so that it can be compared to the appropriate ISO 9000 series standard to determine compliance. Some registrars perform this document review on-site at the facility. However, most registrars perform the review at their own offices, saving travel costs and expenses as well as the time required to host the registrar.

The company should be sure to clearly understand the registrar's policy relative to the cost of manual review and circumstances requiring an additional review. Some registrars may require duplicate review when an additional site under the same quality system applies for certification. Many registrars will require distinct new reviews of quality manuals that have been revised extensively.

Pre-Assessment

Most registrars recommend that a pre-assessment be conducted; some may require it. It is important to understand what a registrar means by the term *pre-assessment.* Some registrars use the term to mean a complete assessment, which is used to determine the current status of an operation. Others use the pre-assessment as a broad overview of a company's operations to determine its initial preparedness for a full assessment and to aid in audit planning, such as determining the number of auditors required and the length of time needed to adequately assess the company.

For some companies, the pre-assessment may be an optional step. A reputable registrar, however, will not recommend a pre-assessment solely for the purposes of gaining additional revenue. Therefore, before a company elects to forgo a pre-assessment, it would be wise to consider the benefits of having one conducted.

A pre-assessment could identify major system deficiencies (or inadequate documentation), thereby alerting the company to the need for additional preparation prior to the full assessment. Conversely, the company may have over-prepared. For example, it may have interpreted that certain documentation would be required and discovered during the pre-assessment that the registrar does not require it. An aggressive response to the pre-assessment will increase a company's chances of passing the full assessment on the first attempt.

A pre-assessment could also result in a smaller audit team, a shorter audit, and thereby reduce the overall cost of the registration process. However, be aware that if a complete pre-assessment is required by the registrar's system, another full assessment with its associated time and expenses may also be required to become registered.

Registrars are prohibited from consulting with the client company during a pre-assessment. The registrar may properly evaluate the state of the supplier's quality system and documentation and indicate the requirements for each ISO 9001, ISO 9002 or ISO 9003 element. However, the registrar is not to provide substantive advice and guidance to the company. An effective pre-assessment may uncover areas for which the company might then enlist the aid of an independent consultant. It is not appropriate that such aid be provided by the registrar, as this constitutes a conflict of interest.

Assessment

After pre-assessment or after the registrar determines that the company's documented quality system conforms to the requirements of the selected ISO 9000 standard, a full assessment is conducted. In a typical assessment, two or three auditors spend two to five days at a facility. Recently, much guidance has been published regarding audit duration. The European Accreditation of Certification (EAC) has issued audit duration guidelines as has the Association of British Certification Bodies (ABCB).[1] The duration will be highly dependent on the size and complexity of the operations to be registered. The client should not hesitate to challenge or question an audit that appears to be overly short or long.

The auditors will hold an introductory meeting with company management, request escorts to assist them during the audit, hold a closing meeting to communicate any deficiencies that were discovered and, as appropriate, leave a draft report containing the audit team's recommendations regarding registration. The client should verify whether the audit teams' recommendation is binding or if further internal review and disposition are required.

During the audit, most registrars conduct a daily review of their findings with the client to keep them apprised of what deficiencies or findings will be documented. This allows the client an opportunity to respond to the stated deficiency, if desired. In most cases, all detected deficiencies, even if rectified in the course of the audit, will be reported.

During the assessment, the auditors will interview all levels of personnel to determine whether the quality system as documented in the quality manual and supporting procedures has been fully implemented within the company.

Registration

There are typically three possible outcomes of an audit:

1) Approval
   - A company can expect to become registered if it has implemented all the elements of ISO 9001, ISO 9002 or ISO 9003, and only minor deficiencies are detected during the assessment.

2) Conditional or provisional approval

A company will probably be either conditionally or provisionally approved if:

- It has addressed all the elements of the standard and has documented systems, but perhaps not fully implemented them.
- A number of deficiencies detected in a particular area show a negative, systemic trend.

Conditional approval requires the company to respond to any deficiencies noted during the time frame defined by the registrar. The registrar, upon evaluating the company's corrective action, may elect to perform an on-site reevaluation or accept the corrective action in writing and review the implementation in conjunction with subsequent surveillance visits.

3) Disapproval

- The final possibility is disapproval, which usually occurs when a company's system is either very well documented but has not been implemented, or when entire elements of the standard such as design control, internal auditing, corrective action or process control, have not been addressed at all. This situation will definitely require a comprehensive reevaluation by the registrar prior to issuing registration.

Once a company is registered, the company receives a certificate and is listed in a register or directory published by the registrar or another organization. The company should also expect to receive rules for use of the certificate and associated quality marks at this time.

The client should be aware of the registrar's policy for publishing registrations, including actions taken when registration is suspended or withdrawn.

Surveillance

It is important for a company pursuing registration to understand the duration and/or validity of its registration. Some registrars offer registrations that are valid indefinitely, pending continuing successful surveillance visits. Others offer registrations valid for a specific time, such as three or four years.

Most registrars conduct surveillance every six months. Those whose registrations expire conduct either a complete reassessment at the end of the registration period, or an assessment that is somewhere between a surveillance visit and a complete re-audit. The client should clearly understand the registrar's policy in this area.

During the interval between surveillance visits, the company should continually ensure that its demonstrated quality systems remain in place, so that the surveillance visit will merely confirm the fact. The internal quality audit (required by ISO 9001, Clause 4.17) and its review by management (required by ISO 9001, Subclause 4.1.3) are mechanisms to aid in this process. (Refer to chapter 5 for further information on the audit process.)

However, rigorous documentation and deployment of an existing system should not stifle continual improvement. If an improvement is identified and requires a modification in the quality system, the company should feel free to make it, so long as the change is specifically documented. Companies should inform their registrars of such changes, however. Some registrars require notification only of major changes to the quality system, while others require that the client apprise them of all changes. The client should clearly understand the registrar's policy in this area, as it can have a profound impact on registration maintenance.

Time and Costs of Registration

The time required to implement an ISO 9000 quality system depends on the company's current status, its commitment to the implementation of the system and the resources it is willing to expend. A good time frame (if a company is starting with no system or a poorly documented system) is 18 to 24 months.

The time required for actual registration depends upon the preparedness of the company and the number of deficiencies detected during the pre-assessment. Registrar lead times are becoming increasingly critical as the demand for registration of quality systems increases. It is important, prior to choosing a registrar, to determine the resources of that registrar and whether it can meet the company's needs for registration. Current registrar lead times range from one or two months to over a year.

Many costs are associated with registration, the first of which is actually developing and implementing the quality system. A company may elect to use internal resources to implement the quality system, to rely on the services of an outside consultant, or to combine both approaches. (Please refer to Chapter 20 for three articles on registration costs from the *Quality Systems Update*/Deloitte & Touche ISO 9000 Survey.)

There is no guarantee, however, that a company will achieve registration using any of these approaches. In fact, fewer than half pass a registration assessment on the first attempt.

When selecting a registrar, companies should assess actual costs of the registration process, becoming familiar with all details of costs associated with the registration process. The company should ensure that it has obtained cost estimates for the following:

- Application and document review
- The pre-assessment visit
- The actual assessment
- Any costs associated with issuing the registration and writing the report
- Surveillance visits.

Furthermore, a company should be aware that some registrars require application fees, listing fees and registration fees in addition to those prices normally quoted for the above actions. A company must ask about all fees to ensure that the full cost of the registration is known.

The company should also be familiar with the registrar's policy on the duration and cost of surveillance visits. A company should know how long the registration is valid, as well as any reassessment or partial reassessment costs that may be required in the future.

The client should feel comfortable openly discussing issues, such as scheduling and qualifications of audit team members, with the registrar. In all cases, although the registrar cannot act as a consultant, it should be willing to guide the client through the registration process.

In conclusion, companies should remember that they are clients of the registrar; they should have no fear of retribution if a complaint is necessary. The registrar on the other hand must operate ethically and in accordance with the requirements of its accreditors. The registrar should actively seek customer feedback in order to continuously improve its operations.

ENDNOTE

[1] The Association of British Certification Bodies can be contacted at the following address: ABCB Secretariat/10th Floor/Norfolk House/Wellesley Road/Croydon CR9 2DT/England. tel. 081-680-1822. fax: 081-681-8146.

MISLEADING ADVERTISING

A July 1993 *Quality Systems Update*/Deloitte & Touche survey conducted of ISO 9000 registered companies in the United States and Canada found that almost 96 percent of respondents said they are using or planning to use registration for public relations or product marketing purposes in the future.

One problem, however, is that many companies may not know how to publicize their registration properly, and they run the risk of creating false or misleading advertisements.

Companies may say that their quality system has been judged by an impartial third party to meet the requirements of the ISO 9000 series, but they are treading on dangerous ground if they try to imply that their products or services have in some way been certified.

According to George Lofgren, president of the Registrar Accreditation Board (RAB), most problems involving misleading advertising usually stem from a wrongful implication that registration to the IS 9000 series standards is an endorsement of the company's products or services.

Lofgren also notes, however, that the RAB can do nothing in cases where a company claiming to be registered is not.

Unlike the RAB, the National Accreditation Council for Certifying Bodies (NACCB) in the United Kingdom requires that a registrar's logo be used in a misleading advertisement before it takes action.

For those companies that do cross the line, there are few sanctions that can be employed, since many ISO 9000 registrars are powerless to take action unless their logo is involved, and awareness about this issue seems limited in the Federal Trade Commission, the agency charged with truth-in-advertising laws.

Editor's Note: *This box was adapted from an article that appeared in the October 1993 issue of Quality Systems Update.*

MAINTAINING CLIENT CONFIDENTIALITY

By James P. O'Neil and Peter Scott

If a company is pursuing registration to the ISO 9000 series standards, to what extent must auditors be given access to proprietary processes and what steps can a company take to ensure confidentiality?

When a company submits itself to the processes of registering to ISO 9000, it extends an open invitation to the personnel of its chosen registrar to delve deeply into the intimate workings of its business processes. Some of these processes may often be proprietary. Hence, the client needs to be assured that the registrar's personnel can be trusted not to reveal any information about its business to any other party.

To satisfy national accreditation requirements, all candidates for a registrar's staff have to pass a security review before they commence full employment with that registrar. Most important, in the case of subcontract assessment staff, in addition to completing a security screening, the staff members are required to endorse a written confidentiality agreement.

This requirement to preserve client confidentiality extends beyond the staff members who are directly involved in the day-to-day activities of the registrar; confidentiality agreements must also be completed by all directors of the registrar's company and certification boards.

To completely close the loop, any representative of the national accreditation organization that may have access to the registrar's client files also is required to endorse a copy of the registrar's confidentiality agreement before he or she is allowed to visit the premises of that registrar.

National accreditation within the United Kingdom also requires that any office of the registrar where client files are kept be protected by an intruder alarm system relayed back to a central station monitored 24 hours a day.

Confidentiality and Certification

The responsibilities of an accredited registrar and the requirements for the preservation of client confidentiality, are fully described in ISO guidance documents. Activities related to auditing a company's documented quality system to ISO 9000 are described in ISO 10011.

The training and experience of the assessors used by the registrar are critical to the effectiveness of quality auditing techniques in such areas as proprietary processes. What are proprietary processes?

Standards maintained and set forth by the Institute of Quality Assurance (IQA) in the United Kingdom and the Registration Accreditation Board (RAB) in the United States assure high levels of competence for assessors. When assessors are competent, the

(continued on next page)

Maintaining Client Confidentiality

(continued from previous page)

subjective nature of auditing is minimized, and an assessor can objectively use his or her skills to record a noncompliance to ISO 9000 without direct reference to that proprietary process.

Throughout his or her career, the experienced auditor will have noted the best ways of auditing proprietary process areas. These high standards and experience—coupled with relationships developed with clients—assure that the quality auditing techniques employed are effective. These aspects are fully covered by the professional conduct requirements of the IQA- and RAB-registered assessor schemes.

Special Cases

A registrar's clients generally fall into four categories:

- **Industrial security**. They provide products or services (e.g., soft drink manufacturers).
- **Personal security**. They provide services to the community (e.g., doctors or lawyers).
- **Civil security**. They work in criminally sensitive sectors (e.g., burglar alarm installers).
- **National security**. They are involved in national security sectors (e.g., manufacturers of nuclear missiles).

Security and confidentiality agreements can easily satisfy the requirements for client confidentiality during certification of organizations involved in the industrial and personal security sectors.

However, only full-time employees of the registrar who have been subject to security screening with background investigations can audit clients in the civil and national security sectors. In the United Kingdom, these employees will either have been "positively vetted" by the Ministry of Defense and will have signed the Official Secrets Act, or they will have been security-screened in accordance with the requirements of BS 7499: Part 1: 1991: Appendix B.

In the United States, these employees will have been issued a confidential, secret, or top secret security clearance by the Department of Defense.

Additionally, each client file is kept in a locked, fireproof safe under the direct control of the registrar's chief executive.

Confidentiality is taken very seriously by an accredited registrar. No company should have to worry that the certification process will be conducted in any way other than in the strictest confidence.

Editor's Note: *This box was adapted from an article that appeared in the May 1993 issue of Quality Systems Update.*

5

THE AUDIT PROCESS

This chapter contains two articles related to the audit process. The first one, by David Middleton, describes the internal quality audit process, including the following:

- Defines an audit and the auditor's role
- Discusses the phases of an internal audit, including the following:
  - o Planning an audit
  - o Executing it
  - o Reporting your findings
  - o Applying the corrective action process.

The second article, by Roger Pratt, discusses communication techniques helpful in both internal and external audits. These techniques will help make the actual audit proceed more smoothly. His article discusses the following issues:

- Putting the auditee at ease
- Helpful techniques to try
- What to do during unusual situations or conflicts
- Ethics involved with auditing.

INTERNAL QUALITY AUDITS

BY DAVID MIDDLETON

The following section is designed to give a brief overview of the key steps in developing, conducting and reporting an internal quality audit.

What Is An Audit?

A quality audit is defined both in *ISO 8402, Quality management and quality assurance—Vocabulary* and in ISO 9001:

Quality Audit

A systematic and independent examination to determine whether quality activities and related results comply with planned arrangements, and whether these arrangements are implemented effectively and are suitable to achieve objectives.

Notes:

1. The quality audit typically applies to, but is not limited to, a quality system or elements thereof, to processes, to products, or to services. Such audits are often called "quality system audit," "process quality audit," "product quality audit," or "service quality audit."

2. Quality audits are carried out by staff not having direct responsibility in the areas being audited but, preferably, working in cooperation with the relevant personnel.

3. One purpose of a quality audit is to evaluate the need for improvement or corrective action. An audit should not be confused with surveillance or inspection activities performed for the purposes of process control or product acceptance.

4. Quality audits can be conducted for internal or external purposes.

ISO 9001 Clause 4.17, Internal Quality Audits

The supplier shall establish and maintain documented procedures for planning and implementing internal quality audits to verify whether quality activities and related results comply with planned arrangements and to determine the effectiveness of the quality system.

Internal quality audits shall be scheduled on the basis of the status and importance of the activity to be audited and shall be carried out by personnel independent of those having direct responsibility for the activity being audited.

The results of the audits shall be recorded [See Clause 4.16 in Chapter 3.] and brought to the attention of the personnel having responsibility in the area audited. The management personnel responsible for the area shall take timely corrective action on deficiencies found during the audit.

Follow-up audit activities shall verify and record the implementation and effectiveness of the corrective action taken. (See 4.16.)

Notes:

1. *The results of internal quality audits form an integral part of the input to management review activities. [See Subclause 4.1.3 in Chapter 3.]*
2. *Guidance on quality system audits is given in ISO 10011.*

Simply stated, an internal audit evaluates a company's quality management capability to determine the following:

1) Does a system exist?
2) Is it implemented?
3) Is it effective?

An internal audit system can also be used to successfully gain ISO 9000 registration, to provide a basis for improving an existing quality system, or to ensure that regulatory requirements are met.

According to ISO 10011-1, Subclause 5.1.2, when determining the audit frequency, a company should consider any changes to its quality system (including changes in management, policy, or technology) and any corrective actions taken for previous audits. Internal quality audits may be scheduled regularly. (See box on next page for an explanation of ISO 10011, Parts 1, 2 and 3.)

The Role of the Auditor

The role of the auditor is to examine whether or not a company or department is meeting the requirements of a declared quality assurance standard and, by collecting objective evidence, verify that the system is implemented and effective. Determining the system's effectiveness is difficult, but it is key to complying with ISO 9001. By questioning and witnessing activities, you can identify whether there is a system and whether it is being followed, but without a frame of reference as to what you expect from an effective system, you cannot evaluate effectiveness.

The auditor's role is not merely to report facts. An auditor obtains information from a variety of different people and interprets the data to make an informed judgment about the effectiveness of the quality system.

Many people think that an audit is a primary policing function that ensures compliance with a set of defined criteria or rules. This perception is often shared by auditors, particularly if they are part of a newly developing audit program within a company. If an audit program has ill-defined objectives or the auditees misunderstand the purpose of the audit, then the "policing" aspect of the audit dominates over evaluating the effectiveness of the quality system.

An example of this misunderstanding is the "gotcha" reaction by an auditor who finds a noncompliance. Unfortunately, some auditors do a little dance of glee and wave a piece of paper, announcing, "It's wrong, it's wrong!" This is perhaps the worst case scenario—an auditor should never express satisfaction in finding a noncompliance.

Involving managers and section heads in the internal audit process means convincing them of its value—convincing them that it won't become a fault-finding exercise. People won't believe that the audit system is designed to improve the process unless they see it; as such, your company's first audits may also be its most critical. Audit preparation should begin with educating everyone in the organization on the following topics:

- What the audit process will involve
- The audit's expected benefits
- How it can be used to measure the effectiveness of the links between internal customers and suppliers within an organization.

ISO 10011: Parts 1, 2 and 3

ISO 10011 offers guidance for establishing a quality audit system, and while the requirements are not mandatory, they are an excellent resource for establishing consistent audit practice worldwide. *ISO 10011, Guidelines for auditing quality systems* consists of the following three parts, which are explained in more detail below:

- Part 1: *Auditing*
- Part 2: *Qualification criteria for quality systems auditors*
- Part 3: *Management of audit programs.*

The three parts of ISO 10011 complement the requirements of ISO 9001 by providing consistent guidance for one critical area of implementing the standards, namely auditing.

As earlier chapters have emphasized, the key role of audits is further strengthened in the Phase 1 revisions. Requirements for internal audits are now present in all of ISO 9001, ISO 9002 and ISO 9003.

ISO 10011-1, Auditing

Part 1 provides guidelines for actually conducting an audit of an organization's quality system including establishing basic audit principles, criteria and practices. It also provides guidelines for establishing, planning, carrying out, and documenting quality systems audits. In addition, it includes guidelines for verifying whether a quality system exists, whether it has been implemented, and whether the system is able to achieve the defined quality objectives.

ISO 10011-1 is general enough that users can tailor the guidelines to suit their needs.

The following definitions are from ISO 10011-1.

Auditor (quality). A person who has the qualifications to perform quality audits.

Notes:

1.   *To perform a quality audit, the auditor must be authorized for that particular audit.*

(continued on next page)

ISO 10011: Parts 1, 2 and 3

(continued from previous page)

   2.   *An auditor designated to manage a quality audit is called a lead auditor. (Clause 3.3)*

Client. A person or organization requesting the audit.

   Notes:

   The client may be:

   a.   *The auditee wishing to have its own quality system audited against some quality system standard;*

   b.   *A customer wishing to audit the quality system of a supplier using his own auditors or a third party;*

   c.   *An independent agency authorized to determine whether the quality system provides adequate control of the products or services being provided (such as food, drug, nuclear or other regulatory bodies);*

   d.   *An independent agency assigned to carry out an audit in order to list the audited organization's quality system in a register. (Clause 3.4)*

Auditee. An organization to be audited. (Clause 3.5)

During internal quality audits, the client and the auditee are the same person; the term "organization" can mean a company, division, branch, department, group, section or function.

ISO 10011-2, Qualification Criteria for Quality Systems Auditors

To ensure that quality systems audits are carried out effectively and uniformly as defined in Part 1, minimum criteria are required to qualify auditors. Part 2 describes these minimum criteria. The criteria upon which an auditor is judged include education and training, experience, personal attributes, management capabilities and competency. ISO 10011-2 also provides a method to judge a potential auditor's compliance with the criteria.

ISO 10011-3, Management of Audit Programs

Companies that conduct ongoing quality systems audits should establish a way to manage the process. Part 3 describes the activities that should be addressed by such an organization and offers basic guidelines for managing them. This guidance document addresses the organization itself, applicable standards, staff qualifications, the suitability of team members, the monitoring and maintenance of auditor performance, operational factors, joint audits, audit program improvement, and a code of ethics.

In addition to the definitions given in ISO 8402 and ISO 10011-1, the following definition applies:

   Audit program management. Organization, or function within an organization, given the responsibility to plan and carry out a programmed series of quality systems audits. (Clause 3)

Phases Of The Audit: PERC

Auditing has four basic phases that are listed below:

1) **P**lanning
2) **E**xecution
3) **R**eporting
4) **C**orrective action

The auditee's perception of the audit is significantly affected by poor planning, inadequate execution, confused reporting or corrective action records. As an internal auditor, you should emphasize each of these four areas to ensure a professional approach.

1) PLANNING

Sufficient planning is especially important. Spending time in this particular phase will reap benefits when trying to ensure a smoothly-run audit process. Planning an audit involves six steps:

1. Select a skilled and capable audit team
2. Confirm the audit's objective and scope together with the specific quality assurance requirements with the auditee
3. Identify information sources on which to base the audit, including the quality system standard itself, the quality manual, procedures, etc.
4. Plan the audit program
5. Confirm the program with the auditee
6. Develop checklists.

Selecting the Team

According to ISO 10011-1, whether an audit is carried out by a team or an individual, a lead auditor should be placed in overall charge. The audit team is best developed from a diagonal cross-section of the organization. People from all levels in the company who perform a variety of tasks from different departments should be included. This team will then audit a function of the company where they are not directly responsible; e.g., marketing should audit manufacturing, sales should audit design, etc. Also, they should have some training in auditing techniques and ethics and remain free of bias. (See chapter 16 for more information on auditor qualifications.)

Objective and Scope

Defining the objective and scope of the audit involves answering the following four questions:

- Where am I auditing from?
- What am I auditing to?
- At what point in the process am I starting?
- At what point in the process am I finishing?

One of the ways to identify the scope of the audit is to obtain the relevant sets of documentation, review the documentation, identify the beginning and ending points of the audit, and then use that initial review to prepare a checklist. However, another strategy is to develop a more proactive approach to preparation; that is, get the auditees involved. It is often more effective to sit down with a department manager, supervisor or section head to identify the key things in their processes that are important to them and then use that as the foundation of your checklist. A checklist should never be a "secret weapon" used to find fault. Rather, preparing and developing the checklist should be part of an open audit process.

Information Sources

Identify the sources of relevant information that should be used in selecting the audit sample to ensure a balanced view of the company's operation. An audit sample is a sample of the documents or processes you may wish to audit; e.g., in purchasing, how many purchase orders will you look at—five, ten or fifteen? In manufacturing, which process will you audit? It is the objective evidence evaluated during the audit itself.

Sources of information from which to develop the audit program/checklists include:

- Quality manual/procedures
- Management priorities
- Quality problems
- Previous audits/outstanding corrective action
- Product information
- Experience of the auditors

Planning an Audit Program

Your audit program should identify the duration of the audit, the areas of the organization that will be subject to assessment, and generally the people who should be available to answer the auditor's questions. Some of the key issues in developing the program follow:

- **Is it well-planned?** Have you thought through the process? Have you identified a beginning and an end? Can you take a sample from the system that will enable you to follow the process in a logical way?
- **Have you set achievable objectives?** Can you verify that something is actually happening? Can you find evidence of an effective system, or are you wasting time following loose ends and trying to establish a pattern? Can you verify that the system or process you are examining is working? If so, how?

  For example, you may be in the receiving area and be told that product is tested to a certain specification. How can you verify that the specification is up-to-date? You can see a date on the specification, but it might not be current. A methodology is necessary to identify a document and to identify whether or not the document is up-to-date. It is far better to identify those difficulties at the audit preparation stage than during the audit itself.
- **How long is the audit?** Is the audit to last one day, two days, one week? The length depends on the objective and scope of the audit.

The audit itself has tight time constraints. It is important to keep the audit program on schedule and yet maintain the flexibility to follow up on any leads that develop. Therefore, you must have a planned approach and a firm idea of how to conduct the audit. During the audit it is too late to make decisions about what and where the sample is to be taken. However, a plan that is changed for valid reasons is far better than no plan at all.

Confirm the Program With the Auditee

Be sure to confirm the audit program, including the dates, time and schedule with the auditee.

Develop a Checklist

Details of the sample and where it will be taken are on the audit checklist. The program is the audit strategy that identifies what areas will be examined and when, whereas the checklist provides the tactical component by identifying how the company complies with ISO 9000.

Thought must be given to structuring the checklist to achieve the stated objective of process improvement. Checklist questions need to be open-ended—ones that will enable the auditee to explain the process and show how that process is documented. Whether the documentation is in a procedure or a flow chart does not matter—as long as it is reflected in the actual process. (See the next section of this chapter for more information on phrasing questions.)

2) EXECUTION

The actual execution of the audit consists of a number of distinct events:

- The opening meeting
- The audit itself: collecting and verifying information
- Recording the discrepancies.

The Opening Meeting

While an opening meeting for an internal audit is far less formal than an opening meeting held for a supplier audit, it still requires preparation. Follow an agenda to ensure that all necessary points are covered in as short a time as possible. Items you should consider putting on the agenda include the following:

- In large organizations it may be necessary to introduce the auditor(s), but departments in medium-sized and small organizations might already know the team
- Explain the audit's purpose and scope as well as the range of activities to be reviewed
- Confirm that the details of the program are acceptable to the auditee and that the necessary employees are available at the scheduled times
- Confirm the status of the procedures and any relevant documents prior to the actual physical audit; clarify any ambiguities
- Explain the manner of identifying and recording nonconformances.

It is also good practice to record those present at the opening meeting.

Collecting Information

The purpose of the audit is to collect objective evidence regarding the effectiveness of the company's quality system. It is a dynamic and practical tour through the company's quality management system along a path prescribed by the auditor's program and checklists.

The team leader's responsibilities during the audit include the following:

- Introduce yourself and the team to the section/department manager
- Develop a rapport with the auditee
- Explain what you want to see
- Focus on the process/understand the objectives
- Investigate as much as necessary
- Get the auditees involved
- Satisfy your sample
- If you don't find any problems, don't panic—some processes might be correct.

You can gain much information by interviewing the staff, by observing activities or by documenting evidence found in a company's records. Staff interviews should not be limited to department heads and senior managers. Everyone in the company has a part to play within the quality system.

When an employee tells you about another employee, however, that information is hearsay evidence and is unacceptable. During one warehouse audit, the manager, who was under increasing pressure from the auditor, finally burst out in exasperation, "Well if you think this place is bad, just wait until you get to Sales!" You cannot use it as a basis for a discrepancy. You can, however, use the information gained to check if a discrepancy indeed exists. But without the "hard" evidence of your eyes, documented proof, or a statement from the person responsible for a particular activity, you must give the auditee the benefit of the doubt.

In gathering information, an auditor should ask open questions—those that cannot be answered by a simple yes or no. For example,

> *"Does this company have a procedure to define the quality audit activity?"*

can be rephrased as,

> *"Can you explain how your audit procedure works?"*

'Yes' and 'No' questions do not allow individuals to elaborate on their work and do not give the auditor confidence that the employees understand their operations. Open questions allow you to ascertain what is not recorded in the procedures and to determine the level of understanding of the people who are responsible for undertaking various functions.

To verify facts, it is permissible and indeed desirable to ask several people the same question to ensure a consistent response. Do not underrate the use of silence. When you think you have received an incomplete answer, you can encourage the auditee to provide more information by using body language or simply remain silent. In general terms, people are anxious to avoid a silent pause and will tend to provide more information to fill that gap.

Remember, however, that it is not necessary to always find something wrong; there are areas that might actually be under control.

Verifying Your Observations

Auditors have to examine samples of documents, equipment, products, etc. to verify their observations. These samples are part of the audit sample, and the auditor determines the size. However, it is not prudent to select only one sample of a system, nor is it possible to select tens or even hundreds of samples. If one sample is incorrect, it would be wise to take another sample to determine whether it is an isolated occurrence or a larger problem.

When following an audit trail or selecting samples for examination, politely insist on selecting the sample rather than asking the auditee to do so at random. The samples taken by auditees are rarely, if ever, random, and likely will be the information that the auditee wishes you to see rather than that you might wish to select.

An empty filing pocket may mean that the record is currently in use, or it could mean the auditee does not want you to examine it. Remember that it is your audit. If a piece of information is missing, you have the right to ask for it, but try to be polite and to remain objective. Also, avoid unduly delaying the audit process by asking for information; you can always return to that point when you have more time.

Nonconformities

Many different words are used to express the same meaning when referring to deficiencies or nonconformities within a company's system. In practice, you are likely to encounter various terms such as discrepancy, deficiency, findings, or nonconformity. All mean the same—in effect, they are the "non-fulfillment of a specified requirement." (ISO 8402, Clause 2.10). The International Standard ISO 8402 standardizes the term nonconformity, but it will take some time for this standard terminology to be adopted on a widespread basis.

Recording Nonconformities

When you identify a nonconformity and can trace and reexamine it to reveal the scale of the problem, stop and record those facts. You do not have to list every single occurrence of a problem, but state that what you witnessed is repeated in other records or in other areas. The audit is very much a "show me" exercise that looks for factual evidence. In this respect, a nonconformity report is a concise record of the facts relating to the nonconformance.

Ideally, a nonconformity should be recorded and signed as agreed at the point of identification. You should explain to the auditee that such an acknowledgment does not necessarily mean that you will issue a corrective action request but that you must evaluate the finding in the context of the entire audit.

How you record those facts is up to you. Remember that phrasing the nonconformity requires some care on the part of the auditor. To stop the audit to write the details in full, well-structured English can destroy the pace and timing of the audit. The actual written nonconformity may not be presented until later in the day.

Some auditors have used recording devices during an audit. In once instance, an auditor decided the best way to use this device was to cover his head with his coat, hide in the corner, and talk into the machine. This activity caused some consternation on the shop floor (not to mention various ribald comments) and isn't recommended.

When recording a nonconformity, statement should be in a format that can be understood by both the auditor and the auditee, including those members of the department who were not necessarily present when the nonconformity was identified. Adequate references should be included to allow the department to reexamine the observations after the auditor has left the department.

The recorded nonconformity should include the following information:

- Where the nonconformity was found
- An exact observation of the facts surrounding the discrepancy
- The reason why the facts constitute a nonconformity
- Sufficient references to allow traceability.

When writing the nonconformity, remember the following suggestions:

- Use local terminology, i.e., work in the language of the department
- Make the information easily retrievable for future reference
- Make it helpful to the auditees
- Make it concise, yet complete.

3) REPORTING

Just as a company has a customer for its product or service, an auditor has a customer for the results of the audit process. With an internal audit, the customer is likely to be the company's own quality assurance manager and the department head of the area under examination. As such, the format of the final report and tone of the closing meeting must be structured to meet the requirements of the department or function.

Before the closing meeting, the audit team may meet to evaluate the information they found during the audit and to ensure their validity as nonconformities. They should then record their findings in a nonconformity report. (See figure 5-1.) At this point, only the "Nonconformance" section should be filled out.

The Closing Meeting

Whether an audit has been an internal or external assessment, the auditor/audit team should meet with the department and/or company management to confirm the results and to identify the subsequent actions required. For an internal audit, discuss the corrective action with the appropriate department manager who is more involved in the process.

The closing meeting should not last longer than 30-45 minutes, and the following items should be covered:

- Thank the auditees for their hospitality and assistance
- Remember to record the attendees of this meeting
- Confirm the scope of the audit
- Identify the audit standard and revision status of the company's documented quality system
- Discuss any corrective action requests (CARs) in the nonconformity report

NONCONFORMITY REPORT

Department/Area Audited:

Department Representative:	**Auditor:**	**Nonconformance Report No.:**

Nonconformance:

Cause Identification/Proposed Corrective Action:

Agreed Time for Implementation:	**Responsibility for Action:**	**Dept. Rep's Signature:**

Auditor's Signature:	**Date:**

Entered in CAR Log by Quality Manager:

Signature: **Date:**

Corrective Action Completed Satisfactorily: ☐ YES ☐ NO
Comments:

                                                    Signature:

© EXCEL Partnership, Inc. 1993.   Form Number

Figure 5-1: Nonconformity Report.

- Explain that the audit has been a sampling exercise of the company's quality system and therefore, the fact that noncompliances have not been identified in a particular area does not mean that none exist
- Ask whether any points need to be clarified
- Confirm future actions.

The last item is an important—if not the most important—element of the audit process. Both internal and external audits are a complete waste of time unless action is taken to correct failures that have been identified within the quality system. (See Corrective Action below.)

The auditee may provide objective evidence that nullifies your claim of nonconformity. The auditor/audit team should evaluate the claim and record it if it is valid. In addition, the auditee might refuse to acknowledge one of your CARs, in which case the auditor should record the refusal. As an auditor, you should leave the corrective action request forms with the department manager at the end of the meeting.

The Formal Audit Report

The formal report should do the following:

- Show a customer or independent third party that the company's quality management system is periodically checked for effectiveness
- Evaluate the adequacy of the company's quality system as compared to its past performance
- Identify the areas of the company's quality management system that need improvement. It should assign responsibilities and apply timetables to monitor the progress of the corrective action.

No auditee expects you to write a dissertation, but your report should provide enough detail to validate your conclusions. A summary statement is a useful way to bring all these facts together.

A summary statement should contain the following applicable information:

- The department audited
- The audit team, auditee representatives
- The duration and extent of the audit and the dates it was conducted
- The audit's scope/objective
- The standard against which the auditee was audited
- The total number of discrepancies and where they were found
- Areas/functions where there were no nonconformities
- The effectiveness of the system
- Recommendations for corrective action
- Report distribution list.

Auditing, by its very nature, looks for areas of noncompliance, and it is important for the auditor to try to provide a balanced report that identifies the positive as well as the negative aspects of a company's systems. Therefore, identify and record acceptable elements of the system. The report should also identify—either by reference to the program, checklists or within the narrative of the report itself—the areas that were visited and the samples that were taken. It should be possible for someone to retrace the auditor's steps and examine the same evidence by referring to the audit report.

4) CORRECTIVE ACTION

An audit uncovers where the system is not functioning in accordance with management's objectives or in regard to the quality standard itself. As such, it can identify the illness, but does not provide the cure. Auditing for the sake of producing a report will serve little purpose. It must be followed by effective corrective action.

In the nonconformity report mentioned earlier, there is a space to record the proposed corrective action. A corrective action/follow-up procedure should include the following elements:

- Identify and agree to the details of the nonconformity between the auditee and auditor
- Agree to the corrective action
- Agree to timetables and dates to accomplish the following:
  - Resolve the problem
  - Implement the solution
  - Evaluate the effectiveness
  - Re-audit to confirm completion (i.e., closeout) of the program
- In the case of serious nonconformities generally associated with observed failures of system or products, it will be necessary to reaudit an activity to verify that the corrective action has been implemented and is effective.

A third party registrar will expect to see evidence that the above points have been addressed.

The corrective action program requires some paperwork—not to create undue bureaucracy, but to provide traceability demonstrating the outcome of an audit, to identify those responsible for its resolution, to monitor progress, and to initiate the "closeout" of the nonconformity.

Another important feature of the corrective action system is a management review (refer to ISO 9001, Subclause 4.1.3) of actions taken. This summary of corrective actions can form the basis on which to judge the entire quality system. It is important to try to quantify the benefits derived from the corrective action program. This can be in the form of increased customer confidence, fewer complaints or operational cost savings.

Some departmental managers within an organization may not respond positively to the need to implement corrective action. A system for escalation to more senior management should be built into the audit procedures when managers fail to act upon audit findings.

Corrective action and follow-up includes the following tasks:

- Identify the discrepancy
- Raise and issue a corrective action request

- Develop timetables for the auditee
- Evaluate the auditee's response
- Maintain accurate records to verify the corrective action has been completed
- "Close out" completed corrective actions requests in the records
- Escalate the issue to senior management if the auditees are not fulfilling their duties.

The corrective action program and its implementation demonstrates the true commitment of a company's management. The corrective action system is a highly visible part of the total quality system, and management must ensure that their actions demonstrate their commitment to the company's quality improvement objectives.

AUDITING THE INTERNAL AUDIT SYSTEM

By Bud Weightman

Must a company's internal audit system be audited itself under ISO 9000 series standards?

Yes. ISO 9001 refers to the requirements for a supplier's quality system. It holds that a supplier shall carry out a compliance system of planned and documented internal quality audits to verify whether quality activities comply with planned arrangements and to determine the effectiveness of the quality system.

There are 20 basic elements in the standard, all of which are applicable to the supplier. Any of these elements is supported by all of the others. You can't take away one of them and say this requirement doesn't apply. Therefore you must also do internal audits of the audit system.

If the quality department, for example, is charged with internal audit scheduling and performance, get a qualified individual from another department, possibly manufacturing, to audit the quality department.

In such a case manufacturing would verify, by using an audit procedure or checklist, that the quality department has implemented the applicable controls established by the quality manual. This is most likely supported by a lower-level procedure and further requirements.

Additionally, manufacturing would verify that those personnel responsible for performing the company's internal audit system were qualified and trained to perform the audits and actually independent from the activities they have audited.

Without such a system in effect, the auditors (in this case the quality department) would get a free ride. Every individual and every department must be counter-checked. That includes the department or individuals charged with performing the audits on everyone else.

Editor's Note: *This box was adopted from an article that appeared in the December 1992 issue of Quality Systems Update.*

INTERVIEW OR INQUISITION: SUCCESSFUL COMMUNICATION TECHNIQUES[1]

BY ROGER C. PRATT

Manager, Quality Training Office
Pacific Northwest Laboratory[2]

Editor's Note: *This paper was presented by Roger C. Pratt at the ASQC's 2nd Annual Quality Audit Conference in Charlotte, NC, in February 1993. It is reprinted with the permission of the American Society for Quality Control.*

The article highlights some interviewing skills that auditors—both internal and external—can use to help smooth communications with the auditee. While it is written from an auditor's point of view, auditees can learn from it as well.

Introduction

Although part of any auditor's time is spent gathering information from documents, a significant portion is spent gathering information from people. This field investigative work is the core of the audit. It is where auditors make observations, collect data and interview employees. Therefore, much of this article addresses the auditing "non-tangibles," so to speak. These include interviewing techniques, body language, and ethical issues.

The point of this article may be a restatement of the golden rule, with a little poetic license: *audit others as you would like to be audited.*

Putting the Auditee at Ease

The announcement that an organization is going to be audited or that a particular function is going to be surveyed automatically creates a fear of the unknown in those being audited. Therefore, auditors must recognize that their early activities will be suspect. Even though the auditees are aware of the ground rules and the scope of the audit, auditees may be concerned that they will be singled out and that areas under their responsibility will be lacking.

Change of any sort can be threatening, causing a defensive or hostile attitude. The auditee will probably spend more time justifying the status quo than listening to suggested improvements. The auditor has to be sensitive to the anxiety of all auditees by considering the audited individual's personal philosophies, motivational characteristics, and individual objectives. An auditor should be able to counter any defensiveness by accepting different methods of compliance to a specific requirement; auditors must avoid the "my way is the only correct way" mentality.

To alleviate some of this stress, the audit team should arrive at the designated locations on time and be mentally and physically prepared to audit. The audit team should appear cohesive and have a leader who sets the tone and pace of the audit. The team should be enthusiastic, unbiased and confident in their ability to assist the organization.

Interview/Communication Techniques

How auditors ask questions will affect the amount and quality of the information they receive. Preparation is the first and most important step; if the auditor knows in advance what should be discussed, the auditor is more likely to ask appropriate questions.

It is up to the auditor to establish an initial atmosphere of trust and open communication. The goal is to obtain as much valid information as possible in the shortest time possible. Some potential conditions that affect the initial interactions include the following:

● The auditee's perceptions of the audit process: "This is a waste of time; I am being evaluated only to fulfill requirements."

● Auditee's initial feelings of fear and skepticism: "Will this clear up the problems; will I come out of this looking OK?" (The auditee might have certain predispositions based on past experiences.)

The auditor must recognize that these factors exist and be aware of them during the audit process.

Auditors should emphasize that they are there to audit the system or program, not the person. Auditors should explain to the auditee's manager that the audit is not a "search for the guilty." It will identify potential problems and assist in correcting them.

Consequently, auditors should take notes throughout the interview process; memory is unreliable, at best. Note-taking may create small pockets of silence which can induce stress, but most auditees will be comfortable if they understand that notes are being taken to ensure that accurate information is being recorded.

The importance of listening cannot be overstressed; it is difficult to gather information while talking. Auditors should not formulate new questions when the individual is responding to the previous ones, and they should listen for more than the "bottom line." It is important to let the auditee respond with as much detail as possible to get the needed information. The best way to accomplish this is to first ask open-ended questions and then move to close-ended questions to get clarification of details.

Questions that can be answered "yes" or "no" should be kept to a minimum. An example of a yes-or-no or close-ended question is, "Do you perform reviews according to your project management procedure Number 51?" The reply would undoubtedly be "yes." One way to rephrase the question in an open-ended format is: "I've read your Procedure 51, which indicates that a particular type of review process is performed. Explain to me in detail how you implement that procedure."

It is important for auditors to communicate at the same responsibility level and knowledge of the person they are interviewing. The discussions may range from quality philosophy with top management to specific manufacturing techniques with the worker on the production line.

There are several clarification techniques that can be used to make sure that the information received from interviewees is clear and complete:

● Probing: Using follow-up questions to further explore something the auditee has said.

● Paraphrasing: Repeating and rewording important points.

● Summarizing: Recapping and repeating a set of major points to make sure all the important information has been noted.

Using these techniques the auditor can demonstrate that he or she is a good listener and is a professional. In addition, the techniques give the auditee a chance to fill in any missing or misunderstood information.

GENERAL CONSIDERATIONS

It is appropriate in a business situation to shake hands with all individuals when they are introduced—both males and females. Auditors should also try to use the person's name occasionally in conversation. This recognizes the auditee as an individual and facilitates the free exchange of information.

Auditors should use appropriate body language to show that they are listening and receiving the message that the individual is sending. This means good eye contact, head nods, etc., as needed. Eye contact should be maintained about 25 percent of the time, as a rule. Too much eye contact, however, makes the auditee feel uncomfortable, and too little makes the interview impersonal. The auditor should smile when appropriate, for it is possible for the auditor to concentrate to such an extent that the auditor appears unfriendly.

The audit team's dress sets the tone for the level of professionalism perceived by the audited organization. A suit projects a power image, while blue jeans set a casual tone. Dress should be appropriate to the organization that is being audited. It would be inappropriate, for example, to conduct an audit of construction activities in a three-piece suit or a silk dress.

DEALING WITH UNUSUAL SITUATIONS OR CONFLICTS

The goal during the interview portions of the audit is to gain information in the best atmosphere possible. There may be times, however, when conflicts or difficult situations arise. This includes situations when the auditee repeatedly fails to answer a question or answers inconsistently, when the auditee tries to dominate the situation, or when the auditee rambles on in an irrelevant monologue. In these cases, it is best to directly confront the individual's behavior and redirect the conversation. The auditor should be persistent and not allow intentional or unintentional avoidance of a topic; it is important to demonstrate control in these types of situations.

It is possible that personnel who are anticipating the audit may develop data, statistics, or other information and offer it to the auditor as evidence of a previous corrective action or as evidence that no problems exist. Some individuals are skilled at using statistical data deceptively. Such data should be used and accepted only if the auditor is convinced that it is valid and appropriate. Usually, obtaining validations from other sources is necessary before such information may be accepted and used in the audit.

Occasionally the auditees will resort to tactics such as showing new products under development, giving tours of the plant, or taking long lunch hours to divert the auditors from their planned activities. The auditor should resist such obvious diversionary tactics.

If a facility is in trouble, and particularly if there are management problems, there may be sincerely ethical people who will indicate an interest in talking to the auditor. This does not mean that these volunteers are necessarily correct in their analysis of the situation. Care must be exercised so as not to be distracted by the side issues. On the other hand, this information should not be ignored and, with proper validation, may give valuable feedback on system effectiveness.

ETHICS

When dealing with the audited organization, there are some key principles to keep in mind that take the above factors into account.

Maintain the self-esteem of the individual—refrain from making cutting or sarcastic remarks. This is important in building rapport between the auditor and the auditee, maintaining an atmosphere of openness and trust, and encouraging the flow of information.

Showing empathy and understanding will also help build rapport. This will ease tension so that the auditor can gain information that would not have been gotten otherwise. To show empathy and understanding, the auditor should listen for both facts and emotions in what the auditee says. Using the technique of "reflecting," the auditor states the emotional content of what the auditee has said to show that the auditor recognizes and understands the auditee. An example might be, "You seem dissatisfied with the manner in which that procedure was implemented."

Also, the auditor should try not to show shock, dismay or surprise if the auditee reveals potentially damaging information; simply indicate that the facts were understood, and communicate an appreciation of openness and honesty.

Check findings and observations against the "so what?" reaction. This means measuring the perceived problem against potential consequences or risks if it is not corrected. If the consequences are small or nonexistent but are symptoms of a larger system problem, the auditor should investigate. They can then be used as facts supporting that more general finding.

The auditor should maintain a conscious objectivity toward the subject being evaluated. Previous practices or personal beliefs can prevent a full understanding of existing conditions. The auditor will be confronted many times with conjecture, suggestions, leading or distracting opinions expressed by those being contacted. It is essential that the auditor keep his or her personal opinions private and concentrate on elements of observed fact.

Concentrate on the relevant facts. The situation should be evaluated in sufficient depth so that the root cause can eventually be determined. It is not, however, the responsibility of the auditing organization to determine the specific source of the problem or to place blame.

Surprises should not be a part of an auditor's evaluation. An ethical audit is not the place for cloak-and-dagger tactics, for witch hunting, or for identifying situations at a critical and embarrassing time (a "gotcha"). These practices violate auditor ethics.

All reported observations and recommendations—including the discussion and supporting data for such recommendations—should be stated in the impersonal tense. Avoid using names; substitute instead a definition of the functions that were evaluated and/or the level of the persons in that function.

The auditor should comply to the greatest extent practicable with the customs of the audited facility. This includes compliance with working hours, mode of dress, observance of lunch hours, and other facility requirements or customary procedures.

Give the benefit of the doubt to the audited organization. When there is significant doubt in the mind of the auditor as to the verifiable facts or the correctness of the auditor's recommendation, the item should be carefully evaluated with other members of the team and the team leader. If, in further evaluation, the item continues to be in doubt, it should be dropped or degree of uncertainty.

Conclusion

Auditing is not a simple task, for an auditor must gather factual information while at times using "intangible" techniques to effectively deal with an organization's employees. It is important that the auditor learn how to interview the auditee, how to handle unusual situations, and how to conduct an ethical audit. The auditor must also be professional, preserve the auditee's self-esteem, and inform the auditee of all information gathered during the audit (i.e., create no surprises). The "amended" golden rule applies: ***audit others as you would like to be audited.***

ENDNOTES

[1] R.C. Pratt, D.E. Ryder, and F.C. Hood, "Auditing Methods for Lead Auditors," Quality Training and Resource Center Course #QLT-180010, Rev. 5, US Department of Energy, Richland Operations Office, Richland, Washington.

[2] Pacific Northwest Laboratory is operated by the Battelle Memorial Institute for the US Department of Energy under contract DE-AC06-76RLO 1830. Pacific Northwest Laboratory, Battelle Boulevard, Richland, WA 99352.

6

A BASIC GUIDE
TO IMPLEMENTING
ISO 9000

BY RODERICK GOULT

This chapter describes the basic steps in the ISO 9000 implementation process. It begins with an overview of the key elements of a quality system and how to make every aspect of the system "visible" to everyone in the company and to external auditors. Next, it presents four important questions every company should consider when beginning an implementation program, such as the anticipated registration date, the scope of the desired registration, the choice of standard and the extent of existing documentation. The chapter lays out a practical approach to implementation that includes the following steps:

- Getting ready for ISO 9000 registration
- How to avoid common ISO 9000 pitfalls
- The registration audit process and the auditee's responsibilities.

INTRODUCTION

The ISO 9000 family of standards provides a series of models that represent a responsible, sensible and practical way to run a company. The basic principles are simple: say what you do, do what you say, write it down, then review and improve the process.

The three separate models represented by ISO 9001, ISO 9002 and ISO 9003 are designed to address the different needs of companies engaged in all activities, from design to post-delivery maintenance—in other words, the 'scope' of a company's activities. The selection of the "scope of registration" will be discussed in some detail later. The essential message at this stage is to recognize that the three independent standards do not represent levels of excellence—they represent types of activity.

It can be argued that the word "quality" has no place in the title of the ISO 9000 series. The standards have nothing to do with product or service quality—they define no requirements or specifications, prescribe no techniques of measurement or test, and insist upon no absolute levels of process or quality control. What they do describe is a set of guidelines for the creation of a management system to ensure that all operations throughout the company occur in a stable manner.

The effective operation of such a system will result in stable processes and, therefore, in a consistent output from those processes—whether they be manufacturing or management processes. Once stability and consistency are achieved, it is possible to initiate improvements. Companies achieving ISO 9000 system registration generally find that the process of implementation has resulted in reduced system redundancy, improved management and production processes and enhanced communication within the organization.

Some companies and commentators, including major quality gurus, complain that the ISO 9000 series is too basic or too open to loose interpretation. These firms and individuals point instead to existing concepts of excellence, and—in the case of some companies—to their training programs and other activities that go far beyond the requirements of the ISO standards. They use these claims as reasons not to invest in quality system registration. In some respects these critics are correct; more often, however, they are misguided and often delude themselves as to how thorough, competent and lasting their programs are.

In addition, much criticism of ISO 9000 rests more on matters of linguistics than substance. This issue will be discussed below. It should be noted, however, that if the quality systems of companies critical to ISO 9000 are in fact as good as their proponents claim, then the process of implementing ISO 9001 or ISO 9002 should be very straightforward.

This chapter is a basic introduction to the concepts, principles and methodologies of implementing a management system—tools that have been developed by the author over many years and that have proven to be effective. The methodology also assures that all the criteria laid out in the ISO 9000 series of standards are met.

MAKING THE QUALITY SYSTEM VISIBLE

Creating a documented management system—usually known in the United States as a quality system—and retaining records of the operation of that system makes the complete management process visible...visible to customers, visible to company staff, and visible to the external auditors. Table 6-1 highlights the key issues that such a system needs to address, and some of the ways and means to address them. These are all key issues defined in the 1987 version of ISO 9001 and ISO 9002 and in all three revised 1994 standards.

Making Quality Management Visible

MAKE THE COMPANY POLICY KNOWN

It is vital that the company policy regarding quality be clearly defined and clearly understood by every employee—from the floor sweeper to the chief executive officer. The ideal quality policy is concise, clear and to the point. Avoid sweeping, high-level statements about "world class quality," "technical leadership" and "the ceaseless pursuit of excellence."

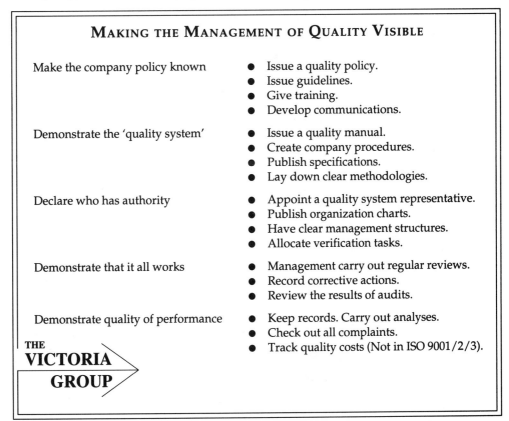

MAKING THE MANAGEMENT OF QUALITY VISIBLE	
Make the company policy known	• Issue a quality policy. • Issue guidelines. • Give training. • Develop communications.
Demonstrate the 'quality system'	• Issue a quality manual. • Create company procedures. • Publish specifications. • Lay down clear methodologies.
Declare who has authority	• Appoint a quality system representative. • Publish organization charts. • Have clear management structures. • Allocate verification tasks.
Demonstrate that it all works	• Management carry out regular reviews. • Record corrective actions. • Review the results of audits.
Demonstrate quality of performance	• Keep records. Carry out analyses. • Check out all complaints. • Track quality costs (Not in ISO 9001/2/3).

THE
VICTORIA
GROUP

Table 6-1: Making the Management of Quality Visible.

Not only are they frequently full of hot air, but they are also completely unauditable either by internal or external auditors and impossible for management to measure. The single most important thing about a quality policy statement is that staff should be able to witness the management living by that statement—in other words, walking the talk.

Policies for quality are like policies for politicians—they need to be supported by clearly defined objectives and strategies for their achievement. A policy lacking a strategy and an objective is not likely to be achieved.

DEMONSTRATE THE QUALITY SYSTEM

The next thing that the company needs to do is document the management system. This is typically done in a four-tier documentation structure, the content and nature of which are discussed later. The 1987 versions of the standards were very open on this issue, but the 1994 revision has become much more specific in defining this system.

DECLARE WHO HAS AUTHORITY

Someone has to be responsible for ensuring the effective maintenance of the quality system. One of the most frequent faults encountered in industry of all types—both service and manufacturing—is the practice of making an individual responsible for an activity without also giving them the authority required to fulfill the task.

The ISO 9000 standards require that the individual charged with the task of ensuring that the system is effectively maintained has both the responsibility and defined authority required. This is one of the places where the 1994 standard has moved forward from the original text. The new version requires that management with "executive responsibility" appoint a member of its own management to be responsible for the system. The wording is unclear as to whether the management representative has to be a member of executive management or not. The implication, however, is quite clear: this task must be overseen at the executive level within the company.

The ISO 9000 standards also require that the "responsibility, authority and interrelation of personnel who manage, perform and verify work affecting quality shall be defined." The question to ask in determining who is covered by this requirement is "who does work affecting quality?"

The answer is obvious—everyone. So there is a need for the documented system to define, in some way, somewhere in its structure, the responsibilities, authorities and interrelationships of all personnel. This may be done through the use of family trees, procedures, work instructions, job descriptions, team structures or any other method that a company chooses to invent or deploy. The method is not the issue—the result is important.

DEMONSTRATE THAT IT ALL WORKS

There is little point in having such a system unless it can all be shown to be working effectively. This is achieved through conducting regular reviews by management—once again, the 1994 version of the standard requires that these be conducted by the executive management of the company. Reviews should not only encompass a system's workings, but also look to see that the system is effectively maintaining the intent of the quality policy...yet another reason for creating a simple, quantifiable quality policy. Records of these reviews are to be kept.

DEMONSTRATE QUALITY OF PERFORMANCE

The management system is of real value only if it enables the company to demonstrate to customers (and to itself) that it is achieving what it is setting out to achieve in terms of service or product performance—not in terms of financial measures.

Most of the performance indicators that management reviews are "lagging indicators." They depend upon historic data to feed management with information upon which actions can be based. The ISO 9000 standards provide the opportunity to build some "leading indicators" into that review process, thereby enabling the management to take action to prevent those problems, rather than to react after they occur.

The 1994 version of the standards also takes all the activities that the 1987 issue had listed as "notes" after *Clause 4.2, Quality System* and turns them into "as appropriate" shall statements. This creates a new requirement: making quality planning an essential element of the management system in some form or another. The standard does not require that formal quality plans be drawn up, simply that the system shall ensure that the necessary planning is carried out.

Making Product or Service Requirements Visible

For any company to operate in a "quality manner" it must ensure that it clearly understands its customers' requirements and that these requirements are properly reflected in design activity being undertaken on behalf of the customer. Table 6-2 takes the essential elements of understanding customer needs and translates them into visible, auditable activities within the company. This table is based on ISO 9001, and therefore includes the activities involved in transferring customer needs through the design process into a product or service. (Those companies that are either ISO 9002 registered or planning to implement a quality system to comply with ISO 9002 can ignore the four elements of the table that mention the word "design.")

The primary elements required to understand the customer's needs are encapsulated in the requirements of the ISO 9000 standards, and they are the following:

- Formal procedures are documented and observed for the performance of contract review
- All the requirements of every contract, tender, and order are adequately defined and documented to the level required by the functional practices of the company
- The company has the capability to meet those requirements, namely through the following:
  - Technical ability
  - Ability to deliver at the agreed time
  - Ability to meet the agreed price.

The 1994 rewrite makes it clear that these requirements have to be met even when there is no written agreement between the two parties.

One more new requirement to be found in the 1994 document concerns the issue of contract changes. There is now a formal requirement for a contract change procedure to be documented within the system.

CONTROL OF THE DESIGN PROCESS

The requirements for formal control of design to ensure that customer requirements are always met have been fairly straightforward, covering the following issues:

- Planning the design
- Allocating tasks
- Providing sufficient trained staff and equipment to meet the desired time frame
- Updating design plans to track the essential milestones
- Providing clear and unambiguous design input
- Including any statutory or regulatory needs that have to be met.

MAKING PRODUCT AND SERVICE REQUIREMENTS VISIBLE

Demonstrate Visibility of
Customer Needs
- Conduct reviews of order input.
- Ensure requirements are understood.
- Validate the capability to meet requirements.

Demonstrate Design Planning
- Implement planning methods.
- Allocate design tasks.
- Ensure adequate skills and equipment.
- Update plans as work proceeds.

Demonstrate the Quality of
Design Input
- Document stated and implied needs.
- Ensure clarity of requirements.
- Conduct regular reviews.
- Control the update of specifications.

Demonstrate Adequacy of Design
Output
- Allocate verification tasks.
- Perform and document design reviews.
- Document test methods and results.
- Establish configuration management.
- Validate against design input criteria.

Demonstrate Control of Designs
- Maintain effective configuration management.

THE
VICTORIA
GROUP

Table 6-2: Making Product and Service Requirements Visible.

The only really significant change made to this section is that of holding formal design reviews. Long advocated by this author, this is now a "shall" requirement in the 1994 text.

The original 1987 requirement for design output to be specified at the input stage has remained unchanged. On the output side, however, the 1994 document sees fit to split the original requirement for design verification into two stages, verification and validation.

The difference between the two is effectively defined within the standard as follows: verification is the activity of ensuring that the output from a design stage meets the input to that same stage—these individual design steps may have little direct linkage to a defined customer need. Validation is seen as a task performed to prove compliance with "defined user needs and/or requirements."

Making the Quality of the Process Visible

The quality of the process should also be visible. Its key elements are shown in Table 6-3.

The effectiveness of the system is seen only when the records of the various processes are regularly and properly analyzed. There are too many companies that start to control processes only once they are in-house, on their own shop floor. This is far too late. If the incoming product is flawed (other than in the business of recycling), then the likelihood of being able to produce fully compliant products is quite remote.

Process control has to start with the raw materials that the company purchases, hence the emphasis that the ISO standards place on selecting, deselecting and verifying vendors.

Once the process is in-house, there are many methods that a company may use to ensure that the process output meets the requirements. Table 6-3 identifies just some of the methods that may be used as a way of making the control of the process visible to all those involved. There are many techniques and methods available, and those selected by the company will depend entirely upon the nature of the product or service that they provide, the level of training enjoyed by the staff, and whether or not the activity is subject to outside regulatory control.

Finally, consideration needs to be given to whether or not there are any special requirements imposed by customers. These are a few of the issues to be considered.

Any company wishing to comply with the ISO standards must—at a minimum—address each of the activities in these three figures, although there are industries where some of those activities might be defined as "not applicable." One example is the concept of calibration in the design and development of applications software. These simple figures are designed to illustrate the overall tasks involved in making the management of quality visible and show some of the actions management can take to promote that goal.

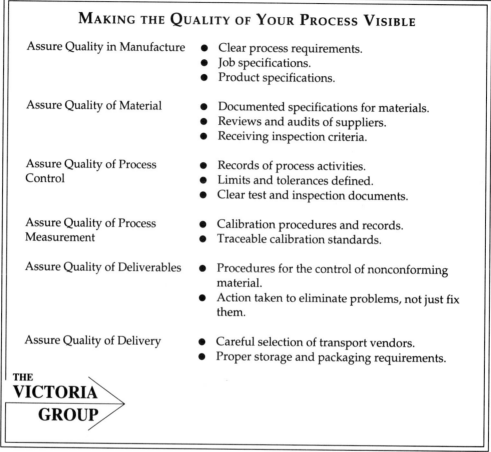

MAKING THE QUALITY OF YOUR PROCESS VISIBLE

Assure Quality in Manufacture	• Clear process requirements. • Job specifications. • Product specifications.
Assure Quality of Material	• Documented specifications for materials. • Reviews and audits of suppliers. • Receiving inspection criteria.
Assure Quality of Process Control	• Records of process activities. • Limits and tolerances defined. • Clear test and inspection documents.
Assure Quality of Process Measurement	• Calibration procedures and records. • Traceable calibration standards.
Assure Quality of Deliverables	• Procedures for the control of nonconforming material. • Action taken to eliminate problems, not just fix them.
Assure Quality of Delivery	• Careful selection of transport vendors. • Proper storage and packaging requirements.

THE
VICTORIA
GROUP

Table 6-3: Making the Quality of Your Process Visible.

ASKING THE RIGHT QUESTIONS

Implementing a structured management system requires a disciplined approach, careful planning, good project control, and regular milestone measurement. Successful implementation of an ISO 9000 program should begin by answering four basic questions.

1. When Is the Anticipated Registration Date?

ISO 9000 implementation is a process, not a quick fix. It requires patience, training, attitude changes, and total commitment from top management. As many companies are discovering, it needs a paradigm shift in corporate outlook—a totally new way of looking at management's role.

One of the major changes that implementation often forces on managers is that of accepting responsibility for their actions. Some companies have completed the registration process in less than a year, including small companies and highly regulated ones that have many existing controls in place. Such an achievement, however, often requires a substantial staff commitment, and the question should be asked whether it is worth that degree of effort.

Companies not operating under such strict controls should not underestimate the registration time line. A large company with a complex management structure should think in terms of at least a 12 to 18 months initial commitment.

Few companies can afford to commit substantial resources full-time to a registration effort. Fitting the required work into busy staff schedules can be difficult. It needs to be recognized that most documentation takes two or three iterations to get right. "Right the first time" may be the target, but it is often an elusive goal. It pays to proceed steadily and carefully, giving due consideration to every aspect of the process, including the decision as to which member of staff is assigned to write any particular document. The individual who performs a particular job is the best person to document how it is done, not that individual's supervisor.

It also pays any company to involve as many staff as possible in the implementation process—this must not be something that is "handed down" from the management, nor should it be something that is created by the quality department. The system must be created by the people who will drive it, and who must take ownership of it if it is to succeed. The best way to achieve this ownership and commitment to the system is for the "user group" to also be the authors. Remember, the primary customer for the management system is the company staff, from floor-sweeper to the president.

2. Register Part of the Organization or the Entire Organization?

This is often a difficult question for a company to answer, particularly if one of the primary reasons for electing to implement ISO 9000 is customer pressure, and that pressure only comes from one particular product sector. A company that produces multiple products for very different markets can often have a much bigger task on its hands in effectively implementing either ISO 9001 or 9002 than the single product company. There has to be a way of simplifying such a decision, and there is. The technique suggested is that of a pressure matrix. An example of such a matrix is shown in Figure 6-1.

If a high customer demand for

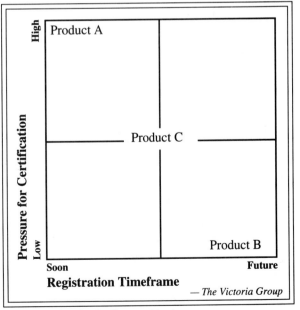

Figure 6-1: Certification Pressure Matrix.

registration exists for Product/Service A and none currently exists for Product/Service B, is registration necessary and prudent for both products? The answer could well be no, unless the two products or services flow through the identical process within the company. Registration refers to the management system, not to the product resulting from that system. It is possible to have multiple systems operating within a company, providing many different products and/ or services.

In the scenario shown by the pressure matrix, with product C in the middle with median pressures for both time and certification, the prudent decision is probably to certify the operational aspects of product A in the first pass, extend to product B in the second pass, and finally reach product C. This multistage operation can be a series of certifications spread over a period of years, or a an extension of business scope arranged to be reviewed at each surveillance visit.

Managing such a situation can have its difficulties, but sometimes it is easier than trying to operate the whole system the same way. Consider as an example a plastics molding company producing high-precision items for the telecommunications industry. This is product A. As a sideline it also makes small plastic toys such as those given away in cereal boxes, and this is product B in the matrix. Product C is a component part used in the manufacture of commercial lap-top computers.

The high-precision telecommunication products will probably face market pressure for both product certification and registration of the quality system. The sideline plastic toy business has only one market pressure—price. The lap-top computer industry, in turn, is facing an increasingly competitive marketplace and is therefore gradually becoming more and more selective about suppliers, hence the pressure for certification.

The stringent quality assurance standards on product A (high-precision telecommunication items) are not the same as those on product B (plastic toys). Therefore, the company may decide to seek a registration that covers, in its scope statement, the close-tolerance, high-grade injecting molding and ignores the high-volume, low-grade plastic toys. By doing so, it first registers the core business scope of the company and retains the flexibility to include other elements at a later date.

3. Should a Company Seek Registration to ISO 9001 or ISO 9002?

ISO 9001 is a more comprehensive standard than ISO 9002. *ISO 9001, Quality systems— Model for quality assurance in design/development, production, installation and servicing*, is used when conformance to specified needs is to be ensured by the supplier throughout the entire cycle, from design to servicing. It is used when the contract specifically requires design effort and the product requirements are stated principally in performance terms, or when the confidence required by the buyer needs to be invested in all stages of the process, from concept to maintenance.

ISO 9002, Quality systems—Model for quality assurance in production, installation and servicing differs from ISO 9001 because it does not include the design function as a significant part of the organization's activity. It is used by industries that work to technical designs and specifications already provided by their customers. It is also used by companies that own the product design. The design, however, is of such a stable nature that the company's manufacturing capabilities are the key quality determinants in purchasing the product—not the product's design.

HOW TO DEFINE "DESIGN"

The chief dilemma faced by many companies in deciding whether to register to ISO 9001 or ISO 9002 results from whether to define the term design in a broad or narrow sense. At one time, design encompassed only organizations that carried out original research and development. Based on that reasoning, few companies would seek the more comprehensive ISO 9001 registration. Current concepts are different.

It is generally accepted that the definition of design can be very broad. Universities and colleges can design training programs for specific curricular requirements. Banks and insurance companies design services for customers. Software houses design computer programs. A computer hardware company designs computers.

Historically, registration bodies have not been consistent in their definition of what constitutes design and when ISO 9001 was really the appropriate standard. There has also been a tendency to allow too many companies that are really ISO 9001 in their scope to register to ISO 9002 on the understanding that ISO 9001 will follow shortly...which has not happened.

The National Accreditation Council for Certification Bodies (NACCB) in the United Kingdom has recognized a growing problem in this area, and in October 1992 decided to take action to tighten up on the issuance of ISO 9002 certificates to essentially ISO 9001 companies. In a letter dated October 21, 1992, the Secretary to the NACCB made it very clear what was expected of certification bodies in this respect. He wrote:

> *Where an individual contract requires design input the assurance which the customer has a right to expect from a certified quality system rests, in part at least, on the capability of the supplier to undertake the design work in such a way that the product or service will meet agreed requirements. To issue a certificate in such circumstances to ISO 9002 risks misleading the market into thinking that the supplier's quality system has been assessed when, in fact, only part of it is assessed.*

> *NACCB, therefore, requires that certificates of compliance to ISO 9002 should not be issued to suppliers whose customers' orders require them to undertake specific design work.*

There is little room for confusion as far as the NACCB is concerned. The next step is up to the registrars, and it will be interesting to see how they react.

TWO KEY QUESTIONS

In making the decision as to whether to register to ISO 9001 or ISO 9002, companies should ask themselves two questions:

- In the continuum from concept to disposal of the product or service offered to customers, to what extent does the design of that product or service determine the effective delivered quality and performance of the product or service supplied to the customer?
- How much control over the product or service offered to the customer is resident in the company offering the product or service?

If a company has complete control over the design of its product or service, and that control is a major factor in ensuring delivered quality, then registration to ISO 9001 is the only choice. However, if a product or service has been an integral and unchanging part of a company for many years, and the principal determining factor in ensuring the quality of the delivered product or service is the manufacturing process, then the company should choose registration to ISO 9002. A manufacturing facility whose design division is off-site can usually choose ISO 9002. (Figure 6-2)

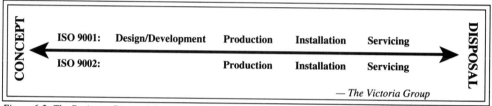

Figure 6-2: The Design to Disposal Continuum.

The 1987 version of ISO 9002 did not include servicing—the 1994 version does. Now the only difference between the two standards is the absence of design and development from ISO 9002.

THE SCOPE STATEMENT

There are many companies where problems exist in getting the design function of a company to support a registration effort. In these situations, companies can write a scope statement that encompasses the entire operation, but contains a design restriction. If the registrar is willing to negotiate these restrictions, a company may specify that at this time only the "manufacturing/procurement/test, etc. areas are operating an ISO 9002 compliant system, and the design elements will be brought into an ISO 9001 system by [a specified date]."

Many companies have followed this path to ISO 9001 registration by declaring intent to embrace the design function at a later date and then doing so. These are not the companies at whom the comments from the NACCB are aimed. If design is critical to the delivered quality of a product or service, ISO 9002 can be used as a starting option, provided that the registrar concurs with an extension to ISO 9001 within a defined time frame.

Registrars need to exercise careful judgment in this area. The NACCB is obviously concerned about the confusion that exists in the marketplace at the present time. Other accreditation boards—including the RAB in the United States—no doubt share this concern but have not yet gone public in addressing the issue.

There is a considerable issue with some Canadian-issued registrations at the present time, where a number of companies hold registrations to ISO 9003, the model for systems covering no more than inspection and test, yet have scope statements that include words about design and manufacture, neither of which are addressed by the ISO 9003 standard. (Please refer to Chapter 20 for more information on the Canadian registration system.)

Fundamentally this becomes an issue of ethics and consumer confidence. Registrars must be free to exercise a degree of judgment in determining with a client company the appropriate section of the standard to be used for registration purposes. Equally, any company must be free to implement its system progressively if that is the approach that makes good business sense, from the point of view of time scales, staff effort and cost of registration.

The real problem is in the fact that many consumers are naive about issues of scope. If the process of registration is to continue to grow and prosper to the ultimate benefit of producers and consumers alike, it is incumbent upon both registrars and accreditation bodies to ensure that their actions do not mislead the consumer about the registration certificate.

The majority of accreditation bodies are subject to some form of government oversight, and this exercises some control over the degree to which they are driven by commercial pressures. This is not yet the case in the United States. Registrars, on the other hand, are primarily private commercial organizations that need to make a profit to survive. This makes them much more subject to financial influences than will usually be the case with an accreditation body.

This is truly one of the most sensitive issues in the entire process and one that is not yet fully mature anywhere. The fact that registrars are commercial organizations means that they are dependent upon their client base of companies for their survival. This must inevitably create pressures for occasional doubtful certifications.

It is to the great credit of the vast majority of registrars in all parts of the world that the system has the degree of respect that it currently enjoys from both the customer and the supplier community. The key to the future continued success of the process of third party certification lies with all those involved, from national accreditation boards to the individual auditors who constantly strive to ensure that this respect continues and grows.

4. How Much Documentation Currently Exists?

In many companies, process documentation does not reside on paper, but in the collective memory of company employees. All companies have systems, but how many systems rely on the memory of trusted key staff members? If a longtime staff member is sick or leaves the job, is it really true that "everyone knows what to do?"

And even more important at this stage of the process: does management's conception of how the system works coincide with what really happens on the shop floor and elsewhere in the company? Not only might these perceptions clash, but the methodology might also be changing at the whim of the individual employee, without any form of review or control. This is not due to any malicious intent of the individual making the changes—it will probably be quite the opposite; the employee may genuinely be trying to improve and perfect the activity.

The point is that all such process changes—whether to manufacturing, design or management processes—should be under control, so that they can be properly assessed for their potential macro impacts on the activity as a whole, as well as for their localized, micro effects on the work being directly performed.

The sort of questions that management needs to ask as it starts to evaluate existing systems begin at the interface between the company and the customer. They include the following:

- Do sales and marketing staff follow systems to ensure that all relevant data needed is collected so that customer needs are met?
- Does the design staff receive all data required to meet customer expectations, and is it always in the same format?
- Does the design staff have control of documents and drawings?
- Do design procedures ensure that constraints of manufacturability, testability, maintainability, reliability and safety are considered, and that no laws are transgressed?

A company trying to determine its optimum level of documentation should also consider these questions:

- Is all the data required to procure, engineer into production, build, inspect, test, store, deliver and maintain a product or service provided in a consistent format?
- Do all these departments have clear instructions as to how the overall tasks are to be performed?
- Is all testing performed to the same specifications on controlled, calibrated test equipment?
- Does the company have records to prove that control exists?

These are just some of the issues companies seeking registration must address when evaluating current documentation. Many companies are shocked by the lack of positive answers to these questions. Experience has shown that even those companies whose commitment to excellence leads them to challenge the efficacy of the ISO standards find that they fall down under this form of examination.

Quality expert Phil Crosby compares the way companies operate by contrasting a game of ice hockey and the art of ballet. Despite the fact that a game of ice hockey operates by a well-defined set of rules, no two games are alike. By contrast, in a ballet such as Swan Lake—which encompasses many elements drawn together under planned, controlled conditions—every Swan Lake performance is essentially the same. Crosby says that running a company can be like ballet, if planning, rehearsal, review and control are part of the corporate score.

GETTING READY FOR ISO 9000 REGISTRATION

The decision to implement a documented quality system based on ISO 9000 series standards affects every element of a company and will significantly change the way a company does business. The buzz-word of the nineties appears to be "reengineering." An effective ISO implementation program will be just that—it revisits, reexamines and often substantially changes the entire way a business is generated, conducted, fulfilled and maintained.

Commitment from Senior Management

The key ingredient is support from senior management. A successful program must be driven by support from committed top management. Whether the effort of analysis and documentation undertaken is used to achieve registration or is used as an internal quality management tool makes no difference to the degree of commitment and effort required.

Obtaining management support is not always easy. When the demand for registration is customer-driven, most senior executives recognize the sensible course of action. When this is not the case, however, the program has to be sold to them in the same way as any other venture that will require an investment in time and money.

Here are the key points to emphasize:

- Registration enables a company to demonstrate visibly to its customers its commitment to quality
- Registration may provide opportunities to enter markets that are open only to registered firms
- An ISO 9000 based system will:
  - Improve the ability to collect quality metrics and thereby improve both quality and the cost of quality
  - Enhance the ability to develop stable processes and eliminate costly surprises
  - Improve overall business efficiency by eliminating wasteful and unnecessary duplication in management systems.
  - Effectively drive the process of continuous improvement through the implementation of a formal, documented corrective action process that is subject to constant review

The use of a structured management system is simply a better way to do business.

Continuous Improvement

It is unfortunate that many commentators who have never worked with the ISO standards continue to bemoan the absence of "continuous improvement" and the concept of defect prevention. Not least among those critics is Dr. Juran. Regrettably, this viewpoint represents no more than an inability to recognize that there is more than one way to speak about "continuous improvement."

The ISO 9000 standards call it "corrective action." Both ISO 9001 and ISO 9002 have a complete section devoted to the requirement for corrective action and ensuring that such action is effective. This is continuous improvement by another name—the constant relentless search for actual and potential causes of nonconformance and following up with corrective actions that are then reviewed for effectiveness. Likewise, in the opening paragraphs, these standards tell us that the primary purpose of the system should be the prevention of nonconformance. In the 1994 version, this emphasis on prevention becomes even more marked, with the addition of a complete new subclause called "preventive action."

Using a Project Management Approach

An effective implementation program requires discipline and determination. Experience shows that the best method is to treat the process as a major corporate project, and to use a project management approach. The following are steps in that process.

ASSIGN RESPONSIBILITY AND AUTHORITY

The first step is to assign to someone the responsibility and authority to drive the project. This person does not necessarily have to be the quality manager. The standard states that the management representative should be a person who, "irrespective of other responsibilities," ensures that the system in support of the standard is effectively maintained. The quality manager will provide input, even if he or she is not the one selected to drive the process. This is a management system for the entire business. Every member of the firm—from the CEO to the janitors—should be involved and provide input.

Remember the comments made earlier about the 1994 version of the standards; these make some specific changes in the description of the management representative. The new version appears to require that the management representative be a member of executive management. This is a philosophical change from the 1987 version, which merely required that the management representative have defined authority and responsibility. This individual need not, however, be the person tasked with the implementation program, merely with responsibility for the maintenance of the system once it is installed.

CREATE A TEAM

Once appointed, the project manager needs a team with whom to work. Volunteers should be drawn from all levels of management and all functional areas of the company. One of the first things that the project manager should undertake is a general program of ISO awareness. Schedule time to enable every member of the company to attend a short awareness session that explains what the ISO 9000 series standards are, how implementation will affect day-to-day work, and what the benefits will be.

This training can either be carried out by the project manager—after he or she has acquired the appropriate training or experience—or by an outside organization. Done properly, the result of this activity should be to generate considerable enthusiasm for the project within the company; the problem will not be obtaining volunteers, rather choosing which volunteers to have on the committee.

The importance of having a wide spectrum of staff grades and disciplines represented on the team cannot be overemphasized—everyone has to feel that they are involved, and every department needs to have a champion for the project. The most effective way of developing that champion is to involve the individual in the strategic implementation program.

DEVELOP MILESTONES

The next step is to develop a set of milestones for the process; a typical set is outlined below. In this example, a five-month set of milestones is described. The time frame will obviously vary, depending on the size and complexity of the company and the sophistication of any existing quality system. It is important to remember that most registrars are reluctant to conduct a certification audit until the management system has been reasonably stable and in use for about six months. There are exceptions to this, but typically this is the time frame needed for sufficient evidence to accrue that the processes are being operated in the manner described.

Month 1

1. Seek good, reliable, well-informed ISO 9000 trainers for the team. Either send key members out for training or bring it in-house. This author's experience is that if there are more than six people to train, then the in-house option will be cheaper. Bringing training in-house also means that the program can be adjusted to meet the specific needs of the company, rather than being a generic training session. The ability of the team to address specifics of its operation can often be very helpful.

   Questions to consider when retaining a training team include the following:

   ● Have the trainers helped other companies achieve registration?

   ● Have the trainers worked in ISO 9000 registered companies?

      Do not use lead auditor training as a means of learning how to implement ISO 9000. Use a proper implementation program or start with a short "What is ISO 9000?" introductory session.

2. Determine whether a consultant is going to be employed to assist the process. Although many companies achieve ISO 9000 registration without using outside consultants, it may be a good investment. A good consultant will effect a speedy transfer of knowledge and skills to the client company, and thereafter will be needed only to provide intermittent guidance to keep the program on track.

   A consultant team should not do the full job of developing a company's documentation; that is the responsibility of the company itself. Never forget the need for ownership—this will not be achieved if the writing has been done by an outsider.

   Avoid publications that offer a "system in a book," or one on an ISO disk. There is no such thing as an effective "off the shelf" set of ISO documentation. Every company is different and does things in its own way. There are few shortcuts other than using a competent consultant. Shortcuts might shoehorn you into a prepackaged system and get you a certificate, but they will not provide you with any of the true benefits that should accrue from the process.

In seeking a consultant, companies should find out if the consultant is a UK or RAB certified auditor. The Certified Quality Auditor (CQA) qualification from the American Society for Quality Control (ASQC) is not the same. The CQA qualification is obtained purely from examination, and the "body of knowledge" contains little or no ISO 9000 expertise. The RAB or UK certified auditor has obtained his or her qualification through demonstrating not only an ability to pass an examination, but also a practical skill as an auditor working with ISO 9001, ISO 9002 or similar standards.

A consultant needs a knowledge and understanding of the ISO standards that comes only from practical experience—not out of books. It is also important that he or she has a reasonable working knowledge of the processes involved in the client's business.

3. Has the consultant helped other companies through the process of registration to one of the ISO 9000 standards?

Companies should ask for and obtain references for the consultants they employ. A good consultant will be more than happy to provide them. Approach the business of buying both consultancy and certification services in exactly the same way as when making any other major purchasing decision that will impact the company for many years!

Remember—the bottom line is not cost of purchase, but cost of ownership. A company will "own" the results of the consultant's work for many years to come...it had better be good!

Months 2 and 3

1. Conduct a business analysis. Will the quality system be a unified system or sectioned to reflect different business units? Analyze and decide.

2. Create a high-level flow chart of the way the company does business. (See Figure 6-3 for a simple example.) How does information flow through the entire business activity, from order placement to customer delivery?

This chart should show the information flow through the company, not the activities associated with departmental response to that data—that activity will come later. It is most important that this chart shows what actually exists—not what should be done. Creating this chart will require sometimes painful honesty on the part of managers. Very often the silliest of activities come to light, along with duplication of unimportant work, and an absence of vital communication links.

3. Review the chart and determine whether the existing system reflects the correct information flow. If not, redraw the flow chart and correct it.

4. Analyze those departments included in the flow chart and determine how many of them are already documented. Keep track of this information for future use.

This initial activity is the start of the process now being called "reengineering." It involves a detailed study of all aspects of business activity to determine whether the right things are being done, in the right sequence and at the right times. It also provides the opportunity to identify how things can be done better—continuous improvement—and to reevaluate whether the company is in fact doing what it should be doing to meet the goal of customer satisfaction.

Month 4

1. Allocate each departmental block to an individual project team member, whose task is to begin working with employees to develop a generalized flow chart of the activities within that department. More detailed analysis comes later in the process.

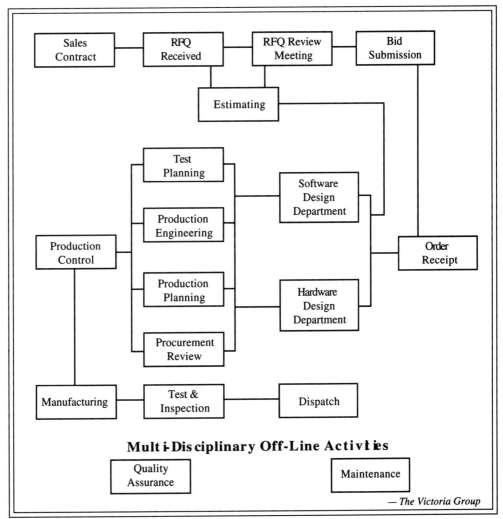

Figure 6-3: High-Level Activity Flowchart.

2. Using the flow charts, establish a record of existing documentation. Frequently, companies discover a significant number of written procedures already in place. Unless they are hopelessly out of date, these documents should never be discarded. Rather they should be incorporated into the new ISO 9001 or ISO 9002 based system. There is no need nor benefit in replacing existing procedures, or in duplicating work already in place; companies should take advantage of and build on these preexisting foundations.

Month 5

Determine what is missing for a system-wide structure of documented procedures. The system should link all departments effectively, thereby ensuring a smooth flow of information through the company.

The Victoria Group, among others, calls this a *gap analysis,* and the methodology the company follows includes a full-scale audit of the current system against both the company documentation and the relevant section of the ISO 9000 standards. Many companies employ an independent consultant to perform this audit to provide a more objective assessment of their system.

Companies would be well-advised to check the ISO 9000 credentials of the consultant used for the gap analysis to ensure the best possible evaluation at this early stage. The non ISO-experienced auditor could hugely over-interpret the standard. It happens often enough with auditors who have some experience. Those not really familiar with the meaning of the standard can cause you major headaches by proposing totally unnecessary work.

Use the same criteria for buying this service as you would for choosing a trainer and consultant—the certified auditor status under the UK or the RAB is even more vital at this stage.

PRODUCE MISSING DOCUMENTS

All employees should begin to produce missing documentation. The best candidate for the task is the employee who performs the job daily. Everyone from the chief executive to the maintenance staff should be involved in flowcharting activities and in writing the procedures and work instructions.

The team should provide a framework—both to help those who are unfamiliar with this sort of activity, and to guide those who have done it before—for producing documents with a unified approach and style. After they have been checked and put into practice, if time and resources permit, every document should be edited to maintain a consistent style.

The author of each document in the system should be the person, or group of people, who will be using it to do their job. These are the people who really know what is going on and which key facts need to be recorded.

This process is true empowerment. It gives each individual the opportunity to participate in determining how his or her particular job should be performed, and provides total participation in creating the management system. (The process of writing documentation is discussed in detail in Chapter 7 of this Handbook.)

SCHEDULE OF CONFORMITY ANALYSIS

Once this stage is completed, the system is complete. Before you move into the full implementation stage of the operation, carry out a *schedule of conformity* analysis. This is used to verify that every section of the relevant ISO 9000 series standard has been effectively addressed. Part of a typical document is shown in Table 6-4.

Procedure Number & Name	ISO 9001—4.1 Management Responsibility					ISO 9001—4.2 Quality System		ISO 9001—4.3 Contract Review			ISO 9001—4.4 Design Control		
	4.1.1	4.1.2.1	4.1.2.2	4.1.2.3	4.1.3	4.2(a)	4.2(b)	4.3(a)	4.3(b)	4.3(c)	4.4.1	4.4.2	4.4.3
QUALITY MANUAL	X	X	X	X	X	X	X	X	X	X	X	X	X
MARKETING MK001 Order Intake								X					
MK002 Review of Quotations									X	X			
MK003 Pricing Policy	—	—	—	—	—	—	—	—	—	—	—	—	—
PROCUREMENT PK001 Pricing Quotes									X	X			
PK002 Vendor Selection													

Table 6-4: Schedule of Conformity.

The schedule of conformity fulfills a number of functions. First, it is a method whereby the company's ISO implementation manager can check that all of the applicable elements of the relevant standard have been covered. This seemingly daunting task becomes relatively straightforward when the matrix approach is used.

The chart should be organized along the lines of the figure shown. For each of the "shall" statements in the subparagraphs of the standard, create a vertical column, and list the procedures down the left hand side. As each procedure is listed on the schedule, an "X" is marked in the appropriate column, indicating that the element is addressed.

You will find that some procedures cross-reference several compulsory elements while others deal only with a single requirement. If all is well with the system, once the schedule is completed every compulsory section ("shall" statement) of the standard will have at least one check mark by it. The only exception to this rule should be if a clause or clauses that have been written out of the system as 'not applicable' to the company.

THE SCOPE OF THE AUDIT

Second, the schedule will probably also highlight the fact that there are a few procedures that fall completely outside the scope of the audit. For example, MK003 in Table 6-4 deals with pricing policies, and as such falls outside the scope of any part of ISO 9000.

The very first section of the standard, paragraph 0.0 Introduction, makes it clear that the requirements can be tailored for individual company requirements, and therefore not every company will need to address each and every "shall" in their chosen ISO model.

When this is the case, it is most important that the tailoring is visible right up front, whether the individual reviewing the company management system is from a registration body, a customer, or the internal audit department. It is important to declare anything novel or unusual about the system at the start of the process, to keep the reviewer from "tripping over" the unusual feature halfway through the process.

One of the most common means adopted for identifying any activity that is outside the scope of the quality management system is to identify the exclusions in the quality manual itself. If the quality manual is formatted to follow the sequence of the standard, then this exclusion can take the form of a written statement in the body of the text when that particular activity is reached.

If the manual is formatted according to the business flow of the company, then a clear written statement in the preamble to the manual is a good approach. Always reference the relevant clause of the standard that is being tailored out of the system, as well as the name of the activity, for company language and the standard's/auditor's language may differ.

Companies that leave the schedule of conformity in the quality manual are showing the exclusions in that way.

One way to write the statement in the preamble is the following:

> *The XYZ Company publishing division provides a design and print service to the parent company and outside clients. There is no post sales maintenance provided for the product, and for this reason Clause 4.19 of ISO 9001 is not addressed within this quality system.*

One thing to bear in mind is that the auditor may not be totally convinced by the argument and may challenge the decision. In the case of a registrar, such a query will be made as soon as you submit your quality manual for evaluation—another good reason for giving any such exclusions high visibility. No one wants the lead auditor of an audit team on site to challenge some basics about the scope of the system that really should have been resolved weeks previously.

HOW TO AVOID COMMON ISO 9000 PITFALLS

The project has now reached a stage where the easy part is completed! The true skill is in making it happen throughout the company, day in and day out, week after week. At this point the management is reasonably committed, the ISO 9000 implementation team have all been trained, the system analysis has been completed and the staff have finished writing all the documents identified as missing by the gap analysis. What happens now? The key questions that must be addressed at this point in the project are the following:

- How is the system going to be properly implemented and controlled?
- How does management ensure that everyone uses all the new procedures and work instructions?
- How are any necessary changes identified?
- How is the management review process to be made meaningful and effective?
- How is the corrective action program going to be used to greatest benefit?
- What can be done to persuade people not to write on controlled documents?

These, and other equally important questions of effective system implementation and maintenance are the issues that mark success from failure. The answer to making the system an integrated part of corporate life does exist, and is not complicated to invoke: the solution to these problems is found in the quality system audit.

The quality system audit is any company's single most powerful tool for both effective system implementation and for driving real, value-added continuous improvement. For the quality system to function properly, a structured audit system needs to be established that will encompass every element of the documented system on a regular, planned basis.

Regular auditing of every aspect of the company detects any changes required in the process, as well as any deficiencies or changes required in the paperwork. Quite apart from the fact that the ISO standards require that a company "shall carry out a comprehensive system of planned and documented internal quality audits to verify whether quality activities comply with planned arrangements and to determine the effectiveness of the system," a thorough and rigorously maintained audit program will also help avoid the problems typically encountered with the five quality failures.

Five Quality Failures

Author Lionel Stebbing, one of the leading UK experts on quality systems, describes the primary problems that constantly recur during management system audits as the Five Quality Failures. All quality system registrars report these five problems as the most common causes of noncompliance during registration audits. Good ISO 9000 consultants will examine these areas of company systems very carefully to ensure that their clients avoid the otherwise seemingly inevitable mistakes.

Editor's Note: *Please refer to Chapter 20 for three articles on the Quality Systems Update/ Deloitte & Touche joint ISO 9000 survey. They discuss the top barriers companies faced in achieving registration.*

1. DOCUMENT CONTROL (ISO 9001, CLAUSE 4.5)

Some typical examples of the inadequacies that are often encountered in document control are given below:

- Out-of-date versions of procedures, work instructions and engineering drawings left in areas where they are available for use

- Marked-up documents—changes made by someone writing on a controlled document either without authority, or with inappropriately defined authority

- Copies of important system documentation not available where they are needed for the effective implementation of the management system

- Changes to documents of all types made without using the approved change procedures

- Local copies of documents kept in a foreman's office that is locked outside "normal" working hours. (This latter procedure may make sense in terms of control, but if the late shift staff are left without access to those documents, the documents may as well not exist.)

Experience shows that frequently the worst offenders in terms of document control are the technical and engineering staffs. These staff will frequently and quite legitimately need copies of drawings and specifications that they will then write and draw upon as changes are developed. This is an obvious and clear need—the technical staff have to be able to mark up drawings and prints both for technical reasons and to develop ideas for production aids, work instructions, test plans and so forth.

The practice is totally acceptable provided the drawing, specification or print is clearly marked with wording such as "uncontrolled copy—not to be used for production purposes," thereby ensuring that anyone examining the document would immediately know that this was not a current print available for any deliverable function.

Another acceptable scenario involving a marked-up document (or "red-line" as it is commonly known), is where there is a formal procedure permitting declared signatories—either by name or job title—to transfer an urgently needed change onto a controlled document and the following two conditions apply:

- The controlled document is then signed and dated with the approval authority, typically also supported by a change note, waiver notice, or other formal temporary change approval

- The effectiveness of the temporary change is limited by time, quantity or contract.

It is almost impossible to imagine a production environment where such a process is not required from time to time (often all the time) if the pressures of delivery schedules are to be met. Such procedures are not a problem provided that they are properly documented, the authority and responsibilities are clear, and the process is not abused to the point of confusion. Where such procedures are used, it is important to ensure that any such temporary configuration changes are reflected across all the relevant parts of the system.

In design and development areas one of the most commonly encountered difficulties is the use of outdated copies of national standards and other externally controlled specifications. There is an inherent tendency to "squirrel" these documents, and they often turn up, months later, during an audit—well out of date, and the cause of another nonconformance report.

2. CALIBRATION (ISO 9001, CLAUSE 4.11)

The range of equipment that a company will identify as requiring calibration is frequently extensive. A careful reading of the standard will enable the cautious implementer to ensure that it is not a gigantic list. The requirement is to calibrate equipment used "to demonstrate the conformance of product to the specified requirements." Items that are for "indication only" or are used only as a means of monitoring a process need not be calibrated to any form of traceable standard.

Subclause 4.11.2, mentions in a note that companies can look to *ISO 10012, Quality Assurance Requirements for Measuring Equipment—Part 1: Management of Measuring Equipment* for guidance. A description of ISO 10012 is included in an Annex to this chapter.

Measurements to Demonstrate Conformance

The key issue identified in paragraph 4.11 of ISO 9001 (4.10 in ISO 9002: 1987) is that the measurement being made is used "to demonstrate conformance." If the measurement being made is not being used to certify a deliverable requirement (a "specified requirement"), then it is the company's choice whether to calibrate. It is not the choice of the auditor or the registrar to determine what should and should not be calibrated.

The concern that many auditors have is that companies will draw the net too skimpily over the system and not calibrate enough items. All too often it is found that measurements are made with uncalibrated equipment at an early stage of the process that are not part of the final specification, but that are critical to the achievement of the final specification, and that are not or cannot be rechecked at a later stage.

In many process environments, highly sophisticated methods of process control are often used almost to the complete exclusion of any testing. In these environments a company has to consider very carefully which of those control measurements are, in fact, critical to the achievement of the "specified requirement," and then calibrate accordingly.

Tracking Calibrated Equipment

Most companies end up with a great deal of equipment in their calibration systems, and it is important to ensure that all calibrated equipment can be efficiently tracked with a sound recall system operating when items become due for recalibration. Outdated calibration stickers and labels, items that have been missed altogether, and certificates that carry no valid traceability to the appropriate national or international standard are some of the more common problems revealed by the audit process.

To protect against these problems, it is important that the system ensure that the individual with assigned responsibility for managing the calibration system has the freedom and authority to make the process work. This may from time to time involve withdrawing equipment from use when it is due for review. All too often the responsibility for managing the calibration system is delegated, but not the authority to make it work. The two things are different, and both must be in place.

Establishing an effective and reliable calibration program these days is not that difficult. Several competent software programs exist that will handle the date-dependent recall requirements as well as the instrument detail, the calibration certificate records, and, if required, the associated procedures contained within interlinked text files within the database. Several of these programs also provide the necessary data storage on pre- and post-calibration measurements to assist in the definition of calibration intervals.

Different departments often purchase test equipment that frequently is not included in the calibration process. The calibration manager is then dependent upon those departments to notify the receipt of such items.

One way around this problem is to require any purchase requisition for test or measuring equipment to carry a signature from the calibration department. In this way at least they know that the kit is going to come in at some stage. Another approach is to insist that all measuring equipment be routed through the calibration area for goods receiving inspection.

Statistical Process Control

When techniques such as Statistical Process Control (SPC) are being used, calibration is essential. If numbers are used to generate charts, and the evaluation of those charts will be used to predict future process requirements, then the validity of the measurements made is vital. A colleague of the author who was involved with a subcontractor assurance program described a visit made to one company that proudly showed an impressive range of SPC activities, covering many aspects of the operation. When questions were asked about the continued variance in the process despite recorded corrective actions, the subsequent audit trail led to the discovery that none of their test equipment had ever been calibrated. The test results, and therefore all SPC data, were suspect.

Equipment Status

An inadequate paper trail of the status of all equipment used in the system is another common problem. Giving the user responsibility is one way efficiently to keep track of all pieces of measuring equipment contained within the system. Whenever tests or inspections are made using equipment that is part of the calibration system, validation of calibration status should be the first item on the test or inspection report. The second entry should be an annotation that work was stopped and the appropriate person contacted if equipment was found out of calibration. The user is the only person who can completely validate that this system works.

An area often overlooked is that of the equipment used by field-service personnel. This must be within the control of the calibration system also. An "out of sight, out of mind" is an easy error.

Equipment for Design

Last but by no means least, remember that a design and development unit is producing and making measurements that affect the deliverables—the equipment that is used for design verification and validation does need to be calibrated, whether the designers think so or not.

3. TRAINING RECORDS (ISO 9001, CLAUSE 4.18, ISO 9002 : 1987 CLAUSE 4.17)

Many organizations fall into the trap of documenting only the training that is provided outside the company, or in-house training that takes place away from an individual's normal place of work. Yet in most companies, this form of "external training" is minimal by comparison with the amount of "on-the-job" training that is carried out—often extremely well and effectively.

The auditors will be looking for evidence of all training given to staff, and at all levels of the company. No one is exempt. The standard tells companies to identify "the training needs and provide for the training of all personnel performing activities affecting quality..." As mentioned earlier, the answer to the question "who does work affecting quality?" is, of course "everyone."

The reality is that training records often are restricted to the production personnel, to career development training, and to other technical staff who participate in external training sessions, which may or may not be of any specific value in the day-to-day work being performed.

The ISO 9000 standard is not, in fact, interested in career development or personal development training unless it has some impact on the work being performed. The requirement states that "personnel performing specific tasks shall be qualified on the basis of appropriate education, training, and/or experience, as required." The training or other means of demonstrating competence must be related to the current task performed, not what an individual may (or may not) be doing next week, next year or next decade. Do not forget that this net should also entrap the executive management.

Key Questions

Auditors will ask the following typical questions regarding training records:

- Are records available for the job-specific skills training received by each employee?
- Do records show which skills were imparted at what time and by whom?
- Does the company routinely provide job-specific training to each employee, and if so, how?
- How is competency assessed for on-the-job training?
- Who is authorized to sign off that the training has been satisfactorily completed?

In most companies, there is a considerable amount of on-the-job training, sometimes called by names such as the buddy system. These forms of training can have immense value if they are properly managed, maintained and documented.

Make sure that all training is properly written up and that records exist to demonstrate who has been trained in which skills. It is important to remember, once again, the concept of authority and responsibility—who has the defined authority to "sign off" on training as having been adequately completed? These structures need not be complicated—a training syllabus may be no more than a list of skills required by an individual fulfilling a specific task, and the record simply an identical list with a name at the top and spaces provided for a date and signature by each skill item.

Training records should be readily accessible to those who need them on a regular basis; this is not usually the human resources department but day-to-day supervisors. Wherever and however these records are maintained, ensure they are readily accessible when and where they are needed.

If the training records are maintained by personnel, make sure that they are kept separate from other personnel records such as salary, performance reviews, medical records, holiday records, disciplinary records, etc. The latter type of information is privileged and is neither subject to nor permitted to be seen by the auditor. This applies whether that auditor is internal, external or extrinsic.

4. PLANNING FOR THE CUSTOMER (ISO 9001, ISO 9002, CLAUSE 4.3)

The ISO 9000 series standards require contract review between the customer and supplier. Make sure evidence exists showing that a review has been made of all orders placed to ensure that the customers' requirements are clearly understood and can be met. This includes delivery and price as well as the technical ability to provide what has been requested. An obligation exists to ensure that any requirements "differing from those in the contract are resolved."

Many businesses do not have a formal process for responding to an invitation to tender, or to a request for quote, followed by an order placement. What often happens is that the customer simply sends in an order for a certain number of items for delivery on a specific date. The response from the supplier accepting the order may reflect a change in the delivery date. This is not, in and of itself, an adequate review.

A mechanism should exist to ensure that any change in delivery date is negotiated and that a new date is agreed to by both parties. The process does not have to be complex, but it should happen and the record should exist.

5. MANAGEMENT REVIEW AND AUDIT (ISO 9001, ISO 9002 CLAUSES 4.1.3. & 4.17; CLAUSE 4.16 IN ISO 9002 : 1987)

The above discussion has identified four of the most common areas of weakness that a comprehensive and effective system of internal auditing would uncover. An inadequate procedure for internal quality system audit and review is the final common weakness revealed by assessments. It is the effectiveness of the internal auditing function in carefully reviewing the level of compliance with the defined procedures that will in large measure determine the efficacy of the corrective action program. Summary audit reports will also provide one of the primary sources of data for management review meetings.

Corrective action must happen in a closed-loop environment. Whenever such action is required it is absolutely vital that all four steps in the well-known "plan - do - check - act" loop are properly fulfilled. Start by carrying out the appropriate level of causal analysis— what is appropriate is determined by the severity of the problem and is a decision for the company, not an auditor.

"Plan" the corrective action based on the findings of the failure analysis and then look at the future. ISO 9000 requires that preventive action is initiated "to a level corresponding to the risks encountered." Taking short-term corrective action to fix a problem without trying to permanently eliminate that problem from the system is pretty much a waste of time. Further- more, the 1994 standard has introduced a complete new section under Clause 4.14 entitled "Preventive action."

The next step is the "do" part of the cycle, where the action is taken to fix the problem and prevent recurrence. The third step is where many organizations totally fall down, and that is the "check" phase. Once an action has been taken, it is most important that there is follow-up to ensure that it was effective.

If the corrective and preventive actions have been effective, then the follow-up checks will reveal that the problem has disappeared. Auditors should look for recurring problems—rest assured that the registration auditors will most certainly do so.

Remember that the corrective action loop identified in the standard is not restricted to product problems, and the process should be operated at all three levels within a company's activities where problems can occur. These are described in Table 6-5.

THE CORRECTIVE ACTION LOOP

On Product:
- Fix the problem, stop the same product failure occurring again.

On Processes:
- If a problem is caused by a process failure, fix it.
- If a process is not being operated correctly, fix it.
- If a process is not producing the desired results, fix it.
- If there is a better process, change it.

On Systems:
- If the system produced the failure, fix it.
- If the system is not being operated properly, fix it.
- If the system is not producing the desired results, fix it
- If there is a better system, change it.

— *The Victoria Group*

Table 6-5. The Corrective Action Loop.

Corrective and preventive action are the two driving forces of continuous improvement. As far as the management system is concerned, one of the adages for any company seeking to constantly drive forward must be the cry—"if it ain't broke, break it." Only in this way can a constant process of improvement happen. The search for better ways of doing everything must be totally relentless—there can be no sacred cows when continuous improvement is the goal.

Corrective action is not restricted to fixing faulty products or services. Management must dedicate resources and support to this process by making the review of internal audit results—and the follow-up and closeout of those audits reports—a matter of high priority. It is the only way to ensure the continued reliability and effectiveness of any quality system. The contribution made by the internal audit and review process to the efficiency and reliability of a management system cannot be overemphasized.

THE REGISTRATION AUDIT PROCESS

The registration or certification audit will often be the first exposure that staff in most companies will have had to a detailed, objective team of auditors whose sole task is to examine the management system for compliance with a standard. A little extra time spent preparing the entire staff for the audit team visit will pay huge dividends, whether the company already had a well-documented system in place before starting down the ISO 9000 road, or if the implementation effort began with virtually nothing on paper.

One of the most important aspects of this stage of the process is that the management team must fully understand what is going to happen during the audit, and equally importantly, what is not going to happen. Unlike many auditors such as those from the EPA, OSHA or the FDA, the registration audit team cannot threaten the survival of the company. No lawsuits or suspension of shipments can follow from their visit, nor should they try to impose changes on the system through whims, fads or fancies. The company staff need not be defensive, protective, confusing or misleading.

The auditors who will appear from the registrar have all been rigorously trained and have been taught to suppress personal bias and focus on facts. The auditee (the company undergoing the audit) is at all times free to challenge any of their findings and should not hesitate to do so if there is any doubt that what is being reported by an auditor is properly supported by objective evidence of noncompliance.

The structure of the accreditation and registration process in the United States, Europe and the United Kingdom is established around the ISO 10011 series standards. *ISO 10011, Guidelines for auditing quality systems*, provides guidelines for the conduct and management of audits and the training of auditors. It also provides the following definition as to what constitutes objective evidence:

> *Qualitative or quantitative information, records or statements of fact pertaining to the quality of an item or service or to the existence and implementation of a quality system element, which is based on observation, measurement or test and which can be verified.*

The importance of this definition is that for a nonconformance to be raised by a registrar, there has to be objective evidence of noncompliance. It must be one of the following three possibilities:

- If one of the "shall" statements in the relevant ISO 9000 model has not been followed.
- If a document is contained within the management system of the company—whether or not that document falls within the scope of the standard—it may be open to audit. (The schedule of conformity discussed earlier adds even more value when it enables a company to identify procedures that are outside the scope of the standard that they therefore wish to exclude from the scope of the audit.)
- If a contract requirement for the auditee to supply a product or service that falls within the scope of activity being audited has not been met.

These are the only three options that are ever appropriate for raising an issue of noncompliance. Under no circumstances should a nonconformance report be written unless there is supporting evidence of a violation of a requirement contained in one of the three types of documents listed.

Auditee's Responsibilities

ISO 10011 requires that the management of the company being audited to carry out a range of activities and make appropriate provision to assist the audit process. The key issues addressed are outlined below.

INFORM RELEVANT EMPLOYEES ABOUT THE OBJECTIVES AND SCOPE OF THE AUDIT

Everyone in the company is involved in some way in the operation of the management system, and any of them could be subject to the auditor's activity. The ISO 9000 coordinator should meet with the management team to explain the scope of corporate activities that will be explored by the auditors and to remind management that they should be open, frank, honest and cooperative with the auditors.

Individual team leaders should then explain the auditing process to the members of their team and ensure that this information is passed on to all the staff in their area.

In Addition to ISO 10011...

In addition to management taking the necessary steps to meet the requirements of ISO 10011, Part 1, listed above, a company can take other actions that will help improve the audit's effectiveness. One such action is to explain the process to **all** employees. Time invested in teaching employees how to respond to auditors is time well spent. Most people are nervous when being audited, and explaining the process in advance can help reduce nervousness and make things run more smoothly.

The company should make sure that each employee has a clear grasp of the following fundamental issues:

● The system—not the staff—is under scrutiny.

● The employee should have all the necessary documentation readily available, including reference materials.

● When asked questions, the employee should respond honestly and concisely about the question asked—not the question he or she thinks the auditor meant to ask.

● The employee need not volunteer information beyond that requested by the auditor.

● If a question is asked that is outside the employee's area of responsibility, the employee should say, "I don't know," or "That isn't something that I am involved with." Most people hate to admit ignorance and will often try to answer questions about things that are not part of their responsibility. Such answers are frequently wrong, and this can confuse the auditor and waste time.

● It is perfectly acceptable for the employee to say "I don't understand your question" when that is the appropriate response. It is OK to ask for clarification when an auditor's questions are not understood. Many auditors have difficulty phrasing their questions in everyday language or will use the words they grew up with rather than the terms used in the company. Other auditors use formal language directly from the standard that some staff might not understand.

A company in Colorado experienced significant problems during an audit due to the way the auditors phrased their questions. According to company officials, the term "nonconforming material" was not one the company used, and shop floor personnel had no idea what the auditor was asking about until the guide translated the question.

- Auditors will take notes, ask for observations to be signed, and sometimes ask for copies of the objective evidence they have seen.

All staff need to understand that an auditor's taking notes does not mean a problem exists. The auditor will annotate evidence of conformance as well as nonconformance. Objective evidence works both ways. Knowing this will make both the auditor and the auditee more comfortable during the audit.

APPOINT RESPONSIBLE MEMBERS OF THE STAFF TO ACCOMPANY MEMBERS OF THE AUDIT TEAM

The company should arrange for guides for the audit team who know the system and the company. Staff members who are trained and active internal auditors are excellent choices. Not only will the company gain good intelligence from these guides as the audit progresses, but such individuals will also be able to ensure that any misunderstanding or miscommunication between any auditor and the interviewee is quickly corrected.

Make guides aware that they should not answer for others, nor interrupt or try to influence the auditor unless something is going wrong. A guide who is helpful and cooperative to the auditor can help the company in making the auditor feel relaxed and comfortable with the environment.

PROVIDE ALL RESOURCES NEEDED FOR THE AUDIT TEAM IN ORDER TO ENSURE AN EFFECTIVE AND EFFICIENT AUDIT PROCESS

The auditors will need to exchange information, trace requests and discuss findings among themselves. Provide a convenient room for these discussions and necessary facilities such as telephone, fax and photocopier. Make arrangements for refreshments and lunch as well. Remember that time is precious, and bringing lunch in to the auditors is often the preferred choice.

The audit team will require access to all areas of the company that influence the activities outlined in the registration scope statement. Do not try to refuse access to areas during the audit by claiming commercial confidentiality. Everything the auditors see during the activity is treated as confidential, and protecting this information is an essential part of the code of conduct of the Registered Assessor (UK) or Certified Auditor (US).

If a company wants certain areas to be off-limits, these must be declared and agreed upon before the auditors arrive. Avoid surprises during the audit—they unsettle everyone and cause unnecessary tension.

As the audit progresses, the company will be asked to produce its records. Declining access to them will damage the process, particularly in the area of training records. As mentioned earlier, everyone must be told that material should be available to the auditors.

COOPERATE WITH THE AUDITORS TO ALLOW AUDIT OBJECTIVES TO BE ACHIEVED

The registrar wants the company to succeed as much as the company wants to succeed. Audit teams normally arrive with a positive attitude, seeking reasons for success, not reasons to be unsuccessful. The registration audit is the start of a long-term relationship between the registrar and the company, and like any other long-term relationship, it is important to get off to a good start.

Make everyone—including security staff—aware that the audit team is going to be on-site, and what the auditors will require. One of the requirements of the ISO 9000 standard is that the quality policy of the company be "understood, implemented and maintained" at all levels of the organization. An auditor who encounters employees who do not know why an auditor is there or what he is doing may wonder how well this section has been implemented.

DETERMINE AND INITIATE CORRECTIVE ACTIONS BASED ON THE AUDIT REPORT

Once the audit is completed and the lead auditor has presented the team findings to the company, corrective actions may be needed. The company should respond promptly and effectively to these requests. The audit team leader will expect to see that a corrective action is solved, the nonconformance reported, and that the company has taken effective action to prevent recurrence. The primary purpose of an ISO 9000 based quality system is the "prevention of nonconformance at all stages..." (Clause 1.1). Respond to the audit finding accordingly.

The standard also requires that corrective actions be effective (Clause 4.14.2(d)). Ensure that the decisions taken in correcting any problems not only fix the problem and endeavor to eliminate the root cause, but provide the ability to ensure future effectiveness (i.e., will be auditable in the future).

The registrar will return at regular intervals—typically two or more times a year—to conduct surveillance audits. The main effort, however, is internal. Constant vigilance by every employee to ensure the ongoing success and progress of the system is essential. Most important of all is management's constant and unwavering commitment to the path they have chosen.

CONCLUSION

When all the audit reports are written and all the corrective actions taken and verified, the company will be a member of the exclusive club of registered firms. This should mean that company executives have committed to the concept of quality as a management issue, and thus have begun the endless journey of continuous improvement.

It also means that the company has a more competitive opportunity in the international marketplace, and that its chances of survival in that marketplace are greatly enhanced. There is one proviso to this—the enthusiasm that took the company successfully through registration has to be maintained indefinitely. The management system will need constant review, constant updating and constant improvement.

There is no such thing as "stable state" in any company. Companies have two options: to grow or to shrink. Management's responsibility is to continually examine the market to ensure that new opportunities to maintain the health and wealth of the company are identified. Remember—survival in the business world is no longer guaranteed.

SURVEILLANCE AUDITS

By Joseph J. Klock

Question

Now that we have completed the registration audit, what's next? How do we prepare for the surveillance?

Answer

Just as most states require periodic auto inspections to assure that you maintain your car, ISO 9000 registration systems require periodic surveillance to assure that you keep your quality system in good running order. Surveillances focus on continued compliance with the ISO 9000 standards and the requirements associated with registration, such as use of the certificate and seal.

In an ISO 9000 surveillance, registrars do not just "kick the tires." They look for evidence that you have maintained the quality system and improved or corrected it where necessary. Continually maintaining and improving your quality system eases the preparation for a surveillance.

As with all elements of the quality system, the auditor will look for evidence that the internal audit process conforms to the standard. Registrars might first go to your customer complaint file to see what the customers are telling you and if you have resolved all complaints.

In an ISO 9000 quality system, improvement often comes through corrective action in response to complaints, internal audit findings, or nonconformities from previous audits by the registrar. The registrar will verify that effective corrections have taken place in conformance with the appropriate standards and your documentation.

Many registrars require companies to notify them of changes to its quality system. Sometimes the company may request a change in the scope of the registration. The registrar then chooses to audit immediately or to wait until the next surveillance, depending on the impact the change may have on products going to the customers.

The registrar has an obligation to verify the correct use of your certificate and use of the registrar's marks. The surveillance provides an opportunity to audit how your company complies with this requirement. Though not covered in ISO 9000, this

(continued on next page)

Surveillance Audits

(continued from previous page)

requirement is a part of the standards used by accreditation boards covering the operation of a registration system.

Review of complaints and internal audits, verification of corrective action, assessment of changes to the quality system, and use of the certificate usually take place during every surveillance. Elements with general applicability, such as those covering management responsibility, the quality system, document control, and recordkeeping, are reviewed during each visit by many registrars as well.

Other elements of the ISO 9000 standard and registration agreement may receive less frequent review. The lead auditor usually will choose a subset of elements of the standard to cover during a surveillance and will cover all elements over a predetermined period.

As with a car, if you have conscientiously maintained your quality system, you can expect to pass a surveillance audit without a follow-up visit. Though the registrar may identify some nonconformities, verifying corrections often can wait until the next surveillance.

On occasion, the surveillance may uncover a major nonconformity or what some call a "hold point," which may require the withdrawal of your certificate until corrective action takes place. If the quality system and its corrective action components function properly, this should not happen. But the registration process provides for the possibility, and your agreement with the registrar specifies what action it will take.

The depth of coverage on a surveillance varies from registrar to registrar. Some do a brief surveillance with a full re-audit every three years or so. Others do a longer surveillance each time rather than periodic complete audits. In any case, most perform surveillances at least twice a year.

You should check with your registrar or the registrars you are considering for specifics about their processes. If you keep the system up-to-date so that you are always ready for a surveillance, you will have little worry when the auditor arrives.

Editor's Note: *The above was adapted from an article that appeared in the June 1993 issue of Quality Systems Update.*

ANNEX 1

Case Study on Surveillance Audits: A.W. Chesterton

This case study is included here mainly because it highlights surveillance audits—an issue that will grow in importance as more and more companies seek to maintain their registration.

Introduction

Groveland and Woburn, MA—When the National Standards Authority of Ireland (NSAI) paid its first surveillance visit to A.W. Chesterton Company's US operations in February 1993, it encountered a typical problem faced by registered companies.

A small number of the 750 employees who work at Chesterton's two registered sites in Massachusetts had been less than diligent about observing the procedures that earned the sealing device manufacturer registration under the ISO 9001 external quality assurance standard six months earlier.

"We were disappointed, I think, that some people weren't following procedures," explained Mary Melia, Chesterton's worldwide project manager for quality systems.

A.W. Chesterton Co.

Employees: 1,500 worldwide

Scope of US Registration: The design and manufacture of mechanical seals, components, spare parts, repairs; pumps and pump related products, components, spare parts and repairs; industrial maintenance products and polymer composites; hydraulic and pneumatic sealing devices and affiliated products at Groveland, Mass. Design and manufacture of mechanical packing, gasketing and affiliated live-loading products at Woburn, Mass.

Registrar: National Standards Authority of Ireland

US Registrar Site Visits: July 6-9, 1992 Groveland, Mass.; January 27-29, 1993 for Woburn and Hydraulic Division at Groveland.

Registration Dates: July 30, 1992 at Groveland; February 25, 1993 at Woburn and Hydraulic Division at Groveland, Mass.

Target Market: Utilities, marine industry, paper and pulp, sewage, chemical processing, petrochemical, petroleum refineries, general industrial sites, and institutions.

The Actual Visit

The surveillance audit was much like the registration audit but not as encompassing. As in the case of a registration audit, no one had any idea beforehand in which direction the auditors would go. Executives strongly suspected, however, that the audit would include areas where previous deficiencies had been identified.

"They went about their business asking their questions in the same way, and we treated them the same way," Melia said. The auditors approached their task in the same manner and upon arriving at the sites arranged meetings with top executives.

Differences in Findings

O'Brien said he noticed a big difference in the type of findings between the registration and surveillance audits. "In the registration audits the breadth of the findings might have impacted on two or three or four organizations," he said. "When we got to the surveillance audit some of the same types of findings occurred, but they were sporadic or isolated."

(continued on next page)

Case Study on Surveillance Audits: A.W. Chesterton
(continued from previous page)

One problem was keeping training records up to date. "If a person moves from one department to another, we need to make sure that their new manager has all his or her paperwork," Melia said. "We also need to make sure that the person receives the training for his or her new position."

For example, one area that was not entirely following procedures was probably doing so even before ISO 9000 registration but had not been previously identified during the internal audit process.

Corrective Action
Company officials were given 30 days to explain how they would correct the problem and to provide documentation to substantiate that the correction was being implemented. O'Brien recalled fearing at first that the problem might be pervasive.

"You have to assume that it's more widespread," he said. "If it happened in this one spot, is it going on elsewhere in the facility? The action taken involved reeducating and retraining all of the work areas, not just the one with the discrepancy."

"The internal audit process was strengthened to improve our ability to detect similar problems [and] was conducted to ensure that the corrective action taken was effective," O'Brien explained.

Audit Results
The nonconformance did not turn out to be systemic, and the company passed its surveillance audit easily. Company officials resisted the temptation to discipline the employees and instead focused on improving the overall quality system.

The problem is common among newly registered companies. Once the goal of registration is attained, it is often difficult to prevent employees and managers from slumping back into familiar work habits. They have a tendency to shift their attention elsewhere or to fail to document all procedural changes, observers have noted.

"Getting registration is hard work but keeping it can be even harder; [although it is] very worthwhile," Melia conceded. The company has invested about $75,000 in registering the two US sites, including the preliminary and final audits and the initial surveillance audits. "We certainly don't wish to lose it," she said.

ANNEX 2

ISO 10012-1, Quality Assurance Requirements for Measuring Equipment—Part 1: Management of Measuring Equipment

ISO 10012 provides requirements for a detailed metrological confirmation system for measuring equipment. This standard contains quality assurance requirements for a supplier to ensure that measurements are made with the intended accuracy. It contains guidance on implementing requirements. The standard specifies the main features of the confirmation system to be used for a supplier's measuring equipment.

ISO 10012-1 is applicable to measuring equipment used in demonstrating compliance with a specification; it does not apply to other items of measuring equipment.

The standard is applicable to testing laboratories, including those providing a calibration service; this includes laboratories operating a quality system in accordance with *ISO Guide 25, General requirements for the competence of calibration and testing laboratories*. It is applicable to suppliers of products who operate a quality system in which measurement results are used to demonstrate compliance with specified requirements, and to other organizations where measurement is used for the same purpose.

The following are key clauses in ISO 10012-1:

- Measuring equipment
- Confirmation system
- Periodic audit and review of the confirmation system
- Planning
- Uncertainty of measurement
- Documented confirmation procedures
- Records
- Nonconforming measuring equipment
- Confirmation labeling
- Intervals of confirmation
- Sealing for integrity
- Use of outside products and services
- Storage and handling
- Traceability
- Cumulative effect of uncertainties
- Environmental conditions
- Personnel.

This standard has not been used routinely, but is called up in some two-party contractual situations. A second part, in the Committee Draft (CD) stage, would expand the standard's perspective to recognize that measuring is itself a process, and that the assurance of measurement integrity requires more than management of measurement equipment.

(continued on next page)

ISO 10012, Quality Assurance Requirements for Measuring Equipment—Part 1: Management of Measuring Equipment

(continued from previous page)

Definitions in ISO 10012-1

Metrological confirmation: Set of operations required to ensure that an item of measuring equipment is in a state of compliance with requirements for its intended use. (**NOTES:** Metrological confirmation normally includes calibration, any necessary adjustment or repair and subsequent recalibration, as well as any required sealing and labeling.) (ISO 10012-1, 3.1)

Measuring Equipment: All of the measuring instruments, measurement standards, reference materials, auxiliary apparatus and instructions that are necessary to carry out a measurement. This term includes measuring equipment used in the course of testing and inspection as well as that used in calibration. (ISO 10012-1, 3.2)

Measurement: The set of operations having the object of determining the value of a quantity. (ISO 10012-1, 3.3)

Traceability: The property of the result of a measurement, whereby it can be related to appropriate measurement standards, generally international or national standards, through an unbroken chain of comparisons.

QUALITY SYSTEM DOCUMENTATION

BY OLLIE YOUNG

This chapter discusses methods for documenting your company's quality system. It covers the following topics:

- Why is documentation important?
- Quality system documentation development
- System documentation and ISO 9000
- The structure of documentation
- Implementation of the system
- Review of the system
- The quality manual: structure and content
- Creating procedures:
  - Procedure planning & development
  - Procedure structure & format
  - Procedure administration & control.

Annexes to the chapter include samples of a quality manual and procedures.

INTRODUCTION

Why document your quality system? A documented quality system sets out in a formal framework the basis of controlling critical activities that affect quality in an organization. A well-documented and effective quality system communicates the following to everyone in the organization:

- The objectives of the system
- The policies of the organization
- Employees' responsibilities within the organization
- The operational procedures (work instructions).

Documentation formalizes the quality system and is necessary because it does the following:

- Encourages consistent action and uniform understanding
- Clearly defines the authority and responsibility of personnel
- Is easily auditable since neither informal nor verbal instructions can be verified
- Is clearly communicated to personnel due to its consistency
- Aids in effectively changing quality policy since documentation is readily updated and changes can easily be incorporated, approved and issued simultaneously
- Is permanent; it ensures consistent performance when personnel changes occur and helps orient new personnel.

Companies must remember that a quality system program belongs to its creators and no other individual or organization. The process of obtaining ISO 9000 registration must be secondary to the real-time organizational benefits of having an effective and fully functional quality system. Always remember these key facts:

- The primary customers for the management system are the company staff.
- Every single document in the system must add value to the company; if there is no added value to any element of the system, discard it. Nothing should ever be done simply to satisfy an auditor. A contract or a customer, yes; an auditor, no.

Documentation, however, need not be excessive. It is not synonymous with paper generation, provided it is well-planned, simple, clear, concise and well-controlled. Quality system documentation and manuals are not required to resemble any standard or conform to any preordained format. Manuals need not be written in formal language or even in the same tense as the ISO 9000 standard. Quality system documentation should reflect the way a particular company operates.

QUALITY SYSTEM DOCUMENTATION DEVELOPMENT

The first question to answer in developing quality system documentation concerns what to document. This requires identifying the scope of the quality system and determining which company functions and areas of activity are critical. Critical areas require a systematic approach, with documented and interfacing procedures. They impact upon the effectiveness of activities, products or services and the efficiency with which they are produced or carried out.

System Documentation and ISO 9000

Which activities, according to ISO 9000, must be controlled by system documentation? *Remember that a quality system is for your company; the ISO 9000 standard is a framework, not an unalterable dictate.*

Also remember that not every clause in the standard will necessarily apply to your company. Whole sections of the standard can be written out as "not applicable," but always provide convincing and clearly stated reasons for doing so.

A list of system documentation for ISO 9001 is shown in the adjoining box. It is typical, not essential. Individual systems may contain many more or many less elements; the list is to help you focus your efforts to identify system documentation needs.

One way to check that every section of the relevant ISO 9000 series standard has been effectively addressed is to create a schedule of conformity. This was discussed in detail in Chapter 6. The schedule of conformity compares your documented system with the requirements of the appropriate standard. It shows the sections of the standard that are addressed by each of your system procedures.

TYPICAL QUALITY SYSTEM DOCUMENTATION IN ISO 9001

4.1 Roles and Responsibilities of Personnel Affecting Quality

- Responsibilities defined in quality manual/job descriptions
- Role and responsibility of the management representative defined in quality manual
- Management review procedure: frequency of meetings; agenda; minutes.

4.3 Contract Review Procedures

- Description of personnel who conduct contract review
- Results of contract review
- Input data necessary for contract review
- Minutes or other records of contract review activity.

4.4 Design Control

- Description of design activity assignment and responsibilities
- Contract files

(continued on next page)

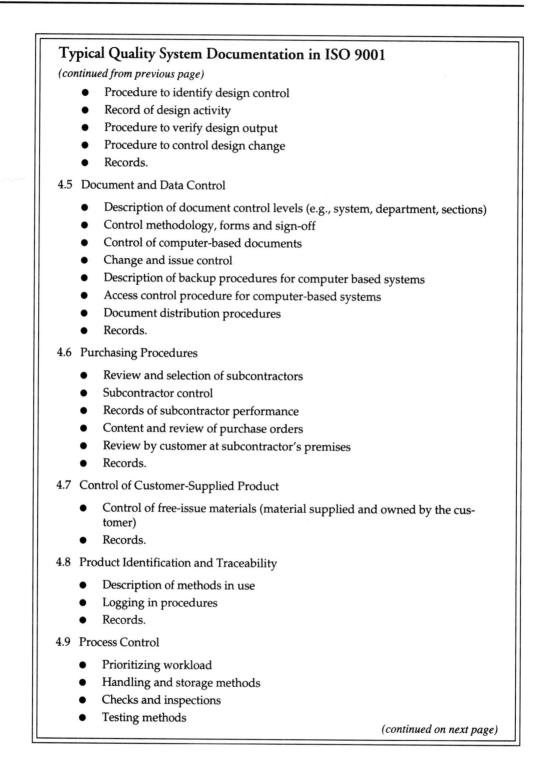

Typical Quality System Documentation in ISO 9001

(continued from previous page)

- Procedure to identify design control
- Record of design activity
- Procedure to verify design output
- Procedure to control design change
- Records.

4.5 Document and Data Control

- Description of document control levels (e.g., system, department, sections)
- Control methodology, forms and sign-off
- Control of computer-based documents
- Change and issue control
- Description of backup procedures for computer based systems
- Access control procedure for computer-based systems
- Document distribution procedures
- Records.

4.6 Purchasing Procedures

- Review and selection of subcontractors
- Subcontractor control
- Records of subcontractor performance
- Content and review of purchase orders
- Review by customer at subcontractor's premises
- Records.

4.7 Control of Customer-Supplied Product

- Control of free-issue materials (material supplied and owned by the customer)
- Records.

4.8 Product Identification and Traceability

- Description of methods in use
- Logging in procedures
- Records.

4.9 Process Control

- Prioritizing workload
- Handling and storage methods
- Checks and inspections
- Testing methods

(continued on next page)

Typical Quality System Documentation in ISO 9001

(continued from previous page)

- Repair techniques
- Release procedures
- Records.

4.10 Inspection and Testing

- Inspection and test of incoming materials
- Identification of incoming material
- Records of receiving inspection
- Procedure for in-process inspection and test
- Records of in-process inspection and test
- Procedure for final inspection or test
- Identification of nonconforming product
- Records.

4.11 Control of Inspection, Measuring and Test Equipment

- Control of inspection test and measuring equipment to full traceability via calibration records to national standards
- Validation of test software
- Records.

4.12 Inspection and Test Status

- Effective identification of all material and product
- Definition of inspection authority for release
- Records.

4.13 Control of Nonconforming Products

- Procedures to isolate material that fails to meet specifications
- Procedures to ensure that a product that does not meet specification cannot be dispatched to customer
- Procedures for the review and disposition of nonconforming material
- Procedures for notifying customers, if contractually specified, of nonconformity
- Records.

4.14 Corrective and Preventive Action

- Procedure for identifying, investigating and resolving nonconformance
- Review and analysis of warranty repairs
- Review of non-warranty repair activity
- Description of interfaces with design and manufacture
- Review and analysis of operational activities for improvement opportunities

(continued on next page)

Typical Quality System Documentation in ISO 9001

(continued from previous page)

- Records.

4.15 Handling, Storage, Packaging, Preservation and Delivery

- Procedures for all product handling to eliminate damage or deterioration
- Storage methods to protect integrity of products and materials
- Procedures for packing all products to ensure safe transit to customers
- Procedures controlling methods of delivery and use of approved transportation
- Records.

4.16 Control of Quality Records

- Procedures that define quality records, where and how they are to be stored, and for how long
- Provisions to back up records stored on magnetic media
- Review of records.

4.17 Internal Quality Audits

- Procedures that provide for the systematic and regular audit of every element of the system, the review and closeout of audit findings, and use of audit reports to constantly improve the system
- Records.

4.18 Training

- Procedures that provide for the proper identification of all training needs and the fulfillment of those needs
- Records.

4.19 Servicing

- Procedures for identifying requirements
- Procedures for controlling servicing
- Corrective action
- Records.

4.20 Statistical Techniques

- Procedures for identifying applications where statistical techniques are in use
- Procedures for assuring that applications using statistical techniques are technically correct and are applied for maximum effectiveness.

The Structure of Documentation

The next requirement in developing a documented quality system is to evaluate how the system will be structured. Documentation is usually structured in a hierarchy, which has four tiers or layers. Each layer develops a steadily increasing level of detail about company operations and methods. These layers are shown in Figure 7-1 and consist of the following:

- The quality manual
- Company operating procedures
- Work instructions
- Records.

The layers in Figure 7-1 are presented as a broad-based triangle. All documentation should cascade from one level to the next to meet traceability and control requirements. Dividing the system in this way applies the political philosophy of "divide and conquer" to managing paperwork. The system should be structured so that changes at one level will virtually never affect a higher level, but may affect the levels below.

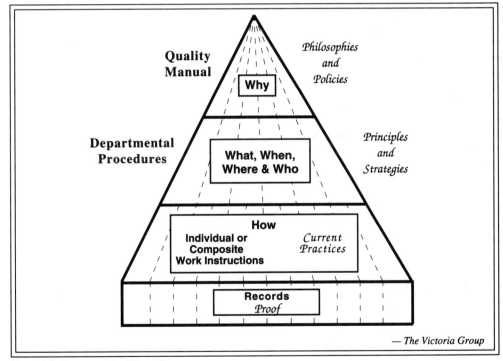

Figure 7-1: Documentation Hierarchy.

LEVEL 1: THE QUALITY MANUAL

A quality manual is "a document stating the quality policy and describing the quality system of an organization" (*ISO 8402, Quality management and quality assurance—Vocabulary*). The quality manual is usually the first indication that a purchaser or prospective client has of a company's approach to quality. It should state the company's total commitment to quality.

LEVEL 2: PROCEDURES

The next level is a set of general operating procedures that describes how the quality system functions. A procedure is defined as "a specified way to perform an activity" (*ISO 8402, Quality management and quality assurance—Vocabulary*).

Procedures reflect the principles and practices defined in the Level 1 documents. They detail the way in which the principles and practices are to be performed and who has the responsibility. A procedure describes what is to be done when, where, why and by whom, whereas a work instruction describes how. When the activity is not very complex, the procedure can describe all of these and separate work instructions are not necessary.

LEVEL 3: WORK INSTRUCTIONS

Within each section or department are several specific job activities. The detailed requirements of any particular task, such as the operating instructions for a piece of equipment may need to be defined to ensure consistent working methods and to achieve required quality standards. With complex activities, it may be useful to develop work instructions that are distinct from the procedures. Work instructions must be traceable back to and be in line with the requirements of the departmental procedures.

LEVEL 4: RECORDS

Records include files, technical standards, statutory regulations, drawings and specifications, as well as the forms that document the output from a procedure or work instruction. These forms and charts are referenced in the individual work instructions and inspection and test procedures, and must be designed to record all of the specified information.

It is preferable to have a coding system for each area of documentation. The system employed must be carefully coordinated to ensure that it does not clash with any existing systems.

Implementation

After the quality system has been designed and documented, it must be implemented. There will almost certainly be an overlap between implementation and documentation since it is highly unlikely that all the required procedures will be written and implemented concurrently.

Throughout implementation, closely monitor the adequacy and effectiveness of the documented procedures. This is best carried out by the quality coordinator in conjunction with any appropriate managers and personnel.

Encourage staff at all levels to scrutinize procedures and instructions relating to their own activities and to provide feedback and constructive criticism. This will help identify and correct errors. Incorporating those suggested improvements will ensure that the system evolves and complies fully with the required standard.

Editor's Note: *When a quality system is already in place, a company may first document the existing system, then improve or redesign the system and implement the improvements. The strategy depends upon each company's starting point.*

Review

When your documented quality system is up and running, make plans for a final, formal review by internal management before inviting ISO 9000 assessment by the approval body. The formal review systematically covers all elements of the quality system and is similar in format to that of the ISO 9000 assessment.

At this stage, you should not find any serious system shortfalls. Nevertheless, you can often uncover minor deficiencies and nonconformances upon which you can implement appropriate actions to fine-tune the system.

QUALITY PLANS

A documented quality system may also include quality plans. A quality plan can be defined as "A document setting out the specific quality practices, resources and sequence of activities relevant to a particular product, project or contract." (*ISO 8402, Quality management and quality assurance—Vocabulary*) A note to this definition emphasizes that a quality plan usually references the applicable parts of the quality manual.

A quality plan is a stand-alone document that defines how quality will be managed on a specific project, contract or product. The quality plan is based on corporate quality procedures, and the quality strategy for a particular application is developed from them. The quality plan should contain:

- A scope statement that defines the boundaries of the quality plan
- The quality strategy, derived from the quality manual and any operating procedures or other core procedures
- The methodology (a detailed definition of how quality will be managed), supported by flow charts, if necessary
- Verification including objective evidence and methods that determine whether the planned controls and procedures have been implemented.

(See Chapter 3 for a discussion of the requirements for quality plans in ISO 9001.)

THE QUALITY MANUAL: STRUCTURE AND CONTENT

Introduction

Subclause 4.1.1 of ISO 9001:1994 states that "The supplier's management with executive responsibility shall define and document its policy for quality including objectives for quality and its commitment to quality." The 1987 version of ISO 9001 did not specifically call for a quality manual. The 1994 version, however, in Subclause 4.2.1 states the following:

> *The supplier shall establish, document and maintain a quality system as a means of ensuring that product conforms to specified requirements. The supplier shall prepare a quality manual covering the requirements of this International Standard. The quality manual shall include or make reference to the quality-system procedures and outline the structure of the documentation used in the quality system.*

In larger companies, the quality manual defines the quality policy and references procedures. In a small business or organization, however, the quality policy, operating procedures and work instructions can be combined into a single "operations manual" type of document.

Can you use an off-the-shelf quality manual? No; your quality manual must describe *your* quality policy and system; the system that you are actually operating, not the one you would like to be operating. Companies manufacture the same products differently, offer different services, and have their own organizational structure.

Quality Manual Structure

A quality manual describes what you do. In larger companies, it usually references but does not include procedures and work instructions. Ideally, it should be a maximum of 20 to 25 pages and comprise 3 sections, as shown below.

SECTION 1: COMPANY QUALITY POLICY

General statement

Policy statement

Details of company organization or structure

Details of the QA organization

Statements of authority and responsibility of department heads

Statement on the manual distribution, amendment and issue.

SECTION 2: SYSTEMS OUTLINE

A brief description of what is done to control the critical activities of the company.

SECTION 3: PROCEDURE INDEX

An index of the company's procedures that support the systems outline.

In a smaller company, where the quality manual includes procedures and work instructions, the manual could be longer. (A more detailed excerpt from a quality manual is included in the Annex to this chapter.)

TWO APPROACHES TO WRITING A QUALITY MANUAL

There are two common approaches to writing a quality manual, and each has its advantages and disadvantages. The first approach is to write the manual following the layout and sequence of the standard. This has the advantage of making the manual very easy for the auditor to follow, but it will not follow the business flow too well. There is also a tendency for such manuals to simply parrot the standard and say nothing company-specific. If those traps can be avoided, this is the easiest approach to ensuring that nothing is left out of the quality manual.

The second approach is to write the manual in a way that follows the corporate business flow, and then cross-map to the standard. If the manual is going to be used to demonstrate conformance to more than one standard, i.e., to both ISO 9001 and Mil-Q-9858A (for example), then this is the better approach. For ease of use, it will need to be backed up by schedules of conformity that cross-reference the manual to each standard, but these are recommended anyway.

— Roderick Goult

Section 1: Company Quality Policy

GENERAL STATEMENT

Often this is a statement as to why the company has decided to introduce a formal quality management system. It may be something about market pressures and the need to improve competitiveness; it may be more general, merely related to the growth and development of the company and the decision by management to formalize and document their commitment to quality products or services.

POLICY STATEMENT

The type of policy statement a company chooses depends upon its specific quality objectives and is particular to that company. (See box, *Sample Policy Statement*) A policy statement should address the following:

- The standard of service provided
- The company's image and reputation for quality
- The approach to be adopted in pursuit of quality objectives.

SAMPLE POLICY STATEMENT

Quality means fitness for intended purpose in all aspects of the company's activities. The company will strive to meet the needs of its customers more effectively than its competitors through a continuous process of quality improvement.

All employees are responsible for quality improvement.

All employees must be able to participate in quality improvement activities.

There will be a measurable annual improvement in quality by setting defined objectives.

Quality improvement will be implemented systematically in every part of the business.

Education and training are vital to the quality improvement process.

Emphasis must be on prevention rather than on control.

The company will involve suppliers in the process of quality improvement.

A quality steering group will exist to coordinate the activities of the quality improvement process.

Issued under the signature of the Senior Executive

COMPANY ORGANIZATION OR STRUCTURE

Usually this is an organizational chart or family tree, showing the interrelationship of departments and personnel. Use job titles on these charts, never names, to keep the chart up-to-date. Identify the management representative responsible for quality.

QUALITY ASSURANCE ORGANIZATION

Similarly, an organizational chart of the quality assurance department personnel, showing the structure and their interrelationship and job titles.

STATEMENT OF AUTHORITY AND RESPONSIBILITY

The standard requires that "The responsibility, authority and interrelation of all personnel who manage, perform and verify work affecting quality shall be defined." Since everyone is fundamentally responsible for quality, there should be some reference to quality related activities in every job specification written within the company.

STATEMENT ON DISTRIBUTION, AMENDMENT AND REISSUE

There should be a distribution and update list that shows who holds which copy of the manual and the issue status of each copy. A short statement would detail how changes are controlled, authorized and implemented.

Section 2: Systems Outline

Always remember that processes, products and services change; therefore the format of Section 2 should facilitate the incorporation of changes or modifications. Briefly detail the control of critical activities. (See box, *Workmanship and Environment*.)

Section 3: Procedure Index

The quality manual describes the quality system; technical data has no place in it, neither has commercially sensitive information. What must be shown is a cross reference to, or index of, the relevant operating procedures. Also stated is:

● Where the procedures are held

● Who is responsible for each procedure or group of procedures

● How they are used, controlled and updated.

WORKMANSHIP AND ENVIRONMENT

The Company has criteria for acceptable workmanship through written standards and/or representative samples. Where applicable, the Company's proposed standard shall be satisfactory to the client.

Job instruction and procedures ensure a correct understanding of the task to be performed and give satisfactory continuity even if the personnel changes. The cleanliness, health and safety of the workplace are important aspects of the quality environment, including the following issues:

● Throughout the organization are available written procedures for matters that affect the quality of the Company products.

● Documentation necessary to achieve product quality is available at the place and time of each manufacturing activity.

● All areas used for the manufacture or storage of material and finished products are maintained in such conditions that avoid contamination, loss of identity and damage.

● Refuse is disposed of in a timely and safe manner.

CREATING PROCEDURES

Introduction

Procedures are part of the quality system documentation and possibly the most important documents in "pulling the system together." A procedure is a document that accurately reflects the operation it describes and who is responsible. The procedure defines how the organization functions in each area. It may also be used as a benchmark to review and improve upon. Procedures are certainly not paper for the sake of paper. They can accomplish the following:

- Provide a reference point to new members of an organization and reduce verbal training
- Clearly define responsibilities
- Allow the identification of error causes
- Prevent subsequent errors by modifying the procedure
- Provide a permanent record.

A procedure is a vital and useful tool; to ensure its credibility, it must be reviewed and updated as necessary to reflect current practice.

Procedure Planning and Development

Management is responsible for developing the overall quality system and for identifying those activities that require a formal procedure. Careful planning is essential to developing and writing logical, well structured and coherent procedures.

IDENTIFY THE NEED

When is a procedure necessary? Wherever its absence would adversely effect quality, since a procedure will ensure that a critical activity is consistently performed. The need for a procedure may arise for several reasons:

- The overall quality system identifies required procedures
- An ISO 9000 standard requires a procedure
- Management wishes to formalize critical activities
- The person responsible for implementing activities may want clear definitions of the procedures involved.

Once the need for a procedure is identified, authorization is required. This is normally given by the head of the department concerned. Those responsible for the critical activities should then nominate the appropriate employees to develop and write individual procedures.

IDENTIFY KEY ASPECTS OF THE ACTIVITY

It is important that someone involved in the activity prepares the procedure. In developing the procedure, that person should consider its scope, objectives, time scale, format and control.

Scope

The author must establish the precise scope covered by the procedure. Consideration should be given to the following:

- Interfaces with other procedures or intended procedures
- Whether the critical activity being addressed can be contained in only one procedure
- What procedural information already exists for the activity.

Objectives

Management must define the specific objectives of the activity covered by the procedure.

Time Scales

To keep the project on track, it is important to establish a time scale for each aspect of procedure preparation. Time scale considerations should include the following:

- Getting authorization to proceed
- Defining the scope
- Collecting information relating to the activity
- Preparing a draft procedure
- Circulating the draft for comment
- Getting agreement from those concerned
- Getting authorization for issuing the procedure
- Incorporating it into the control system.

Format and Control

When producing a procedure, the format used is normally described in a company standard. That is, there should be a "procedure for procedure formats." This procedure defines such things as standard headings, type faces, title indents, line justification, contents sheets, page layouts, etc. When the procedure has been written, it will require administration and control.

PREPARING THE PROCEDURE

Preparing the actual procedure involves the following:

- Establishing current practice
- Documenting current practice
- Reviewing current practice
- Writing the procedure
- Approving and issuing the procedure.

Establish Current Practice

The first step in preparing a procedure is to review the existing activity to determine how it is currently performed. It is essential to do the following:

- Establish what procedural information already exists for the activity

- Establish and record the routine methods of performing the activity
- Identify responsibilities
- Determine the current standards, if any, and how effectively they are being achieved
- Identify those aspects that significantly impact on quality and how efficiently this is achieved.

Document Current Practice

Document the existing methods of performing an activity for revision and agreement before preparing the procedure. It is important to understand how each activity is carried out, how each step is initiated, and how it leads to the next step. A flow chart can assist in this process.

Information and instructions given in the procedure must be easy to find. The process of documenting the existing activities may itself identify potential changes and improvement in working methods.

Review Current Practice

Review the current practice with appropriate and responsible personnel to evaluate and determine the following:

- If the specified objectives are being achieved
- The best methods of achieving the agreed levels of quality
- If those levels are adequate
- Gaps, duplications and areas of weakness, especially a lack of interfacing between departments
- Potential improvement.

Write the Procedure

The next step is to write the procedure. Keep the following in mind:

- The ultimate test of an effective procedure is its ability to provide the control necessary to achieve the desired result. When considering a procedure or the need for one, take into account the effect it is likely to have on performance.
- When writing a procedure, use tools such as a flow chart for reference.
- Include only instructions specific to the activity controlled by the procedure; these should be defined by means of the "Purpose" and "Scope" statements.
- Where appropriate, include references to procedures that address related activities. If the information contained in one procedure is too lengthy, more than one procedure may be required.
- The degree of detail required in a procedure depends upon the personnel for whom the procedure is written and their level of training.
- Those effected by the implementation of the procedure should be involved as much as possible during the drafting stage. This will create a sense of ownership and will assist in the implementation of the procedure.
- The appropriate person, together with related departments, should review the initial draft

procedure to see if it is workable. Consideration must be given to all comments received regarding the workability of the procedure. Modifications or additions should be incorporated if pertinent.

- Any revisions agreed at this stage should be recorded, documented in the standard format and then checked for errors.

- For a procedure to be auditable, it should be possible to take a clause from the procedure and convert it into a question. For example, the clause "the document controller shall ensure that all master files are kept in lockable cabinets" should be easy to convert to the checklist question, "does the document controller ensure that all master files are kept in lockable cabinets?" When you are implementing this clause in your company, a "yes" answer would demonstrate that it is auditable.

Approve and Issue the Procedure

The appropriate, responsible person should approve the procedure once it has been checked. Then it can be issued and distributed to the relevant employees, according to document control procedures. It's up to sectional or departmental management to ensure that relevant personnel effectively implement the procedure.

To summarize, the evolution of a procedure from its inception to its withdrawal can be summarized as the following:

- Identify the need for a procedure
- Prepare a procedure
- Check and review the procedure
- Authorize the procedure
- Issue and distribute the procedure
- Regularly review the procedure
- Rewrite the procedure as necessary
- Withdraw the procedure from the system when it is no longer applicable.

Procedure Structure and Format

Effective procedures are uniform in structure and consistent in presentation. Experience has shown a seven-section format to be most effective. The sections include the following:

- Purpose/objective
- Scope
- Responsibilities
- References
- Definitions
- Procedures
- Documentation.

(Two examples of procedures are shown in the Annex to this chapter.)

PURPOSE

The purpose outlines the objective or intention of the document. For example, if a procedure is being written to control documentation, the phrase outlining the purpose of the procedure could be written as follows:

The purpose of this procedure is to provide instruction on and assign responsibility for systematically controlling the issue, receipt, revision and withdrawal of all documents.

SCOPE

This section will outline the area, department, group or personnel to which the procedure applies. Using the document control procedure again as an example, the scope could be phrased as:

This procedure applies to all documentation generated as a result of implementing the requirements of both the quality assurance program of the company and a quality plan developed by the company for a contract.

REFERENCES

The references section lists documents that have a bearing on and that refer to the activities within a procedure. (See Table 7-1 for an example.)

DEFINITIONS

Words, abbreviations or actions that may be ambiguous or that may not be readily understood by the reader should be clearly defined. For example, documents and procedures may be defined as follows:

Documents are written statements that shall individually or collectively include procedures, specifications, work instructions, drawings and correspondence.

A procedure is a specified way to perform an activity.

Wherever possible, use terms defined in ISO 8402.

Table 7-1: Document List	
Document Number	**Title**
QA-PROC-001	Preparation and administration of procedures
QA-PROC-002	Document numbering and identification
QA-PROC-003	Document change control

PROCEDURE(S)

A procedure describes the personnel involved in an activity. It should also explain the activity and include how, where, when and possibly why the activity is carried out. As stated earlier, a procedure should be auditable, which means it should be possible to take a clause from the procedure and convert it into a question. Remember, however, that the auditability of a procedure is a measure of how effectively the procedure has been written, but not a measure of the effectiveness of the procedure itself.

DOCUMENTATION

All documentation referred to within a procedure and generated as a result of implementing the procedure is listed under the documentation section.

Copies or examples of such documents should be attached to the procedures as an appendix. Documents relating to a given procedure should bear a reference number linking that document to the procedure.

Procedure Format

A consistent format aids readability and comprehension. It can be achieved by using standard templates or a standard layout. The details of the required format are defined in the "Procedure for Procedures." (See above.) Templates on which to produce procedures should include the following:

● The company name, division and logo
● Provision for the document title
● Provision for the document number
● Provision for the document revision and date.

To ensure uniformity of document presentation, the layout should be defined. Some aspects to consider include the following:

● The columns on which the text should start and finish
● The setting of tab spaces to define indents for sections and sub sections
● The typefaces to be used
● The use of upper and lower case for headings
● What is to be used.

A standard layout is shown in the Annex to this chapter.

Procedure Administration and Control

Procedure administration and control are important aspects of the process and should be considered before writing a procedure. Decisions should be finalized before procedures are issued. The key issues include the following:

- Defining responsibilities
- Developing a procedure numbering system
- Controlling distribution
- Amending and revising the procedures.

SUGGESTIONS FOR WRITING DOCUMENTATION

In writing the text, remember the KISS principle: *Keep It Short and Simple.* Use straightforward words and terms; do not use this documentation to demonstrate a vast and sophisticated command of the English language. Follow novelist George Orwell's suggestion to ask six questions before writing begins:

- What am I trying to say?
- What words will best express it?
- What image or idiom will make it more clear?
- Is this image fresh enough to have an effect?
- Could I have put it more shortly?
- Have I said anything that is ugly?

More ground rules to follow include:

- Make the meaning very clear.
- Sift out all irrelevant material.
- Ensure that the text is grammatically correct; avoid the use of passive verbs and split infinitives.
- Search out errors in spelling and punctuation.
- Avoid jargon and "committee language."
- Use the simplest language to convey the thought.
- Use clear words and phrases.
- Use short sentences.
- Use punctuation thoughtfully and in a way to aid understanding.
- Separate ideas into individual sentences or paragraphs.

Remember that these are documents written to enable coworkers to perform their tasks more efficiently and consistently. Also remember that documentation users are intelligent; they just have different skills. Therefore:

- Do not write in an antagonistic manner.
- Do not write in a condescending manner.
- Do not write in a supercilious manner.

PROCEDURES AS BRIDGE BUILDERS

Procedures build bridges between departments—lines that are essential for the effective management of any organization. One of the fundamental problems in most businesses' management structures is that they are organized in functional, vertical operational lines; this is the most efficient way to perform tasks. Satisfying customer needs, however, requires that a series of processes be fulfilled that essentially run horizontally across the organizational structures, trying to bridge the gaps between functional departments. These gaps are almost always where the problems lie. The task of the procedures is to ensure that the "gaps" are as seamless as possible.

Anyone who has worked in any size company—sometimes even in small companies—will know that "turf wars" between functional departments are common, and the manager who spends most of his or her time playing interdepartmental politics poses a problem. As a result, it is most important for procedures to clearly define responsibilities and authorities to ensure that work will be completed despite the management. It is quite rare to find problems within the vertical structures of an organization—it is also quite rare to find those horizontal lines functioning unless a company is complying with ISO 9000 or a similar system. It is a case of managing the white space, and Figure 7-2 highlights the danger zones.

The process of achieving customer satisfaction can be thought of as building a vast jigsaw puzzle. Each employee in the company holds one piece of the jigsaw, and the task is to complete the picture on time, every time, with every piece of the jigsaw puzzle correctly placed to create a masterpiece. Imagine trying to do that if the pieces are randomly distributed—which they usually are—and there are no instructions as to how to make the picture up. The system numbers each piece and tells the experienced jigsaw-puzzle solver how to complete the task.

— *Roderick Goult*

DEFINING RESPONSIBILITIES

Three primary areas of responsibility regarding procedures should be defined. They are: identify, review and authorize procedures; prepare and write procedures; and administer and control documents.

Identify, Review and Authorize Procedures

All personnel should be responsible for identifying the need for a procedure, but it is usually senior management that verifies the need for a procedure. Once written, a review of procedures is necessary to ensure the following:

- Any conflicts within or between existing procedures are identified and resolved
- The procedure reflects current practice and provides adequate direction
- Interfaces at both departmental and interdepartmental levels are defined and agreed by means of detailed reviews at both these levels.

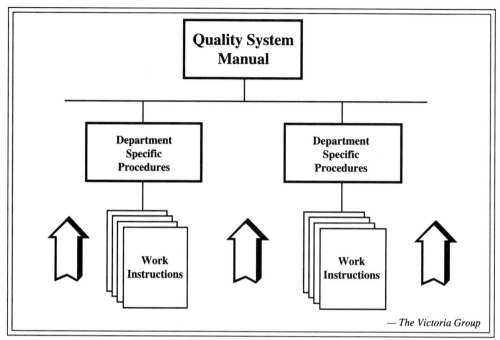

Figure 7-2: The Classic "White Space" Danger Zones.

To become an official document, the procedure must be approved by a nominated or authorized person. Typically, a procedure may require approval from personnel such as a department head or manager, a quality assurance manager, or the CEO.

Prepare and Write Procedures

The quality assurance department should not write procedures for activities outside their direct authority. This should be undertaken by personnel familiar with the activities and functions to be controlled. Procedures should be written using the company's accepted format, but need not be written in formal language, as long as they are clearly understood by the affected employees.

Administer and Control Documents

Management should determine those who will be responsible for procedure administration and control. This should specify the following:

- The format in which procedures shall be written
- The numbering system for procedures
- How procedures will be reviewed and the steps to follow in case of approval, amendment and revision
- Document storage, distribution and retrieval.

PROCEDURE NUMBERING SYSTEM

Develop a numbering system for procedures that allows adequate room for including new procedures. A typical procedure numbering system could be structured as followed:

PROD-WI-001, where:

      PROD = Code for the particular department (Production)

      WI = The level of the document (i.e. work instruction = WI)

      001 = Sequential Number.

It's a good idea to have a central register of documentation for *all* organizations. It may be advantageous to employ a master record index system, particularly where project work is involved. For the smaller company, a log will suffice under the control of a responsible person and in a readily accessible position.

DISTRIBUTION CONTROL

Document distribution should be on a "need to know," not a "want to know" basis and should be planned, documented and controlled. The first issue of a set of procedures is in the form of controlled copies; that is, each manual is numbered and signed out to a specified individual.

Procedure holders can be audited periodically to ensure that copies are kept up to date and that superseded copies or unofficial versions are destroyed.

A document control procedure should prevent unauthorized duplication of documents. This identifies how and by whom document reproduction is carried out and the method used to identify controlled copies.

PROCEDURE AMENDMENT AND REVISION

Procedures are living documents that require amendment or revision from time to time. When amending or revising a procedure, consider including the following:

- A request for change note
- Procedure revision numbers
- A revision record sheet
- The manner in which the revised procedure is issued.

Request for Change

Before a procedure is changed, it is important that the person wishing to make the change request the change in writing. The request should indicate the required change, the reason for the change, what will be effected, and who is making the request. Authorization for the change will be necessary and the request must be signed by either the author of the procedure or the manager responsible.

Procedure Revision Numbers

Each page of the procedure should contain a revision indicator. Revisions can be referred to numerically and changes within the document can be indicated alphabetically. For example, the initial procedure is Issue 1. If page 25 of Issue 1 is revised, it can be numbered "25-1a." The date of the revision should be included. Whichever system is chosen for identifying the revision status of documents, it should be consistent throughout the organization.

The extent of any revisions made within the text of the procedure can be highlighted. This can be done by means of a revision number placed in brackets at the point in the margin where the revision starts. A line is extended down from this point to the end of the revised text. Alternatively, you can underline the revised material or use any other consistent method.

Revision Record Sheet

It is customary to include a record of the revisions made at the front of each procedure, or at the front of a manual containing a separate set of procedures. This is done to ensure that the user is in possession of the latest revision and that this can be verified.

A record of procedure revisions may be displayed in a revision box on the cover page of the procedure or by an amendment or revision record sheet immediately after the cover page. As a minimum, the record sheet should identify:

- The revision indicator (1, 1a, 1b, as described above)
- The date of the revision
- The specific revision made
- The affected pages or procedures
- Authorizing signature.

Departments responsible for issuing revisions should maintain an index of all revisions to procedures. The index itself should be traceable by having a revision number and date.

Revision Issue

Companies vary in the way they issue procedure revisions. Some favor reissuing the entire procedure, using the next revision number; others issue only the affected pages, with the alphabetic revision indicator, until a major revision is carried out.

Revisions are issued to all holders of the procedure(s) and should be accompanied by a transmittal document. The transmittal document allows the recipient to acknowledge receipt and to incorporate the revision into his or her copy of the procedure.

PAPERLESS MASTERS

Many document masters are now held on computer; this makes them especially vulnerable to unauthorized change or tampering. There should be an authorization mechanism (e.g., passwording or structured access) to prevent this from happening, a log or other means of tracing who accessed the document, what changes were made, when, and why.

The intangibility of software can cause problems. Think of software as just another type of document; the same requirements apply regarding authority, revision status, etc.

A master copy should be kept in a fireproof safe, or if this is not available, at a separate location and one or two working copies at the place of use: the same rules apply regarding removal of obsolete copies.

CONCLUSION

In summary, your documented quality system, when completed, should help customers and auditors understand how your quality management system addresses the requirements of ISO 9001, ISO 9002 or ISO 9003. Remember, however, that your quality system belongs to you and no other individual or organization. The process of obtaining ISO 9000 registration should always be secondary to the benefits to your company from having an effective, fully functional and well-documented quality system.

ANNEX 1

Quality Manual Sample Content

The following is an excerpt from an actual, complete manual. It is included in this Annex for illustration purposes.

Section 1: Quality Policy

1. COMPANY PROFILE

As one of the industry's leading and largest contract electronics systems manufacturers, the Company offers a complete service, from surface mount to full production and complete systems built, to all customer specifications.

ISO 9000 registration has been awarded.

Computer-assisted automatic component insertion, computer-controlled in-circuit test, functional testing, and automatic flow soldering add to the technical and manufacturing expertise of the Company.

2. QUALITY POLICY

This quality manual contains the Company's quality objectives endorsed by the senior management. It has been formulated to serve as a reference base for the policy and procedures for quality assurance and controls within the Company. The quality system is designed to ensure the maintenance of product quality standards through the provision of evaluation, inspection and verification of processes at all stages of manufacture.

It is company policy to manufacture and market goods which comply with the customer's needs and the designer's specification. Responsibility for the implementation of this policy has been delegated to all staff through their senior management. Compliance with the provisions and objectives of this manual are mandatory on all personnel.

Chief Executive Officer: _____

3. ORGANIZATION

The Company has appointed a management representative, independent of other functions, to be responsible for implementation of the quality policy, and has the necessary authority to execute such responsibilities. The structure of the Company is shown in the overall organization chart, and that of the quality department is shown separately.

4. RESPONSIBILITIES

Senior management responsibilities are defined as follows. Responsibilities for other positions are fully detailed in the relevant job descriptions held by personnel department.

1. Quality Manager

The quality manager is responsible to the chief executive officer for the definition, mainte-

(continued on next page)

Quality Manual Sample Content
(continued from previous page)

nance and implementation of quality standards for the Company's specifications and the requirements specified by individual customers.

The quality manager is responsible for the functioning of the quality department, and is the management representative for quality.

The quality manager has the authority to define methods and procedures that are mandatory and to reject those procedures and products that do not conform to the Company or customer quality standards.

2. Materials Manager
The materials manager is responsible for the planning, purchasing, expediting and control of materials to facilitate cost-effective manufacture and for providing a cost-effective, timely delivery service to customers.

3. Manufacturing Manager
The manufacturing manager is responsible for entering orders to provide feasible production schedules, coordination, motivation and control of staff and for using capital resources to ensure cost effective, timely achievement of production schedules.

4. Engineering Manager
The industrial engineering manager is responsible for providing effective, estimating, planning and engineering-support services to manufacturing and providing facilities service to the factory in order to maximize contributions to Company profitability.

5. Sales Manager
The sales manager is responsible for the company image in the electronics market that is conducive to the quality and business strategy of the organization and is responsible for direct sales from initial inquiry to contract receipt, review and delivery.

6. Human Resources Manager
The human resources manager is responsible for all personnel matters including recruitment, industrial relations and conditions of employment. The human resource manager administers training at all levels.

5. AMENDMENTS
In order that the manual reflects the current practices and requirements of the Company, amendments to the manual may be necessary, and these must be recorded. Amendments to this quality manual shall be done in accordance with document change procedure DOC-PROC-001.

Amendment or changes to this manual shall be published in accordance with the document change policy. Proposed amendments to the Manual shall be submitted to the quality manager for

(continued on next page)

Quality Manual Sample Content

(continued from previous page)

consideration under the documentation change control procedure. The manual shall be formally reviewed at intervals of no more than 12 months by the quality manager to reaffirm its adequacy to current company requirements. The control, revision and distribution of this manual shall be the quality manager's responsibility. A list of amendments shall be included in each controlled copy of the manual.

Section 2: Systems Outline

1. REVIEW & AUDIT

A system of management review and quality audit has been established. The audit shall be performed in accordance with a specified plan that states upon which items an audit shall be undertaken, how it shall be performed and when it shall be carried out.

A quality audit includes both the Company and suppliers' quality assurance where this is required.

The audit shall be carried out by competent personnel who are not directly responsible for the activity being audited.

In order to maintain an effective quality assurance system, an internal audit of all procedures that affect the quality of the Company products and services shall be undertaken twice each year. The quality manager is responsible for implementing and controlling the audit system. Audits may be delegated to any responsible employee of the Company. No sectional audit shall be delegated to persons responsible for that section.

The quality manager shall ensure that where necessary, corrective action is taken. Audit reports shall be compiled into an annual report for senior management and discussed at the annual management review. The management review shall be chaired by the chief executive officer and attended by the senior manager and shall discuss the effectiveness and achievement of the Company quality policy.

Upon receipt of an order, the sales manager shall ensure that a contract review is initiated. The aim of this meeting is to establish the contract requirements, establish specific quality requirements and highlight differences from the tender.

2. RECORDS

The Company maintains records of all controls and inspections or tests performed to substantiate conformance to specified requirements. Subcontractors' records and procurement specifications are elements of that data. Records that substantiate conformance to the specified requirements are retained for five years.

Records shall be prepared as evidence of compliance with the contents of the quality manual, Company procedures and contractual agreements. There shall be records showing the extent and findings of inspection of goods inward, work in progress, final inspection and test, dispatch of goods and calibration of measuring equipment. Records shall be retained in the department most suited to them.

(continued on next page)

Quality Manual Sample Content

(continued from previous page)

3. DOCUMENTATION AND CHANGE CONTROL

A system is established that ensures control of validity, publishing and distribution of documentation required in accordance with this standard.

Documentation means not only drawings and specifications but also other documents necessary for satisfactory quality assurance (i.e., procedures, job instructions and standards).

Established procedures ensure that changes to documents essential to the control and monitoring of manufactured processes are carried out in a controlled and authorized manner.

Established procedures ensure that only correct editions of relevant documents are available where and when an activity is being carried out.

Records shall be maintained for all changes, updates and replacements of essential documents for the system of recalling outdated documents.

4. CONTROL OF TEST AND MEASURING EQUIPMENT

The Company is responsible for providing, controlling, calibrating and maintaining inspection, testing and measuring equipment suitable to demonstrate the conformance of material and service to the specified requirements.

The degree of confidence in measuring and testing procedures depends on the accuracy and reliability of the equipment. Measuring and testing equipment does not only include general measuring instruments but also special instruments used with specific products for measuring purposes.

Calibration of measuring equipment will cover all items of equipment used within the Company that are the property of other organizations and persons.

Calibration shall be carried out at intervals established by stability and usage and in accordance with the calibration procedure.

Calibration records shall be maintained, showing the calibration history and condition of each item.

All measuring equipment within the calibration system shall indicate the validity of calibration.

Section 3: Procedure Index

DEPARTMENT PROCEDURE MANUALS

Specific company procedures are detailed in department procedure manuals. The designated managers are responsible for generating, authorizing and controlling the following procedures. Master copies are held as detailed, and working copies are available at the place of use.

Sales   **Responsibility: Sales Manager**
Sales Department Procedures Manual   SAL-PROC-001
Location: Sales Office

(continued on next page)

Quality Manual Sample Content
(continued from previous page)

Engineering
Planning Department Procedures Manual
Estimating Department Procedures Manual
Manufacturing Process Procedures
Location: Engineering Office

Responsibility: Engineering Manager
ENG-PROC-001
ENG-PROC-002
ENG-PROC-003

Manufacturing
Manufacturing Department Procedures
Location: Manufacturing Office

Responsibility: Manufacturing Manager
MAN-PROC-001

Materials
Purchasing Manual
Stores Manual
Packing and Despatch Procedures
Goods Inward Manual
Location: Purchasing Office

Responsibility: Materials Manager
MAT-PROC-001
MAT-PROC-002
MAT-PROC-003
MAT-PROC-004

Personnel & Training
Personnel Department Manual
Location: Personnel Office

Responsibility: Human Resources Manager
PER-PROC-001

Quality
Quality Procedures Manual
Receiving Inspection Manual
Location: Quality Office

Responsibility: Quality Manager
QA-PROC-001
QA-PROC-002

ANNEX 2

Sample Procedure 1—Document Control Procedure

Purpose

This document describes the procedure to be followed for the approval, issue and maintenance of all controlled documentation.

Scope

This procedure shall apply to all controlled documentation relating to all company products and services.

References

Document Change Procedure	DOC-PROC-001
Document Register	DOC-REG-001

Procedure

All controlled documentation shall be subject to approval by the following before issue and release:

a) Originator

b) Originator's manager

c) Quality manager.

Released documentation can only be changed in accordance with the Change Control System DOC-PROC-001.

A record of all controlled documentation shall be maintained by the quality manager indicating the following:

a) Reference number

b) Issue number

c) Disposition of copies.

Details of controlled document holders shall be held on the Document Register.

Officially distributed copies of the documents shall be identified by a red "Official Distribution" stamp giving date of distribution. Action affecting product quality shall only be taken on the basis of information contained in officially distributed copies of controlled documents.

Master copies of all controlled documentation shall be held by the quality manager.

All copies of documentation that become obsolete by reissue shall be promptly removed from distribution. One copy shall be archived by the quality manager; all other copies shall be destroyed.

ANNEX 3

Sample Procedure 2—Corrective Action Procedure

Scope
This procedure defines the corrective action process.

Purpose
To ensure the effective tracking, reporting and control of all corrective action within the manufacturing unit of the ABC Company.

Responsibilities
1. The senior production engineer is responsible for the effective management of the corrective action procedure.
2. All other managers are responsible for ensuring that any CARs (corrective action reviews) forwarded to them for investigation are responded to within the defined time scales.
3. Shop floor supervisors and operators are responsible for raising a CAR whenever a production problem cannot be resolved on the shop floor, or where a problem is repetitive.

Procedure
1. Any problem that cannot be resolved by shop supervision, or that is found to be repetitive, is to be reported on a CAR form. All relevant parts of the form are to be completed with the information indicated. The CAR will be signed by the individual who has raised the problem, and passed to the shop supervisor. (See Appendix A for the CAR form.)
2. The shop supervisor will examine all CARs submitted, and endeavor to identify a solution. Any CAR which is resolved at this stage will be signed off by the shop supervisor and passed on to production engineering for recording. CARs which cannot be resolved by shop supervision will be initialed as such and passed to production engineering.
   2.1 The shop supervisor is responsible for determining whether or not the subject of the CAR is such that a production permit/waiver is required to enable production to continue during the investigation. If this is the case, the supervisor will notify Quality accordingly and request the waiver, referencing the CAR.
3. Production engineering will log each CAR received and allocate a serial number from the CAR serial number list. The pink copy will be filed in the OPEN file. CARs which have been closed by shop supervision will be filed in numeric order, and the green copy returned to the originator.
4. Open CARs will be passed to the senior production engineer, who will classify them as A, B, or C, and determine which department is best equipped to resolve the problem. This will be noted on the form as indicated. The CAR will then be passed to the identified department or individual for resolution.

   Category A requires a response within 24 hours, Category B within 72 hours, and Category C within five working days.

(continued on next page)

Sample Procedure 2—Corrective Action Procedure

(continued from previous page)

5. The recipient of a CAR is responsible for ensuring that a response is generated within the designated timeframe. The relevant sections of the form should be completed as indicated, and the form returned to the production engineering department.

   5.1 Any CAR which requires longer than the designated timeframe for a response should be annotated accordingly, and the yellow copy returned to production engineering. Production engineering will notify the originator accordingly.

   5.2 Once the CAR is completed, the response will be approved by the appropriate departmental manager. If an engineering change is required to resolve the problem, the investigating engineer will initiate the change in accordance with the appropriate procedure and annotate the Request for Change form with the number of the CAR. The completed CAR will then be returned to the production engineering department.

6. Production engineering will log the completed CAR, and the senior production engineer will review the response. Satisfactory responses will result in the CAR being closed out, filed in the CLOSED file, and a copy sent to the originator. If production engineering does not accept the response, the CAR will be resubmitted to the relevant department with an explanation for the rejection. The re-submission will be logged in the OPEN log, and a new category noted and advised to the recipient.

7. The senior production engineer is responsible for producing a monthly summary report on all currently open CARs, and a quarterly analysis report. These reports will be circulated to all departmental managers.

Related documents

1. Production Permit/Concession or Waiver procedure
2. Engineering Change Request procedure

Records

1. Production engineering CAR Log.
2. Production engineering OPEN CAR file.
3. Production engineering CLOSED CAR file.
4. Monthly summary report.
5. Quarterly analysis report.

The CAR log will be maintained on a rolling three-year basis.

Closed CARs will be kept on active file on a rolling twelve-month basis, and archived for two years prior to disposal.

Reports will be retained for twelve months.

ANNEX 4: Sample Procedure Format

	Procedure for the Preparation and Administration of Procedures	Issue 1	12/12/92
		DOC-QP-001	

1.0 PURPOSE

This procedure describes the format, preparation, numbering, revision, distribution and administration of all company procedures, applicable to the quality and operating systems.

This procedure shall also be used as an example of how a procedure shall be prepared, formulated and presented.

2.0 SCOPE

This procedure shall apply to all documents that identify the activities of a department or group and shall be observed by all departments and groups without exception.

3.0 REFERENCES

DOC-QP-002 Document numbering system.

4.0 DEFINITIONS

An example of a definition is a word or action not universally understood or that may have a specific interpretation in the procedure.

Copyright the XYZ Company Ltd.

Page 4 of 9

ANNEX 5

ISO/DIS 10013: Guidelines for developing quality manuals

The revised ISO 9001 standard requires a quality manual. In Subclause 4.2.1, a note refers companies to ISO 10013 for guidance on quality manuals.

The contents of ISO/DIS 10013 include the following sections:

1. Scope
2. Normative reference
3. Definitions
4. Documentation of quality systems
5. Process of preparing a quality manual
6. Process of quality manual approval, issue and control
7. What to include in a quality manual

The Annex to the standard includes a description of the typical quality system document hierarchy, examples of a procedure format, and a section of a quality manual. The following are some key points from the standard.

Internal or External Purposes

In *Clause 3, Definitions*, the standard makes a distinction between a quality management manual and a quality assurance manual. The former is designed for internal use only and may contain proprietary information, while the latter does not contain such information and may be used for customers and third-party assessors. The same issue is discussed in *Clause 4.3, Special applications of quality manuals* where the standard points out that where there are internal and external manuals, they must describe the same quality system and not conflict.

Procedural Scope (4.1.1)

"Each documented procedure should cover a logically separable part of the quality system, such as a complete quality system element or part thereof, or a sequence of interrelated activities connected with more than one quality system element."

Structure and Format (4.2)

There is no required structure or format for quality manuals, so long as they convey the quality policy, objectives and governing procedures of the organization clearly, accurately and completely. A quality manual may:

- Be a direct compilation of quality system procedures
- Be a grouping or section of the quality system procedures
- Be a series of procedures for specific facilities/applications
- Be more than one document or level
- Stand alone or otherwise

(continued on next page)

ISO/DIS 10013: Guidelines for Developing Quality Manuals

(continued from previous page)

● Be other numerous possible derivations based upon the particular organization's need.

Preparing a Quality Manual (5)

Clause 5 suggests the following process for preparing a quality manual:

● List existing applicable policies, objectives and procedures
● Decide which quality system elements apply according to the selected standard
● Gather information about the existing quality system
● Obtain additional documentation or references from operational units
● Determine the format and structure of the intended manual
● Classify existing documents in accordance with intended format and structure.

The actual writing of necessary procedures follows the above process.

What to Include in a Quality Manual (7)

Clause 7 lists the suggested contents of a quality manual, including the following:

● Title, scope and field of application
● Table of contents
● An introduction to the organization and the manual
● Quality policies and objectives
● Description of the organization, responsibilities and authorities
● Description of the quality system elements and/or references to quality system procedures
● A definitions section, if appropriate
● A guide to the quality manual, if appropriate
● An Appendix that contains data necessary to support the quality manual.

A QUALITY SYSTEM CHECKLIST

BY ROBERT W. PEACH

The generic list that follows offers concise instruction and guidance for translating ISO 9000 requirements into a full-fledged quality system. Together with the previous detailed chapters on implementation and documentation, this "starter list" traces a logical path from the standards to system documentation.

INTRODUCTION

Early in the registration process, it is important to understand the ISO 9000 standard that you have selected for registration and to develop quality system documentation.

Teams responsible for developing ISO 9000 documentation face the challenge of making the analysis and developing the documentation—a task they likely have never done before. Not only must they determine how to start the process, but also how to develop a schedule of activities and how to keep on that schedule while remembering how thorough the documentation process should be.

The list that follows offers specific guidance for team members faced with translating the requirements of the ISO 9000 standard into a comprehensive quality system. Together with documentation (quality manual, quality procedures, and operator instructions), it provides an orderly journey from the standards to system documentation.

Team members should recognize that these lists are generic. The team should first review the content of the implementation lists and then modify them to meet their particular needs. This is a "starter list" to aid teams in their initial task of defining and guiding their assignment.

Management Responsibility (4.1)

1. Establish a quality policy:
   - Assign responsibility for someone/some team to develop the quality policy
   - Ask for input from across the company to ensure "ownership" of the quality policy
   - Develop comprehensive objectives
   - Consider organizational goals
   - In the policy, mention a commitment to the following:
   - Quality
   - Products
   - Services
   - Customers (expectations and needs)
   - Personnel
   - Safety
   - Responsibility to society.

2. Develop a plan to ensure that the policy is understood, implemented and maintained at all levels:
   - Conduct an orientation for new employees
   - Display copies of the policy
   - Hold departmental meetings/discussions
   - Reinforce/follow-up on the ideas in the policy

- Verify its effectiveness.

3. Define responsibility, authority and how the assignments are interrelated:
   - Prepare organizational charts
   - Review and expand job descriptions for personnel whose work affects quality and who have authority over the following:
   - Identifying problems
   - Generating solutions
   - Initiating corrective action to prevent recurrence of the problems
   - Verifying implementation of the corrective action
   - Controlling nonconforming product.

4. Identify resources:
   - Management
   - Work performance
   - Verification activities.

5. Appoint a management representative to:
   - Ensure that quality system is established
   - Report on performance.

6. Provide for management review of the quality system:
   - Assess quality audit results
   - Maintain records.

Quality System (4.2)

1. Determine the requirements of the standard, including the following:
   - Documentation
   - Implementation.

2. Determine which ISO standard applies.

3. Plan the structure of the documentation:
   - Manual
   - Operating procedures
   - Instructions
   - Records, forms and specifications.

4. Establish the existing company practices by using the following:
   - Flow charts
   - Procedures (written and unwritten)
   - Instructions.

5. Evaluate resources (present and needed):
   - Personnel
   - Instrumentation
   - Specifications and acceptance standards
   - Quality records.

6. Establish a plan for implementing the quality system. Consider the following:
   - Quality plans/quality manual
   - Needed resources
   - Updating procedures and instrumentation
   - Identifying extreme measurement requirements
   - Clarifying acceptance standards
   - Compatible elements
   - Quality records.

Contract Review (4.3)

1. Document the customer's requirements.
2. Identify pre-contract practice.
3. Establish contract review procedures.
4. Verify the capability to meet requirements.
5. Internalize customer's requirements and resolve any differences.
6. Maintain control of purchase orders that are written under one contract.
7. Develop a plan for deployment.
8. Establish purchase order review procedures.
9. Obtain customer agreements.
10. Revise/improve procedures.
11. Evaluate revisions.

Design Control (4.4)

1. Document all customer requirements (input).
2. Establish a plan for design control and assign responsibilities.
3. Assign qualified staff; provide adequate resources.
4. Obtain input from all cross-functional activities to establish interfaces.
5. Document the control procedures, with milestones required by the standard. Design output to do the following:
   - Meet input requirements
   - Contain reference data

- Meet regulations
- Consider safety
- Review documentation before release.

6. Provide output verification through the following:
   - Alternative calculations
   - Comparison with proven design
   - Qualification tests
   - Review of documents before release.

7. Validate design:
   - Assure that design verification is successful
   - Confirm that the final product meets user needs
   - Assess the need for multiple validations.

8. Develop change control procedures:
   - Identification
   - Documentation
   - Review
   - Approval.

Document and Data Control (4.5)

1. List all documents.
2. Establish a control plan for each category of document:
   - Document original procedures
   - Verify review and approval of documents
   - Consider the pros and cons of hard copy versus electronic media.
3. Investigate conformity to a control plan.
4. Assure availability at operations.
5. Establish control over documents that become obsolete.
6. Establish/implement change control procedures.
7. Investigate conformity to change procedures.

Purchasing (4.6)

1. Evaluate existing purchasing specifications and requirements:
   - Review the process for development and approval
   - Update the procedures.
2. Begin upgrading specifications as required. Prioritize by criticality.

3. Prepare, review and approve purchasing documents based on updated specs.
4. Establish criteria for establishing subcontractor acceptability based on the following:
   - Product quality history
   - Delivery dependability
   - Quality system capability (via quality audit/ISO 9000).
5. Develop a subcontractor classification system.
6. Establish a record system.
7. Deploy the plan through the following:
   - Develop a schedule
   - Coordinate with receiving inspection
   - Assign responsibility for administration.
8. Revise/improve procedures.
9. Evaluate revisions.

Control of Customer-Supplied Product (4.7)

1. Determine existence of customer-supplied product (including test equipment).
2. Document existing practice for:
   - Verification
   - Storage
   - Maintenance.
3. Revise/improve procedures.
4. Evaluate revisions.

Product Identification and Traceability (4.8)

1. Establish customer and/or regulatory requirements.
2. Document the existing traceability practices to include the following:
   - From subcontractor
   - In plant
   - To customer
   - Installation.
3. Revise/improve traceability procedures.
4. Consider types of traceability/identification:
   - Unit identification (serial number)
   - Lot identification
   - Production date code.

5. Consider methods of identification:
   - Paper versus electronic
   - Labeling
   - Bar codes.

6. Determine the following about the records to be kept:
   - Availability
   - Retention times
   - Responsibility.

Process Control (4.9)

1. Base process control on the quality plan.
2. Identify critical control points.
3. Define factors affecting key processes (production/installation and servicing):
   - Equipment
   - Work environment
   - Hazardous material control.
4. Identify the following product requirements:
   - Specifications
   - Workmanship standards
   - Regulatory standards and codes.
5. Review existing monitoring techniques.
6. Develop control and approval procedures.
7. Develop work instructions.
8. Develop control equipment maintenance procedures.
9. Identify special processes.
10. Implement process change control.
11. Revise/improve procedures.
12. Evaluate revisions.

Inspection and Testing (4.10)

Establish a separate plan or procedure for the following:
   - Receiving inspection and testing (consider the existing level of supplier control)
   - In-process inspection and testing
   - Final inspection and testing.

1. Determine the policy (i.e., "do not use until verified").
2. Identify categories of the product affected.

3. List all quality characteristics subject to inspection and test.
4. Ensure that the procedures for identifying specified requirements are available.
5. Provide for complete and current procedures at point of inspection/test.
6. Provide for positive product identification/recall for urgent release.
7. Release only when successful tests/records are complete.
8. Revise/improve procedures.
9. Evaluate revision.

Control of Inspection, Measuring and Test Equipment (4.11)

1. Identify all inspection and test requirements (Clause 4.10).
2. List equipment available to conduct inspections/tests (fixed and portable):
   - Laboratory equipment
   - Inspection and test equipment
   - Production machinery
   - Jigs, fixtures, templates
   - Test software.
3. Identify recognized calibration requirements for each piece of equipment:
   - Both fixed and portable equipment
   - Required measurement capability
   - Known measurement uncertainty.
4. Review and flow chart existing procedures and documentation for the following:
   - Measurements to be made
   - Calibration procedures
   - "Measurement uncertainty"
   - Identification of calibration status on equipment
   - Out of calibration action
   - Work environment control
   - Handling, storage
   - Safeguarding against unauthorized adjustment
   - Rechecking intervals.
5. Revise/improve procedures regarding hard copy versus electronic.
6. Establish an effective record system.
7. Evaluate revisions.

Inspection and Test Status (4.12)

1. Identify locations where inspection status is critical, such as the following areas:

- Receiving
- Production
- Post production
- Installation
- Servicing.

2. Flow chart all processes.
3. Determine the means of identification/status:
   - Marking, stamps
   - Tags, labels
   - Routing cards
   - Hard copy versus electronic records
   - Physical location.

4. Review positive release procedures and responsibility.
5. Revise/improve the quality plan or procedures.
6. Evaluate revisions.

Control of Nonconforming Product (4.13)

1. Review and document procedures for the following:
   - Identification
   - Documentation
   - Segregation
   - Prevention of inadvertent use/installation.

2. Document procedures for disposition, notification and classification to do the following:
   - Rework
   - Accept
   - Regrade
   - Reject.

3. Assign authority for disposition approval.
4. Document procedures for reinspection of repairs/rework.
5. Document concession reporting and handling procedures.
6. Revise and approve procedures.
7. Evaluate revisions.

Corrective and Preventive Action (4.14)

Separately identify procedures for corrective action (actual nonconformities) versus preventive action (potential nonconformities).

CORRECTIVE ACTION

1. Assign responsibility.
2. Review the number and significance of complaints and returns.
3. Prepare flow chart of the present system.
4. Evaluate the effectiveness of present practice.
5. Provide resources:
   - Expertise
   - Records, instruction procedures
   - Defective product (for analysis).

6. Revise/improve procedures to:
   - Investigate the cause of nonconformities
   - Analyze all processes
   - Determine a final "fix" (i.e., an action plan)
   - Initiate action to prevent recurrence
   - Apply new controls.

7. Evaluate revised procedures.

PREVENTIVE ACTION

1. Assign responsibility.
2. Review existing preventive action activities.
3. Prepare flow chart of present system.
4. Evaluate the effectiveness of present practice.
5. Identify appropriate sources of information:
   - Processes
   - Concessions
   - Audit results
   - Quality records
   - Service reports
   - Customer complaints.

6. Identify activities in which preventive action activities can be established or enhanced. Examples include:
   - Product design
   - Process development
   - Process control.

7. Modify/improve procedures to:
   - Identify potential nonconformities
   - Initiate action to prevent occurrence

- Apply new controls
- Revise/improve procedures.

8. Evaluate revised procedures.

Handling, Storage, Packaging, Preservation and Delivery (4.15)

1. Identify critical points in process.
2. Review available information (damages rates, etc.).
3. Generate documentation for the following:
   - Packaging designs
   - Unique customer packaging requirements
   - In-process handling procedures
   - Packing, packaging and marking processes
   - Warehouse procedures
   - Transportation techniques/carrier selection
   - Storage, preservation and segregation methods
   - Environmental impact.
4. Revise/improve procedures.
5. Evaluate revisions.

Control of Quality Records (4.16)

1. Review the list of documents (4.5).
2. For each category (function) of documents review procedures to:
   - Identify
   - Collect
   - Index
   - Provide access
   - File
   - Store
   - Maintain
   - Dispose.
3. Include a review of the following:
   - Supplier records
   - Subcontractor records
   - Installation and servicing.

4. For each document category, establish the following issues about the document:
   - Legibility
   - Identification with a product
   - Ability to be retained
   - Storage environment
   - Retention needs
   - Availability to customer.

5. Review requirements for quality records under the following clauses:
   - 4.1.3, 4.2, 4.3.4, 4.4, 4.6.2, 4.7, 4.8, 4.9, 4.10, 4.11, 4.12, 4.13, 4.14, 4.17 and 4.18.

Internal Quality Audits (4.17)

1. Identify the activities to be audited.
2. Establish the qualifications of audit personnel, including the following:
   - Experience
   - Training
   - Availability.

3. Develop (or update) audit procedures to include:
   - Planning
   - Documentation.

4. Conduct an initial (trial) quality audit:
   - Evaluate the adequacy of procedures
   - Determine their effectiveness
   - Verify compliance
   - Suitability of working environment.

5. Establish a permanent quality audit program:
   - Schedule the audit frequency
   - Document any follow-up
   - Report to management
   - Initiate Corrective action
   - Verify effectiveness of action.

Training (4.18)

1. Identify training needs:
   - List all job functions
   - Establish training requirements for each function

- Include the requirements in job descriptions.

2. Provide training based on the following:
   - Quality plan elements
   - Process knowledge requirements: methods/equipment
   - Product knowledge requirements: specifications/workmanship standards
   - Cross-training
   - Other requirements: internal customer/delivery.

3. Establish/record personnel qualifications in individual personnel file to include the following:
   - All required training completed
   - Education (initial, additional)
   - Previous experience
   - Physical characteristics/limitations
   - Special training (safety, SPC)
   - Medical records
   - Awards/rewards/promotions
   - Cross-training.

4. Develop and document a training plan (matrix) to include:
   - Required training
   - Optional additional training
   - Periodic evaluation of effectiveness.

Servicing (4.19)

1. Identify customer service requirements.
2. Document the service requirements:
   - Establish procedures
   - Perform the service
   - Report and verify that the requirements are met.
3. Revise/improve procedures.
4. Evaluate revisions.

Statistical Techniques (4.20)

1. Identify existing statistical applications and procedures.
2. Review status/correctness/effectiveness of statistical technique applications such as in:
   - Establishing process capability
   - Verifying product characteristics.

3. Examine the quality plan for additional applications.
4. Provide for additional statistical applications.
5. Establish a training plan.
6. Select training personnel.
7. Conduct training sessions.
8. Evaluate the effectiveness and value of new applications.

QUALITY IN THE DEVELOPMENT AND USE OF SOFTWARE

This chapter examines the role of quality in developing and using software. It provides an overview of software quality challenges and discusses ISO 9001 and its relation to ISO 9000-3. The chapter describes the British TickIT scheme, discusses developments in the United States and highlights general issues concerning software sensitivity. The chapter concludes with a look at three other software quality arrangements and predictions for future trends.

SOFTWARE QUALITY CHALLENGES

Software is increasingly important to the successful, efficient operation of American business. Its use varies widely and includes the following:

- As a stand-alone product (whether mass-marketed "shrink wrap" software or a customized one-of-a-kind application);
- As embedded software (where the software on board a product provides its essential functionality);
- As support software (woven into the business process as a provider of information and as a basis for decision making).

Many opportunities exist for quality improvement in the development and use of software. Anecdotal evidence suggests that software quality has not improved much in the past decade or more, and corrective maintenance is typically of the same order of magnitude as the original development effort for most large software-based systems. Horror stories abound, in which there are spectacular instances of multimillion dollar costs, millions of affected customers, bankrupted companies, and occasional loss of life.

Until recently there has been little direct consideration of the special needs of software developers and users. Quality in the development and use of software, however, is no longer merely optional—it is mandatory.

Software demands different quality management emphases than "traditional" products, however. Software is immaterial, intangible. Its flexibility is legendary but ultimately frustrating if not properly identified and controlled. Unlike other products, the production phase (replication) can be performed with arbitrarily high precision. On the other hand, its design phase calls for more discipline and insight than perhaps any other intellectual activity. Software doesn't wear out, so all failures are the result of faults injected during design.

Software auditing is also different. It requires insights into the unique aspects of the design process and of the particulars of software development. If value is to be added in a software audit, the auditor must be sensitive to these issues. He or she must know which quality principles are directly applicable, which may be treated by analogy, and which are not directly applicable at all.

The United States is now moving toward a software quality systems registration arrangement. (See below.) The software-specific arrangement would incorporate an internationally recognized guidance document, *ISO 9000-3, Guidelines for the application of ISO 9001 to the development, supply and maintenance of software.* It would ensure that registrars act responsibly in adding software to their scope of supply and would facilitate identifying auditors who are competent not only in audit skills but also in addressing software issues.

An assessment arrangement can add value for both suppliers and their customers to the extent it is sensitive to the particulars of an industry and responsive to market demands. A software-specific scheme known as TickIT is already a business reality in the United Kingdom and is gaining some acceptance in the international community. The US approach would recognize that reality and build upon it.

SOFTWARE DEFINITIONS IN ISO 9000-3

Software .... Intellectual creation comprising the programs, procedures, rules and any associated documentation pertaining to the operation of a data processing system. (Software is independent of the medium on which it is recorded.)

Software Product: .... Complete set of computer programs, procedures and associated documentation and data designated for delivery to a user.

Software Item .... Any identifiable part of a software product at an intermediate step or at the final step of development.

Development .... All activities to be carried out to create a software product.

Phase .... Defined segment of work.

Verification .... The process of evaluating the products or a given phase to
(for software) ensure correctness and consistency with respect to the products and standards provided as input to that phase.

Validation .... The process of evaluating software to ensure compliance
(for software) with specified requirements.

USE OF ISO 9001

Consider how some of the key areas of quality management, as exemplified in the requirements of ISO 9001, address software's unique aspects. The ISO 9001 standard has several key clauses that are most directly applicable to software: Contract Review (4.3), Design Control (4.4), Product Identification and Traceability (4.8), Inspection and Testing (4.10), Servicing (4.19), and Statistical Techniques (4.20). (See Table 9-1.)

The life cycle for development of a software-based product differs markedly from that of more production-oriented items, which seem to be the primary focus of ISO 9001. Software methodologies are based on a phased (often repetitious) progression through development. Design—not production—is the challenge.

Mapping 9001 to 9000-3

ISO 9000-3 provides guidance for the application of ISO 9001 to software development. Strictly speaking, the 9000-3 guidelines do not establish a so-called sector scheme, not in the sense that there are specific sectors such as the automotive, aviation, banking, or health care industries. The guidelines exist to bridge the gap between the high level requirements of ISO 9001, which describe the obligations of all quality management systems, and the specifics of applying those principles to software development and use.

Table 9-1:
ISO 9001 Clauses That Are Applicable to Software

Aspect	Approach/Response	ISO 9001 Reference
Customized	Customer Requirements	Contract Review (4.3)
Design-Intensive	Phased Development	Design Control (4.4)
Evolutionary	Sustaining Engineering	Servicing (4.19)
Difficulty of Evluation	Inspections, Reviews	Inspection & Testing (4.10)
Plastic	Configuration Management	Identification, Traceability (4.8)
Intangible	Visibility Through Metrics	Statistical Techniques (4.20)

ISO 9000-3 essentially expands the design stage of the generic ISO 9001 life cycle into a multi-phase software development process, sequenced as follows:

- Contract review
- Purchaser's requirements specification
- [Project-specific] development planning
- [Project-specific] quality planning
- Design and implementation
- Testing and validation
- Acceptance
- Replication, delivery, and installation
- Maintenance.

It also recognizes other software activities (quality systems elements) that are not dependent on any particular development phase:

- Configuration management
- Document control
- Quality records
- Measurement
- Rules, practices, and conventions
- Tools and techniques
- Purchasing

- Included software product
- Training.

Many paragraphs of the 1987 version of ISO 9001 are simply reprinted within 9000-3, presumably to make the guidelines readable as a stand-alone document. Material copied verbatim is printed in italics, with the citation to 9001 placed directly at the end of each block of text.

These transcribed sections represent areas for which the authors had no software-specific guidance to provide. There is, for instance, no guidance in the clauses addressing "Internal Quality System Audits," "Corrective Action," and "Quality Records." There also is little that is software-specific in the clauses for "Document Control" and "Training." The guidelines do add clauses on Purchaser's Management Responsibility and Joint [supplier-purchaser] Reviews under "Management Responsibility." Clearly, these clauses could not have been added to a requirements standard, since the supplier has no means of enforcing purchaser behavior.

The following clauses of 9001 correspond more-or-less directly to one or more clauses of 9000-3. For example, "Design Control" (4.4) expands in the guidelines to the clauses in the heart of its design life cycle: "Purchaser's Requirements Specification" (5.3) through "Testing and Validation" (5.7). "Inspection and Testing" (4.10) overlaps somewhat by corresponding to the back end of the cycle: "Testing and Validation" (5.7) through "Replication, Delivery, and Installation" (5.9). The last life cycle phase, "Maintenance" (5.10), corresponds to "Servicing" (4.19). Two key phase-independent activities, "Configuration Management" (6.1) and "Measurement" (6.4), contain software-specific guidance on "Product Identification and Traceability" (4.8) and "Statistical Techniques" (4.20), respectively. (Table 9-2 maps all the ISO 9001 clauses to those in 9000-3.)

The author is suitably cautious in introducing life-cycle-based activities (5.1), where the claim is made that what follows can be applied regardless of the particular life cycle model in use by the developers. "Should any description, guidance, requirement or structure be read differently [they add], this is unintended and should not be read as indicating that the requirements or guidance is restricted to a specific life-cycle model only." Under the heading of Product Measurement (6.4.1), they are similarly restrained in stating, "there are currently no universally accepted measures of software quality."

The ISO 9000-3 document concludes with two cross-reference mappings: Annex A maps the clauses of 9000-3 one by one onto corresponding clauses of 9001, and Annex B does the same from 9001 onto 9000-3. In most cases the mappings are sensible and useful, but some are dubious. For example, the cross-references do not properly restrict "Process Control" to the straightforward replication of software; it is "Design Control" that should be applied to the software development process itself. Another confusion is failing to recognize that "Document Control" (4.5) applies to requirements of the standard necessary for the effective functioning of the quality management system (quality manual, procedures, work instructions, quality plans, external requirements), in contrast to "Design Control" for the intermediate products of software development/design. An updated mapping of the 1994 version of ISO 9001 to 9000-3 is shown in Table 9-2.

Table 9-2: ISO 9001 and ISO 9000-3 Cross Reference		
ISO 9001 Clause	Quality System Elements	ISO 9000-3 Clause
4	Quality System Requirements	4, 5, 6
4.1	Management Responsibility	4.1
4.2	Quality System	4.2, 5.5
4.3	Contract Review	5.2, 5.3
4.4	Design Control	5.3, 5.4, 5.5, 5.6, 5.7, 5.10, 6-5
4.5	Document and Data Control	6.2
4.6	Purchasing	6.7
4.7	Control of Customer-Supplied Product	6.8
4.8	Product Identification and Traceability	6.1
4.9	Process Control	5.9
4.10	Inspection and Testing	5.7, 5.8, 5.9
4.11	Control of Inspection, Measuring and Test Equipment	5.7, 6.6
4.12	Inspection and Test Status	6.1
4.13	Control of Nonconforming Product	5.7, 5.9, 5.10, 6.1
4.14	Corrective and Preventive Action	4.4
4.15	Handling, Storage, Packaging, Preservation and Delivery	5.8. 5.9
4.16	Control of Quality Records	6.3
4.17	Internal Quality Audits	4.3
4.18	Training	6.9
4.19	Servicing	5.10
4.20	Statistical Techniques	6.4

The TickIT Scheme

In the late 1980s, the United Kingdom's Department of Trade and Industry (DTI) commissioned studies that highlighted both the crucial role of information technology (IT) and the need to address quality problems within IT. Out of these efforts came a project to apply ISO 9000-based assessment and registration to the particular nature of IT. The project was dubbed

TickIT, a visual/verbal play on the "tick" (check mark) for IT being an admission *ticket* to higher quality. TickIT is fully explained in the *Guide to Software Quality Management System Construction and Certification Using EN 29001.*[1]

TickIT is mainly a certification scheme, but this is not its primary purpose. TickIT seeks to harmonize the way registrars and their auditors approach the assessment of quality management systems in an IT setting. It also aims at achieving true "value added" in the audit process, something that seemed problematical if auditors were not suitably knowledgeable through experience and training. TickIT designates 9000-3 as the "definitive interpretation" of 9001, and obliges registrars to use TickIT-certified auditors when addressing the software elements of their assessments.

The TickIT effort was sponsored by DTI with close cooperation from the British Computer Society. It established specific experience and training requirements for quality management system auditors to provide more software-knowledgeable individuals. If a registrar wants to include IT within its scope, it has to use only auditors qualified specifically within the TickIT scheme. Similarly, so-called TickIT training courses—which are Lead Auditor classes with software case studies—can be offered only by approved course providers.

OTHER SOFTWARE ARRANGEMENTS

In addition to the software arrangements discussed in this chapter, others do exist. The Institute of Certification of Information Technology (ICIT) is one such example.[2] ICIT has been operating as the RvC's coordinating committee since 1989. Six of the 32 registrars accredited by the RvC have IT scope.

In addition, other European arrangements exist such as those used by registrars in the Information Technology Sector (ITQS). The following registrars participate in ITQS and can be contacted for further information:

AFAQ	Paris, France
AIB-Vincotte	Brussels, Belgium
BSI QA	Milton Keynes, England
ElektronikCentralen	Horsholm, Denmark
IMQ	Milan, Italy
KEMA N.V.	Arnhem, the Netherlands
RW-TUV	Essen, Germany
TUV-Bayern	Munich, Germany
TUV-Rheinland	Cologne, Germany

An American Software-Specific Arrangement

The Registrar Accreditation Board has recognized the need for software-specific assurances throughout the assessment and registration process. RAB-accredited registrars are now seeking to extend their scope to include software. New training courses are being offered and presented to the RAB for evaluation and approval. Auditors are preparing to obtain a specific endorsement in software for their credentials.

The RAB chartered and then later received the recommendations of the Software Quality Systems Registration (SQSR) committee. The committee has been at work since October 1992 to establish minimum requirements for the management of quality in the development and use of software.

Committee members include software purchaser representatives, developers, suppliers, quality assurance managers, registrars and consulting/training organizations. The SQSR committee is chaired by Jim Roberts of Bell Communications Research. Meetings of the full committee have been held at three-month intervals, with much work done in the interim by several working groups.

A strong consensus emerged early that registrars not exclude software from the scope of any assessment they are asked to undertake. Some organizations have been asking for hardware-only registrations because there were no definitive interpretations of the ISO 9000 standards (which are manufacturing-oriented) when applied to software.

The committee undertook to remedy this situation by providing the RAB with a complete software-specific arrangement. This committee approved the final draft of a guide book in April 1994. The document, called *A Guide to Software Quality System Registration Under ISO 9001*, is primarily advisory in nature. It does not impose additional requirements beyond ISO 9001, but it helps clarify implementation issues for companies where software is a crucial part of their end products or services.

The TickIT scheme from the United Kingdom was chosen as the baseline for SQSR efforts because it has a good track record and is being adopted/adapted by several countries. Working groups organized to study TickIT material on customers, suppliers and auditors, and spent time making the TickIT materials applicable in the United States.

The Software Division of the American Society for Quality Control (ASQC) has also played a significant role, especially in the effort to establish auditor qualifications. They have recruited panels of experts who can evaluate proposed course offerings as well as scrutinize individuals who present themselves as candidates for certified auditor. The goal has been to have the arrangements fully implemented during 1994.

Staffing Up with Software Auditors

The SQSR committee developed a short-term strategy to bootstrap the program and to establish mutual recognition with the TickIT scheme and other nations' software registration programs. Once established, the arrangement could develop into a more comprehensive system, which can include additional elements such as the Software Engineering Institute's capability assessment methodology. (See below.)

There is likely to be a large demand for software-certified auditors as soon as any arrangement is established. From the beginning, individuals applying for certification as software quality system auditors will be required to possess qualifications such as the following:

- Academic degree or additional supplementary workplace experience if less than bachelor's (Two more years for associate degree or five more years for secondary diploma)
- At least five years of relevant software workplace experience, with at least two of the past four years in quality activities ("relevant" means addressing full software life cycle, software quality management systems, software auditing or detailed knowledge of one area of software expertise)
- Experience in quality system audits against ISO 9001, ISO 9002 or equivalent national, industry or company standards
- Completion of a week-long approved Software Quality System Auditor training course.

Individuals with no quality system audit experience would enter as Provisional Auditors and could advance to the status of Auditor with suitable software audit experience. Similarly, individuals could advance to Lead Auditor with additional software audits and audit leadership experience.

Software Sensitivity

The software quality system registration arrangement is intended for companies that produce software as an end-product and for producers of other products that depend on software for their functionality. The arrangement will require auditors of software developers to hold an endorsement/specialization in software. However, the pervasiveness of software in *all* businesses means that training *all* quality system auditors in aspects of software quality shouldn't be neglected.

There is a need to create awareness and sensitivity to fundamental software concerns among all individuals performing quality system assessments. During the upcoming renewal cycle for auditor training courses, there may be an additional requirement that each course add such material, as specified in the outline below. Existing auditors would then be required to take this training during their recertification cycle.

Software sensitivity issues include the following:

- Impact of software on development and delivery of products or services
- Issues in configuration management, including identification and status accounting, access control, and change control
- A high-level appreciation of the software development life cycle
- How software can assist quality management for any product or service.

Certified auditors who wish to add the software endorsement will already have taken an approved 36-hour auditor training course. They may need to supplement that training with material devoted to software-specific guidelines and practices. Unlike the 16-hour courses currently available to CQAs, there will probably not be approved courses for this information, but the subject matter to be mastered by non-software-knowledgeable auditors is shown as follows:

- The software development process
- Quality standards for software
- *ISO 9000-3, Guidelines for the application of ISO 9001 to the development, supply and maintenance of software*
- Interpreting the *Guidelines*—life-cycle activities
- Interpreting the *Guidelines*—supporting activities
- Using established software tools and techniques
- Addressing emerging computing technologies

A candidate who has not previously trained as an ISO auditor could obtain the software endorsement by taking a full 36-hour auditor training course that covers ISO 9000-3 and suitable software case studies. It would address audit skills, the ISO standards, and all the software specifics outlined above. This course would also satisfy the training requirements for the existing RAB auditor arrangement, so upon completion of all requirements, the auditor would be certified for the corresponding RAB classification *plus* the software specialization.

Several UK-based training firms are preparing Americanized versions of the TickIT training course and have indicated they will submit them for RAB approval. Other trainers are modifying their existing Lead Auditor courses to include software case studies and treatment of 9000-3.

In the future, all auditors may well have fundamental "software sensitivity training" and be able to determine the extent to which additional expertise is required for a given assessment. The software endorsement would be required of auditors who evaluate any quality management system where software is a crucial element. If the scope of the registration is for delivered software, the lead auditor would be expected to have the software endorsement.

Other Software Standards and Models

IEEE SOFTWARE ENGINEERING STANDARDS

For nearly 15 years the Computer Society of the Institute of Electrical and Electronics Engineers (IEEE) has sponsored a growing family of so-called software engineering standards, all under the umbrella of the *IEEE Standard for Software Quality Assurance Plans* (ANSI/IEEE Std 730). This standard requires developing a range of intermediate software products (software requirements specifications, software design descriptions, user manuals, etc.) and plans for various support and evaluation activities (configuration management, verification and validation, testing, etc.) for crucial software applications.

A mapping of both the IEEE Software Quality Assurance standard and its references is shown below. These standards provide a valuable additional level of detail on how one might satisfy the high-level requirements of ISO 9001 within the guidance of 9000-3.

Table 9-3: Mapping the ISO 9000-3 Guidelines Against ANSI/IEEE Standard 730, Software Quality Assurance		
ISO 9000-3 Guidelines: Section 4	**IEEE 730 Section**	**Referenced IEEE Standard(s)**
.1	3.6.2.1, 3.6.2.8	1028 (Reviews & Audits)
2	3.3	1002 (Standards Taxonomy), 1058.1 (Project Management)
3	3.6.2.7	1028
4	3.8	
ISO 9000-3 Guidelines: Section 5	**IEEE 730 Section**	**Referenced IEEE Standard(s)**
.1		
2		
3	3.4.2.1	830 (Requirements Specifications)
4	3.4.3	
5	3.3	1002, 1058.1
6	3.4.2.2	1016 (Design Descriptions)
.7	3.7	829 (Test Documentation), 1008 (Unit Testing)
8		
9		
.10	3.4.3	
ISO 9000-3 Guidelines: Section 6	**IEEE 730 Section**	**Referenced IEEE Standard(s)**
.1	3.4.2.6, 3.10	829, 1042 (Configuration Mgt.)
2	3.13	
3	3.13	
4	3.5	
5	3.5	
6	3.9	
.7	3.12	
8	3.12	
9	3.14	

SEI CAPABILITY MATURITY MODEL

A popular model for process evaluation and improvement is the Capability Maturity Model (CMM) of the Software Engineering Institute (SEI), a Department of Defense-funded organization housed at Carnegie-Mellon University in Pittsburgh.[3] This model consists of five categories into which a software development organization may be placed and through which it can progress. The categories are called levels and are arranged as follows:

Table 9-4: Five Levels of the Capability Maturity Model	
Level 1, Initial	Ad hoc, rather chaotic performance with no consistent ability to meet schedule, budget or quality commitments
Level 2, Repeatable	Able to meet commitments, but dependent on personalities and intuitive approaches
Level 3, Defined	Institutionalized processes, defined in qualitative fashion
Level 4, Managed	Processes are controlled quantitatively
Level 5, Optimizing	Feedback of improvements continually refines processes

Evaluating a software developer's maturity level may be accomplished in one of two modes: as a Software Process Assessment or as a Software Capability Evaluation. A process assessment is typically done as part of an in-house process improvement effort, and may involve use of one of the commercial firms licensed by the SEI to apply the methodology. It looks at a broadly representative set of development projects in different application domains.

In contrast, a capability evaluation is performed by an acquisition agency (usually military) to evaluate risks in awarding a major software-based system development project. It focuses on previous work done with software similar to that of the new project to understand how the organization is likely to perform on that particular job. Different ratings of the same organization might well result from evaluations that were focused on different project needs.

Because there is no direct correlation between the elements of ISO 9001 and the key practices with the CMM, it is not possible to state exactly which level an ISO 9001-compliant software developer would attain. Conversely, it is not certain that an organization rated at any particular level within the CMM would necessarily satisfy ISO 9001 requirements.

AUSTRALIAN STANDARD: SOFTWARE QUALITY MANAGEMENT SYSTEM

Late in 1992, the IEEE Standards Board adopted a document from Standards Australia entitled *Software Quality Management System, Part 1: Requirements*. (A *Part 2: Implementation* is anticipated.)[4] The Australian standard, designated AS 3563.1-1991, represents a revision of AS 3563-1988, the original Australian document applying ISO 9001 to the software development arena. This 1991 revision restructured the document to map directly to Clauses 4.1 through 4.20 in ISO 9001. There is also a twenty-first clause, "Control of Development Environment," which addresses software-unique concerns not readily mapped to any of the 20 clauses of 9001.

This document is a strange hybrid that mixes requirements paragraphs ("The developer shall ....") with guidance material ("Developers should choose ...." or "The effect of such changes can be ....") under most of its 21 clauses. Several clauses (such as Process Control , Inspection and Test Status, and Control of Nonconforming Product) impose no requirements, claiming "This quality system element has no direct equivalent in a software development quality management system." Clearly, this model is restricted to the very narrow case of stand-alone software products without any larger system considerations.

The IEEE balloting group was not exclusively American, and a number of both US and overseas voters raised objections to diverging from the separately established ISO requirements and guidelines documents already available. In fact, national standards bodies are adopting not only 9001 but also 9000-3; in the United States, 9000-3 is undergoing a final review process before being formally proposed for ASQC approval and ultimate ANSI designation. In October 1993, the American National Standards Institute (ANSI) Board of Standards Review disapproved the submission of this document to become an American national standard. They ruled that the IEEE had not respected the due process rights of those who objected to the document's technical content. The document now bears the designation IEEE Std 1298-1992. It is far from clear what role it will play in subsequent efforts to evaluate and improve software quality management systems.

Emerging Trends

The quality of software is increasingly affecting the quality of everyday life, and there is a pressing need to ensure that software is sufficiently fit for use. The inherent complexity of such applications, however, means there is great uncertainty that a given software product will satisfy its requirements while not introducing significant new failure modes. Decreasing that uncertainty to an acceptable level is the task of quality management.

Well-designed and well-conducted quality evaluations can establish an adequate level of confidence in the fitness of the software for its intended use. Such *a priori* assurance needs to be certified to public bodies before software can be given control of key, potentially life-threatening processes. Market forces cannot always be relied upon to efficiently or expeditiously isolate items of poor quality, particularly if the problems reside in software.

So-called regulated industries—electric utilities, medical-device manufacturers, commercial aviation, and so on—offer products and services sufficiently widespread and visible that the "public good" is seen to be impacted by poor quality. It is accepted public policy that quality in such industries be evaluated and documented before granting them approval to offer their goods and services. Even customers of the more market-driven industries may demand advance notification of the quality they expect to receive.

If regulatory agencies and, ultimately, the public are to be confident that software technology has been appropriately and safely applied to critical processes, comprehensive quality assessment must be planned, implemented and documented. The ISO 9000 standards provide a firm foundation for designing and performing such assessments.

At the end of the day, the question remains: How are we improving the quality of software through all these efforts? The better developers and users may indeed not go much beyond their previous good practices. But everyone should benefit from a better-disciplined, better-documented software development effort. Sponsors, regulators, end users should all become more confident in the claims made for software quality.

It is becoming increasingly clear that many people no longer tolerate a hands-off attitude toward the quality of software. Existing and emerging efforts to qualify software will depend, at least in part, on quality management system assessment and registration. Quality professionals now have the opportunity to establish certification standards that will enhance confidence in software applications. Use of the ISO 9000 standards, so well received in other industries and applications, should be expected to grow within the software arena as well.

ENDNOTES

[1] To obtain more information about this guide, call or write to the following: DISC TickIT Office/2 Park Street/London W1A 2BS/England. Tel. 44-71-602-8536, Fax 44-71-602-8912.

[2] More information on ICIT is available through Mr. Jan Sauer/Ryvoortshoef 110/NL-4941VD Raamsdonksveer/The Netherlands.

[3] Version 1.1 of the Capability Maturity Model for software is available through Research Access Incorporated/3400 Forbes Avenue/Suite 302/Pittsburgh, PA 15213. Tel. 800-685-6510, Fax 412-682-6530.

[4] The IEEE Standard Software Quality Management System and related information are available through IEEE Customer Service/445 Hoes Lane/PO Box 1331/Piscataway, NJ 08855-1331. Tel. 800-678-IEEE, Fax 908-981-9667.

ANNEX 1

TickIT Case Study: Terminal Data Corporation

Moorpark, CA—Jeffrey A. Wilson, President and CEO of Terminal Data Corporation (TDC), considered himself an advocate of the quality movement, but when a major European client first asked him about ISO 9000, Wilson didn't know how to respond. In fact, recalled Rebecca J. Crites, the Moorpark, California firm's director of quality assurance: "He wasn't sure what they were talking about."

That was in July 1991. Over the next six months—as other customers and potential customers also began inquiring about ISO 9000—Wilson started mapping out plans for TDC's registration to the ISO 9001 external quality assurance standard.

The Decision to Go With TickIT

There was just one hitch. The more Wilson learned about the ISO 9000 series, the more he realized that TDC, which designs and manufactures high-tech computer imaging equipment and related software, would probably do well to seek registration through the UK's TickIT program.

Terminal Data Corporation

Employees: 180

Date of Registration: August 23, 1993

Registrar: Lloyd's Register Quality Assurance Ltd.

Registrar Site Visit: August 11-12, 1993

Scope: Design and manufacture of electronic imaging and micrographics equipment and associated software designed and developed in accordance with TickIT.

Target Market: Original equipment manufacturers, resellers, system integrators, large corporate users of computer imaging equipment.

In TDC's case, TickIT was neither an explicit nor an implicit customer requirement, but company executives felt it would provide some needed structure to TDC's software design element.

At first glance, Crites said, the nearly 200-page TickIT document looked imposing by comparison to the succinctly written ISO 9000 series. "The ISO 9001 standard is about a seven-page standard and the TickIT standard that complements ISO is a lot more detailed," explained Crites.

Getting Started

The initial thrust of the registration effort revolved around training. All company employees would undergo general training on ISO 9000, and each department was to be given specialized training.

The overall registration effort was coordinated by a five-person implementation team lead by Crites. By January 1992, the team had finished reviewing all key areas of the company for compliance and concluded that employees had become quite knowledgeable about ISO 9000 requirements.

That was the good news. "The bad news was that TDC was not nearly as compliant as its management

(continued on next page)

TickIT Case Study

(continued from previous page)

had initially imagined it to be," Crites said. "Everybody dug in a bit harder. Every process and associated page of documentation was being reviewed."

Knowing that most registrars were booked months in advance, the implementation team turned its attention to selecting a registration body in March 1992. After soliciting bids from five firms, Lloyd's Register Quality Assurance Ltd. got the nod on the recommendation of Siemens' executives.

That's the TickIT

The actual TickIT requirements arrived in June 1992 and were thought to hold promise for improving the company's software design process.

According to Valerie Coffman, a senior program manager, "Complying to ISO 9001 without TickIT would have required less effort on our part, but based on the market's increasing demands for better software products and our internal requirements for a more structured software development model, TickIT seemed to be the means to that end."

Coffman, also a software engineer, said that TickIT provided the fundamentals for developing a basic product life cycle model. "Initially, many of the engineers balked at the emphasis on more frequent design reviews and the associated documentation. However, when all was said and done, I think everybody felt that it was an excellent guideline for our software development efforts."

Final Audit

The registration audit was scheduled for February 1992. The internal audits had shown some weaknesses in the system, but executives were hopeful that the deficiencies would not prohibit the company from attaining registration.

The audit was conducted by a team of three auditors over a three-day period. The first day went smoothly with the auditors turning up no nonconformances.

That all changed on the second day, however, as the auditors turned up several areas that would prevent the company from becoming registered. Day three of the audit brought more disappointment with the auditors turning up additional findings. In all, the auditors noted seven serious issues standing in the way of registration, and 11 minor ones.

Crites said the results were not completely unexpected. "We knew that we were not fully prepared within the area of software based on our internal audits," Crites explained. "We thought it would just be healthy for us to proceed with the third-party audit at that point."

Most of the nonconformances dealt with the software area, Crites said. "Our software configuration system was in place but not well documented," she said. "Our functional specifications were being used but not all of them were in the same format with the same information."

For example, she said, the company had drafted specific requirements for releasing new software, but they were not being followed in every case. "We still had people who felt the release notes' contents should be unique to their projects."

(continued on next page)

TickIT Case Study

(continued from previous page)

The engineering department was required to do much more planning and design work prior to writing software rather than focusing on correcting problems after the fact. Engineering was also required to keep daily log books, documenting all product development activity, whereas in the past they often passed such information along verbally.

Second Try

With its work clearly cut out for it, the implementation team pushed hard to correct the nonconformances. A member of the team was detailed to work full time with the software group.

By the time Lloyd's returned for another round of audits in August 1993, executives felt they had addressed all the outstanding issues.

Even though the follow-up audit was primarily to reassess the nonconformances, it was clear that the entire operation would once again be fair game. "Everybody was prepared to represent the entire facility," Crites said.

This time the auditors did not find a single nonconformance, and TDC executives were stunned by the good news. "People couldn't believe that we came through without even a scratch," Crites explained. "Practically everybody wanted to celebrate this great accomplishment."

Benefits

Company president and CEO Wilson said that the registration should strengthen TDC's position in the marketplace for sophisticated document capture systems. "We firmly believe we have the system in place to produce the highest quality, best built imaging products on the market," he said.

The implementation effort has resulted in a number of tangible benefits for the company, according to Crites. The company is now much more focused on customer requirements and makes fewer mistakes, she said. Since 1991, the price of nonconformance, which is calculated by a number of key quality indicators, has dropped significantly.

In 1991, for example, the price of nonconformance totaled 13.9 percent of total sales dollars. The following year the number dropped to 10.7 percent and in 1993 it fell to 8.5 percent.

"This is the type of payback that a good, sound quality system yields," she said. "Much of the reduction can be tracked to a product being designed correctly in the first place. We are able to catch mistakes or problems a lot earlier in the process. We do a lot more testing on the front end than we used to."

USING ISO 9000 IN
SERVICE ORGANIZATIONS

This chapter examines the use of ISO 9000 by service organizations. It highlights
factors affecting ISO 9000's popularity and some special characteristics of
service organizations. It also discusses the use of process control and guidance
from ISO 9004-2 for managing service quality. Lastly, it describes, clause-by-
clause, how to apply ISO 9001 or ISO 9002 to service organizations.

INTRODUCTION

The concepts and principles in ISO 9001 and ISO 9002 are as applicable to service organizations as they are to the physical production aspects of hardware manufacturers. However, the standards do not yet enjoy the same widespread acceptance in service organizations as they do in industrial sectors.

One exception is in the United Kingdom, where service organizations represent the fastest growing segment of registrations. The UK experience demonstrates that application of the ISO 9000 standards to service organizations is practical, and it suggests that the present level of use is more a reflection of motivation than lack of compatibility with service organization needs.

FACTORS AFFECTING USE OF THE ISO 9000 STANDARDS

The relatively low application of the standards by services appears to have three causes:

- Until recently, many service organizations—even service departments in manufacturing companies with a quality strategy—have not been pushed to implement systematic, disciplined approaches to quality management. This is changing. Interest by service organizations in quality management has been spurred by the transition to a service economy in the United States and other developed countries.

  Increasing competition at the local regional, national and international levels is fostering management interest in customer satisfaction and lower costs, coupled with faster response times. Even companies that have traditionally focused on the technical quality of their hardware, software or processed materials are now beginning to improve the service component of their "product" to differentiate themselves from competitors. They recognize that service quality is critical to customer satisfaction.

- Most managers in service organizations are not familiar with quality management principles and quality system concepts. This is particularly true in small and medium-sized service organizations. This unfamiliarity makes it difficult for such companies to understand the value of the standards and the benefits that could accrue. Recently, however, leading companies in the commercial and industrial sectors are focusing explicitly on service quality. This strategic focus will likely encourage more managers to become educated about quality system concepts.

- The original versions of the core standards in the ISO 9000 family, published in 1987, use a language and structure drawn from manufacturing, particularly hardware manufacturing. ISO Technical Committee 176 identified the language and structure of the standards as an area for improvement in 1985. *ISO 9004-2, Guidelines for services*, a supplement to the 1987 issue of ISO 9004, was published in September 1991. It provides guidance on quality management and quality system elements for service organizations.

The 1994 version of the core standards explicitly notes the relevance and applicability of the standards to combinations of four generic product categories: hardware, processed material, software and services. While the basic structure and content remains the same, language in the revised standards has been modified to make the relevance to all four product categories more obvious. For example, hardware-oriented terms such as parts, material, batches and lots has been changed to a more generic word such as product. A key objective of future revisions is to make the standards user-friendly for producers of all four generic product categories.

Nonetheless, the growing use of the standards by service organizations indicates that companies need not wait for these revisions to apply the ISO 9000 standards to services, service delivery processes, and service organizations.

ISO DEFINITIONS

Service .... The results generated by activities at the interface between the supplier and the customer and by supplier internal activities, to meet customer needs.

> *Notes:* 1. *The supplier or the customer may be represented at the interface by personnel or equipment.*
>
> 2. *Customer activities at the interface with the supplier may be essential to the service delivery.*
>
> 3. *Delivery or use of tangible product may form part of the service delivery.*
>
> 4. *A service may be linked with the manufacture and supply of tangible product.*

Service Delivery .... Those supplier activities necessary to provide the service.

Supplier .... The organization that provides a product to the customer.

> *Notes:* 1. *In a contractual situation, the "supplier" may be called the "contractor."*
>
> 2. *The "supplier" may be for example the producer, distributor, importer, assembler, or service organization.*
>
> 3. *The "supplier" can be either external or internal.*

Customer .... The recipient of a product provided by the supplier.

> *Notes:* 1. *In a contractual situation, the "customer" may be called the "purchaser."*
>
> 2. *The "customer" may be for example the ultimate consumer, user, beneficiary or purchaser.*
>
> 3. *The "customer" can be either external or internal.*

From ISO 8402, Quality management and quality assessment—Vocabulary.

SPECIAL CHARACTERISTICS OF SERVICES

The ISO 9000 standards differentiate service from servicing.

- *Service* covers non-tangible aspects of the market offering and contact with customers, including responding to initial inquiries, delivering the "product," billing and invoicing, and conducting after-sales follow-up.
- *Servicing* is a particular type of service that focuses primarily on after-sales maintenance and support.

Hardware, processed material and software components may be involved in a service to varying degrees. These components may be part of the transaction, such as automotive repair, or in support of the service, such as computer system support for catalog sales.

Table 10-1: Examples of Services	
Administration Personnel, computing, office services.	**Professional** Building design (architects), surveying, legal, law enforcement, security, engineering, project management, quality management, consultancy, training and education.
Communications Airports and airlines, road, rail and sea transport, telecommunications, postal, data.	**Purchasing** Contracting, inventory management and distribution.
Financial Banking, insurance, pensions, property services, accounting.	**Scientific** Research, development, studies, decision aids.
Health Services Medical staff/doctors, hospitals, ambulances, medical laboratories, dentists, opticians.	**Technical** Consultancy, photography, test laboratories
Hospitality Services Catering, hotels, tourism, entertainment, radio, television, leisure.	**Trading** Wholesale, retail, stockist, distributor, marketing, packaging.
Maintenance Electrical, mechanical, vehicles, heating systems, air conditioning, buildings, computers	**Utilities** Cleansing, waste management, water supply, grounds maintenance, electricity, gas and energy supply, fire, police, public services.
NOTE: Manufacturing companies also provide internal services in their marketing, delivery systems, and after-sales activities.	*Table 10-1 based on Annex A from ISO 9004-2*

Service delivery processes range from the highly automated, such as automatic teller machines (ATM), to the highly personalized, as with some branches of medicine. In a few cases, service may be the only component of the product. The ISO 9004-2 definition of service clearly indicates the broad coverage of this component of the total product. Examples of service organizations are shown in Table 10-1.

One difference between services and other types of products is the relative importance of qualitative or subjective quality characteristics versus more quantitative characteristics. For example, directly measurable physical characteristics for hardware often take precedent over more aesthetic requirements. The opposite may be true for services. This tends to make the requirements for services harder to define. This more qualitative nature, coupled with the involvement of customers in the service delivery, usually dictates that customers will also be involved in subjectively evaluating the quality of service they receive.

MANAGING SERVICE QUALITY THROUGH PROCESS CONTROL

The inherent nature of the service determines the appropriate approaches to managing service quality. To the extent that the service is generated by activities at the interface between the customer and supplier, (in health services, for example) traditional "produce, inspect, sort and fix" approaches to quality control are not usable. In these cases, controlling service and service delivery characteristics can only be achieved by controlling the process(es) that deliver(s) the service. In the language of ISO 9001, these would be "special processes."

In addition, internal activities within the supplier organization usually involve real-time creation of internal products for internal customers. For example, chefs produce meals for serving people to deliver to restaurant patrons. These internal products may be essential to providing high quality service to external customers, and their processes require control.

This means that control of service delivery processes must be the primary basis of quality systems for services. Process control requires knowledge and stability of the delivery processes. Consequently, the actual operation of all processes must be formally documented and not modified without appropriate approval. Unfortunately, many managers in service organizations are not familiar or comfortable with process control and process management techniques.

A useful discussion of the importance of process is in ISO 9000-1, the revised version of ISO 9000. The basic premise is that all work is accomplished through processes. This premise is illustrated in Figure 10-1. Every "product," whether intermediate or delivered to an external customer, is the output of a process. A process is a set of interrelated resources and activities that add value by transforming or changing specific product-related inputs into specific outputs. This transformation usually requires information-related inputs as well, e.g., product requirements, feedback on product performance and measurements of process and product characteristics.

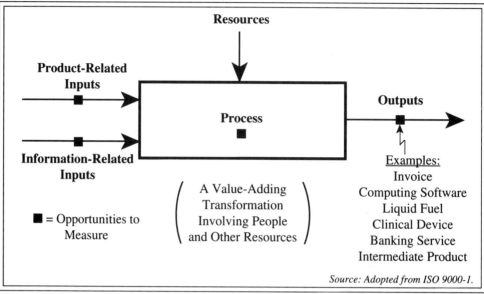

Figure 10-1: All Work Is Accomplished by a Process.

In practice, most organizations have evolved a complex network of processes that cut across functional departments to create and deliver their marketable products to customers. Effective management of product quality and customer satisfaction requires that this network of processes be defined, organized, measured and controlled. This would include defining customer-supplier relationships at internal interfaces as well as controlling local processes that are within the purview of a single department. Managing the processes in an organization is critical to the success of service organizations.

ISO 9004-2, GUIDELINES FOR SERVICES

ISO 9004-2 builds on the quality management principles of ISO 9000-1, ISO 9001 and ISO 9004-1 and provides guidance on establishing and implementing a quality system for services. It uses language and concepts that are familiar to service organizations. Managers in service organizations should consult this standard—whether they are developing a new quality system or refining an existing one—for the advice is useful both for newly offered services and those already in the market. ISO 9004-2, however, cannot be used for registration.

Topics covered in ISO 9004-2 include:

● Management of customer relations

● Measurement of customer satisfaction

● Emphasis on the critical need for process management, especially across departments

- Dependence of service quality on employee knowledge, skills and motivation, in addition to the formal quality system
- Employee involvement and teamwork
- Quality planning and life-cycle management of services
- Prevention-oriented systems (versus find-and-fix approaches)
- Importance of continuous improvement based on quantitative measurements.

The concept of managing the network of processes in service organizations is illustrated by Figure 10-2, taken from ISO 9004-2. Three functional processes are shown:

- The marketing process
- The design process
- The service delivery process.

Measurements of service quality by the customers and the supplier are used both to control the service delivery process and to improve all processes.

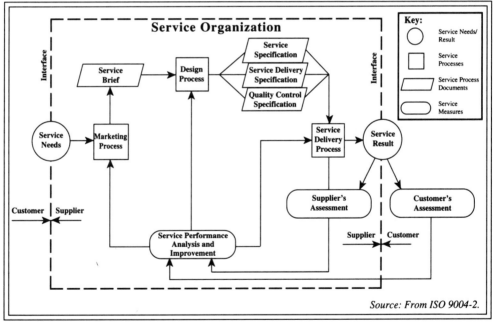

Figure 10-2: Service Quality Loop.

USE OF ISO 9001 OR ISO 9002 BY SERVICE ORGANIZATIONS

The self-discipline that comes from the use of ISO 9001 or ISO 9002 can provide major benefits to service organizations, apart from improved customer satisfaction. Data collected

Table 10-2: ISO 9004-2 and ISO 9004-1—Cross Reference of Quality System Elements and Causes

Clause (or Subclause) in ISO 9004-2: 1991	Title	Corresponding Clause (or Subclause) in ISO 9004-1: 1994
4	Characteristics of service	7.2
4.1	Service and service delivery, characteristics	7.2
4.2	Control of service and service delivery, characteristics	11.4
5	Quality system principles	5
5.1	Key aspects of a quality system	5.1.1
5.2	Management responsibility	4
5.2.2	Quality policy	4.2
5.2.3	Quality objectives	4.2
5.2.4	Quality responsibility and authority	5.2.2
5.2.5	Management review	5.5
5.3	Personnel and material resources	5.2.4
5.3.2	Personnel	18
5.3.2.1	Motivation	18.3
5.3.2.2	Training and development	18.1, 18.2
5.3.2.3	Communications	7.3
5.3.3	Material resources	5.2.4
5.4	Quality system structure	4.4, 5.2.1
5.4.2	Service quality loop	5.1
5.4.3	Quality documentation and records	5.2.5, 5.3, 17
5.4.3.1	Documentation system	5.3.2
5.4.3.2	Documentation control	17.2
5.4.4	Internal quality audits	5.4
5.5	Interface with customers	7.3
5.5.2	Communication with customers	7.3
6	Quality system operational elements	5
6.1	Marketing process	7
6.1.1	Quality in market research and analysis	7.1, 19
6.1.2	Supplier obligations	8.2.4
6.1.3	Service brief	7.2
6.1.4	Service management	8.7
6.1.5	Quality in advertising	7
6.2	Design process	8
6.2.2	Design responsibilities	8.2
6.2.3	Service specification	16.4

(continued on next page)

(continued from previous page)

Table 10-2: ISO 9004-2 and ISO 9004-1—Cross Reference of Quality System Elements and Causes

Clause (or Subclause) in ISO 9004-2: 1991	Title	Corresponding Clause (or Subclause) in ISO 9004-1: 1994
6.2.4	Service delivery specification	16.2
6.2.4.2	Service delivery procedures	16.2
6.2.4.3	Quality in procurement	9, 12.1
6.2.4.4	Supplier-provided equipment to customers for service and service delivery	13.3
6.2.4.5	Service identification and traceability	11.2, 19
6.2.4.6	Handling, storage, packaging, delivery and protection of customers' possessions	16
6.2.5	Quality control specification	12.2
6.2.6	Design review	8.5, 8.5.2
6.2.7	Validation of the service, service delivery and quality control specification	8.4, 8.5.3, 8.7, 8.9
6.2.8	Design change control	8.8
6.3	Service delivery process	12.3, 16.2
6.3.2	Supplier's assessment of service quality	12
6.3.3	Customer's assessment of service quality	7.3
6.3.4	Service status	11.7
6.3.5	Corrective action for nonconforming services	11.8, 14, 15
6.3.5.1	Responsibilities	15.2
6.3.5.2	Identification of nonconformity and corrective action	14, 15
6.3.6	Measurement system control	11.3, 13
6.4	Service performance analysis and improvement	16.3
6.4.2	Data collection and analysis	15.5
6.4.3	Statistical methods	20
6.4.4	Service quality improvement	

during registrations by British Standards Institution Quality Assurance (BSI QA) indicate that sampled service organizations saw reductions in costs ranging from 15 percent to 60 percent. This is consistent with other studies on the cost of rework, expediting, and other non-value adding activities in service organizations.

These studies indicate that frequently one-half to two-thirds of the work in service-type organizations is devoted to fixing or responding to problems caused within the organization itself, often by poorly functioning processes and systems. An ISO 9001 or ISO 9002-based quality system helps improve efficiency by reducing problems and increasing customer satisfaction.

Understanding the relevance of ISO 9001 (or ISO 9002) to service organizations can be facilitated by grouping the 20 clauses into three categories:

- Leadership and Improvement
- Quality in Line Organizations
- Quality System Infrastructure.

The elements in these categories, and their relation to different phases of the product realization cycle is shown in Table 10-3. (Line organizations are directly involved in creating products for external customers. Support organizations support the line organizations.)

Editor's Note: *Given the harmonization of clause numbers among ISO 9001, ISO 9002 and ISO 9003 in the revised 1994 versions, only ISO 9001 clause numbers are referenced.*

This depiction of the relationship of the elements is useful for all organizations. It is especially helpful to managers in service organizations, for it allows them to pay special attention to elements that apply to their operation rather than be distracted by quality system elements that may not be relevant.

The need for process management and control means that ISO 9003, with its emphasis on final inspection and testing, is not appropriate for service organizations.

Leadership and Improvement

The seven elements of ISO 9001 covered under this category are equally applicable in all organizations, regardless of their size or primary product offerings.

(4.1)   Few quarrel about the need for a clear quality policy and objectives that are understood throughout the organization, or about the importance of regular management reviews of quality system performance and areas for improvement.

(4.17)   Objective, internal audits of quality system adequacy, compliance and effectiveness are essential for these management reviews. Clause 4.17 intends that quality systems audits be conducted on behalf of senior management.

(4.14)   For the services industry, sustained reduction in quality problems requires a systematic analysis based on quantitative information. A structured approach should do the following:
- Identify and prioritize problems
- Analyze root causes
- Postulate remedial action
- Evaluate possible solutions
- Monitor the effectiveness of actions taken.

(4.2)   A formalized approach to managing quality, including documented descriptions of policies, responsibilities and procedures, is necessary to move beyond traditional levels of quality and productivity. Even very small, single-location companies find that clarity and improved communications result from documenting how they want to function.

Table 10-3: Phases of the Product Realization Cycle	
Leadership and Improvement	Management Responsibility (4.1)
	Internal Quality Audits (4.17)
	Corrective and Preventive Action (4.14)
	Quality System (4.2)
	Control of Quality Records (4.16)
	Statistical Techniques (4.20)
	Document and Data Control (4.5)
Quality in Line Organizations	Contract Review (4.3)
	Purchasing (4.6)
	Design Control (4.4)
	Process Control (4.9)
	Inspection and Testing (4.10)
	Handling, Storage, Packaging, Preservation, and Delivery (4.15)
	Servicing (4.19)
Quality System Infrastructure	Product Identification and Traceability (4.8)
	Inspection and Test Status (4.12)
	Control of Nonconforming Product (4.13)
	Control of Customer-Supplied Product (4.7)
	Control of Inspection, Measuring and Test Equipment (4.11)
	Training (4.18)
	Source: Copyright 1993, Service Process Consulting.

(4.16) Process measurements are essential to process control, which is critical to managing service quality. Records provide internal evidence that requirements are being satisfied and procedures followed. More important, they provide the key to understanding when something goes wrong.

(4.20) Most raw records are of limited value, however. Analysis is needed to turn these data into useful information, including comparison with past performances and related parameters.

(4.5)   Any dependence on a documented system requires that everyone have access to appropriate, up-to-date documents and confidence that the documents are correct.

Quality in Line Organizations

Contract Review, Purchasing, and Process Control elements have obvious application in service organizations. Design control can apply to both the service product itself and to the service delivery processes. These elements must form the heart of an effective quality system for service organizations.

(The other three elements under "Quality in Line Organizations" (4.10, 4.15, and 4.19) may not be fully applicable to service organizations.)

(4.3)   A clear understanding of the customer needs and requirements is the *sine qua non* of quality. Given the personalized nature of many services, determining customer needs and satisfying them may require more careful efforts than determining customer requirements for other products.

(4.4)   Design control applies both to the service delivery process(es) as well as the service itself.

(4.6)   To the extent that purchases of goods or services affect the quality of the service offered, the requirements of Clause 4.6 apply.

(4.9)   The importance of process management and control has already been discussed. While process control requires effective internal measurement of the process performance, customer assessment is the ultimate measure to validate the internal measures.

In addition, a quality plan for each service or class of services should be developed. This quality plan can be a critical component of employee training as well as operation of the service delivery process(es).

Quality Systems Infrastructure

With the exception of training, the importance of the clauses that describe the infrastructure elements will depend on the particular service. Please note the following examples:

(4.8)   Product identification and traceability is critical in certain kinds of distribution services. It may not be a factor in utilities.

(4.12) Inspection and test status may be important in medical practices, but not some hospitality services.

(4.13)   Control of nonconforming products will be important for services that have critical hardware, software or processed material components.

(4.7)   Customer-supplied product is critical in the airline industry and overnight delivery services. It may not be important in certain kinds of communication services.

(4.11)   Many service delivery processes do not use inspection, measuring and test equipment that require calibration. Control of these processes may only require simple counts of events of activity rates; time can be measured with everyday clocks or watches. However, medical laboratories may use instruments that require calibration on a daily basis.

(4.18)   The importance of employee knowledge of the service products, the service delivery processes, and the systems that support the processes is amply discussed in ISO 9004-2. Employee interpersonal skills—as well as technical skills—may also be critical to customer satisfaction.

SUMMARY

Carefully reading the Clause elements in ISO 9001—while paying attention to the underlying intent—will reveal how most requirements apply to a particular service organization. At the same time, it may become clear that a few of the elements are not applicable. Understanding the clause's intent is aided by studying ISO 9004-2 and ISO 9000-1.

Experience of service organizations in the United Kingdom and a growing number of US companies with registration to ISO 9001 or ISO 9002 indicates that not only are the ISO standards applicable to service organizations, but that using the standards yields beneficial results both for the customer and the supplier.

REVIEW AND REVISION OF ISO STANDARDS

BY DONALD W. MARQUARDT

ISO directives provide for review and revision of standards approximately every five years. In the case of the ISO 9000 series, the ISO Technical Committee 176 (TC 176) has developed a two-phase strategy for the first two review and revision cycles. The details of the ISO 9000 series first-phase revisions, published in 1994, are described throughout this handbook.

This chapter contains two sections addressing the revision process. The first, entitled *Updating the ISO 9000 Quality Standards: Responding to Marketplace Needs*, provides a comprehensive overview of all major changes and the general strategy behind the phase-one revision. It is a slightly revised and updated version of an article that first appeared in the July 1993 issue of *Quality Progress* magazine. This article is a general summary of the 1994 ISO 9000 series revisions. For more detailed information on changes to specific clauses please refer to Chapter 3.

The second section, entitled *Vision 2000: The Strategy for the ISO 9000 Series Standards in the 90s*, describes the entire two-phase strategy and the concepts upon which it is based. It was first printed in *Quality Progress* magazine's May 1991 issue.

In addition, this chapter contains a section entitled *TC 176 Standards Issued and Being Developed*, which describes the various other standards that TC 176 has published or is preparing.

Updating the ISO 9000 Quality Standards: Responding to Marketplace Needs

by Ian G. Durand, Donald W. Marquardt, Robert W. Peach and James C. Pyle

Directives of the International Organization for Standardization (ISO) require that all standards be reviewed every five years. Based on inputs from member countries, ISO Technical Committee 176 (TC 176) has reviewed and revised the five standards. The revisions have been given overwhelming approval by the member bodies representing the countries participating in this TC 176 work and were published in 1994.

The widespread use of the standards focuses attention on the responsibilities of TC 176 in this effort. To respond fully to marketplace needs, the revisions must simultaneously meet the following objectives:

- Ensure that the standards reflect experience in practical applications and acknowledge best current practices
- Ensure that the series remains stable and consistent to facilitate training and continuity of use
- Facilitate the use of the standards by all companies, regardless of size, industry or product offering.

Standards always lag behind the cutting edge of technology or practice in any field, but periodic review and revision prevent them from lagging so much that they become a nontariff trade barrier.

The 1994 revisions incorporate changes that do not alter the basic approach and structure of the 1987 standards but instead enhance their usability. The changes reflect the progress in the quality field and companies' experience using the 1987 standards.

The revised standards are the result of more than four years of international negotiation, in which all nations participating in TC 176 have had multiple opportunities to propose, comment on, and vote on changes. This consensus-forming approach is a systematic, proven route to developing standards that adequately meet the needs of all parties and satisfy the first two of the three objectives listed above.

The current revisions are an interim step toward achieving the third objective. Improvements in language reduce the strong hardware manufacturing flavor of the 1987 versions.

MODIFICATIONS COMMON TO ALL FIVE STANDARDS

Several modifications are common to the revisions of all five standards in the series. ISO 9000-1 and the three models for quality assurance—ISO 9001, ISO 9002 and ISO 9003—now recognize their important use for third-party registration.

All five standards also explicitly incorporate the concept of generic product categories, which were first described in "Vision 2000: The Strategy for the ISO 9000 Series Standards in the '90s." (See the next article in this chapter.) Combinations of the four generic product categories (hardware, software, processed materials and services) encompass all of the kinds of product offerings supplied by organizations.

The premise is that quality system requirements are essentially the same for all product offerings, although the terminology, management system details and emphasis might vary. In the revised standards only intended products are addressed; the environmental aspects of unintended by-products are not included.

The revised standards also move toward general harmonization of terminology, while maintaining continuity with the 1987 versions. For example, the supply chain terminology is modified, as shown in Table 11-1.

Table 11-1: Relationship of Organizations in the Supply Chain			
	Companies Supplying Products to You	**Your Organization**	**Companies to Whom You Provide Products**
ISO 9000-1	Subsupplier	Supplier or Organization	Customer
ISO 9001	Subcontractor	Supplier	Customer
ISO 9002			
ISO 9003			
ISO 9004-1	Subcontractor	Organization	Customer

(Note in Table 11-1 that the requirements to ISO 9001, 9002 and 9003 are addressed to the supplier, while ISO 9004-1 addresses the organization. The supplier receives goods and services from either subsuppliers or subcontractors and provides products/services to the customer.)

Modifications in ISO 9000-1

ISO 9000-1, Quality management and quality assurance standards—Part 1: Guidelines, helps organizations select and use all standards in the ISO 9000 family—that is, all the international standards produced by TC 176, which include the ISO 9000 series. This road map to the ISO 9000 family has been expanded substantially in the revision. In particular, it includes concepts that are fundamental building blocks for modern quality systems. These concepts place in perspective the traditional quality system elements required in the quality assurance standards.

A critical role of the 1987 version of ISO 9000 was to introduce the new, internationally defined term "quality management" and to emphasize international harmonized definitions for "quality assurance" and "quality policy." In the 1987 version, these terms were included in Clause 3, Definitions; now they are in Annex A at the end of the standard because they are accepted and used worldwide.

New terms important to understanding and applying the ISO 9000 family are now defined in Clause 3. The terms include "industry/economic sector," "stakeholder," "ISO 9000 family," and the four generic product categories.

Clause 4, Principal concepts, is expanded significantly. It now describes:

1. Five key objectives and responsibilities for quality (Clause 4.1).

   A strong emphasis on quality improvements in products and operations, and confidence that quality system requirements are being fulfilled have been added. This builds on the three objectives in the 1987 version that focused on achieving and sustaining the product quality.

2. Four facets that are key contributors to product quality (Clause 4.5).

   Articulation of these facets is new in international standardization:

   - Quality due to definition of needs for the product
   - Quality due to product design
   - Quality due to conformance to product design
   - Quality due to product support throughout its life cycle.

3. Process orientation.

   In contemporary use of quality concepts, emphasis is placed on preventing nonconformance rather than on inspecting and segregating product based on conformance. Operationally, this implies that the processes in an organization must be controlled in the broadest sense of the term.

Clause 4.6 defines "process" and discusses related concepts, such as the following:

- All work is accomplished by a process
- Processes involve people and other resources and apply to products in all generic product categories
- Process inputs and outputs can be products or information.

(See box on Concept of a Process.)

EXAMPLES OF INPUTS AND OUTPUTS OF PROCESSES

Type	Examples
Product-related	• Raw materials
	• Intermediate product
	• Final product
	• Sampled product.
Information-related	• Product requirements
	• Product properties and status data
	• Support function communications
	• Feedback on product performance and needs
	• Measurement data from sampled product.

Clause 4.7 points out that every organization accomplishes its work through a network of processes. This network must be identified, organized, and managed to provide consistent output. Clause 4.8 discusses the quality system in relation to the network of processes.

4. The concept of a supplier's stakeholders. (Clause 4.2)

Stakeholders include customers, employees, owners, subsuppliers, and society. (See box.)

STAKEHOLDERS AND THEIR EXPECTATIONS

Supplier's Stakeholders	Typical Expectations or Needs
Customers	Product Quality
Employees	Career/Work Satisfaction
Owners	Investment Performance
Subsuppliers	Continuing Business Opportunity
Society	Responsible Stewardship

---

5. The distinction between quality system requirements and product technical requirements. (Clause 4.3)

The subject of the ISO 9000 standards is the quality system itself. This crucial distinction was not clear in the 1987 version, which led to many misunderstandings in practical use.

6. Role in evaluating quality systems.

The ISO 9000 series is intended as a means to evaluate the effectiveness of quality systems, but the standards have not previously given a big-picture view of this role. Clause 4.9 presents three areas to be addressed for every process being evaluated: process definition and documentation, process deployment, and process effectiveness. This clause also clarifies the roles of management review and quality system audits in the evaluation.

Clause 5, Roles of documentation, is a new clause that stresses that documentation is a high-value-adding activity. Documentation is objective evidence for quality audits, is the starting point in quality improvement efforts, and provides support for such efforts.

Clause 6, Quality system situations, is an expansion of the information in Clause 5 of the 1987 version, *Characteristics of quality system situations*. Clause 6 identifies and clarifies four situations for which the ISO 9000 series is intended to be used:

- Guidance for quality management
- Contractual agreements between first and second parties
- Second-party approval or registration
- Third-party certification or registration.

This clause also points out that a supplier can choose to use the ISO 9000 standards as a response to internal (management) or external (stakeholder) motivation.

Clause 7, Selection and use of International standards on quality, replaces and expands the information in Clauses 6 and 7 in the 1987 version, which covered types and uses of international standards for quality systems. It is now a definitive source for guidance on selecting appropriate standards from the growing ISO 9000 family. The five revised standards are described along with 11 additional standards that have been published since 1987.

Clause 8, Selection and use of International Standards for external quality assurance, gives explicit attention to quality system situations in which there are contractual agreements or second-party approval or registration. This attention emphasizes that both customers and suppliers must benefit from the standard selected and applied.

With third-party registration, the selection of the quality assurance standard should be agreeable to both the supplier and the registrar, taking into account customer needs and supplier objectives.

Typical means of demonstrating conformance to requirements and explicit additional considerations in contractual situations are discussed.

Clause 8 also clarifies how the process perspective discussed earlier leads to documented procedures that satisfy requirements such as those in ISO 9001 that are typically phrased: "The supplier shall establish and maintain documented procedures...."

Three new annexes have been added to ISO 9000-1.

Annex A includes terms and definitions from *ISO 8402, Quality management and quality assurance—Vocabulary*. Annex B discusses product and process factors that should be considered in applying the ISO 9000 standards. Annex C provides information and guidance on the types of standards that are appropriate in international, multinational regional, and national as well as industry/economic sector domains. This guidance is provided with a view toward minimizing proliferation of standards that create nontariff trade barriers.

Modifications in ISO 9001, ISO 9002 and ISO 9003

The quality assurance standards ISO 9001, ISO 9002 and ISO 9003 specify three sets of quality system requirements that can be used for external quality assurance purposes. *The requirements in these external quality assurance standards are viewed as minimum good business practices for a supplier company in any industry/economic sector.* The requirements are stated mainly in terms of what the supplier shall accomplish, leaving considerable flexibility on the method of implementation.

Since their first publication, these quality assurance standards have been adopted worldwide, providing a source for valuable feedback from major users. The revisions to these standards address many of the reported difficulties.

One improvement priority was to make the clause structures of the three quality assurance standards identical (See Table 11-2). Here is what has and hasn't changed:

● The structure of ISO 9001 remains unchanged.

● The ISO 9002 structure was changed by adding a heading for *Clause 4.4, Design control*, followed by the statement: "The scope of this International Standard does not include quality system requirements for design control."

● Requirements for servicing have been added in ISO 9002 as Clause 4.19.

● The ISO 9003 structure was changed by adding headings that act as "place keepers" for four clauses that do not contain requirements (Clause 4.4, 4.6, 4.9, and 4.19). ISO 9003, however, now includes additional quality system elements for contract review (Clause 4.3), corrective action (Clause 4.14), and internal quality audits (Clause 4.17).

The additional requirements ensure that all three quality assurance models embrace a core set of quality system elements (within their defined scopes) that address customer requirement evaluation and adequate demonstration of product conformity.

The following additional changes have been incorporated as appropriate, given the respective scopes of the standards:

● Ensuring continuity with the 1987 versions of the standards

● Modifying some subclause titles to make them consistent among the standards

● Ensuring consistency of subclause content among the standards

● Clarifying the requirement text

● Enhancing the scope of some existing quality system requirements.

Here are the specific changes to the quality system requirements:

● In *Clause 0, Introduction*, the reference to quality systems being "suitable for two-party contractual purposes" has been replaced by the phrase "quality system requirements for use where a supplier's capability to design and supply conforming product needs to be demonstrated."

● *Subclause 4.1.1, Quality policy*, has been enhanced with respect to its relevance to customers' expectations and needs, and the supplier's internal organizational goals for meeting policy requirements.

- *Subclause 4.1.2.2, Resources*, has been expanded to include management, work performance, and verification activities.

- *Subclause 4.2.1, Quality system-General*, now includes a requirement for a quality manual that defines the documentation structure of the quality system.

- *Subclause 4.2.2, Quality system procedures*, has been enhanced to clarify the degree of documentation required for the quality system. The subclause now states that the extent of documented procedures required for work activities shall depend on the skills needed, the

---

Table 11-2:
Contents of ISO 9001, ISO 9002 and ISO 9003

To reflect the narrower scope, some subclause details in ISO 9003 are modified from the corresponding subclauses in ISO 9001 and ISO 9002.

0   Introduction
1   Scope
2   Normative reference
3   Definitions
4   Quality system requirements
    4.1   Management responsibility
    4.2   Quality system
    4.3   Contract review
    4.4   Design control #*
    4.5   Document and data control
    4.6   Purchasing*
    4.7   Control of customer supplied product
    4.8   Product identification and traceability
    4.9   Process control*
    4.10 Inspection and testing
    4.11 Control of inspection, measuring and test equipment
    4.12 Inspection and test status
    4.13 Control of nonconforming product
    4.14 Corrective and preventive action
    4.15 Handling, storage, packaging, preservation and delivery
    4.16 Control of quality records
    4.17 Internal quality audits
    4.18 Training
    4.19 Servicing*
    4.20 Statistical techniques

Annex A: References

 # Not a requirement of ISO 9002   ** Not a requirement of ISO 9003*

methods used, and the training acquired by the personnel involved in performing the activity.

- *Subclause 4.2.3, Quality planning*, has been added. It covers quality system planning and product quality plans. The requirement states that the quality plan for a product, project, or contract may be in the form of a detailed reference to those documented procedures of the quality system that are appropriate to providing complete assurance of product quality.

- *Subclause 4.3, Contract review*, now includes precontract tender arrangements as well as contract and ordering requirements.

- *Clause 4.4, Design control*, has been expanded to include design validation, and separate requirements for design review and design verification.

- *Clause 4.9, Process control*, includes additional requirements for maintaining process equipment to ensure continuity process capability.

- *Clause 4.14, Corrective and preventive action*, now includes separate requirements for corrective and preventive action. Corrective action is directed toward eliminating the causes of actual nonconformities, and preventive action is directed toward eliminating the causes of potential nonconformities.

Modifications in ISO 9004-1

ISO 9004-1, Quality management and quality system elements—Part 1: Guidelines, helps organizations design and implement a quality system so that they can meet their marketplace needs and achieve overall success. The guidance in ISO 9004-1 generally goes beyond the requirements in the quality assurance standards ISO 9001, ISO 9002, and ISO 9003.

The 1987 version of ISO 9004 was developed in parallel with ISO 9000, ISO 9001, ISO 9002 and ISO 9003 and it was intended as a separate standard that organizations could use internally to improve their quality management practices. The revised standard retains this role. As a guidance document, it more thoroughly identifies effective quality management practices without mandating requirements. Table 11-3 presents the table of contents for ISO 9004-1.

The role of ISO 9004-1 is clarified by an additional sentence in the *Foreword*: "ISO 9004 is a document for internal use by an organization. It is not intended as guidance to ISO 9001, ISO 9002 or ISO 9003, for which ISO 9000-2 is available."

In practice, many organizations use both ISO 9004-1 and ISO 9001 or ISO 9002. Some organizations use ISO 9004-1 for designing and implementing their quality systems, even though their systems are later assessed and registered to ISO 9001 or ISO 9002. This is appropriate as long as organizations recognize that ISO 9004-1 is a guideline and should not be used to interpret ISO 9001. In other cases, organizations structure their internal quality systems around ISO 9004-1, while using ISO 9001 or ISO 9002 when working with subcontractors.

To further clarify the intended usage of ISO 9004-1, the introductory clauses note that although the standard presents quality system elements it does not specify the way those elements should be implemented. It is not the purpose of the standard to enforce uniformity of quality systems among different companies.

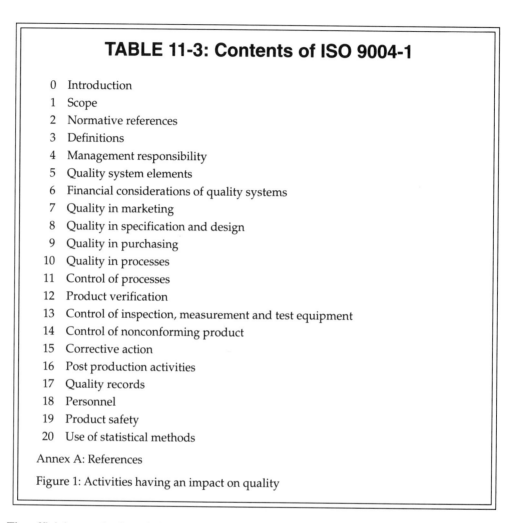

TABLE 11-3: Contents of ISO 9004-1

0 Introduction
1 Scope
2 Normative references
3 Definitions
4 Management responsibility
5 Quality system elements
6 Financial considerations of quality systems
7 Quality in marketing
8 Quality in specification and design
9 Quality in purchasing
10 Quality in processes
11 Control of processes
12 Product verification
13 Control of inspection, measurement and test equipment
14 Control of nonconforming product
15 Corrective action
16 Post production activities
17 Quality records
18 Personnel
19 Product safety
20 Use of statistical methods

Annex A: References

Figure 1: Activities having an impact on quality

The official renumbering of ISO 9004:1987 as ISO 9004-1 positions it as the overall guidance standard in a set of quality management guidance standards. Three additional guidance standards have been published that are numbered parts of ISO 9004. These additional standards treat in greater depth many elements contained in the revised ISO 9004-1 standard.

The following are the modifications to the standard's content:

● A new clause has been added on quality improvement (Clause 5.6) to coordinate with the newly developed standard ISO 9004-4

● Clause 6 has been retitled *Financial considerations of quality systems* and draws on the content of a new standard being developed on the economics of quality

● Contents related to configuration management have been revised to be consistent with another new draft international standard

● Additional references to environmental considerations have been added

- The diagram and description of the quality loop has been replaced with a diagram of the typical life-cycle phases of a product to make it more consistent with the content of ISO 9004-1. The life-cycle phases are: marketing and market research; product design and development; process planning and development; purchasing; production or provision of service; verification; packaging and storage; sales and distribution; installation and commissioning; technical assistance and servicing; post-market surveillance; and disposal or recycling at the end of useful life.

- Additional references to marketplace input and feedback as a means of improving the quality system have been made. The structure of the clauses related to handling and storage has been revised to make it consistent with ISO 9001 and ISO 9002. These activities were previously treated as post-production elements along with maintenance and servicing. As revised, they are recognized as relevant throughout the production processes.

In addition to content enhancements, virtually every clause in ISO 9004-1 contains some changes in wording for clarification or consistency with other standards in the ISO 9000 family. For example, "develop and state" has been changed to "define and document" and references to "quality management systems" have been changed to "quality systems."

IMPACT OF THE REVISIONS

The revisions of the ISO 9000 series standards will enhance the utility of these basic quality standards, providing requirements and guidance without becoming prescriptive. The generic requirements and guidance provide customers with the confidence they need. Supplier organizations can then improve specific aspects of their quality and management systems to achieve marketplace differentiation and competitive advantage.

REFERENCES

Donald Marquardt, Jacques Chove, K.E. Jensen, Klaus Petrick, James Pyle, and Donald Strahle. "Vision 2000: The Strategy for the ISO 9000 Series Standards in the '90s." Quality Progress, May 1991, pp. 25-31.

Vision 2000: The Strategy for the ISO 9000 Series Standards in the '90s

by Donald Marquardt, Jacques Chove, K.E. Jensen, Klaus Petrick, James Pyle and Donald Strahle

INTRODUCTION

This article is adapted from the report of the Ad Hoc Task Force of the International Organization for Standardization (ISO) Technical Committee 176 (TC 176). The task force was commissioned to prepare a strategic plan for ISO 9000 series architecture, numbering, and implementation. The task force report, which has become known as *Vision 2000*, was prepared by the authors of this article. TC 176 adopted unanimously the strategic principles of the report at its meeting in Interlaken, Switzerland, in October 1990. This article is part of a worldwide communication effort to gain broad acceptance of these principles and to globally influence standardization activities in the quality arena.

This article contains four major sections:

1. The Stake
   - The ISO 9000 series standards
   - Global trends
   - The critical issues

2. Basic Concepts
   - Generic product categories
   - Industry/economic sectors

3. Analysis of the Marketplace
   - Preventing proliferation
   - Segmenting the markets

4. Vision 2000
   - Migration to product offerings involving several generic product categories
   - Implications for standards development
   - Recommendations on implementation

1. THE STAKE

The ISO 9000 Series Standards

In the years just prior to 1979, when TC 176 was formed, quality was rapidly emerging as a new emphasis in commerce and industry. Various national and multinational standards had been developed in the quality systems arena for commercial and industrial use and for military and nuclear power industry needs. Some standards were guidance documents. Other standards were for contractual use between customer and supplier organizations.

Despite some historical commonalities, these various standards were not sufficiently consistent for widespread use in international trade. Terminology in these standards and in commercial and industrial practice was also inconsistent and confusing.

The publication of the ISO 9000 series in 1987, together with the accompanying terminology standard (ISO 8402), has brought harmonization on an international scale and has supported the growing impact of quality as a factor in international trade. The ISO 9000 series has quickly been adopted by many nations and regional bodies and is rapidly supplanting prior national and industry-based standards. This initial marketplace success of the ISO 9000 series is testimony to the following two important achievements of TC 176:

- The ISO 9000 series embodies comprehensive quality management concepts and guidance, together with several models for external quality assurance requirements. Using an integrated systems architecture, the standards are packaged under a harmonized, easily memorized numbering system. These features have high value in meeting the commercial and industrial needs of current international trade.
- The ISO 9000 series was published in time to meet the growing need for international standardization in the quality arena and the wide adoption of third-party quality systems certification schemes.

More recently, TC 176 has been preparing additional international standards in quality management, quality assurance, and quality technology. Some of these will become part numbers to the 9000 series, while others will be in a 10000 series that has been reserved by ISO for use by TC 176.

Global Trends

GLOBAL COMPETITION

Globalization has become a reality in the few years since the ISO 9000 series was published. Today, all but the smallest or most local commercial and industrial enterprises are finding that their principal marketplace competitors include companies headquartered in other countries.

Consequently, product development and marketing strategies must be global to reckon with global competition. Quality continues to grow in importance as a factor in marketplace success.

THE EUROPEAN UNION

The rapid implementation of the European Union (EU) single-market arrangement, targeted for full operation in 1992, has become a major driving force. EU 92 has global significance in quality because it places new marketplace pressures on all producers worldwide that wish to trade with European companies or even compete with European companies in other markets.

The EU 92 plan rests on the use of TC 176-produced standards as the requirement documents for its third-party certification scheme for quality systems registration, and for auditing compliance to the requirements.

Under such certification schemes, a company arranges to be audited by a single accredited independent (third-party) registrar organization. If the company's quality systems documentation and implementation are found to meet the requirements of the applicable ISO 9000 series international standard, the registrar grants certification and lists the company in its register of companies with certified quality systems. All purchasers of the company's products can then accept the third-party certification as evidence that the company's quality systems meet the applicable ISO 9000 series requirements.

Such a third-party certification scheme provides a number of benefits. Certification demonstrates that a company has implemented an adequate quality system for the products or services it offers. By this, better internal commitment as well as enhanced customer confidence can be achieved.

In the EU 92 scheme, quality system certification often will be a prerequisite for product certification or product conformity statements. In addition, from a broader national viewpoint, the scheme will result in improvements in the quality capability of a large fraction of commercial and industrial organizations.

An important corollary benefit for any organization is reduction of the costs of multiple assessments by multiple trading partners. In practice, customer organizations often audit portions of the quality systems of their suppliers, but because of supplier quality system certification, the customer does not have to duplicate the, say, 80 percent that has already been audited by the third-party auditor.

QUALITY AS A COMPETITIVE WEAPON

Quality assurance continues to be a competitive weapon for companies, even in markets where third-party certification has become widespread. The competitive advantage can be achieved by means of second-party (customer) quality system requirements and audits that supplement (i.e., go beyond) the requirements of the ISO 9000 series contractual standards. This approach can be carried another step by setting up mutually advantageous partnership arrangements between customer and supplier, supplementing third-party audits.

Such partnerships focus on mutual efforts toward continuous quality improvement and the use of innovative quality technology. In instances where customer-supplier partnerships are fully developed, third-party certification often plays an important early role but might become relatively less important as the partnership develops and progresses beyond the requirements of the ISO 9001, ISO 9002 or ISO 9003 contractual standards. Various quality awards conferred at the company, national, or multinational level also provide further motivation for excellence in quality.

Critical Issues

PROLIFERATION OF STANDARDS

The ISO 9000 series standards—in particular, those for contractual use (ISO 9001, ISO 9002 and ISO 9003)—are being employed in many industries for many different kinds of products and services. Some groups are evaluating or implementing local or industry-specific adaptations of the ISO 9000 series for guidance, for certification, for auditing and for documentation.

These include national or regional bodies (such as CEN/CENELEC, the European regional standardization organization) and international standards committees for industry sectors (such as other technical committees of ISO and IEC). These developments are indicators of success of the ISO 9000 series and indicators of concerns that TC 176 must address.

If the ISO 9000 series were to become only the nucleus of a proliferation of localized standards derived from, but varying in content and architecture from the ISO 9000 series, then there would be little worldwide standardization. The growth of many localized certification schemes would present further complications. Once again, there could be worldwide restraint of trade because of proliferation of standards and inconsistent requirements.

INADEQUACIES OF THE ISO 9000 SERIES STANDARDS

Careful study of the ISO 9000 series standards by certain major groups of users or potential users has identified a number of needs that are not easily met with the ISO 9000 series contractual standards in their present form. One example of such users or potential users is large companies, such as electric power providers or military organizations that purchase complex products to specific functional design.

These users request, for example, a requirement for a quality plan to document how the generic requirements of the ISO 9000 series standards will be adapted to the specific needs of a particular contract. The requirement for a quality plan can improve the consistency of audits.

The position of such purchasers in the supply chain and their size enable their actions to expedite or hinder the worldwide implementation of harmonized external quality assurance standards. Moreover, there appears to be a large number of other users that would optionally want some of the same changes to the standards.

At the same time, it is important to preserve simplicity of ISO 9000 series application for smaller companies.

At its meeting in Interlaken, Switzerland, in October 1990, TC 176 took actions to reckon with these critical issues in formulating future policy for international standards. To understand the basis for the TC 176 actions, some terminology and concepts must be introduced.

2. BASIC CONCEPTS

A Terminology Distinction

A product can be classified in a generic sense in two separate ways. The task force has introduced two terms to describe this important distinction. The first term is *generic product category*. The second term is *industry/economic sector* in which the product is present.

Generic Product Categories

The task force has identified the following four generic product categories:

- Hardware
- Software
- Processed Materials
- Services.

Table 11-4: Generic Product Categories

Hardware .... Products consisting of manufactured pieces, parts or assemblies thereof.

Software .... Products, such as computer software, consisting of written or otherwise recordable information, concepts, transactions or procedures.

Processed Materials .... Products (final or intermediate) consisting of solids, liquids, gases, or combinations thereof, including particulate materials, ingots, filaments or sheet structures.

NOTE: *Processed materials typically are delivered (packaged) in containers such as drums, bags, tanks, cans, pipelines or rolls.*

Services .... Intangible products which may be the entire or principal offering or incorporated features of the offering, relating to activities such as planning, selling, directing, delivering, improving, evaluating, training, operating or servicing a tangible product.

NOTE: *All generic product categories provide value to the customer only at the times and places the customer interfaces with and perceives benefits from the product. However, the value from a service often is provided primarily by activities at a particular time and place of interface with the customer.*

These four generic product categories are described in Table 11-4. At the present time, Subcommittee 1 of TC 176 is developing formal definitions based on the descriptions of the four generic product categories in this table.

Subcommittee 1 has developed and submitted for international comment definitions for *product* and the generic product category *service*. *Product* is defined as the result of activities or processes. Notes to the definition point out that a product can be tangible or intangible or a combination thereof, and that, for practical reasons, products can be classified in the four generic product categories introduced in Table 11-4.

Service is defined as the results generated by activities at the interface between the supplier and the customer, and by supplier internal activities to meet the customer needs. Notes to the definition point out that the supplier or the customer may be represented at the interface by personnel or equipment, that customer activities at the interface may be essential to the service delivery, that delivery or use of tangible products may form part of the service delivery, and that a service may be linked with the manufacture and supply of tangible products.

We believe the four generic product categories are all the kinds of product that need explicit attention in quality management and quality assurance standardization.

Industry/Economic Sectors

The term *industry/economic sector* applies to all sectors of the economy, including service sectors. The dual use of *industry sector* and *economic sector* recognizes that each term is used for the intended meaning in specific countries or languages. Such sectors include administration, aerospace, banking, chemicals, construction, education, food, health care, insurance, medical, retailing, telecommunications, textiles, tourism, and so forth. The number of industry/economic sectors and potential subsectors is extremely large.

An industry/economic sector can be described as a grouping of suppliers whose offerings meet similar customer needs and/or whose customers are closely interrelated in the marketplace.

Required Combinations of Generic Product Categories

Two or more of the generic product categories have to be present in the marketplace offerings of any organization, whatever the industry/economic sector in which the organization operates.

An electric power utility is an example where the offering combines many characteristics of a service with delivery of a form of processed material (electric current) via a conducting cable.

Project management is another example where the offering typically combines many characteristics of a service with production and/or delivery of a hardware and/or software product.

Analytical instruments are examples where hardware, software, processed materials (such as titrating solutions or reference standard materials), and services (such as training) might all be important features of the offering.

GOALS FOR THE ISO 9000 SERIES AND RELATED STANDARDS

The Ad Hoc Task Force of the International Organization for Standardization Technical Committee 176 (TC 176) set forth four strategic goals for the ISO 9000 series standards and their related ISO 10000 series standards developed by TC 176:

- Universal acceptance
- Current compatibility
- Forward compatibility
- Forward flexibility.

In the following table, informal illustrative tests are described for each strategic goal. These tests are not meant to be strict requirements but only examples of indicators as to whether a strategic goal has been satisfied adequately.

These goals and tests are intended to apply particularly to standards used for external quality assurance. They are important but less critical for quality management guidance documents.

These four strategic goals for TC 176-developed standards will require constant managerial attention by the participants in TC 176 as well as affected user communities. Proposals that are beneficial to one of the goals might be detrimental to another goal. As in all standardization, compromises and paradoxes might be needed in specific situations. Experience continues to show that, when all viewpoints are put forth objectively, a harmonized standard can result, providing benefits to all parties.

Strategic Goals and Illustrative Tests for TC 176 Standards

Goal	Tests
Universal Acceptance	• The standards are widely adopted and used worldwide. • There are few complaints from users in proportion to the volume of use. • Few sector-specific supplementary or derivative standards are being used or developed.
Current Compatibility	• Part-number supplements to existing standards do not change or conflict with requirements in the existing parent document. • The numbering and the clause structure of a supplement facilitate combined use of the parent document and the supplement. • Supplements are not stand-alone documents but are to be used with their parent document.
Forward Compatibility	• Revisions affecting requirements in existing standards are few in number and minor or narrow in scope. • Revisions are accepted for existing and new contracts.

(continued on next page)

Goals for the ISO 9000 Series and Related Standards

(continued from previous page)

Forward Flexibility

- Supplements are few but can be combined as needed to meet the needs of virtually any industry/economic sector or generic category of products.

- Supplement or addendum architecture allows new features or requirements to be consolidated into the parent document at a subsequent revision if the supplement's provisions are found to be used (almost) universally.

Market Need

In managing the ISO 9000 series standards during the 1990s, market need also must be kept in focus. There is no value in a standard that is not wanted or not used in the marketplace. We encourage TC 176 to expedite the process of identifying and balloting internationally proposed new work items for new standards documents to meet new market needs. TC 176 must always apply the test of market need before embarking on a new standards project, however.

Confusion Due to Intermixing Terms

It has been common practice to intermix the terms for generic product categories and the terms for industry/economic sectors. The result has been confusion and misunderstanding.

A prime example involves the terms "process industries" and "hardware industries." In retrospect, these terms are seen to be collective names for the industry/economic sectors where processed materials and hardware, respectively, are the primary kinds of product. All products are produced by processes.

People in the process industries know from experience that the classic quality management approaches, especially the quality control techniques and quality technology from the hardware industries, are not adequate to deal with the complexities they regularly encounter in the production processes and measurement processes for processed materials. In the language of ISO 9001 and ISO 9004, almost all processes in the process industries are special processes. These differences are crucial matters of degree and emphasis in a quality systems sense.

Terms such as *process industries* and *hardware industries* will continue to be useful when discussing collections of industry/economic sectors. However, for purposes of standardization in the quality arena, we recommend precise use of the four generic product category terms in written documents and oral communication.

3. ANALYSIS OF THE MARKETPLACE FOR THE ISO 9000 SERIES STANDARDS

Preventing Proliferation

The strategy regarding proliferation of supplementary or derivative standards must face up to a political and marketplace reality. TC 176 cannot legislate that industry groups, regional bodies, or other standards organizations will not produce supplementary or derivative documents.

This implies that to continue to influence the marketplace it serves, TC 176 must design its products and provide them in a timely way to prevent (or at least minimize) unhealthy proliferation of industry/economic sector schemes based upon supplementary or derivative documents.

Fortunately, the current global trends are driving many standard users toward strategic recognition that they need and should conform to international standards. This suggests that the marketplace will resist proliferation if TC 176 meets the marketplace needs in a timely way.

It is easy to see why people in various industry/economic sectors would be motivated to create supplementary or derivative documents when confronted with implementing the initial ISO 9000 series standards published in 1987. The initial series is truly generic in scope and is applicable to all four generic product categories.

Nevertheless, the language and many details refer mainly to products in the hardware generic category. People in industry/economic sectors that involve products in the other generic product categories could easily conclude that what they need is a supplementary or derivative document for their specific industry/economic sector. This turns out, in our opinion, to be the wrong solution for the right problem.

We believe the proliferation of supplementary or derivative documents and industry-sector-specific schemes can be prevented or minimized by recognizing criteria that segment the markets for standardization in quality management and external quality assurance.

We recommend a development path for ISO 9000 series architecture that mirrors these market segmenting criteria. This path will allow sufficient flexibility in the ISO 9000 series to meet the needs of users in all generic product categories and all industry/economic sectors. There are, in our view, three criteria that are important to segment the markets.

MARKET-SEGMENTING CRITERION 1: GENERIC PRODUCT CATEGORIES

Having distinguished generic product categories and industry/economic sectors as ways of classifying, we found an unanticipated commonality of our viewpoints on standardization policy. The members of the *ad hoc* task force represent a variety of national standards systems, generic product categories, industry/economic sectors, areas of personal experience, and current functional roles within our own organizations.

From all these points of view, we conclude the following:

- Guidance standards written by TC 176 should explicitly deal with the special needs of each generic product category. In fact, at the October 1990 meeting of TC 176, supplementary documents (guidelines) for services and software were advanced to international standard status and work continued on a supplementary document for processed materials. Only these four generic product categories are represented by such formal work items. This reflects, we believe, a heretofore unarticulated international consensus on generic product categories.

- Neither TC 176 nor other groups should write supplementary or derivative standards (whether guidance standards or quality assurance requirements standards) for specific industry/economic sectors. In fact, experience in several nations has been that their industry-specific schedules or guidance documents have soon fallen into disuse because they had only transient tutorial value.

MARKET-SEGMENTING CRITERION 2: COMPLEXITY OF PURCHASER NEED AND PRODUCT AND PROCESS CHARACTERISTICS

A second dimension that segments the market for quality management and quality assurance standards has to do with the differing complexities of customer need and product characteristics as well as the differing complexities of designing and operating the process for producing and delivering the product or service. These differences are most obvious in external quality assurance situations.

The existing ISO 9000 series deals with this market-segmenting criterion by having three levels or models for external quality assurance requirements (ISO 9001, ISO 9002 and ISO 9003) and by providing guidance for selecting the appropriate model (ISO 9000, Clause 8.2) and for tailoring the model within a particular contract (ISO 9000, Subclause 8.5.1).

In some industry/economic sectors, the options available in the existing ISO 9000 series are felt to be insufficient to meet all the critical needs. These deficiencies, for example, underlie the unmet needs of certain large organizations that purchase complex products to specific functional design, as discussed previously.

We believe that modest additions and revisions of the existing ISO 9000 series contractual standards can resolve these unmet near-term needs while preserving the necessary compatibility and flexibility.

MARKET-SEGMENTING CRITERION 3: CONTRACTUAL VERSUS NONCONTRACTUAL

For completeness, we remark that the distinction between contractual and noncontractual situations is a fundamental market segmenting criterion. The distinction is built into the existing ISO 9000 series architecture: ISO 9001, ISO 9002 and ISO 9003 are contractual requirements for quality assurance, and ISO 9004 provides guidance to a producer for implementing and managing a quality system. We believe the existing architecture meets the needs of this market-segmenting criterion.

COMBINED USE OF THE MARKET-SEGMENTING CRITERIA

Market-segmenting criteria 1, 2 and 3 currently provide an opportunity for many options of requirements to meet the needs of the various industry/economic sectors. When the recommendations of the *ad hoc* task force report are implemented, additional options will be provided. We believe that the need for sector-specific supplementary or derived standards and schemes will disappear with this added flexibility of implementation.

4. VISION 2000

The background, analyses, and goals discussed in the previous sections provide the basis for anticipating some critical features of standardization in the quality arena by the year 2000. We call this *Vision 2000*. We believe our recommendations will enhance progress toward *Vision 2000*.

Migration to Product Offerings Involving Several Generic Product Categories

Underlying *Vision 2000* is recognition of where current marketplace trends are leading. In all industry/economic sectors, there is an across-the-board migration toward product offerings that are combinations of two or more of the generic product categories (hardware, software, processed materials, and services).

For example, many products today involve the production of processed materials that are then incorporated into manufactured parts and into hardware assemblies in which computer software also is an incorporated feature and the service aspects of selling, delivering and servicing are important features of the total offering. A related example is firmware, where computing software is an integral part of the hardware of a product.

During the 1990s this migration will continue. This means that organizations will have to learn about and must implement the quality management and quality assurance terminology, skills, and emphases for all four generic product categories.

Global competition will be a powerful driving force in this process. Various requirements of society will also be a driving force, including laws, statutes, rules and regulations, codes, environmental considerations, health and safety factors, and conservation of energy and materials.

The boundaries for standardization program responsibilities will have to be worked out as a strategic issue in the 1990s. In this context, government agencies are one group representing the society as a customer whose needs and requirements must be satisfied and for whom appropriate quality management and quality assurance tools must be available.

Today, there is the impression that quality management and quality assurance for hardware, software, processed materials, and services are substantially different from each other. It is true that the relative emphases of quality system elements might differ and the sophistication of the quality technology being applied might differ, but the underlying generic quality system elements and needs are the same.

Today, there is the impression that quality systems and quality technology for hardware products is most mature because that has been the predominant kind of product in earlier standards and quality technology literature. However, we believe that the most rapid development of new quality technologies will occur in the other three generic product categories during the 1990s.

Implications for Standards Development

The standards now under development by TC 176 include a generic guidance document for implementing ISO 9001, ISO 9002, ISO 9003, and guidance documents for software, processed materials, and services. All of these reflect, in their detailed content, the migration we have described. All of these are expected to be published within a couple of years. It can be expected that the 1990s will be a transition period in standards development. During the early 1990s, we will need these separate documents for the various generic product categories.

As product offerings continue to migrate toward combinations of two or more generic product types, suppliers will find it increasingly necessary for employees in different functional activities to refer to different (but interrelated) supplementary standards, each written in a somewhat different style and format. Organizations have the managerial task of achieving compatibility in their quality systems for their offerings containing combinations of several generic product categories. This will be state-of-the-art and acceptable for the early 1990s, but a more strategic approach is needed for the longer term.

We envision that, by the year 2000, there will be an intermingling, a growing together, of the terminology, concepts, and technology used in all four generic product categories. This vision implies that, by the year 2000, the need for separate documents for the four generic product categories will have diminished. Terminology and procedures for all generic product categories will be widely understood and used by practitioners, whatever industry/economic sector they might be operating in.

Consequently, our *Vision 2000* for TC 176 is to develop a single quality management standard (an updated ISO 9004 that includes new topics as appropriate) and an external quality assurance requirements standard (an updated ISO 9001) tied together by a road-map standard (an updated ISO 9000). There would be a high degree of commonality in the concepts and architecture of ISO 9004 and ISO 9001. The requirements in ISO 9001 would continue to be based upon a selection of the guidance elements in ISO 9004. Supplementary standards that provide expanded guidance could be provided by TC 176 as needed.

Multiple models of external quality assurance (now exemplified by ISO 9001, ISO 9002 and ISO 9003 in accord with the complexity criterion) might still be needed.

ISO standards must be reaffirmed or revised at approximately five-year intervals. At its October 1990 meeting, TC 176 adopted a two-phase strategy to meet the needs for revision of the ISO 9000 series. The first phase is to meet near-term needs for the (nominal) 1992 revision, with no major changes in architecture or numbering. Work on the second phase will begin during 1991, with the intent of implementing *Vision 2000*.

The target date is 1996—intentionally earlier than the nominal five years for the second cycle of revision. Working groups were set up within TC 176 to do these revisions. Formal comments have already been received from many nations as a basis for the revisions and additional comments are being received.

Vision 2000 emphatically discourages the production of industry/economic-sector-specific generic quality standards supplemental to, or derived from, the ISO 9000 series. We believe such proliferation would constrain international trade and impede progress in quality achievements. A primary purpose of the widespread publication of this article is to prevent the proliferation of supplemental or derivative standards.

It is, however, well understood that product-specific standards containing technical requirements for specific products or processes or describing specific product test methods are necessary and have to be developed within the industry/economic sector.

A Visual Portrayal of International Quality Standardization

Figure 11-1 shows graphically how the evolving system of standards meets the combined needs for quality management and quality assurance from both the producer's and the purchaser's viewpoints during the early 1990s.

Recommendations on Implementation

This section discusses some recommendations that are not entirely within the responsibility of TC 176. Nevertheless, reasonable conformance to these recommendations will be critical to success of the ISO 9000 series in the 1990s international environment. The recommendations include the following:

- TC 176 is encouraged to prepare standards that might be needed for an intermediate period for the four generic product categories. At the same time, TC 176 and all other standards-writing bodies are discouraged from writing standards for specific industry/ economic sectors. The rationale for this recommendation was given earlier in this article.

    Comment: This recommendation is not intended for standards dealing with technical requirements for specific products, processes or measurements that are outside the scope of TC 176.

- Quality system certification schemes worldwide should register suppliers only to ISO 9001, ISO 9002, ISO 9003, and other ISO 9000 series requirements documents that might hereafter be published and to their national equivalents translated exactly from the ISO 9000 series.

- There should be no industry/economic-sector-specific external quality system standards used as the assessment documents for such certification schemes. This recommendation applies to both third-party and second-party accredited assessment organizations.

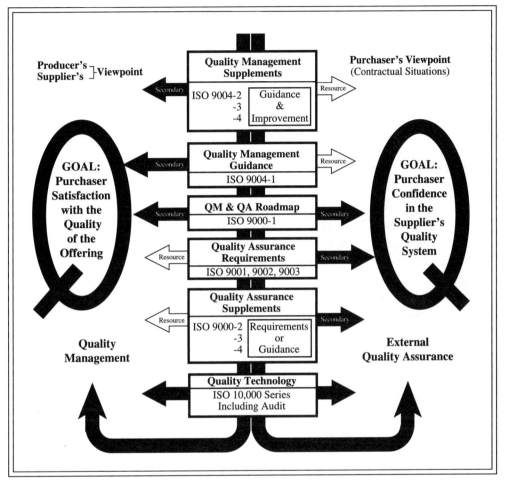

Figure 11-1: ISO 9000—Future Architecture.

- Auditor accreditation (certification) schemes worldwide should be based on the ISO 10011 series audit standards.
- Auditors should be accredited (certified) generically, not on an industry/economic-sector basis. Each audit team should include at least one person knowledgeable in the industry/economic sector(s) involved in a particular audit. This knowledge might reside in the accredited auditors on the team or in technical experts on the audit team.
- TC 176 should help promote the development of mutual recognition arrangements among national quality system certification schemes worldwide. Fairness and consistency must be satisfied adequately, but failure to accomplish mutual recognition could severely restrain trade.
- The European Union has adopted a series of European standards (EN 45000 series) dealing with general criteria for operation, assessment and accreditation of laboratories;

certification bodies relating to certification of products, quality systems, and personnel; and suppliers' declaration of conformity.

Preexisting ISO/IEC guides also deal with these topics. Implementation of the ISO 9000 series and ISO 10000 series standards interfaces with such criteria. At the October 1990 meeting, TC 176 requested its chairman and secretary to investigate the desirability and options to harmonize the European standards in the EN 45000 series and the relevant ISO/IEC guides and transform the results into international standards.

ACKNOWLEDGMENTS

We acknowledge our indebtedness to R.N. Shaughnessy, TC 176 Chairman, for his early appreciation of the strategic issues and his leadership in causing this task force to be formed, and to K.C. Ford, TC 176 Secretariat, for his continuing and incisive support for our work. We also acknowledge the suggestions made by H. Kume and K. A. Rutter. Many other people have contributed indirectly through participating in other TC 176 activities or through contacts with task force members.

Donald Marquardt, Du Pont, United States; Jacques Chove, Conseil, France; K.E. Jensen, Alkatel Kirk A/S, Denmark; Klaus Petrick, DIN, Germany; James Pyle, British Telecom, United Kingdom; and Donald Strahle, Ontario Hydro, Canada, are members of the Ad Hoc Task Force of the International Organization for Standardization Technical Committee 176. Marquardt is the Chairman of the task force.

TC 176 STANDARDS ISSUED AND BEING DEVELOPED

The numerical sequencing of ISO standards has been designated by the International Organization for Standardization. Approved and published ISO standards are designated ISO XXXX. Because of the importance of the ISO 9000 series, the ISO Central Secretariat has set aside a block of numbers in the 90xx range beginning with 9000, and a block of numbers in the 100xx range beginning with 10001, to be used by TC 176 as new standards are formulated.

Drafts of proposed standards go through several stages. Initially, while the Working Group is developing a standard, it is called a *Working Draft (WD)*. When the Working Draft is circulated internationally for formal ballot, it is called a *Committee Draft (CD)*. When sufficient consensus is achieved to seek approval as an international standard, the document is called a *Draft International Standard (DIS)* and is circulated internationally for ballot and approval. This process is illustrated in Figure 11-2.

The architecture of the ISO 9000 series maintains ISO 9001, ISO 9002 and ISO 9003 as standards with no "Part Numbers." Therefore their numerical designations do not have dashes and part number identifiers after the main number. ISO 9000 itself does have a number of supplementary "parts" which are:

- External quality assurance guidance for the proper use of ISO 9001, ISO 9002 and/or ISO 9003
- Potential supplemental quality management guidance to ISO 9000 itself
- Potential optional external quality assurance requirements that are supplemental to the requirements in ISO 9001, ISO 9002, or ISO 9003.

Part 1 (ISO 9000-1) has been reserved for the designation of successive revisions of ISO 9000 (1987) itself.

ISO 9004 has a number of supplementary "parts" which are expanded quality management guidance that relates to the existing or potential subject matter of ISO 9004. Part 1 (ISO 9004-1) has been reserved for the designation of successive revisions of ISO 9004 (1987) itself.

The ISO 100xx series is reserved for quality technology standards.

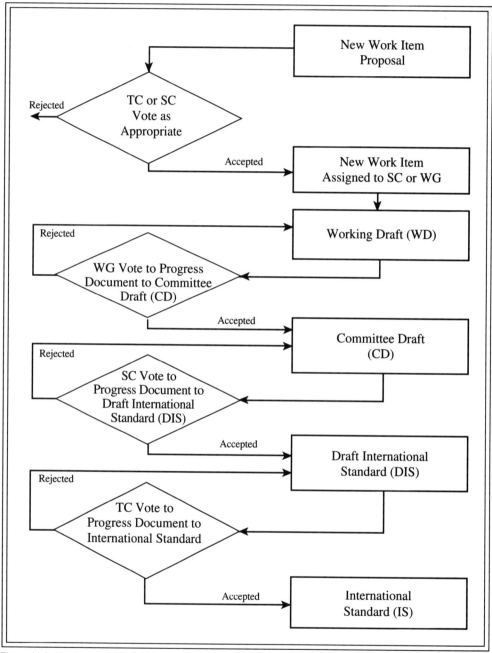

Figure 11-2: ISO Standards Development Process.

Status of Each Document as of Mid-1994

Existing Standards

ISO 8402, Quality - Vocabulary (1994)

ISO 9000, Quality management and quality assurance standards

  Part 1, *Guidelines for selection and use* (1994)

  Part 2, *Generic guidelines for the application* of ISO 9001, ISO 9002, and ISO 9003 (1993)

  Part 3, *Guidelines for the application of ISO 9001 to the development supply and maintenance of software*
  (1993)

  Part 4, *Guide to dependability program management* (1993)

ISO 9001, Quality systems - Model for quality assurance in design, development, production, installation and servicing (1994)

ISO 9002, Quality systems - Model for quality assurance in production, installation and servicing (1994)

ISO 9003, Quality systems - Model for quality assurance in final inspection and test (1994)

ISO 9004, Quality management and quality system elements

  Part 1, *Guidelines* (1994)

  Part 2, *Guidelines for services* (1993)

  Part 3, *Guidelines for processed materials* (1993)

  Part 4, *Guidelines for quality improvement* (1993)

ISO 10011, Guidelines for auditing quality systems

  Part 1, *Auditing* (1993)

  Part 2, *Qualification criteria for quality systems auditors* (1993)

  Part 3, *Management of audit programs* (1993)

ISO 10012: *Quality assurance requirements for measuring equipment*

  Part 1, *Management of measuring equipment* (1992)

Work in Progress

ISO 9004 Part 5, *Guidelines for quality assurance plans* (DIS)

ISO 9004, Part 6, *Guidelines for quality assurance for project management* (WD)

ISO 9004, Part 7, *Guidelines for configuration management* (DIS)

ISO 9004, Part 8, *Quality Management Principles* (WD)

ISO 10012, Part 2, *Control of measurement process* (CD)

ISO 10013, Guidelines for developing quality manuals (DIS)

ISO 10014, Guide to the economic effects of quality (CD)

THE LEGAL LIMITATIONS OF ISO 9000 REGISTRATION AND EU PRODUCT LIABILITY AND PRODUCT SAFETY

BY James Kolka and Gregory Scott

This chapter examines legal issues related to ISO 9000 registration. It covers the following four areas:

- The role of ISO 9004-1
  - Voluntary standard
  - Product safety
- ISO 9000 Registration and its limitations
- EU (formerly EC) liability and safety directives
  - Product liability
  - Product safety
  - Machinery safety
  - Services liability
- Product Liability Prevention.

INTRODUCTION

ISO 9000 registration is playing an increasingly larger role in global trade. Manufacturers are becoming aware that ISO 9000 registration is important—sometimes vital—to their company's success.

Thousands of company sites worldwide have already become registered to one of the standards in the ISO 9000 series. Countless others are working toward registration. In this move toward registration, many companies may not have given enough consideration to the legal aspects of ISO 9000 registration. This chapter discusses the following key legal issues raised by ISO 9000 registration:

- What is the legal role of ISO 9004-1?
- What is the relationship between ISO 9000 requirements and those of the liability and safety directives?
- Is ISO 9000 registration a legal defense to a product liability suit?
- Is ISO 9000 registration a separate source of liability?

Finally, this chapter will discuss the role of product liability prevention. The European Union has stated that its purpose in creating liability and safety directives is not to encourage lawsuits but to encourage companies to prevent possible lawsuits by manufacturing safe products.

THE ROLE OF ISO 9004-1, QUALITY MANAGEMENT AND QUALITY SYSTEMS ELEMENTS—GUIDELINES

The ISO 9000 series contains five distinct standards: ISO 9001, ISO 9002 and ISO 9003 are prescriptive registration standards; ISO 9000-1 and ISO 9004-1 are voluntary guidance standards. These standards do not contain prescriptive language; companies do not register to ISO 9004-1. They should, however, pay special attention to the guidance standard from a legal standpoint.

Voluntary Standard

US courts have used voluntary standards to establish a manufacturer's "duty of care." Failure to conform to voluntary standards does not constitute negligence *per se,* but it may be considered by the court as evidence of negligence or as evidence of a design defect. This means that the plaintiffs' attorneys can present ISO 9000 standards as an integrated series—including ISO 9004-1—to the court.

Under Clause 19 of ISO 9004-1, certain steps and analyses are set forth that a company should consider to improve product safety. (Clause 19 is described below.) This paragraph has been revised under the recently approved 1994 revisions, and all explicit references to liability have been removed. The focus on product safety, however, remains and the 1994 version would not change a court's interpretation of ISO 9004-1. If anything, it amplifies the issue of product safety to reduce liability exposure.

A company will be hard-pressed to explain to a court that it decided that ISO 9001 was important enough to comply with for registration purposes but considered ISO 9004-1 to be purely voluntary and advisory. The money, time, and effort spent on obtaining ISO 9000 registration flies in the face of an argument that companies somehow deem ISO 9004-1 to be unimportant or nonbinding.

The plaintiff's attorney will likely argue that ISO 9004-1 sets forth the proper conduct of a reasonable and safety-conscious company because it codifies what a company should do to deal with product liability issues.

The only safe and logical way for a company to deal with the critical issues of safety and liability is to develop a product liability prevention program that responds to the guidance language of ISO 9004-1 as well as to the prescriptive language of ISO 9001, ISO 9002 or ISO 9003.

ISO 9004-1 and Product Safety

Clause 0.1, General of ISO 9004-1 describes the objectives of an organization to offer products that meet various goals and expectations of customers and society. In order to be successful, an organization should offer products that:

- Meet a well defined need, use or purpose
- Satisfy customers' expectations
- Comply with applicable standards and specifications
- Comply with requirements of society
- Reflect environmental needs
- Are made available at competitive prices
- Are provided economically.

Clause 19.0 of ISO 9004-1 specifically addresses product safety. It reads as follows:

Clause 19.0, Product Safety

Consideration should be given to identifying safety aspects of products and processes with the aim of enhancing safety. Steps can include:

a) Identifying relevant safety standards in order to make the formulation of product specifications more effective;

b) Carrying out design evaluation tests and prototype (or model) testing for safety and documenting the test results;

c) Analyzing instructions and warnings to the user, maintenance manuals and labeling and promotional material in order to minimize misinterpretation, particularly regarding intended use and known hazards;

d) Developing a means of traceability to facilitate product recall (see 11.2, 14.2 and 14.6);

e) Considering development of an emergency plan in case recall of a product becomes necessary.

This 1994 language is slightly different than the 1987 version. The word "liability" has been removed from the clause, and reference to minimizing liability has been removed from the text. In its new format, however, the issue of company responsibility for product safety has been amplified.

If anything, the emphasis on product safety heightens the requirement for product safety and thus highlights the issue of liability exposure when safety has been ignored. The failure to respond to these issues increases a company's liability exposure.

A plaintiff's attorney would argue that, although Clause 19 is guidance language, the steps set forth in it should be followed long before a company seeks to register under any other standard in the series. This type of analysis is basic to ensuring the safety of a company's products.

A plaintiff's attorney would use this clause to cross examine in-house engineers and quality people on precisely what the company did to comply with this clause. Attempting to defend noncompliance by arguing that ISO 9004-1 is advisory and nonbinding might suit the drafters of the standard but probably will not play well with the court.

Clause 19 and ISO 9004-1 in general seem to codify product liability prevention and describe the procedures necessary to create safe products. To the extent the court believes that this is nothing more than a codification of what a reasonable company would do, noncompliance could be disastrous.

The prevention theme is echoed in other parts of ISO 9004-1 as well. For example, Subclause 5.2.5: *Operational Procedures* of ISO 9004-1 provides in part that:

The quality system should emphasize preventive actions that avoid occurrence of problems, while maintaining the ability to respond to and correct failures should they occur.

Editor's Note: *As detailed in Chapter 3 of this handbook, the 1994 versions of ISO 9001, ISO 9002 and ISO 9003 place more explicit emphasis on preventing nonconformity in products and services than did the 1987 version of the standard.*

ISO 9004-1: Answering the Tough Questions

The guidance language in ISO 9004-1 raises several other questions that companies would do well to address when preparing to register to ISO 9001, ISO 9002 or ISO 9003:

- What will the company be able to tell the court in terms of its quality manual (Subclause 5.3.2.1), its quality plan (Subclause 5.3.3), and its quality records (Subclause 5.3.4)? The impact of not having these documents fully in place prior to registering to another part of the standard may be devastating.

- What can the company tell the court about the customer feedback system established in compliance with Clause 7.3? Much of this information should be part of an information-gathering network set up to monitor post-sale issues. This, too, is part of a well-designed prevention program.

- What will the company be able to tell the court regarding its designers' obligation to give consideration to the requirements relating to safety, environmental and other regulations, including items in the organization's quality policy which may go beyond existing statutory requirements?" (Subclause 8.2.4.)

- Can the company document its design function? Has it done a hazard analysis as part of a design process? Did it do prototype testing specifically focusing on the safety and environmental concerns?

- Precisely what does it mean to give due consideration to "safety" and "environmental and other regulations?" Does this mean a company must also consider EU product liability-related directives such as the Directive on Product Safety, the Machinery Safety Directive or the proposed Civil Liability Directive for damage caused by environmental waste?

- Further, will the company be able to demonstrate that due consideration for safety is equal among all of its plants? For example, a US court could site "state of the art" and "due diligence" if a company was manufacturing to higher safety standards under EU law than it was in the United States.

- What has the company done to consider "fitness for purpose" and "safeguards against misuse," as required in Subclause 8.2.5?

- In that same clause, what has the company done to analyze the "dependability and serviceability (of the product) through a reasonable life expectancy, including benign failure and safe disposability, as appropriate?"

- What can the company tell the court about the testing that it did under Clause 8.4 to evaluate the performance, durability, safety, reliability and maintainability under expected storage and operation conditions?

- How could a company possibly register to ISO 9001 without first having complied with the provisions of Clause 8.4? Will the company be able to show the court that it performed the design reviews, design verifications and validations provided for in Clauses 8.4, 8.5 and 8.6? How did these requirements relate to ISO 9001?

- Clause 8.7 provides for a market readiness review. The review includes the availability and adequacy of installation, operation, maintenance and repair manuals. Can the company document its efforts to review the manuals for its product as part of a market readiness review?

- How can a company become registered to ISO 9002 without first having implemented the provisions of Clause 10.0 of ISO 9004-1 dealing with quality of processes?

A company that decides to pay attention to the guidance language in ISO 9004-1 will face quite a task. It contains provisions that may greatly expand liability as well as provisions that seem to conflict with current liability. For example, *Clause 0.4, Benefits, costs and risks*, seems to conflict with certain parts of the EU Product Liability Directive (to be described below). It states, in part:

> *Benefit, cost and risk considerations have great importance for both the organization and customer (0.4)...Consideration has to be given to risks related to deficient products...(0.4 c)). Consideration has to be given to increased profitability and market share (0.4 a)).*

This language suggests some type of risk-benefit analysis. The EU Product Liability directive has specifically rejected a risk-benefit analysis in considering whether a product is defective and supports instead a consumer expectation test.

This raises significant issues as to whether what a company does under ISO 9004-1 will translate into an adequate defense under the EU Product Liability Directive. Apparently, a company that complies with ISO 9004-1 might nonetheless find itself in trouble with the consumer expectation test under the EU Product Liability Directive.

REGISTRATION AND ITS LIMITATIONS

Quality assurance registration can confer significant benefits, whether as a regulatory, contractual or market requirement. Registration to ISO 9001, 9002 or 9003, however, is not a legal shield; it will not prevent lawsuits. Companies should consider the following issues concerning the legal character of ISO 9000 registration.

Documentation as a Paper Trail

ISO 9000 registration can be a double-edged sword. On the one hand, an ISO 9000 registered company has a well-documented quality assurance program to help it defend itself in the event of a lawsuit. But this same documentation can expose it to attack. Evidence of a failure to comply with its documented quality assurance procedures may expose the company to liability. From a quality standpoint, documentation is helpful in achieving consistency. But if documents are not properly drafted, they could become potential smoking guns that will come back to harm companies.

All Registrars Are Not Equal

All registrars are not equal; their costs and quality can vary widely, and cost is no guarantee of quality. A neophyte auditing team can breeze through a complex operation, overlook problems, and register a company that otherwise would not comply with the standard.

A manufacturer who was led to believe that its registration was complete—only to be challenged or sued—can in turn sue the registrar and other appropriate parties to recover damages.

A quality system is only as good as its construction, and an audit only as competent as the auditors. Since these activities do not occur in a vacuum, parties who are financially injured will seek recompense for incompetence and/or sue quality assurance professionals for malpractice.

The Potential Liability of Consultants and Registrars

If a consulting firm, registrar or notified body fails to inform a client fully about potential liability and safety issues, can it be sued for negligence or faulty performance?

Since there is no law exempting private firms from liability exposure in the United States and the European Union, this issue may be raised by unhappy clients. Courts will decide each claim on its merits. Misleading a client can occur in different ways, including implying that registration means more than it does, or by failing to suggest that registration is a limited entitlement and that legal counsel should be sought to deal with questions of liability and safety.

An indication of the European Community's viewpoint on this issue can be found in the adopted and proposed new-approach EU directives that apply to medical devices (Active Implantable Medical Devices Directive, Medical Devices Directive and In-Vitro Diagnostics Directive).

The language in these directives stipulates that notified bodies must take out liability insurance unless liability is assumed by the state in accordance with national law, or the member state itself is responsible for controls. No less measure of responsibility can be expected from registrars and consultants whose work precedes the notified bodies.

ISO 9000 Is Not a Complete Defense to a Claim

Simply achieving ISO 9000 registration for a facility is not a complete defense to any product liability claim. Nor is it a defense to claims that a program was improperly certified, or that certain procedures that should have been employed as part of the quality process were not employed.

In a strict liability case, the question is whether the **product itself** is defective. The focus is on the product, not on the nature of the quality assurance system. For example, if a company is registered to ISO 9001 in the European Union and a customer sues because a defective product causes injury, ISO 9000 registration will not preclude the lawsuit. The question will be: "Is the product defective?"

The legal benefits of quality assurance registration do not cover the issues of product liability, product safety and services liability. These issues are the subject of specific directives with separate legal requirements that will be used to judge whether a product is unsafe or defective.

How to Limit Exposure

Companies can limit their exposure to litigation by avoiding certain language in documentation that may directly or indirectly imply wrongdoing. Words that should be avoided include: "defect" or "defective," "negligent," "unsafe," "unreasonably dangerous," "hazardous," "reckless," and "misrepresentation."

Often the most damning evidence in a product liability case comes from written criticisms of a product by design engineers or sales representatives. Even the most common work procedures may be worded in such a way that a jury could form a negative impression.

For example, documentation might state that a particular procedure is being imposed to avoid the possibility of a defective product finding its way into the market place. Use of the word "defective" has a negative connotation. The word "nonconforming" has a more positive connotation. These are subtle things that make a big difference when a company finds itself in the courtroom.

Companies also run a risk if they try to downplay the consequences of not following a particular procedure. Being candid and open is not inconsistent with being careful with the words a company uses to describe its processes and products.

The focus should be on prevention. If you're going to demonstrate to someone that you're concerned about safety, then you need to figure out what it takes to make safe products. In this regard, collective judgment is more easily defended than individual judgment.

In the case of committees, however, its members must truly have input into the decision-making process to be of use in litigation. In the case of a safety committee, for example, who's on the committee? Did they report to management? Was there a key management representative on the committee? A company should consider all of these issues when trying to limit exposure.

For a legal defense, a company should have ready the appropriate documentation that would allow the use of one of the legal defenses available under the Product Liability Directive (see below). Absence of this documentation could mean an automatic loss in the suit.

EU LIABILITY AND SAFETY DIRECTIVES

This section briefly discusses the EU Product Liability Directive, Product Safety Directive, Machinery Safety Directive, and the proposed Services Liability Directive.

ISO 9000 REGISTRATION AND COMPLIANCE WITH US LAWS AND EU DIRECTIVES

What does ISO registration mean for complying with US laws or with EU directives? This issue deserves careful study. In the case of US agencies, such as the DOD or the FDA, each agency provides quality assurance criteria with which companies must comply. A company's quality assurance program must be tailored to meet the agency requirements.

An approved quality assurance program that follows an agency's guidelines will not save a company from being sued for product liability and product safety. An agency such as the FDA, for example, monitors self-certification by companies seeking FDA approval. Self-certification is an imperfect process. An inadequate response that escapes the scrutiny of the FDA monitoring process can still lead to liability suits.

Similarly, ISO 9000 registration does not guarantee a perfect quality assurance program and does not offer absolute protection from a liability suit. Liability would exist and the question for a consumer that is suing would be whether to include the consultants and registrar along with the corporation in the lawsuit.

In the case of EU-harmonized, new-approach directives, close study will be required of the specific directive(s) and standards drafted by CEN, CENELEC or ETSI (e.g., toy safety, active implantable medical devices, simple pressure vessels, etc.). This will reveal whether ISO 9000 is required or optional, and, if optional, it will reveal the range of options described by the conformity assessment procedures.

For example, in the case of the Toy Safety Directive it will be necessary to study *Annex II: Essential safety requirements for toys,* and *Annex IV: Warnings and indications of precautions to be taken when using toys.* In addition, Articles 3, 5, 8, 10 and 11 describe necessary steps for compliance and certification necessary to affix the CE mark. It also will be necessary to study standards EN 71 and HD 271 H1. Finally, since the Toy Safety directive provides for options, it will be necessary to study the appropriate conformity-assessment procedures.

As mentioned earlier, it may be necessary to meet more than one EU directive. In such an instance, ISO 9001 full-quality-assurance certification may be the preferred and perhaps only way to satisfy the directives, and obtain approval from the appropriate EU-notified bodies.

Product Liability Directive

The European Union entered a new era when it adopted the Product Liability directive on July 24, 1985. Prior to this directive, EU product liability protection did not exist, and European consumers were protected under only a few national laws. Generally, if a consumer was injured by a defective product, the old Latin principle of *caveat emptor* ("let the buyer beware") prevailed.

The Product Liability directive changes this situation radically. If a consumer is injured and can prove that a defective product caused the injury, then the manufacturer responsible for putting the product on the market is strictly liable—regardless of fault.

The Product Liability directive defines what is meant by a defective product and identifies the acceptable legal defenses a manufacturer could use to defend against a legal action. The fact that a CE mark exists, conformity assessment to an EU directive applicable to the product has been achieved, and that a quality system is ISO 9000 registered is irrelevant. The Product Liability directive provides the legal authorization, logic and statutory language that will be used by an EU court to determine whether a product is defective.

The Product Liability directive also provides the legal defenses a manufacturer will have to use to reject a consumer's claim that a product is defective. In short, it is the Product Liability directive that a manufacturer should study in conjunction with the applicable technical directive (e.g., toy safety, medical devices, construction products, etc.) to understand the nature of the manufacturer's product liability exposure.

The success of any possible lawsuit will depend on a company's ability to defend its actions under the Product Liability directive. The European Union will not allow jury trials or contingency fees. It will control damages for pain and suffering and has set upper limits for recovery. The upper limits are generous, however, and strict liability may be easier to prove. Further, the issue of contingency fees to allow for greater access to the courts is under review.

Under the EU system, it is not necessary to prove that a product is both defective and unreasonably defective, leading some experts to suggest that proving a defect is easier under EU product liability law than under US product liability law.[1]

Product Safety Directive

The European Union adopted the Product Safety directive on June 29, 1992. The European Union considers product safety a key requirement for creating the single internal market. The directive lays out basic principles of product safety and is meant to complement the Product Liability directive.

According to Article 3 of the directive, "producers shall be obliged to place only safe products on the market." The positive obligations that this entails are listed in Article 3. The Product Safety directive provides the following information:

- Defines what is meant by a safe product
- Provides that products shall not present "unacceptable risks"
- Establishes product-labeling and monitoring requirements
- Requires that manufacturers develop procedures for product disposal if the product is deleterious to the environment
- Establishes a community framework for the standardization of product safety requirements and a special procedure to deal with emergencies at a community level
- Imposes a general obligation on manufacturers, distributors and importers to market only safe products

- Provides for procedures among member state or community authorities to intervene in the marketing of dangerous consumer products.

These provisions give a new dimension to product safety law.

If there are specific rules of EU law containing provisions imposing safety requirements on the products they govern, then provisions of Articles 2-4 of the product safety directive do not apply. Where specific rules govern only certain aspects of product safety or categories of risk, those provisions apply.

Thus, a manufacturer should examine the Product Safety directive in conjunction with any applicable new-approach directives and with the Product Liability directive.

An important feature of the directive is that it covers all products and provides a legal safety net to ensure that a consumer always has legal redress against the suppliers of a dangerously defective product. No new EU standards on product safety are to be introduced, except for the specific safety requirements set forth by each new-approach directive.

The Product Safety directive introduces a general ban on anything that might create an unacceptable risk to consumers. To achieve this, the directive sets out a set of rules and procedures that many companies will have to follow—from the time their goods are put on the market to the end of their foreseeable time of use. Manufacturers will be responsible for permanently monitoring their products to ensure they do not present an unacceptable risk.

The other important provision in the directive is the emergency procedure to remove unsafe products from the markets. A committee on product safety emergencies is to be established that will be composed of government representatives and European Commission officials. This body will decide whether to remove a product from the market or to temporarily suspend the marketing of the product. The withdrawal of the product will initially be for up to three months. The manufacturer concerned, however, will be given the right of redress against the removal or suspension.

COUNCIL REGULATION 339/93 ON PRODUCT SAFETY CONFORMITY

This EU regulation was approved on February 8, 1993, published in the *Official Journal* on February 17, 1993 and went into full effect on March 17, 1993.

It stipulates that a document physically must accompany all products through customs indicating compliance with EU product safety legislation. Products also must display proper safety marking and labeling in accordance with EU product safety legislation. Products that fail to meet these requirements shall be suspended by customs, and the national authority responsible for monitoring the product shall be immediately notified.

This new regulation is now being put into effect. Customs officials will conduct spot checks on all imported products. If there is a concern about the safety of a product, it will be suspended until a company can prove conformity with EU and/or national safety laws. While this regulation applies to all products, the initial list of high-risk products includes toys, food stuffs, and pharmaceutical products. (It is worth noting that the inclusion of toys as a first priority in part stems from manufacturer abuse of self-certification under the Toy Safety Directive.)

Machinery Safety Directive

In 1989, the EU Council adopted the Machinery Safety directive. The directive creates uniform design and safety requirements for machinery. It has two purposes: to promote safety and to eliminate barriers to trade that arise from the differing safety standards of the member states.

When understood in conjunction with the EU Product Liability directive, the Machinery Safety directive has significant ramifications for US companies selling machinery in the European Union. The directive requires manufacturers or their authorized EU representatives to certify that their products comply with Community safety standards in accordance with specified procedures. The precise certification procedures to be followed depend upon the type of product involved, with certain types of machines subject to more restrictive certification procedures.

In 1991, the European Union adopted amendments to the Machinery Safety directive that expanded its scope. Unless a type of machine is specifically excluded and/or covered by a specific new-approach directive (e.g., commercial refrigeration equipment), it is covered by the Machinery Safety directive.

Two classifications exist under the directive: *Annex IV Machinery,* which requires special safety steps outlined in the directive, and *Non-Annex IV,* which might allow for self-certification. Of particular interest are the warnings, cautions, instructions, maintenance instructions, etc. that are explained in *Annex I, Essential Health and Safety Requirements Relating to the Design and Construction of Machinery.*

The Machinery Safety Directive becomes mandatory on January 1, 1995. After that date, **all** machines, including those in stock, must have a CE mark to be sold in the European Union.

Proposed Services Liability Directive

Finally, the European Union has proposed a Services Liability directive. The service sector in Europe is seen as critical to the European Union's economic success. The proposed directive seeks to protect consumers of services and to resolve legal differences between member states.

The proposed directive includes the concept of strict liability as the theory of recovery against service suppliers. The commentary to the preliminary draft directive made clear that the aim is to introduce objective liability on the part of the supplier of defective services—regardless of any concept of fault.

The directive applies to any commercial transaction—whether or not payment was involved. The definition of a *supplier of services* under this directive is quite broad. Among the examples cited are engineers, electricians, mechanics, hotel-service providers and dry-cleaning establishments.

The proposed directive would be extended to damages from services provided by health clinics, doctors, quality assurance professionals, registrars and notified bodies. (New directives will be developed in the future that may remove the liability of specific service sectors from this general rule and create new specific liability rules for those sectors (e.g., medical services).

Liability and Safety Directives: Implications for Companies

The liability and safety directives described above have important implications for any company that exports to the European Union, one of which is obvious: companies exporting to the European Union must comply with the new EU directives as well as the national liability and safety laws within each EU member state. Further, conformity with product safety laws must be declared at customs, backed by full documentation if requested.

Remember that these directives apply to all products—both regulated and non-regulated. Each manufacturer of a regulated product must study the product liability and product safety laws in conjunction with the appropriate EU directive that applies to its products.

The product safety directive constitutes a significant increase in the regulation of producers, who are now exposed to obligations throughout the foreseeable lives of their products. With these new liability and safety laws, the European Union is becoming more consumer-oriented. The litigation climate can be expected to resemble more closely that of the United States.

PRODUCT LIABILITY PREVENTION

As the above discussion indicates, ISO 9000 registration and legal issues of liability and safety will require specific responses to distinct laws. The parties involved in ISO 9000 registration need to understand this clearly. A failure to address legal concerns of liability and safety—when a party knows or should have known—could be as risky as overtly leading a corporation to believe falsely that ISO registration provides liability protection.

The European Union has made clear that its principal focus in the product liability arena is on product safety and product liability prevention, not on liability *per se*. In other words, the focus is on requiring manufacturers to prevent accidents, not on creating undue liability. (An example of this focus can be seen in the Council's new regulation 339/93 on product safety conformity, discussed earlier.)

The preparation process for an ISO 9000 registration audit includes close analysis of a company's existing quality system. This is the perfect opportunity not only to document which procedures are currently being followed, but to analyze critically which procedures should be followed to prevent product liability problems. Documented preventive actions create defenses in the event of legal action.

It is possible to synchronize the technical documentation required for ISO registration with the legal documentation required to comply with the product liability, product safety, machinery safety or services liability directives. Comprehensive documentation would provide a powerful legal defense against future legal claims. In the European Union, such documentation would be invaluable and would help reduce liability exposure.

Increasingly, product liability prevention is focusing on potential post-sale obligations and the creation of post-sale safety committees. These committees analyze and synthesize relevant data received on a daily basis from warranty returns, claims, lawsuits, and salespeople to determine whether some type of post-sale action is necessary. The availability of data that was analyzed by an appropriate safety committee makes it much easier to defend against an allegation that the company failed to take some type of post-sale action.

Product liability prevention also entails document retention policies that will allow the manufacturer to defend itself in litigation and take whatever post-sale action might be necessary.

A prevention program can be a full-scale audit of the entire process—from design through servicing—or a focused project such as warning labels and instruction manuals. The most prudent approach for doing business on a global basis is to start with a full-scale product liability audit at the same time that ISO 9000 certification is achieved. Through periodic checks and periodic updates, the systems put into place following the audit can be updated.

THE FUTURE

Obtaining ISO 9000 registration is becoming critical to selling products in a global marketplace. It does not, however, in and of itself, provide a defense to product liability claims. Implementing product liability preventive procedures will reduce the likelihood of accidents and place a company in an excellent position to defend product liability claims.

ENDNOTE

[1] Sara E. Hagigh, US Department of Commerce, as referenced in *Business America* (January 1992).

EMERGING STANDARDS FOR ENVIRONMENTAL MANAGEMENT SYSTEMS

Just as the ISO 9000 series of quality management system standards have been adopted by thousands of companies worldwide, another potentially more powerful set of standards is now emerging to address the state of environmental management systems (EMS).

These environmental management system standards are being developed on several fronts by organizations such as the British Standards Institution (BSI), the European Community's Environmental Commission, the Chemical Manufacturers Association (CMA), the International Organization for Standardization (ISO), and the American National Standards Institute (ANSI).

This chapter does the following:

- Provides an overview of the forces driving the development of an international EMS standard
- Reports on the work being done by the various parties involved in developing EMS standards
- Discusses the potential results of this effort and the implications for business and industry.

What is now a chapter in this handbook may—in a year or two—become a book itself. The potential impact of an international EMS standard on global business practices is tremendous. The public, the international business community, and governments worldwide are intensely interested in establishing a balance between the health of industry and the protection of the world's ecosystems. A useful international EMS standard will go a long way towards helping establish and maintain just such a balance.

WHAT IS DRIVING THE EMS MOVEMENT?

Public concern over industry's impact on the world's environment is increasing. Politically-minded bodies such as environmental advocacy organizations, watchdog groups and the so-called "green" parties that have established footholds in most European parliaments are urging businesses to take responsibility for their impact on the environment. This pressure from the public sector has led to a rash of environmental legislation and regulation enacted worldwide.

Over the past 15 years, in response to this wave of new environmental legislation, many companies voluntarily began unilateral "environmental auditing" programs to both ensure compliance and to demonstrate good will. While some firms undertook environmental self-audits with an open mind and took corrective actions based on their own findings, others saw the effort as little more than a public relations move.

As the public began to see the differences between these approaches, challenges to the "green" claims made by businesses became more and more common. This created new markets for goods and services that are demonstrably "friendly" to the environment. However, it also became apparent that the consumer was not willing to trust industry alone to decide what is and is not friendly.

The list of reasons for adopting an environmental management system includes the following:

- Insurance companies' unwillingness to issue coverage for pollution incidents unless the firm requesting coverage has a proven environmental management system in place
- Pressure from shareholder groups
- Community goodwill
- Improved internal management methods
- Interest in attracting a high-quality work force
- Desire to profit in the market for "green" products
- "Whistle blowing"
- Legislative and regulatory requirements, including requirements that certain information relating to environmental performance be made public.

THE NEED FOR A SINGLE EMS STANDARD

Due to growing interest in the health of the global environment, the undeniable evidence of harm from past practices, and the market opportunities created by these factors, industry is feeling more pressure than ever to clean up its act and prove it. Companies now see the value of installing an EMS, but that may not be enough. The public wants proof that these systems are more than just artifice. One way to truly verify a firm's commitment to environmental issues is by adopting an international generic EMS standard and by establishing a third-party auditing system to ensure that the standard is being met. This is a logical way for the world's businesses to quell consumer fears, meet customer requirements, and take advantage of new global market opportunities all at once.

The question that remains is whether a range of unrelated—and sometimes competing—standards should be allowed to take root as they did in the quality management systems arena before ISO 9000 came along. To avoid a confusing proliferation of duplicative or redundant standards, a common internationally recognized generic EMS standard must be agreed upon.

A single generic internationally recognized EMS standard would do the following:

- Facilitate international trade and commerce
- Ensure the uniformity of the registration burden placed upon all companies required to meet the standard
- Reduce the incidence of multiple audits conducted by customers, regulators or registrars.

EMS INITIATIVES UNDER DEVELOPMENT

Assuming that all interested parties wish to avoid unnecessary proliferation of standards, a single internationally recognized standard by which any EMS could be measured is the ultimate goal. Experience in the quality arena makes it clear that the eventual EMS standard will most likely result from some combination of a handful of existing initiatives currently in various stages of development by various organizations.

Though it is impossible to predict the final form of any international EMS standard, it is safe to say it will be largely influenced by the following emerging initiatives.

BS 7750: Environmental Management Systems

Perhaps the most visible predecessor to any future internationally recognized generic EMS standard is an existing standard called *BS 7750, Environmental Management Systems*.

First published in March 1992, British Standards Institution's standard BS 7750 was designed to be compatible with the ISO 9000 series. It can be folded into existing ISO 9000 practices and applies to all industry sectors. It can be used for certification and quoted as a contract requirement, if necessary.

The basic goals of BS 7750 are to assure a company's compliance with its stated environmental policy and to require that the company demonstrate that compliance to others.

Since BS 7750 was designed as a stand-alone standard, it is not necessary for companies that wish to adopt it to have already been registered to ISO 9000. However, it is possible to extend existing ISO 9000 practices to incorporate elements from   BS 7750. The two series of standards share the following features:

- Requirements for documentation
- Supplier assessment
- System auditing.

Since both systems share these elements and others, anyone familiar with ISO 9000 should be able to understand BS 7750. However, BS 7750 does have some elements not found in ISO 9000, especially those specifically related to environmental issues.

Requirements of BS 7750

The specific requirements of an EMS as put forth by BS 7750 include the following:

- The organization must develop a full environmental plan that specifically details the objectives and targets of the EMS and the means that will be used to achieve them
- The organization must be in compliance with all applicable environmental legislation
- The organization's EMS must be able to respond quickly to the ever-changing world of environmental legislation
- The organization must compile a register of all environmental regulation and legislation that affects their business and must use it to ensure that the previous requirement is met
- A full review of the environmental impact of the organization's operations, including site assessment, must be performed
- The organization must assign environmental management responsibilities to staff employees, defining exactly who will manage the EMS
- Personal environmental targets for individual employees must be assigned
- The organization must train its employees to understand the potential problems that may arise if they stray from the defined EMS
- Proof of continuous improvement in environmental performance is required
- Specific procedures must have environmental targets that must either be met over time or be reviewed and have changes made
- Records regarding the achievement of objectives and targets, including the disposal of waste materials, must be kept
- Internal audits must be conducted
- The organization must periodically review its EMS and its compliance with the standard.

Eco Management and Audit (Eco Audit)

At about the same time BSI was developing BS 7750, the EU (formerly the European Community) Environmental Commission was developing a set of mandatory EMS regulations applicable to about 12,000 sites in the European Union that came under the Environmental Commission's "most polluting industries" designation.

These regulations, commonly referred to as the Eco Audit, made adherence to a formal environmental management system mandatory and required that organizations make annual, independently verifiable public statements regarding their environmental performance.

After protests regarding the number of companies and sites affected and the mandatory nature of the Eco Audit regulations, the Eco Audit was revised and republished in March 1992 as a voluntary scheme. Though participation is voluntary, the EC's Environmental Commission hopes market pressures will act as an inducement.

Meanwhile, the regulation does require a mandatory framework for monitoring participation in the scheme to be put in place in each EU member state by 1995. That means that within a few years, all EU member states will have a body in place dedicated to overseeing the auditing of environmental management systems.

The main requirements of the Eco Audit include the following:

- Establishment of an EMS
- A complete environmental assessment of each site
- An easy-to-understand environmental statement must be prepared from the assessment and be made available to the public
- Both the assessment and the statement must be approved by an "Eco-Verifier"
- All EU member states, through a Competent Authority, must maintain registers of approved sites and Eco-Verifiers.

The main differences between the Eco Audit scheme and BS 7750 are the Eco Audit's public statement requirement and the fact that the Eco Audit scheme will only allow manufacturing sector organizations to be registered.

E4, the Emerging US Standard

In the Fall of 1989, the American National Standards Institute (ANSI) and the American Society for Quality Control's (ASQC) Environmental Quality Division (EEQD) began an initiative to produce a US consensus standard on environmental management designed to make it easier for companies doing business with the government to comply with environmental requirements.

The proposed US standard is called *ANSI/ASQC-E4, Specifications and Guidelines for Quality Systems for Environmental Data Collection and Environmental Technology Programs* (E4). E4 harmonizes differing requirements used by various federal agencies to establish quality assurance and quality control procedures associated with environmental data operations at hazardous chemical and radioactive waste sites. E4 describes minimum quality management elements needed for programs that involve environmental data collection and evaluation, and environmental technology design, construction and operation.

The standard is organized into three parts. Part A describes general quality management elements applicable to all types of environmental programs. Part B describes quality system elements related to the collection, analysis and evaluation of environmentally-related data. Part C provides additional quality system elements that relate to design, construction and operation of environmental technology.

The US Environmental Protection Agency (EPA) plans to adopt much of the E4 standard within its government quality assurance framework for environmental programs. The US Department of Energy (DOE) is already applying the standard to contracts, and the Department of Defense (DoD) is also using the standard in contracts for its installation restoration program. In January, 1994, the proposed standard was submitted to ASQC for approval by the ASQC Standards Committee. Approval of the standard is anticipated by the end of 1994.

Responsible Care®

While standards-writing groups and governmental (or quasi-governmental) bodies work to develop comprehensive guidelines for environmental management systems, perhaps the most complete set of guidelines already in place is the product of an industry association—the US-based Chemical Manufacturers Association (CMA). The CMA's program is called Responsible Care®, and participation by individual businesses is an obligation of membership in the CMA.

Responsible Care®, which was adopted by the CMA Board of Directors in 1988, was launched as a response to public concern that the chemical industry was a potential threat to health and safety. Believing that self-imposed industry-driven guidelines would be preferable to externally imposed ones, the chemical industry's leaders began a search in the early 1980s for a program that would at once make the industry safer, address public fears, and not impinge too much on the industry's ability to turn a profit.

CMA's Responsible Care® program establishes the following goals:

- Improved chemical process
- Enhanced practices and procedures
- Reduction of every kind of waste, accident, incident and emission
- Reliable communication and dialogue
- Heightened public involvement and input.

Responsible Care® is built around six Codes of Management Practices and 10 Guiding Principles. Following the six codes will automatically result in the guiding principles being followed as well:

- Product Stewardship
- Community Awareness and Emergency Response

- Process Safety
- Employee Health and Safety
- Pollution Prevention
- Distribution.

Responsible Care's 10 Guiding Principles are as follows:

1) To recognize and respond to community concerns about chemicals and company operations
2) To develop and produce chemicals that can be manufactured, transported, used and disposed of safely
3) To make health, safety and environmental considerations a priority in planning for all existing and new products and processes
4) To report promptly to officials, employees, customers and the public, information on chemical-related health or environmental hazards and to recommend protective measures
5) To counsel customers on the safe use, transportation and disposal of chemicals
6) To operate plants and facilities in a manner that protects the environment and the health and safety of employees and the public
7) To extend knowledge by conducting or supporting research on the health, safety and environmental effects of products, processes and waste materials
8) To work with others to resolve problems created by past handling and disposal of hazardous substances
9) To participate with government and others in creating responsible laws, regulations and standards to safeguard the community, workplace and environment
10) To promote the principles and practices of Responsible Care® by sharing experiences and offering assistance to others who produce, handle, use, transport or dispose of chemicals.

One of Responsible Care's fundamental themes is that the implementation of the program will never be complete at any site. It is designed to be approached as an ongoing way of managing a chemical company's environmental impact. Four other themes are consistently stressed in each of the six codes that make up Responsible Care®:

Accountability. The program both recognizes the need for and broadens the definition of accountability. Traditionally, product accountability lasted only until the point of sale. In the Responsible Care® program, members are expected to take responsibility for their products' performance during and after its use, including its performance as a recyclable and its suitability for disposal.

Dialogue. The program helps businesses realize that the chemical industry does not function in a vacuum. It is interrelated with suppliers of raw materials, end users, regulators, lawmakers, shareholders and employees. The importance of effective communication and mutually beneficial dialogue is paramount.

Teamwork. Just as Responsible Care® puts an emphasis on working closely with those outside the chemical industry, it also stresses the need for cooperation within it.

Continuous Improvement. Responsible Care® is designed to be an ongoing commitment for those who undertake it. It is a way of doing business, not an end result.

In addition to the codes, principles and themes of Responsible Care®, the program includes several adjunct panels, processes and groups responsible for keeping Responsible Care® current and continuously improving. These include the following:

- A Public Advisory Panel designed to critique the development and implementation of the program and to provide public feedback
- Executive Leadership Groups that provide a forum where senior management can exchange information
- A mutual assistance strategy designed to identify and address the mutual assistance needs of member companies
- A self-evaluation process designed to determine how well member companies are applying the codes and to evaluate the performance of the industry as a whole.

Another important aspect of the Responsible Care® program is that it incorporates the management aspects of quality, environmental protection, and health and safety into one overall management system.

This all-in-one approach to management systems may eventually be reflected in the development of an international generic management system standard that combines the existing quality elements of the ISO 9000 series with elements from environmental and health and safety management systems.

Eco-labeling

In the late 1980s, the EU Commission announced the development of a product labeling scheme designed to give governmental approval to accurate claims that a product was manufactured, shipped and/or packaged in such a way as to reduce its negative impact on the environment. The need for such a system arose from pressure brought to bear by consumers who wanted to know which products were "environmentally friendly" but were not willing to trust the claims of manufacturers. An official Eco-label—a logo printed on the approved product's label—gives governmental backing to the manufacturer's claim.

Through the Eco-labeling scheme, each EU member state was to establish a national board to organize and administer the granting of the label to products that deserved it.

Since it was first envisioned, however, the Eco-labeling scheme has run into some problems. Methods for judging products have created disagreements within industries and between environmental groups and manufacturers. The Commission's initial goal was to have five different products bearing an Eco-label on store shelves at the time of the scheme's official launch. When that launch finally occurred in July 1993, there were no labeled products on the market.

The appearance of an Eco-label on a product was never intended to be an assurance that the manufacturer had a complete and auditable EMS in place. It is strictly a product certification scheme, designed to help consumers weed through the thousands of accurate and inaccurate environmental claims that appear on product labels. Still, Eco-labeling is an interesting attempt to reward those manufacturers really working to reduce the environmental impact of their products by giving them a competitive advantage in the marketplace. As such, it may well be incorporated—in one form or another—into a future internationally recognized EMS standard series.

THE SEARCH FOR AN INTERNATIONAL EMS STANDARD

The International Organization for Standardization's Strategic Action Group on the Environment (SAGE), which was established in 1991 to make recommendations regarding international standards for the environment, spent more than year studying BS 7750 as the possible basis for an ISO version. In 1993 SAGE recommended the formation of an ISO Technical Committee dedicated to developing a uniform international EMS standard.

That committee, ISO TC 207, met for the first time in June 1993, at which point SAGE was disbanded. At TC 207's first meeting, some 200 delegates representing about 30 countries expressed a desire to move as rapidly as possible to complete a first draft of the international standard. In March 1994, Working Group 1 of Subcommittee 1, approved a preliminary "strawman" working document that served as a starting point for discussions. TC 207 is striving to complete its work by 1996.

Canada is the Secretariat of TC 207, and six other countries head the committee's six subcommittees. The United States heads the subcommittee on environmental performance evaluation, the United Kingdom is responsible for the environmental management systems subcommittee, the Netherlands chairs the subcommittee on environmental auditing, Australia leads the subcommittee on environmental labeling, France is responsible for life-cycle analysis, and Norway heads the subcommittee on terms and definitions. In addition, Germany is the convenor for a working group addressing environmental aspects in product standards.

It is important to note that although BS 7750 was used as a starting point in the search for an international standard, it is not guaranteed to be the model for the standard that eventually emerges. The eventual standard may be a combination of many existing or developing EMS guidelines, including some or all of those mentioned above. BS 7750 is, however, the most fully realized attempt yet to bring the features that have well-served the ISO 9000 series to EMS standards-writing.

The key features of ISO's developing EMS standard include the following:

● Guidelines for performance indicators
● Appraisal of relative environmental performance
● Objectivity, measurability, repeatability and user-friendliness

- Performance orientation—not specification orientation.

Since other areas of business management are being targeted for new standards (health and safety standards are reportedly next on ISO's agenda), it is fair to talk in terms of harmonizing all of the eventual international standards in such a way that they share similar structures, wording and philosophy. If business is to end up with a quality standard (ISO 9000), an environmental standard, a health and safety standard and perhaps others, then it is extremely important that they can harmonize as a single program for those companies wishing to become certified to all of them. Achieving this kind of harmony is never easy in the field of standards-writing, and it may be many years before such a system is in place.

Until then, organizations wishing to develop their own EMS should take a good look at the models currently available. The chemical industry's Responsible Care® program, for example, already integrates quality, environmental and health and safety management issues and is highly regarded by standards writers and industry players alike.

Pilot programs for both the BS 7750 and Eco-Audit schemes were conducted in 1993. The results showed that just as with ISO 9000 registration, registration to an EMS standard is a time-consuming, documentation-heavy process. Both programs seem workable, however, and with modifications, both should improve with time as revisions to the standards are written.

The single most important finding of the pilot programs seems to be that most of the participating organizations think that BS 7750, Eco Audit and the Responsible Care® program are all compatible. This is strong evidence that a single international EMS standard is a realistic goal.

The next step may be to integrate the quality, environmental, and health and safety components into one unified series of management standards. This process may take years. It is now—during this formative stage—that standards-writers, industry players, government representatives and environmental activists should make their concerns known to ISO, ANSI or others involved in the development of an international EMS standard. Only with the carefully considered input of all parties can a standard emerge that is both workable and valuable.

COMPARING ISO 9000 QUALITY REQUIREMENTS, MALCOLM BALDRIGE NATIONAL QUALITY AWARD GUIDELINES AND DEMING/ SPC-BASED TQM PRACTICE

BY JOEL S. FINLAY

This chapter compares ISO 9000 to the Malcolm Baldrige National Quality Award guidelines and to TQM. It provides an overview of the three quality initiatives, compares each to the other two, and compares their various elements, including the following:

- Documentation and control
- Required degree of prescriptiveness
- Theory/application.

INTRODUCTION

The intent of the ISO 9000 series requirements is simple. The standards require that a basic quality system be implemented to ensure customers that suppliers have the capabilities and systems to provide quality products and/or services.

A major goal of the Malcolm Baldrige National Quality Award (MBNQA) is to increase US competitiveness worldwide. This is consistent with W. Edwards Deming's concerns about the competitive global marketplace. In his 1986 book, *Out of the Crisis*, Deming warned that the western world needs a "transformation of the American style of management" and not merely a "reconstruction" or "revision." He further pointed out that this new way "requires a whole new structure, from foundation upward."

Comparing ISO 9000 requirements, the MBNQA guidelines, and Deming-based Total Quality Management (TQM) practices is a difficult task. To use a simple analogy, the ISO 9000 standards are like three starched, white business shirts—small, medium, and large—form-fitting but not expected to cover the whole body. MBNQA is like a giant, one-size-fits-all T-shirt with 28 pockets in which specific articles are to be placed. Deming-based TQM is like a whole wardrobe from which the user is expected to select a set of clothing to fit his or her organization.

OVERVIEW OF THE THREE SYSTEMS

ISO 9000

ISO 9000 series requirements are clearly defined, but how the requirements are to be met is left largely to the organization. Clear documentation of all work processes affecting quality is required, but that documentation can be written as work instructions—provided and documented as basic training for employees—or even displayed as a process flow chart in a work area.

The ISO 9000 series concentrates almost exclusively on results criteria, although process criteria may meet some ISO 9000 series requirements. Registering to the ISO 9000 series probably requires the least change in organizational involvement. A traditional, mass-inspection-oriented organization may be readily registered.

MBNQA

The Malcolm Baldrige National Quality Award guidelines are clearly defined and the methods for meeting the guidelines are fairly well-defined. MBNQA guidelines are documentation-dependent. An organization committed to basing its quality initiative upon the MBNQA guidelines must expect a high level of documentation in many areas.

MBNQA guidelines are somewhat more results-oriented than process-oriented, but the organization is required to follow both results and process criteria. MBNQA requires specific organizational involvement and change.

Deming-Based TQM

Deming-based TQM is much more open than MBNQA or ISO 9000. It has no firm requirements other than to meet and/or exceed customer needs through an understanding of the organization and the effects of current management practices and by the use of applied statistics. It expects the senior managers of an organization to consider management style through a scientific examination of Deming's 14 points, and then prove or disprove those points as they apply to the organization.

Deming expects senior managers to establish a controlled, customer-focused, continuously improving organization. That kind of organization has requirements, but practical application must define these requirements in a Deming-based TQM system. That is, form should follow function. Documentation showing how processes are to be accomplished is necessary. It is up to an organization to document processes to communicate effectively with those who need to know or might benefit from knowing. Deming-based TQM involves the most organizational involvement and organizational change of the three systems.

ISO 9000 COMPARED TO MBNQA

MBNQA is a larger overall system than the ISO 9000 series. Several MBNQA requirements are either not covered or receive only a cursory mention in the ISO 9000 series. Spreading knowledge about quality to other organizations is not an ISO 9000 series requirement, but it is a clear requirement of the MBNQA. The ISO 9000 series has no requirement for quality leadership benchmarking. It makes little provision for employee recognition and performance, employee morale, quality-results benchmarking, customer-relationship management, and customer-satisfaction benchmarking.

While the ISO 9000 series is the smaller system, there are several requirements of ISO 9000 that are given only limited attention in MBNQA guidelines. Document control is at the heart of the ISO 9000 series, but one of a number of MBNQA requirements. Product identification and traceability is a much larger part of ISO 9000 series requirements than it is in the MBNQA guidelines.

For the most part, however, the two systems cover much of the same material, although sometimes in different ways. Table 14-1 identifies the extent to which ISO 9000 series requirements align with MBNQA guidelines.

Most of the line items in Table 14-1 for each system are aligned in multiple fashion, indicated by the large number of "highly aligned" symbols. An even larger number of "somewhat

Table 14-1: Extent to Which ISO 9000 Requirements Align with MBNQA Guidelines

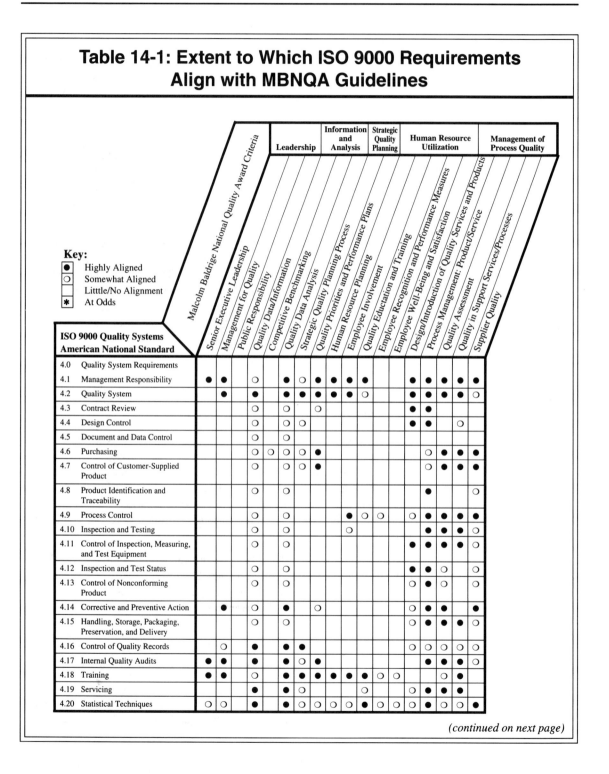

Key:
- ● Highly Aligned
- ○ Somewhat Aligned
- ☐ Litttle/No Alignment
- ✱ At Odds

Columns grouped under **Malcolm Baldrige National Quality Award Criteria**:

ISO 9000 Quality Systems American National Standard	Leadership			Information and Analysis			Strategic Quality Planning		Human Resource Utilization					Management of Process Quality				
	Senior Executive Leadership	Management for Quality	Public Responsibility	Quality Data/Information	Competitive Benchmarking	Quality Data Analysis	Strategic Quality Planning Process	Quality Priorities and Performance Plans	Human Resource Planning	Employee Involvement	Quality Education and Training	Employee Recognition and Performance Measures	Employee Well-Being and Satisfaction	Design/Introduction of Quality Services and Products	Process Management: Product/Service	Quality Assessment	Quality in Support Services/Processes	Supplier Quality
4.0 Quality System Requirements																		
4.1 Management Responsibility	●	●	○	●	○	●	●	●	●					●	●	●	●	●
4.2 Quality System		●	●	●	●	●	●	●	○					●	●	●	●	○
4.3 Contract Review			○	○			○							●	●			
4.4 Design Control			○	○	○									●	●	○		
4.5 Document and Data Control			○	○														
4.6 Purchasing			○	○	○	○	●							○	●	●	●	
4.7 Control of Customer-Supplied Product			○	○	○	●								○	●	●	●	
4.8 Product Identification and Traceability			○	○										●			○	
4.9 Process Control			○	○					●	○	○			○	●	●	●	●
4.10 Inspection and Testing			○	○		○								●	●	●	○	
4.11 Control of Inspection, Measuring, and Test Equipment			○	○										●	●	●	●	○
4.12 Inspection and Test Status			○	○										●	●	○	○	
4.13 Control of Nonconforming Product			○	○										○	●	○		○
4.14 Corrective and Preventive Action		●	○	●		○								○	●	●		●
4.15 Handling, Storage, Packaging, Preservation, and Delivery			○	○										○	●	●	●	○
4.16 Control of Quality Records		○	●	●	●									○	○	○	○	○
4.17 Internal Quality Audits	●	●	●	●	○	●								●	●	●	○	
4.18 Training	●	●	○	●	●	●	●	●	●	○	○				○	●		
4.19 Servicing		●		●	○			○						○	●	●	●	
4.20 Statistical Techniques	○	○	●	●	○	○	○	○	○	●	○	○		○	●	○	○	●

(continued on next page)

(continued from previous page)

Table 14-1: Extent to Which ISO 9000 Requirements Align with MBNQA Guidelines

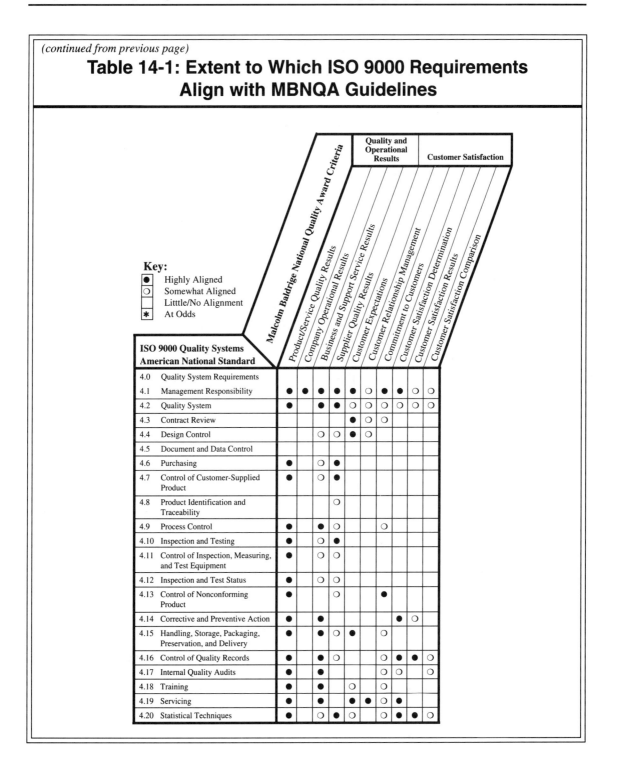

Key:
- ● Highly Aligned
- ○ Somewhat Aligned
- ☐ Litttle/No Alignment
- ✻ At Odds

Column headings (Malcolm Baldrige National Quality Award Criteria):

Quality and Operational Results: Product/Service Quality Results · Company Operational Results · Business and Support Service Results · Supplier Quality Results · Customer Quality Results

Customer Satisfaction: Customer Expectations · Customer Relationship Management · Commitment to Customers · Customer Satisfaction Determination · Customer Satisfaction Results · Customer Satisfaction Comparison

ISO 9000 Quality Systems American National Standard	Product/Service Quality Results	Company Operational Results	Business and Support Service Results	Supplier Quality Results	Customer Quality Results	Customer Expectations	Customer Relationship Management	Commitment to Customers	Customer Satisfaction Determination	Customer Satisfaction Results	Customer Satisfaction Comparison
4.0 Quality System Requirements											
4.1 Management Responsibility	●	●	●	●	●	○	●	●	○	○	
4.2 Quality System	●		●	●	○	○	○	○	○	○	
4.3 Contract Review					●	○	○				
4.4 Design Control		○	○		●	○					
4.5 Document and Data Control											
4.6 Purchasing	●		○	●							
4.7 Control of Customer-Supplied Product	●		○	●							
4.8 Product Identification and Traceability			○								
4.9 Process Control	●		●	○			○				
4.10 Inspection and Testing	●		○	●							
4.11 Control of Inspection, Measuring, and Test Equipment	●		○	○							
4.12 Inspection and Test Status	●		○	○							
4.13 Control of Nonconforming Product	●			○				●			
4.14 Corrective and Preventive Action	●	●						●	○		
4.15 Handling, Storage, Packaging, Preservation, and Delivery	●	●	○	●			○				
4.16 Control of Quality Records	●	●	○				○	●	●	○	
4.17 Internal Quality Audits	●	●					○	○		○	
4.18 Training	●	●		○			○				
4.19 Servicing	●	●			●	●	○	●			
4.20 Statistical Techniques	●	○	●	○			○	●	●	○	

aligned" symbols exist, further indicating the multiple alignment of line items in the two systems. No "at odds, potentially" symbols occur on Table 14-1, suggesting harmony between them.

ISO 9000 COMPARED TO DEMING-BASED TQM

The ISO 9000 series has clear requirements that may or may not be particularly significant in Deming-based TQM. ISO 9000 series requirements dictate that contract review be addressed in very specific terms, while a Deming-based TQM system leaves the details entirely up to the organization. Design control, document control, and product identification and traceability are aligned with, but not required, in Deming-based TQM. Requirements in those areas are derived from specific customer needs rather than by fiat.

The ISO 9000 series has several highly specific concerns about inspection and testing that could be at odds with Deming-based TQM. Deming emphasizes that an organization should "cease dependence on inspection to achieve quality." Deming says that companies should "eliminate the need for inspection on a mass basis by building quality into the product in the first place." ISO 9000 provides for cases in which in-process control makes later inspection unnecessary, but also recognizes circumstances where inspection is needed.

The ISO 9000 series and Deming are in agreement that when inspection and testing are required, those doing the work should be trained and provided with appropriate equipment to perform the inspection or testing.

Deming urges companies to: drive out fear, eliminate slogans and exhortations, eliminate management-by-objective, remove barriers that rob people of pride in workmanship, and institute education. These points are not addressed in the ISO 9000 series.

ISO 9000 does not emphasize statistical techniques. If statistical process control methods are used, the ISO standard requires that procedures for SPC tools be documented and implemented as documented with appropriate training provided. The basis of Deming-based TQM is statistical understanding, and the ISO 9000 series supports statistical process control but does not require SPC use. Table 14-2 provides a graphic identification of the alignment of ISO 9000 with Deming-based TQM.

DEMING-BASED TQM COMPARED TO MBNQA

Deming-based TQM and MBNQA differ greatly in their approaches to benchmarking. Deming recommends that companies spend "time and effort focusing on what customers want and need, not what competitors are doing." Deming says that if you treat your customers right, and continuously improve in what you provide to them, your competitors will be watching you, and you will always be ahead of those competitors, because you will be continuously improving while they are trying to catch up to you.

Table 14-2: Extent to Which ISO 9000 Requirements Align with Deming Principles

Key:
- ● Highly Aligned
- ○ Somewhat Aligned
- ☐ Litttle/No Alignment
- ✱ At Odds

To the extent that the inspection is necessary, the Deming philosophy supports SO 4.10, 4.11, 4.12, and 4.13. The Deming philosophy stresses movement towards process control, eliminating the need for mass inspection.

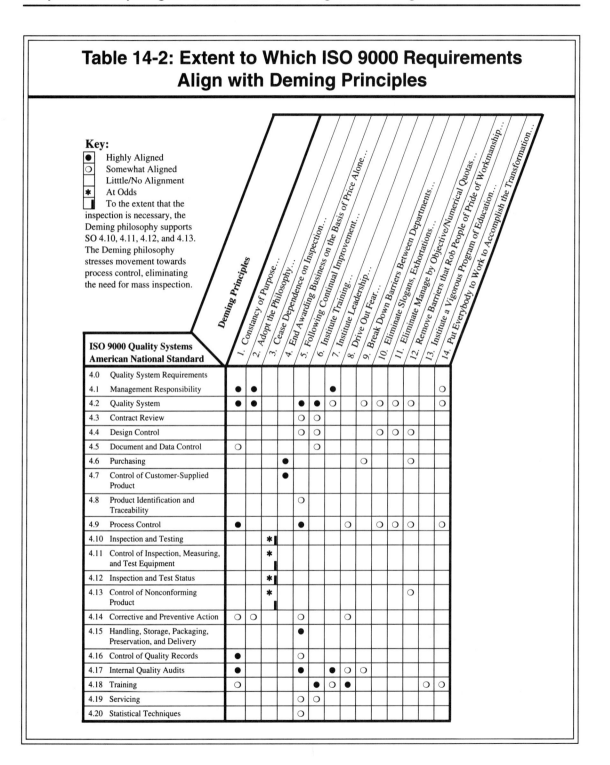

Deming Principles:
1. Constancy of Purpose...
2. Adopt the Philosophy...
3. Cease Dependence on Inspection...
4. End Awarding Business on the Basis of Price Alone...
5. Following Continual Improvement...
6. Institute Training...
7. Institute Leadership...
8. Drive Out Fear...
9. Break Down Barriers Between Departments...
10. Eliminate Slogans, Exhortations...
11. Eliminate Manage by Objective/Numerical Quotas...
12. Remove Barriers that Rob People of Pride of Workmanship...
13. Institute a Vigorous Program of Education...
14. Put Everybody to Work to Accomplish the Transformation...

ISO 9000 Quality Systems American National Standard

ISO 9000 Requirement	1	2	3	4	5	6	7	8	9	10	11	12	13	14
4.0 Quality System Requirements														
4.1 Management Responsibility	●	●			●									○
4.2 Quality System	●	●			●	●	○		○	○	○	○		○
4.3 Contract Review					○	○								
4.4 Design Control					○	○				○	○	○		
4.5 Document and Data Control	○					○								
4.6 Purchasing				●					○			○		
4.7 Control of Customer-Supplied Product				●										
4.8 Product Identification and Traceability						○								
4.9 Process Control	●				●			○		○	○	○		○
4.10 Inspection and Testing			✱											
4.11 Control of Inspection, Measuring, and Test Equipment			✱											
4.12 Inspection and Test Status			✱											
4.13 Control of Nonconforming Product			✱									○		
4.14 Corrective and Preventive Action	○	○			○			○						
4.15 Handling, Storage, Packaging, Preservation, and Delivery					●									
4.16 Control of Quality Records	●				○									
4.17 Internal Quality Audits	●				●		●	○	○					
4.18 Training	○					●	○	●					○	○
4.19 Servicing					○	○								
4.20 Statistical Techniques					○									

Deming favors comparison of quality results and comparison of support-system quality results, but recommends that this comparison be made against the organization's previous record, not as a benchmarking device against competitors' results.

Deming is less concerned about measuring customer satisfaction and more concerned about developing a focused, continually improving relationship with customers and suppliers. While Deming supports organizational leaders helping improve public quality awareness, it is not a requirement as expressed by MBNQA.

THREE-WAY COMPARISON OF DOCUMENTATION AND CONTROL

The requirements for documentation are high for both MBNQA and ISO 9000. MBNQA includes elements such as benchmarking to other organizations (not required by ISO 9000) while ISO 9000 identifies specifics such as equipment calibration, only incidentally referred to in MBNQA.

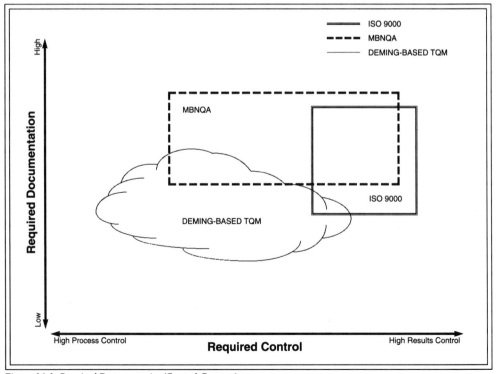

Figure 14-1: Required Documentation/Control Comparison.

Both ISO 9000 and MBNQA have high requirements for results measurement; MBNQA requires evidence of high quality, but ISO 9000 does not. The MBNQA requires measured process control; ISO requires documentation of process control where it exists, but does not necessarily require measured control. Perhaps MBNQA does not require process control to the extent encouraged in a Deming-based TQM system. These comparisons are shown in Figure 14-1.

THREE-WAY COMPARISON OF THE REQUIRED DEGREE OF PRESCRIPTIVENESS

The degree of prescriptiveness inherent in the three approaches to quality is defined by what work is to be done and how that work is done. MBNQA guidelines spell out what must be done to attain a high score. It also spells out how each area should be approached.

The ISO 9000 series requirements define what work should be done, but avoid offering much guidance on how the system should be set up and or how it should operate. Deming-based TQM offers little guidance on either the nature of the work or how to set up a system. These comparisons are shown graphically in Figure 14-2.

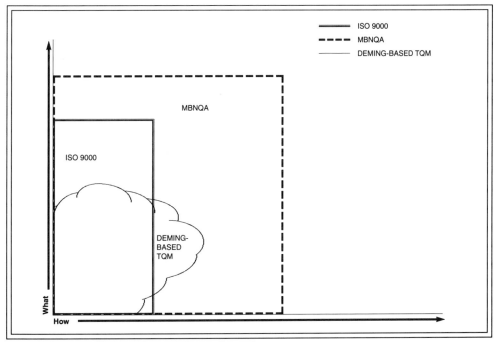

Figure 14-2: Required Degree of Prescriptiveness Comparison.

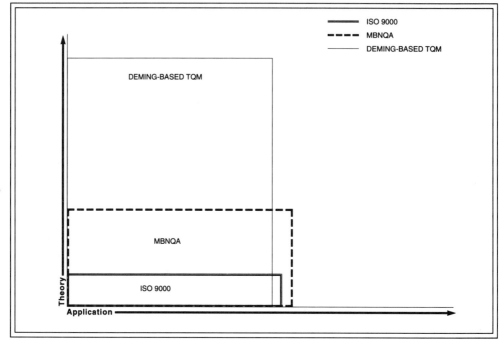

Figure 14-3: Theory/Application Comparison.

THREE-WAY COMPARISON OF THEORY/APPLICATION

Deming-based TQM emphasizes theory and practice to a greater degree than either MBNQA or the ISO 9000 series.

ISO 9000 is a quality system based largely on traditional quality control theory, identifying elements such as design control, supplier control, process discipline, inspection, close management and training to achieve quality results for the customer.

MBNQA guidelines are a mixture of traditional theories—plus the theory developed by Crosby, Deming, Feigenbaum, Juran and others. MBNQA guidelines emphasize application of various pieces from the theories behind the approach. Figure 14-3 illustrates this graphically.

SUMMARY

ISO 9000 series registration and instituting TQM principles are two effective beginnings for a quality journey.

A Deming-based TQM initiative requires the substantial commitment of personal time and resources of senior managers in transforming the organization. Quality cannot be just another aspect of the business—it must become the way business is conducted.

While ISO 9000 series registration does require support and involvement by senior management, it is not nearly so demanding as a Deming-based TQM transformation initiative.

A Deming-based TQM organization creates a learning organization. This learning tenet of TQM makes selecting a Deming-based approach to TQM even more persuasive. Deming provides depth of theory as well as application. Deming points out, "There is no learning without theory." He goes on to say:

> *All theory is wrong. Some is useful. Of course all theory is wrong! If it were right, it wouldn't be theory, now would it? It would be fact. But without theory, we cannot learn. Experience alone teaches nothing. If we have a theory, then experience can help us to learn.*

After an organization has become effective through TQM transformation and has become a learning organization, the use of MBNQA quality criteria—even if you don't actually apply for the award—can be an excellent means to improve an already effective organization. An organization that applies for the Baldrige Award is likely to put more pressure on itself than one using criteria internally.

It is a good idea for a company to spend a year working internally with the MBNQA criteria. The MBNQA criteria are self-descriptive. Even if it is difficult to measure the number of points achieved when self-scoring, the practice is worthwhile. Winning the Baldrige award should not be a company's goal. The intent should be to improve.

No matter what route a company takes on its quality journey, the most important step is the first. In the words of Bob Killeen, retired UAW official, "I call TQM training 'retirement parties' because the fact that your company is doing TQM means it will be in business when you're ready to retire."

REFERENCES

ANSI/ASQC Q90-1987: Quality Management and Quality Assurance Standards—Guidelines for Selection and Use, American Society for Quality Control, Milwaukee, WI (1987).

ANSI/ASQC Q91-1987: Quality Systems—Model for Quality Assurance in Design/Development, Production, Installation, and Servicing. Milwaukee, WI: American Society for Quality Control (1987).

W. E. Deming, *Out of the Crisis* (Cambridge: Massachusetts Institute of Technology Center for Advanced Engineering Study, 1986).

W. E. Deming, author's notes from attending the *Quality, Productivity, and Competitive Position* seminar, Houston, TX (October 1990).

W. E. Deming, Author's notes from attending the *Quality, Productivity, and Competitive Position* seminar, Nashville, TN (October 1991).

R. Killeen, Author's notes from attending *Understanding the Total Quality Movement*, sponsored by the Hubert H. Humphrey Institute of Public Affairs, Minneapolis, MN (April 1992).

1994 Application Guidelines, Malcolm Baldrige National Quality Award, National Institute of Standards and Technology, Gaithersburg, MD.

EUROPEAN UNION
CONFORMITY ASSESSMENT

BY JAMES KOLKA

This chapter provides the reader with a broad overview of conformity
assessment by addressing the following topics:

- An explanation of conformity assessment
- The European Union's single internal market
- Conformity assessment's four major components
- EU-wide directives
- Harmonized standards
- Consistent conformity assessment procedures
- Competent certification and testing bodies
- The European Union and other countries.

INTRODUCTION

This handbook has focused on the ISO 9000 series international standard and on the process of implementing the standard in companies that seek ISO 9000 registration. ISO 9000 is a global phenomenon, and companies around the world are registering to one of the ISO 9000 standards. For many companies the European Union's (formerly the European Community) single internal market (EC 92) has been a key impetus for ISO 9000 registration. Although ISO 9000 registration is required only for some regulated products, the European Union is stressing ISO 9000 registration as an integral part of its overall goals. One of the European Union's overall objectives is to develop a complex and comprehensive regulatory and product certification framework that may become a model for other regional groups of nations.

This chapter takes a closer look at the system of standards and product certification in Europe. It discusses the goals of the European Union and describes its conformity assessment procedures in detail. For US companies seeking to do business in the European Union, it is important to keep up-to-date with the EU's efforts to establish Community-wide directives, standards and certification procedures.

WHAT IS CONFORMITY ASSESSMENT?

Conformity assessment includes all activities that are intended to assure the conformity of products to a set of requirements. These activities can include the following:

- Approving product designs
- Testing manufactured products
- Registering a company's quality system
- Accrediting organizations that perform testing and assessment procedures.

In general, conformity assessment includes all market access processes for a product or service that must be followed to bring that product or service to a market.

Governments use conformity assessment procedures to ensure that products sold in their countries meet their laws and regulations and to protect their citizens, public systems and the environment from harm caused by products that enter their country.

Customers benefit from conformity assessment for the same reasons as do governments. Purchasers of products and services can use conformity assessment to identify suppliers whose products can be relied on to comply with critical requirements. Manufacturers, in turn, use conformity assessment procedures to demonstrate to their customers that their products comply with requirements.

THE EU'S SINGLE INTERNAL MARKET

The goal of the European Union's single internal market is to promote economic competitiveness and to become a powerful economic trading bloc by removing physical, technical and fiscal barriers to trade. The free internal movement of goods, services, people and capital from one member state to another is essential to economic growth.

During the past few years, the European Union has been developing a new approach to regulating products as one way to unify the European market. It has enlisted the aid of key European regional standards organizations to develop EU-wide, "harmonized" standards. The purpose of these standards is to eliminate the jumble of standards of the individual twelve member states. The European Union has drafted nearly 300 regulations to implement the single internal market.

Technical Trade Barriers

The trade barriers of most concern to US companies wishing to do business with the European Union are technical barriers. These include different standards for products, duplication of testing and certification procedures for products and differences in the laws of EU member states. These restrict the free movement of products within the European Union.

Goals of the New System

The European Union recognized that, as technical barriers were lowered, a new framework must replace them. The goal of this new framework is to create confidence among the member states in the following:

● Quality and safety of products sold in the European Union

● Overall competence of manufacturers, including their quality procedures

● Competence of the testing laboratories and certification bodies that assess the conformity of products.

The new framework would involve EU-wide directives issued by the European Commission that would replace individual member state regulations. It would also involve a comprehensive approach to conformity assessment.

This developing system encompasses all aspects of conformity assessment. The European Union refers to it as its Global Approach to Product Certification and Testing. The approach has four major components:

1. EU-wide directives
2. Harmonized standards
3. Consistent conformity assessment procedures
4. Competent certification and testing bodies.

Each component is discussed in detail as follows.

1. EU-wide Directives

As mentioned in Chapter 1, products in the European Union are classified into two categories: Regulated products and non-regulated products.

NON-REGULATED PRODUCTS

Most products sold in the European Union are non-regulated products such as paper and furniture. The European Union's strategy for removing technical barriers to non-regulated products is to rely on the principle of mutual recognition of national standards established by the European Court of Justice in the *Casis de Dijon* decision. According to the principle of mutual recognition, products that meet the requirements of one EU member state can freely circulate in other member states.

Thus, an EU purchaser of an unregulated product (such as cardboard boxes or manually operated hand tools) can continue to purchase US products specified in terms of US standards. Even if the product remains regulated at the national level and is not subject to harmonized standards, a US product that meets the national requirements of one EU member state may enjoy free circulation throughout the entire European Union through mutual recognition.

REGULATED PRODUCTS

Only a small percentage of the total number of products sold in the European Union are regulated. Regulated products such as medical devices, pressure vessels and personal protective equipment, however, make up approximately 50 percent—or $95 billion—of US exports to the European Union, according to US Department of Commerce estimates. They include those products that the European Union believes are associated with significant safety, environmental or health concerns.

The EU Council of Ministers is working to remove technical trade barriers for regulated products by issuing Union-level directives. A *directive* is the official legislation promulgated by the European Commission and binds all members of the European Union who are required to convert the directive into national legislation and regulations. Existing laws and rules that conflict with the directive are invalid and are superseded by EU directives. After a transition period, the regulated products must meet the requirements of the directive.

OLD-APPROACH DIRECTIVES AND NEW-APPROACH DIRECTIVES

Prior to 1989, the European Union issued directives that are now known as *old-approach* directives. These directives were highly specific, detailing and defining all technical characteristics and requirements of a product. The problem with old-approach directives is that they are complicated, it is expensive to comply with them and they are easily outdated due to technological advances. The term "old approach" is confusing, because the European Union continues to adopt these types of directives. The 1992 automotive type approval directives, for example, are old-approach directives.

Nevertheless, these directives are binding on all manufacturers. If a company's product falls within the scope of an old-approach directive, it must meet the directive's requirements.

The European Union soon realized that the detailed blueprint it was drafting was slowing its progress in meeting the goals of EC 92. To expedite the process, the European Union began issuing more "generic-type" directives, known as *new-approach* directives.

New-approach directives are based on the following four key elements:

- Essential environmental, health and safety requirements
- Presumption of conformity
- Mutual recognition
- Voluntary standards.

Essential Requirements

New-approach directives stipulate the environmental, health, and safety requirements a product must meet to be considered safe for the marketplace. Technical requirements—or the "how-to" specifications—are left to be "spelled out" by European regional standards organizations and by the member states themselves. The directives do not specifically list these technical requirements, but they do provide references for all appropriate supporting technical documentation. The number of standards per directive can be considerable. For example, 40 technical committees have drafted 560 technical standards for the Machinery Safety Directive.

Presumption of Conformity

If a product conforms to the specific technical standards, it is assumed that the product conforms to the essential requirements contained in the applicable directive. For example, if a company declares that its product conforms to CEN or CENELEC technical standards referenced in the directive that applies to the company's product, the product is presumed to conform with the applicable EU directive. (CEN and CENELEC are described in detail below.)

Mutual Recognition

Member states must accept products that are lawfully manufactured in any other member state, provided that the product meets EU-wide standards and/or the health, safety and environmental concerns of the receiving state.

The European Union is seeking to apply this principle not only to the acceptance of products, but also to test results and certification activities. Further, it intends to push for Mutual Recognition Agreements (MRAs) with non-EU nations to mutually accept test results and product certifications.

Voluntary Standards

Each new-approach directive provides companies with various options to comply with the essential requirements of the directive. These include a range of conformity assessment procedures. To determine which conformity assessment procedure applies to a product, manufacturers should study the appropriate directive or directives, review the options for conformity assessment, and choose the preferred or acceptable option. Depending on the type of product and its potential safety risk, the choices can range from manufacturer self-certification to the implementation of a full quality assurance system. (The options are discussed below.)

Companies also have choices regarding the technical standard(s) to which their product can conform. These include the following:

● They can comply with the technical standard referenced in the directive. Conformance to the technical standard may involve a third-party evaluation; it depends on the specific directive and the procedure chosen for conformity assessment.

● They can conform to a non-European standard or to no standard at all. In this case, the company still must demonstrate that its product meets the requirements of the directive.

   This is accomplished by submitting the product to a testing organization for third-party evaluation. In cases where there is a low safety risk, directives will allow a company to self-certify its product. However most conformity assessment options require some third-party involvement in testing and certification.

   Some manufacturers have abused the self-certification options of the Toy Safety Directive. This may lead to some involvement by the testing organization with all conformity assessment procedures, including the self-certification option.

To be able to assess product compliance with EU legislation, it is important for manufacturers to identify relevant European standards and, where appropriate, third party testing or certification entities authorized to assess product conformity to the requirements of specific directives.

This information is published in the European Union's *Official Journal*. For example, the first EU technical harmonization directive to be implemented, covering toy safety, came into effect on January 1, 1990. Reference standards were formally identified in the Official Journal on June 23, 1989. Lists of bodies authorized to carry out EU-type examination as referred to in the toy safety directive were published over a period of months, beginning June 23, 1990. (See Appendix B for a list of key EU directives.)

TRANSITION PERIOD

In the case of some directives, provisions have been made for a transition period between the implementation of the directive and the date by which companies must comply. The purpose is to allow time for reference standards to be completed and sufficient testing facilities to be qualified and authorized.

For example, under the medical devices directives, transition periods have been established, ranging from two to four years from the date the directive is implemented. This transition period allows manufacturers to continue meeting existing national standards during the transition period. However, they can market only to countries where their product complies with national standards. Under these circumstances, they cannot affix the CE mark and are not guaranteed free circulation for their products among all EU member states.

Manufacturers that meet the new EU-wide directives immediately will be able to sell medical devices throughout the European Union and European Free Trade Association (EFTA).

Consequently a number of EU and US medical device manufacturers are ignoring the transition period and are moving to complete certification as soon as possible. This gives them an edge over competitors, allows them to advertise compliance with new EU safety standards, establish an EU-wide marketing presence, and increase their market share.

With other directives, such as construction products and personal protective equipment, there is no transition period. Since the construction products directive covers a vast range of products and the system for product certification is not fully operational, the lack of a transition period is causing difficulties in that industry. Interim procedures are now being developed.

REQUIREMENTS MAY INCLUDE SEVERAL DIRECTIVES

It is possible that a company must conform to more than one directive. For example, a commercial air conditioning manufacturer would have to meet the requirements of four different directives, Machinery Safety, Electromagnetic Compatibility, Pressure Vessels and Construction Products (which covers equipment installed in buildings and building materials).

In another example, compressor-generators are covered by the requirements of the machine safety directive. However, the air tank component of this equipment must also meet the requirements of the simple pressure vessel directive. The same is true for suppliers of air brakes that are incorporated into mobile industrial or construction equipment. Thus, manufacturers who supply components to other producers for incorporation into a product that is then exported to the European Union may find that they themselves are expected to meet the technical requirements of EU legislation.

The European Union has also issued directives that apply not to a specific class of products but to all industry sectors. These include directives on product liability and product safety. Manufacturers will be required to comply with these as well. (See Appendix B for a list of major EU directives.)

NOTIFIED BODIES

In addition to requirements, directives also list the appropriate government-appointed organizations, known as *notified bodies*, that are authorized to certify that a particular product conforms to the requirements of a directive. A notified body might be a testing organization, testing laboratory, the operator of a certification system, or even a government agency itself.

A notified body is designated by the competent authority of a member state from among the bodies under its jurisdiction. A *competent authority* is the national authority in each member country that has overall responsibility for the safety of products.

The name *notified body* comes from the fact that member states notify the EU Commission as to which bodies in their country are qualified to perform the specific evaluations stipulated in individual directives.

The duties of notified bodies are clearly spelled out in each directive, and lists of notified bodies vary depending on each directive. Every EU country must accept the results of conformity assessments by notified bodies in all other EU countries unless there is cause to believe the product was improperly tested.

The Competence of Notified Bodies

Each member state must have confidence that its notified bodies are competent to declare conformity to a directive. In order to ensure members of the competence of notified bodies, the European Union has developed the Community-wide EN 45000 series standards for certification and testing. The European Union also is developing a Council regulation to guide the creation of notified bodies and their compliance with the EN 45000 series. (Chapter 16 discusses the EN 45000 standards in more detail.)

PRODUCT CERTIFICATION VERSUS ISO 9000 REGISTRATION

To satisfy the conformity assessment requirements of most EU new-approach directives and to affix the EU mark, a company must receive third-party approval from an EU notified body.

Since this product certification approval is not the same as ISO 9000 registration by a registrar, it is critical to ascertain the quality assurance requirements of a directive and establish contact with an EU notified body to make certain that everything is in order. Some US manufacturers have presented ISO 9000 registration to EU authorities and have been denied access to the marketplace because directive requirements and notified body approval have not been met.

It is possible that at least three elements will be necessary. For example, the new EU medical devices directives will require a registered ISO 9000 quality assurance system, augmented by compliance with the EN 46000 requirements as guided by an EN medical devices guidance document. A simple registration to ISO 9001 will not fulfill the requirements of the medical device directive. A company will require certification of its product to the EN 46000 requirements, in addition to the essential requirements set forth in Annex 1 of the directive. Similar essential requirements are set forth in each EU new-approach directive.

A 1993 notified body working paper now is being circulated by the EU Commission. When it is approved, it will outline the operating procedures and requirements for notified bodies. It will be a chapter in a new-approach guidance publication that is being finalized by the EU Commission.

THE CE MARK

The final result of the product certification process is the *CE mark*. A notified body is authorized to permit manufacturers to affix the CE mark, which signifies proof that a company has met essential health and safety requirements and the specific conformity assessment requirements to market its product in the European Union.

The CE designation, French for "Conformite Europeene", is required in order to sell any product manufactured or distributed under the new-approach directives. The CE mark will replace all national marks now used to show compliance with legislated requirements for regulated materials and products.

The requirements for affixing the CE Mark are set forth in each directive. (See Figure 15-1.) Basically, four steps are needed to obtain the mark. They are:

- Conformance with the requirements of the appropriate EU directives
- Official registration **with a notified body** to the appropriate ISO 9000 standard (ISO 9001, ISO 9002 or ISO 9003), if quality system registration is required by the directive
- Documentation of any test data required by the directives
- Necessary certification by the appropriate notified bodies to verify compliance with the directive(s).

Each member state must allow products with the CE mark to be marketed as conforming to the requirements of the directive. The same rules apply—regardless of the product's origin. Products that have been improperly certified will be refused entry or withdrawn from the market.

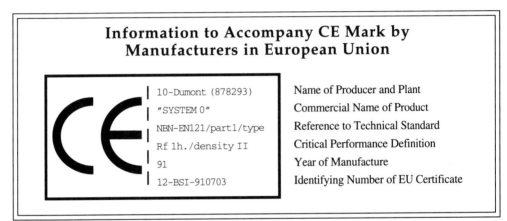

Information to Accompany CE Mark by Manufacturers in European Union

10-Dumont (878293)	Name of Producer and Plant
"SYSTEM 0"	Commercial Name of Product
NBN-EN121/part1/type	Reference to Technical Standard
Rf 1h./density II	Critical Performance Definition
91	Year of Manufacture
12-BSI-910703	Identifying Number of EU Certificate

Figure 15-1: Information to Accompany CE Mark by Manufacturers in European Union.

Old-Approach Directives

Old-approach product safety directives, such as those for motor vehicles, tractors and chemicals, contain detailed requirements for standards and test methods, and specify required marks which must be applied to indicate conformance. Products subject to product safety requirements in these areas—as well as to new-approach directives—must bear both the CE mark and other marks required under EU legislation.

CE Mark Directive

Generally, the CE mark indicates compliance with mandatory EU-wide legal requirements related to product safety and consumer protection. However, there are differences between one EU product safety directive and another regarding what the CE mark signifies, who is responsible for affixing the CE mark, and what the mark is intended to look like. The EU Commission is aware of these inconsistencies and has proposed a directive on the use and protection of the CE mark, which would harmonize and clarify the provisions of all directives requiring the mark on products.

According to the draft directive, the manufacturer, or its authorized representative in the European Union, is responsible for affixing the CE mark to the apparatus, or else to the packaging, the instructions for use, or the guarantee certificate. The CE mark is to be accompanied, where appropriate, by a numerical code identifying the approved body that issued the EU type examination certificate. The mark indicates that the manufacturer has followed all of the conformity assessment procedures laid down in all directives requiring the CE mark that are relevant to the product. The CE mark indicates only compliance with relevant EU legal requirements; it is not a quality mark and does not indicate conformance with particular standards.

Additional Marks

The CE mark alone is sufficient to market a product in the European Union. In some cases, however, customer acceptance of materials and products may hinge on the appearance of one or more additional certification and/or quality marks issued by bodies in that member state.

The CE mark does not preclude the continued existence of national quality or performance marks representing levels of quality, safety or performance higher than those specified in EU legal requirements. Member states cannot require that products bear these marks as a condition of market access, but they can continue to exist on a voluntary basis and can be specified in private commercial contracts.

In addition, there are aspects of a CE-marked product that may also require national marks in order to be placed on the market in an EU member state, e.g., to signify compliance with environmental control, ergonomics or workplace safety requirements.

If a product incorporates a safety element subject to EU legislation requiring the CE mark but is also subject to national environmental control requirements (recycling, disposal, etc.), manufacturers could be required to obtain additional national marks in order to market the product in a specific EU member state. The EU Commission is examining the need to obtain authority to harmonize technical requirements in these areas to avoid technical barriers to trade.

2. Harmonized Standards

The second key component of the European Union's conformity assessment system is harmonized standards. Harmonization refers to the process of creating uniform, EU-wide standards. The European Union believes that harmonized standards are essential to promote trade, not only in Europe but around the world. Standards have been steadily growing in importance and are becoming a strategic issue for business.

Ultimately, the aim of harmonization is a global system, where manufacturers could produce to a single standard, be assessed by a single assessment or testing body and the resulting certificate would be accepted in every market. This is the goal of "make it once, test it once, sell it everywhere."

EU STANDARDS AND REGIONAL STANDARDIZATION ORGANIZATIONS

The essential requirements in the EU directives are broad guidelines only. In addition to issuing directives, the European Union is seeking to harmonize technical requirements by mandating the use of *harmonized standards* whenever possible. The task of developing specific technical standards to harmonize the many differing national standards of the EU countries into one set of common standards is carried out primarily by three European standard-setting organizations.

These include the Committee for European Standardization (CEN), the European Committee for Electrotechnical Standardization (CENELEC), and the European Telecommunications Standards Institute (ETSI). A fourth organization, the European Organization for Technical Approvals (EOTA), assesses the technical fitness of construction products for their intended use, even when no EU-wide harmonized standard or national standard exists for that product. (The four organizations are discussed in more detail below.)

These four organizations develop standards according to priorities set by the European Union and its member states. They also consult with existing national and international standardization organizations. CEN and CENELEC have negotiated agreements with the two international standards organizations, the International Organization for Standardization (ISO) and the International Electrotechnical Commission (IEC) to develop new standards.

CEN and CENELEC will develop a new standard when:

● A standard does not already exist under ISO or IEC auspices
● The standard cannot be developed at the international level
● The standard cannot be developed at the international level within a specific time frame.

All member states must conform to each standard once it is formally adopted.

Committee for European Standardization (CEN)

CEN is the Committee for European Standardization (or Normalization, hence the "N"). This nonprofit organization is the world's largest regional standards group. It comprises delegates from 18 Western European countries—the 12 European Union nations plus six member nations of the European Free Trade Association (EFTA). CEN is composed of the national standardization institutes of these 18 countries.

CEN's main objective is to prepare a single set of European standards in place of numerous national standards. CEN works to remove any standardization differences among its 18 members.

Roles in Testing and Certification

CEN promulgates standards when the European Union passes a directive. It also responds to EU requests to develop a standard when no directive has been issued. When necessary, CEN promulgates new standards which the member countries are obligated to adopt as their own national standards. CEN also creates and implements procedures for the mutual recognition of test results and certification schemes.

CEN and ISO

CEN adopts ISO standards whenever possible and promotes the implementation of ISO and IEC standards. As far as possible, CEN avoids any duplication of work. CEN also works with ISO to draft new standards and has formal agreements with ISO for the exchange of information and for technical cooperation. CEN and ISO share common planning and have parallel votes during the development of standards.

Types of CEN Standards

CEN publishes its standards in one of the following three ways.

European Standards (or European Norm, hence the EN designation) are totally harmonized, and the 18 member nations of CEN are obligated to adopt these standards as their own national standards. An EN must be implemented at the national level as a national standard and by withdrawing the conflicting national standard.

Manufacturer compliance with European standards is voluntary. But if an EN is met, it is presumed that this also fulfills the requirements of the directive that applies to the manufacturer's product. ENs for a new technology are prepared following specific requests from the European Union and EFTA.

Harmonization Documents (HD) allow for some national deviations in standards. The HD must be implemented at the national level, either by issuing the corresponding national standard or, as a minimum, by publicly announcing the HD number and title. In both cases, no conflicting national standard may continue to exist after a fixed date.

European Pre-standards (ENV) are guidelines for expected ENs or HDs, or guidelines for rapidly developing industries. ENVs may be established as prospective standards in all technical fields where the innovation rate is high or where there is an urgent need for technical advice. CEN members are required to make the ENV available at the national level in an appropriate form and to announce their existence in the same way as for ENs and HDs. However, any conflicting national standards may be kept in force until the ENV is converted into an EN.

European Committee for Electrotechnical Standardization (CENELEC)

The European Committee for Electrotechnical Standardization (CENELEC) is CEN's sister organization and is also based in Brussels, Belgium. CENELEC is a nonprofit technical organization working to harmonize standards among its 18 EU and EFTA member countries and is composed of delegates from those countries.

While CEN works closely with ISO to adopt standards on everything but technical issues, CENELEC works with its international counterpart, the International Electrotechnical Committee (IEC). CENELEC maintains an active working agreement with IEC, and 85 percent of the European standards adopted by CENELEC are IEC standards.

The procedures for the development of CENELEC standards are the same as those described for CEN. CENELEC publishes its standards in the same manner as CEN: as European Standards (EN), Harmonization Documents (HD), and European Pre-standards (ENV).

CENELEC Priorities

CENELEC's areas of priorities for developing standards are low-voltage areas, other electric equipment, and agreed-upon mandates for standardization from EU and EFTA countries. As mentioned earlier, manufacturers do not have to meet CENELEC standards if their products fulfill the essential requirements of the applicable directive(s). Products which meet CENELEC standards, however, are presumed also to fulfill the requirements of EU directives.

European Telecommunications Standardization Institute (ETSI)

The European Telecommunications Standardization Institute (ETSI) is the third sister organization in the CEN/CENELEC/ETSI regional triumvirate. It promotes European standards for a unified telecommunications system.

ETSI membership is open to all relevant organizations with an interest in telecommunication standardization that belong to a country within the European Confederation of Posts and Telecommunications Administrations. Users, research bodies and others may participate directly in standardization work for Europe.

The process of publishing final ETSI standards is almost identical to the methods used by CEN and CENELEC. The three groups have formed a Joint Presidents' Group to handle common concerns regarding policy and management. The three groups also have signed a cooperation agreement to prevent overlapping assignments and to work together as partners.

Non-European organizations interested in telecommunications are sometimes invited as observers to the technical work of ETSI. In addition, ETSI and the American National Standards Institute (ANSI), the US standardization body, have agreed to an exchange of information concerning their respective work.

3. Consistent Conformity Assessment Procedures

The third component of the EU's overall conformity assessment approach is consistent conformity assessment procedures. The main principle is that, rather than adopting certification procedures on an *ad hoc* basis, directive-by-directive, as in the past, the European Union in the future will choose from a set of detailed conformity-assessment procedures. This plan is called the *modular approach.*

THE MODULAR APPROACH

The *modular approach* to conformity assessment offer several procedures for a manufacturer to demonstrate compliance with directives. These range from a manufacturer's self-declaration of conformity to assessment of a quality system; to type-testing of the product by a third party, depending on the health, safety and environmental risks of the product. All future conformity assessment procedures will be based on one or more of these options.

The EU Council outlines the combination of procedures it considers appropriate for each directive and sets the conditions of application. The manufacturers themselves, however, have the final choice as to which of the procedures they will follow.

Figures 15-2 and 15-3 illustrate the certification options available to comply with the directives. If one or more directives is applicable to a particular product, the directives indicate whether a notified body must be involved, and if so, the extent of that involvement. Apart from Module A, the supplier has to involve a notified body for all other modules. The supplier is responsible for maintaining the conformity of its product to all relevant essential requirements. As noted earlier, due to abuse of Module A by some toy manufacturers, the EU Commission is considering notified body involvement with manufacturer self-certification.

	MODULES						
	A	B+C	B+D	B+E	B+F	G	H
PRODUCT SURVEILLANCE: Samples:	○	○			●		
Each Product:	○				● (OR)	●	
Q.A. Surveillance:			● EN 29002	● EN 29003			● EN 29001
Type Testing:		●	●	●	●	○ Design	
Technical Documentation:	①	②	②	②	②	②	③
CE MARK AFFIXED BY: Manufacturer:	CE	CE	CE ⋆	CE ⋆	CE ⋆		CE ⋆
Third Party:					CE ⋆ (OR)	CE ⋆	

○ Supplementary Requirements ① Required to Be Available CE CE Mark

● Action by Third Party ② Required by Notified Body CE ⋆ CE Mark with the Notified Body Identification Symbol

③ Part of Quality System

Figure 15-2: Overview—EC 92 Conformity Assessment Procedures—The Modules.

As stated earlier, ISO 9000 registration alone, without product testing, is not sufficient to meet EU directive requirements. Quality system registration is a component of the conformity assessment requirements for some regulated products. The directives, however, require that products be tested to ensure compliance with the minimum requirements of the directive. In some directives, if a manufacturer has an ISO 9001-registered quality system, they can then self-declare conformity with the technical requirements of the directive.

DESCRIPTION OF MODULES IN MODULAR APPROACH

There are two main phases in the modular approach: the design phase and the production phase. Both phases are covered by modules, which are further broken down into four types of examination:

● Internal control of production

- Type-examination
- Unit verification
- Full quality assurance—EN 29001.

These are examined in more detail below. (See Figure 15-4.)

Internal Control of Production (A)

Internal control of production allows manufacturers to self-declare conformity to the specific standard. Self-declaration is possible for toys, electromagnetic compatibility, weighing instruments for noncommercial use, and most types of machinery, as well as for some types of personal protective equipment, pressure vessels and equipment, recreational craft and low risk medical devices.

During the design phase, the manufacturer may carry out the procedure for conformity assessment itself. The manufacturer, however, must keep the technical documentation available for review by the national authorities for at least ten years after production of the product. This way, assessments and checks can be carried out to determine whether the product complies with the directive.

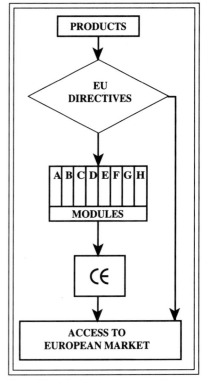

Figure 15-3: Conformity Assessment Process.

The producer has to provide insight into the design, the manufacturing process and the performance of the product. The manufacturer must take all the steps necessary to ensure the manufacturing process guarantees that the product constantly complies with the essential requirements.

During the production phase, a notified body carries out testing on specific aspects of the product at random intervals. This module is designed for the manufacturer who chooses to produce, not in accordance with the European standards, but directly in accordance with the essential requirements of the applicable directive.

Type-Examination (B)

In type-examination, the design phase involves verification by a third party. In this module, the manufacturer has to present the technical documentation and one *product type* (typical example) to a testing organization of its choice. The testing organization assesses and draws up a declaration. This module must be supplemented by modules C, D, E or F.

Conformity to Type (C)

The manufacturer can self-declare conformity to type with no quality system requirement. The manufacturer draws up a declaration of conformity for the approved type from module B, and keeps this for at least ten years after manufacture of the last product.

DESIGN	PRODUCTION
A. INTERNAL CONTROL OF PRODUCTION — **Manufacturer** ●Keeps technical documentation at the disposal of national authorities **Aa** ●Intervention of notified body	**A. Manufacturer** ●Declares conformity with essential requirements ●Affixes the CE-Mark **Aa** ●Tests on specific aspects of the product ●Product checks at random intervals
B. TYPE EXAMINATION — **Manufacturer submits to notified body** ●Technical documentation ●Type **Notified body** ●Ascertains conformity with essential requirements ●Carries out tests, if necessary ●Issues EU type-examination certificate	**C. CONFORMITY TO TYPE** — **Manufacturer** ●Declares conformity with approved type ●Affixes the CE-Mark **Notified body** ●Tests on specific aspects of the product ●Product checks at random intervals
	D. PRODUCT QUALITY ASSURANCE — **EN 29002 • Manufacturer** ●Operates approved QS-production & testing ●Declares conformity with approved type ●Affixes the CE-Mark **EN 29002 • Notified body** ●Approves the QS ●Carries out surveillance of the QS
	E. PRODUCT QUALITY ASSURANCE — **EN 29003 • Manufacturer** ●Operates approved QS-production & testing ●Declares conformity with approved type or essential requirements • Affixes CE-Mark **EN 29003 • Notified body** ●Approves the QS ●Carries out surveillance of the QS
	F. PRODUCT VERIFICATION — **Manufacturer** ●Declares conformity with approved type or with essential requirements ●Affixes the CE-Mark **Notified body** ●Verifies conformity ●Issues certificate of conformity
G. UNIT VERIFICATION — **Manufacturer** ●Submits technical documentation	**Manufacturer** ●Submits product ●Declares conformity ●Affixes the CE-Mark **Notified body** ●Verifies conformity with essential requirements ●Issues certificate of conformity
H. FULL QUALITY ASSURANCE — **EN 29001 • Manufacturer** ●Operates an approved QS for design **EN 29001 • Notified body** ●Carries out surveillance of the QS ●Verifies conformity of the design ●Issues EU design examination certificate	**Manufacturer** ●Operates an approved QS for production & testing ●Declares conformity ●Affixes the CE-Mark **Notified body** ●Carries out surveillance of the QS

Figure 15-4: Conformity Assessment Procedure Modules.

Production Quality Assurance (D)

This module requires third-party certification to ISO 9002. ISO 9002 includes the entire production process, except for design. The manufacturer's quality system for production is approved by a testing organization. Then the manufacturer declares that his product matches the approved type.

Product Quality Assurance (E)

This module requires third-party certification to ISO 9003, for inspection and testing. Module E is the same as Module D, except that the quality system concerns only the end-production checks.

Product Verification (F)

This module requires testing the product and certifying conformity by a third party. The manufacturer ensures that the production process guarantees the product meets the requirements. Then the manufacturer declares conformity. An approved testing organization checks this conformity. This can take place sometimes by testing each product separately and sometimes by random testing. Finally, the testing organization issues a certificate of conformity.

Unit-Verification (G)

Unit-verification requires the manufacturer to submit technical documents and a prototype product to regulatory authorities. A notified body must certify by checking the product that the production process conforms with essential requirements.

Full Quality Assurance (H)

Full quality assurance requires the manufacturer to operate an approved quality system for design, production and testing, and to be certified to the European quality standard EN 29001/ ISO 9001 by a notified body. Manufacturers can avoid expensive, time-consuming product testing by instituting a full quality assurance system according to ISO 9001.

DEGREE OF COMPLEXITY

As a general rule, the greater the safety risk associated with a product, the more complex the conformity assessment process. For example, in the EU Council *Directive on Personal Protective Equipment*, a manufacturer can probably choose to self-certify a product where the model is simple, the risks are minimal, and the user has time to identify those risks safely. Some examples are gardening gloves, gloves for mild detergent solutions, seasonal protective clothing, and gloves or aprons for moderate exposure to heat.

Manufacturers, however, must choose either ISO 9001, full quality assurance, or EU type approval plus EU verification in cases where personal protective equipment is of a complex design, "intended to protect against mortal danger or against dangers that may seriously and irreversibly harm the health..." of individuals.

Given a choice between EU type approval plus EU verification or ISO 9001, most manufacturers will choose ISO 9001 registration. Under ISO 9001, the manufacturer submits the full quality system for approval, a preferable alternative to the more intrusive EU process of continuously submitting representative samples to a third party for screening.

ADDITIONAL REQUIREMENTS

In addition to using the basic framework of the ISO 9000 series, some EU directives have supplemental requirements. For example, to certify under the EU Construction Products directive, a manufacturer must also comply with the additional requirements of the EN 45000 series of standards. These standards apply to laboratory, testing, and certification organizations.

Other product sectors for which additional guidelines have been developed are medical devices (*EN 46001, Particular requirements for the application of EN 29001 (ISO 9001) for medical devices*) and aerospace products (EN 2000, EN 3042). Most likely, similar special requirements will be developed for other directives.

4. Competent Certification and Testing Bodies

The fourth and final component of the EU's comprehensive framework for conformity assessment is the role of certification and testing bodies. The goal of the European Union is to increase confidence of member nations in the work of these organizations so that the results of testing will be accepted throughout the European Union.

In its 1989 presentation, entitled *The Global Approach to Certification and Testing*, the European Union outlined the following major elements of its program for certification and testing bodies:

● The credibility of the manufacturer must be reinforced. This can be achieved by promoting the use of quality assurance techniques.

● The credibility of and confidence in testing laboratories and certification bodies must be enhanced. This can be achieved by developing the EN 45000 series of standards to evaluate the competence of testing laboratories.

● The competence of laboratories and certification bodies is established through an accreditation process based on EN 45000 standards. This accreditation process involves a third-party evaluation and is discussed in more detail in Chapter 16.

   According to this system, notified bodies must produce documentation proving they conform to the EN 45000 series. If the notified bodies are not formally accredited, the appropriate national authority in the state where the notified body is located must produce documentary evidence that the notified body conform to the relevant standards of the EN 45000 series.

● Finally, there is a testing and certification organization at the European level. This organization, called the European Organization for Testing and Certification (EOTC), has the role of promoting mutual recognition agreements in the non-regulated sphere. The EOTC is discussed in detail in Chapter 16.

THE EUROPEAN UNION AND OTHER COUNTRIES

As the European Union moves toward its goal of a unified market and maps out its comprehensive system for product regulation and certification, it is also defining its future relationship with other countries. One of the key components of this relationship is *nondiscrimination*. This means the same rules apply, regardless of the product's origin. A corollary to this is acceptance of test reports or certificates of conformity from countries outside the European Union. These relationships, however, are still in a developmental phase. The issues discussed in this section include the following:

- Can notified bodies subcontract any of their activities to bodies outside the European Union? How much can be subcontracted?
- Are ISO 9000 registration certificates recognized throughout the European Union?
- Can a notified body be located outside the European Union?

Subcontracting

Can notified bodies subcontract any of their activities to bodies outside the European Union? To some extent, yes. The European Union has proposed new rules for subcontracting and is moving to permit more extensive use of subcontracting. The European Union's proposed general guidelines for subcontracting as stated in a 1993 working document follow:

- EU notified bodies will need to hold subcontractors to the EN 45000 series of standards, including the requirements to maintain records
- Subcontractors must contract with notified bodies and test to the same standards as the notified body
- EU notified bodies "cannot subcontract assessment and appraisal activities"
- EU notified bodies remain responsible for any certification activity.

Notified bodies can subcontract quality assessment audits, provided that they retain responsibility for the audit assessment. Still up in the air are issues such as how widely EU notified bodies will exercise their subcontracting capabilities and whether subcontracting arrangements will give US-based manufacturers sufficient low-cost access to the EU market.

A new-approach guidance document is due from the EU Commission in early 1994 that will discuss notified bodies, subcontracting, mutual recognition agreements, etc.

Mutual Recognition

Currently, US companies that achieve ISO 9000 registration obtain whatever recognition that their accrediting entity has in the country in which the accreditation entity (i.e., NACCB in the United Kingdom, RAB in the United States) is located. Other countries in the European Union and elsewhere can voluntarily choose to recognize the registration certificate. The registration certificates are not yet governed by EU legislation, and EU-wide recognition is not yet mandatory. Presently, a few national accreditation entities are negotiating mutual recognition agreements to recognize one another's ISO 9000 registrations.

Although the term *mutual recognition agreement* fairly describes what has been negotiated, it should not be confused with the EU legal term. The EU legal term—*Mutual Recognition Agreement*—will be governed by an EU legal document and will refer to product-sector Mutual Recognition Agreements, negotiated between the European Union and third countries (United States, Canada, Japan, etc.).

(Issues of registrar accreditation and the recognition of registration certificates are discussed in more detail in Chapter 16.)

Non-EU Notified Bodies

Under the EU system, member states can designate only notified bodies from within the European Union. No subsidiaries or related enterprises located in a third country can perform full third-party product certification and quality system registration except under a legal Mutual Recognition Agreement (MRA) between the European Union and the government authorities of that country. In addition, their competence must be assessed by third parties, according to the provisions of the EN 45000 series.

At the present time, an EU Commission 1993 working document and a Commission communication on MRAs are in circulation regarding this issue. When a directive is finalized it will state the general criteria for negotiating MRAs that allow notified bodies to reside in a non-EU country.

An MRA would allow US testing and certification organizations to act as notified bodies in the product areas covered by the MRA. In this way, non-EU notified bodies could award the CE mark for regulated products under the negotiated industry sector.

The US government is actively exploring the prospects for concluding MRAs with the European Union in areas where interest has been indicated on the part of the US private sector. These include medical devices, pressure vessels, recreational craft and electromagnetic compatibility.

The European Union and US Conformity Assessment

Increasingly, the global economy is exercising an influence on the standards process. While both the European Union and the United States are major players in international conformity assessment talks, the European Union's influence now takes center stage as it works to harmonize standards and eliminate national barriers to trade.

Initially, the European Union directed its energies to critical health and safety issues in the 1985 EU White Paper, *Completing the Internal Market, White Paper from the Commission to the European Council.* More recently, however, EU standards activity is moving beyond the White Paper to new areas of concern. In part, this process is being aided by various EU "green papers" that address topics from transportation to telecommunication. It is reasonable to expect this activity to continue and examine most every area of standards activity over the next twenty to thirty years.

The US Response to the European Union

The critical issue for the United States is how to respond to these developments. On the one hand, the European Union and EFTA and their constituent member states have developed a standards structure which uses regional European quasi-legal standards organizations (CEN, CENELEC, ETSI, EOTC) to flesh out product standards. It is a process that fits comfortably into the framework of the EU and European legal code traditions of seventeen EU and EFTA member states (only Ireland and the United Kingdom share the English legal system found in the United States). Furthermore, the remaining European nations and most Asian and Latin American nations share those same legal code traditions.

By way of contrast—except for areas of health and safety, where federal or state agencies have entered the conformity assessment process through regulatory procedures—most American products are manufactured in accordance with industry standards. Industry product sector associations such as API, SAE, NEMA, etc., have established voluntary quality standards which must be met and approved before a company is entitled to stamp that it has met association standards.

Quite clearly, the two systems do not provide an easy match. The EU system is quasi-legal in structure and a significant part of the US system is private and voluntary. The European Union has made it clear that it wants to interact directly with the US government through a federal agency.

Whether NIST, DOC or some other federal entity takes on the role of interfacing with the European Union, it will be a US governmental entity. How the United States structures its conformity assessment process is a US concern. Whether it is a shell or a structure is for the United States and its voluntary agencies to decide.

Whatever the decision, if a conformity assessment procedure is put forth as the US procedure, it will have to be sanctioned by the United States. Likewise, only the European Union can sanction its conformity assessment procedures, government to government.

The Critical Role of Conformity Assessment

The critical role of conformity assessment procedures worldwide is just beginning to emerge. A company's decision to seek ISO 9000 registration should be part of an overall conformity assessment strategy. For example, a company's choice of an ISO 9000 series registrar might be limited by an EU directive or US law. Approval of conformity assessment procedures for a specific product might also be required by the European Union.

In the United States, the regulatory process is guided by federal agencies, such as the FDA, the Environmental Protection Agency and the Consumer Product Safety Commission. These agencies drive much conformity assessment activity. Most US products, however, are manufactured to private industry standards such as those adopted by the American Petroleum Institute and the Society of Automotive Engineers.

Despite the complexity of the issues, US business must understand and prepare conformity assessment strategies for the products it sells. While ISO 9000 registration is a significant accomplishment for any company, it may not be sufficient to constitute a comprehensive global market access program.

CONCLUSION

For those people reading about the European Union and its new structure for the first time, it probably seems like one of Bob Newhart's early comedy routines in which he has Abner Doubleday call a company that sells party games and try to describe his new idea, a game called "baseball."

Naturally, the description of a baseball diamond, outfield, batter, pitcher, home plate, three bases, balls, bats, outs, innings and nine players to a team sounded like total gibberish to the party game company. But what may have been gibberish in 1839 is now called our national pastime.

The European Union's new game may seem confusing and unsettled. From our US perspective, it may not appear to be a level playing field. But it is becoming *the* playing field. Not understanding its dynamics could mean that a company's team is suited up for football only to discover that the other team is playing baseball.

To understand the EU system, it will be necessary to read the directives in depth and more than one directive or set of laws likely will be involved. Understanding the process will be crucial to becoming an effective competitor in what may become the world's largest market. For those companies that get there early and establish a presence, the monetary rewards could be substantial.

ANSI's Conformity Assessment Activities

The American National Standards Institute (ANSI) is taking the lead in educating US business about the importance of conformity assessment and in fostering international consensus on standards use and development ANSI has identified four principal conformity assessment goals, according to a 1993 policy paper. The goals are:

1) To provide a policy forum to represent US constituency interests at the domestic, regional and international levels. Issues emphasized are the mutually supportive roles of the public and private sectors; fostering cooperation and coordination with US government representation of US interests in relevant multilateral and bilateral trade negotiations; providing US access mechanisms to foreign conformity assessment systems; and defining the role of manufacturers' declarations vis-a-vis independent third-party assessment activities.

2) To provide and assure full use of the US access mechanisms to the private-sector international and regional organizations. ANSI seeks to set requirements for conformity assessment programs and to operate such programs.

3) To collect and disseminate on behalf of its constituents timely, accurate information on conformity assessment developments nationally, regionally and internationally.

4) To provide a private-sector-based national accreditation mechanism for conformity assessment programs. These mechanisms would facilitate sectorial approaches to satisfy US needs for products and services to flow freely in the marketplace (domestic, regional and international). These assessment programs include product certification, quality system registration and assessment of laboratories.

EC 92 Leadership

ANSI has also recognized that European Union (EU) requirements will be a significant factor for individual product sectors subject to EU directives. ANSI's three-year dialogue with the European Commission and private-sector European Organization for Testing and Certification (EOTC) has produced the most timely, comprehensive and relevant information for US businesses on these issues that exists in the United States.

One of the goals for these ongoing talks is to promote the greatest possible use of manufacturers' declarations of conformity assessment consistent with the degree of product risk involved. ANSI is working to assure that US manufacturers' declarations will be accepted on the same terms as European manufacturers' declarations. Third-party certifications should be required only when appropriate. If a third-party assessment is a requirement, US manufacturers should have the option of using recognized US testing and certification or quality system registration entities.

ANSI also promotes the concept of a flexible government-to-government approach that will allow for different industry sectors to take advantage of existing private-

(continued on next page)

ANSI's Conformity Assessment Activities

(continued from previous page)

sector accreditation mechanisms. In Europe, the European Organization for Testing and Certification (EOTC) is the private-sector focal point in Europe for all issues relating to conformity assessment. ANSI serves as a catalyst to promote such sector-specific discussions between interested parties and sectorial committees within EOTC.

For more information about ANSI conformity assessment activities, contact: ANSI, 11 West 42nd Street, New York, NY 10036, (212) 642-4900, Fax: (212) 398-0023.

REGISTRAR ACCREDITATION

BY JOSEPH TIRATTO

As explained in earlier chapters, auditing a company's quality system may be performed by the company (self-audit), by the customer who requires quality system assurance (second-party evaluation), or by a third party. Third-party assessment of a company's quality system and registration to ISO 9000 standards is performed by a registrar.

The role of the registrar is to perform on-site audits of companies' quality systems and to issue registration certificates. The accreditation of these registrars and the recognition of the certificates they issue are critical matters. This is the foundation of the ISO 9000 registration system.

Chapter 16 examines the following topics:

- Registrar accreditation
  - In Europe
  - In the United States
  - In Canada
- Criteria for accrediting certified bodies—the EN 45000 series
- Recognition of registration certificates
- Auditor certification.

The discussion focuses on registration and accreditation in the European Union (formerly the European Community) and the United States. It describes the developing relationship between the two and highlights the problems and differences that must be worked out along the road to mutual acceptance of registration and accreditation practices.

REGISTRAR ACCREDITATION

Companies seek registration for different reasons; the specific needs of the would-be registered company determine the type of registration, and therefore the type of registrar required. Some seek registration to meet mandatory requirements for the sale of government-regulated products. Others do it to gain strategic advantage in the marketplace, or simply as a means of improving their quality system by subjecting it to the vigorous self-inspection that the audit process requires.

Different registrars are qualified in different ways to assess the needs of the would-be registered company. Some are more respected than others in certain regions of the world and in certain industries. Some have more experience than others in certain areas, or have auditors better trained for specific types of audits. But the primary way in which various registrars differ is in how they are accredited—or whether they are accredited at all. Accreditation is the initial evaluation and periodic monitoring of a registrar.

The issues surrounding accreditation remain largely unsettled. Not all registrars are accredited, and unaccredited registrars can be as fully competent to conduct quality system audits and to award ISO 9000 certificates as accredited registrars. Nor is accreditation in and of itself a guarantee of quality auditing services. The general trend, however, is moving toward accrediting registrars to provide confidence to industry regarding their competence.

Registrars also can be accredited by more than one accrediting body. In this case, companies have the opportunity to choose the registration scheme under which they wish to participate. Thus, if most of a company's customers are in the United Kingdom and those customers value UK accreditation, the company may choose the registration scheme accredited by the National Accreditation Council for Certification Bodies (NACCB) in the United Kingdom.

Accreditation Bodies in Europe

Who accredits European registrars? In Europe, third-party assessors are regulated by governmental or quasi-governmental agencies. The Dutch Council for Certification (RvC) in The Netherlands and the NACCB in the United Kingdom are two quasi-governmental bodies that certify organizations to perform third-party quality system audits.

Other accreditation bodies in Europe include AFAQ in France, UNICEI in Italy, and AENOR in Spain. The RvC, the first body to be established, is the only accreditation body in Europe at this time that will accredit certification bodies outside its own country.

ACCREDITATION AND REGULATED PRODUCTS

For companies selling products not regulated by the European Union, it may not matter whether the registrar is accredited. In this case the value of a registration certificate is determined solely by the marketplace. If a nonaccredited registration is acceptable to a company's customers or otherwise allows it to meet whatever goals it had for registration, then it has served its purpose.

On the other hand, if the product produced by the company being registered is regulated by the European Union, then the company must undergo a quality systems audit performed by a registrar that is an EU notified body. (Please refer to Chapter 15 for more information on notified bodies.) Registrars can become accredited to register firms selling any or all of the various regulated products. They can also become accredited in non-regulated areas, and it is sometimes felt that an accredited registration carries more weight in the marketplace than a nonaccredited one, whether or not regulated products are involved.

Companies producing regulated products that enlist the services of registrars must be confident that the registrar is authorized by an accreditation agency to provide acceptable audit services and that the results of its audit—the registration certificate—will be accepted in those countries where the company seeks to do business.

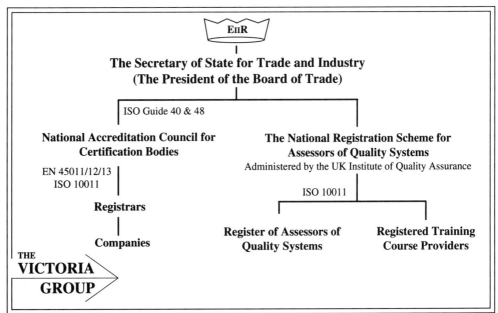

Figure 16-1: Accreditation in the United Kingdom.

Accreditation in the United States

Until recently the United States did not have an accreditation system. Several important reasons to develop such a system existed:

- To establish credibility for US-based registrars
- To follow the precedent set by an EU resolution that calls for implementing accreditation bodies throughout the European Union
- To keep pace with the worldwide move to establish accreditation bodies in each country.

In response to these needs and to the proliferation of third-party certifiers in the United States, the Registrar Accreditation Board (RAB) was established as an affiliate of the American Society for Quality Control (ASQC) in late 1989 to develop a joint ANSI/RAB American national accreditation program. The program is called the American National Accreditation Program for Registrars of Quality Systems.

REGISTRAR ACCREDITATION BOARD

The RAB is a national board that accredits registrars in the United States. The RAB performs initial audits of registrars, issues certificates of accreditation, performs regular follow-up surveillance and maintains a directory of accredited registrars. The RAB performs complete reassessments of accredited registrars every four years.

The RAB has established a group of qualified auditors to perform the audits, an accreditation council to evaluate the audit results and to make accreditations, an operations council, a board of directors and an administrative office.

RAB Accreditation Criteria

The criteria used by RAB to accredit registrars are the same as those used by the EU and EFTA accreditation organizations. A common basis for accreditation will enhance the mutual recognition of accreditation systems between the United States and European countries and eventually with other US trading partners.

It is anticipated that mutual recognition of accreditations will lead to international acceptance of individual supplier quality system registrations. The RAB has incorporated the following international criteria into its own criteria:

- *ISO 10011: Guidelines for auditing quality systems*
- *ISO/IEC Guide 40: General requirements for the acceptance of certification bodies*
- *ISO/IEC Guide 48: Guidelines for third-party assessment and registration of a supplier's quality system*
- *EN 45012: General criteria for certification bodies operating quality system certification.*

RAB Recognition

The RAB is seeking formal recognition of its registrar accreditation scheme in both the United States and in Europe. Since the system to establish broad mutual recognition of accreditation bodies throughout Europe is not functioning at this time, the RAB has negotiated with European countries on a bilateral basis to achieve mutual recognition of accredited registrars.

In August 1992, the RAB signed a Memorandum of Understanding (MOU) with the RvC that its supporters say will eventually lead to mutual acceptance of registrar accreditations performed on both sides of the Atlantic.

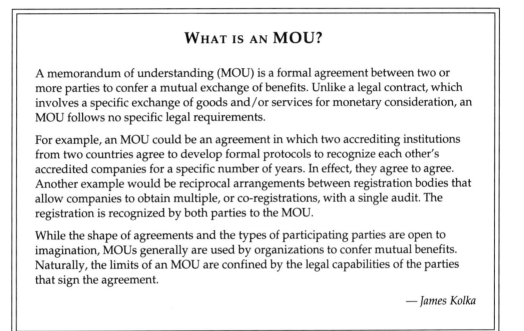

WHAT IS AN **MOU?**

A memorandum of understanding (MOU) is a formal agreement between two or more parties to confer a mutual exchange of benefits. Unlike a legal contract, which involves a specific exchange of goods and/or services for monetary consideration, an MOU follows no specific legal requirements.

For example, an MOU could be an agreement in which two accrediting institutions from two countries agree to develop formal protocols to recognize each other's accredited companies for a specific number of years. In effect, they agree to agree. Another example would be reciprocal arrangements between registration bodies that allow companies to obtain multiple, or co-registrations, with a single audit. The registration is recognized by both parties to the MOU.

While the shape of agreements and the types of participating parties are open to imagination, MOUs generally are used by organizations to confer mutual benefits. Naturally, the limits of an MOU are confined by the legal capabilities of the parties that sign the agreement.

— James Kolka

Figure 16-2: Accreditation in the United States.

NIST AND THE NVCASE PROGRAM

In setting up its EU-wide accreditation structure, the European Union prefers to work on a government-to-government basis. The RAB is not a government organization. The US Department of Commerce, however, has designated the National Institute of Standards and Technology (NIST) to establish criteria for conformity assessment in the United States.

NIST has proposed its own program for accrediting registrars where an acceptable accrediting program does not already exist—the National Voluntary Conformity Assessment Systems Evaluation (NVCASE) program. More than two years after it was first proposed, the NVCASE program went into effect in May 1994. The purpose of the program is to establish criteria and a system to evaluate and recognize specific conformity assessment activities. Under the program, bodies such as the RAB can apply for and gain government recognition through NIST. The program is intended to boost the acceptance of US products abroad.

The scope of NIST's involvement under the NVCASE program does not extend to the actual registration of individual firms. That would be left to registrars. It only extends to the evaluation of a testing laboratory, certification body or quality system registrar when directed by law or requested by another federal agency.

It also responds to a specific industrial or technical need relative to a mandatory foreign technical requirement where there is no accreditation alternative available and where the absence of any alternative would result in significant public disadvantage. NIST's operation at the recognition level at the top of the pyramid, however, is unconditional. NIST is responsible for evaluating bodies that accredit testing laboratories, certification bodies and quality system registrars.

NVCASE is organized as a separate office within NIST. It is fully funded by fees charged to accredit conformity assessment organizations.

DESIGNATING US NOTIFIED BODIES

Is the NVCASE program authorized to designate notified bodies in the United States? The US government currently is awaiting an EU directive regarding Mutual Recognition Agreements (MRA) that will address the question of notified bodies in countries outside the European Union.

Until the directive is issued and until MRAs are negotiated along industry sector lines to allow US conformity-assessment bodies to act as notified bodies, the question of which US organization will be responsible for designating notified bodies remains unanswered. Since the European Union has not yet defined the ground rules for naming US organizations as notified bodies, it is premature to speculate on the sort of role—if any—NVCASE or NIST may play in designating notified bodies.

INDEPENDENT ASSOCIATION OF ACCREDITED REGISTRARS

Accredited registrars operating in the United States have formed a body called The Independent Association of Accredited Registrars (IAAR). The IAAR seeks to promote consistency among the registrars and to ensure the integrity of the registration process. Among the issues that IAAR is addressing are consistent interpretation of the ISO 9000 series standard and conflict of interest.

In order to make the ISO 9000 series registration process more uniform for US and Canadian companies, the IAAR has established a technical committee to consider offering common interpretations of the ISO 9000 series standards. The committee may accept interpretation questions from member companies as well as the general public. The committee also will select issues that are deemed to have a significant affect on the IAAR.

Another issue on the IAAR agenda is conflict of interest—specifically, how to avoid it in organizations that offer both consulting and registration services. The association has created a subcommittee to study the issue and to make recommendations.

Accreditation Bodies in Canada

The Standards Council of Canada (SCC) has a registrar accreditation program called *Accreditation of Organizations that Register Suppliers' Quality Systems*. It was approved by the SCC on December 9, 1991. The program's Registration Accreditation Subcommittee (RASC) performs the assessment of the applicant registrar.

The recommendation to accredit is left to an advisory committee. The final decision to accredit, however, is made by the SCC's Executive Committee. SCC will conduct yearly surveillance audits of accredited registrars. The schedule for conducting full-scale reassessments of accredited registrars has not been determined.

The accreditation program is open to non-Canadian registrars as well. The criteria for the program, spelled out in SCC document CAN-P-10, allows for the accreditation of non-Canadian registrars so long as certain conditions are met. A non-Canadian registrar's country of origin must operate a similar accreditation scheme that is open to Canadian companies. That country would eventually have a mutual recognition agreement to recognize accredited Canadian registrars.

By receiving government funds and by reporting to Parliament through the Minister of Consumer and Corporate Affairs, the SCC has implicit government recognition in its programs.

CRITERIA FOR ACCREDITING CERTIFIED BODIES

How does a company that receives ISO 9000 series standard registration know that the registrar that awarded the registration is competent?

The European Union is developing a framework for evaluating notified bodies, using the EN 45000 series of standards. (See box.) CEN/CENELEC adapted the EN 45000 series of standards from existing ISO/IEC guides to increase the level of confidence in the certification, inspection and testing bodies of the European Union.

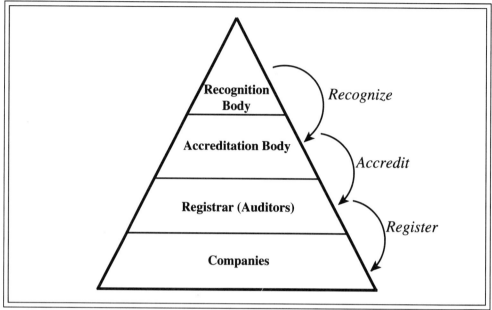

Figure 16-3: Accreditation Pyramid.

Of this series, *EN 45012, General Criteria for Certification Bodies Operating Quality System Certification*, is important to companies seeking ISO 9000 series standard registration. (See the Annex to this chapter for an outline of EN 45012 requirements.)

EN 45012: Criteria for Registrars

Organizations that perform quality system certification activities must be evaluated against the requirements of EN 45012, which sets out the criteria for registrars. These criteria address the requirements for certified bodies at a national or European level. Implementation of this standard is the responsibility of EQNET.

Further guidance related to EN 45012 implementation is contained in the *ISO/IEC Guide 40, General Requirements for the Acceptance of Certification Bodies*, and *ISO/IEC Guide 48, Guidelines for Third-party Assessment and Registration of a Supplier's Quality System.*

Manufacturers or suppliers involved in ISO 9000 registration efforts should make sure that their quality system registrar has been accredited according to EN 45012.

When the framework for evaluating notified bodies in Europe is in place, each notified body will be assessed by a third party against the requirements of EN 45000, to ensure its notification within the Union. These standards will form the foundation for a system of mutual recognition within the European Union.

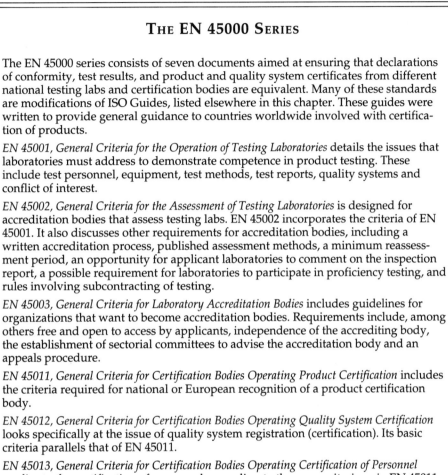

THE EN 45000 SERIES

The EN 45000 series consists of seven documents aimed at ensuring that declarations of conformity, test results, and product and quality system certificates from different national testing labs and certification bodies are equivalent. Many of these standards are modifications of ISO Guides, listed elsewhere in this chapter. These guides were written to provide general guidance to countries worldwide involved with certification of products.

EN 45001, General Criteria for the Operation of Testing Laboratories details the issues that laboratories must address to demonstrate competence in product testing. These include test personnel, equipment, test methods, test reports, quality systems and conflict of interest.

EN 45002, General Criteria for the Assessment of Testing Laboratories is designed for accreditation bodies that assess testing labs. EN 45002 incorporates the criteria of EN 45001. It also discusses other requirements for accreditation bodies, including a written accreditation process, published assessment methods, a minimum reassessment period, an opportunity for applicant laboratories to comment on the inspection report, a possible requirement for laboratories to participate in proficiency testing, and rules involving subcontracting of testing.

EN 45003, General Criteria for Laboratory Accreditation Bodies includes guidelines for organizations that want to become accreditation bodies. Requirements include, among others free and open to access by applicants, independence of the accrediting body, the establishment of sectorial committees to advise the accreditation body and an appeals procedure.

EN 45011, General Criteria for Certification Bodies Operating Product Certification includes the criteria required for national or European recognition of a product certification body.

EN 45012, General Criteria for Certification Bodies Operating Quality System Certification looks specifically at the issue of quality system registration (certification). Its basic criteria parallels that of EN 45011.

EN 45013, General Criteria for Certification Bodies Operating Certification of Personnel applies to the certification of personnel, according to the same criteria as in EN 45011.

EN 45014, General Criteria for Declaration of Conformity goes into detail about the process of actually preparing the Declaration of Conformity to demonstrate conformance with a directive's requirements.

EN 45019, Guidance on Specific Aspects of Testing and Certification.

EN 45020, Definitions.

[*To obtain the above standards, contact the American National Standards Institute, 212-354-3300.*]

INTERPRETING EN 45000

The EN 45000 series addresses several controversial issues. Among the most significant are the definition of certification, the technical competence of assessors, the potential conflict of interest between consultancy and registration operations, and the peer review program.

In an effort to establish norms by which all European accreditation bodies should conduct their business, the European Accreditation of Certification (EAC) has published its interpretations of the EN 45000 series of standards. This process involves the definition of certain terms and the interpretation of particularly crucial or vague areas of the standards.

Definition of Certification

Quality systems certification has a different meaning to customers, suppliers and registrars within and outside the European Union. The EAC, realizing that mutual recognition of accreditation and quality systems certification requires that a certificate have similar meaning and value to all parties affected by it, has tried to harmonize these differences by defining the meaning of a quality systems certificate.

The EAC interprets EN 45012 *Clause 2, Certification of Conformity*, as follows:

> *The certification should give the market confidence that the supplier is capable of systematically meeting agreed requirements for any product or service supplied within the field specified on the certificate, the 'scope of the supplier.'*

This interpretation affirms that a supplier should give the market confidence that a product or service will meet the agreed-upon requirements. A customer who places an order with a certified supplier should expect consistency.

This does not imply that the product or service will meet the requirements of a specific technical standard. The supplier and the customer must understand that quality system certification and supplier conformance to agreed-upon customer requirements go hand in hand. Demonstrated product conformity to a technical standard is a separate issue.

Assessor's Technical Competence

The most effective way to ensure and promote market confidence in a certified supplier—and to increase industry belief in the value of the certificate—is for the certifying registrar to employ technically competent assessors.

The EAC interpretation of EN 45012 *Clause 7, Certification Personnel,* clarifies what is meant by competency. The EAC guidelines state:

> *The assessment team needs a background which ensures that they understand the requirements relating to the system they are auditing. Each assessment team should have a general understanding and background in each technological and industrial sector in which it operates. It should be able to determine whether or not a particular quality system adequately covers the requirements of the standard in the area that it covered.*

An assessor's technical competence should be demonstrated by his or her understanding of how the product is used, a general knowledge of the product's critical characteristics, the process by which the product is manufactured and tested, and his or her familiarity with the appropriate product standards.

This competence can be demonstrated by a recognized industry certification, prior work experience or technical society participation. The ability of a quality systems registrar to employ assessors with the necessary audit skills, technical depth, and product use knowledge ensures marketplace confidence in a certified supplier.

Consultancy

Consultancy is an area of extreme importance to the EAC, registrars, suppliers and customers alike. Conflict of interest problems spawn a wide range of opinions among both EU and US conformity assessment experts.

In the guidelines, the EAC has clarified its position on consultancy. They state that if a certification body is owned by a person or holding company that also engages in consultancy, then that person or company is regarded as a consultant and the certification body must have an appropriate structure to prevent that entity from influencing certification.

In addition, the EAC understands that even the perception of conflict is as harmful as the actual act. Thus the guideline also states that consultancy and accredited certification should never be marketed together.

These guidelines clarify that the registrar and its representatives have a duty to make clear to the supplier that using both consulting and registration services will bring no business advantages.

Peer Review

The EAC's harmonized interpretation for applying the EN 45012 standard offers a mechanism for assuring that signatories of the EAC are complying with these guidelines. A peer review method will be used by the EAC to demonstrate this assurance.

While the policies are still being discussed, peer review will ensure that the certificates issued by an accreditation board and accredited registrar are "valid" within the EAC community. "Valid" may be loosely defined as a certificate that provides the necessary marketplace assurance.

RECOGNITION OF REGISTRATION CERTIFICATES

The international acceptance of registration certificates is a crucial issue, though still developing.

The key issue is this: If a registrar performs a quality system audit based on the ISO 9000 series standards and subsequently registers a facility, will the registration certificate be recognized within the industry and in the rest of the world?

As mentioned earlier, in the private sector, recognition of the certificate by a company's customers is the primary determinant of a certificate's acceptability. The accreditation status of the registrar itself and how this is viewed by the marketplace is another key factor.

At the member state level in the European Union, a registration obtained in one EU member state for a regulated product may not necessarily be accepted in other EU states on a bilateral basis. Other member states in the European Union can voluntarily choose to recognize the registration certificate.

Europeans and Americans are currently working on these issues, which most agree will take years to be resolved. This work is progressing largely through the efforts of the International Organization for Standardization's Committee on Conformity Assessment (CASCO), the International Accreditation Forum (IAF), the European Network for Quality System Assessment and Certification (EQNET), and the European Committee for Quality System Assessment and Certification (EQS).

ISO's Council Committee on Conformity Assessment (CASCO)

The goals of CASCO, the International Organization for Standardization's Council Committee on Conformity of Assessment, are the following:

- Study the means of assessing the conformity of products, processes, services and quality systems to appropriate standards or other technical specifications
- Prepare international guides relating to the testing, inspection and certification of products, processes and services and to the assessment of quality systems, testing laboratories, inspection bodies, and certification bodies, including their operation and acceptance
- Promote mutual recognition and acceptance of national and regional conformity assessment systems
- Promote the appropriate use of international standards for testing, inspection, certification, quality systems and related purposes.

CASCO reached a consensus while meeting in Spring 1993, agreeing to begin resolving the many complex technical problems affecting global recognition of ISO 9000 series registrations. CASCO members recommended that an international system be established to promote this recognition, though just who would set up the international system is still unclear.

CASCO members also recommended the following:

- Accreditation bodies that enter mutual recognition agreements with other accreditation bodies should address issues affecting both the national and multinational levels
- The identity and traceability of conformity certificates—including ISO 9000 registrations—should be maintained through use of certificates
- Such certificates should be adequately supported if necessary by requiring that audit reports be made available.

International Accreditation Forum (IAF)

The IAF was formed in January 1993 when ten representatives of various international standards bodies and registrars met to begin a series of discussions on how international accreditation bodies could better cooperate with one another in the effort to establish a complete network of mutual recognition agreements. The goal is a system whereby accreditations are recognized throughout the world.

At an April 30-May 1, 1993 meeting, the IAF considered a master list of 22 topics that members felt should be addressed and whittled it down to the following 9 primary areas of focus:

ISO/IEC GUIDES PERTINENT TO CERTIFICATION, REGISTRATION AND ACCREDITATION

Guide 2 .... *General terms and definitions concerning standardization and related activities*

Guide 7 .... *Requirements for standards suitable for product certification*

Guide 16 ...... *Code of principles on third-party certification systems and related standards*

Guide 22 ...... *Information on manufacturer's declaration of conformity with standards or other technical specifications*

Guide 23 ...... *Methods of indicating conformity with standards for third-party certification systems*

Guide 25 ...... *General requirements for the competence of calibration and testing laboratories*

Guide 27 ...... *Guidelines for corrective action to be taken by a certification body in the event of misuse of its mark of conformity*

Guide 28 ...... *General rules for a model third-party certification system for products*

Guide 38 ...... *General requirements for the acceptance of testing laboratories*

Guide 39 ...... *General requirements for the acceptance of inspection bodies*

Guide 40 ...... *General requirements for the acceptance of certification bodies*

Guide 42 ...... *Guidelines for a step-by-step approach to an international certification system*

Guide 43 ...... *Development and operation of laboratory proficiency testing*

Guide 44 ...... *General rules for ISO or IEC international third-party certification schemes for products*

Guide 45 ...... *Guidelines for the presentation of test results*

Guide 48 ...... *Guidelines for third-party assessment and registration of a supplier's quality system*

Guide 49 ...... *Guidelines for development of a quality manual for a testing laboratory*

Guide 53 ...... *An approach to the utilization of a supplier's quality system in third-party product certification*

Guide 54 ...... *Testing laboratory accreditation systems—General recommendations for the acceptance of accreditation bodies*

Guide 55 ...... *Testing laboratory accreditation systems—General recommendations for operation*

Guide 56 ...... *An approach to the review by a certification body of its own internal quality system*

1) Requirements of complete reevaluation of a supplier's quality system, separate and distinct from surveillance
2) Sphere of influence for accreditation bodies
3) Structure of registrars, including role and makeup on the independent advisory board
4) Use of satellite offices of an accredited registrar and the conditions for issuing registration certificate bearing the registration mark
5) Mutual recognition of accreditation
6) Minimum level of registration activity required before accreditation is granted
7) Misleading ISO 9000 advertising
8) Public announcement of applications for accreditation
9) Allowing registrars to offer suppliers a choice of accreditation body marks and use of a quality mark system on packaging.

A working paper will be developed on each area and the issues will be discussed at the IAF's planned Spring 1994 meeting.

European Network for Quality System Assessment and Certification (EQNET)

EQNET was founded early in 1990 by eight certification institutions: AFAQ (France), AIB-Vincotte (Belgium), BSI (Great Britain), DQS (Germany), DS (Denmark), N.V. KEMA (The Netherlands), SIS (Sweden), SQS (Switzerland). More institutions from the remaining EU and EFTA countries are expected to join EQNET as soon as they comply with EN 45012 and comply with the additional European harmonization criteria. For now, cooperation among individual members is based on analogous bilateral sets of agreements. The intention is to further expand the EQNET network with the aid of multilateral contracts as soon as possible.

The main tasks of EQNET include the following:

• Cooperate to recognize the certificates issued by other members on the basis of existing contracts and to promote the recognition of certificates
• Coordinate the certification of border-crossing groups of companies/organizations and the joint conduct of the said certificates in a competent and efficient way
• Issue several certificates at the same time on the basis of joint certification audits.

European Committee for Quality System Assessment and Certification (EQS)

EQS was formed to achieve the following primary goals:

• Harmonization of rules for quality system assessment and certification
• Overall recognition of quality system certificates
• Efforts to permit mutual recognition of the certificates of quality system certification bodies.

The group's ultimate aim is to avoid multiple assessment and certification of an organization's quality system and to develop confidence in quality system assessment and certification carried out by competent bodies.

The ongoing work of CASCO, IAF and EQNET and EQS will eventually lead to a larger if not complete network of mutual recognition agreements.

The European Accreditation of Certification (EAC)

The European Accreditation of Certification is an association of accreditation bodies from the European Union (EU) and the European Free Trade Association (EFTA). The EAC's goal is the creation of a single European accreditation system covering products, quality systems and personnel. The EAC has published its own interpretations of the EN 45000 standards. (See below.) By harmonizing the definitions and interpretations of these rules, the EAC hopes to bring the business practices of all registrars into closer alignment.

The European Organization for Testing and Certification (EOTC)

The European Organization for Testing and Certification (EOTC), proposed by the European Union for the purpose of dealing with conformity assessment issues, was created in April 1990. Its role is to promote mutual recognition of test results, certification procedures, and quality system assessments and registrations in non-regulated product areas throughout the European Union and EFTA. Its primary goal is to encourage equivalency of certificates and to avoid the duplication caused by multiple certifications.

The EOTC will also be responsible for providing technical assistance to the EU Commission in the implementation of some EU legislation, especially in the preparation of Mutual Recognition Agreements with non-EU countries.

EOTC AGREEMENT GROUPS

EOTC aims to recognize the technical competence of the certification bodies (i.e., registrars and laboratories) in certain industry agreement groups. The purpose of an agreement group is to promote mutual recognition of test certificates by certification bodies throughout the EU, EFTA and third world countries. These agreement groups assure mutual recognition of test reports and certificates by the certification bodies that participate in the agreement group. The EOTC also is considering extending the conformity assessment modular approach to old-approach directives and certain non-regulated products.

The EOTC has recognized ten agreement groups. The industry sectors these groups cover vary from fire and security to information technology.

The EOTC's agreement groups bring value to the marketplace and benefit both the customers and agreement group participants by helping establish shared confidence in the test procedures and product and quality system evaluation procedures.

EOTC'S STATUS

The EOTC previously was under the auspices of the European Commission, However, the EOTC signed an agreement with its 23 founding members to establish its independence as a private association. The founding members will continue to serve a leadership role in the non-regulated product conformity assessment scheme, but the association may help to organize agreement groups among notified bodies.

One of the EOTC's sectorial committees, the European Committee for Information Technology Testing and Certification (ECITC)—which oversees the agreement groups for information technology—is primarily responsible for this activity.

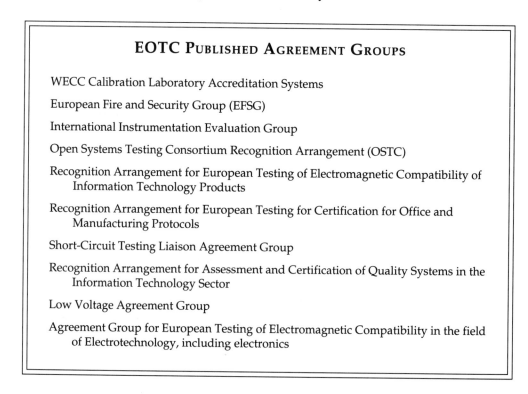

EOTC PUBLISHED AGREEMENT GROUPS

WECC Calibration Laboratory Accreditation Systems

European Fire and Security Group (EFSG)

International Instrumentation Evaluation Group

Open Systems Testing Consortium Recognition Arrangement (OSTC)

Recognition Arrangement for European Testing of Electromagnetic Compatibility of Information Technology Products

Recognition Arrangement for European Testing for Certification for Office and Manufacturing Protocols

Short-Circuit Testing Liaison Agreement Group

Recognition Arrangement for Assessment and Certification of Quality Systems in the Information Technology Sector

Low Voltage Agreement Group

Agreement Group for European Testing of Electromagnetic Compatibility in the field of Electrotechnology, including electronics

AUDITOR CERTIFICATION

A final issue of interest to companies who are considering registration to ISO 9000 standards is the qualification of auditors. Who certifies auditors and according to what criteria?

ISO 10011, Guidelines for auditing quality systems, has been accepted by ISO as the qualifica-

---

RECOGNITION ARRANGEMENT FOR THE ASSESSMENT AND CERTIFICATION OF QUALITY SYSTEMS IN THE INFORMATION TECHNOLOGY SECTOR (ITQS)

ITQS is one of several agreement groups that EOTC has formally approved, and is a good example of how an agreement group contributes to the harmonization process. Agreement groups are set up along industry lines and allow companies to rely on just one test or assessment that will be accepted throughout Europe.

The assessments carried out by the certification bodies (registrars) cooperating in ITQS will be carried out in a harmonized way, using common standards, techniques and guidance material. ITQS membership is open to any EU or EFTA organization, provided the organization accepts and applies ITQS regulations, including an auditor guide.

The ITQS auditor guide is "unique because instead of being a guidance document for the certification applicant, it is mainly designed to be used by the certification bodies," according to Paul Caussin of AIB-Vincotte. AIB-Vincotte is the ITQS secretariat.

The auditor guide "tells the auditors what to look for when auditing an information technology firm, covers software and hardware development, and production and service activities," said Caussin. The purpose of an auditing guide is to ensure that information technology firms certified by an ITQS member are assessed on an equivalent basis. Quality managers at some US information technology firms have cited the lack of experienced information technology auditors as one of the reasons the United States does not, as yet, have a strong formalized system for information technology quality assurance.

Criteria for information technology auditors under the ITQS system include a professional education or training, or practical experience in information technology, as well as specific training in the understanding of quality control techniques applicable to information technology. "ITQS regulations also require that the auditors be evaluated on a regular basis by an evaluation panel, possibly from a professional society," according to Caussin.

---

tions criteria for auditors. It contains three parts (*10011-1, Auditing, 10011-2, Qualification criteria for quality systems auditors, and 10011-3 , Management of audit programs*). The *ISO 10011* series of guidelines has been widely accepted internationally, and while it is not a mandatory requirement, it is an excellent resource for establishing consistent audit practice worldwide.

While ISO 10011 guidelines cover all aspects of the conduct and management of an audit and the training of auditors, perhaps their most important requirement is that only certified lead assessors can lead the audit team and perform the assessment of your company's quality systems. (ISO 10011 is discussed in more detail in Chapter 5.)

Auditor Certification Programs

THE INSTITUTE FOR QUALITY ASSURANCE

The Institute for Quality Assurance (IQA) in the United Kingdom is currently the only organization outside of the United States that governs and controls the assessor training and certification process.[1] Its program is known as *The National Registration Scheme for Assessors of Quality Systems*. The aim of the scheme is to recognize the integrity and competence of quality systems auditors as measured against the criteria found in international standards.

Under the IQA scheme, auditor certification is reviewed every three years, with renewal dependent upon the ability of the registered auditor to meet criteria for assessment experience required at the time of the renewal.

REGISTRAR ACCREDITATION BOARD

In the United States, the Registrar Accreditation Board (RAB) has its own program for auditor assessor certification, *The Certification Program for Auditors of Quality Systems*. In addition, the RAB has published a program to train ISO 9000 series auditors, called *Requirements for the Recognition of an Auditor Training Course*.

This program is the final piece of a complete ISO 9000 series registration and accreditation scheme that includes the accreditation of registrars, certification of auditors and lead auditors, and the recognition of training courses.

Certification under RAB's Certification Program for Auditors of Quality Systems requires training in an approved course. Two types of courses may be offered to meet RAB training requirements for RAB auditor certification:

1) A 36-hour Lead Auditor Training Course that includes ANSI/ASQC Q90 (ISO 9000) series training, quality system audit training, and an examination that covers this information. An ability to communicate, both orally and in writing, and the personal attributes and audit management capabilities are necessary to conduct and lead an audit.

2) A 16-hour Lead Auditor Training Course for Certified Quality Auditors that includes ANSI/ASQC Q90 (ISO 9000) series training and an examination. The applicant's ability to communicate both orally and in writing will also be evaluated. The 16-hour course and an ASQC Certified Quality Auditor certificate meet general auditor training requirements for RAB certification.

The Certified Quality Auditor rating currently offered by the ASQC means that an applicant to the program has fulfilled requirements and has demonstrated knowledge of auditing.

The CQA rating does not exempt the candidate from the other experience required by RAB, including audit experience. A CQA rating, together with a 16-hour course, along with appropriate ISO 9000 training given by the RAB-approved training organizations, will exempt the candidate from the standard 36-hour course.

The CQA program will not be affected by RAB's quality system auditor certification program. RAB and ASQC are separate organizations with separate goals for auditor certification.

AMERICAN SOCIETY FOR QUALITY CONTROL

The ASQC has an auditor certification program that offers a CQA rating as described above. This rating signifies that an applicant has education and/or work experience in a specified field and demonstrates knowledge through the successful completion of a written examination.

MUTUAL RECOGNITION OF AUDITOR CERTIFICATION

In March 1994, the RAB and the IQA reached an agreement that allows students who complete a lead assessor, or lead auditor's course sanctioned by one of the organizations to apply for certification through the other. The agreement also means that auditors who have been certified through one accreditation body are recognized by the other.

In September 1993, 16 nations met in Singapore to develop a plan to create a single, internationally accepted set of requirements for ISO 9000 series auditor certification and related course accreditation. Under such a system, it would not be necessary for providers of ISO 9000 series lead auditor training to receive more than one accreditation of their courses, or for auditors to seek certification from more than one body. It would also mean that an individual could take lead auditor training under one accreditation program and apply for auditor certification under another. For course providers it would mean that a single accreditation from an approved body would suffice for global recognition of training courses.

CONCLUSION

Registrar accreditation issues are far from settled. Issues concerning international acceptance (i.e., between the United States and the European Union) of registration practices also remain unresolved. Some have been addressed above under the focus areas of CASCO, IAF, EQNET or EQS. Other questions include:

- If the European Union accepts ISO 9000 certificates issued by US registrars, is there any way to guarantee that the United States would recognize certificates issued by EU notified bodies?
- Who in the United States would be required to recognize certificates issued by EU notified bodies?

What assurances could be provided by the EU regarding the competence of their notified bodies and vice-versa? These and many other areas that touch on the activity of registrars remain unsettled.

ENDNOTE

[1] For more information on the IQA scheme, write to: The Scheme Manager/The Registration Board for Assessors/PO Box 712/61 Southwark Street/London, SW1W 0DQ, England; tel. 071-401-2988, fax 071-401-2725.

ANNEX 1:

EN 45012 General Criteria for Certification Bodies Operating Quality System Certification—Outline of Requirements

1. **Object and field of application**—general criteria for a certification body operating quality system certification.

2. **Definitions**—definitions applicable to EN 45012.

3. **General requirements**—states that all suppliers have access to the services of the certification body and that the procedures under which the body operates shall be administered in a nondiscriminatory manner.

4. **Administrative structure**—requires the certification body to do the following:
    - Be impartial
    - Choose the members of its governing board from among the interests involved in the process of certification without any single interest predominating
    - Safeguard impartiality and enable participation from all parties concerned in certification system functions
    - Have permanent personnel under the senior executive to carry out the day-to-day operations in a way that is free from control by those who have a direct commercial interest in the products or services concerned.

5. **Terms of reference of governing board**—addresses the functions of the governing board of the certification body through the following:
    - Formulation of policy
    - Overview of policy implementation
    - Overview of the finances
    - Setting up committees as required.

6. **Organizational structure**—addresses the requirements for a certified body's organizational structure by calling for the following:
    - A chart showing the responsibility and reporting structure of the organization and in particular the relationship between the assessment and certification functions
    - A description of the means by which the certified body obtains financial support
    - A documented statement of its certification systems, including its rules and procedures for granting certification
    - Documentation clearly identifying its legal status.

7. **Certification personnel**—requires the following:
    - Personnel be competent for the functions they undertake
    - Information be maintained regarding relevant qualifications, training, and experience
    - Records of training be kept up-to-date
    - Personnel have available clear documented instructions pertaining to their duties and responsibilities

(continued on next page)

EN 45012

(continued from previous page)

- Personnel of subcontracted sources meet the requirements of EN 45012.

8. **Documentation and change control**—requires the following:
   - That the certified body maintain a system for controlling documentation related to the certification system. This means that:
   - Current issues of the appropriate documentation must be available at all relevant locations
   - Changes to documents must be covered by the correct authorization and processed in a way that ensures direct and speedy action at the effective point
   - Superseded documents be removed from use throughout the organization and its agencies
   - Certified suppliers be notified of changes that could be accomplished through direct mailing or by issue of a periodic publication.

9. **Records**—addresses the requirements for the following:
   - Maintaining a record system to demonstrate the way in which each certification procedure was applied, including assessment and surveillance
   - Storing records for an adequate period
   - Holding records secure and in confidence to the client, unless otherwise required by law.

10. **Certification and surveillance procedures**—addresses the following requirements:
    - That the certification body have documented procedures to enable the assessment, certification, and surveillance of quality systems to be carried out
    - That the certification body require the supplier to have a documented quality system
    - That the certification body maintain regular surveillance of the supplier's quality system.

11. **Certification and surveillance facilities**—address the following requirements:
    - That the certification body have the required facilities in terms of certification personnel expertise and equipment to perform assessment, certification, and surveillance of the supplier's quality system
    - That the certification body ensure that external bodies conform to the above requirement and that a properly documented agreement covering the arrangements, including confidentiality, be drawn up.

12. **Quality manual**—addresses the requirements that the certification body have a quality manual and documented procedures setting out the way in which it complies with the following criteria:
    - A quality policy statement
    - A brief description of the legal status of the certification body
    - A statement about the organization of the certification body, including details regarding the governing board, its constitution, terms of reference, and rules of procedure
    - Names, qualifications, experience, and terms of reference of the senior executive and other certification personnel, both internal and external
    - Details of training arrangements for certification personnel
    - An organizational chart showing lines of authority, responsibility and allocation functions

(continued on next page)

EN 45012

(continued from previous page)

stemming from the senior executive

- Details of the documented procedures for assessing and auditing supplier quality systems
- Details of documented procedures for surveillance of suppliers
- A list of subcontractors and details of the documented procedures for assessing and monitoring their competence
- Details of appeals procedures.

13. **Confidentiality**—addresses the requirements that the certification body ensure confidentiality of the information obtained in the course of its certification activities at all levels of its organization, including committees.

14. **Publications**—addresses the requirements that the certification body produce and update, as necessary, a list of certified suppliers with an outline of the scope of the certification of each supplier, and the requirement that the list be available to the public. This section further requires that a description of the certification system(s) be available in published form.

15. **Appeals**—addresses requirements that the certification body have procedures for considering appeals to its decisions.

16. **Internal audit and periodic review**—addresses the requirement that the certification body undertake internal audits and periodic reviews of its compliance with the criteria of EN 45012. The reviews are to be recorded and are to be made available to persons having the right of access to this information.

17. **Misuse of certificates**—addresses requirements that the certification body exercise proper control on the use of its quality system certificates. This section also requires that incorrect references to the certification systems or misleading use of certificates found in advertisements, catalogs, etc., be dealt with by suitable actions. A further notation states that such actions include corrective action, publication of the transgression and, if necessary, legal action.

18. **Complaints**—addresses requirements that the certification body require the certified suppliers to keep a record of all complaints and remedial actions relative to the quality system.

19. **Withdrawal and cancellation of certificates**—addresses the requirement that the certification body have documented procedures for withdrawal and cancellation of quality system certificates.

CREDIBILITY OF QUALITY SYSTEMS CERTIFICATION: HOW TO DEAL WITH SCOPES OF CERTIFICATION, CONFLICTS OF INTEREST AND CODES OF CONDUCT

BY DONALD W. MARQUARDT

This chapter addresses the issue of credibility of quality systems certification. This chapter was prepared as a document for the Registrar Accreditation Board (RAB). Part 1 is a white paper that discusses the scope of registration of a supplier's quality system. Parts 2 and 3 include policy statements that have been adopted by the RAB Board of Directors and have been implemented in RAB procedures. Specifically, this chapter discusses the following:

- Ways to properly define the scope of registration of a supplier's quality system
- Policy regarding conflict of interest by RAB-accredited registrars
- Registrar Code of Conduct.

These points are first briefly addressed and are followed by their full text in the annex (parts 1, 2 and 3).

INTRODUCTION

Programs for third-party certification/registration of quality systems have grown worldwide and the impact on the global economy has become enormous.

Existing international, regional and national standards and guides for implementation of such third-party programs are providing support for developing programs worldwide. This support includes requirements standards and supplementary guidance standards.

One focal point is the ISO 9000 series and ISO 10000 series standards prepared by the ISO/ TC 176 committee. Another focal point is the implementation guides, such as ISO/IEC Guides 40 and 48, prepared by the ISO Committee on Conformity Assessment (CASCO). The elements of these various standards and guides have been adopted by regional bodies such as the European Community and by many nations worldwide.

In addition, many nations have set up implementation programs that reflect the three-level concept of certification, accreditation and recognition.

- Quality systems certification bodies (registrars) evaluate suppliers' quality systems for conformity to the requirements standards.
- Accreditation bodies evaluate the managing systems of certification bodies for conformity to international guides.
- Recognition bodies, usually government affiliated, provide national recognition of the quality systems certification (registration) and accreditation program, and thus facilitate the establishment of mutual recognition among nations in regulated areas.

The marketplace credibility of this developing network of international programs rests upon the elements of assurance and ethical principles incorporated in the various standards and guides and their implementation. The high degree of success to date in implementing registration programs worldwide indicates that the base of assurance elements and ethical principles is sound, at least in broad outline.

As the registration programs have become widespread and involve multiple business/economic sectors and multiple cultures, new and unanticipated complexities are revealed. It is therefore timely to reexamine the details of the assurance/ethical infrastructure of the evolving registration programs.

The RAB has evaluated carefully the elements of assurance and ethical principles to ensure a credible program giving due consideration to the complexities of the international system.

The following three components of these elements are entitled:

1. Defining the scope of registration of a supplier's quality system (defining which standard, which geographic sites, which products, which portions of the supply chain)
2. Policy, Principles and Implementation Regarding Conflict of Interest by RAB-Accredited Registrars
3. Code of Conduct (for persons working on behalf of RAB).

All three components are considered essential to achieve the goal of marketplace credibility. The full text of the components, contained in a White Paper, is included in the annex at the end of this chapter. Some of the key points described in the first component are discussed below.

SCOPE OF CERTIFICATION/REGISTRATION OF A SUPPLIER'S QUALITY SYSTEM

In current practice worldwide there is great variability in the documented definitions of the scopes of supplier quality system registrations. This variability is observed from supplier to supplier for a given registrar, from registrar to registrar in a given nation, and from one nation to another. The term "registrar" is used in North America; the term "certification body" is used in Europe. RAB believes that greater consistency in defining and documenting this scope is an essential prerequisite to do the following:

● Establish marketplace credibility of quality system certification/registration to the ISO 9000 series standards

● Negotiate meaningful mutual recognition arrangements among nations.

Beyond the benefits of marketplace credibility, there are important benefits to registrars if the ground rules for defining scope are consistent for all parties. To adequately describe the scope of certification/registration of a supplier's quality system, four basic questions must be answered:

● **Which standard?**

The statement of scope should identify the ISO 9000 series standard whose requirements have been the basis for evaluating conformity leading to the registration of the supplier's quality system (i.e., ISO 9001, ISO 9002, ISO 9003).

The customer must be confident that the joint selection of the appropriate standard by the supplier and the registrar has taken adequately into consideration the amount and nature of product design activity that is involved in the products produced by the supplier, as well as the nature of the production processes through which the supplier adds value to the product.

● **Which geographic sites?**

The statement of scope should identify the boundaries of the registered supplier quality system, in terms of the geographic location(s) of the facilities and activities. The procedure should inform the customer whether the product the customer receives is processed within the registered quality system, even in situations where the supplier may have multiple sites dealing with the same product, not all of which may be registered.

● **Which products?**

The statement of scope should identify the boundaries of the registered supplier quality system in terms of the commercial product(s) that are processed. The term "products" includes all four generic product categories: hardware, software, processed materials and services.

The customer should be informed whether the product the customer receives is processed within the registered quality system, even in situations where the supplier may deal with multiple products at the same site, and not all of the products may be processed within the registered quality system.

● **Which portions of the supply chain?**

The statement of scope should identify the boundaries of the registered supplier quality system, in terms of supply-chain criteria, specifically the starting points and ending points of the registered quality system. Specification of boundaries in terms of supply-chain criteria is not part of established procedures.

There appear to be many instances where the registered quality system represents only a small fraction of the supplier's operations, or a small fraction of the total value added in the product. This is not stated in registration documentation, and, as a consequence, customers are not aware of this fact.

In practice today virtually all certificates of quality system registration are deficient because they do not provide definitive answers to all four questions. Part 1 of the White Paper goes on to suggest ways that registrars can implement the above requirements. Four steps in this process are proposed:

1. Each accredited registrar provides information on the four elements discussed above on the face of each registration certificate issued.
2. All publishers of registration lists show the same information.
3. Each registered supplier maintains a mechanism to inform customers about the four elements, such as providing copies of the certificates when appropriate.
4. Each registrar establishes and maintains procedures and records regarding the above elements.

Part 2, Policy, Principles and Implementation Regarding Conflict of Interest by RAB-Accredited Registrars and Part 3, Code of Conduct (for persons working on behalf of RAB) are discussed in the Annex to this chapter.

CONCLUSION

ANSI-RAB and the US program do not stand alone. The issues discussed in the White Paper are of international concern. They are intended to serve as a basis for discussion and consensus development by interested parties in the United States and worldwide.

The implementation of the ethical principles and elements of assurance incorporated in the various standards and guides is clearly important to the credibility of quality systems registration. Who should take responsibility for these? At a fundamental level, every person involved in any facet of quality system registration should take personal responsibility.

Specific organizations must have clear responsibilities for implementing the recommended procedures. For example, the code of conduct discussed in Part 3 is to be implemented at the accreditation body level, but corresponding codes of conduct are required of organizations operating at the registration level. The Registrar conflict of interest policy and principles discussed in Part 2 is to be implemented at the registration level. The scope of registration definition discussed in Part 1 is to be implemented jointly by suppliers and registrars.

In each instance there are other organizational entities that have defined roles. For example, registrars audit suppliers for conformance, accreditation bodies audit registrars, and recognition bodies have formal processes to establish credibility for recognition.

Those who write international standards (e.g., ISO/TC 176) and guides (e.g., ISO CASCO) have their own defined responsibilities. They set the ground rules by means of the standards and guides. ISO Central Secretariat has recently formed a special group to study the international procedures for implementing quality systems registration and related matters. A variety of involved constituencies are represented on this group.

The suggestion also has been made to incorporate the scope of accreditation elements, as discussed in Part 1 of this paper, into the revisions of the ISO 9000 series standards as part of their guidance with respect to third-party registration.

The Registrar Accreditation Board stands ready to facilitate international discussion and consensus formation to enable international systems to continue to meet the growing needs for credibility of quality systems certification and registration.

ACKNOWLEDGMENTS

Members of the RAB Board of Directors have contributed to the discussions leading to the policy statements and proposals in this paper. G.Q. Lofgren and R.W. Peach provided helpful comments in the preparation of this paper. J.H. Hooper and others also provided comments and suggestions on Part 1.

ANNEX 1

Part 1: A Registrar Accreditation Board (RAB) White Paper— Defining the Scope of the Certification/Registration of a Supplier's Quality System

1. INTRODUCTION

Background

RAB observes that there is great variability in the documented definitions of scope of registration of suppliers' quality systems. This variability is observed from supplier-to-supplier for a given registrar, from registrar-to-registrar in a given nation, and from one nation to another. The term "registrar" is used in North America; the term "certification body" is used in Europe.

Benefits

RAB believes that greater consistency in defining and documenting this scope is an essential prerequisite for the following:

- Establishing marketplace credibility of quality system certification/registration to the ISO 9000 series standards

- Negotiating meaningful mutual recognition arrangements among nations.

Beyond the benefits of marketplace credibility, there are important benefits to registrars if the ground rules for defining scope are consistent for all parties.

2. PURPOSE OF THIS WHITE PAPER

The purpose of this White Paper is to do the following:

- Analyze the concept of "scope" and define its elements

- Describe for each element of scope, a recommended approach, the current status in relation to the recommended approach, and the unresolved issues

- Propose a principle upon which implementation procedures should be based

- Propose implementation procedures for describing and publishing the scope of registration of a supplier's quality system

- Provide guidelines for describing scope.

This White Paper is intended to serve as a basis for discussion and consensus development on these issues by interested and affected parties in the United States and worldwide.

3. THE CONCEPT AND ELEMENTS OF SCOPE

To adequately describe the scope of certification/registration of a supplier's quality system, four basic questions must be asked:

- Which standard?

- Which geographic sites?

- Which products?

(continued on next page)

ANNEX 1

(continued from previous page)

● Which portions of the supply chain?

In practice today virtually all certificates of quality system registration are deficient because they do not provide definitive answers to all four questions.

The four basic questions lead to the four elements of scope:

3.1 Which Standard?

The statement of scope must identify the ISO 9000 series standard whose requirements have been the basis for evaluating conformity leading to the registration of the supplier's quality system (i.e., ISO 9001, ISO 9002, ISO 9003).

3.2 Which Geographic Sites?

The statement of scope must identify the boundaries of the registered supplier quality system, in terms of the geographic location(s) of the facilities and activities.

3.3 Which Products?

The statement of scope must identify the boundaries of the registered supplier quality system in terms of the commercial product(s) that are processed. The term "products" includes all four generic product categories: hardware, software, processed materials and services.

3.4 Which Portions of the Supply Chain?

The statement of scope must identify the boundaries of the registered supplier quality system, in terms of supply-chain criteria, specifically the starting points and ending points of the registered quality system.

4. RECOMMENDED APPROACH, CURRENT STATUS AND ISSUES

4.1 Selection of Standard

Approach

The procedure should provide confidence to the customer that the joint selection of the appropriate standard by the supplier and the registrar has taken adequately into consideration the amount and nature of product design activity that is involved in the products produced by the supplier, as well as the nature of the production processes through which the supplier adds value to the product.

Status

The majority of quality systems today are being registered to ISO 9001 or ISO 9002. Most choices seem to be appropriate to the circumstances. In most cases the identification of the standard selected is visible to the customer.

Issue

In some cases ISO 9003 or ISO 9002 has been selected when it appears that a more comprehensive quality assurance model would be more appropriate. In some cases the mismatch may not readily be apparent to the customer. *(continued on next page)*

ANNEX 1

(continued from previous page)

4.2 Specification of Boundaries in Terms of Geographic Location

Approach

The procedure should inform the customer whether the product the customer receives is processed within the registered quality system, even in situations where the supplier may have multiple sites dealing with the same product, not all of which may be registered.

Status

Most customers today seem to be informed on this element of scope, and are, when they deem it important, requiring suppliers to supply product processed at registered sites.

Issue

The lack of consistent procedures sets the stage for misrepresentation.

4.3 Specification of Boundaries in Terms of Product(s) Processed

Approach

The procedure should inform the customer whether the product the customer receives is processed within the registered quality system, even in situations where the supplier may deal with multiple products at the same site, and not all of the products may be processed within the registered quality system.

Status

Most customers today seem to be informed on this element of scope.

Issue

The lack of consistent procedures sets the stage for misrepresentation.

4.4 Specification of the Boundaries in Terms of Supply-Chain Criteria

Approach

The procedure should inform the customer regarding the following:

- The starting points of the supplier's registered operations (e.g., the raw materials, parts, components, services and intermediate products that are provided by sub-suppliers)
- The ending points of the supplier's registered operations (i.e., the remaining steps on the way to the ultimate consumer that are excluded from the supplier's registered operations)
- The nature of the value added that has been provided by the supplier's registered operations.

Status

Specification of boundaries in terms of supply-chain criteria is not part of established procedures. There appear to be many instances where the registered quality system represents only a small fraction of the supplier's operations, or a small fraction of the total value added in the product. This is not stated in registration documentation, and, as a consequence, customers are not aware of this fact.

(continued on next page)

ANNEX 1

(continued from previous page)

Issue

This situation invites suppliers who wish to be registered, but want to exclude portions of their operations from scrutiny by the registrar, to declare the excluded portions to be subcontractor operations. It does not matter whether the excluded portions are in another nation, elsewhere in the same nation, or simply in another part of the same production site. It is possible that a supplier can be registered for the supply of an end product, when only a small portion of the value added has been provided by the operations that have been subject to the registrar audit and evaluation. The lack of procedures in this element of scope appears to be providing a significant opportunity for misrepresentation by some suppliers, in various nations.

5. PRINCIPLE UPON WHICH IMPLEMENTATION PROCEDURES SHOULD BE BASED

5.1 Principle

There are many registrars; each is registering many supplier quality systems. Each supplier is dealing with many customers. It is impractical to monitor adequately the operations of such a system solely by periodic audits.

Consequently, RAB supports the following principle regarding scope:

> *Primary reliance must be placed on the concept of "truth in labeling" by means of which every customer has routine, ready access to the information upon which to judge all four elements of the scope of a supplier's registered quality system.*

5.2 Relation to International Criteria

The first three elements of scope are dealt with in ISO/IEC Guide 48 in generic terms. The last (supply-chain boundaries) is new, but equally important.

Certificates of registration are the original records from which other records (e.g., lists of registered quality systems) are derived. Examination of samples of certificates and registers shows that even the first three elements are not universally or uniformly documented today.

6. FORMAT AND IMPLEMENTATION PROCEDURES FOR DESCRIBING SCOPE

To implement the principle supported by RAB, four types of requirements are proposed:

6.1 Each accredited registrar shall show on the face of each registration certificate it issues clear, specific and sufficient information for **all** four elements of the quality system scope, as discussed in this document:

- Standard selected
- Geographic sites
- Products
- Supply chain boundaries.

6.2 All parties who publish registers that list certified quality systems shall show for each registered system, information on all four elements as required in item 6.1.

(continued on next page)

ANNEX 1

(continued from previous page)

6.3 Each supplier with a registered quality system shall establish, maintain and implement a mechanism to inform customers, as appropriate, about all four elements of its registered quality system, such as providing copies of applicable certificates to a customer prior to consummation of a sales agreement.

6.4 Each accredited registrar shall establish procedures and maintain records regarding its implementation of requirements 6.1 and 6.2, and its notification of suppliers and other parties to whom it provides information, regarding requirements 6.2 and 6.3.

7. IMPLEMENTATION GUIDELINES REGARDING ELEMENTS OF SCOPE

RAB proposes the following guidelines for "clear, specific and sufficient information" on each of the elements of scope. The information should be concise. Concise description of the boundaries for item 6.1 will often depend in part upon the interrelations of the boundaries defined for elements 3.1, 3.2, 3.3 and 3.4.

7.1 Selection of Standard (See 3.1 and 4.1)

Guideline

For the requirement in 6.1 simply show the number of the ISO 9000 series standard whose requirements were the basis for verifying conformity of the supplier's quality system (i.e., ISO 9001, ISO 9002 or ISO 9003).

7.2 Boundaries in Terms of Geographic Locations (See 3.2 and 4.2)

Guideline

For the requirement in 6.1 identify each of the facilities and sites in sufficient detail to distinguish those facilities comprising the registered quality system from other facilities owned, operated or controlled by the supplier and other parent, subsidiary or affiliated organizations. In most cases a full street address is not necessary.

7.3 Boundaries in Terms of Product(s) (See 3.3 and 4.3)

Guideline

For the requirement of 6.1 identify the products in sufficient detail to distinguish those products processed by the registered quality system from other products processed by the supplier and other parent, subsidiary or affiliated organizations. In many cases a listing of generic product names, types and/or trade names will be clear, specific and sufficient.

7.4 Boundaries in Terms of Supply-Chain Criteria (See 3.4 and 4.4)

Guideline

For the requirement of 6.1 identify the processes that are provided by sub-suppliers and are not part of the supplier's registered operations. This is normally accomplished by specifying in sufficient detail which raw materials, parts, components, services or intermediate products of any

(continued on next page)

ANNEX 1

(continued from previous page)

generic product category (hardware, software, processed materials and services) are provided by sub-suppliers. Specify only those that are critical to the requirements for quality of the final product.

- If the starting and ending points in the supply-chain are different for the various products covered in a single registration certificate, the specifics should be made clear.

- If intermediate steps are done by a sub-supplier, creating multiple starting and ending points, the specifics should be made clear.

- If, from one shipment to another, the situation may change, the specifics should be made clear. An example is an intermediate product or component sometimes produced by the supplier and sometimes purchased from a sub-supplier.

If the quality systems of some sub-suppliers are separately registered, then that information may be provided to customers, but should not be shown on the supplier's certificate.

8. EDUCATION OF CUSTOMERS

The "truth in labeling" principle will function most effectively when customers are educated in the issues and criteria. RAB recommends that educational materials be developed by accreditation bodies for distribution to customers. For example, the materials could suggest questions for customers to ask their potential suppliers, and discuss the scope issues related to those questions. Registrars could audit suppliers to verify that the information provided to customers is reasonable.

RAB welcomes comments on this White Paper. Address your comments to:

George Q. Lofgren, President
Registrar Accreditation Board
PO Box 3005
Milwaukee, WI 53201-3005
FAX: 414-765-8661

(continued on next page)

ANNEX 1

(continued from previous page)

Part 2: Registrar Accreditation Board (RAB)—
Policy, Principles and Implementation Regarding
Conflict of Interest by RAB-Accredited Registrars

POLICY

An RAB-accredited registrar, its employees and its agents shall not be involved in activities that constitute a conflict of interest, nor any activities that may reasonably be perceived to constitute a conflict of interest, with the registrar's registration services for any supplier.

PRINCIPLES

1. Consulting, or the giving of advice to a supplier, or any of its employees or agents, by a registrar or any of its employees or agents (whether engaged as agents of the registrar, or as individual consultants) is considered a conflict of interest when the consulting or the giving of advice is provided under circumstances that are conducive to the fact or perception that the acceptance of the consulting or advice enhances the likelihood of a favorable outcome of the registration services provided to the supplier.

2. Teaching activities may create or may be perceived to create the likelihood of concomitant consulting or the giving of advice when provided for a student group consisting exclusively or significantly of employees or agents of the supplier, or when provided on premises owned or arranged by the supplier, or when the supplier provides substantial funding or sponsorship.

3. Consulting, or the giving of advice to a supplier may create, or may be perceived to create, the likelihood of conflict of interest, if any parent, subsidiary, or affiliate organization (or division thereof) of the registrar, or their employees or agents also provide registration services to the same supplier, or a parent, subsidiary or affiliate organization (or division thereof) of the supplier.

4. A pre-audit of a supplier by a registrar to assess readiness for a full audit that could lead to registration is not in itself a conflict of interest, if the results provided to the supplier consist only of audit findings in relation to the requirements of the applicable quality system standard, and do not include consulting or advice on how to remedy any deficiencies encountered in the pre-audit.

5. If a registrar is itself a unit of a supplier and wishes to engage in first party registration (i.e., to register other units of the supplier) or second party registration (i.e., to register sub-suppliers of the supplier) such registration cannot be done under RAB accreditation.

6. A conflict of interest may exist, or be perceived to exist, where a registrar shares the same marketing organization, marketing procedures or facilities, and/or market plan with any parent, subsidiary or affiliate organization that provides consulting.

7. A conflict of interest may exist, or be perceived to exist, where the organizational units, employees or agents, of the registrar organization have a significant financial ownership relation to the supplier organization or any of its parent, subsidiary or affiliate organizations.

(continued on next page)

ANNEX 1

(continued from previous page)

IMPLEMENTATION

1. Where a registrar seeking accreditation or re-accreditation by RAB does not have any potential conflicts of interest under Principles 1 through 7, the registrar shall do the following:

   - Attest to that fact in writing as part of the documentation supplied to RAB for accreditation or re-accreditation, and

   - Inform RAB whenever any change in this status may occur.

   This is subject to verification by RAB auditors on any audit of the registrar.

2. Where a registrar engages in consulting activities as described in Principles 1, 2, 3 or 6, the registrar must take special steps in addition to attestation as in Implementation item 1, to assure the absence of conflict of interest.

   The following steps are required:

   a. Option 1

   An RAB-accredited registrar (including any of its parent, subsidiary or affiliate organizations) shall not provide consulting to an organization and issue a certificate of quality system registration to a supplier unit that includes the organization for which consulting is provided, unless the time interval during which consulting is provided and the time interval during which registration services and subsequent surveillance are provided are separated by at least one year, and the registrar's procedures provide documentation and demonstration of that separation.

   Option 2

   The registrar's procedures, organizational assignments, and documentation thereof shall ensure and demonstrate that the employees or agents involved in the consulting have no part in, nor give nor receive information relating to, any of the activities leading to certification, registration and subsequent surveillance for the supplier, nor is there any other communication regarding the supplier between those doing consulting and those doing certification and registration services, where the information, activities or communication could reasonably be perceived to constitute a conflict of interest.

   b. The registrar's advertising and other written materials for suppliers must disclose the nature of the dual consulting and registration services, and the nature of the organizational, procedural and other steps the registrar has taken to ensure the absence of conflict of interest.

   These provisions are subject to verification by RAB auditors in any audit of the registrar. RAB registration fees may reflect the additional effort required to audit items a, b.

   c. The registrar shall, upon engaging the services of each employee or agent, and at least once per year thereafter, inform the employee or agent of the provisions in this policy, and obtain the signature of the employee attesting to the absence of personal involvement in any conflict of interest under this policy, or documenting the circumstances if any such conflict or potential conflict has existed since the prior signature. These records shall be retained for RAB audit.

(continued on next page)

ANNEX 1

(continued from previous page)

3.   This statement shall be included by RAB in its "Procedures for Accreditation" and shall be supplied therewith to every registrar seeking accreditation or re-accreditation.

Part 3: Code of Conduct—Registrar Accreditation Board (RAB)

SCOPE
This Code of Conduct applies to members of the RAB Board of Directors, its Councils (e.g., on Operations and Accreditation), its employees, and auditors and others working on behalf of RAB.

CODE OF ETHICS
RAB, being an affiliate company of the American Society for Quality Control (ASQC) adopts the ASQC Code of Ethics for all RAB personnel within the Scope of this Code of Conduct. (The ASQC Code of Ethics is shown on page 20 of this document.)

GENERAL STATEMENT OF THE RAB CODE OF CONDUCT
All persons within the Scope, in promoting high standards of ethical conduct shall:

a)   Conduct themselves professionally, with truth, accuracy, fairness and responsibility to their publics

b)   Not misrepresent their qualifications, competence or experience, nor undertake assignments beyond their qualifications

c)   Treat all accreditation and registration-related information as confidential, unless authorized in writing by the registrar company and the RAB Board of Directors to disclose such information, and do the following:

  ●   Do not discuss such information with anyone outside those who have a need to know the information (e.g., for legitimate purposes of the accreditation or registration process)

  ●   Do not disclose the names, or otherwise reveal the identities of registrar companies, or any part of assessment findings, both during and after the assessment process until or unless the names of successfully accredited registrars are made public by RAB and the registrars, (but will not disclose assessment findings at any time)

d)   Not accept retainers, commissions or valuable considerations from past, present, or potential registrars, or past, present or potential accredited auditor training organizations, or other interested parties, except where the person's other employment or consulting affiliations do not constitute a conflict of interest or a likely perception of a conflict of interest, and either

  ●   These other employment or consulting affiliations are disclosed and available to interested and affected parties

  ●   If not disclosed and available, the person attests in writing that no such conflict of interest or likely perception of a conflict of interest exists

(continued on next page)

ANNEX 1

(continued from previous page)

e) Acknowledge that the provisions of clause d) apply to situations where the person may provide services to such registrars, training organizations, or other interested parties, and also apply to situations where the person may provide confidential information or disclosures which may in any way influence an assessment process currently or in the future

f) Not serve any private or special interest in fulfillment of RAB duties, for example:

- Unduly influencing the registration or assessment of any supplier company, division or business unit of which the person is employed or of which a consulting arrangement is in effect

- Unduly influencing actions concerning a primary competitor of any supplier company, division or business unit of which the person is employed or of which a consulting arrangement is in effect

g) Not intentionally communicate false or misleading information which may compromise the integrity of the assessment and registration processes or decisions therein.

IMPLEMENTATION OF THE CODE OF CONDUCT

1. Any person within the Scope, upon perceiving or being informed competently of the existence of a conflict of interest under any of a) through g), or the ASQC Code of Ethics, shall self-exempt from deliberations and decisions of RAB that relate to the conflict of interest.

   For example, a conflict of interest or a likely perception of a conflict of interest within this Code exists when a person within the Scope accepts compensation from an organization for which the person has a direct influence as to whether the organization is accredited by, or accreditation is continued by, RAB as a registrar or as an auditor training organization. In particular, members of the RAB Councils and auditors have a direct influence on accreditation whereas members of the RAB Board of Directors only have a direct influence in the event that an organization appealed a decision by the RAB Councils which would then be decided by the Board of Directors.

   In implementing provisions d), e), f) a conflict of interest would be presumed not to exist for employment or consulting affiliations that have been terminated for at least one year.

2. All persons within the Scope shall annually sign a statement attesting to their understanding of this Code of Conduct, and state that either:

   - They have no instances of conflicts of interest since the last such statement they signed

   - They will describe in sufficient detail each such instance, and how each has been dealt with, and these records will be retained in RAB files.

3. Annually, RAB shall conduct training and/or discussions of the Code of Conduct and its applications for all persons within the Scope, and will retain records of the fact of such training and/or discussion.

(continued on next page)

ANNEX 1
(continued from previous page)

ASQC Code of Ethics

To uphold and advance the honor and dignity of the profession, and in keeping with high standards of ethical conduct I acknowledge that I:

FUNDAMENTAL PRINCIPLES

I.   Will be honest and impartial, and will serve with devotion my employer, my clients, and the public.

II. Will strive to increase the competence and prestige of the profession.

III. Will use my knowledge and skill for the advancement of human welfare, and in promoting the safety and reliability of products for public use.

IV. Will earnestly endeavor to aid the work of the Society.

RELATIONS WITH THE PUBLIC

1.1 Will do whatever I can to promote the reliability and safety of all products that come within my jurisdiction.

1.2 Will endeavor to extend public knowledge of the work of the Society and its members that relates to the public welfare.

1.3 Will be dignified and modest in explaining my work and merit.

1.4 Will preface any public statements that I may issue by clearly indicating on whose behalf they are made.

RELATIONS WITH EMPLOYER AND CLIENTS

2.1 Will act in professional matters as a faithful agent or trustee for each employer or client.

2.2 Will inform each client or employer of any business connections, interest or affiliations which might influence my judgment or impair the equitable character of my services.

2.3 Will indicate to my employer or client the adverse consequences to be expected if my professional judgment is overruled.

2.4 Will not disclose information concerning the business affairs or technical processes of any present or former employer or client without his consent.

2.5 Will not accept compensation from more than one party for the same service without the consent of all parties. If employed, I will engage in supplementary employment or consulting practice only with the consent of my employer.

RELATIONS WITH PEERS

3.1 Will take care that credit for the work of others is given to those to whom it is due.

3.2 Will endeavor to aid the professional development and advancement of those in my employ or under my supervision.

3.3 Will not compete unfairly with others; will extend my friendship and confidence to all associates and those with whom I have business relations.

ISO 9000
AROUND THE WORLD

Increased global competition and the proliferation of trade agreements have piqued international interest in the ISO 9000 series standards. Once thought of as a European standard, ISO 9000 is making its mark on the rest of the world.

One reason for global interest in ISO 9000 is the development of a multinational manufacturing system. In this system, large organizations buy components and subsystems for complex equipment from companies in different countries. As labor costs rise in industrialized nations, these large companies will purchase increasingly more components from developing countries. ISO 9000 registration is one key factor in ensuring the quality of the products and services supplied by companies in the developing countries.

This chapter examines recent ISO 9000 developments in Mexico and South America, Canada and the Pacific Rim.

ISO 9000 IN MEXICO AND SOUTH AMERICA

Mexico's interest in quality systems management began in the early 1980s with the Deming and Crosby philosophies, and it adopted the ISO 9000 series standards in 1990. While only a handful of companies are registered to the ISO 9000 series standards, interest in ISO 9000 is growing.[1]

Mexican suppliers are interested in the ISO 9000 series in response to EU, US and Canadian activity. In addition, the ISO 9000 series can help strengthen Mexico's industrial and economic growth.[2]

Small and medium-size businesses make up 90 percent of Mexican industry. Mexico and its neighboring countries realize the importance of educating these companies on quality management principles, and regional quality organizations and standards bodies are trying to accomplish this through their information campaigns. Both the Comité Ténico Nacional de Normalización de Sistemas de Calidad (CONNSISCAL) and the Mexican National Laboratory of Industrial Promotion (LANFI) have geared their campaigns toward such companies.[3]

Growing Interest in South America

Interest in South American countries is growing as well. ISO 9000 is the "first mile in the TQM marathon," according to Hernán Pavez Garcia, executive director of the Instituto Nacional de Normalización (INN), the Chilean standards body. He sees it as the baseline for developing quality.[4] In Venezuela, ISO 9000 application is driven mostly by market forces.[5] In Colombia, the national standards body Instituto Colombiano de Normas Técnicas (ICONTEC) attributes companies' improvements in quality and economic performance to the ISO 9000 series.[6]

International Acceptance of Registration Certificates

While interest in ISO 9000 is increasing, so is concern about a larger issue—whether or not registration certificates are accepted in international markets. Companies in all developing nations—and also in industrialized countries for that matter—are asking this question.

Developing nations were among the first to recognize a need for global acceptance of ISO 9000 series registration. The International Organization for Standardization's Development Committee (DEVCO) asked ISO to address the issue. DEVCO is made up of representatives from developing countries and liaisons from six developing country regions.[7] ISO's Committee on Conformity Assessment (CASCO) agreed to examine the issue.

Companies in developing nations often conduct most of their business in small shipments to multiple purchasers. These nations rely more heavily on exports than do developed countries, and they market to a broader array of countries. As a result, registered companies in developing countries run the risk of being subjected to more than one registration audit to satisfy all of their international customers.[8]

They want a registrar that is recognized and whose certificates are accepted in many markets. While some regional registrars do exist in Mexico, companies fear that those certificates are not as valued as ones from registrars in industrialized nations. As a result, most Mexican companies are using international registrars for their registrations.[9]

Companies in developing countries also face an unwarranted perception that they perform to lower standards, which in turn could lead to growing skepticism about the value of their ISO 9000 certificates.[10] In Mexico, for example, exports account for more than half the products manufactured by many companies. Mexicans hope the standard will become a tool for improving the perception of quality in their exported sector.[11]

In the absence of a global system of mutual recognition of ISO 9000 series certificates, the international quality assurance standards could pose a trade barrier for some developing countries.[12] However, ISO 9000 series registration could also present an opportunity to enter new markets. According to Manuel Diaz Portocarrero, this is the case for many small and medium-sized industries.[13]

Conclusion

These issues are far from settled, and universal acceptance of ISO 9000 registration is critical to overcoming these burdens and misperceptions. But despite the potential roadblocks, companies in Mexico and South America are well on their way to achieving ISO 9000 registration. Not only will it help improve their industrial growth and economic strength, but it will also help improve the perception of quality in their products. John Hinds, president of ISO, said that developing countries "may offer highly competitive prices, but they won't make the sale if their products and commodities don't meet the standards buyers impose."[14]

FOR FURTHER READING...

The International Trade Centre UNCTAD/GATT and ISO have published a book, *ISO 9000 Quality Management Systems: Guidelines for Enterprises in Developing Countries.* Published in 1993 and 231 pages long, the book is free to developing countries. Write to: ISO/1 Rue de Varembe/CH-1211 Geneva 20, Switzerland or call: 011-41-22-749-0111.

In addition, ISO has published a *Directory of Quality System Registration Bodies: Third-Party Bodies Operating Quality System Registration Programs.* The second edition was published in October 1993 and includes information on national programs operating in ISO member countries. Write to ISO Central Secretariat/Case Postale 56/CH 1211 Geneva 20 Switzerland or call 011-41-22-749-0111.

THE CANADIAN ISO 9000 REGISTRATION SYSTEM

BY BOHDAN DYCZKOWSKY

History of Quality Standards in Canada

In the mid-1960s Canada's largest electrical utility company, Ontario Hydro, recognized the need to exercise more effective control over its purchased items. On a mega-project such as a nuclear generating station, for example, it is costly and time consuming to inspect every piece of purchased equipment. A mechanism was needed to make the suppliers responsible for product quality, and the most effective way to do so was to contractually require vendors to develop and implement quality systems.

During this period, many quality system standards were developing in Canada, the United States and Europe. In 1975, the Canadian Standards Association (CSA) published the Z299 series of standards and established the first quality registration system in 1979. These standards specified generic quality requirements and were intended for use by a wide range of manufacturers. They contain four tiers, in contrast to the three levels of ISO 9000 series standards. (See Table 18-1.)

In 1987, the International Organization for Standardization published the ISO 9000 series standards. Canada has actively participated in drafting the ISO 9000 standards, including *ISO 10011, Guidelines for auditing quality systems* and *ISO 9000-3, Guidelines for the application of ISO 9001 to the development, supply and maintenance of software*. Delegates from Canada serve on ISO Technical Committee 176 (TC 176) and hold the positions of international chairman and secretariat.

Canadian industry was slow to accept ISO 9000, for the Z299 series is considered more stringent than the 1987 version of ISO 9000. But as the requests for registration grew, Canadians began to recognize the international standard's importance. Due to the emergence

Table 18-1: Canadian Quality Standard Equivalents					
ISO 9000	ISO 9001	ISO 9002		ISO 9003	ISO 9004
Z299.0	Z299.1	Z299.2	Z299.3	Z299.4	
	Q9001	Q9002		Q9003	Q9004

of the European Union (formerly the European Community) and increasing global competition, Canada adopted the ISO 9000 series in 1991 as its national quality standard.

The Canadian version is called the CSA Q9000 series. It consists of two parts. The first is an identical copy of the corresponding ISO 9000 standard. The second contains additional requirements from Z299 that were added to retain the distinctive features of the series. The Q9000 series was intended to be an interim measure until the ISO 9000 series become as stringent as the Z299s—possibly by the third revision of the ISO 9000 series in the late 1990s.

Canadian Market Acceptance of ISO 9000

Because the Z299 series is considered more stringent, Canadian companies began complying with ISO 9000 by seeking dual registrations to ISO 9003 and Z299.3. Canadians viewed such dual registrations as complete quality systems suitable for manufacturers, and they were more comprehensive than ISO 9003 alone. (See Table 18-1.) This not only satisfied local customers, but also international customers requiring ISO 9000 registration.

The international community failed to recognize dual registrations, however, and Canadians realized that despite the comprehensiveness of their own system, they needed to meet a standard acceptable to their customers. As a result, Canadian companies began registering solely to one of the ISO 9000 standards. Most chose to register to 9003, partly because the Z299 series is more stringent, and partly because there was no real pressure to register to ISO 9001 or 9002.

The pressure to register to ISO 9001 and 9002 has increased, however. The prevailing viewpoint is that the 1987 version of ISO 9003 does not offer sufficient benefits to manufacturers.

Some Canadian registrars have dual accreditations with both the Standards Council of Canada (SCC) and Raad voor de Certificatie (RvC), for example. The SCC believes that companies should be allowed to register to the standard they choose, whereas the RvC believes that if a company includes a manufacturing or design process in its scope, then it should register to 9001 or 9002.

As a result, one Canadian registrar is offering its clients two alternatives: companies with a domestic market that have no interest in upgrading may keep their ISO 9003 registration under a special marking that is recognized only by the SCC. On the other hand, companies that want to maintain their registration recognition in international markets must upgrade their certificates to ISO 9001 or 9002.

Editor's Note: *The perception of ISO 9003 as a "less stringent" standard might change, since the 1994 version includes some changes to existing clauses and adds new quality system elements for contract review, control of customer-supplied product, corrective action and internal quality audits. (See Chapter 11 for more information on the revisions to ISO 9003.)*

SMOOTH TRANSITION

Companies that are easily making the transition to ISO 9000 are regulated industries, primarily because the standard is comparable to Z299, and manufacturers have experience with regulatory authorities. Industries with comparable standards include the pharmaceutical and medical devices industries and the military.

In non-regulated industries, the pace of ISO 9000 activity has been increasing as well. Requests for registration of Canadian companies are coming from around the world—not just from European customers. As companies become registered and recognize the benefits of requiring their suppliers and sub-suppliers to become ISO 9000 registered, they will specify

---

THE ISO 9000 SERIES: THE CANADIAN PERSPECTIVE

Editor's Note: *Several public and private organizations have developed programs to support the registration process throughout Canada. The following information was drawn from a paper that Michael McSweeney, executive director of the Standards Council of Canada, presented at the Quality Expo International in Rosemont, Illinois on April 20, 1993. The paper was titled, "The ISO 9000 Series: The Canadian Perspective."*

The Canadian Manufacturer's Association (CMA) and the Canadian government have established a program that should register more than 100 small and medium-sized companies to ISO 9000. The Department of Industry, Science and Technology is financing the program. If the project is successful, the CMA hopes to see it expanded so that 7,500 firms will be registered by 1998.

In addition, the National Quality Institute and its affiliate organization, the Canadian Network for Total Quality, were established to function as Canada's "quality headquarters," and to maintain information on the country's quality organizations, respectively. Both organizations, which have strong government backing, hope to educate Canadians and to serve as a resource for information on quality.

The government has internal interest in ISO 9000 as well. The Department of National Defense has begun using ISO 9000 in its procurement contracts in hopes of improving the competitiveness of Canadian defense contractors in the global market.

The government's purchasing division, Supply and Service Canada, also plans to require many of its suppliers to become registered. This is a powerful incentive for the private sector, since the government consumes roughly $9.4 billion in goods and services each year. Although no timetable has been set, it will probably be implemented gradually, sector by sector, starting with sectors that have a high percentage of registered companies. Internally, Supply and Service Canada is considering implementing the guidance document *ISO 9004-2, Quality management and quality systems elements-Part 2: Guidelines for services.*

Several other departments and agencies might also follow suit. As Michael McSweeney said, "If government is to preach ISO 9000 and require ISO 9000, then it should live by ISO 9000."

the standard in their purchase orders. This will dramatically increase the number of ISO 9000 registrations.

Canadian Registrars and Registrar Accreditation

Due to this increase in registration activity, the Standards Council of Canada established an accreditation system for the quality systems registrars that operate in Canada. (Refer to Appendix D for a list of registrars that operate in the United States and Canada.)

The Standards Council uses standard CAN-P-10 to accredit a registrar. The CAN-P-10 Standard was published by the Standards Council of Canada in December 1991 and has been adopted as the national standard of Canada for accreditation of quality system registrars. It embodies *ISO/IEC Guide 48, Guidelines for third-party assessment and registration of a supplier's quality system*; *EN 45012, General criteria for certification bodies operating quality system certification*; and *ISO 10011, Guidelines for auditing quality systems*.

Conclusion

Because the Canadian Z299 quality standards and a quality registration system have been in place since the late 1970s, Canadian companies did not immediately adopt ISO 9000. Yet the overwhelming global acceptance of the ISO 9000 series is causing Canadians to adopt the international standards in lieu of the Canadian standard. The use of the ISO 9000 series has been accelerated by the Canadian federal and provincial governments, which are encouraging companies to become quality-conscious.

PACIFIC RIM COUNTRIES

Interest in ISO 9000 among the Pacific Rim countries has increased recently. Japan's quality systems registration efforts seem to be the most developed, with China, Singapore, Taiwan, Hong Kong and others involved as well. These countries are concerned about the increasing global importance of ISO 9000 and want to bolster their position in the world market.

Japan's Quality Revolution

Japan's strict quality control standards were implemented as early as 1954, when W. Edwards Deming and Joseph M. Juran introduced to the Japanese what was to become the backbone of modern Japanese quality management. They suggested that the Japanese establish programs that would foster continuous quality improvement. Japanese companies did so by incorporating the following three strategies:

● The senior executives of Japanese companies accepted responsibility for managing quality
● Company engineers began to use statistical methods for quality control

- Companies included quality goals in their overall business strategy.

Because each of these strategies had never been implemented in industry, they amounted to a significant change in direction and have served Japan well.[15]

Although Japan has been slower to embrace the ISO 9000 standard, the Japanese did not entirely ignore it. Japan actively served on ISO TC 176, and the Japanese version of the ISO 9000 series, JIS Z 9900-9904, was published by the Japanese Industrial Standards Committee (JISC) in October 1991.[16] JISC is a trans-ministerial organization in the Japanese government and the only representative to ISO and the International Electrotechnical Commission (IEC).

In addition, some Japanese companies were ahead of the rest of the country. The Japanese companies that export electronics parts to Germany were familiar with the standard as early as 1989. In fact, the country's electronics industry decided that year to comply with the standards to maintain their access to the European markets. Although the Japanese auto makers are not actively pursuing registration, parts suppliers are more likely to do so to maintain their international market share.[17]

JAPAN'S LATE REGISTRATION START

So why was the rest of Japan slow to embrace the ISO 9000 series of quality management standards? A number of reasons exist. Some Japanese executives believed that ISO 9000 wasn't critical to their companies, which already had strict quality control standards in place. How would ISO 9000 contribute anything to their already efficient and productive management systems? Others wanted to compare ISO 9000 against their current practices before deciding whether to comply with the standards.[18]

Despite these reasons, Japan realizes the advantages to the international standard, and it is trying to harmonize ISO 9000 with Japan's own quality management approach.[19]

JAPAN'S QUALITY MANAGEMENT AND ASSURANCE (QMA) SYSTEM

As Japanese industry considers ISO 9000 registration, the Japanese have been developing other aspects of a third-party certification system. In June 1992, JISC submitted a proposal to the government to introduce its quality management and assurance (QMA) system.[20] The QMA system, which is based on the ISO 9000 series, includes the following:

- Recommendations on the QMA system's basic scheme
- The basis for an accreditation body
- Criteria for quality systems (QS) assessment bodies
- Criteria for QS auditors
- Mutual recognition with accreditation bodies overseas.

The proposed accreditation body, a not-for-profit organization, would be financed by contributions from major industrial federations, standardization organizations, and other groups. It would be independent of the Japanese government and offer the following services:

- Accredit auditor training bodies
- Evaluate QS auditors to be registered

- Formulate criteria for accrediting QS assessment bodies and for evaluating QS auditors in conjunction with ISO/IEC Guide 40 and ISO 10011-2, respectively
- Remain open to QS assessment bodies abroad that apply for accreditation.

The proposal indicated that this system may be used by the government for procurement and for future regulatory certification systems. It also hopes to extend the scope of the accreditation body to include the following:

- Product certification bodies
- Testing/inspection bodies
- Personnel-proficiency qualifications bodies.

Although the Japanese haven't entirely embraced the standards as quickly as other countries, they are actively establishing a credible ISO 9000 registration and accreditation system.

Other Asian Quality Initiatives

The countries of China, Singapore, Taiwan, Malaysia, Korea and Thailand have also formally adopted the ISO 9000 series standard. Hong Kong is home to several registered companies, and the Hong Kong Quality Assurance agency has been promoting ISO 9000 since early 1990.

Both the governments of Taiwan and Singapore encourage companies to become registered to ISO 9000. Taiwan's main reasons for adopting the standards include meeting the demands of international customers, fulfilling corporate policy, and satisfying product certification and export requirements for EU and government procurement. [21]

In Singapore, companies are using quality management systems not only to improve their competitiveness, but also to improve their internal efficiency. The Singapore Institute of Standards and Industrial Research (SISIR) has targeted the information technology, construction and food industries. It helps these industries by sharing their knowledge of standards and certification, by developing guidelines to meet ISO 9000 standards, and by signing MOUs with eight overseas registrars to promote joint recognition of each other's certificates. [22]

Emerging Trends

Although Asian countries might not have thousands of companies registered to ISO 9000, their behind-the-scenes registration activity is building a firm foundation upon which to progress quickly. Executives in Asian companies recognize the impact of ISO 9000 on their businesses, which is why they are seriously pursuing quality systems registration and verification.

CONCLUSION

The ISO 9000 series is growing in popularity around the world. Companies in Mexico and

South America, Canada and the Pacific Rim are considering registration, and organizations in those areas are developing registration schemes and support groups to foster the standard's acceptance. These regions are confronted with some of the same problems regarding acceptance of registration certificates and accreditation schemes as other countries with more established programs in place. The ISO 9000 series is an international standard in more ways than one.

ENDNOTES

[1] Paul Scicchitano, "Mexican Government May Announce National ISO 9000 Program as Industry Interest Grows," *Quality Systems Update* Vol. 2, No. 10 (October 1992): 1.

[2] Neil P. Cook, "'Leave the Door Open'—DGN Director General," *ISO 9000 News* (February 1993): 7.

[3] *ibid.*

[4] *ibid.*

[5] Tito Zambrano, speaking at the *The ISO 9000 Forum Application Symposium*, November 1992, as reported in "'Leave the Door Open'—DGN Director General," *ISO 9000 News* (February 1993): 7.

[6] Neil P. Cook, "'Leave the Door Open'—DGN Director General," *ISO 9000 News* (February 1993): 7.

[7] Paul Scicchitano, "Developing Nations Seek Global ISO 9000," *Quality Systems Update* Vol. 3, No. 6 (June 1993): 7.

[8] Gene A. Hutchinson, as quoted in "Developing Nations Seek Global ISO 9000," *Quality Systems Update* Vol. 3, No. 6 (June 1993): 7.

[9] Neil P. Cook, "'Leave the Door Open'—DGN Director General," *ISO 9000 News* (February 1993): 7.

[10] Paul Scicchitano, "Developing Nations Seek Global ISO 9000," *Quality Systems Update* Vol. 3, No. 6 (June 1993): 7.

[11] Miguel Garcia Altamirano, as quoted in "Mexican Government May Announce National ISO 9000 Program As Industry Interest Grows," *Quality Systems Update* Vol. 2, No. 10 (October 1992): 1.

[12] Paul Scicchitano, "Developing Nations Seek Global ISO 9000," *Quality Systems Update* Vol. 3, No. 6 (June 1993): 7.

[13] Manuel Diaz Portocarrero, as quoted in "Developing Nations Seek Global ISO 9000," *Quality Systems Update* Vol. 3, No. 6 (June 1993): 7.

[14] John Hinds, speaking at a November 1992 conference, as reported in "World Bank Might Hasten Global Standardization," *Quality Systems Update* Vol. 2, No. 12 (December 1992): 1.

[15] Joseph M. Juran, "What Japan Taught Us About Quality," *The Washington Post,* 15 August 1993, section H, p. 1.

[16] Kevin Cooper, "The Japanese Are Gaining Lost ISO 9000 Ground," *Quality Systems Update* Vol. 3, No. 1 (January 1993): 11.

[17] Kevin Cooper, "The Japanese Are Gaining Lost ISO 9000 Ground," *Quality Systems Update* Vol. 3, No. 1 (January 1993): 11.

[18] Kevin Cooper, "The Japanese Are Gaining Lost ISO 9000 Ground," *Quality Systems Update* Vol. 3, No. 1 (January 1993): 11.

[19] Hitoshi Kume, "ISO 9000 Implementation in Japan." Paper presented at the Joint ISO, ANSI, and ASQC ISO 9000 Forum Application Symposium, Washington, DC, 7-8 October 1993.

[20] The following details of Japan's new system were provided by Takashi Ohtsubo, "Japanese Ready to Launch Accreditation System," *Quality Systems Update* Vol. 3, No. 8 (August 1993): 14.

[21] Susanto Halim, as quoted in "Asia/Pacific Countries Embrace ISO 9000," *Quality Systems Update* Vol. 2, No. 5 (May 1992): 1.

[22] "What ISO 9000 Has Done for Us," *ISO 9000 News* (February 1993): 11.

ISO 9000 IN US GOVERNMENT AGENCIES

This chapter briefly highlights some of the US government agencies that are considering implementing ISO 9000, are using it as a guideline, or are registering to the standard. Many agencies see ISO 9000 as a viable option to replace and/or supplement their current quality standards.

The following information on ISO 9000 activity in federal agencies was adapted mostly from the National Institute of Standards and Technology's (NIST's) clearinghouse on federal ISO 9000 activities and in part from articles in *Quality Systems Update* newsletter. The information was current as of publication but is subject to change. For the most up-to-date information, please call the contacts listed for each agency.

Department of Agriculture (USDA)

The USDA's AMS is approaching the ISO 9000 standards on many fronts. The standards are being considered for use in both internal and external applications.

Following an initial investigation conducted by the Livestock and Seed Division (LS), an agency-wide ISO 9000 action team was formed. The purpose of the team is to develop a strategic plan for using the ISO 9000 standards in new and existing programs within the agency. The AMS/LS is implementing ISO 9002 in its Meat Grading and Certification Branch (MGC). Although formal outside registration is not being considered at this time, MGC plans to become fully compliant with the standard by early 1995.

The MCG implementation project will lay the groundwork for a Quality System Certification Program (QSCP) for meat production systems. This program, for which MGC graders will act as auditors, is designed to supplement end-item examinations MGC currently performs. These assessments will form a part of the Branch's third-party quality certification service.

Department of Commerce (DOC)

INTERNATIONAL TRADE ADMINISTRATION (ITA)

The Office of European Community Affairs (OECA) coordinates US participation in the US/EU talks designed to establish one or more mutual recognition agreements (MRAs) covering testing and certification of EU-regulated goods and (where relevant) the approval/registration of the quality systems under which such goods are produced.

OECA also tracks references to the use of the ISO 9000 series (or their equivalent—the EN 29000 series) in EU directives and assesses the potential impact on US-EU trade.

Contact: Charles Ludolph, Office of EC Affairs, ITA/DOC, Herbert C. Hoover Bldg., Room 3036, Washington DC 20230, tel. 202-482-5276, fax 202-482-2155.

NATIONAL INSTITUTE OF STANDARDS AND TECHNOLOGY (NIST)

In response to queries from customers of NIST's Office of Measurement Services, NIST managers have been holding discussions related to quality and the need for an internal quality policy in specific program areas, particularly with respect to the ISO 9000 series. These discussions indicate considerable support among both managers and staff for articulating such a policy. NIST is currently exploring its available options.

Contact: William Reed, NIST, TRF Bldg., Room 112, Gaithersburg MD 20899, tel. 301-975-2015, fax 301-926-4751.

National Voluntary Laboratory Accreditation Program (NVLAP)

The NIST National Voluntary Laboratory Accreditation Program (NVLAP) operated by the Office of Standards Services is doing the following:

● Working towards internal compliance with ISO 9000 requirements

● Planning to offer its accredited laboratories (as an option) quality system registration to ISO 9002.

The assessment processes would be combined to provide NIST-accredited laboratories with a cost-effective option for obtaining laboratory accreditation and quality system registration at the same time. Staff members are completing training in ISO 9000 requirements and how to conduct assessments.

Contact: Albert Tholen, NVLAP, NIST, TRF Bldg., Room 112, Gaithersburg MD 20899, 301-975-4017, 301-926-2884.

National Voluntary Conformity Assessment System Evaluation (NVCASE)

NIST has proposed its own program for accrediting registrars where an acceptable accrediting program does not already exist—the National Voluntary Conformity Assessment Systems Evaluation (NVCASE) program. More than two years after it was first proposed, the NVCASE program went into effect in May 1994. The purpose of the program is to establish criteria and a system to evaluate and recognize specific conformity assessment activities. Under the program, bodies such as the RAB can apply for and gain government recognition through NIST. The program is intended to boost the acceptance of US products abroad.

The scope of NIST's involvement under the NVCASE program extends to the evaluation of a testing laboratory, certification body or quality system registrar when directed by law or requested by another federal agency. It does not extend to the actual registration of individual firms.

Contact: John Donaldson, Standards Code and Information Program, NIST, Building 101, Room A629, Gaithersburg MD 20899, tel. 301-975-4030, fax 301-926-2871.

Office of Standards Services' Weights and Measures Program

During 1992, the Office of Standards Services' Weights and Measures Program began upgrading the State Laboratory Accreditation Program in cooperation with the National Voluntary Laboratory Accreditation Program. Technical criteria are being developed based on *ISO/IEC Guide 25, General Requirements for the Competence of Calibration and Testing Laboratories.* New requirements include a revision of laboratory quality manuals to meet ISO/IEC Guide 25 requirements. The Weights and Measures Program believes that once laboratories are accredited under the new criteria, they will fully meet customer ISO 9000 service requirements.

Contact: Georgia Harris, Weights and Measures Program, NIST, Building 101, Room A617, Gaithersburg MD 20899, tel. 301-975-4014, fax 301-926-0647.

NATIONAL OCEANIC AND ATMOSPHERIC ADMINISTRATION (NOAA)

The unit responsible for electronic and digital charts is planning to become internally compliant with applicable ISO 9000 requirements.

Contact: Russell Kennedy, NOAA/NOS, N/CG 2232, SMC 3 Station 6558, 1315 East West Hwy, Silver Spring MD 20910, tel. 301-713-2719, fax 301-713-4543.

Department of Defense (DoD)

The DoD, in conjunction with NASA, published *Guidance on the Application of ISO 9000-ASQC Q90 Series Quality System Standards* in February 1994. The document officially approved the use of the ISO 9000 series standards in contracts to eliminate unnecessary quality system requirements and to create a single system. The decision gives contractors the option of deciding if they want to use ISO 9000 to satisfy government contractual requirements for quality systems.

DoD program offices are authorized to use the ISO 9000 series standards in contracts for new programs instead of MIL-Q-9858-A and MIL-I-45208-A. (Applying ISO 9000 to existing contracts will be considered on a case-by-case basis.)

In addition, third party registration will not be required nor will it be a substitute for government quality surveillance at the present time. Both DoD and NASA purchasing offices have the authority to require compliance with the international quality assurance documents, but the DoD does not intend to force ISO 9000 on contractors.

Contact: Frank Doherty, chief of industrial quality and productivity, Department of Defense, OASD (P&L) PR/IEQ, Pentagon (Suite 2A318), Washington, DC 20301, tel. 703-695-7915, fax 703-693-7038.

Department of Education (DOEd)

While DOEd has no plans at present for using the ISO 9000 standards within its programs, DOEd is collecting information on the possible applications of the ISO 9000 series standards within the education and training fields.

Contact: Ron Hunt, Special Assistant to the Director, US Dept. of Ed., 400 Maryland Ave SW, Room 3061, Washington DC 20202-3643, tel. 202-401-1953.

Department of Energy (DOE)

The DOE plans to endorse aspects of the ISO 9000 series standards, which will be referenced in their safety guide series. This series provides supplemental information regarding acceptable methods for implementing specific provisions of the DOE orders and rules. The ISO 9000 series has already been used as one of the models for DOE's quality assurance order 5700.C, which spells out requirements for DOE personnel and contractors.

The department is also looking at the ISO 10000 series, which includes guidelines for auditing quality systems and quality assurance requirements for measuring equipment. In addition, the DOE is looking at other non-government standards developed by organizations such as the American Society of Mechanical Engineers and the American Society for Quality Control.

Contact: Gustave Danielson, Department of Energy, Group Code EH62, 19901 Germantown Road, Germantown, MD 20874, tel. 301-903-2954.

Department of Health and Human Services (DHHS)

CENTER FOR DISEASE CONTROL (CDC), NATIONAL INSTITUTE FOR OCCUPATIONAL SAFETY AND HEALTH (NIOSH)

NIOSH is considering ISO 9000 quality standards for implementation in its certification programs.

Contact: Richard Metzler, M/S 1138, NIOSH, 944 Chestnut Ridge Road, Morgantown WV 26505-2888, tel. 304-284-5713, fax 304-284-5877.

FOOD AND DRUG ADMINISTRATION (FDA), CENTER FOR DEVICES AND RADIOLOGICAL HEALTH (CDRH)

Domestic Use. FDA is revising its medical device Good Manufacturing Practice (GMP) regulations to include requirements related to design control. The revised GMP was published in the *Federal Register* on November 23, 1993. The comment period has ended, and the FDA is making some changes to the proposed rule. The final rule should be published by the end of 1994, with an effective date 180 days after publication.

The GMP will be reorganized and some of its language modified to harmonize it with ISO 9001. The revised GMP regulations will incorporate the requirements of ISO 9001 plus supplemental requirements specific to medical devices that are found in the present GMP regulations.

Global Harmonization. A Global Harmonization Task Force composed of government and industry representatives from the European Union, Canada, Japan, and the United States has been established to harmonize supplementary device requirements to ISO 9001 and 9002 and to examine the need for new documents and/or programs to encourage uniformity of inspections of quality systems. The first meeting was held in January 1993 in Brussels, where representatives discussed harmonizing FDA, Canadian, EU and Japanese GMPs and guidelines. They also formed three study groups:

(1) Comparison of Regulatory Schemes

(2) Harmonization of FDA and EU GMP Requirements (contained in EN 46001)

(3) Harmonization of Guidance Documents.

This third group's goal is to develop a generic guideline for applying EN 46001 to medical devices. It should reflect any differences between the proposed, revised GMP and EN 46001. Overall, the task force is developing a common GMP that will be used as a foundation for harmonization, and to develop a guideline to ensure that the GMP is uniformly interpreted. If successful, these actions will form a solid foundation for a mutual recognition agreement.

Contact: Pam Wojtowicz, FDA/ Center for Devices and Radiological Health, 12720 Twinbrook Parkway, Rm. T123, Rockville MD 20857, tel. 301-443-3426, fax 301-443-4196.

Department of Interior (DOI)

OFFICE OF ACQUISITION AND PROPERTY MANAGEMENT (PAM)

The Office of Acquisition and Property Management has been assigned responsibility for this issue since February 1993, though no specific activities other than information collection are underway. Preliminary discussions are currently being held with other DOI personnel involved in quality assurance and environmental matters to better assess the proper placement of standards-related responsibilities, including the ISO 9000 series standards, within the department.

Contact: Wiley Horsley, Automated Systems Division, DOI, MS-5512, 1849 C Street NW, Washington DC 20240, tel. 202-208-3347, fax 202-208-6301.

Department of Labor (DOL)

MINE SAFETY AND HEALTH ADMINISTRATION (MSHA)

MSHA's Approval and Certification Center's (A&CC) has ISO 9000-related activities in four areas:

Research. A committee was formed to study and compare the ISO 9000 standards with other popular quality assurance standards. The committee found that the standards parallel other national and international standards and are clearly becoming the world's benchmark quality assurance standards. Information reported by the committee will be used for future regulatory review activities.

Education. A training seminar was held at the A&CC for 24 employees by an accredited ISO 9000 registrar. The seminar covered a wide variety of ISO 9000 topics including: history; a discussion of each element in ISO 9001; and registration processes and auditing.

Evaluation. A regular part of the Quality Assurance Division (QAD) activities is the evaluation of quality assurance (QA) manuals. More companies are submitting QA manuals which follow the elements of the ISO 9001 and 9002 standards, and QAD employees are becoming familiar with these elements.

Accreditation. The A&CC is considering seeking accreditation by a third party to demonstrate compliance with the requirements of ISO/IEC Guide 25. As part of this process, the A&CC is currently focusing on two areas: documented procedures, and calibration. A committee was formed to thoroughly review all A&CC policies and procedures. A contractor has been hired to assist the A&CC in updating the calibration program.

Contact: Ken Sproul or John Fain, MSHA/DOL, Industrial Park Road, RR 1 Box 251, Triadelphia WV 26059, tel. 304-547-0400, fax 304-547-0400.

OCCUPATIONAL SAFETY AND HEALTH ADMINISTRATION (OSHA)

OSHA in its rulemakings and written documentation requirements is seeking consistency with quality management objectives. The documentation requirements of ISO 9000 have been used, in part, as a guide to the documentation requirements in the Process Safety Management Standard. The relationship between the ISO 9000 series and process safety is being addressed on a limited basis in outreach presentations on the OSHA Process Safety Management Standard.

Contact: Thomas Seymour, USDOL, OSHA, 200 Constitution Ave NW, Room N3605, Washington DC 20210, tel. 202-219-8061.

Department of State

OFFICE OF INTERNATIONAL COMMUNICATIONS AND INFORMATION POLICY

While the Office of International Communications and Information Policy has no plans at present for using the ISO 9000 standards within its activities, the Office is continuing to collect information on the requirements and applications of the ISO 9000 series standards.

Contact: Earl Barbely, State Department/CIP Bureau, Room 6317, 2201 C Street NW, Washington DC 20520, tel. 202-647-0197, fax 02-647-7407.

Federal Trade Commission (FTC)

The FTC is collecting information on the requirements/applications of the ISO 9000 series standards and the use of ISO 9000 registration claims in advertising and labeling.

Contact: Sidney Steinitz, FTC (H-200), 6th and Pennsylvania NW, Washington DC 20580, tel. 202-326-3282, fax 202-326-2050.

General Services Administration (GSA)

The Office of Business, Industry, and Governmental Affairs is coordinating GSA's ongoing study of ISO 9000 in collaboration with members of the GSA working group on quality management system registration. Included in the GSA action plan are discussions with trade associations, corporations registered to ISO 9000, the Small Business Administration (SBA) and colleagues in other federal agencies.

Contact: Jo McLaughlin, GSA/Office of Business, Industry, and Governmental Affairs, 18th and F Streets NW, Washington DC, 20405, tel. 202-501-4177, fax 202-501-2806.

International Trade Commission (USITC)

While the USITC does not participate in any standards developing groups or become involved in procurements requiring the use of such standards, USITC is interested in the impact of the development and application of international standards, such as the ISO 9000 series standards, on international trade and competitiveness.

Contact: David Rohr, USITC, 500 E Street NW, Washington DC, 20436, tel. 202-205-3041, fax 202-205-2338.

National Aeronautics and Space Administration (NASA)

NASA, in conjunction with the DoD, published *Guidance on the Application of ISO 9000-ASQC Q90 Series Quality System Standards* in February 1994. The document officially approved the use of the ISO 9000 series standards in contracts to eliminate unnecessary quality system requirements and to create a single system. The decision gives contractors the option of deciding if they want to use ISO 9000 to satisfy government contractural requirements for quality systems.

NASA's current policy, as described in NHB 5300.4 (1B), "Quality Systems—Quality Program Provisions for Aeronautical and Space Systems Contractors" (dated April 1969), will be phased out. The ISO 9000 series, supplemented with the NASA Augmentation Requirements that were developed during the October 1993 Johnson Space Center ISO 9001 working group meeting, will become the basis for contractual quality assurance requirements. Applying ISO 9000 to existing contracts will be considered on a case-by-case basis.

Third party registration requirements are optional for NASA applications. It remains the responsibility of the procuring NASA organization to assess their suppliers' quality management systems.

Contact: Charles Harlan, director of safety reliability and quality assurance, NASA, Lyndon B. Johnson Space Center, Houston, TX 77058, tel. 713-483-3191.

Nuclear Regulatory Commission (NRC)

The NRC has not initiated program/activities to formally review the ISO 9000 series standards. The focus of NRC activities in the area of quality assurance is the requirements contained in 10 CFR 50, Appendix B, and the related NRC regulatory guides and industry standards.

Typically, a formal NRC review would be conducted in response to a request from a licensee (an organization licensed by NRC to operate a commercial nuclear power plant) who sought to use or rely on the ISO 9000 series in order to comply with NRC regulations and/or license commitments. To date, the NRC has not received a request from a licensee. Absent a request, the NRC staff is monitoring the development and implementation of the quality assurance standards in the ISO 9000 series standards.

Contact: John Craig, deputy director, or Owen P. Gormley, Division of Engineering, Office of Nuclear Regulatory Research, NRC, Washington DC, 20555-0001, tel. 301-492-3872, fax 301-492-3696.

Office of Management and Budget (OMB)

The Office of Management and Budget issued a revised version of OMB Circular A-119, "Federal Participation in the Development and Use of Voluntary Standards," to the heads of executive departments and agencies on June 25, 1993. Closing date for final review and comments was July 30, 1993. Section 7a(2) of the circular states the following:

International standards should be considered in procurement and regulatory applications in the interests of promoting trade and implementing the provisions of the Agreement on Technical Barriers to Trade and the Agreement on Government Procurement (commonly referred to as the 'Standards Code' and the 'Procurement Code,' respectively).

Annual OMB reporting requirements on the implementation of this circular by agency heads are also included in the revised circular.

Contact: Chris Jordan, Office of Federal Procurement Policy, OMB, Washington DC, 20503, tel. 202-395-6812, fax 202-395-5105.

US Postal Service

The Postal Service has recently initiated an effort to determine how ISO 9000 will/could impact US postal activities.

Contact: Donald J. Burke, manager of quality assurance, or Mark Nepi, US Postal Service, N.B. 4000, 475 L'Enfant Plaza, Washington DC 20260, tel. 202-268-4166 (Burke), 202-268-4642 (Nepi), fax 202-268-4012.

ISO 9000 IN VARIOUS INDUSTRY SECTORS

As ISO 9000 grows in popularity, more and more industries are being affected. Not only are companies in certain industry sectors becoming registered, but some sectors are also starting to implement ISO 9000 policies on an industry-wide level. The big three American automakers, for example, are developing a system that will incorporate ISO 9000 into their supplier audits.

This chapter focuses on a few industries and includes the following types of information:

- Information from the joint *Quality Systems Update*/Deloitte & Touche ISO 9000 survey. Conducted in July 1993 of registered companies in the United States and Canada, it contains valuable information broken down by industry sector. Three survey articles are included in this chapter:
  o A general analysis of the survey
  o An industry-specific analysis
  o An analysis of companies based on size.
- Contributor-written articles.
- Case studies of companies that have been registered or are in the process of becoming registered.

Information on "small companies" is also included in this section. While not technically an industry, smaller companies have characteristics distinct from those of corporate giants. The section attempts to highlight some of those differences through a case study and the survey comparison of small and large companies.

The following industry sectors—and any applicable articles—are included in this chapter:

- *QSU/Deloitte & Touche Survey: Overview*
- *QSU/Deloitte & Touche Survey by Industry*
- Chemical Industry
  - *The Chemical Industry: Past and Present,* by Dr. Robert Belfit
  - *ISO 9000: Problems Facing the Chemical Industry,* by William Ferguson
  - Betz Laboratories, Inc.
  - Monsanto Chemical Company
- Computer Industry
  - Unisys
- Auto Industry
  - *The AIAG and Joint Quality Initiatives*
  - *ISO 9000: What Every Supplier Must Know,* by William Harral
  - Ford of Europe
- Steel Industry
  - *Quality Systems Assessments in the Steel Industry,* by Peter Lake
  - Taylor-Wharton Cylinders
- Small Companies
  - *QSU/Deloitte & Touche Survey of Companies by Size*
  - Techni-Test.

GENERAL INTRODUCTION AND OVERVIEW OF THE QSU/DELOITTE & TOUCHE SURVEY

Introduction

US and Canadian companies that have achieved registration under the ISO 9000 series standards report an average annual savings of $179,000 as a consequence, according to a joint *Quality Systems Update*/Deloitte & Touche survey.

The survey, conducted in July 1993, canvassed companies in the United States and Canada that had one or more registration certificates. It had a 37 percent response rate based on a total distribution of 1,679 copies—620 companies responded.

The eight-page survey, the first of its kind for registered companies in the United States and Canada, provides a statistically significant snapshot of the registration process and addresses many of the most commonly asked questions of companies considering registration and those that have already attained it.

Table 20-1: Reasons to Attain ISO 9000 Registration	
Customer Demands/Expectations	27.4%
Quality Benefits	21.8%
Market Advantage	15.6%
Requirements of EC Regulations	9.0%
Corporate Mandate	8.9%
Part of Larger Strategy	8.9%
Competitive Pressures	2.4%
Reduced Costs of Production	1.5%
Non-EC Government Requirements	0.8%
Other	1.0%
No Answer	2.7%

Reasons to Pursue Registration

The results of the survey contradict a widely held assertion that the explosion of ISO 9000 series registrations in the United States and Canada has been fueled by European requirements for exporting regulated products.

Only nine percent of all respondents said their principal reason for pursuing registration was to comply with EU requirements. But nearly 28 percent cited meeting customer demands and expectations and almost 22 percent cited the quality benefits. (See Table 20-1.) Companies in all industries are feeling customer pressures to seek registration. Two-thirds of all respondents ranked it among their top three reasons, along with quality benefits (at 62 percent) and market advantage (60 percent).

SUPPLIER INVOLVEMENT

The 35-question survey also bolsters projections that the number of registrations will continue to grow at a

Table 20-2: Factors in Selecting a Registrar		
Reputation	155	25.0%
Country Affiliation/Accreditation	153	24.7%
Prior Experience with the Registrar	87	14.0%
Industry Expertise	69	11.1%
Registrar "Philosophy" on Quality Management Systems	54	8.7%
Corporate Dictate	35	5.6%
Geographic Proximity	13	2.1%
Independence from Consulting	9	1.5%
Cost	8	1.3%
Size/Resources	7	1.1%
Other	25	4.0%
No Answer	5	0.8%

quantum rate for the foreseeable future. Nearly 83 percent of the respondents indicated that they are encouraging their suppliers to seek registration and 34 percent are encouraging all suppliers. Some 80 percent of the respondents indicated that ISO 9000 registration does influence their selection of suppliers. Nearly 84 percent anticipated reducing the number of audits they conduct of suppliers registered to the ISO 9000 series standards.

Table 20-3: Satisfaction With Registrars	
Very Satisfied	52.1%
Satisfied	38.4%
Neither Satisfied nor Dissatisfied	7.3%
Dissatisfied	1.5%
Very Dissatisfied	0.3%
No Answer	0.5%

Selecting Registrars and Consultants

Two of the most important choices companies face include selecting an ISO 9000 series registrar and deciding whether to retain the services of a consultant. The survey showed that when choosing a registrar, companies put the most weight on reputation, country affiliation, and accreditation. (See Table 20-2.)

One area that apparently was not high on the companies' lists of concerns involved possible conflicts in organizations that offer both consulting and registration services. Overall, only 1.5 percent of companies said they viewed independence from consulting as the most important criterion for selecting a registrar.

Companies as a whole, regardless of sales volume, said overwhelmingly that they were satisfied or very satisfied with their registrars. Less than two percent of the respondents indicated they were at all dissatisfied with their choices. (See Table 20-3.)

Asked if they relied on consultants, about half said they had and the other half said they had not. Overall, companies that employed consultants did not report a greater savings than those that relied on internal resources. However, companies that used consultants for project management fared better than those that entrusted their entire implementation to outside sources, according to the survey results. Many ISO 9000 series experts have maintained that company commitment is critical to a successful registration effort.

Table 20-4: Barriers to Registration		
Procedure Creation	122	19.7%
Document Development	116	18.7%
Lack of Management Commitment	59	9.5%
Not Following Set Procedures	50	8.1%
Employee Resistance	49	7.9%
Conflicting Interpretations	46	7.4%
Training Requirements	27	4.4%
Mandated Time Frame	23	3.7%
Policies or Procedures "Inherited" from Other Divisions/Locations	22	3.5%
Implementation of Corrective Action	21	3.4%
Lack of Information	21	3.4%
Calibration of Instruments/Equipment	20	3.2%
Document Approval Process	10	1.6%
High Preparation Cost	5	0.8%
Registrar Selection	2	0.3%
Other	17	2.7%
No Answer	10	1.6%

Overall Barriers

Among the most time-consuming aspects of registration, according to the respondents, were preparing documentation and developing procedures. Some 35 percent listed documentation as the single most time-consuming activity while about 28 percent identified procedure development as the most time-consuming. (See Table 20-4.)

Accordingly, the greatest challenge in attaining ISO 9000 series registration is creating procedures and developing the necessary documentation. Companies overwhelmingly cited both factors as the greatest barriers from a list of 16 choices. A lesser but still substantial number of companies also cited lack of management commitment and not following set procedures high on their list.

The survey results confirm the standards' reputation for placing a heavy emphasis on documentation during registration but show that calibration is not nearly as great a problem as many observers have maintained. Selecting a registrar is likewise not a significant barrier, with only two respondents of 620 citing that as the greatest hindrance.

Table 20-5: External Benefits of Registration		
Higher Perceived Quality	208	33.5%
Improved Customer Satisfaction	165	26.6%
Competitive Edge	133	21.5%
Reduced Customer Quality Audits	53	8.5%
Increased Market Share	28	4.5%
Quicker Time to Market	4	0.6%
Other	6	1.0%
No Answer	23	3.7%

Costs of Registration

Companies paid an average of $245,200 for costs associated with registration, including auditing fees and internal expenses. Registrar fees alone averaged $21,000. It took most of them slightly longer than a year to prepare for their first registration audit. The survey also found that more than half of the respondents recouped or anticipated recouping the cost of registration in less than 40 months.

Editor's Note: *Respondents were asked to indicate the total* ***domestic*** *cost expended to achieve their current level of registration. The implication is that these figures represent company-wide, domestic registration expenditures— not expenses for individual sites.*

Table 20-6: Internal Benefits of Registration		
Better Documentation	201	32.4%
Greater Quality Awareness	159	25.6%
Positive "Cultural" Change	93	15.0%
Increased Operational Efficiency/Productivity	56	9.0%
Enhanced Intercompany Communications	45	7.3%
Reduced Scrap/ Re-Work Expenses	41	6.6%
Other	8	1.3%
No Answer	17	2.7%

Benefits

When choosing the top three benefits of registration, about 75 percent of the respondents noted greater quality awareness; 72.7 percent pointed to improved documentation; 48 percent listed positive cultural change; and 39 percent pointed to enhanced intercompany communications.

As for external benefits, nearly 34 percent of respondents cited higher perceived quality. Almost 27 percent ranked improved customer satisfaction on top, and nearly 22 percent identified gaining a competitive edge as the main external benefit of registration. (See Table 20-5.)

Regarding internal benefits, nearly 33 percent of all respondents cited better documentation as the primary advantage. Almost 26 percent pointed to greater quality awareness, and 15 percent ranked a positive cultural change as the main internal benefit. (See Table 20-6.)

REGISTRATION AS A CRITICAL MARKETING TOOL

The survey confirms suspicions that many suppliers to larger companies will be required to seek registration in the coming years, and that more and more companies view registration as a critical marketing tool. Almost 96 percent said they either were now using, or planned to use registration for those purposes in the future.

Savings

While most companies that achieved registration under the ISO 9000 series standards report significant annual savings, not all companies found the same return on their investments. Some 26 percent of companies responding to the survey estimated their domestic annual savings to be $10,000 or less. The average annual savings, however, was nearly $179,000.

Conclusion

The results of the survey support what up until now has been only conjecture: ISO 9000 registration is rapidly being viewed as another routine cost of doing business in the United States and Canada.

Please refer to the following two survey articles for further information. The first, *QSU/ Deloitte & Touche Survey of Companies by Industry*, immediately follows this article and highlights three of the main industries discussed in this chapter:

- SIC code 2800: Chemicals and Allied Products
- SIC code 3400: Fabricated Metal Products, Except Machinery and Transportation Equipment
- SIC code 3500: Industrial and Commercial Equipment and Computer Equipment.

The second article, *QSU/Deloitte & Touche Survey of Companies by Size*, is at the end of the chapter. It highlights some of the differences between large and small companies. Please note that both survey articles contain general charts and graphs that apply to all companies. Companies that are either registered or are pursuing registration can find them helpful.

QSU/DELOITTE & TOUCHE SURVEY OF COMPANIES BY INDUSTRY

Introduction

Companies that responded to the joint *Quality Systems Update*/Deloitte & Touche survey fell into 33 Standard Industrial Classification (SIC) codes, some of which are presented in this chapter. (Please refer to the discussion in the first survey article of this chapter for more information on the survey itself and for results that apply to all industries.)

Unfortunately, however, not all of the SIC codes represented in the survey had a significant response rate. For example, several different SIC codes had only one respondent for that entire industry. It would be inaccurate to infer general industry information from a single company's answers. This article, therefore, highlights only those industries with significant response pools.

The following three industries had high response rates, representing nearly half of the entire survey respondents:

● 2800—Chemicals and Allied Products, representing 17.7 percent of all respondents
● 3400—Fabricated Metal Products, Except Machinery and Transportation Equipment, with 14 percent
● 3500—Industrial and Commercial Equipment and Computer Equipment, with 17.4 percent of the responses.

This article provides a comprehensive look at a variety of issues associated with ISO 9000 registration: reasons for registering, the barriers companies face, the costs of registering and the potential savings.

Reasons to Register

US and Canadian companies that sought registration to the ISO 9000 series standards did so for a variety of reasons. Companies in SIC codes 2800, 3400, and 3500 overwhelmingly cited customer demands/expectations and quality benefits as high on their lists. (See Table 20-7.)

Table 20-7: Two Primary Reasons for Registering by SIC Code				
	Primary Reason		**Secondary Reason**	
2800 (Chemicals)	Customer Demands/Expectation	25.5	Quality Benefits	22.7
3500 (Computers)	Customer Demands/Expectation	25.9	Quality Benefits/Corporate Mandate	15.7
3400 (Metal)	Customer Demands/Expectation	29.3	Quality Benefits	22.4
Survey Average	Customer Demands/Expectation	27.4	Quality Benefits	21.8

One slight discrepancy in the industries highlighted was in SIC code 3500, where "corporate mandate" was also a top reason for registering. Companies in SIC code 3500 ranked it equally with quality benefits at 16 percent, whereas overall, corporate mandate was cited by only 8.9 percent of companies as the most important reason for attaining registration.

Barriers to Registration

Companies in SIC codes 2800, 3400, and 3500 overwhelmingly cited document development and procedure creation as the main barriers to successful registration efforts. A lesser but still substantial number of respondents also cited lack of management commitment and not following set procedures high on their list of barriers. (See Table 20-8.)

Table 20-8: Main Barriers to Registration by SIC Code				
	Primary Reason		**Secondary Reason**	
2800 (Chemicals)	Document Development	23.6	Procedure Creation	15.5
3500 (Computers)	Procedure Creation	29.6	Lack of Management Commitment	13.9
3400 (Metal)	Procedure Creation	22.4	Document Development	15.5
Survey Average	Procedure Creation	19.7	Document Development	18.7

Costs

Companies in SIC code 2800 had a higher average cost of $348,000, while those in SIC code 3500 spent just under the overall average at $242,000. The fabricated metal industry had considerably lower costs, averaging $99,000. SIC codes 2800 and 3500 each spent roughly $23,000 on registrar fees alone, while SIC code 3400 spent less—$16,800. (See Table 20-9.)

Table 20-9: Average Internal, External, Registrar and Total Costs Associated with Implementing ISO 9000 by SIC Codes				
	Average Internal Cost	**Average External Cost**	**Average Registrar Cost**	**Average Total Cost**
2800 (Chemicals)	$301,500	$50,500	$23,300	$347,900
3500 (Computers)	$164,200	$43,200	$23,200	$241,600
3400 (Metal)	$72,000	$15,900	$16,800	$99,000
Survey Average	$180,000	$60,100	$21,000	$245,200

Editor's Note: *Respondents were asked to indicate the total **domestic** cost expended to achieve their current level of registration. The implication is that these figures represent company-wide, domestic registration expenditures—not expenses for individual sites.*

Savings

In general, the higher the sales figure, the greater the annual savings. One notable exception involved companies in SIC code 3400. Those companies' total average costs were $99,000, and they had annual savings of over $206,000. On the other hand, companies in SIC code 3500 spent nearly $242,000 on average and had annual savings of only $182,400. Companies in SIC code 3400 realized a greater average annual savings than did those in SIC code 3500. (See Table 20-10.)

Table 20-10: Average Annual Domestic Savings by SIC Codes		
	Average Domestic ANNUAL Savings	Average TOTAL Cost
2800 (Chemicals)	$223,800	$347,900
3500 (Computers)	$182,400	$241,600
3400 (Metal)	$206,600	$99,000
Survey Average	$178,900	$245,200

One confusing result of the survey involves the average number of years companies predicted to recover their costs. For example, companies in SIC code 2800 had an average total cost of $348,000 and an average annual savings of nearly $224,000. Using these figures, one could estimate that it would take the company less than two years to recover the costs. However, respondents from SIC code 2800 predicted 13.6 years to recover them. (See Table 20-11.)

Why the difference? First, it is a mistake to compare the averages, for the respondents did not all answer each of the three registration cost questions and the one savings question. All companies would have had to answer all of these questions for the statisticians to accurately calculate the average number of years to "recover" the costs.

Table 20-11: Average Number of Years to Recover Costs by SIC Codes	
2800 (Chemicals)	13.6
3500 (Computers)	11.8
3400 (Metal)	6.2
Survey Average	11.2

In addition, the "recover" calculation was not an average of the "costs" and "savings" averages, but was calculated by each respondent's own "costs" and "savings" answers. These answers were then totaled and averaged to produce the dollar amounts in Table 20-11.

Conclusion

This survey points to both similarities and differences among the various industries regarding registration costs and anticipated savings, reasons for registering and barriers to registration. Although the article does not highlight all industries, readers can nevertheless apply this information to their own companies.

THE CHEMICAL INDUSTRY

The Chemical Industry: Past and Present

BY DR. ROBERT BELFIT

THE BEGINNING OF ISO 9000 IN THE CHEMICAL INDUSTRY

During the first few years of ISO 9000 series implementation in the United States, the chemical industry took the lead in the number of registrations for several reasons. The chemical industry has been a leader in a favorable balance of payments for many decades—a balance of about $20 billion dollars[1] annually for the last ten years. The industry immediately recognized the need to maintain this balance. A half dozen well-known chemical giants led the United States' charge into ISO 9000. These companies started a trend that continues today. Several factors influenced their early decision to register.

● Companies with considerable capital investments around the world quickly recognized that ISO 9000 registration would help them maintain their market position

● Other companies that shipped their products from the United States into the European Union, Australia, or other countries, rapidly recognized the value of the market-driven concept of ISO 9000 management. In many instances they were urged to register by their European customers or by their European divisions or branches. They were particularly concerned that the European Union might erect a barrier against nonregistered companies.

As a result, chemical companies implemented and continue to implement the ISO 9000 quality management system, and in most cases seek ISO registration.

THE CHEMICAL INDUSTRY TODAY

The early leaders, while perhaps experiencing a few bumpy campaigns, were clearly committed to ISO 9000 and had strong senior management support. There are signs that some of the newer entrants may not possess the same enthusiasm.

Most people familiar with ISO 9000 understand how to develop an ISO quality manual and how to organize a campaign. Yet those personnel who require the organizational freedom to initiate action often have little authority and poorly defined responsibilities. They are unable to identify and record, to verify and control, and to ascertain the corrections that need to be implemented. Perhaps there is a reluctance to delegate responsibility to others or a failure to recognize that everyone in the organization has an impact on the company's quality management system. This lack of clearly defined responsibilities and authority can translate into a lack of empowerment. As a result, employee input is limited, and managers are not sufficiently involved.

The management representative or ISO coordinator often carries too big a load and tries to do the job for others, rather than coaching employees into defining the system statements and establishing procedures themselves. Consequently, responsibility is diluted and gaps are prevalent. In such cases, the site management or senior management believes that it need not get involved and thus has not fully understood the ISO 9000 concept. Managers would undoubtedly become more enthusiastic if they better comprehended what ISO 9000 could do for them.

Following are some of the key concerns of chemical companies—or at least what should be of concern to them—and how companies can address those concerns and conform to the various elements of the ISO standards.

Contract Review

Contract review, while a simple concept, is frequently given inadequate attention due to a historical lack of problems in the chemical industry. Yet with today's changing values in terms of products, economics, safety and the environment, regulations affecting the chemical industry will require more attention. For example, the management concept embodied in the ISO 9000 standards is an ideal mechanism to implement the OSHA 29CFR1910.119 safety management regulation for the chemical process industries.

Design Control

The design control section of 9001 is one of the most important elements of the ISO 9000 series standards. Its requirement for documenting design inputs, outputs, verification, change control, and organizational and technical interfaces affords one of the most effective approaches to introducing new products. Many organizations see design control as too burdensome and avoid it by registering to ISO 9002. This system approach to new products, however, will accelerate new-product decision making and improve effectiveness if properly executed.

Document and Data Control

In the chemical industry, poor document control is not unusual. Frequently employees fail to destroy obsolete copies and to update appropriate procedures.

Purchasing

Purchasing from a chemical industry standpoint has undergone a dramatic change from the 1970s and early 1980s when low-cost raw materials were the emphasis, and there was less regard for raw material quality. Raw materials such as those easily mined from the ground or brine wells were inexpensive. Today, however, the need to be more specific about impurities and their impact on the operation has increased company costs. Thus, companies should implement the requirement for documented purchasing procedures.

Process Control

Documented work instructions and compliance with standard codes and quality plans have improved significantly over the past two years as the benefits of process control have become more apparent. According to this author's experience, 50 percent of the procedures are in good condition, compared to less than 25 percent three years ago.

Receiving Inspection and Testing, In-process Control, Final Inspection Testing

Receiving inspection and testing, in-process control, and final inspection testing have been at the center of the chemical industry for decades. These systems and procedures are usually in good condition. However, quantitative validation that shows "how good the numbers are" is often lacking. As a result, rework and shipping decisions are sometimes made based on numbers of unknown validity. Such a process highlights the need for calibration in the chemical industry.

Control of Nonconformances, Nonconformance Review, Corrective Action

Control of nonconformances, nonconformance review, and corrective action are at the heart of continuous improvement when internal auditing is included. Nevertheless, chemical companies sometimes claim that ISO 9000 does not mention continuous improvement. This interpretation fails to properly interpret the standard and its systems requirements.

Handling, Packaging, Delivering Chemicals

Handling, packaging, and delivery of chemicals has undergone significant improvement over the last decade. The chemical industry has focused on this area intensively through OSHA 29CFR1910.119 and the CMA Responsible Care® program. In fact, many chemical businesses are using the safety and risk elements from the ISO 9004-1 guidance standard to strengthen their management programs. (Refer to Chapter 13 for more information on Responsible Care®.)

CONCLUSION

Two of the key ingredients for a successful and efficient ISO campaign are proper training and understanding/commitment from senior management. The older generation of chemical industry leaders is enthusiastic about ISO 9000. Improving training and increasing management's involvement will generate enthusiasm among the newer generation of quality professionals.

The true value of ISO 9000 has grown more apparent as the chemical industry has become more involved with the standard. Ronald C. Spillers, president of Arkansas Eastman Division (AED), has summarized this value most simply and concisely by saying the following:

> *Despite AED's excellent TQM activities, ISO 9000 registration has been one of the best quality moves we have ever made because:*
>
> ● *It helped instill within us the discipline and the contagious pride of a winner*
>
> ● *It enhanced our company's image—not only with our worldwide customers, but within our own ranks...within our company*
>
> ● *It is bringing us significantly new business.*

Indeed, implementing ISO 9000 has prepared many chemical sites and businesses for the next decade, both by developing new products and by meeting society's needs in the areas of environment and process safety management.

FOR FURTHER READING...

For further reading on guidelines for the chemical industry, refer to:

- *ANSI/ASQC Q90/ISO 9000 Guidelines for Use by the Chemical and Process Industries.* ASQC Quality Press, Milwaukee, Wisconsin, 1992. ISBN: 0-87389-196-1.

- ASQC Chemical and Process Industries Division, Chemical Interest Committee, *Quality Assurance for the Chemical and Process Industries—A Manual of Good Practices.*

- Chemical Industry Association, London, England, *ISO 9001, EN 29001, BS 5750: Part 1: 1987: Guidelines for Use by the Chemical and Allied Industries.*

SUPPLIER QUESTIONNAIRE: THE *CMA CRITERIA FOR CONTINUOUS IMPROVEMENT*

A supplier questionnaire based in part on the ISO 9000 series standards is saving the chemical industry thousands of dollars each day and its use may spread to other industries. Companies have found that the survey not only reduced the amount of time spent auditing suppliers, but it also decreased the amount of time consumed by customer audits. It has received widespread attention throughout the industry.

The survey was created by the Total Quality Council of the Chemical Manufacturers Association (CMA), which comprises 35 industry representatives. The questionnaire is intended to assist industry in verifying basic quality system requirements. Known as the *CMA Criteria for Continuous Improvement,* it provides customer assurances and is intended to lead to continuous improvement of the quality system. The survey is divided into five main sections: leadership, strategic planning, human resources, product service quality systems, and customer satisfaction.

The document is based partly on ISO 9000 and partly on Malcolm Baldrige National Quality Award criteria. The focus on ISO 9000 is in recognition of the growing segment of US chemical companies that have undergone registration.

Typically, companies send out a questionnaire to potential suppliers and then follow up with a site visit. In many cases, before they began using the CMA document, companies were asking for the same information in slightly different ways. Using the survey eliminates redundancies.

CMA officials hope the survey will catch on outside the chemical industry, since the questionnaire is general enough that it can be used by any industry with minor modifications. [2]

To receive a copy of the questionnaire, contact Trish Messenger, Chemical Manufacturers Association, 2501 M Street NW, Washington, DC 20037; tel. 202-887-1169.

ISO 9000: Problems Facing the Chemical Industry

BY WILLIAM FERGUSON

INTRODUCTION

A misconception exists that because the chemical industry is somewhat unique, its operations are not compatible with the ISO 9000 series standards. Fortunately, the experience of those chemical companies that have successfully achieved registration is helping to dispel this misconception. This, of course, does not mean that no problems exist in implementing ISO 9000 in the chemical industry.

This article attempts to highlight problems the chemical industry could encounter when developing a documented quality system under ISO 9000.

Although the clauses of ISO 9001 are used for comparison in this article, the majority of companies will need to satisfy only the requirements of ISO 9002. Only companies supporting research and design will be required to satisfy the requirements of ISO 9001—if they decide to include these activities within their scope of registration.

Editor's Note: *The 1994 version of ISO 9002 is identical to ISO 9001, except that ISO 9001 references design—a topic that does not appear in ISO 9002. (The 1987 version of ISO 9002 did not include servicing.)*

The major problems facing the chemical industry at the moment are not only implementing ISO 9000, but also complying with the requirements of Responsible Care®. These issues are further compounded by the possible development of an ISO standard on environmental management. Fortunately, in a number of instances there is considerable overlap between the requirements of the ISO standard and those of Responsible Care®. (See Chapter 13 for more information on Responsible Care®.)

ISO 9001: PROBLEM CLAUSES FOR THE CHEMICAL INDUSTRY

4.1 Management Responsibility

No real difficulties appear to exist in satisfying the requirements of Clause 4.1 of ISO 9001, since it is concerned with the organization of the company. In general, most organizations have a well-defined hierarchical structure. Difficulties may arise in defining responsibilities for controlling nonconforming product. It is usual for the operator to be responsible for correcting minor deviations from the normal operating conditions. This must be recognized when responsibilities are defined.

4.2 Quality System

Both the 1987 version and the 1994 versions of the standard indicate that in developing a quality system, timely consideration should be given to preparing quality plans. (The 1994 version also refers more specifically to quality planning.) Within the chemical industry, difficulty could arise in accepting the philosophy of quality plans, for some think that such plans are more appropriate to a repetitive, mass-producing operation and are inconsistent with the methods of operation in the chemical industry. (Please refer to Chapter 7 for more information on quality plans.)

Generally in the chemical industry, "frequency of sampling" and "testing the product" are well defined at all stages of the process. For example, the frequency of testing the incoming raw materials and the final inspection of the product are usually defined in laboratory procedures, and the frequency of in-process inspection is defined in the process control procedures. Such procedures define the tests that should be conducted and explain how to ensure product quality at all stages of the process. These procedures should therefore satisfy this requirement of the standard.

4.3 Contract Review

A considerable proportion of orders and contracts are processed by telephone and, as a result, little or no objective evidence exists to show that the details have been confirmed. It is therefore necessary to build some process into the system that provides evidence that the accuracy of each telephone order has been confirmed.

A majority of complaints from customers are as follows:

● The customer did not receive what was ordered
● The customer did not receive what was required
● The material did not arrive on time
● The delivery was either short or duplicated.

Such problems can be greatly reduced with an effective method of verifying customers' orders.

4.4 Design Control

This clause is one of the most extensive and is divided into subcategories. These sub-clauses require preparation of documented procedures that describe the way design activity is controlled—from the conception of the project through its development and ending with verification or validation to confirm that the design inputs have been satisfied. While this clause presents no problems unique to the chemical industry, uncertainty exists over where and when it is necessary to begin documenting the design activity.

In basic research, considerable activity can be devoted to identifying new materials or compounds—some of which may never be developed beyond that basic stage. One question is whether or not such research needs to be documented to satisfy the requirements of this clause. Its wording does not help to identify the point at which such documentation should commence. It does, however, appear to indicate that documentation should begin when the identified material could be developed to meet a market need or to satisfy a potential customer requirement (i.e., when it has become a potential product).

Another possible "gray area" centers around whether is it necessary to calibrate equipment that is used in basic research activity. Clause 4.11—which deals with calibration of inspection, measuring and test equipment—indicates that equipment used to demonstrate conformance of the product to specified requirements must be calibrated. Equipment used at the basic research stage does not need to be calibrated to meet the requirements of this clause, but towards the end of the design activity—once definitive values are established—the equipment used to define these values should be calibrated.

4.5 Document and Data Control

Clause 4.5 of the standard is concerned with all aspects of document control. The documentation required may be slightly more extensive than in other industries, since it will require the following:

- Specifications for both raw materials and finished products
- Test methods used in laboratories and other areas where testing is conducted
- Material and safety data information.

4.6 Purchasing

The requirements in relation to the purchasing of material and services from approved subcontractors should present no problems, nor should approving subcontractors and monitoring the performance of these subcontractors. (The term "suppliers" has been changed in the 1994 version to "subcontractors.")

One change is that the 1994 standard appears to require more positive definition of the type and extent of control exercised by the supplier over subcontractors. In addition, it now takes account of the inspection of purchased product by the supplier at the subcontractor's premises.

Toll manufacturing is a common activity in the chemical industry. A toll manufacturer is a subcontractor who undertakes a prescribed part of the manufacturing process. Where the work is undertaken, it must be undertaken by an approved subcontractor. Neither of these changes should affect the chemical industry in any unique way.

4.7 Customer-Supplied Product

Processing customer-supplied material within the chemical industry is not uncommon, but the way in which the processing is undertaken does present some problems in relation to documenting the activities. (The term "purchaser-supplied" has been replaced with "customer-supplied.")

In a straightforward case where a discrete amount of material is received and processed before being returned to the customer, the requirements to identify the amount received, the amount returned and any amount lost can be documented in a fairly simple fashion. In such cases, title to the material remains wholly with the customer.

In a number of cases, however, this simple arrangement does not exist. The material received from the customer may be commingled with the company's own material and, therefore, the customer's material loses its unique identity. In such cases it would be necessary to have documentation available to show that an agreement existed with the customer that required an agreed quantity of product to be prepared against each quantity of delivered material.

Theoretically, the customer can still lay title to the material and, therefore, this activity would be considered a customer-supplied product. It would be necessary to develop procedures showing how the requirements of Clause 4.7 were satisfied for these transactions.

In other cases the customer may supply material for conversion, but the agreement will cover the purchase of the material supplied by the customer and the repurchase of the converted material—in agreed quantities—by the customer. Since the customer loses title to the material, processing such material would not lie within the sphere of customer-supplied material.

4.8 Product Identification and Traceability

Clause 4.8 of ISO 9001 is concerned with product identification and traceability. In general, satisfying the requirement for product identification presents no great difficulty, since each product—intermediate or final—usually has some form of unique identification that may be a name or number.

In a batch process where product is manufactured in discrete quantities, full traceability is achieved by identifying the batch/lot numbers of the ingredients against the unique identification of the batch.

In continuous manufacture—especially where the feed stock is taken from a continuously replenishing source such as a pipeline—achieving full traceability is very difficult, if not impossible. In such instances it may be possible to provide traceability to only a particular day or period of time unless recourse is made to some form of continuous monitoring.

Similarly, in continuous manufacture where product tanks are being depleted and replenished at the same time, it will be possible to achieve traceability to only a particular period of time. The use of statistical process control (SPC) can provide some confidence in the quality of the product, but in itself does not achieve traceability.

In some cases material from a continuous process may be fed into run-down tanks and subjected to some form of checking. If satisfactory, the material is then passed into a product tank. The accumulation of material from several run-down tanks (in a product tank) then constitutes a discrete quantity, but even in these circumstances full traceability can be related to only a period of time.

It should be noted that traceability is a requirement of the standard only when it is called up in the contract. In general, contracts placed within the chemical industry do not specify traceability, although in some sensitive areas—such as materials used in food manufacture or in pharmaceuticals—it may well be a requirement. In such cases it would be necessary to develop procedures and practices that fully satisfy these requirements.

4.9 Process Control

Meeting the requirements of Clause 4.9 should not pose problems within the industry, since clear instructions covering the process or processes usually exist. This is an area where the requirements for Responsible Care® and the ISO standards overlap. In general, however, the requirements of the former tend to be more stringent than those of the latter, with Responsible Care® addressing safety that is not covered in ISO 9000. If desired, it should be possible to cover both sets of requirements by one set of procedures.

4.10 Inspection and Testing

Clause 4.10 is concerned with inspecting incoming raw materials, materials in process, and finished products to ensure that the specifications are being satisfied at all stages of the process.

If the raw materials are in continuous supply from a pipeline, some difficulty could arise in satisfying the requirements of Clause 4.10. The problem could be solved by introducing some form of statistical sampling or some form of continuous monitoring in the line. Delivery of materials in rail cars, road tankers, drums and packages should present no problems, since these are discrete amounts.

Although testing in-process material should present no unique problems, the same cannot be said for finished product. Here again, if the finished product is discharged into a pipeline or into a tank that is continuously depleted and replenished, it would be necessary to resort to some type of sampling plan (in the absence of on-line continuous sampling) to give confidence in the quality of the product.

This sampling plan approach would present problems if the customer requires a certificate of analysis instead of a certificate of conformity, because the former relates to a discrete amount of material. It may be that in such circumstances changes to the method of operation or special steps would be required to satisfy the customer's requirements.

4.11 Control of Inspection, Measuring and Test Equipment

Clause 4.11 of ISO 9001 addresses calibration of instrumentation. Among other things, it requires that all instrumentation used in releasing the product must be calibrated in such a way that the calibration can be related to national standards. This can pose various problems within the chemical industry—especially when the calibration requires techniques beyond the basic parameters of length, mass and time.

In the laboratory, calibrating the simpler pieces of equipment—such as balances, pH meters, viscometers and hydrometers—presents no great problem, for any calibration undertaken on these instruments can easily be traced to national standards.

Problems do arise, however, when it is necessary to consider some advanced techniques, such as gas chromatography with its various additions, infrared spectrophotometry, nuclear magnetic resonance, etc. In a number of cases these instruments can be calibrated before use by using standards prepared by weighing out quantities of a standard material or a group of material on a traceable balance.

In other cases, the calibration could consist of analyzing at regular intervals a standard batch of material or a standard sample with the results plotted on a graph to indicate consistency in the instrumentation. Clause 4.11 allows for such calibrations but requires defining the method used.

In the plant itself a problem exists in deciding whether or not a particular instrument should be calibrated. It could be argued from the quality point of view—provided the laboratory equipment is calibrated and is used to release the product—that there is no need to calibrate any equipment in the plant. This philosophy, however, is really continuing a concept of quality control that has been shown very conclusively to be an inefficient way to conduct business.

The entire concept of quality assurance is to build quality into the product at all stages of manufacture to prevent the production of nonconforming product. This implies control, and almost without exception, control in the chemical industry generally relies on instrumentation.

Given that instrumentation must be calibrated, the problem arises in deciding which instrumentation should be included within the calibration system. There are no hard and fast rules. Every instrument or group of instruments must be examined individually. The following questions can help in deciding which instruments to include:

● Does the actual instrument control the operation?
● What direct effect does it have on the final quality of the product?

For example, if there is a pH meter in the process line that itself automatically controls the pH within clearly defined limits as a part of the operation, then it is an instrument that must be calibrated. Similarly, an instrument that is used to control the temperature within very fine limits must also be calibrated.

On the other hand, flow meters used to measure quantities of liquids entering tanks or weigh cells (which are used to measure quantities of material being added to tanks) do not in themselves control the operation. Nevertheless, if not calibrated, these could lead to production of nonconforming product. It therefore seems logical to include flow meters in the calibration system.

There are numerous instruments in the control room of any plant that enable the operator to tune the plant to achieve the optimum output. While it may be desirable to calibrate these instruments, the lack of such calibration should not cause problems at an assessment.

4.12 Inspection and Test Status

The requirements of Clause 4.12 address the way the inspection status of material is identified at all stages of the process. There is no problem with drums, packages and tanks of material since these are discrete quantities that can be marked to show the inspection status. Difficulties arise in a continuous process and, in such circumstances, the only course of action is to consider all material satisfactory unless it is identified otherwise or is located in an area that is set aside for nonconforming material. The standard allows the inspection status of material to be established by means of marking, location or associated paperwork.

4.13 Control of Nonconforming Product

Clause 4.13 of the standard is concerned with the way a product is controlled when it is found to be nonconforming. Within the chemical industry this usually refers to a product that cannot be suitably adjusted and that must either be mixed off in small quantities, recycled or put to waste. Documenting such problems presents no difficulties, but problems can arise when physically separating the product—especially in a continuous process. For example, in a tank that is being continuously replenished or in a pipeline where commingling can occur, it may be necessary to separate some satisfactory product to ensure that all of the nonconforming product has been separated.

4.15 Handling, Storage, Packaging, Preservation and Delivery

The requirements relating to storage, handling, packaging, preservation and delivery of the product are detailed in Clause 4.15 of the standard. Generally, the way chemical material is stored, packaged and transported is controlled by state or federal regulations. The way material is handled within the plant is usually determined by the nature of the material and the rules drawn up for the safe operation of the plant. While some of the requirements are unique to the chemical industry, these would not present any problems in satisfying the requirements of Clause 4.15.

4.18 Training

The standard ensures that all personnel who perform activities affecting quality training are properly trained to undertake their tasks. Clause 4.18 requires that records of training be maintained, and that the training needs be identified.

Consideration should be given to training personnel such as customer service representatives who receive orders, personnel who purchase material and laboratory personnel responsible for analyzing the materials, since these people perform activities affecting quality.

4.19 Servicing

This clause of the standard indicates that where servicing is specified in the contract, procedures must be developed to show how the servicing will be performed and how it will be verified—whether it is satisfactory and meets the specified requirements. It is generally accepted that this clause is not relevant within the chemical industry. An exception may be in the plastics industry where it may be necessary to assist a customer with the use of a particular plastics product.

4.20 Statistical Techniques

Statistical techniques are very valuable tools—especially in the chemical industry—and while the standard does not make their use mandatory, it does indicate in Clause 4.20 that, where appropriate, the supplier shall identify adequate statistical techniques. Statistical process control can be used for the following:

- To identify process variability
- To assess changes in the operating procedures on the variability in the final product
- To determine the operation of an instrument within acceptable limits
- To give assurance of the quality of material deliveries to customers that do not result from the analysis of discrete batches of material.

CONCLUSION

A major problem facing the chemical industry in implementing the requirements of ISO 9000 centers around the swap deals and product transfers that are extremely common in the industry. In a swap deal, for example, one firm accepts an order for a product and then arranges that another firm should supply and deliver against that order. The standards themselves make no reference to such activities, and in general, it is left to the assessment bodies to define their policy.

The policy appears to vary from one assessment body to the next. One assessment body has regulations that such activities be undertaken outside the scope of registration, unless it can be shown that the material has been obtained from a registered company and that the items are within that company's scope of registration. Other assessment bodies look on such activities as subcontractor operations and place responsibility for the control on the company applying for registration. This variation in assessment body policies is somewhat confusing, but each assessment body should be able to provide a clear definition of its policy.

This article does not pretend to identify each and every ISO 9000 issue, for it is impossible to do this when addressing general issues. It highlights some of the problems that several petrochemical companies have faced in implementing ISO 9000. In some cases, the problems were difficult to overcome and required changes to long-established practices. Most will agree, however, that ISO 9000 registration has ultimately been a valuable exercise.

ISO 9004-3: GUIDELINES FOR PROCESSED MATERIALS

ISO/9004-3, Quality management and quality system elements—Part 3: Guidelines for processed materials is modeled generally after the 1987 edition of *ISO 9004, Quality management and quality system elements—Guidelines* and other guidance standards. The standard defines processed materials as the following:

Products (final or intermediate) prepared by transformations, consisting of solids, liquids, gases, or combinations thereof, including particulate materials, ingots, filaments or sheet structures. (Clause 3.5)

One of the key organizational goals for processed materials manufacturers is control of the process itself. ISO 9004-3 offers the following guidance for the application of ISO 9000 to the processed materials industry:

4 Management Responsibility
5 Quality system principles
6 Economics—quality-related cost considerations
7 Quality in Marketing
8 Quality in specification and design/development
9 Quality in procurement
10 Quality in production
11 Control of production
12 Product verification
13 Control of measuring and test equipment
14 Nonconformity
15 Corrective action
16 Handling and post-production functions
17 Quality documentation and records
18 Personnel

(continued on next page)

ISO 9004-3: Guidelines for Processed Materials

(continued from previous page)

19   Product safety and liability
20   Use of statistical methods

The following are some key points from the standard that apply directly to processed materials.

Quality in Marketing: The Product Brief (7.2)

In Clause 7.2, the standard recommends a product brief as a way to outline the product requirements. Among the elements that apply to process industries are "performance characteristics including strength, durability, corrosion resistance, thermal resistance and workability, as well as other measurable properties of the process output."

Planning and Objectives of Design/Development (8.2)

Management should establish a time-phased design/development program that could include the following stages:

- Research and development at a laboratory stage
- Trial at the plant to ensure that pilot plant output can be scaled up to predict commercial plant output
- Tentative use by customer or in-market
- Initial production at commercial plant
- Mass production
- Design of monitoring and process control systems.

The product definition may include "process capability, durability and reliability, processability, homogeneity, impurities, foreign substances, changes in quality over time, deterioration, safety and disposability."

Process and Product Design Qualification and Validation (8.4)

The design process should provide for periodic evaluation, including trial samples from the pilot plant and commercial plant. Evaluation methods can include Failure Modes and Effects Analysis (FMEA), Fault Tree Analysis (FTA) or risk assessment.

Requirements for Specifications, Drawings and Purchase Orders (9.2)

Purchasing documents should be specific and include elements such as the following:

- Precise identification of grade
- Inspection instructions and applicable specifications
- Quality system standard to be applied
- Requirements for evidence of process control from the supplier
- Precise descriptions of chemical composition and physical properties
- Packaging, labelling, transportation and delivery timing requirements
- Laboratory method specifications and analysis instructions

(continued on next page)

ISO 9004-3: Guidelines for Processed Materials

(continued from previous page)

- Advance notification when the supplier makes materials composition or significant process changes.

Planning for Controlled Production (10.1)

Companies should consider verifying the quality status of a product or process throughout the production sequence to "minimize effects of errors and to maximize yields. By their nature, processed (bulk) material manufactured by continuous processes may be difficult to sample. This situation increases the importance of the use of statistical sampling and evaluation procedures with processed materials."

Product Verification: Incoming Materials and Parts (12.1)

"Both bulk and packaged materials should be segregated and/or marked to avoid consumption before being accepted. Introduction of new bulk materials into the inventory of existing materials raises the potential of cross-contamination (intermixing of materials). In some cases (e.g., pipeline shipments), raw materials proceed directly from the supplier's process, without going into inventory, and are immediately consumed in the consumer's process." In such cases, the supplier should provide assurance on quality.

Completed Product Verification (12.3)

It is important to develop appropriate sampling plans to provide quality assurance since "it is often difficult to designate or identify precise lots or batches from a continuous process." Even in the case of a batch process, "the batch producer needs to carefully address these issues..." The sampling plan should consider:

- The cost of the test
- Whether the test is meaningful in relation to customer requirements
- Whether the test is destructive
- The stability of the process
- The measurement error in proportion to total variability
- The time to complete test
- Customer or statutory requirements.

Identification of Nonconforming Products (14.2)

Sometimes it is not possible to directly identify a nonconforming product, "due to the complexity of the required storage conditions (e.g., extremes of temperature or pressure or corrosive nature of the product)." In these situations, companies can use documented or computer-based control systems, "provided the system is designed for the prevention of inadvertent use or shipment (i.e., a low-customer-risk segregation system).

Disposition of Nonconforming Products (14.5)

The guidance standard notes that "nonconforming products may be blended with conforming products, under controlled procedures which ensure that the resulting mixture is in full compliance with specified requirements."

(continued on next page)

ISO 9004-3: Guidelines for Processed Materials

(continued from previous page)

Handling and Storage (16.1.2)

Handling of processed materials should be designed to prevent damage due to "vibration, shock, abrasion, corrosion, temperature or moisture..." Stored process materials "should be checked periodically to detect possible deterioration contamination, undesirable separation, or reaction."

Identification (16.1.3)

Companies should seek an appropriate method for identifying products that are delivered as a continuous flow, where no marking and labeling is possible.

After-sales Servicing (16.2)

The standard suggests that suppliers "provide customers with end-use application information for correct use and handling" and should obtain detailed information about the "purpose, methods, and conditions about product use, to be able to provide proper advice."

Marketing Reporting and Product Supervision (16.3)

Companies should establish an early warning system for "reporting instances of product failure or shortcomings, as appropriate, particularly for newly introduced products, to ensure rapid corrective action."

Chemical Industry Case Study: Betz Laboratories, Inc.

Trevose, PA—When Steven D. Haberly was attempting to sell senior management on the ISO 9000 series at Betz Laboratories Inc., he assured them that the company would undergo fewer customer audits once it became registered.

Instead of reducing the number of audits, however, registration seemed to have the opposite effect. More customers than ever wanted to audit Betz, which posted net sales of more than $7 million in 1992-1993.

Haberly was clueless as to the reason for the requests. "It was a zoo for the first 60 to 90 days after we got certification," recalled Haberly, then assistant vice president for quality. "We thought, 'Oh, no, what have we done!'"

After an initial wave of audits the mystery was solved. Most of the customers were not interested in verifying Betz's quality system; they wanted information. "They wanted to pick our brains about how we got certified,"

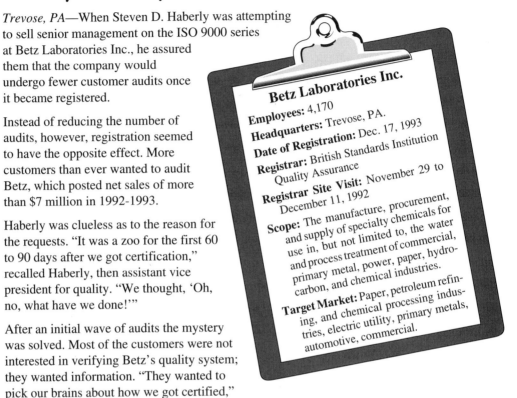

Betz Laboratories Inc.

Employees: 4,170
Headquarters: Trevose, PA.
Date of Registration: Dec. 17, 1993
Registrar: British Standards Institution Quality Assurance
Registrar Site Visit: November 29 to December 11, 1992
Scope: The manufacture, procurement, and supply of specialty chemicals for use in, but not limited to, the water and process treatment of commercial, primary metal, power, paper, hydro-carbon, and chemical industries.
Target Market: Paper, petroleum refining, and chemical processing industries, electric utility, primary metals, automotive, commercial.

Haberly said. Once that was understood, Haberly, who now has other responsibilities, made it known that he was willing to discuss the registration process without the formality and cost of full-blown audits.

It was only a matter of months before the audit phenomenon reversed itself, according to B.C. Moore, a senior vice president with the specialty chemical company. Eventually, the number of customer audits dropped to half as many as in previous years. "Before ISO, we used to have customers coming in here once a week to audit us," Moore said. "Every one of them was different. Every one of them was time-consuming and sometimes adversarial."

DECISION TO PROCEED

Even without Haberly's assurances, Moore said, senior management was keen on ISO 9000 series registration from the start.

"Obviously there's always one skeptic, but by and large" most were signed onto the effort, Moore explained. The company had made a commitment to improving quality in the late 1980s, and ISO 9000 fit the game plan. Its emphasis on documentation and process control would also give the company a leg up on meeting quality assurance aspects of the Malcolm Baldrige National Quality Award criteria.

Customer Survey

Before committing to the project, Betz had each of its 10 US marketing divisions survey their top 25 customers. The customers were asked if they planned to pursue ISO 9000 series registration.

"There was really no pressure from our customers at the time or from anyone else to get certified," Haberly explained. "We decided to evaluate what it meant in the marketplace. Was it a competitive advantage and was it a way to improve our quality system?"

The answer was "yes" to both questions. In two of the company's largest marketing divisions, at least half of the major customers were pursuing registration or intended to do so.

Reassured by the survey, senior management gave its blessing to the registration effort in early 1992. In a letter that went out to Betz's 4,000+ employees, the company's chief executive officer and chairman made ISO 9000 registration one of the top priorities for 1992. He set a one-year goal to attain it.

CHOOSING SITES

Management had to decide which aspects of the company to register. Since Betz has 12 production and distribution sites throughout the United States, a given order might have been filled from any one of the sites. It was decided that partial registration of these sites would not reap benefits for the system as a whole for some time.

Company executives decided to register all 12 production and distribution sites simultaneously, as well as its quality assurance, purchasing, traffic, and materials management operations.

There was no question that these sites would pursue registration under ISO 9002, which covers all elements of the standards except design. The design function would be registered separately as warranted by each of the company's seven US operating units. Each of these units specializes in a different aspect of the company's business and each houses the design function for that particular segment of the market. One of those business units—Betz Equipment Systems—later attained ISO 9001 registration for the design, development, manufacture, assembly and service of its chemical feed and control equipment. Betz executives selected British Standards Institute Quality Assurance (BSI QA) as the registrar.

INTERNAL AUDITS

Betz trained 39 of its own people to be internal auditors, including nine lead auditors. Each of the lead auditors who were chosen from senior management would be held accountable for the registration of two production and distribution sites. They were given responsibility to schedule internal audits and maintain records of nonconformances. Several other executives, including Haberly, were appointed to a management team that would coordinate the entire effort.

Haberly said the organizational structure was key to the company's ability to meet the one-year registration deadline. "There was an absolute line of authority to get it done," Haberly said. "I hate to admit it but in some way it almost developed into a competition. ... Nobody was going to have a plant that got turned down."

The internal auditors performed a preliminary audit of the company in August 1992. They turned up more than 250 minor nonconformances, but no major ones. All were taken seriously and addressed quickly. Their goal was to fix everything that they could possibly fix before BSI QA arrived for another pre-assessment in September 1992.

One of the biggest problems involved a lack of detailed training records. Most of the records were just notes in a file rather than something that was easy to read, Haberly explained. Company executives developed a chart that would allow each plant manager to have a better understanding of the training level of each employee at any given moment. This would also ease the process of prioritizing training.

Through the audits, company officials also discovered that some calibration records could not be located easily. They created central storage locations at each site to solve the problem.

One of the unexpected benefits of the process was an opportunity for plants to run benchmarks against one another. "Plants began to compare procedures to procedures," Haberly said. "We'd compare and actually pick best-possible practices."

DOCUMENTATION

Much of the company's documentation had to be rewritten to conform to the ISO 9000 series requirements. There was no corporate-wide quality manual. Each site had been responsible for maintaining its own quality manuals, and in most cases that meant that information was distributed among several documents.

"Our quality manuals would cover an entire table because our documentation was so spread out," Haberly said. As part of the registration effort, the company pared the overall number of manuals to one per production facility, and one for the corporation as a whole.

This allowed the 68-year-old company to eliminate some of the inefficiencies that had been built into the system over the years. One of the processes that benefited most from the approach was that of bringing a new product to market. In the past it took 54 separate steps to bring a product on line after research was completed.

"We all knew it was complex but none of us had ever taken the time to count all of the steps," Moore explained. "The first conclusion you come to is 'How did this get to be so complex?'" Now there are only 12 steps, and the time it takes to bring a new product to market has been reduced by 25 percent.

BSI QA performed its preliminary audit in September 1992, and by that time the company had already corrected most of the nonconformances identified by the internal audits, according to Haberly. As a result, BSI QA's preliminary assessment turned up only about 20 minor nonconformances for all sites combined.

FINAL AUDIT

The final audit lasted two weeks. In some ways it was anticlimactic since most of the nonconformances were thought to have been identified and addressed in the internal and preliminary audits.

A team of three auditors visited all 12 plants and the corporate headquarters during the final audit. The auditors traveled separately and each was assigned a company escort who was chosen from the pool of internal lead auditors based on the division of plant responsibility.

The final audit proved grueling for the BSI QA auditors. Their typical day began at dawn when they observed the first shift in action, and often ended when the night shift came on. Then the auditors would be driven to the airport where they would board a plane to repeat the process at another Betz site the next morning.

Communication among the plants was ongoing. "The minute that the audit was over with we knew if there were any nonconformances," Haberly said. The final audit turned up only 15 minor nonconformances throughout the company.

Everything they found was of no consequence, Haberly said. "In some ways our lead auditors were much more aggressive than the BSI people because we knew the system."

Registration was granted effective December 17, 1992.

When it was all over, Betz had spent about $500,000 on internal costs and another $100,000 on external costs, most of which was the registrar's fee. The auditors logged some 400,000 air miles traveling among sites and their base of operations in the United Kingdom. Internal costs translated into 1,200 work hours for internal audits, 6,500 work hours for writing and rewriting documentation, and 5,500 work hours for other aspects of implementation, including training employees on new procedures and educating the workforce about ISO 9000.

Haberly recommended the approach of assigning internal auditors to accompany the registrar auditors. This prevented incorrect interpretations and misunderstandings, he said. "We took them to task on everything," Haberly explained. "If the internal auditors felt that a BSI QA auditor was making a bad call, they challenged it."

Apparently this practice did not go unnoticed by the audit team. Haberly recalled one of the BSI QA auditors later telling company officials: "Arguing with an [internal] auditor is like wrestling with a pig in the mud. At some point you begin to realize that the pig is enjoying himself."

MAINTAINING REGISTRATION

The company not only met its goal of becoming registered in one year, it finished early, completing the process in about nine months.

As a result, Haberly said, he was concerned that it might be difficult to maintain the level of enthusiasm and effort that it took to attain registration. "I think we were worried because we had pushed them really hard," Haberly said. "I spent a lot of time away from my family. A lot of us did. Then we got this prize that we had been searching for."

He thought it was only natural for the process to falter. But fortunately, he said, that never happened. Company executives knew there would be a surveillance visit in six months and, while not nearly as comprehensive as the final audit, it still meant that the company's registration would be on the line.

Betz tried to minimize any tendency to ease off by scheduling additional management training on ISO 9000 in February 1993. "We pretty much kept it in front of their faces," Haberly said.

"I think you have to have a strong internal system in order to make sure that you keep things on the same track."

Internal audits began again from March to May 1993. They turned up very few nonconformances and the first official surveillance visit in June 1993 confirmed the company's findings.

Haberly said the fear of losing registration is enough to keep the process running smoothly in between audits. "I'm not convinced that getting certification is going to get you business, but losing certification is definitely going to lose you business," he said.

Chemical Industry Case Study: Monsanto Chemical Company

Sauget, IL—Monsanto Chemical Company's W. G. Krummrich facility used a rigorous internal auditing schedule to prepare for ISO 9002 registration.

Thirty-two internal audits were performed in less than a year using ISO 9000 criteria. The company hired Bywater of the United Kingdom to perform in-house auditor training. Fourteen Krummrich employees are now auditors approved by the Institute for Quality Assurance (IQA).

The Krummrich facility, just across the Mississippi River from St. Louis, achieved ISO 9002 registration November 7, 1991, after a final audit by British Standards Institution (BSI). The registration was for the manufacture and distribution of Santoflex, ACL and chlorobenzenes.

Monsanto Chemical Company
W.G. Krummrich Facility

Location: Sauget, IL.
Scope: The manufacture and supply of 4-nitro diphenylamine, para-phenylene diamines (Santoflex), chlorobenzenes/nitrochlorobenzenes, trichloro-zenes/nitrochlorobenzenes, trichloro-s-triazinetrione (ACL 90 Plus), phosphorus pentasulfide, and nitroanilines.
Registrar: British Standards Institution Quality Assurance.

BEGINNING THE PROCESS

In May 1990, plant manager Bill Boyle hired Tom Kreinbrook, who had previous ISO 9000 experience, to implement a quality system and to lead the facility to ISO registration.

"Initially, our driving force was external (and) we thought we'd need to do this to compete in the European Economic Community," said Boyle, noting that Krummrich's chemical products are shipped all over the world. However, once the benefits of ISO were realized, the value of the system itself, and not the market implications of registration, became the driving force.

GAINING COMMITMENT

From May until early Autumn 1990, Kreinbrook met with every unit at the Krummrich facility to explain ISO and "to gain commitments to be involved in the registration effort." The facility employs 600 workers.

The Krummrich site is composed of six distinct manufacturing units. Kreinbrook met with all six in October 1990 to set up timeliness and to delegate responsibility for ISO registration. Development of the procedures that describe the quality system also began.

In late 1990, "we were not making significant progress toward registration," said Kreinbrook. ISO coordinators were designated and made the "focal point for the implementation of a quality system."

An ISO coordinator was named in all six manufacturing units as well as in each of the service units (purchasing, distribution, laboratory, and the maintenance group). Nearly 80 percent of these coordinators' time was spent on ISO activities leading up to registration.

In addition, each of the units had a full-time trainer who spent approximately 50 percent of his or her time on ISO activities before registration. The trainers are operators whose responsibilities include training employees and updating operating instructions in the respective units.

QUALITY SYSTEMS LAUNCHED

Krummrich bought a computer scanner, hardware and software packages for documentation, and hired a full-time document control employee. The extra training and staff paid off. Krummrich did not bring in any consultants during the ISO 9000 effort, nor did it undergo a formal BSI pre-assessment. BSI was chosen for the registration audit.

INTERNAL AUDITING: KEY TO SUCCESS

After a three-month grace period, internal audits began in March 1991. Along with the extremely close scrutiny of the system came the inevitable revisions to the procedures.

"We put a lot of effort into getting people trained as lead auditors," said Gary Johnson, superintendent of customer service. Both Johnson and Kreinbrook view Krummrich's internal auditor program as key to the successful ISO implementation. Krummrich currently has 14 trained auditors, with five more employees slated for in-house training.

The commitment to the internal audit process extended from the top down. Krummrich's internal auditors visited some of the employee training classes to question and reinforce the employees on registration practices. In addition, plant manager Boyle accompanied Kreinbrook on every audit he performed. The audits "were structured to be positive experiences and to be opportunities to improve, not exercises in identifying flaws," said Johnson.

INDIVIDUAL UNIT TRAINERS SHARE INFORMATION WITH OTHER MONSANTO UNITS

According to Jeff Scharringhausen, a full-time trainer at the unit, the units wanted to be drilled and questioned, and they asked for help from the other registered units. He views this kind of intra-site communication and willingness to seek help as a benefit of ISO.

Scharringhausen has made the updating of statistical process control (SPC) charts a job definition. "It's no longer just someone's hobby," he said. Implementing ISO also has led to a better appreciation and understanding of others' jobs within the same unit, he said.

BENEFITS

Implementing ISO enabled Krummrich to more efficiently track nonconforming material. In a chemical plant, this had not been viewed as a great problem because the nonconforming product can often be reprocessed. Since registration, the plant has a better system of gauging how much rework material it produces.

Krummrich has distributed its procedures to several locations to use as a model; major customers undergoing the ISO 9000 registration process have visited Krummrich.

Kreinbrook also said that Krummrich uses ISO criteria in its supplier audits. The suppliers that are registered are audited less frequently and receive higher scores. In addition, customers have indicated that supplier audits of the facility will now be less frequent, or perhaps not conducted at all.

THE COMPUTER INDUSTRY

Computer Industry Case Study: Unisys

Tredyffrin, PA—When Unisys executives first announced plans to seek registration of their East Coast design facility to the ISO 9001 external quality assurance standard, a number of engineers and systems designers balked at the idea.

There are as many different approaches for designing computer software and hardware products as there are workers at the sprawling East Coast Development Center not far from Philadelphia, and the engineers were concerned that design freedom would become the first casualty of the standard's heavy emphasis on documentation.

"We heard how we're going to stifle innovation, that you can't really take the design mentality and put it down on paper," recalled Daniel Ziobro, the facility's ISO 9001 coordinator. The engineers felt strongly that the design process should not be placed on a path toward rigidity.

Unisys East Coast Design Center
Employees: 1,500
Location: Tredyffrin, PA.
Date of Registration: Oct. 17, 1992
Registrar: National Standards Authority of Ireland.
Registrar Site Visit: Sep. 14-18, 1992.
Scope: Design, development and servicing software for mainframe computers, work stations, communication processors and open system environments.
Target Market: Users of open systems.
Parent Company: Unisys Corporation.
Location: Blue Bell, PA.
Primary Focus: Information technology.

The 1,500 employees who work at the 200,000-square-foot site were not the only ones with reservations. The facility was to be the first without a manufacturing element to undergo registration in the Unisys organization, an $8 billion-a-year corporation, and it soon became apparent to Ziobro and others charged with carrying out the effort that gray areas outnumbered black-and-white ones.

CORPORATE MANDATE

The push toward registration began in June 1991 following a corporate-wide directive that all manufacturing and engineering sites pursue registration to an "appropriate" ISO 9000 series standard. Unisys has incorporated registration into its Total Quality Management program— Unisys Total Quality Process.

GEARED TO MANUFACTURERS

"The terminology of the standard very much relates to a manufacturing organization," explained Jim Stevenson, the ISO 9001 management representative. They initially thought that writing a quality manual that related to their site's activities would suffice. As company officials learned more about the process, however, they realized that partial implementation of the standard would be of no value to the operation. "We started to realize that we couldn't [register] a part of this organization," Stevenson said. "It had to cover both hardware and software development."

That involved seven major organizations representing both software and hardware development: A Series Networking, East Coast Software Development Organization, Systems Engineering, CSG Power Supply Engineering & Mechanical Packaging, Computer Telephony Group, Software Products Group and LINC Products Group.

Company officials had to convince the engineers and systems designers that they were looking beyond the process of putting a design on paper, according to Ziobro. "I want to know how you take that paper and transfer that information to the manufacturing arm, and ensure that when problems come in, those fixes get back into root cause."

Attempting to retain as much flexibility as possible, the seven organizations were permitted to write separate procedures as long as those procedures did not conflict with the overall goals of the corporation.

STARTING OUT

Ziobro's first mission after being named coordinator in June 1991 was to learn as much as he could about the standards. He traveled to the Unisys facility in nearby Flemington, NJ, which had been operating under British Standard 5750, one of the forerunners of the ISO 9000 series. (Unisys no longer operates that facility.)

Initially, Ziobro said he didn't have a clue as to what he was getting into. "We thought, 'We'll just go to Flemington, find out what they did, get a copy of their quality manual, and [wherever] it said Flemington, we'll put in Tredyffrin.'"

It was not until some months later and a visit to another ISO 9000 company, that Ziobro realized why his New Jersey colleagues had been unwilling—and unable—to help. He couldn't take a custom-designed system and force-fit it into a completely different matrix.

He talked to others familiar with the registration process and attended an in-house training program on ISO 9000 familiarization and process definition, which was held for about 300 key employees. Ziobro's knowledge filtered down to the remaining workforce through several less intensive one-hour presentations.

Procedure Development

Soon department heads were implementing new procedures and dusting off old ones in anticipation of the coming audits. By March 1992, the facility had trained 16 internal volunteer auditors and was conducting the first of 58 departmental audits in preparation for a July pre-assessment.

The company discovered that many of the departments had been relying on outdated procedures. Some documentation history was missing. All equipment was not being calibrated at regular intervals, and some departments had been better at following procedures to protect delicate equipment than others.

Corrections had to be made to the system. "We stepped up our activity based on our initial findings," Stevenson said. "More management started to get involved in making sure that their departments and organizations were going to come up squeaky clean."

Unlike many large companies, Unisys chose not to rely on outside consultants for guidance and training. Instead it made available the in-house expertise of Dr. Phil Miller, who was tasked with overseeing all of the corporation's registration efforts. This approach not only saved money, but it also underscored the corporate commitment to the program.

Quality Manual

One of the major hurdles for the Tredyffrin facility was writing a quality manual. With Miller's guiding hand, company officials settled for a minimalist approach. "This was one of our guiding principles," Ziobro said. "You don't want a big quality manual. If you have 100 pages in it, that's too many. What you want is a big picture view of your organization."

A snapshot may have been a more apt description. Formatted to correspond with each of the clauses in the 9001 standard, the manual has only 42 pages. It functions much like an index, referring the reader to a host of other documents.

Therein lies the beauty of the system, according to Stevenson. "Our quality manual isn't constantly undergoing change in itself," he said. "It's the detailed areas that are undergoing change" to keep pace with technology.

SELECTING A REGISTRAR

Selecting a registrar also was made at the corporate level. Unisys retained National Standards Authority of Ireland (NSAI) for most of its registrations, including the Tredyffrin facility.

As a result, Unisys received a group rate and scheduling preferences. The Tredyffrin facility paid about $15,000 for registration services.

PRE-ASSESSMENT AND FINAL AUDIT

The pre-assessment was handled by Miller, who oversaw four teams of auditors—mostly from other Unisys facilities. The audit lasted five days, turning up 77 minor non-conformances. Company officials attribute the lack of major problems to the fact that they sought the experience of other Unisys registered companies—including one that failed its final audit on the first attempt.

Based on the findings of the pre-assessment, Miller told company officials that the Tredyffrin facility would have no difficulty passing the scrutiny of a third-party registrar.

On the morning of September 14, 1992, a team of NSAI auditors began their official five-day audit. To smooth the process, Stevenson said the company arranged its high-level process documents on one table for easy access by the auditors. "If the auditors wanted to see how the A Series Networking group did something, they went to [that] document."

By Friday afternoon the auditors had turned up a total of 79 minor non-conformances, but no major ones. Many of the non-conformances had to do with problems with documentation, such as incorrectly numbered pages, missing signatures on engineering change orders, and signatures written in pencil instead of ink.

The auditors recommended unconditional registration later that afternoon. The official certificate was awarded on October 17, 1992.

BENEFITS

One of the early benefits of registration has been improved record keeping. Because of the kinetic nature of design work, the task of keeping records up to date can be monumental at a large facility.

"We're constantly producing new documents," Stevenson said. "As rapidly as technology advances, we're changing processes and procedures to keep all these things going in step with that. To be absolutely up to date across the board everywhere is certainly very difficult." That is one of the problem areas that regular auditing should all but eliminate.

Another benefit, according to company officials, is that it is now easier to make changes to the system since all processes are spelled out in detail. At least one department manager was preparing to make changes only weeks following registration.

Registration also opens up the possibility for benchmarking with other companies. "To actually do a benchmarking exercise with another company, it is first of all essential that you understand what you've got," Stevenson explained. "ISO 9000 imposes this discipline of documenting processes and in turn enables us to go and share our processes both within the company and with other companies."

THE AUTO INDUSTRY

The Automotive Industry Action Group and Joint Quality Initiatives

INTRODUCTION

A common complaint among passenger-vehicle and truck suppliers has been the difficulty and cost of complying with customer quality-system requirements. Various company standards often differ in intent, philosophy, approach and detail. In addition, the strong competition in the automotive industry hasn't helped efforts to harmonize quality system requirements. Customers have been aware of the problems but lacked a means to reach a mutually agreeable set of criteria.

THE AUTOMOTIVE INDUSTRY ACTION GROUP

In response, major North American automotive manufacturers and suppliers formed the Automotive Industry Action Group (AIAG) in 1982. The not-for-profit organization supports efforts to increase productivity, improve quality and eliminate non-value-added costs throughout the automotive industry by standardizing the industry's business practices and technologies. For example, the group addresses differing requirements among the big three in shipping, transportation, electronic data and manufacturing support. The AIAG more than 700 member companies that include most North American highway, off-road and heavy vehicle manufacturers and their major suppliers. AIAG's board has representatives from 15 suppliers in addition to Chrysler, Ford and General Motors.

A project team was initiated at AIAG member requests in the 1980s to develop strategies for continuous quality improvement through leading-edge technologies and methodologies. Unfortunately, the strong automotive market at that time reinforced resistance to change and eliminated an apparent need for cooperation.[3]

There were other reasons for resistance to change:

● A belief that differences in a quality system provide a company with a competitive advantage

● Third-party assessments might expose extremely sensitive plans, operations performance data, or other critical information, which is unacceptable, especially in light of Japan's "time to market" advantage

● A misidentification of the ISO 9000 series as a European standard instead of a global standard—and a possible link to traditional European cost disadvantages

● A lack of understanding about the ISO 9000 series as minimal requirements to be augmented with additional requirements

● ISO 9000's lack of emphasis on planned continuous improvement, TQM, or other statistical methods

● An unfamiliarity with the descriptive rather than prescriptive approach to quality systems requirements

● A concern about abilities of suppliers and in-house quality managers to comprehend and apply specific requirements appropriate to individual quality systems based solely on ISO 9000 documents.[4]

In an attempt to increase cooperation, the big three—along with the AIAG and the ASQC—established the Supplier Quality Requirements Task Force in 1988. One of its main goals is to improve industry productivity by eliminating redundancy and reducing the costs associated with the big three's individual quality programs.

COMMON SUPPLIER MANUALS

As a result, the big three developed four reference manuals for suppliers. The first manual, published in 1990, is entitled *Measurement Systems Analysis*. In 1991 they introduced *Fundamental Statistical Process Control*. Two additional manuals have been published more recently, entitled *Production Part Approval Process* and *Potential Failure Mode and Effects Analysis*. These manuals were mailed free to more than 13,000 suppliers, and an additional 10,000 copies of each manual have been printed.[5]

JOINT QUALITY INITIATIVES

Each of these manuals has lead to reduced system costs and significant benefits to suppliers and consumers, and the big three is in the process of developing more initiatives to harmonize their practices. On December 17, 1992, the then-vice presidents of supply and quality—Norman Ehlers of Ford, Thomas Stallkamp of Chrysler, and Jose Ignacio Lopez de Arriortua of General Motors—agreed to incorporate the ISO 9001 external quality assurance standard in a combined quality system.

The Supplier Quality Requirements task force unveiled a draft of the "Chrysler, Ford, General Motors Quality System Standard" in late 1993. The document stops short of requiring ISO 9000 registration of the big three's estimated 12,000-13,000 suppliers, but states unequivocally that registration will be considered as a criteria for supplier selection. The task force will officially publish the standard once the revisions to the ISO 9000 series standards are approved, these revisions are incorporated in the task force document, and internal reviews of the task force document are finalized.

The new system will replace existing quality programs for each of the big three and will be imposed throughout the supply chain. In terms of which types of suppliers will be affected, first-tier suppliers will be expected to extend the standard to their suppliers. The joint system could be extended to the entire pool. The new document might be sold as a model for an industry-wide supplier assessment instrument.[6]

CONTENT OF THE STANDARD

The joint quality systems standard consists of an introduction, three main sections, four appendices, a bibliography and a glossary.

● The first main section addresses elements of ISO 9001 and other industry-specific requirements

● The second discusses additional requirements by the big three with respect to production parts approvals, continuous improvement and manufacturing capabilities.

- The last main section covers unique requirements by each of the automakers.[7]

There are still unanswered questions with respect to the role of ISO 9000 series registrars. At a February 1994 meeting, big three representatives met with more than ten registrars to discuss a variety of issues, such as ways to qualify accredited registrars and provide auditors with specialized training.[8]

OVERCOMING OBSTACLES

The release of the combined quality system came as a surprise to some industry insiders, who theorized that the big three were having difficulty working out details of the combined system.[9]

One obstacle to accepting the ISO 9000 series in the automotive industry has been that its approach to process control differs from existing standards. Existing automotive standards prescribe specific requirements for control of processes. The 9000 series, on the other hand, describes requirements for management systems and allows suppliers themselves to define the process control techniques to be used.[10]

Another issue involves the competitiveness of automotive manufacturers and suppliers. The big three agreed to develop a joint quality initiative based on the following two conditions:

- The initiative must result in real cost-of-quality benefits.
- It must not impact on any strategic competitive advantages that each of the big three companies has or may be developing.[11]

The auto industry is one of the most competitive in the United States. Some people fear that using a generic quality systems standard would level the playing field. According to Thomas Stallkamp of Chrysler, "Each of us in the big three has their own strategy for supplier relations...some of which, I would add, are more effective than others." He stressed that those differences help each company's competitive advantage and shouldn't be discarded in the search for commonality.[12]

Yet despite this fear, executives are feeling the pressure to do something to help their estimated 13,0000 suppliers, many of whom have been looking for ways to cut costs as the industry tries to rebound from record losses. Stallkamp said, "There is a time and a place for cooperation. But there is a time and a place for competition. And somewhere between these two places is, I believe, enough common ground on which OEMs and suppliers can stand and decide, together, what works best for all of us."[13]

ISO 9000: What Every Supplier Must Know

BY WILLIAM HARRAL

INTRODUCTION

ISO 9000 is here to stay. Suppliers who understand and accept the new standard will have a head start on their competition.

The ISO 9000-9004 series and its technical equivalent, the ANSI/ASQC Q9000-9004 series (formerly Q90-94), have generated a good deal of confusion among automotive suppliers. Most wonder about the series' role and impact on their business. They are concerned about acquiring basic knowledge and learning the differences between ISO 9000 requirements and traditional automotive requirements. While this brief article cannot go into significant detail, it highlights some of these areas and offers a view of the overall situation to assist those developing individual action plans.

WORLDWIDE ISO 9000 AUTOMOTIVE ACTIVITIES

The AIAG Truck Advisory Group (TAG) Quality Committee of truck manufacturers and suppliers has completed draft and committee approval of an Industry Sector Quality System Standard based on the ISO 9001 model and augmented with 13 additional elements or expected activities. Review by the AIAG and companies was planned for the fourth quarter of 1993 with publication sometime in 1994. Since this is a voluntary standard, companies may adopt it and require their suppliers' conformance according to their individual timetables. Most of this standard has already been incorporated into the requirements of several truck original equipment manufacturers (OEMs) and major supplier organizations for their suppliers over the past year or so.

In July, the TAG committee and the big three decided to pursue a joint effort for all automotive vehicles. Truck OEM representatives were identified to work with the big three standardization committee and to pursue a common document. As a result, several truck manufacturers—including Freightliner, MackTrucks, Navistar, Paccar, Transportation Manufacturing Corp. and Volvo/GM—are using the big three draft quality standard discussed in the previous article.

Automotive Directive

Beginning January 1, 1996, automakers will be able to satisfy a new type approval directive and sell automobiles throughout the European Union. The 14 annexes of the automotive type approval directive explain the approval procedures, steps for a certificate of conformity, and the Annex IV list of requirements that identifies the 52 subordinate directives covering safety requirements for vehicle components such as brakes, emissions, headlights, etc.

The authorization for this new EU-wide law comes from a June 18, 1992 directive entitled "Type Approval of Motor Vehicles and their Trailers" (92/531), which amends a 1970 directive that allowed each member state to develop its own type approval procedures.

The 1992 directive allows automakers to begin using the new EU type approval procedure on January 1, 1996 for complete vehicles and on January 1, 1998 for completed vehicles involving a multistage approval process. A two-year transition period exists, but if a company decides to use the transition period, it can only sell automobiles in those member states where it has approval.[14]

EU-based automakers and their suppliers are already using ISO 9001 and ISO 9002 to organize their response to the directive. These initiatives should convince the most diehard resister that ISO 9000 is not going away. The choice is to either move forward or find yourself left behind.

UNIQUE ASPECTS OF ISO 9000

Prior to implementing the ISO 9000 series, suppliers must understand some differences between ISO requirements and traditional automotive requirements.

First, the ISO 9000 series requirements are complementary to statutory and customer requirements—not substitutes for them. Current customer requirements may only cover about 75 percent of ISO requirements. Consequently, the number of requirements from any individual customer could increase, since customers probably won't waive existing requirements.

However, this increase should be more than offset by harmonization efforts between customers. Suppliers should realize significant benefits as soon as customers start recognizing other second- and third-party audits for basic quality system evaluations.

The ISO 9001 and 9002 models represent good basic business practices that can serve as a framework and initial approach to Total Quality Management (TQM). Augmenting the selected model can provide a customized, comprehensive, robust system while maintaining conformance to the original model.

A second difference is that the ISO 9000 series is fundamentally different from current automotive quality standards. The ISO 9000 series is descriptive—it tells **what** a company should do, not **how** it should comply. The standards identify goals while allowing the supplier to determine the best way to achieve those goals. Current automotive standards, on the other hand, are prescriptive. They identify specific methods of accomplishment and often demand specific levels of achievement. For example, ISO 9001 and 9002 require the supplier to satisfy contract requirements and carry out production under controlled conditions, whereas an automotive requirement might specify, for example, 1.67 as minimum Cpk. For the near future, expect to see both types of requirements. Prescriptiveness should decline over time as confidence is established in suppliers' abilities to effectively interpret and implement descriptive requirements.

Third, contrary to the claims and advertised offers of assistance from consultants, there is no required "ISO format" for documents. The only mandate is to address all the requirements. A list or matrix satisfies this mandate by identifying your procedures against each requirement. Some requirements, such as Customer-Supplied Product, may not apply to your operation. These can be addressed with a short statement that you are both aware and knowledgeable of the requirement, but no controls exist because the situation itself doesn't exist. This cross-reference or matrix is a very useful early exercise for identifying which areas need the most effort and for estimating the general size of the task. (Please refer to Chapter 6 for a Schedule of Conformity matrix.)

Finally, the ISO 9001 and 9002 models apply systematic requirements to more of the total business cycle and supporting staff functions than many automotive company requirements. This will cause more widespread responsibility for quality and facilitate implementation of many new quality and competitive concepts, such as simultaneous engineering, agile manufacturing and time-based manufacturing.

FUTURE DEVELOPMENT OF ISO 9000

The automotive industry has always been a demanding, competitive one, and the current quality challenges should be well within industry capabilities. While the situation with ISO 9000 may seem overwhelming, suppliers should not be discouraged. This new approach brings some distinct advantages. The industry should experience a reduction in non-value activities; encouragement of systemic thinking; and more widespread quality involvement within our organizations. The industry will be better able to demonstrate North American quality to the global and domestic automotive markets, and even to potential domestic customers outside the automotive industry that are pursuing suppliers whose quality systems comply with ISO 9000.

Auto Industry Case Study: Ford of Europe

Brentwood, UK—Ford of Europe was at a crossroads in June 1991. Its most important customer was moving toward an ISO 9000 series mandate, and the automotive giant had to decide whether it could afford to snub its nose at registration.

At stake was not only a large chunk of Ford's European fleet sales, but also its very backbone—the Q101 quality system. Every Ford plant in the world adheres to the same quality tenets and any changes, even modest ones, have global implications.

Like other automakers, Ford of Europe was feeling the sting of the recession, and it was a particularly bad time to be faced with the prospect of lost business. European operations in 1992 posted an operating loss of $1.2 million.

Ford of Europe

Employees: 93,000

Headquarters: Brentwood, U.K.

Date of Registration: Pending.

Registrar: Vehicle Certification Agency.

Registrar Site Visit: March 1993 to ?.

Scope: Design and manufacture of passenger and estate cars, light and medium commercial vehicles and their related power trains.

Parent Company: Ford Motor Co.

Target Market: Purchasers of passenger and estate cars, commercial vehicles.

Along with three other senior quality executives, John Ford, the company's quality systems specialist, had the task of making the case for ISO 9000 series registration in Europe. They were pushing for registration to either ISO 9001 or 9002, for either would satisfy the customer mandate by the United Kingdom's Ministry of Defense (MOD).

Anticipating that other clients might follow MOD's lead and wanting to take no chances with registration, Ford of Europe president William Fike opted to pursue ISO 9001. He disseminated a letter to the company's then 110,000 employees spread across six European countries—the United Kingdom, Spain, France, Germany, Portugal and Belgium. The letter advised the workforce that Ford was moving ahead with ISO 9001 registration and asked for a commitment to support the effort.

FIRST STEP

Because of the company's large size, the initial thrust of the registration effort was on studying the complex processes involved in producing and delivering the end products. The approach was first to examine top-level documentation and then to progress downward to plant levels.

The company had quality manuals but they would have to be rewritten to reflect ISO 9001 and to withstand the scrutiny of outside auditors. "They were tailored specifically for Ministry of Defense requirements," Ford said. "What is required for ISO 9000 is much more comprehensive."

The manuals took about a year to complete. Even though most of the documentation was similar at the plant level, there were nuances from site to site. "We tried to get across that what we were looking for was this tiering effect where the European manual would say broadly how the quality system operated," Ford said.

TRAINING

The first large training event was held in November 1992—five months from the time Fike started the company's mighty wheels churning. An outside consultancy was retained to facilitate the three-day seminar for key personnel from throughout Europe. The attendees were selected for their knowledge of quality systems. Most had led successful efforts to attain Ford's Q1 quality award at various sites throughout the organization.

Attendees also left with an understanding of the differences between the company's existing quality system and ISO 9001. Once that initial training was completed, attendees then were expected to pass their newly acquired knowledge on to colleagues back at each respective site.

The plan met with some internal resistance, but even skeptics of ISO 9000 soon became convinced of its necessity to maintain sales to fleet markets.

COMMUNICATING INFORMATION

For many large organizations the act of building consensus can be a time-consuming exercise in bureaucracy, but this was not the case at Ford. Executives relied heavily on the company's sophisticated electronic-mail system to overcome distance barriers and obtain swift approvals for various aspects of implementation. They also relied on an internal television network and in-house publications to raise employee awareness of ISO 9000 series registration.

FLAT ORGANIZATION

One of the major decisions that executives wrestled with during the course of implementation was whether to pursue separate certificates for each major site or to move toward registration as a single entity. It chose the latter approach, although each site will be issued its own copy of the corporate certificate to promote ownership of the system.

"It was felt that if you go the other way you tend to get competition between plants rather than cooperation," Ford said. "They all rely on each other to ensure that everybody gets through."

INTERNAL AUDITS

In all, some 100 internal auditors were trained to ensure that Ford was performing to ISO 9000 series specifications. Previous audits had been limited to manufacturing areas of the company. ISO 9000 series registration marked the spread of auditing to other areas of the organization, such as sales and marketing, which were unaccustomed to such scrutiny. This posed relatively few problems for the organization, according to Ford.

REGISTRAR SELECTION

After interviewing five of the UK's major registrars, company officials selected one that was relatively new to the field but had a relationship with Ford through its role with the British government.

The Vehicle Certification Agency (VCA), part of the Department of Transport, also serves as the notified body on motor manufacturing in the United Kingdom, according to Ford. As such, the company could be assured that VCA auditors would have an unmatched familiarity with the industry.

DOCUMENT REVIEW

By February 1993, Ford's documentation was in place and its internal audits had turned up no major problems. The company was deemed ready for registration. A decision was made to bypass the preliminary audit, which is optional, and move directly to the final stage of the audit process.

FIRST AUDIT

The European headquarters was the first stop for the auditors in March 1993. After that they would evaluate remaining UK sites before covering the rest of Europe. The UK sites were selected for the initial phase because they were thought to be the most vulnerable to customer mandates.

Typically, auditors arrived in two-person teams. As they visited each new site, they were introduced to key personnel before starting the actual audits. Their findings were announced at daily meetings. Any nonconformances that were identified were raised at the conclusion of the visit and auditors noted at that time if the company would be recommended for registration.

The most critical observation had to do with how the company could be assured that each foreman had the latest document revisions, Ford said. "In essence, that was our first test of Ford's quality system by an outside body," Ford explained. "Since we use exactly the same systems throughout all of our facilities, we knew that we had the ability to pass."

GREATEST CHALLENGES

The area that required the most attention, according to Ford, was document control. "The essence of ISO 9000 is all about documenting your system, and obviously it's very easy on the paper trail to find those kinds of concerns," he said.

"We started [documenting our processes] at the beginning with how we receive a customer's order and we tracked it all the way through the system until we actually delivered." The exercise promoted introspection. "What has been the greatest involvement for us was to rethink the way our quality system is set up," Ford explained. "It's far too big. That's what's taking a lot of effort."

For the most part the system was already fine-tuned. There was little duplication of effort. Some documents, such as the quality system manual, were put under tighter control.

Another barrier to registration was the natural tendency to resist change. Ford's internal quality system was so steeped in tradition that many executives advocated staying the course and riding out the "ISO 9000 wave." Like the other members of the big three—Chrysler and General Motors—Ford's preexisting quality system had a differing approach to process control than does the ISO 9000 series. It prescribed specific requirements for control of processes while the 9000 series describes requirements for management systems. It also gives users the power to define process control techniques to be used.

SAVINGS

The registration effort has not been the great savings vehicle that other companies have found. In fact, company officials have been hard-pressed to cite any savings as a result. Many automakers are pioneers in the field of quality and will most likely not see the same level of savings that other types of companies have seen as a result of ISO 9000 registration. "Our quality systems have been around for so many years and we're so cost-effective," he said, "for the core business of making motor cars it would be honest to say that ISO 9000 will not do anything for us."

Even so, Ford estimated, the money spent on registration will come back to the automaker in new business or by maintaining existing contracts. One area where the company expects to realize significant savings is in customer audits. Once the company attains registration, Ford said, MOD and other customers may spend less time verifying the quality system and more time looking at control plans.

The US industry experience will likely be similar, according to Ford. Customer mandates may be the driving factor. "For anybody wishing to put their products into Europe, I think this will be a prerequisite in the future," he said.

ADVICE

The best advice Ford has for other automakers is to avoid debating the benefits and disadvantages of ISO 9000. "It takes an awful lot of time to attain registration," Ford said. "The largest proportion of the time is involved with understanding your system, describing your system, and ensuring that the documentation is up to date and that people are working to it." Ford said that's where most of the resources should be expended. Time spent arguing over the better system is wasted effort. "The actual certification process is relatively short and sweet," he said.

SURVEILLANCE VISITS

Following registration audits at six-month intervals, the registrar will conduct surveillance audits—less intensive efforts that nevertheless place the same pressures on management. If for any reason a site does not pass a surveillance visit, the company's entire registration would be delayed, something which Ford expects will not happen.

Ironically, parts of the company will undergo their first six-month surveillance visits before the company receives its registration certificate. "It just shows you the size of the organization," Ford said.

FUTURE TRENDS

Many of Ford of Europe's UK suppliers are already registered to the ISO 9000 series standards. So are a number of its suppliers in Holland and Belgium, according to Ford. In time, he added, the company will make registration mandatory for its suppliers. Ford of Europe also is pushing for a common quality program among the European manufacturers, but progress has been slow, he said.

One reason is cultural differences. The European initiative crosses international borders and involves not only obtaining a consensus with the British, but also the Japanese, Germans, French and Spanish automakers. Such a consensus is much easier to achieve in the United States, he said. "Obviously you all speak the same language and you're all from the same country," Ford said.

THE STEEL INDUSTRY

Quality Systems Assessments in the Steel Industry

BY PETER B. LAKE

THE STEEL INDUSTRY: OVERVIEW

The steel industry remains among the largest industries in the United States in aggregate value of shipments. In the last ten years, annual sales have averaged over $40 billion. In turn, the industry spends more than $25 billion annually on materials equipment and services and is the largest industrial consumer of energy in the United States. The US steel industry currently consists of about 300 companies operating in 34 states.

QUALITY SYSTEM ASSESSMENT

The steel producers of North America have been much involved in supplier quality system assessments for over a decade, including undergoing audits by the many original equipment manufacturers (OEMs) to which the steel industry is a major supplier.

Table 20-12: SISAP Audit Criteria	
Supplements:	Leadership and Total Quality Management Strategic and Business Planning Human Resources Work Environment, Health and Safety Cost Reduction Management Continuous Improvement Customer Satisfaction Customer Service Scheduling and Delivery Inventory Control Product and Process Innovation Preventive Maintenance Software Control
Base:	ISO 9001

In 1990, under the auspices of the American Iron and Steel Institute, a quality improvement subcommittee of 14 major steel companies and key suppliers developed a shared audit program, in which third-party assessors conducted an ISO 9001-based TQM assessment of voluntarily participating suppliers. This program, now called the Steel Industry Supplier Audit Process (SISAP) provides an assessment report for each of the 13 subscribing steel companies as well as for the participating supplier. Each can then use the results of the assessment accordingly.

Steel subscribers and suppliers from various industries, including steel production and steel fabrication, have adopted SISAP criteria to evaluate their systems. ISO 9001 is the foundation of SISAP, with supplements taken from Malcolm Baldrige and other TQM programs. (See Table 20-12 for the SISAP audit criteria.) These SISAP/ISO 9000-based efforts in many ways parallel the ongoing ISO 9000-based standardization efforts by the big three automakers. The synergy should further reduce redundancies and costs for suppliers to both industries.

The SISAP audit criteria and methodology take a top-down look at the approach, deployment and results of each management system. The assessor not only evaluates whether the system is in place, but also if key indicators are tracked and reviewed and whether the system is working.

With the SISAP approach, the steel subscriber and the supplier share the third-party assessment costs. The third party, SRI Quality System Registrar, Inc., conducts the assessments. Training, experience and auditor qualifications are important. SISAP requires that the registrar's auditors not only meet all ISO 9000 registrar accreditation requirements, but also pass a four-day SISAP training course and test that focuses on assessing all TQM systems.

BENEFITS

Despite on-going industry-wide downsizing and restructuring, these steel companies have benefited from this arrangement in the following ways:

- Fewer supplier audits
- Fewer assessment resources, such as manpower
- Lower internal costs
- Benefits from receiving a documented, broad-based ISO 9000 and TQM assessment.

The suppliers enjoy several of the same and some additional benefits:

- Fewer customer assessments
- Reduced preparation and resource costs
- Ability to help reduce customer costs
- Ability to satisfy the broader assessment requirements of its steel customers
- The option to provide the SISAP report to any other customers
- The option to obtain internationally recognized ISO 9000 registration.

ISO 9000 REGISTRATION AND ITS RELATION TO SISAP

Because the SISAP assessment and ISO 9000 are closely related, four situations can arise:

- The supplier can receive a SISAP assessment only. Many suppliers who undergo a SISAP audit use the experience as a pre-assessment to a later ISO 9000 audit.
- The supplier can achieve ISO 9000 registration only.
- A supplier can try to register to ISO 9000 and receive a SISAP evaluation simultaneously.
- If a supplier wants to participate in SISAP but is already registered to ISO 9000, the steel companies subscribing to SISAP accept ISO 9000 registration in lieu of an assessment of the ISO 9000 elements. In this instance, the SISAP assessment only involves those supplemental TQM areas shown above in Table 20-12.

Despite their overlap, an important distinction exists between SISAP and ISO 9000. Under ISO 9000, a registrar will audit a site to determine whether that company has a documented quality system in place that conforms to the appropriate standard. If so, the registrar gives that company a certificate of registration.

SISAP, however, is not a pass/fail assessment. The assessor provides written observations and ratings, and the 13 subscribing steel companies make decisions based on that assessor's report. The assessor provides the information; each of the 13 companies individually use the assessor's evaluation.

CONCLUSION

Across most sectors of the steel industry, the ISO 9000 standards continue to provide a base for internal quality systems and supplier quality assessments as the majority of producers seek ISO 9000 registration.

Steel Industry Case Study: Taylor-Wharton Cylinders

Harrisburg, PA—The manufacture of high-pressure cylinders is a hands-on operation. Square billets of highly refined steel are plucked by a masked worker one by one from a huge furnace, before an army of skilled workers shapes, cuts, inspects, cleans, x-rays, tests, paints and loads the finished products onto trucks.

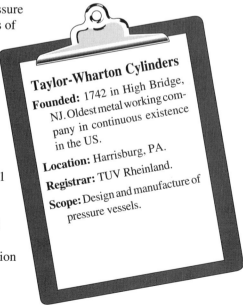

Taylor-Wharton Cylinders

Founded: 1742 in High Bridge, NJ. Oldest metal working company in continuous existence in the US.

Location: Harrisburg, PA.

Registrar: TUV Rheinland.

Scope: Design and manufacture of pressure vessels.

Taylor-Wharton Cylinders vice-president and general manager Clark Hall believes that ISO 9000 series registration is also a hands-on operation. He said the decision to seek ISO 9001 registration was driven not only by pressing European Union product and quality system compliance requirements, but by the committed involvement required of every employee to successfully complete a quality system registration effort.

MANAGEMENT INVOLVEMENT

"I feel very strongly that [the drive for the ISO 9000 effort] must come from management," Hall said. Delegating and directing the effort is not enough. Management must "participate in and lead" the effort. He said too many "fundamental business decisions are made during the registration process that should not be delegated to the quality assurance department."

Hall admitted that he was the "chief cheerleader" for Taylor-Wharton's registration drive. But his enthusiasm for the ISO 9000 series' common sense standard had a practical side. He said he liked the procedure and documentation discipline offered by ISO 9000 series registration. In addition, high-pressure vessels—like medical products and several other product categories—will require quality system assurance to enter the EU market. "It was obvious that ISO 9000 certification was coming, and we wanted to do it sooner rather than later," Hall said.

Currently, a "substantial" portion of Taylor-Wharton's production is exported to Europe. Taylor-Wharton also has a related cryogenic cylinder manufacturer located in Husum, Germany. The Germany connection made the choice of TUV Rheinland of North America, Inc., a logical registrar for the facility. TUV Rheinland also verifies conformance to various German product codes at the Harrisburg site, along with other US government and third-party inspectors verifying domestic product code enforcement such as Department of Transportation codes.

WORLD CLASS COMPANY

The quality system base offered by ISO 9000 series registration will assist Taylor-Wharton's stated goal of creating a world-class manufacturer that manages quality using ISO 9000 and Total Quality Management (TQM) principles. The inspection-driven quality assurance department is using more process controls, despite the large number of required inspections for high-pressure vessels.

The bottom-line result of Taylor-Wharton's quality improvement efforts will be increased profitability, Hall pointed out. "We have put in considerable time figuring out the cost of quality and the consequences of not doing it right the first time. We have a good idea what those costs are. No one in the organization needs to be convinced of that."

FAST-TRACK REGISTRATION EFFORT

Taylor-Wharton Cylinder's ISO 9000 registration effort began in earnest in mid-August 1991. The background work and planning began earlier. "I am not sure that I would recommend it [a fast-track registration drive]," Hall said. "It was an intense couple of months."

During the months before Taylor-Wharton's ISO 9000 series full-court-press registration effort, a review committee coordinated task identification and duty assignments that created a policy and quality manual as well as manuals for procedures and control documents. The process also created an extremely long "to-do" list for procedure documentation.

At Taylor-Wharton, the ISO 9000 series registration effort revealed that the company's written procedures and process documentation were not adequate. "Before [registration] virtually everything was verbally communicated and much of the training [of hourly workers] was done by other hourly workers," Hall said. All training is now performed by supervisors who use a controlled, centralized document.

"TO-DO" LIST

The procedures "to-do" list was broken down into assignments. Two guide procedures were written to give managers and supervisors a model to create their own procedure documentation for every item on the assignment list.

All the procedures were submitted to Rick Grande, who served as editor for the review committee. After all members of the review committee were satisfied that the procedures matched the job described, these procedures became part of the official procedure manual. Policy and control documents were created using the same methodology.

Hall said regular Friday management staff meetings were used to keep the process on track and to provide information about the registration process. Some managers used monthly meetings with the workforce as a platform to explain registration requirements. "It was almost a constant training and communications process," Hall said.

AUDITING

After the preparatory procedure and documentation work was accomplished, auditing teams examined the entire company. In October 1991, two employees took an ISO 9000 auditing training course, and an internal auditing program was written.

Over the months leading up to registration, five three-member teams made sure that the new quality policies implemented remained in effect. The auditing effort allowed employees from diverse divisions of the company to audit each other. "It made everyone learn about the entire company's operations," Hall said. (See Chapter 5 on internal auditing.)

Reaction from the plant workforce was positive as audit teams from different departments learned how co-workers contributed to the overall production and quality control process. He noted that any resistance to the process came from supervisors who had to make radical changes to a system that had not previously required extensive documentation.

The internal auditing process was such a success that about 85 percent of the nonconformances found by TUV auditors reviewing submitted completed manuals were matched by Taylor-Wharton auditors.

When Hall felt the registration effort was nearly complete, he called TUV in for a pre-assessment. The TUV auditor spent two days interviewing managers and reviewing the process. Two meetings were held with key managers. The first, at the beginning of the process, brought more information about the registration process. The second meeting, after the audit was complete, pointed out nonconformances found.

Two TUV Rheinland representatives spent one week at the Taylor-Wharton facility. The company received the recommendation for ISO 9001 registration on December 13, 1991.

SMALL COMPANIES

QSU/Deloitte & Touche Survey of Companies by Size

INTRODUCTION

Companies that responded to the joint *Quality Systems Update*/Deloitte & Touche survey range in size from the smallest to the largest. Their annual earnings are anywhere from under $11 million to more than $1 billion.

This article provides a comprehensive look at ISO 9000 registration by company size. Issues include: the reasons for choosing a registrar and for registering, the barriers companies face in doing so, the costs of registering and companies' potential savings.

(Please refer to the discussion in the first survey article of this chapter for more information on the survey itself and for results that apply to companies of all sizes.)

REASONS TO REGISTER

As was evident in the survey by industry, US and Canadian companies that sought registration to the ISO 9000 series standards did so for a variety of reasons, but only nine percent did so to satisfy European requirements for exporting regulated products. The explosion of ISO 9000 series registrations is fueled mainly by customer demands or expectations, better quality, and market advantage.

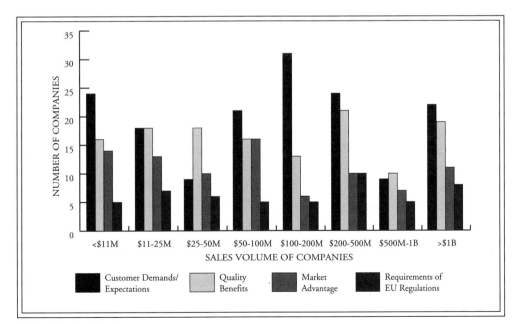

Figure 20-1: The Most Important Reason for Attaining ISO 9000 Registration, by Company Sales Volume.

The survey also highlights an interesting phenomenon: the largest companies—those reporting annual sales of $1 billion or more—are feeling customer pressures to seek registration to the same extent as small companies. In all, 22.4 percent of respondents from large companies identified customer demands and expectations as their principal reason for pursuing registration, and 49 percent of them cited it among their top three reasons. (See Figure 20-1.)

The survey highlights another key difference between small to midsize companies and the corporate giants. Many of the companies with annual sales of $500 million or more—some 37 percent of them—sought registration as part of a larger strategy. Of the larger companies, 44 percent identified pursuit of the Malcolm Baldrige National Quality Award as being among their top three reasons for seeking registration.

In contrast, only 27.5 percent of the smaller companies—those with annual sales of less than $500 million—cited registration as being part of a larger strategy.

REGISTRAR CHOICE

Companies that don't do their homework before selecting an ISO 9000 series registrar face the prospect of not having their registration certificates honored by all overseas and domestic customers. Companies overwhelmingly pointed to reputation and country affiliation or accreditation as the two most important factors in selecting a registrar. (See Table 20-13.)

On the other hand, some groups of companies, depending on their annual sales, placed greater weight on other factors. For example, 22.4 percent of companies reporting annual sales greater than $1 billion said their primary concern in the selection process was having prior experience with the firm they chose. In comparison, only 14 percent of the total respondents listed prior experience as the most important factor.

Similarly, companies with annual sales between $500 million and $1 billion placed a greater weight on registrar philosophies regarding quality management systems than did the other groupings. Some 13 percent of those companies ranked philosophy as the single most important factor, while only 8.7 percent of the companies overall gave registrar philosophy the highest mark. A significantly greater number of those same companies said their selection of a registrar was based on a corporate dictate—13.3 percent listing it as their principal rationale compared with only 5.6 percent of all companies.

Companies as a whole, regardless of sales volume, said overwhelmingly that they were satisfied or very satisfied with their registrars. Less than two percent of the respondents indicated they were at all dissatisfied with their choices. One aberration appeared, however: 16.7 percent of companies with annual sales of $11 million and less reported feeling neutral about their registrars.

Table 20-13: Factors in Selecting a Registrar		
Reputation	155	25.0%
Country Affiliation/Accreditation	153	24.7%
Prior Experience with the Registrar	87	14.0%
Industry Expertise	69	11.1%
Registrar "Philosophy" on Quality Management Systems	54	8.7%
Corporate Dictate	35	5.6%
Geographic Proximity	13	2.1%
Independence from Consulting	9	1.5%
Cost	8	1.3%
Size/Resources	7	1.1%
Other	25	4.0%
No Answer	5	0.8%

BARRIERS

Smaller companies tended to cite procedural problems more frequently than larger companies when responding to the question of what constituted the greatest barrier in preparing for a successful ISO 9000 registration effort. (See Figure 20-2.)

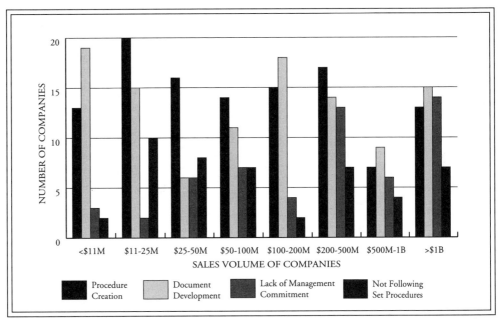

Figure 20-2: The Greatest Barrier to Preparing for Successful ISO 9000 Registration Effort, by Company Sales Volume.

For example, 25.3 to 25.4 percent of the companies with sales volume between $11 million and $50 million cited "procedure creation" as their greatest barrier compared to an average of roughly 20 percent of all companies and 13.3 to 15.6 percent of companies in the top two sales categories (over $500 million).

This tendency also showed up with nearly 13 percent of companies having sales of $11 million to $50 million citing "not following set procedures" as the greatest barrier, compared to an average of 8.1 percent overall.

"Lack of management commitment," the third most noted barrier, is cited more frequently by larger companies, with 13.3 to 15.9 percent of companies having sales volume over $200 million citing this problem. Overall, 9.5 percent of companies noted this barrier. It would appear that the larger companies, with their more extensive organizational structures, have a more difficult time enlisting full support among all managers than do the smaller and more compact organizations.

These results confirm empirical evidence gathered from companies that have attained registration. Many quality managers at these companies have noted that nonconformances that must be corrected before the final audit often relate to document development and procedure creation.

COSTS

In general, costs tended to be higher for larger companies than for small to midsize firms. Variations in cost from one class of company to another often appeared to be commensurate with greater annual sales. (See Table 20-14.)

Companies overall reported spending an average of slightly more than $21,000 for registrar fees alone. Typical fees ranged from about $8,000 for companies in the $11-million-and-less category to almost $39,000 for companies with sales of $1 billion or more.

Table 20-14: Average Internal, External and Registrar Costs by Company Sales Volume			
Company Sales Volume	Average Internal Cost	Average External Cost	Average Registrar Cost
< $11M	$40,600	$17,900	$8,200
$11-25M	$91,000	$28,800	$11,600
$25-50M	$110,600	$28,500	$16,300
$50-100M	$107,700	$104,000	$17,800
$100-200M	$140,300	$46,900	$19,400
$200-500M	$242,400	$70,900	$23,400
$500M-$1B	$239,100	$75,700	$32,800
Over $1B	$465,100	$134,800	$38,600
Survey Average	$180,000	$60,100	$21,100

While costs for larger companies were generally higher than smaller firms, some smaller businesses actually spent more than did billion-dollar corporations. Variations were reported

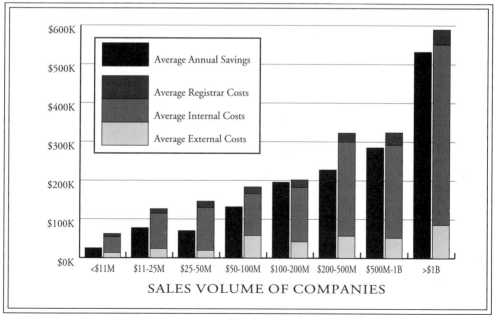

Figure 20-3: Average Domestic Annual Savings Associated with Implementing ISO 9000 Compared with Average Domestic Costs Expended to Achieve Current Level of Registration, by Company Sales Volume.

under the category of external expenses, which primarily covers auditing and consultancy fees. Out of 620 respondents, 28.6 percent of the smaller companies spent between $25,000 and $50,000 on external expenses, while 24.4 percent of companies posting $1 billion or more in sales paid only $10,000 or less.

Such a wide gap between the larger and smaller companies' external costs might imply that registration and consulting bodies are attempting to strengthen their position in a developing market with price incentives.

Editor's Note: *Respondents were asked to indicate the total **domestic** cost expended to achieve their current level of registration. The implication is that these figures represent company-wide, domestic registration expenditures—not expenses for individual sites.*

SAVINGS

Although most companies that achieved registration report significant annual savings, not all companies had such a high return. (See Figure 20-3.) Some 26 percent of companies responding to the survey estimated their annual savings to be $10,000 or less, including 28.9 percent of those companies generating sales of $500 million to $1 billion a year.

In general, the higher the sales figure the greater the annual savings. Companies with total sales of $11 million or less reported average annual savings of $25,000. At the other end of the spectrum, companies with annual sales of $1 billion or more reported average savings of $532,000 each year, the survey found. (See Table 20-15.)

Overall, the rate of increased savings was consistent with the increase in annual sales. One notable exception involved companies with sales between $11 million and $25 million. Those companies actually realized a greater average annual savings than did those with sales between $25 million and $50 million.

Table 20-15: Average Total Annual Domestic Savings, by Company Sales Volume	
Company Sales Volume	**Average Total Domestic Annual Savings**
< $11M	$25,100
$11-25M	$77,200
$25-50M	$69,900
$50-100M	$132,100
$100-200M	$195,700
$200-500M	$227,700
$500M-$1B	$284,900
Over $1B	$532,000
Survey Average	$178,900

In this case, the smaller companies reported average savings of slightly more than $77,000 a year while companies in the larger category reported an average of only $69,900 a year. The variation can be attributed largely to the experience of a single smaller company in the $11-25-million bracket. That company reported an annual savings of between $1 million and $1.5 million, which was at least $250,000 more than any company reported in the larger class.

One confusing result of the survey involves the average number of years companies predicted to recover their costs. (See Table 20-16.) For example, the average total internal and external costs for companies earning more than $1 billion was $607,600, while their average annual savings was 532,000. Using these figures, one could estimate that it would take the company less than two years to recover the costs. However, companies earning more than $1 billion predicted an average of 14.2 years to recover them.

Why the difference? It is a mistake to compare the averages, for the respondents did not all answer each of the three registration cost questions and the one savings question. All companies would have had to answer all of these questions for the statisticians to accurately calculate the average number of years to "recover" the costs.

In addition, the "recover" calculation was not an average of the "costs" and "savings" averages, but was calculated by each respondent's own "costs" and "savings" answers. These answers were then totaled and averaged to produce the dollar amounts in Table 20-16.

Table 20-16: Average Number of Years to Recover Costs, by Company Sales Volume	
Company Sales Volume	**Average Number of Years to Recover Costs**
< $11M	4.6
$11-25M	9.1
$25-50M	6.5
$50-100M	18.4
$100-200M	7.6
$200-500M	15.1
$500M-$1B	12.1
Over $1B	14.2
Survey Average	10.7

CONCLUSION

This article highlights some of the differences associated with ISO 9000 registration between large and small companies. Variations occur with registration costs and the amount companies can save. Similarities exist among the reasons for choosing a registrar, the reasons for registering, and the barriers companies face in doing so. Examining these similarities and differences can better guide companies through the registration process and serve as a method of comparison for companies already registered.

Small Company Case Study: Techni-Test

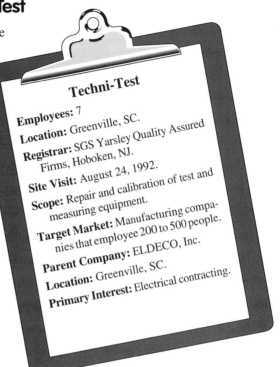

Greenville, SC—With only seven full-time employees and revenues approaching $500,000 a year, Techni-Test is probably one of the last firms you'd expect to raise the ISO 9000 series flag outside its unassuming brick headquarters.

"It's trickled down to a point that mom-and-pops are being affected by ISO 9000," said Tim Benjamin, manager of the calibration and repair facility that is located about 150 miles northeast of Atlanta.

In September 1992, Techni-Test became one of the smallest, if not the smallest US firm to achieve registration. It signals the growing acceptance of ISO quality standards in this country, and illustrates the ripple effect being felt by businesses that employ fewer than 100 people.

Techni-Test

Employees: 7
Location: Greenville, SC.
Registrar: SGS Yarsley Quality Assured Firms, Hoboken, NJ.
Site Visit: August 24, 1992.
Scope: Repair and calibration of test and measuring equipment.
Target Market: Manufacturing companies that employee 200 to 500 people.
Parent Company: ELDECO, Inc.
Location: Greenville, SC.
Primary Interest: Electrical contracting.

"Major manufacturing firms [have] 27,000 people in the quality department," said Benjamin jokingly. Techni-Test repairs and calibrates test and measuring equipment for some of those larger firms, such as Michelin Tire Co., 3M Co., and Toledo Scale. "Here at Techni-Test we only have two people in our quality department, and they're basically part-time positions."

COST JUSTIFIED

Even so, Benjamin said Techni-Test was able to more than justify the $10,000 expenditure over three years for ISO certification. In fact, he said Techni-Test couldn't afford not to spend the money with so many of its primary clients seeking registration.

"I felt it would benefit us to get registered first and be the first kids on the block," he said. "My philosophy there is if you've got the customers on hand, if you give them good service at a good price, why would they look to change?"

NO CONSULTANTS

As manager, Benjamin took it upon himself to work out the details. A consultant might have been helpful, but Techni-Test had only limited resources to spend on the project. With all the bells and whistles, the company could easily have been out $20,000 to $30,000. But as Benjamin puts it, "for the small business that we are, the juice probably wasn't worth the squeeze."

The first priority for Techni-Test was to identify a registrar. Using a magazine article as a reference point, Benjamin began making phone calls and writing letters. His first investment of $49.95 got him a copy of the ISO 9000 series standards from the American Society for Quality Control.

CHOOSING A REGISTRAR

Most of the registrars Benjamin contacted were either booked well in advance or were unfamiliar with the type of operation he ran. "Everybody was just bogged down," he said. "I just called around, compared cost versus timing."

He chose SGS Yarsley Quality Assured Firms of Hoboken, New Jersey. From that point on, the process moved quickly. Over the following month, Benjamin worked to develop a quality manual in accordance with ISO 9000 series standards. That proved difficult because Benjamin could only devote limited time to the project.

AUDITS NOT NEW

Though new to ISO 9000 series registration, Techni-Test was no stranger to the process. It already was certified under MIL-STD-45662A Calibration System Requirements. Benjamin also had a copy of ISO Guide 25, which is a requirement of independent laboratories and laboratories testing to European regulatory requirements.

He found the military standards and Guide 25 to be similar but less encompassing than the ISO 9000 series in certain areas. "There were other areas such as management responsibility …that didn't come up" in the other standards, but are addressed by the ISO 9000 series, he said.

The first draft of the quality manual, totaling about nine pages, missed its mark. "They said it was too vague," he explained. For example, where Benjamin referred to Techni-Test personnel, the registrar wanted to know which specific personnel he was talking about. Benjamin said he was initially uncertain whether all clauses applied. "But my understanding is that whether it applies or not, it needs to be addressed," he said.

Benjamin's final draft was three times as thick as the original. The additional material was just what the registrar wanted. With some minor suggestions, the registrar felt the time had come to pencil in a date for final assessment.

AUDIT IN AUGUST

Benjamin spent the last six weeks before the final audit making revisions to the manual and preparing the staff for a site visit. After incorporating the changes, Benjamin passed out copies of the revised quality manual to everyone in the office.

One benefit of having such a small firm is the ability to involve the entire staff in the process. For example, Benjamin called a staff meeting to review the document line by line. "Everybody had some questions, some input, constructive criticism," he said. "If we had a question, everybody heard it at the same time and we made a corrective change at the same time."

THREE FINDINGS

Five months after he signed on with SGS Yarsley, the 11-hour site visit began. Two auditors "went through all the procedures. They went through everything, the whole nine yards," Benjamin said. Benjamin stayed with one of the auditors while his lab supervisor went with the other.

The visit turned up only three inconsistencies:

● Techni-Test had not yet performed any internal audits as required by the ISO 9000 series.

● Another finding related to the forms the firm uses to log its asset control and test equipment. Techni-Test had not updated its procedures with respect to changes in the forms.

● The last finding dealt with documenting out-of-tolerance conditions, which merely required some more paperwork.

BENEFITS

One of the most tangible benefits that resulted from the certification process was a tagging system to keep track of incoming equipment. Under the old system, it was difficult to trace equipment when the assigned technician was unavailable. Now, all items remain tagged from the time they are received until they are shipped back to their owners.

Benjamin said it is too soon to tell if his firm will generate any additional business as a result of the certification, but some existing customers are already beginning to ship more equipment as they attempt to meet ISO 9000 series standards. He has also noticed an increase in requests for more detailed documentation.

"If they're going for the ISO 9000 series registration they have to have it," he said, referring to the more in-depth reports.

Techni-Test plans to take advantage of its status. "The European market is going to be wide open," he said. "Companies are not going to demand it, but [they will] suggest you have that certification to do business with them."

ENDNOTES

[1] James E. Emanuel, "US Industrial Outlook 1993—Chemicals and Allied Products," International Trade Commission.

[2] Paul Scicchitano, "Short Document Long on Results for Chemical Companies," *Quality Systems Update* Vol. 3, No. 8 (August 1993): 1.

[3] William M. Harral, Arch Associates, Northville, MI.

[4] *ibid.*

[5] Thomas Stallkamp . "Teaming Up for Quality," paper presented at the University of Michigan Automotive Management Briefing, Traverse City, MI (August 1993).

[6] Paul Scicchitano, "Big Three Draft Quality Standard Forces Suppliers to Consider ISO 9000 Registration," *Quality Systems Update* Vol. 4, No. 1 (January 1994): SR-1.

[7] *ibid.*

[8] Paul Scicchitano, "Big Three Make Progress with Registrars," *Quality Systems Update* Vol. 4, No. 3 (March 1994): 8.

[9] Paul Scicchitano, "Big 3 Automakers Reach Long-Awaited Consensus on Joint ISO 9000-Based Quality System," *Quality Systems Update* Vol. 3, No. 8 (August 1993): 12.

[10] *ibid.*

[11] Thomas T. Stallkamp "Teaming Up for Quality," paper presented at the University of Michigan Automotive Management Briefing, Traverse City, MI (August 1993).

[12] *ibid.*

[13] *ibid.*

[14] David V. Fette "Industry Standards Reports—Automotive," *The EC Report on Industry* (January 1994): 17.

Appendix A

CONTRIBUTORS TO THIS BOOK

This appendix lists all the contributors to the second edition of *The ISO 9000 Handbook* and is grouped into two sections.

PART A

This first section highlights people who have written material specifically for this Handbook—some of the articles have never before been published. They are longer pieces and usually comprise complete chapters or parts of chapters.

Bohdan Dyczkowsky (PE) is director of MOYE Company Limited and served as secretary of the Canadian Advisory Committees to ISO and the IEC—most notably TC 176 as it was developing the ISO 9000 standards. He also helped develop the Canadian National Standards on Quality and helped establish Strategic Training Solutions for the Province of Ontario on ISO 9000 training. In addition, Mr. Dyczkowsky has helped two Canadian registrars establish their ISO 9000 registration systems, has conducted ISO 9000 audits on behalf of Canadian registrars and has led companies through to ISO 9000 registration. A frequent speaker on the subject of quality, he has been quoted in various trade magazines and has broad manufacturing experience in construction, steel fabricating, nuclear piping and electronics.

Mr. Dyczkowsky is a native of Toronto, Ontario, Canada and graduated from the University of Toronto with a BASC in Mechanical Engineering. He is a registered Professional Engineer, a registered auditor with the IQA and RAB, an active member of the ASQC, and a past member of the Advisory Committee on Quality Engineering at Humber College in Toronto. *MOYE Company Limited, 59 Breadner Drive, Suite 102, Toronto, Ontario M9R 3M5, Canada, Tel/Fax: 416-248-9187.*

Bud Weightman is president of Qualified Specialists, Inc. (QSI) and an international consultant who has extensive experience designing, implementing and assessing quality management systems, particularly ISO 9000 and similar standards.

Mr. Weightman is a registered lead assessor (UK), RAB lead auditor, Texas Quality Award Examiner (1993), Houston Awards for Quality Assessor (1993) and an ASQC CQA. He has personally assisted more than 50 companies worldwide achieve third party quality system/product registration/licensing. In addition, he is an active member of the US Technical Advisory Group to TC 176. Mr. Weightman has had several of his articles on ISO 9000 published in national and international trade magazines. He has over 20 years experience in quality systems, and he engages in public speaking and training on the subject of auditing, quality, ISO 9000 and registration. *Qualified Specialists, Inc., 13231 Champion Forest Drive, Suite 104, Houston, TX 77069, Tel: 713-444-5366, Fax: 713-444-6127.*

David N. Middleton is president and director of Excel Partnership, Inc., an international training and consulting organization. He is responsible for managing EXCEL's activities in the United States. Mr. Middleton's experience in quality management consultancy and in the application of ISO 9000 extends over several years, particularly in the textile, packaging, apparel, transport and process industries. He guided a wise cross section of industrial and service companies to registration, including a number of organizations first in their field. His practical approach to implementing quality systems is supported by earlier experience in production and commercial management in the Middle East, Far East, the United States and Europe. *Excel Partnership, Inc. 75 Glen Road, Sandy Hook, CT 06482, Tel: 203-426-3281, Fax: 203-426-7811.*

Donald W. Marquardt has been active in TC 176 since its inception in 1980. He leads the US delegation to TC 176 and is a member of the TC 176 Chairman's Advisory Group. He served as a convener of several working groups, including those responsible for ISO 9000:1987, ISO 9000-2 and ISO 9000-1. Mr. Marquardt chaired the TC 176 task force that developed Vision 2000 and is on the board of directors of the RAB. After 39 years with Du Pont, he is now president of Donald W. Marquardt and Associates in Wilmington, DE. He is a fellow of the American Association for the Advancement of Science (AAAS), the American Statistical Association (ASA) and the ASQC. His awards include the ANSI Meritorious Service award and the ASQC Shewhart Medal. *Donald W. Marquardt and Associates, 1415 Athens Road, Wilmington, DE 19803, Tel: 302-478-6695, Fax: 302-478-9329.*

Elizabeth A. Potts is president of ABS Quality Evaluations, Inc., an accredited third-party registrar of quality systems to a variety of standards, including the ISO 9000 series standard. Ms. Potts was most recently Quality Assurance Manager for the American Gas Association Laboratories where she was responsible for product registration and follow-up inspections, ISO 9000 quality system registrations, and internal quality control program development. She was also employed as a Quality Control Manager with Babcock & Wilcox, where she developed and implemented quality control programs for nuclear reactor and other defense-related components. Ms. Potts is a member of the Executive Committee of the ANSI ASC Z-1 on quality assurance and is also a member of the US Technical Advisory Group to TC 176 on quality assurance and quality management. She is a registered ASQC Certified Quality Auditor (#445) and an IQA Registered Assessor (A003493). *ABS Quality Evaluations*

Inc., 16855 Northchase Drive, Houston, TX 77060-6008, Tel: 713-873-9400, Fax: 713-874-9564.

Gregory G. Scott (Esq.) is shareholder in the Minneapolis office of Popham Haik Schnobrich & Kaufman, Ltd. where he specializes in preventive law, corporate compliance and product liability. He also advises clients worldwide on international product standards and product liability prevention strategies. He leads the firm's Globalization / International Practice Group and is a member of the Preventive Law Practice Group, Product Liability Practice Group, Liability Management Practice Group and Healthcare Practice Group.

Mr. Scott is a member of the Product Liability Committee and the International Law committee of the American Bar Association, and he chairs the International Law Subcommittee of the Product Liability Committee at the ABA level. He is a frequent writer and lecturer on prevention and product liability in the United States and Europe and has given seminars in Japan and Korea. Mr. Scott received a J.D. *magna cum laude* from William Mitchell College of Law and a B.A. from St. Johns University. *Popham Haik Schnobrich & Kaufman, Ltd. 222 South Ninth Street, Suite 3300, Minneapolis, MN 55402, Tel: 612-333-4800, Fax: 612-334-8888.*

Ian G. Durand is president of Service Process Consulting, Inc., which he founded after 31 years with AT&T Bell Laboratories. He has been active as a US delegate to TC 176 since 1986—he facilitates the TC 176 Advisory Group responsible for the consistency and compatibility of standards in the ISO 9000 family. Initially, this group focused on the revisions of the five core standards. More recently, it is addressing all existing and planned standards written by TC 176. In addition, Mr. Durand was a major contributor in drafting *ISO 9004-2: Guidelines for Services* and was the lead US delegate to the ISO working group responsible for its publication. He has also served as a senior examiner for the Malcolm Baldrige Award. He has a master's degree in electrical engineering from New York University in New York and is a member of the ASQC. *Service Process Consulting, Inc., 76 George Avenue, Edison, NJ 08820, Tel: 908-321-0045, Fax: 908-549-9117.*

James W. Kolka has a Ph.D. in political science/international affairs from the University of Kansas and a J.D. with a background in product liability and environmental law from the University of Wisconsin-Madison. An international legal consultant, he has served as a full professor, published numerous articles, and has served as vice president both at Drake University and in the University System of Georgia. He has held senior management positions in the University of Wisconsin System, developed Wisconsin's statewide Adult Extended Degree Program and was instrumental in creating the Center for International Standards and Quality at Georgia Tech. Dr. Kolka has conducted seminars and consulted on topics including product liability, product safety, services liability, EC product certification, environmental planning, global liability and strategic planning. Dr. Kolka is fluent in Spanish and conversant in German, Portuguese and Italian. He has worked throughout the United States, Canada, Europe and Latin America. *2193 Spearpoint Drive, Marietta, GA 30062, Tel: 404-977-4049, Fax: 404-651-9185.*

Joel S. Finlay is a senior consultant with Process Management International, a Deming-based Total Quality Management consulting firm, where he has worked full-time since 1987. He has been involved in training for several Malcolm Baldrige National Quality Award winners, including Xerox and Zytec, and he has assisted several companies in ISO 9000 series certification, including leading the team to certify his own company, Process Management International. Dr. Finlay has a Ph.D. degree in communications from the University of North Dakota, an M.A. degree in small-group communication applied to the creative process from the University of Cincinnati, and is presently a Ph.D. candidate in total quality management leadership at Walden University. He has authored more than three dozen publications, including a book on applied creativity, and he has edited book on organization development. Dr. Finlay is certified as a registered organization development consultant (RODC)—only about 100 people worldwide hold the RODC certification. He was recently honored as an "Outstanding Researcher in Quality" for inclusion in the *International Who's Who in Quality.*

Joseph Tiratto (PE) is an international consultant on quality systems, an IQA Lead Assessor and a European Engineer (EUR. ING). Tiratto is a member of the RAB, the US Technical Advisory Group to TC 176 and other international and national standards groups. He has conducted audits of quality systems in 15 countries worldwide and has also directed the development of a registrar quality system that would meet both RAB and RvC requirements. *Joseph Tiratto and Associates, 5 N Longview Road, Howell, NJ 07731-1701, Tel: 908-367-0837, Fax: 908-549-9117.*

Ollie Young is a director of The Victoria Group. His background is electronics—from military to commercial—including designing and manufacturing avionic equipment and high volume communication products. A quality manager for over 12 years, Mr. Young has extensive experience in implementing quality systems. He has worked with major US and UK high-tech companies in various quality and TQM programs and has successfully achieved ISO 9001 and 9002 registration for companies. In addition, he has gained the IBM Vendor of the Year Award as well as AQAP, BABT, British Telecom, UL and CSA approvals. His special areas of expertise encompass small companies, service industries, and general manufacturing/engineering. *The Victoria Group (Management Consultants) Ltd., 10529 Braddock Road, Suite D, Fairfax, VA 22032, Tel: 800-845-0567, 703-250-4990, Fax:: 800-845-0767, 703-250-5523.*

Peter B. Lake is president of Steel Related Industries Quality System Registrar, Inc., which registers companies in many basic manufacturing and services industries. He is the director of the Steel Industry Supplier Audit Process (SISAP) that involves ISO 9000-based TQM assessments of steel suppliers as part of a "shared audit" program. In addition, Dr. Lake is a steel industry representative to TC 176 and is vice president of the independent association of accredited registrars, a newly formed organization of registrars working in North America. He served as a Malcolm Baldrige Senior Examiner in 1991 and 1992 and previously was National Steel's corporate quality manager, director of the Product Application Center in Detroit and chairman of the quality improvement committee (AISI). *SRI Quality System Registrar, Inc., 2000 Corporate Drive, Suite 450, Wexford, PA 15090; Tel: 412-935-2844, Fax: 412-935-6825.*

Robert W. Belfit is president and chairman of Omni Tech International, Ltd., quality systems consultants. He is the principal author of Omni Tech's "Implementing ISO 9000" and "Principles of

Auditing" seminars and has developed another course, "Implementing ISO 9000 and OSHA's Regulation 29 CFR 1910.119." Dr. Belfit was actively involved for 20 years at Dow Chemical in designing and implementing Dow's global quality systems. He is an ASQC Certified Quality Auditor and an IQA Provisional Assessor. *Omni Tech International Ltd., 2715 Ashman Street, Suite 100, Midland, MI 48640, Tel: 517-631-3377, Fax: 517-631-7360.*

Roderick S.W. Goult is chairman and chief executive of The Victoria Group (Management Consultants) Ltd. in the United Kingdom, and president and chief operating officer of The Victoria Group, Inc. in the United States. His specialist areas are electronics and software, although he has also worked with paper mills, banking, aircraft fastenings stockists, chemical companies and mechanical engineering. He has been a quality professional for nearly twenty years. Before leaving industry for the world of consultancy, Mr. Goult spent six years as a quality manager in an AQAP-1 military communications design and manufacturing environment.

As a consultant he has successfully completed a number of ISO 9000 development projects for the United Kingdom's Department of Trade and Industry Quality Initiative and has assisted manufacturers in the United Kingdom and Sweden to obtain BABT approvals. Mr. Goult is a Lead Assessor registered by the Governing Board of the UK International Registration Scheme for Assessors of Quality Systems, and the author of several training programs, including a UK registered assessor training program.

Mr. Goult was a commentator in the development of the RAB's auditor training and registration program and currently sits on the Software Quality System Registration committee established by the RAB to investigate, establish and advise upon the creation of a software specific registration program in the United States. *The Victoria Group Incorporated, 10529 Braddock Road, Suite D, Fairfax, VA 22032, Tel: 800-845-0567, 703-250-4990, Fax: 800-845-0767, 703-250-5523.*

Taz Daughtrey is in quality engineering at Babcock & Wilcox in Lynchburg, Virginia, where he has managed the acquisition, installation, and qualification of analytical software used in designing systems such as nuclear reactors. He has been active for more than ten years in developing software quality engineering standards under the sponsorship of professional societies such as the IEEE Computer Society, the American Nuclear Society, and the American Society of Mechanical Engineers. Daughtrey was a founding officer of the Software Division of the ASQC, which he chaired from 1990 to 1992. He is currently active on the Software Quality Systems Registration committee for the RAB, heading the working group for industry awareness and support. *Babcock & Wilcox, PO Box 785, Lynchburg, VA 24505-0785, Tel: 804-522-5137, Fax: 804-522-5922.*

William Ferguson (C.Eng., F.inst.E., FIQA) is director and principal consultant of Wickham International Management Services, Ltd. He has been in the quality assurance field for 20 years, during which time he has been involved with the following: defining the quality requirements for chemicals, papers and textiles used by the UK Ministry of Defense; evaluating the quality systems of chemical, paper and textile suppliers to subsequently approve and monitor their performance; and conducting assessments to defense standards in the United Kingdom that preceded the ISO 9000 standards.

Mr. Ferguson has conducted more than 350 assessments and has provided advice to several multinational companies—all of whom have achieved registration. He is a Fellow of the IQA and a lead assessor registered by the UK Registration Board for Assessors. *Wickham International Management Services, Ltd., PO Box 86, Sugar Land, TX 77487, Tel: 800-486-4138, Fax: 713-242-6462.*

William M. Harral (QS-LA, RLA, CQE, CQA, CRE, PEIT) is director of Arch Associates, a TQM and ISO 9000 consulting and training firm. He has 20 years experience in various engineering, manufacturing, planning, and quality management positions at Ford Motor Company prior to founding Arch Associates in 1983. He is an active ASQC Fellow, past chair of the Greater Detroit section, Region 10 deputy director, Automotive Division councilor, Quality Management Division Technology Group chair, and executive secretary of the General Technical Council. At the Automotive Industry Action Group, he has served on the Continuous Quality Improvement Project Team since 1984. Mr. Harral currently chairs the Standards Committee and serves as the ISO 9000 series technical advisor to the Truck Advisory Group. He is also a corporate member of the IQA and a company voting representative to ANSI.

Mr. Harral has authored numerous articles,

books and handbooks on quality and has been named in five Who's Who publications. He holds an MBA from the University of Michigan and a BS in industrial and systems engineering from Ohio State University. *Arch Associates, 15770 Robinwood Drive, Northville, MI 48167, Tel: 313-420-0122, Fax: 313-420-0122.*

Part B

The second section of contributors includes those whose work was published elsewhere first—such as in *Quality Systems Update* or as a conference paper. These articles are usually shorter and appear in this Handbook as boxes of additional information.

Dennis Abarca is an account manager with P-E Handley-Walker Inc., which offers consulting and training assistance on ISO 9000. Abarca helps clients establish a strategy for implementing ISO 9000 quality systems. The company has helped more than 1,600 companies attain registration worldwide.

Tom Bair is managing director of Tom Bair & Associates, which offers a broad range of quality control services. He is an ASQC certified quality auditor and has completed an ISO 9000 lead auditor course. He is in the process of seeking certification as an ISO 9000 lead auditor from the Registrar Accreditation Board.

Charles McRobert is president of Quality Practitioners, Inc., which provides training and consulting in the application of the ISO 9000 series. He has developed and implemented ISO 9000 systems and has taken companies to ISO 9000 series registration. He is also an accredited auditor in the United States and Canada.

Peter Melville is the ISO 9000 project manager with Butler Quality Services. He is an IQA registered assessor and a mechanical engineer. He specializes in implementing ISO 9000 quality systems in a manufacturing environment and has assisted clients in attaining ISO 9001 and ISO 9002 registration in Europe and North America

Dan Epstein is an independent consultant who assists both large and small companies in preparing for ISO 9000 registration. He was an examiner for the 1992 Malcolm Baldrige National Quality Award and for the 1993 Governor's Excelsior Award. He is also a certified ISO 9000 lead assessor.

David Ling (P.E.) is currently the ISO 9000 coordinator for Hewlett-Packard Corporate Quality and participates in the US Technical Advisory Group for TC 176 and TC 207. Mr. Ling has had extensive engineering experience in production at HP Sonoma County division and product regulations at HP Corporate.

Dean W. Stamatis (Ph.D., CQE, CMfgE) is president of Contemporary Consultants Company. With more than 25 years of experience in the quality field, he is a specialist in management consulting, quality science, and organizational development. He is active in the ASQC and has written numerous papers on quality.

Dennis Arter of Columbia Quality, Inc. is a Senior Member of ASQC and is active in the Quality Audit Division. He has written a book, *Quality Audits for Improved Performance*, and he teaches two courses for the ASQC Professional and Technical Development series.

Donald Strahle of Ontario Hydro in Canada is a member of the Ad Hoc Task Force of TC 176.

Dr. James Lamprecht is an accredited assessor with the IQA of London, and has been consulting on ISO 9000 implementation with numerous companies in the US and Europe. He is the author of *ISO 9000: Preparing for Registration* and *The ISO 9000 Phenomenon.*

Foster Finley is a senior consultant in the Atlanta office of Deloitte & Touche. He is a registered professional engineer with seven years of experience in manufacturing, quality systems, and management consulting. He specializes in helping manufacturers implement and realize the maximum benefits of ISO 9000 registration.

Ira Epstein is vice president of Government Services at STAT-A-MATRIX. He is a member of the US Technical Advisory Group to TC 176 and was formerly the manager of quality assurance with the Department of Defense.

Jacques Chove of Conseil in France is a member of the Ad Hoc Task Force of TC 176.

James C. Pyle has been active in TC 176 since 1980. He served as convener of three working groups, including those responsible for the original version and the draft international standard of ISO 9001, ISO 9002, and ISO 9003. After 40 years with British Telecom, he is now an independent consultant in London.

James Highlands founded Management Systems Analysis, Inc. in 1986 and serves as president. He is a member of TC 176 on Quality Management and the ANSI/ASQC Z-1 Quality Management Committee. He is a TQA certified lead assessor, an RAB certified lead auditor, an ASQC quality auditor, and a certified nuclear lead auditor.

James P. O'Neil is president of NQA (USA), Inc.

Jeffrey P. Tuthill is president of EC Technical Compliance, which specializes in implementing quality systems. He was the first US representative of the NSAI and is an active member of the US Technical Advisory Group to TC 74, IEC 950, the IEC committee for the Safety of Information Technology Equipment.

John Cachat is president of IQS, Inc. He is an expert in quality systems development and computerization. He lectures on and has authored publications on TQM systems. He is also a Certified Quality Engineer, and a former chairman of the ASQC Management Division Quality Information Systems (QIS) Committee.

Joseph A. Chiaramonte is a senior staff engineer in corporate quality and reliability with Underwriters Laboratories, Inc. He is a lead auditor for UL's ISO 9000 registration program with more than 14 years of experience in quality system auditing and is a member of the US Technical Advisory Group to TC 176.

Joseph DeCarlo is division manager of corporate QA services for TUV Rheinland of North America, Inc. He is also a registered lead assessor with the RAB and the IQA.

Joseph J. Klock is quality registrar director of AT&T Quality Registrar.

K.E. Jensen of Alkatel Kirk A/S in Denmark is a member of the Ad Hoc Task Force of TC 176.

Kevin Drayton is principal and senior consultant of Kevin Drayton Associates. He has spent more than 12 years in the aerospace industry and has served as laboratory quality coordinator, quality assurance engineer, and senior purchased materials analyst for General Electric.

Kirk Eggebrecht is an executive manager with Geo. S. Olive & Co. He heads the manufacturing consulting division and helps clients develop and implement ISO 9000 systems and is a frequent speaker on quality and ISO 9000-related topics.

Klaus Petrick of DIN in Germany is a member of the Ad Hoc Task Force of TC 176.

Michael McSweeney is the executive director of the Standards Council of Canada.

Peter M. Malkovich is the director of ISO 9000 consulting and training services for Process Management International (PMI). He has extensive business background and assists organizations in quality systems and in total quality.

Peter Scott is managing director and founder of NQA Worldwide.

Ralph D. Schmidt is a director of Thornhill USA, consultants on business excellence in North and South America. Thornhill specializes in ISO 9000 consulting and pre-audits and furnishes personnel under contract to registrars.

Raymond P. Cooney, Ph.D. is principal quality management consultant of R.P. Cooney & Associates. He has 15 years' experience, including ISO 9000 series registrations with Exxon Chemical Co. He serves on the accreditation council of the American Association for Laboratory Accreditation (A2LA).

Robert D. Bowen is president of r. bowen international, inc. He has spent more than 18 years as a quality professional with E.I. du Pont de Nemours & Co. Inc. He is certified by the ASQC as a quality engineer and quality auditor and sits on the Electronics Industry Association's Committee for Quality and Reliability Engineering.

Robert Hammil is a senior staff consultant with Perry Johnson, Inc. He is one of the leading in-house authorities on the ISO 9000 series standards and is a presenter and instructor in ISO 9000-related topics at the Perry Johnson Quality Institute and at client sites.

Roger C. Pratt is manager of the Quality Training Office at Pacific Northwest Laboratory in Richland, Washington. The Laboratory is operated by the Battelle Memorial Institute for the US Department of Energy.

Ronald Muldoon is a quality consultant on quality systems and audits with Brown & Root, Inc. He is an ASQC certified quality auditor, an RAB certified quality systems lead auditor and an IQA accredited assessor. He is a senior member of the ASQC and is a member of the US Technical Advisory Group to TC 176.

Serge E. Gaudry is a senior consultant with FED-PRO, Inc., which offers ISO 9000 series training and computer software.

Stephen Gousie is a partner with Information Mapping, Inc. He is responsible for business relations and is an expert in performance technology, training and education, and quality programs with expertise in the petrochemical industry.

Stephen Hedman is president of Hedman Consulting Services, which specializes in ISO 9000 series implementation.

Stephen Nicholas is president of Experts in ISO 9000, Ltd. His firm has assisted numerous subcontractors to successfully achieve registration.

Stephen S. Keneally is president and founder of Scott Technical Services, Inc., which focuses on ISO 9000, re-engineering and new product development cycle time reduction. He has more than 15 years of experience in quality assurance working for various Fortune 50 firms in the aerospace, defense, and medical electronics manufacturing industries.

Terry Heaps is Project Administrator, QA Services for Vincotte USA, Inc., an ISO 9000 series quality systems auditing company.

Victoria Group, The is a management consulting company in the quality field. Established in the UK in 1989, The Victoria Group offers public programs, in-house training and private consulting on all aspects of the ISO 9000 series of standards and lead auditor training. The company incorporated in Virginia in 1993.

William Cox is president of TQM Consulting, which offers consulting services and training for implementation of ISO 9000 and broader TQM processes with an emphasis on the petrochemical industry. Cox is a certified auditor by the IQA and ASQC. He also is on the board of examiners for the Texas Quality Award.

William J. Deibler, II is a founding partner of Software Systems Quality Consulting (SSQC). He is a member of the Software Quality System Registration (SQSR) committee of the RAB, which is developing the US equivalent of the UK's TickIT scheme.

Harvey S. Berman is manager of corporate quality and reliability with Underwriters Laboratories. He is a member of the Technical Advisory Group to the International Organization for Standardization (ISO) Technical Committee 176, and is an American Society for Quality Control Fellow, a registered professional engineer, and an ASQC-certified reliability engineer. He also chairs the International Electrotechnical Commission's Quality Assessment System for Electronic Components.

Michael P. Enders is principal of American Quality Resources (AQR), which specializes in ISO 9000 implementation and internal training. He has completed course requirements for lead assessor certification and is a former senior account manager with Intertek Testing Services.

Jeffry J. Omelchuck is principal of International Quality Associates, which specializes in quality systems consulting, training, and implementation support. He has completed training requirements for the lead assessor certification.

Chuck Rhodes is executive director of the Management Resource Group, which specializes in ISO 9000 and Malcolm Baldrige National Quality Award issues. He has been a quality consultant for more than 20 years.

Robert Kennedy is US national director of operations with Quality Management Institute, an ISO 9000 series registrar. Kennedy is a US delegate to the International Organization for Standardization (ISO) Technical Committee 176.

Larry Bissell is vice president of Management Standards International Ltd., which provides ISO 9000 training, consulting, and support services. He is an RAB-certified lead auditor, an ASQC-certified quality engineer and a 1994 Malcolm Baldrige National Quality Award examiner. He has helped more than 12 clients attain ISO 9000 registration.

Ren Verasco is assistant vice president of quality management with Chubb Services Corp., the consulting arm of the Chubb Group of Insurance Companies. He specializes in ISO 9000 implementation.

Graham Cartwright is managing consultant with MRA International, which offers ISO 9000 consulting services. Cartwright has been consulted by more than 150 organizations in the UK, Europe, North America, and Scandinavia.

Appendix B

STANDARDS AND DIRECTIVES

This appendix contains sources for information about EU standards and directives, including the following information:

- ISO 9000 and ANSI/ASQC/Q9000 Standards
- EU Directives
  - General Overview
  - Selected Status Charts
  - Sources for Directives & Further Information
- Additional EU Standards
  - Information Sources for EU Standards (US and EU)
  - Hotlines
- EC 1992 Single Market Information.

ISO 9000 STANDARDS

To order the ISO 9000 standards, call ASQC or ANSI at the addresses and phone numbers listed below:

American Society for Quality Control (ASQC)

611 East Wisconsin Avenue, Post Office Box 3005
Milwaukee, WI 53201
Tel: 414-272-8575 or 800-248-1946

ASQC sells the 1994, fully revised American (Q9000) version of the ISO 9000 series :

The ANSI/ASQC Q9000-1—9004-1 *Complete Set*. (Item T3000) is sold as a complete set for $49.00 for members and $59.00 for non-members.

ANSI/ASQC Q9000-1 *Quality management and quality assurance standards—Guidelines for selection and use.* (Item T9000) Member: $11.00, List Price: $13.00

ANSI/ASQC Q9001 *Quality systems—Model for quality assurance in design, development, production, installation and servicing.* (Item T9001) Member: $14.00, List Price: $16.00

ANSI/ASQC Q9002 *Quality systems—Model for quality assurance in production, installation, and servicing.* (Item T9002) Member: $12.00, List Price: $14.00

ANSI/ASQC Q9003 *Quality systems—Model for quality assurance in final inspection and test.* (Item T9003) Member: $10.00, List Price: $12.00

ANSI/ASQC Q9004-1 *Quality management and quality system elements—Guidelines.* (Item T9004) Member: $20.00, List Price: $22.00

American National Standards Institute (ANSI)

Attention: Customer Service
11 West 42nd Street, New York, NY 10036
Tel: 212-642-4900; Fax: 212-302-1286
(Some orders require a 7 percent handling charge. Operating hours: 8:45 am to 4:45 pm EDT.)

ANSI Products:

ISO 9000 Compendium

Includes the entire ISO 9000 (1987) series, 10011 and 10012 series standards, 8402 vocabulary standards, draft international standards, guideline documents and *Vision 2000, A Strategy for International Standards Implementation in the Quality Arena during the 1990's.* 224 pages. $235.

ISO 9000 (1987): *Quality management and quality assurance standards—Guidelines for selection and use.* ANSI version ANSI/ASQC Q90 (1987). $31.

ISO 9001 (1987): *Quality systems—Model for quality assurance in design/development, production, installation and servicing.* ANSI version ANSI/ASQC Q91 (1987). $34.

ISO 9002 (1987): *Quality systems—Model for quality assurance in production and installation.* ANSI version ANSI/ASQC Q92 (1987). $31.

ISO 9003 (1987): *Quality systems—Model for quality assurance in final inspection and test.* ANSI version ANSI/ASQC Q93 (1987). $22.

ISO 9004 (1987): *Quality management and quality system elements—Guidelines.* ANSI version ANSI/ASQC Q94 (1987). $47.

ISO 9000-3 (1991): *Quality management and quality assurance standards—Part 3: Guidelines for the application of ISO 9001 to the development, supply, and maintenance of software.* $47.

ISO 9004-2 (1991): *Quality management and quality system elements—Part 2: Guidelines for services.* $51.

ISO/Draft International Standards (ISO/DIS):

ISO/DIS 9000-1.2: *Quality management and quality assurance standards—Guidelines for selection and use.* $51.

ISO/DIS 9001.2: *Quality systems—Model for quality assurance in design/development, production, installation and servicing.* $40.

ISO/DIS 9002.2: *Quality systems—Model for quality assurance in production and installation.* $36.

ISO/DIS 9003.2: *Quality systems—Model for quality assurance in final inspection and test.* $34.

ISO/DIS 9004-1.2: *Quality management and quality system elements—Guidelines.* $59.

ISO/DIS 9004-2: *Quality management and quality system elements—Part 2: Guidelines for services.* $70.

EUROPEAN UNION DIRECTIVES

Overview

Demonstrating conformity with a directive or with a European standard is not a straightforward process, mainly because the European product standards and certification system is not fully in place. Despite the uncertainties, it is a good idea to develop a strategy for learning about standards and directives that affect your products and how to comply with them.

One place to start is to obtain, read, and understand *A Global Approach to Certification and Testing* (COM (89)209), the policy statement of the European Commission referred to in Chapter 15 of this handbook. This useful document will help you understand the specific conformity

assessment sections in particular directives. It is available from ANSI.

In its report, *ANSI Global Standardization, News Volume 2,* ANSI provides strategy and tactical recommendations for complying with all EU requirements. Key questions to consider and steps to follow in the strategy include the following:

- First, is your product regulated or unregulated, based on EU requirements?

- If it is regulated, is there an EU directive that will affect your products? If so, obtain the directive and analyze it.

- How many directives apply?

  Contact your industry's trade association to determine European Community 92 activities or contact the US Department of Commerce, Office of European Community Affairs, for lists and status reports on EU directives.

- Does the scope of the directive include your product?

- What are the essential requirements invoked by the directives?

- What are the required methods for demonstrating conformity? Review the conformity assessment section of the directive. This is usually Section 8.

- What is the effective date? What grandfathered provisions have been made for products on the market at the time of implementation?

- If the directive is final, has the EU Commission published any lists of related standards? If not, determine whether the Commission has mandated the preparation of any European standards.

- For final directives, determine how member states have implemented the directive and what organizations have been named as notified bodies.

- If the product is regulated in the United States, consult ANSI, your trade association, the US Department of Commerce, Office of European Community Affairs, the National Institute of Standards and Technology*, or the applicable regulatory agency in the United States to determine if there are any official agreements—completed or in process—that would allow you to comply with the European requirements as a by-product of complying with the applicable regulations.

- If the product is not regulated in the United States, consult the same sources mentioned above and any applicable private sector testing organization(s) in the United States to determine whether there are any private-sector agreements between testing and certification bodies and their counterparts in Europe, such that certificates from the private body could be used to demonstrate conformity with the European requirements.

(*Addresses and phone numbers of these organizations are listed after the following tables.)

Table B-1: Selected EU New-Approach Directives

Adopted Directives	Implementation Date	Transition Period
Toys	1/1/90	None
Simple Pressure Vessels	7/1/90	7/1/92
Construction Products	6/27/90	Indefinite
Electromagnetic Compatibility	1/1/92	12/31/95
Gas Appliances	1/1/92	12/31/95
Personal Protective Equipment	7/1/92	12/31/92
Machinery	12/31/92	12/31/94
Non-Automatic Weighing Instruments	1/1/93	1/1/2003
Active Implantable Medical Devices	1/1/93	12/31/94
Type Approval of Telecommunications Terminal Equipment	11/6/92	None

Proposed Directives	Implementation Date	Transition Period
Medical Devices	7/1/94	6/30/97
Elevators	1/1/95	12/31/97
Equipment for Use in Explosive Atmospheres	7/1/93	12/31/02
Recreational Craft	7/1/95	None

Planned Directives

In-vitro Diagnostics
Flammability of Furniture
Pressure Equipment
Measuring and Testing Instruments
Cable Ways
Amusement Park and Fairground Equipment
Playground Equipment (includes sports equipment)
Used Machinery
Fasteners

Table B-2: EU Product Directives

Referencing ISO 9000 (EN 29000) Standards as a Component of the Product Certification Process

ISO 9000 (EN 29000) Reference   ISO 9000 (EN 29000) Reference

Adopted Directives

Construction Products .... 29002 or 29003
Gas Appliances 29002
Personal Protective Equipment .... 29002 or 29003
Non-Automatic Weighing
    Instruments 29002
Active Implantable Medical Devices .... 29001 or 29002
Telecommunications Terminal
    Equipment.................................. 29001 or 29002

Proposed Directives

Medical Devices .... 29001 or 29002
Elevators .... 29001 or 29002
Equipment for Use in Potentially
    Explosive Atmospheres
    (mines, surface extractions) .... 29001 or 29002
Recreational Craft .... 29001 or 29002

Planned Directives

Flammability of Furniture 29002
Pressure Equipment .... 29001 or 29002
Measuring and Testing Instruments .... 29001, 29002 or 29003
Cable Ways Equipment 29001
Amusement Park and Fairground
    Equipment 29003
Fasteners 29002

Table B-3: EU Legal Requirements for Industrial Equipment and Consumer Goods

Directive	Citation Number	Official Journal	Date of OJ	Current Status	Date of Implem.
General					
Extension of information procedures on standards and technical rules	83/189	L 100	4/26/83	Adopted	
Amendment to Directive 83/189	88/182	L 81	3/26/88	Adopted	1/1/89
Second Amendment	92/400	L221	8/6/92	Adopted	
Proposed Amendment	Com(92)491	C340	12/12/92	Proposal	1/1/94
Green Paper on European Standardization Action for a faster technological integration in Europe (L 247)	(91) 521		11/27/91	Proposal	N/A
Appliances					
Appliances burning gaseous fuels (L 223)	90/396	L 196	7/7/90	Adopted	1/1/92
	(88)786	C 42	2/21/89	Common Position	12/31/92
	(88)459	C 260	10/13/89	Amendment	12/31/92
Civil Aviation					
Council regulation on technical requirements in civil aviation	3922/91	L 373	12/31/91	Adopted	1/1/92
Construction Products					
(L 140)	89/106	L 40	2/11/89	Adopted	6/28/91

(continued on next page)

Table B-3

(continued from previous page)

Electrical Equipment

Electrical equipment for use in potentially explosive
atmospheres/certain types of protection -
standards and marking (amends 79/196).
Certificates of conformity (L 147) .... 84/47 .... L 31 .... 2/2/84 .... Adopted 1/1/85
.... 88/571 .... L 311 .... 11/10/88 .... Adopted 12/31/89
(see also L 382,88/665)
.... 90/487 .... L 270 .... 10/2/90 .... Amendment 7/1/92
.... 82/490 .... L 218 .... 7/27/82 ... Recommendation ....

Low Voltage: electrical appliances: standards (L 185) .... 73/23 .... L 77 .... 3/26/73 .... Adopted 8/75

Commission communication on notified bodies, marks
and standards .... 88/C168/02 ...... C 168 .... 6/27/88 .... Communication ....

Update to '88 Communication .... C210 .... 8/15/92 .... Communication ....

Electromagnetic Compatibility

Radio Interference (L 127) (Electromagnetic compatibility) 89/336 .... L 139 .... 5/23/89 .... Adopted 1/1/92

Reference Standards .... 92/C44/10 .... C 44 .... 2/19/92 .... Communication ....
.... 92/C90 .... C 90 .... 4/10/92 .... Communication ....

Amendment - Transition Period .... L 126 .... 5/12/92 .... Adopted 10/28/92

Notified Bodies .... C271 .... 10/20/92 Communication ....

Instruments

Non-automatic weighing instruments (L 213) .... 90/384 .... L 189 .... 7/20/90 .... Adopted 7/1/92

Council Directive on Measuring Instruments and methods
of metrological control (L 315) .... 71/316 .... L 202 .... 9/6/71 .... Adopted 3/26/73
.... 83/575 .... L 332 .... 11/28/83 ...... Amendment 1/1/85
.... 87/355 .... L 192 .... 7/11/87 .... Amendment 12/31/87
.... 87/354 .... L 192 .... 7/11/87 .... Amendment 12/31/87
.... 72/427 .... L 291 .... 12/28/92 ...... Amendment 1/1/73
.... 88/665 .... L 382 .... 12/31/88 ...... Amendment .... Immed.

Lifts

Standards applied to electrically operated lifts
(amends 84/529/EEC) (L 226) .... 90/486 .... L 270 .... 10/2/90 .... Adopted ....

Proposal for a Council Directive on safety requirements
for lifting appliances for persons .... COM(92)35 .... C 62 .... 3/11/92 .... Proposal ....

Medical Devices

Active Implantable Medical Devices (L 212) .... 90/385 .... L 189 .... 7/20/90 .... Adopted 7/1/92

Proposal for a Council Directive concerning medical
devices (C 328) .... (91) 287 .... C 237 .... 9/12/91 .... Proposal 12/31/93

Amended Proposal .... (92)356 .... C251 .... 9/28/92 .... Proposal ....

(continued on next page)

Table B-3

(continued from previous page)

Product Liability

Directive on liability of defective products (L 110)	85/374	L 210	8/7/85	Adopted	7/1/88

Safety

Household Appliances: airborne noise (L 50)	86/594	L 344	12/6/86	Adopted	12/4/89
(Noise Standards)	90/C28/20	C 28	2/7/90	Amendment	
Lawnmower noise (L 79)	84/538	L 300	11/19/84	Adopted	
	88/180	L 81	3/27/88	Adopted	7/1/91
Safety of Toys (including chemical properties and electrical toys)	88/378	L 187	7/16/88	Adopted	6/30/89
	(88)201	C 155	6/23/89		
Reference Standards		C 154	6/23/90		
List of Notified Bodies (L 85)	90/162/14	C 162	7/3/91	Communication	
	90/278/03	C 278	11/6/90	Communication	
	90/320/03	C 320	12/20/90	Communication	
	90/32/06	C 32	2/7/91	Communication	
	90/68/03	C 68	3/16/91	Communication	
	91/155	L 76	3/22/91	Extension	6/18/91
		L 321	11/21/90	Corrigendum	
	91/307/03	C 307	11/27/91	Communication	
	91/279/04	C 279	10/26/91	Communication	
	92/25/03	C25	2/1/92	Communication	
	92/91/02	C91	4/10/92	Communication	
	92/97/03	C97	4/6/92	Communication	
Machine Safety (L 128)	89/392	L 183	6/29/89	Adopted	12/31/92
Amendment to include Mobile Machinery	91/368	L 198	7/22/91	Amendment	1/1/93
Amendment - lifting/loading	COM(91)547	C 25	2/1/92	Proposal	7/1/94
Amended Proposal	COM(92)363	C252	9/29/92		
Reference Standards		C157	6/24/92	Communication	
Notified Bodies		C271	10/20/92	Communication	
Minimum safety and health for work equipment used by workers at the workplace (second directive under 89/391/EEC) (L 187)	89/655	L 393	12/30/89	Adopted	12/31/92
		L 59		Corrigendum	
Minimum safety and health for personal protective equipment in the workplace (third directive under 89/391/EEC) (L 188a)	89/656	L 393	12/30/89	Adopted	12/31/92
		L 59		Corrigendum	
Commission communication for implementing Directive on safety aspects of personal protective equipment (L 188b)	89/328/02	C 328	12/30/89	Communication	12/31/92
Council Directive on laws relating to personal protective equipment	89/686	L399	12/30/89	Adopted	12/1/91

(continued on next page)

Table B-3

(continued from previous page)

Reference standards - respiratory protective devices (L 181)		C 44	2/19/92	Communication	12/1/91
		C240	9/19/92	Communication	
Minimum safety and health on visual display units (Visual Display Units - CRT) (L 220)	90/270	L 156	6/21/90	Adopted	12/31/92
Approximation of laws concerning general product safety (L320)	92/59	L228	6/1/92	Adopted	
Proposal for a Council Directive on safety requirements for equipment for use in potentially explosive atmospheres	COM(91)516	C 46	2/20/92	Proposal	7/1/93
Proposal for a Council Directive on safety of recreational craft	COM(92)141	C 123	5/15/92	Proposal	

Simple Pressure Vessels

(L28)	87/404	L 220	8/8/87	Adopted	7/1/90
Amendment-Transition period	90/488	L 270	10/2/90	Adopted	7/1/92
Reference Standards	92/C104	C 104	4/24/92	Communication	
Reference Standards	92/C328	C328	12/12/92	Communication	
Notified Bodies	93/C76/08	C76	3/18/93	Communication	

Telecommunications Terminal Equipment

Directive on the initial stage of the mutual recognition of type approval for telecommunications terminal equipment (L 96)	86/361	L 217	8/5/86	Adopted	7/24/87
Approximation of member state laws concerning telecommunications terminal equipment, including mutual recognition of conformity (L 280)	91/263	L 128	5/23/91	Adopted	11/6/92

Testing and Certification

Global approach to certification and testing: Quality measures for industrial products (C153)	(89)209	C267	10/19/89	Communication	N/A
Council Resolution of 12/21/89 on a global approach to conformity assessment		C10	1/16/90	Resolution	
Council decision concerning the modules for various phases of conformity assessment procedures (L245)	90/683	L380	12/31/90	Adopted	
Proposal for a council directive harmonizing CE marking requirements for new approach directives (C322)		C28	2/3/93	Proposal	1/1/95

Informal Draft EU Commission Documents

- Council directive on furniture flammability safety requirements
- Essential requirements for safety in pressure equipment
- Interpretation of standards for construction products: Eurocodes
- European standards for procurement

- Safety requirements for cableway equipment
- Safety requirements for playground equipment (includes sports equipment)
- Safety requirements for in-vitro diagnostics
- Safety requirements for measuring instruments

Where to Get EU Directives

European Union Depository Libraries in the United States

The European Union has established a network of libraries in the United States to provide access to all official EU publications. All depositories automatically receive—free of charge—one copy of each EU institution's periodical and non-periodical publications. The collection is available to the public during the library's regular working hours, free of charge and without any conditions. Many of the libraries also offer interlibrary loan services. The libraries listed below are included in this network.

Of particular importance for businesspeople and lawyers is the *Official Journal of the European Communities* (OJEC), the equivalent of the US *Federal Register.* The "C" section of the OJEC includes proposed legislation and other important notices; the "L" section has the final texts of legislation. Annual indexes and the *Directory of Community*

Legislation in Force provide subject and numeric reference access to legislation. Depository collections also contain the legislative proposals and communications of the Commission in their original, "COM" document form, as well as reports and debates of the European Parliament, opinions of the Economic and Social Committee, and decisions of the Court of Justice.

Subscriptions to the Official Journal are available in the United States and Canada through UNIPUB, the North American representative of the European Union for all publications. Daily publications of the OJEC are sent to subscribers at the close of each week's business. The annual subscription costs for the L and C Series are $750 surface mail and $1100 airmail (1994 prices in effect). The Journal is also available on microfiche for $525 (surface rates only).

UNIPUB
4611-F Assembly Drive
Lanham, MD 20706-4391
800-274-4888 (USA)
800-233-0504 (Canada)

European Union Depository Libraries

American University
Law Library
4400 Massachusetts Avenue, NW
Washington, DC 20016
Tel: 202-885-1000

Arizona, University of
International Documents
University Library
Tucson, AZ 85721
Tel: 606-621-2211

Arkansas, University of
Documents Department, UALR Library
33rd & University
Little Rock, AR 72204
Tel: 501-569-3000

California, University of
International Documents
Public Affairs Service
Research Library
Los Angeles, CA 90024
Tel: 310-825-4732

California, University of
Documents Department
General Library
Berkeley, CA 94720
Tel: 510-642-6000

California, University of
Documents Department
Central Library
La Jolla, CA 92093
Tel: 619-534-2230

Chicago, University of
Government Documents
Regenstein Library
1100 E 57th Street
Chicago, IL 60637
Tel: 312-702-1234

Colorado, University of
Government Publications
University Library
Box 184
Boulder, CO 90309-0184
Tel: 303-492-1411

Council on Foreign Relations
Library
58 E 68th Street
New York, NY 10021
Tel: 212-734-0400

Duke University
Public Documents Department
University Library
Durham, NC 27706
Tel: 919-684-2323

Emory University
Law Library
School of Law
Atlanta, GA 30322
Tel: 404-727-6123

Florida, University of
Documents Department
Libraries West
Gainesville, FL 32611
Tel: 904-392-3261

George Mason University
Center for European Community Studies
4001 N Fairfax Drive, Suite 450
Arlington, VA 22203
Tel: 703-993-8200

Georgia, University of
Law Library, Law School
Athens, GA 30602
Tel: 706-542-1922

Harvard University
Law School Library
Langdell Hall-Law 431
Cambridge, MA 02138
Tel: 617-495-1000

Hawaii, University of
Government Documents
University Library
2550 The Mall
Honolulu, HI 96822
Tel: 808-956-7204

Illinois Institute of Technology
Law Library
77 South Wacker Drive
Chicago, IL 60606
Tel: 312-567-3000

Illinois, University of
Law Library, School of Law
504 E Pennsylvania Avenue
Champaign, IL 61820
Tel: 217-333-1000

Indiana University
Government Documents
University Library
Bloomington, IN 47405
Tel: 812-332-0211

Iowa, University of
Government Publications Library
Iowa City, IA 52242
Tel: 319-335-3500

Kansas, University of
Government Documents and Maps
University Library
6001 Malott Hall
Lawrence, KS 66045
Tel: 913-864-2700

Kentucky, University of
Government Publications
Margaret I. King Library
Lexington, KY 40506
Tel: 606-257-9000

Library of Congress
Serial Division
Madison Building
10 First Street, SE
Washington, DC 20540
Tel: 202-707-5000

Maine, University of
Law Library
246 Deering Avenue
Portland, ME 04102
Tel: 207-780-4141

Michigan State University
Documents Department
University Library
East Lansing, MI 48824-1048
Tel: 517-355-1855

Michigan, University of
Serials Department
Law Library
Ann Arbor, MI 48109-1210
Tel: 313-764-9324

Minnesota, University of
Government Publications
Wilson Library-409
Minneapolis, MN 55455
Tel: 612-625-5000

Nebraska, University of
Acquisition Division, University Libraries
Lincoln, NE 68588-0410
Tel: 404-472-7211

New Mexico, University of
Social Science Coll. Dev.
Zimmerman Library
Albuquerque, NM 87131
Tel: 505-277-0111

New Orleans, University of
Business Reference, Earl K. Long Library
New Orleans, LA 70148
Tel: 504-286-6000

New York Public Library
Research Library, Ecn & Pub Aff.
Grand Central Station
PO Box 2221
New York, NY 10017
Tel: 212-930-8800

New York, State University of
Government Publications, Library
1400 Washington Avenue
Albany, NY 12222
Tel: 518-442-3300

New York, State University of
Government Documents
Lockwood Library Building
Buffalo, NY 14260
Tel: 716-645-2000

New York University
Law Library, School of Law
40 Washington Square South
New York, NY 10012
Tel: 212-998-1212

Northwestern University
Government Publications
University Library
Evanston, IL 60201
Tel: 708-491-3741

Notre Dame, University of
Document Center, Memorial Library
Notre Dame, IN 46556
Tel: 219-631-5000

Ohio State University
Documents Division, University Library
1858 Neil Avenue Mall
Columbus, OH 43210
Tel: 614-292-6175

Oklahoma, University of
Government Documents
Bizzell Memorial Library, Room 440
401 W Brooks
Norman, OK 73019
Tel: 405-325-2151

Oregon, University of
Documents Section, University Library
Eugene, OR 97403
Tel: 503-346-3111

Pennsylvania State University
Documents Section, University Library
University Park, PA 16802
Tel: 814-865-4700

Pennsylvania, University of
Serials Department, Van Pelt Library
Philadelphia, PA 19104
Tel: 215-898-5000

Pittsburgh, University of
Gift and Exchange
Hillman Library G 72
Pittsburgh, PA 15260
Tel: 412-624-4141

Princeton University
Documents Division, Library
Princeton, NJ 08544
Tel: 609-258-3000

Puerto Rico, University of
Law School Library
Rio Piedras, PR 00931
Tel: 809-763-7199

South Carolina, University of
Documents/Microforms
Thomas Cooper Library
Columbia, SC 29208
Tel: 803-777-4866

Southern California, University of
International Documents
Von Kleinschmidt Library
Los Angeles, CA 90089
Tel: 213-740-1767

Stanford University
Central Western European Coll.
The Hoover Institution
Stanford, CA 94305
Tel: 415-723-2300

Texas, University of
Law Library
School of Law
727 East 26th Street
Austin, TX 78705
Tel: 512-471-3434

Utah, University of
International Documents
Marriott Library
Salt Lake City, UT 84112
Tel: 801-581-7200

Virginia, University of
Government Documents
Alderman Library
Charlottesville, VA 22903
Tel: 804-924-0311

Washington University
John M. Olin Library
Campus Box 1061
1 Brookings Drive
St. Louis, MO 63130
Tel: 314-935-5000

Washington, University of
Government Publications
University Library FM-25
Seattle, WA 98195
Tel: 206-543-2100

Wisconsin, University of
Documents Department
Memorial Library
728 State Street
Madison, WI 53706
Tel: 608-262-1234

Yale University
Government Documents Center
Seeley G. Mudd Library
38 Mansfield
New Haven, CT 06520
Tel: 203-432-4771

ADDITIONAL EU STANDARDS

Information Sources

To find out whether your product is covered by harmonized (EU-wide) standards, first call:

Office of European Community Affairs
International Trade Administration
Department of Commerce
Room H-3036
Washington, DC 20230
Tel: 202-482-5276
Fax: 202-482-2155

Charles Ludolph, Director, Office of European Community Affairs

Lori Cooper, Director of Single Internal Market Information Services

Direct line Tel: 202-482-5279

The office will send the standard to you if it is in the EU office files. If the standard is in the "proposal and commentary stage," it will be necessary to examine *Information and Notices,* an almost daily publication of the *Official Journal of the European Community.* This publication can be found in any state's EU full depository library or any partial depository library. The OJEC can also be found in many law libraries.

For information on various aspects of EU activities related to standardization, contact the Office of European Community Affairs at the Department of Commerce above, or:

National Center for Standards & Certification Information (NCSCI)
TRF Building, Room A163
Gaithersburg, MD 20899
Tel: 301-975-4040; Fax: 301-926-1559

Office of the US Trade Representative
Technical Barriers to Trade
Winder Building, 600 17th Street, NW, Room 513
Washington, DC 20506
Tel: 202-395-3063

European Community Information Service
2100 M Street, NW, Suite 707
Washington, DC 20037
Tel: 202-862-9500

European Community Information Service
305 East 47th Street
3 Dag Hammarskjold Plaza
New York, NY 10017
Tel: 212-371-3804

For further information on European standards, the National Institute of Standards and Technology has prepared a more extensive summary of the EU initiatives on standards and other related materials. These can be obtained by contacting:

Department of Commerce, National Institute of Standards & Technology (NIST), National Center for Standards and Certification Information (NCSCI)
TRF Bldg. Room A163
Gaithersburg, MD 20899
Tel: 301-975-4040; Fax: 301-926-1559
NCSCI provides assistance in obtaining current standards, regulations and certification information for the manufacture of products.

Other US and European sources for EU standards and standardization information are listed below.

United States and Canadian Contacts

The American National Standards Institute (ANSI)
11 West 42nd Street, 13th Floor
New York, NY 10036
Tel: 212-642-4900; Fax: 212-302-1286
Other ANSI offices:

ANSI Brussels Office
Avenue des Arts 50
BTE 5, 1040 Brussels, Belgium
Tel: 011 322 513 6892; Fax: 011 322 513 7928

ANSI Washington Office
655 15th Street, NW, Suite 300
Washington, DC 20005
Tel: 202-639-4090; Fax: 202-347-6109

American Society for Quality Control (ASQC)
611 E Wisconsin Avenue
Milwaukee, WI 53202-4606
Tel: 414-272-8575 or 800-248-1946

Canadian Standards Association
178 Rexdale Boulevard
Rexdale, ON M9W 1R3 Canada
Tel: 416-747-4000; Fax: 416-747-4149

Compliance Engineering
629 Massachusetts Avenue
Boxboro, MA 01719
Tel: 508-264-4208; Fax: 508-635-9407

Defense Printing Service
700 Robbins Avenue, Building 4, Section D
Philadelphia, PA 19111-5094
Tel: 215-697-2179 or 697-2667; Fax: 215-697-2978

Document Center
1504 Industrial Way, Unit 9
Belmont, CA 94002
Tel: 415-591-7600; Fax: 415-591-7617

General Services Administration (GSA)
Federal Supply Service Bureau, Specifications Branch
470 East L'Enfant Plaza, SW, Suite 8100
Washington, DC 20407
Tel: 202-755-0325 or 755-0326; Fax: 202-205-3720

Global Engineering Documents
1990 M Street, NW, Suite 400
Washington, DC 20036
Tel: 202-429-2860 or 800-854-7179; Fax: 202-331-0960

Information Handling Services (IHS)
PO Box 1154
15 Inverness Way East
Englewood, CO 80150
Tel: 303-790-0600 or 800-241-7824;
Fax: 303-397-2599 (Literature Dept.)

Intertek Technical Services
9900 Main Street, Suite 500
Fairfax, VA 22031
Tel: 703-591-1320

Standards Sales Group (SSG)
9420 Reseda Boulevard, Suite 800
Northridge, CA 91324
Tel: 818-831-3456 or 800-755-2780; Fax: 818-360-3804

Technical Standards Services
4024 Mount Royal Boulevard
Allison Park, PA 15101
Tel: 412-487-7007; Fax: 412-487-7027

European Union Contacts

Commission of the European Communities Directorate General Information, Communication
Culture Rue de la Loi 200 B-1049
Brussels, Belgium
Tel: 235 11 11

Council of Ministers
General Secretariat
Rue de la Loi 170
B-1048 Brussels, Belgium
Tel: 234 61 11

**European Committee for Standardization (CEN),
European Committee for Electrotechnical Standardization
(CENELEC),* European Organization for Testing and
Certification (EOTC)**
2 Rue de Brederode, Boite No. 5
1000 Brussels, Belgium
Tel: 011 32 25 196811; Fax: 011 32 25 196819
* More on CEN and CENELEC can be found in the next
section of this Handbook

EC Committee (On Behalf of the AMCHAM Council)
American Chamber of Commerce in Belgium
avenue des Arts 50, bte 5
B-1040 Brussels, Belgium
Tel: 32 2 237 65 60 11; Fax: 32 2 513 79 28

European Free Trade Association
Brussels Office
118 rue D'Arlon
B-1040 Brussels, Belgium
Tel: 32 2 230 12 23; Fax: 32 2 230 34 75

European Parliament
Seat of the Secretariat
Centre European, Plateau de Kirchberg
L-2929 Luxembourg
Tel: 352 430 01; Fax 352 437 009
or:
Brussels Office
rue Belliard 97-113
B-1040 Brussels, Belgium
Tel: 284 21 11; Fax: 23 69 33

or:
Strasbourg Office
Palias de L'Europe, Place Lenotre
F-67006 Strasbourg, France
Tel: 33 88 37 40 01; Fax: 33 88 25 65 01

**European Telecommunications Standards Institute
(ETSI)**
C-O/CEPT
Telecommunication
CMSN
British Telecommunications International
BT 1-10
120 Holborn, London
E C1N, UK

International Chamber of Commerce
Secretariat
38, Cours Albert ler
F-75008 Paris, France
Tel: 33 1 49 53 28 28; Fax: 33 1 49 42 25 86 63

International Electrotechnical Commission (IEC)
3 Rue de Varembe
Case Postale 131
CH-1211 Geneva 20, Switzerland
Tel: 011 41 22 7340150; Fax: 011 41 22 7333843

International Organization for Standardization (ISO)
Rue de Varembe 1
CH-1211 Geneva 20, Switzerland
Tel: 011 41 22 7490111; Fax: 011 41 22 7333430

GATT
Centre William Rappard
154 Rue de Lausanne
1211 Geneva 21, Switzerland

Access To EU Standards Development

Membership in CEN and CENELEC is limited to the EU
member state standards bodies, as well as the national
standards bodies from the EFTA (European Free Trade
Association) members. The US government and some US
industries have, however, requested *observer status*, wherein
interested US parties could maintain a voteless participation
in CEN and CENELEC meetings on standards issues. To
date, US requests for formal observer status have been
rejected. In some instances, interested parties receive

invitations to attend CEN and CENELEC committee
meetings.

Interested US parties may formally request meetings with
CEN and CENELEC technical committees. Requests may
either be made directly though CEN or CENELEC or
through the American National Standards Institute
(ANSI).*

* Addresses and phone numbers for CEN, CENELEC and
ANSI are available earlier in this appendix.

HOTLINES

EU Hotline

This hotline reports on draft standards of the European Committee on Standardization (CEN), the European Committee for Electrotechnical Standardization (CENELEC) and the European Telecommunications Standards Institute (ETSI). It also provides information on selected EU directives. The recorded message is updated weekly and gives the product, document number and closing date for comments. The hotline telephone number is 301-921-4164.

GATT Hotline*

This hotline provides current information, received from the GATT Secretariat in Geneva, Switzerland, on proposed foreign regulations which may significantly affect trade. The recorded message is updated weekly and gives the product, country, closing date for comments (if any) and Technical Barriers to Trade (TBT) notification number. The hotline telephone number is 301-975-4041.

On-line database services are available in Appendix E of this Handbook.

EC 1992 SINGLE MARKET INFORMATION

For information on the 1992 Single Market program, background information on the European Union, or assistance regarding specific opportunities or potential problems, contact the Office of European Community Affairs' Single Internal Market Information Service at 202-482-5276.

In addition, Department of Commerce industry experts assigned to the 1992 Single Market program are indicated below. Write to the Department of Commerce, Washington, DC 20230:

Aerospace, Deborah Semb, Office of Aerospace, Room 2104, Tel: 202-482-4222.

Autos, Stuart Keitz, Office of Automotive Affairs, Room 4036, Tel: 202-482-0554.

Basic Industries, Claudia Wolfe, Office of Basic Industries, Room 4043, Tel: 202-482-0614 or Mary Ann Smith 202-482-0575.

Chemicals and Allied Products, Fred Siesseger, Office of Basic Industries, Room 4043, Tel: 202-428-0128.

Computer Equipment, Tim Miles, Office of Computer Equipment, Room 2806, Tel: 202-482-2990.

Consumer Goods, Harry Bodansky, Office of Consumer Goods, Room 3013, Tel: 202-482-5783.

Forest Products, Building Materials and Industrial Machinery, Chris Kristensen, Room 4043, Tel: 202-482-0385.

Industrial Trade Staff, Heather West, Room 3814 A, Tel: 202-482-2831.

Microelectronics, Medical Equipment & Instrumentation, Marge Donnelly, Office of Microelectronics, Medical Equipment & Instrumentation, Room 1015, Tel: 202-482-5466.

Telecommunications, Myles Denny-Brown, Office of Telecommunications, Room 1009, Tel: 202-482-4466.

Service Industries, Fred Elliott, Office of Service Industries, Room 1124, Tel: 202-482-3575.

Textiles and Apparel, Office of Textiles, Apparel and Consumer Goods Industries, Room 3001, Tel: 202-482-3737.

US & Foreign Commercial Service, Room 3802, Tel: 202-482-5777; District Office: 800-343-4300, ext. 940.

Additional US Government Contacts

Additional US government contacts for information on European Union matters include:

Office of the US Trade Representative
600 17th St., NW
Washington, DC 20506
Tel: 202-395-3074

European Commission
Delegation of the European Communities
2100 M St., NW
Washington, DC 20037
Tel: 202-862-9500

Department of Agriculture, Foreign Agricultural Service
AG, PO Box 1063
Washington, DC 20250-1063
Tel: 202-720-5267

Small Business Administration, Office of International Trade
409 3rd St., SW, 6th Floor
Washington, DC 20416
Tel: 202-205-6720 or 800-UAS-KSBA (827-5722)

Department of State
Office of European Community and Regional Affairs
Room 6519
Washington, DC 20520
Tel: 202-647-2395; Fax: 202-647-9959

Department of State
Office of Commercial, Legislative & Public Affairs
Room 6822
Washington, DC 20520
Tel: 202-647-2395; Fax: 202-647-5713

US Export-Import Bank
811 Vermont Ave., NW, Room 1207
Washington, DC 20571
Tel: 202-566-8990; Fax: 202-535-3838

For advice or information about any aspect of exporting to the European Union, contact a local International Trade Administration (ITA) District Office or speak to the appropriate desk officer at the US Department of Commerce's International Trade Administration:

Belgium, Luxembourg, Netherlands
202-482-5401

Denmark
202-482-3254

France
202-482-6008

Germany
202-482-2434

Greece, Portugal
202-482-3944

Ireland, Italy
202-482-2177

Spain
202-482-4508

United Kingdom
202-482-3748

Appendix C

ISO 9000 CONSULTANTS AND TRAINING SERVICES

This section profiles 100 companies that provide ISO 9000 consulting and training services. While it is not a comprehensive or official list, it gives a sampling of the ISO 9000 services available to companies seeking information about the registration process.

The section is divided into the following three parts:

- Companies providing ISO 9000 training
- Companies providing ISO 9000 consulting
- Companies providing both services.

Acronyms used by consultants and trainers are listed on the following page.

Editor's Note: *This listing is provided for your information and consideration. CEEM Information Services does not endorse any of the consultants or trainers by including them in this Handbook. CEEM Information Services has made every effort to verify the accuracy of the information contained in this section. Please notify CEEM of any errors.*

ACRONYMS USED BY CONSULTANTS AND TRAINERS

ANSI .... American National Standards Institute

API .... American Petroleum Institute

ASME........... American Society of Mechanical Engineers

ASQC........... American Society for Quality Control

ASTM .... American Society for Testing and Materials

CMC .... Certified Management Consultant

CQA............. Certified Quality Auditor

CQE .... Certified Quality Engineer

CRE .... Certified Reliability Engineers

CSA .... Canadian Standards Association

DoD .... Department of Defense

DOE .... Department of Energy

EQA .... Effective Quality Workshop

FCC .... Federal Communications Commission

GMP .... Good Manufacturing Practices

IAEI.............. International Association of Electrical Inspection

IEEE .... Institute of Electrical and Electronic Engineers

IIE .... Institute of Industrial Engineers

IQA .... Institute for Quality Assurance

ISO .... International Organization for Standardization

MBNQA .... Malcolm Baldrige National Quality Award

NACCB .... National Accreditation Council for Certification Bodies (UK)

NIST .... National Institute of Standards and Technology

PE .... Professional Engineer

PQA .... Preproduction Quality Assurance

QA .... Quality Assurance

QMS .... Quality Management System

RAB .... Registrar Accreditation Board

RBA.............. Registration Board for Assessors

SPC .... Statistical Process Control

TAG .... Technical Advisory Group

TC .... Technical Committee

TQM .... Total Quality Management

COMPANIES PROVIDING ISO 9000 TRAINING

ASQC

611 E Wisconsin Avenue
PO Box 3005
Milwaukee, WI 53201-3005, USA
Tel: 800-248-1946/414-272-8575; Fax: 414-272-1734
Contact: Lori Meisinger Lupton, Manager, Professional
and Technical Development
Services: ASQC provides a variety of professional,
educational and informational programs that reflect
the changing demands of American business and
industry. ASQC operates a series of business groups
that provide leading-edge technology and information
not only to members but to any individual, company
or group interested in improving quality of products
and services. These groups provide books, courses, the
monthly magazine Quality Progress, certification
programs and conferences.
In Business: 47 years
Clients: Northwest Airlines; Viking Laboratories; M&F
Case Company, Inc.; AT&T; TTX Company; I/N
TEK; AFG Industries; US Army; US DOE; Hybricon
Corp.; Acuson; Siemans Solar Industries.
Qualifications/Certifications: ASQC has been a quality
improvement organization in the United States for
almost 50 years. The Society is currently composed of
over 100,000 individual members and over 900
sustaining members in the United States, Canada and
63 other nations. ASQC is the administrator of the
George M. Low Trophy, NASA's Quality and
Excellence Award and the Malcolm Baldrige National
Quality Award. The Professional and Technical
Development department includes nine dedicated
professionals providing services in course development, instructional design, meeting planning,
registration and marketing.

B-K EDUCATION SERVICES

2505 Locksley Drive
Grand Prairie, TX 75050, USA
Tel: 214-660-4575; Fax: 214-641-1327
Contact: Laurie Miller, Director
Services: B-K Education Services' approach translates the
course materials' significance into strategies and tactics
to improve company effectiveness, while concentrating
on techniques that have proven to be effective. The
courses are presented by highly qualified instructors
with diverse backgrounds and experience gained from
designing, directing, implementing and measuring
quality systems in a wide variety of businesses

worldwide. Workshops include the following:
- Effective Quality Auditing Workshop (EQA)
- ISO 9000 Quality Management System Design
  (ISO 9000)
- Effective User Friendly SPC Workshop (SPC)
- ASQC (CQA Examination Refresher Courses)
- Business Process Improvement.

In Business: 7 years
Clients: DuPont, American Airlines, Mobil, Goodyear,
Sandoz Chemical, Occidental Chemical, ALCOA,
Amoco Chemical, AT&T, Federal Express, US Postal
Service, IBM, Nabisco, Johnson & Johnson, Department of Defense.
Qualifications/Certifications: The course authors, Clyde
Brewer, Dick Kleckner and Claude Westbrook, have
over 90 years combined experience in quality systems
management, including 45 years encompassing all
aspects of the certification/accreditation process. They
have conducted hundreds of audits for qualification
and certification of quality systems to worldwide
recognized standards, including the ISO series
standards. Clyde and Dick were instrumental in the
development and initial operations of Quality Systems
Registrars, the first US company to be accredited as a
quality system registration body.

BREWER EDUCATION SERVICES

2505 Locksley Drive
Grand Prairie, TX 75050, USA
Tel: 214-660-4575; Fax: 214-641-1327
Contact: Clyde Brewer, President
Services: Full service quality education specializing in ISO
9000 training. Training is designed to help organiza-
tions learn how to design quality systems for success
rather than just meeting customer or industry
mandates.
In Business: 7 years
Clients: Essex, American Airlines, Asten, Westvaco, Air
Canada, Canadian Airlines, G-Tech, Motorola,
Federal Express, Occidental Chemical.
Qualifications/Certifications: Clyde Brewer has been
involved in training over 6,000 people in six countries
on ISO 9000 and quality system auditing. Clyde is
chairman of the ASME main committee on quality
system accreditation for safety and pollution prevention equipment. In 1983, Clyde wrote the original
draft of API Q1, quality specification for the American
Petroleum Institute.

CARMAN GROUP, INC., THE
1600 Promenade Tower, Suite 950
Richardson, TX 75080, USA
Tel: 214-669-9464; Fax: 214-669-9478
Contact: Jim Carras, President
    Jim Talley, ISO Program Director
    Susi Walworth, Office Manager
Services: The Carman Group, Inc. provides services in the following areas:
- Process management
- ISO 9000
- Cost of quality
- Total Quality Management.

In Business: 6 years
Clients: Pacific Bell, Microwave Networks, Estee Lauder, GTE, Chevron, Campbell Soup, more than 100 small-to-medium-sized companies.
Qualifications/Certifications: The Carman Group's staff include the following: a Texas Quality Award examiner, ASQC fellow, IQA Registered Lead Assessor/auditor and seasoned senior staff executives.

CEEM INFORMATION SERVICES
10521 Braddock Road
Fairfax, VA 22032-2236, USA
Tel: 800-669-1567/703-250-5900; Fax: 703-250-5313
Contact: Leila Martin, Director of Programs
Services: CEEM offers ISO 9000 series quality system management courses, seminars and publications. Course offerings include internal auditing processes, quality systems certification and laboratory quality assurance. Conferences and seminars range from one to five days, depending on the topics and audience. While CEEM designs and sponsors many of its own course offerings, it also co-sponsors courses and seminars with respected national and international organizations. Through its newsletters, guidebooks, handbooks, reports and videos, CEEM Information Services provides executives and managers with up-to-date information on an array of topics, including critical environmental issues, international product standards, laboratory certification and ISO 9000 quality systems registration developments.
In Business: 14 years
Clients: CEEM's co-sponsors include American Association for Laboratory Accreditation (A2LA); American Management Association (AMA); American Petroleum Institute (API); British Standards Institute (BSi); Business Publishers, Inc. (BPI); Inside Washington Publishers; National Association of Manufacturers; Production Consulting & Construction; The Victoria Group.

Qualifications/Certifications: CEEM's staff has extensive experience and expertise in conference management, journalism, marketing and training programs. CEEM is also seeking ISO 9000 certification.

GEORGIA TECH
Center for International Standards & Quality
Georgia Institute of Technology
Atlanta, GA 30332, USA
Tel: 800-859-0968/404-853-0968; Fax: 404-853-9172
Contact: David Clifton, Jr., Director
Services: The Georgia Tech Center for International Standards & Quality (CISQ) offers comprehensive ISO 9000, quality management and international standards information retrieval services. Its full range of services include ISO 9000 open-enrollment courses, in-plant training, assessments, ISO 9000 User Networks and SQUIRE, an international standards information retrieval service.
In Business: 3 years
Clients: CISQ is a national organization serving industries primarily in the Southeast.
Qualifications/Certifications: Drawing on the expertise of private consultants, Georgia Tech research faculty and other quality assurance organizations, CISQ can give your firm the specific assistance it needs to better compete in today's dynamic global arena.

QUALITY FOR AMERICAN COMMUNITIES
1600 Promenade Tower, Suite 955
Richardson, TX 75080, USA
Tel: 214-669-9588; Fax: 214-669-9478
Contact: Jim Carras, President
    Jim Talley, ISO Program Director
    Susi Walworth, Office Manager
Services: Quality for American Communities provides the following services:
- Process management
- ISO 9000
- Cost of quality
- Total Quality Management
- Education quality programs
- Health care quality programs
- Government quality programs.

In Business: 1 year
Clients: Eaton Corporation, Auqua Process, ASOMA Corp., High Strength Steel, Perry Scale, Colcom Corp., AirBorn, Austron, Gruen Corp., PC Dynamics, PM Circuits, The Gammon Group.
Qualifications/Certifications: Quality for American Communities has staff with the following qualifications: a Texas Quality Award examiner, ASQC fellow, IQA Registered Lead Assessor/Auditor and seasoned senior staff executives.

SKILL DYNAMICS
An IBM Company
500 Columbus Avenue
Thornwood, NY 10594, USA
Tel: 800-IBM-TEACh (800-426-8322); Fax: 408-256-5216

Contact: Customer Education/Info Number
5600 Cottle Road, 31K/025
San Jose, CA 95193, USA
Tel: 408-256-1047; Fax:408-256-5216
Gisela E Norwood, ISO 9000 Program Manager

Services: Skill Dynamics, the IBM Education Company provides comprehensive education offerings and services to corporations and institutions in the United States as well as to IBM internal organizations. The ISO 9000 training courses include the following:
- ISO 9000 Executive Overview
- ISO 9000 Series Interpretation
- ISO 9000 Implementation, Documentation and Registration
- ISO 9000 Internal Quality Auditor Training
- ISO 9000 Lead Assessor/Assessor Training.

In Business: 2 years

Clients: Client list available upon request.

Qualifications/Certifications: Skill Dynamics has provided ISO 9000 training to approximately 75 IBM organizations, numerous private businesses and government organizations. Skill Dynamics' services provide its clients with the opportunity to acquire skills and knowledge that will help them implement the ISO 9000 Quality Management System (QMS). Skill Dynamics' links to the IBM consultancy network enables clients to integrate ISO 9000 into their business.

COMPANIES PROVIDING ISO 9000 CONSULTING

ANDERSEN CONSULTING
One Detroit Center
500 Woodward Avenue
Detroit, MI 48226, USA
Tel: 313-596-9400; Fax: 313-596-9731

Contact: Mike J Sovel, Manager of Personnel & Operations
Tel: 313-596-9460; Fax: 313-596-9731

Contact: Robert Denner
Tel: 313-596-9466; Fax: 313-596-9731

Contact: Jeffrey Smith

Services: Andersen Consulting helps its clients change to be more successful. The mechanisms for the change include information technology, business re-engineering, strategic planning, organizational change and manufacturing productivity.

In Business: Andersen Consulting's parent Arthur Andersen & Co. has been in business since 1913. Andersen Consulting became a separate entity in 1989.

Clients: Caterpillar, Ford Motor Company, Harley-Davidson, Steelcase, General Motors, Dow Chemical, Upjohn Corporation, Georgia-Pacific, Domino's Pizza, Philip Morris.

Qualifications/Certifications: Andersen Consulting is ISO 9000 certified in London, Sweden and Australia and has certified auditors on staff. Andersen Consulting is a Baldrige Award finalist.

BREWER & ASSOCIATES, INC.
2505 Locksley Drive
Grand Prairie, TX 75050, USA
Tel: 214-641-8020; Fax: 214-641-1327

Contact: Mike Cobb, President/CEO

Services: Brewer & Associates, Inc. has found that many programs being designed for ISO 9000 introduce pressures and changes that are costly and unnecessary. Brewer & Associates, Inc. offers a full range of quality consulting services, with a specialty in design of quality systems to fit the organization and to operate in conjunction with other quality enhancements, such as TQM, Baldrige, etc.

In Business: 10 years

Clients: Brewer & Associates, Inc. has clients in the United States, Canada, Mexico, Indonesia, Singapore and Malaysia. Clients include: ALCOA, Amtech Systems, Champion Technologies, Honeywell, Huffy Bicycles, Occidental Chemical Corporation, Paxton Polymer Corporation, Hoechst Celanese, Sandoz Chemical, Asten Technologies, Potlatch Corporation, Texas Process Equipment Company, G-Tech Corporation.

Qualifications/Certifications: Brewer & Associates, Inc. has been involved in quality system certification accreditation with the ASME program for Safety and Pollution Prevention Equipment (SPPE) for Offshore Oil and Gas Operations for 14 years. They created the original draft of the Q-1 Specification for a Quality System for the American Petroleum Institute (API) in 1983. They have designed ISO 9000 and equivalent quality system standards for over 300 companies worldwide.

DELOITTE & TOUCHE

285 Peachtree Center Avenue, Suite 2000
Atlanta, GA 30303-1234, USA
Tel: 404-220-1500; Fax: 404-220-1300
Contact: Don Swann, Principal
Services: Deloitte & Touche provides a broad range of
consulting services that help clients implement and
realize the maximum benefits of ISO 9000 registra-
tion. Specific services include the following:
- Strategic evaluation
- Registration preparedness assessment
- Program development
- Implementation management.

In Business: 98 years
Clients: Deloitte & Touche has an international base of
clients from small manufacturers to Fortune 50
companies in a variety of industries. More than 600
clients have annual sales in excess of $1 billion.
Qualifications/Certifications: Deloitte & Touche and its
international affiliates are composed of 56,000
professionals including lead auditors, registered
professional engineers and certified quality engineers
with experience in manufacturing, services and
information technology.

EC TECHNICAL COMPLIANCE

13 Westborn Drive
Nashua, NH 03062, USA
Tel: 603-880-8256; Fax: Available on request
Contact: Jeffrey P Tuthill
Services: EC Technical Compliance offers assistance in
achieving ISO 9000 quality management system
registration and referral of a quality registrar that will
be recognized in the EC Single Market. EC Technical
Compliance assists in developing awareness on the
elements of ISO 9000 series standards within a
company, through seminars and workshops, that are
customized to suit a corporation's needs. Specific
services include the following:
- Planning sessions for quality system registration
  and further implementation of TQM
- In-company workshop for ISO 9000 implementation
- Internal auditor training
- Preliminary audits of company quality system
- Assistance in corrective action planning and
  selection of a quality registrar
- Assistance in documenting the quality system with
  optimum efficiency in mind (review, editing or
  writing quality documentation).

In Business: 2 years
Clients: G.W. Lisk Co., Exide Electronics, Union
Specialists, Krebs Engineers, Ametek Process &

Analytical Controls Division, Barksdale Controls,
Baird Division of IMO, Cybermation Corporation,
Brown & Sharpe, Keithley Metrabyte, Stratus
Computer.
Qualifications/Certifications: Jeffrey Tuthill was previously
employed with the National Standards Authority of
Ireland (NSAI) and set up operations for NSAI in
Merrimack, NH. During his two-year tenure with
NSAI, he received an in-depth education on compliance with the EC Single Market Technical Requirements. With this knowledge, he has developed
programs of complying with the essential requirements
of EC "New Approach" directives, utilizing the Firm
Registration Scheme to ISO 9000/EN 29000 series
standard. Mr. Tuthill offers additional consulting
services related to this proactive program as a
compliance tool in the EC single market, and
promotes utilizing ISO 9000 as a platform for TQM.

INFORMATION MAPPING, INC.

300 Third Avenue
Watham, MA 02154, USA
Tel: 617-890-7003; Fax: 617-890-1339
Contact: Jerry Paradis, Director of ISO 9000 Services
Services: Information Mapping, Inc. (IMI) offers custom
services for ISO 9000 in four areas:
- IMI offers a number of training and consulting
  modules to help clients at every step of the ISO
  9000 certification process. These range from
  executive briefings to strategy sessions to documentation training to pre-certification audits.
- IMI experts work in close collaboration with clients
  to create documentation that meets ISO 9000
  standards, with the goal of helping clients achieve
  ISO certification on their first attempt. This is a
  results-oriented service, based on Information
  Mapping's proprietary, research-based methodology for analyzing, organizing and presenting
  information
- IMI works with clients to establish a logical,
  structured ISO 9000 document control system.
  This ensures that employees, managers, and
  knowledge workers have quick, efficient access to
  all quality systems documentation
- IMI's performance improvement specialists work
  with clients to implement quality management
  systems. This helps clients move beyond ISO 9000
  certification to the organization-wide implementation of a quality management system, focusing on
  performance improvement by linking individual
  job performance to organizational goals.

In Business: 26 years
Clients: AT&T, Bell Atlantic, Dow Chemical Co.,
Eastman Kodak, Intel Corp., Shell Oil Co., Monsanto

Chemical, Allergan, ACT Manufacturing, Exxon, Bausch & Lomb.

Qualifications/Certifications: IMI experts have made presentations at many ISO 9000/quality conferences, including ASQC regional conferences, BOSCON, Northeast Quality Control Conference (10/92), and the American Quality Congress national conference (5/92). IMI staff maintains membership in many ISO/quality organizations, including ASQC. IMI consultants include RAB Accredited Lead Assessors.

ISO 9000 COMMUNICATIONS

PO Box 1110
Amherst, VA 24521, USA
Tel: 804-946-2211/804-845-5271;
Fax: 804-946-2411 (call first)/804-847-2029
Contact: Louise C Rozene, President
James B Kohler II, Director of Marketing
Karen Lupton, Art Director
Services: ISO 9000 Communications provides customized internal communications services, including newsletters, brochures, audit tip cards, handbooks and videos, to companies pursuing ISO certification, continuous improvement and Total Quality Management, as well as post-certification marketing pieces. ISO 9000 Communications also provides newsletters and marketing pieces to ISO consultants and auditing agencies.
In Business: 2 years
Clients: National Quality Assurance, USA, Ericsson GE Mobile Communications, GE Drive Systems, Limitorque Corp.
Qualifications/Certifications: Principals in the company have more than 15 years of experience each in journalism, public relations, graphic design and marketing, the last two of which have been spent solely in quality communications in business.

LAW ENGINEERING

396 Plasters Avenue, NE
Atlanta, GA 30324, USA
Tel: 404-873-4761; Fax: 404-881-6635
Contact: Alpesh Maurya, Staff Engineer
Kenneth B Green, Senior Engineer
R.W. "Bill" Wright, Principal Engineer
Services: Law Engineering provides the following services:
- Pre-audit assessment of organizational structure
- Comparison of existing quality assurance program to ISO 9000 standards
- Modification of existing program to meet ISO 9000 standards.
In Business: 45 years
Clients: Law Engineering has limited experience with ISO 9000 consultation. Its emphasis has been in the area of accreditation for its laboratories. Individual experience within our firm has included military, manufacturing, laboratory and construction audits.
Qualifications/Certifications: Law Engineering was established in 1948 as a testing firm. They are currently an international full service engineering firm with over 4,500 employees. Recognized throughout the world for its engineering consultation, Law Engineering has offered quality assurance program development and implementation services for the past 20 years. Law Engineering currently employs an ISO 9000 lead auditor and has offices registered under the ISO 9000 system.

LEADS CORPORATION

230 N Elm Street
Greensboro, NC 27401, USA
Tel: 800-626-1832/919-275-9989; Fax: 919-275-9952
Contact: J. Michael Crouch, President
Services: LEADS' consultants work closely with senior management to ensure their personal involvement and participation in: assessing their current quality and productivity status, establishing desired business-quality goals, developing a customized implementation plan and strategy, identifying specific improvement opportunities for immediate action, and defining and executing management actions which underscore their commitment.
In Business: 10 years
Clients: Arizona Department of Transportation; Department of Labor, Office of Employment and Unemployment Statistics; Office of Personnel Management; US Air Force Academy; Dow Corning; Empressa Naviera Santa; Hughes Simulation; Life Technologies, Inc.; New York Telephone; Oxford Industries.
Qualifications/Certifications: The experience of the LEADS' consultants includes senior management expertise in the service, manufacturing, human resources, aerospace, and engineering areas. LEADS Corporation is certified by the US Federal Government and the Arizona Department of Transportation to provide ISO 9000 consulting and training services. All consultants bring "hands-on" experience to every task and client.

LEVITT, CONFORD & ASSOCIATES

PO Box 653
Fresh Meadows, NY 11365, USA
Tel: 718-969-1111; Fax: 718-454-7855
Contact: Alan M Levitt, Principal and Managing Director
Services: LC&A provides a full range of integrated, comprehensive consultancy services in information management, information security, data protection and disaster contingency planning. LC&A assesses needs and vulnerabilities, formulates procedures and design, writes and publishes manuals and instructions. LC&A creates forms, paperwork, and datawork (its term for computer-based paperwork) systems vital to implement processes and procedures. LC&A also designs and installs paperwork and datawork simplification programs and business methods improvements that ensure compliance and conformity to established standards.
In Business: 10 years
Clients: All categories of domestic and international businesses, professional firms and organizations (small, medium and large) in the private and public sectors.
Qualifications/Certifications: LC&A are independent consultants, offering a full range of comprehensive, integrated consultancy services in information management, contingency planning and business continuation. The firm's principals and professional staff have earned advanced degrees in business management, engineering, computer and communications technology. Its staff participate as members, officers and advisors to professional societies, learned organizations, and lecture and publish internationally in their various competencies.

MEDICAL TECHNOLOGY CONSULTANTS EUROPE LIMITED (MTC EUROPE)

Arndale House
The Precinct
Egham, Surrey TW20 9HN, England
Tel: 44 784 432233; Fax: 44 784 470026
Contact: Susan Whittle, Ph.D., Senior Consultant
161 Boulevard Reyers
Brussels 1040, Belgium
Tel: 32 27 32 6070; Fax: 32 27 32 5575
Services: MTC Europe offers assessment, auditing and consulting on the implementation of quality systems in the medical device industry. The company recognizes that the quality route (ISO 9001/2 + EN 46001/2) is often the most efficient and satisfactory route to obtaining a CE Mark under the European Medical Device Directive. MTC Europe has, on its permanent staff, an experienced UK Department of Health Lead Assessor registered with the UK Institute

of Quality Assurance. She can assess a manufacturer's present quality status and advise on the steps required to meet quality standards. Medical Technology Consultants Europe, has an integrated advisory and information service, offering accurate, objective, up-to-date data and interpretation as well as practical guidance on what to do and how to do it. This multi-national and multi-lingual team is made up of specialists who offer services in the following areas:
- Business strategy
- Clinicals and monitoring
- Quality Systems
- Product evaluation and submission for regulatory approval
- European standards information
- Regulatory Affairs with particular emphasis on current European regulations and the future Medical Device Directive.

In Business: 4 years
Clients: Several of the world's top 20 health care manufacturers.
Qualifications/Certifications: See Services section.

MILLER COMPANY

3331 Cochran Drive
Lancaster, PA 17601, USA
Tel: 717-898-7971; Fax: 717-285-4426
Contact: Ted A Miller, Consultant
Services: Miller Company specializes in quality systems, manufacturing and general business consulting. These efforts include the establishment of a quality mission, management policies and process documentation. Ted Miller, of Miller Company, has also developed and presented Total Quality Management curriculums including Executive, Middle Management and Technical Training sessions. Prior experience by Mr. Miller has included 15 years of management both domestically and off-shore. In addition, he has successfully implemented total quality systems in commercial and DoD environments. ISO 9000 services provided by Miller Company include the following:
- ISO 9000 assessment and strategy development
- Gap analysis
- Implementation planning
- Education and training
- Implementation support
- Registrar selection
- Pre-assessment audits.

In Business: 4 years
Clients: IBM, Martin Marietta, Hughes Aircraft.
Qualifications/Certifications: Lead assessor training for ISO 9000 certified by the Assessor Registration Board for Assessors of the United Kingdom.

QUALITY IMPROVEMENT CORPORATION

2225 Central Avenue, Suite 3
Columbus, IN 47201, USA
Tel: 812-372-7618; Fax: 812-378-3299
Contact: Robert L Bilz, President
Services: Quality Improvement Corporation specializes in helping companies improve product quality and reduce waste, especially small-to-medium-sized-companies that do not have quality improvement specialists on their payroll. Services include the following:
- Orientation to ISO 9000
- ISO 9000 strategic planning consultation
- Organizational structuring for effective ISO 9000 implementation
- Quality system documentation for ISO 9000
- Quality system evaluation relative to ISO 9000 requirements
- Determination of work required to become registered.

In Business: 9 years
Clients: Decatur Mold, Cairnsair, Survivair, Respiratory Systems, Dayco, Scott Aviation, Interspiro, Cummins Engine Co.
Qualifications/Certifications: Robert L. Bilz, president of Quality Improvement Corporation, has 34 years of experience in the quality field. This experience includes all aspects of quality engineering, quality auditing, inspection, supplier quality improvement, customer quality improvement, and implementation of quality standards such as ISO 9000 and quality management. Mr. Bilz is a registered professional quality engineer, an ASQC Certified Quality Engineer and an ASQC Certified Auditor.

QUALITY INTERNATIONAL, L.L.P.

16009 Country Club Court, Suite 200
Houston, TX 77040, USA
Tel: 713-849-2953; Fax: 713-890-1808
Contact: Bruce Kennedy, Vice President
Services: Quality International (Qi) was formed to meet the special quality system needs of industrial manufacturing clients, with an emphasis on metalworking. Not affiliated with any registrar, Qi is a completely independent consulting firm offering consulting services in the following areas:
- ISO 9000 quality systems design & implementation
- Supplier audits and assessments
- ISO registrar selection assistance
- Product design review
- Failure analysis
- Inspection, test and metrology consulting
- TQM implementation

- Product liability litigation support.

In Business: 2 years
Clients: Metalworking, fabrication, metal plating and finishing, plastic molding, industrial services, distribution.
Qualifications/Certifications: All clients work with Qi principals who have experience in the appropriate industrial sector and are registered quality auditors or professional engineers. Qi staff have worked as line or staff managers in industry with backgrounds in manufacturing operations, material selection, purchasing, industrial design, patent law and critical component failure analysis.

QUALITY MANAGEMENT ASSISTANCE GROUP (QMAG)

1528 Ballard Road
Appleton, WI 54911, USA
Tel: 800-236-7802; Fax: 414-738-7802
Contact: Roy E Rodgers, Principal
Services: QMAG provides guidance in planning, documenting and auditing quality management systems for ISO 9000 and other standards. QMAG also has special programs for smaller businesses.
In Business: 8 years
Clients: Appleton Mills, Schlafer Supply Co., Mercury Marine, Dover Industries, H.G. Weber, Temple Island, International Paper, James River Corp., Wisconsin Cetrifugal, Sargento Foods.
Qualifications/Certifications: Principals have IQA Lead Assessor training, over 10 years experience as quality managers and are ASQC Certified Quality Engineers. Associates have IQA Lead Assessor training and are ASQC Certified Quality Engineers or Certified Auditors. Staff members are represented on quality committees of ASM and TAPPI.

SOFTWARE ENGINEERING PROCESS TECHNOLOGY

2725 NW Pine Cone Drive
Issaquah, WA 98027, USA
Tel: 206-451-1051; Fax: 206-557-9419
Contact: Stan Magee, President
Services: Software Engineering Process Technology is a software consulting firm that specializes in the field of software engineering technology for US and international corporations and organizations. SEPT's mission is to consult with companies concerning national and international software engineering standards that will affect the sales of a company's product. SEPT also consults in the area of software processes improvements. Consulting services are provided in the following areas:
- ISO 9001/9000-3 consulting services

- Life cycle
- Maturity models
- Metrics
- Quality assurance
- Configuration management
- Project management.

In Business: 2 years

Clients: Client list available on request.

Qualifications/Certifications: Stan Magee is president of Software Engineering Process Technology Company and is a member of the US SC-7 TAG (Technical Advisory Group) which determines the US position on international (ISO) software engineering standards. He has been a US delegate to the International Plenary meetings since 1986 and chaired the delegation during the 1987 Paris meeting. Mr. Magee is co-author of the book *Software Engineering Standards and Specifications*, Global Publications, 1993. He lectured on the Impact of International Standards on World Trade at the International Computer Conference in Hong Kong. Mr. Magee is a member of the Software Quality System Registration Committee, which is preparing an American system for certification of ISO 9001 software auditors. He gives seminars on meeting the requirements of ISO 9001/9000-3 to medical device firms. Mr. Magee is active on many governmental, educational and professional boards, and holds a BS from the School of Engineering from Oregon State University and an MBA in international business from the University of Puget Sound.

THOMAS F. BRANDT ASSOCIATES
Innovative Technology Management
PO Box 24765
Edina, MN 55424, USA
Tel: 612-926-9222; Fax: 612-925-2278

Contact: Thomas F Brandt, Principal

Services: Thomas F. Brandt Associates specializes in assisting manufacturing companies use quality as a competitive weapon by:
- Briefing management and employee teams on the content of ISO 9000
- Facilitating design and implementation of ISO 9000-based quality management systems
- Performing pre-assessments of ISO 9000 systems
- Identifying additional resources for specific ISO 9000 system elements
- Coaching implementation teams.

In addition, Thomas F. Brandt Associates work with companies to improve their new product development and introduction processes.

In Business: 5 years

Clients: Despatch Industries, Inc., Harmon Contract

W.S.A., Inc., APG Cash Drawer Company, Cornerstone International Group, BVQI (NA), Inc., Gas Research Institute, Precision Gasket Company, Teltech, Riverside Electronics Ltd., TSI Plastics, Inc.

Qualifications/Certifications: As principal, Thomas F. Brandt consults with manufacturing companies focusing on ISO 9000 quality management, new product development processes and international technology transfer. Mr. Brandt also participated in ISO 9000 pre-registration, registration and surveillance assessments as a sub-contractor to BVQI (NA). He is an IQA Certified Assessor of quality systems and a RAB quality systems provisional Auditor. He was a 1992 and 1993 Senior Examiner for the Minnesota Quality Awards and is a member of the Minnesota High Technology Council, the ASQC, the Minnesota Council for Quality, and a senior member of IEEE.

TQM CONSULTING
9718 Braesmont Drive
Houston, TX 77096, USA
Tel: 713-723-6390; Fax: 713-721-5401

Contact: William E Cox

Services: Total Quality Management (TQM) Consulting offers ISO 9000 quality management systems design and implementation assistance as well as general consulting on any quality improvement process based on principles of Deming, Juran, Ishikawa, Crosby, TQM, SPC, the Baldrige award criteria, or ISO 9000. TQM Consulting takes a flexible approach, designed to tailor a system to fit a company's existing culture and quality improvement process, rather than prescribing a standard "one size fits all" approach. Areas of ISO 9000 expertise include both services and manufacturing, the petrochemical and refining industries, engineering and construction, and research and development.

In Business: 3 years

Clients: Exxon Chemical Co.; Callaway Chemical Co.; Cole Chemical & Distributing, Inc.; Lyondell Petrochemical Co.; Union Carbide Chemicals & Plastics Co. Inc.; Petrolite; KRC Rolls, Inc.; Haltermann, Ltd.; Reliability, Inc.; Data Point, Inc.; International Colombia Resources Corp.; Kirby Corp.; Lagoven, S.A.

Qualifications/Certifications: William Cox has eighteen years of experience in the petrochemical industry, the last eight being dedicated to quality management. Mr. Cox is certified as a quality systems assessor by both the IQA and the ASQC. He is a member of the Board of Examiners for the Texas Quality Award, which is based on the criteria of the Baldrige Award. He has a BSChE degree from the University of Tennessee and has been a member of the ASQC since 1987. TQM

Consulting is a member of The Baldwin Group, an alliance of independent consultants who are able to apply expertise and guidance to businesses on a wide variety of issues. Through this association, specialists are available in strategic planning, productivity, morale, compensation, leadership, development, crisis communications, diversity management, dispute mediation, succession planning and a variety of other issues.

COMPANIES PROVIDING
ISO 9000 TRAINING AND CONSULTING

3C TECHNOLOGIES, INC.
122 Shaffer Blvd.
Bryan, OH 43506, USA
Tel: 800-3C SOLVE; Fax: 419-636-7248
Contact: Devan R Capur, Executive Director
Services: The 3C Consulting Group is dedicated to helping organizations achieve performance excellence by implementing customer-focused, globally-competitive change. Services include the following:
- ISO 9000 implementation assistance and training
  - facilitating ISO 9000 strategic planning
  - organizational ISO 9000 readiness assessments, "gap analysis" and project plans
  - customized training, including internal auditor training
  - consulting and facilitation services for reengineering quality processes
- Total Quality Management (TQM)
- Global diversity and change management
- Business process reengineering.

In Business: 5 years
Clients: The 3C Consulting Group works internationally as well as domestically in the automotive, industrial, software and distribution industries. Clients include: Honda, Ingersoll-Rand, Ferro Corp., Ohio Art, Poly Craft, Component Finishing Corp., the state of Ohio and the federal government.
Qualifications/Certifications: Devan R. Capur, Executive Director of the 3C Consulting Group, has applied TQM, teamwork, business process reengineering and innovative technology to improve organizational performance for more than ten years. Mr. Capur's experience spans both the private and public sector, and he has facilitated ISO 9000 implementations at all levels and functions of organizations. He holds a degree in Industrial Engineering and Operations

Research and has in-depth knowledge of different types of industries, functions, technologies, techniques and international experience. The 3C Consulting group has ASQC RAB Registered Lead Auditors, specialists in the automotive, industrial, software, distribution and international business segments, and experienced implementors and trainers.

ABS CONSULTING SERVICES, INC.
16855 Northchase Drive
Houston, TX 77060-6008, USA
Tel: 800-874-8174/713-873-6800; Fax: 713-874-5991
Contact: Marietta Dar, Market Coordinator
Tel: 800-874-8174/713-874-6426
Contact: Ed Grober, Director, Quality Consulting
Services: ABS Consulting Services, Inc. is a subsidiary of the ABS Group of Companies, Inc. which can provide a wide range of services from consulting on the implementation of a quality system to certification by an internationally recognized registrar. ABS Consulting Services can guide a company in the selection of the appropriate ISO 9000 standard for registration and help establish the system for compliance. To assure success in the shortest time with minimum cost, ABS combines several strengths: knowledge of the standard, experience working with registrars, an effective training program and a proven project management system. ABS Consulting's services include the following:
- Status assessment to compare an existing quality system with the applicable requirements
- Preparation of the plan needed to implement a quality management system and guide a company to successful certification
- Assistance in the development of manuals and procedures

- ABS Consulting Services can conduct ISO 9000 management overviews and detailed training programs on all phases of compliance.

In Business: 24 years

Clients: The ABS Group of Companies is helping hundreds of businesses with their efforts to achieve ISO 9000 certification. The industries ABS works with include: oil field equipment, metals, chemical processing, electronics, computer hardware and software, engineering services, medical diagnostics and transportation.

Qualifications/Certifications: The ABS Group of Companies has been a leader in ISO 9000 implementation for several years. The senior consultants and certified auditors at ABS have guided many businesses, large and small, in achieving ISO 9000 certification and developing effective quality management systems.

ADVANCE CONSULTING INTERNATIONAL LTD.

Unit 8B, Ricebridge
Brighton Road, Bolney
Haywards Heath, West Sussex, England
RH17 5NA
Tel: 44 444 417482; 44 444 881083; Fax: 44 444 414301

Contact: Noel White, Director
751 Oaknoll Drive
Springboro, OH 45066, USA
Tel: 513-885-3919; Fax: 513-885-4319

Contact: Eleanor Roach

Services: ACI's goal is to improve the profitability of client companies. ACI achieves quality and performance improvement at all levels by emphasizing improvement through people and preventive systems. ACI offers a full range of ISO 9000 training and consulting services to prepare all companies, despite their knowledge of ISO 9000, for registration. Their skill base includes TQM, JIT, MRP, QFD, SPC and other quality tools so that ISO 9000 is successfully integrated with these environments. Specific services include the following:

- ISO 9000 strategic planning
- ISO 9000 awareness training (all employee levels)
- Initial benchmarking and gap analysis
- Internal auditor training
- Lead assessor training
- Training to become ISO 9000 trainers
- Documentation review and report
- Pre-registrar assessment and report
- Registrar selection advice
- On-site implementation support.

In Business: 4 years (previously Advance Consulting Services). Active in the United States for two years.

Clients: GTE Concord; BP British Petroleum; SmithKline Beecham; Premark, PMI FEG; Rubbermaid; Reike Corporation; Nucor Steel; Wangtek; HA Guden; Tellabs; Roband.

Qualifications/Certifications: Noel White has extensive quality consulting and training experience spanning 12 years. He holds a post graduate degree in business management studies. His early career included successfully implementing BS 5750 (ISO 9000) and TQM systems, and he has held senior quality positions in blue chip and fortune 500 companies, including GTE and PA Consulting Group. He was the author of BP's Pinnacle Quality Book and he trains lead assessors. He has completed the IQA Lead Assessor Course. Noel spends much of his time in the United States conducting ISO 9000 training and consulting. He is Director of Quality for a UK manufacturing company, and his professional qualifications include: ASQC full member, LicIQA, ISO 9000 Forum member, BSI member and British Institute of Management committee member.

ADVENT MANAGEMENT ASSOCIATES, LTD.

PO Box 3203
West Chester, PA 19381-3203, USA
Tel: 215-431-2196; Fax: 215-431-2641

Contact: Hugh C Lovell, Vice President

Services: Advent's services include a complete ISO 9000 package providing the client with all management assistance and training services necessary to prepare for certification. Since Advent is not involved in the actual certification, total energy is devoted to the implementation of the right mix of quality programs that make sense for the clients' business. Key elements of the service include the following:

- Initial assessment of current quality policies
- Management training in the fundamentals of ISO 9000
- Development of a total quality system
- Policies and procedures
- Auditor training and scheduling of internal audits
- Development of customer and market focus for the organization
- Development of implementation plans
- Training programs for company employees
- Assistance in application for certification
- Pre-assessment audit
- Post-assessment recap and corrective actions
- On-going consulting for recertification and continuous improvement beyond ISO 9000.

In Business: 15 years

Clients: Osram/Sylvania; Johnson Matthey; Courtney Industries; Connecticut Steel; SHW, Inc.; Durham

Industries; Dri-Print; Sartomer International; Schenkers International Forwarders; Omni North America; BDP, Inc.; Intertrans; Pegasus; A. Rifkin; Action Technologies.

Qualifications/Certifications: Advent consultants come from a broad range of backgrounds. Credentials include: PE, IQA Lead Auditor, CQA Lead Auditor and Certified Management Consultant (CMC). Each ISO engagement is lead by a trained lead auditor and supported by trained internal auditors and supporting specialists with a variety of credentials. Staff includes 10 lead auditors, 16 internal auditors and more than 20 consultants.

ALLAN SAYLE ASSOCIATES
Redruth
The Shrave
Four Marks, Hampshire GU 34 5BH
United Kingdom
Contact: Allan Sayle
Services: Allan Sayle Associates offers audits and assessments (internal and external), provides ISO 9000 compliance system development, integrates ISO 9000 systems with customers' TQM programs, and provides training and advice during implementation, as well as providing total quality programs. Self-audit training is available through videos and workbooks. Four-day quality assurance audit training course is available.
In Business: 10 years
Clients: Digital Equipment, British Standards Institution, British Nuclear Fuels, New Zealand Dairy Board, Datachecker USA, Mobil, Sir Alexander Gibb & Partners, Norsk Air, Rolls Royce, Foxboro, James Williamson & Partners.
Qualifications/Certifications: Allan Sayle's qualifications include: BSc (Hons) from the University of Strathclyde, Fellow of the Institute of Quality Assurance, Member of the American Society for Quality Control. He has been a quality assurance professional for over twenty years and held positions of increasing seniority including Corporate QA Manager of a well-known international engineering company. An internationally-known speaker on quality management, he has had many papers published. Mr. Sayle still performs internal and external audits for clients all over the world. Until June 1991 he was a Member of Council of the Institute of Quality Assurance and a past member of its Editorial Committee. He is a member of the Editorial Board of Managerial Auditing Journal, a premier publication in that field; a member of the Canadian Standards Association's Auditing Standards Committee and of its Software Quality Assurance Standards Committee;

and a member of the ASQC's Quality Audit Technical Committee. He is special adviser to the Singapore Quality Institute for its Assessor Registration Scheme and a member of its Board of Certification & Accreditation. A Lead Auditor qualified in accordance with the requirements of ANSI N45.2.23 since 1977, Mr. Sayle is also an accredited Lead Assessor with the British National Registration Scheme for Assessors of Quality Systems. Mr. Sayle is also one of the officially designated Lead Auditors for the Standards Association of New Zealand.

APPLIED QUALITY SYSTEMS
2845 Hamline Avenue N
St. Paul, MN 55113, USA
Tel: 612-633-7902; Fax: 612-633-7903
Contact: Mark Ames, Chief Executive Officer
Peter Ryhn, President
Services: Applied Quality Systems offers ISO 9000 and Total Quality Management consulting and education for clients in the manufacturing, service and public sectors. Headquartered in Minneapolis/St. Paul, its professional staff provides services to clients from coast to coast. Applied Quality Systems is committed to tailoring its services to meet the unique needs of an organization. From planning and basic education, to successful implementation guidance, Applied Quality Systems is committed to its clients' success. Its approach to ISO 9000 focuses on interactive learning through employee knowledge and participation. This strategy is designed to add value to an organization in addition to compliance with ISO 9000. Applied Quality Systems quality offerings include the following:
- RAB accredited lead auditor training
- ISO implementation
- Documenting an ISO 9000 system
- ISO internal auditing
- Basic concepts of quality for leaders and teams
- Total Quality Management assessment
- Total Quality Management implementation
- Team building
- Strategic thinking and planning
- Basic and advanced leadership training
- Problem solving
- Train-the-Trainer skills
- Quality functional deployment.

In Business: 6 years
Clients: Colder Products Company, Houston Atlas, Perkin-Elmer (Physical Electronics Division), Phoenix International, Ramsey Technology (A Baker Hughes Company), Seagate Technology, Spectrace Instruments (A Baker Hughes Company), Texas Nuclear (A

Baker Hughes Company), Viking Press (Banta Corporation), Young Manufacturing, US Navy, Alcon Surgical.

Qualifications/Certifications: Applied Quality Systems' instructors are professional and experienced practitioners. Their backgrounds include extensive experience in the manufacturing and service sectors. Certifications include: CQE, CQA and RAB Lead Assessor. All staff members are ASQC members.

ARC PROFESSIONAL SERVICES GROUP, INC.

1340 Ashton Road, Suite E
Hanover, MD 21076, USA
Tel: 410-850-5411; Fax: 301-621-1930
Contact: Stephen T Gaw, Principal
Services: ARC provides evaluation and training to assist companies in becoming certified to ISO 9000 standards. ARC provides information for management and employees to facilitate an understanding of the ISO 9000 quality management system requirements. This can assist companies to compete in the global market place.

In Business: 20 years
Clients: Fortune 500 companies, medium and small businesses. ARC provides government agencies the same services. Emphasis is in the area of information technology.
Qualifications/Certifications: ARC draws on its worldwide staff to assist companies in preparation for becoming ISO 9000 compliant. ARC personnel and specialized consultants provide customers with cost effective service, and have been trained by accredited organizations in the areas of lead auditor, internal audits and document preparation.

ARCH ASSOCIATES

15770 Robinwood Drive
Northville, MI 48167-2041, USA
Tel: 313-420-0122; Fax: 313-420-0122
Contact: William M Harral, Director
Services: Arch Associates provides comprehensive, customized total quality support based on the ISO 9000 series and applicable regional, national, industry, product, market sector and customer requirements. The goal is to implement global competitiveness within client organizations that is aligned with their strategy, vision and culture. Arch Associates' scope of support services ranges from a complete cycle of strategic planning, quality system planning, development, documentation, training, implementation and ongoing oversight to specific projects for training, system enhancement or independent assessments against numerous standards. Assessments may focus

on needs assessments, facilitate qualification/ certification to different customer or public standards, or support EN45014 self-declaration for manufacturers of EC-regulated products. Arch provides an RAB accredited, 16-hour ISO 9000 training course that fulfills certification training requirements for CQAs.

In Business: 10 years
Clients: Clients are primarily in the following industries: automotive, general manufacturing, basic metals, metal fabricating or forming, machinery/tools design and manufacture, electromechanical, plastic, microbiology, contracted design and other service industries. Client size ranges from small organizations such as Continental Carbide and McQuade Industries that have been featured in Detroit Business and Nation's Business as outstanding examples of small-organizations with high quality-based growth during the recession, to the over 3000-person GM-Cadillac Grand Blanc Stamping Plant which received the Malcolm Baldrige National Quality Award.
Qualifications/Certifications: William M. Harral, QS-LA, CQE, CQA, CRE, PEIT, has 20 years experience in various engineering, manufacturing, planning and quality management positions at Ford Motor Company prior to founding Arch Associates in 1983. Mr. Harral is author of numerous articles, books and handbooks on quality. He is an active ASQC fellow, past-chair of the Greater Detroit section, Region 10 section's deputy director, Automotive Division councillor, Audit Division standards committee, Quality Management Division Technology Group chair and Executive Secretary of the General Technical Council. At Automotive Industry Action Group (AIAG), he has served on the Continuous Quality Improvement Project Team since 1984. He currently chairs the Standards Committee and serves as ISO 9000 series technical advisor to the Truck Advisory Group. He is a corporate member of Institute of Quality Assurance in the UK and company voting representative to American National Standards Institute (ANSI). Mr. Harral holds an MBA from the University of Michigan and a BS in industrial and systems engineering from Ohio State University.

ASSOCIATED BUSINESS CONSULTANTS, INC.

201 E Kennedy Boulevard, Suite 715
Tampa, FL 33602, USA
Tel: 813-223-3008; Fax: 813-223-5406
Contact: Malcolm Harris, President
1916 14th Street
Tampa, FL 33605, USA
Tel: 813-223-3008; Fax: 813-223-5406
Contact: Steve Pearson, Vice President

Services: Associated Business Consultants, Inc. provides consulting in ISO 9000 preparation, quality auditing, procedures development, and quality systems. Registered lead assessors from the United Kingdom and the United States are on staff to perform quality system assessments. They provide consulting and training in SPC, ISO 9000 and BS7750 compliance and auditing techniques.

In Business: 7 years in the United Kingdom, 2 years in the United States

Clients: Clients are involved in bulk materials, plastics, metals, wood, electronics, equipment, accounting, construction, distribution and computers.

Qualifications/Certifications: Staff members are registered lead assessors, CQAs and CQEs.

BOOZ•ALLEN & HAMILTON, INC.

4330 East West Highway
Bethesda, MD 20814, USA
Tel: 301-907-4070; Fax: 301-951-2255
Contact: Joyce Doria, Vice President
Services: Booz•Allen & Hamilton, Inc. provides consulting services for preregistration assessment, registration support and strategic quality planning as well as training workshops.

In Business: 79 years

Clients: Fortune 200 firms, small and medium-size companies, and all federal government agencies.

Qualifications/Certifications: Booz•Allen & Hamilton, Inc. staff is composed of lead auditors, quality professionals, and subject matter experts from a wide range of industries and technologies located through-out the world. Booz•Allen & Hamilton, Inc. is not affiliated with any ISO 9000 registrar.

BQS, INC.

110 Summit Avenue
Montvale, NJ 07645, USA
Tel: 800-624-5892/201-307-0212; Fax: 201-307-1778
Contact: Peter Melville, Director of Consulting
Services: BQS, Inc. is a quality assurance organization that specializes in consulting, training, auditing and source inspection. Services include the following:
- Preparation for ISO 9000 registration
- Internal Auditing Training Program
- Document Control Workshop
- Corrective Action Workshop
- First article, in-process and final inspection
- Audits: government or customized.

In Business: 8 years

Clients: BP Chemical, Allied Bendix Aerospace, Hoechst Celanese, ITT Cannon, Eastman Kodak, Ingalls Shipbuilding, Bradfoote Gear, Unaform, Fanfield

Manufacturing, Sikorsky Aircraft.

Qualifications/Certifications: BQS, Inc. is involved with various industries providing quality assurance services. BQS, Inc.'s expertise is in the following listed industries: gear manufacturing, heavy equipment, computer, paper, chemical and related process industries. Each facilitator has specific training and background in assessing, installing and operating ISO 9000 registered systems.

BTI SERVICES, INC.

1815 Ironstone Manor, Suite 16B
Pickering, Ontario L1W 3W9, Canada
Tel: 416-839-4697; Fax: 416-839-0752
Contact: Massey Ghatavi, Quality Management Practitioner
2100 Roosevelt Avenue
PO Box 2208
Springfield, MA 01102-2208, USA
Tel: 413-747-3341; Fax: 413-747-3576
Services: BTI Services, Inc. provides the following services:
- ISO 9000 quality system strategy and planning
- ISO 9000 quality management and assurance development
- ISO 9000 implementation and coaching
- ISO 9000 education and training in the following areas:
  - quality planning and implementation steps
  - quality system documentation
  - internal quality auditing
  - ISO 9000 lead auditor training (RAB and IQA)
  - ISO 9000 for service industry
  - ISO 9000 for software development
  - ISO 9000 for environmental, food and health care industries.

In Business: 10 years

Clients: Chicago Engineering, Society for Plastics Industry of Canada, Enviro Care, Emphenol, Horn Plastics, NCR, Smith & Wesson, Calcutron, Welland Chemical, Phillips and several more in both the service and manufacturing industries.

Qualifications/Certifications: BTI Services, Inc. was established to focus on assisting organizations make the transition into a competitive market environment across many sectors of industry and commerce in North America. The principals of BTI bring extensive experience in providing organizations, both in the service and manufacturing industries, the required framework and discipline to achieve their business goals and objectives. The senior principals of BTI have experience in industry and as management consultants working with major international organizations with whom BTI Services still maintains an associate relationship.

- IQA Certified ISO 9000 Lead Assessor
- RAB Certified ISO quality systems Lead Auditor
- American Society for Quality Control (ASQC)
- Association for Manufacturing Excellence (AME).

BYWATER

Two Stamford Landing
68 Southfield Avenue
Stamford, CT 06902, USA
Tel: 203-973-0343/4; Fax: 203-973-0345
Contact: Vic Allum, Vice President Marketing
Phil Midgley, Principal Consultant
119 Guildford Street
Chertsey Surrey, KT16 9AL, England
Tel: 44 932 567866; Fax: 44 932 568157
Contact: Mike Carton, Marketing Coordinating
Services: Bywater is dedicated to services in quality
management, providing a wide range of consulting,
training and associated services to all sectors of
industry. Bywater's consulting services include the
following:
- Benchmarking
- Strategic guidance
- Process management
- ISO 9000 implementation
- Managing continuous improvement.
Bywater's training courses include the following:
- Introduction to Quality Management and ISO
9000-Series
- Planning and Implementing a Quality System
- Quality Assurance Auditor Training.
In Business: 11 years
Clients: Aer Lingus, BP Nutrition, British Steel, Cincinnati
Bell, ICI (C & P), Monsanto, Philips USA, Rank
Hovis, Shell International, Smith & Wesson.
Qualifications/Certifications: Bywater's consultants and
trainers are permanent salaried staff, operating from
bases throughout the United Kingdom, Europe,
North America and Australasia. They are all experienced, professionally qualified practitioners with
substantial hands-on experience in turning quality
management principles into practice. In addition,
many are registered lead assessors with specialist
knowledge in the automotive, chemical, electronics,
food, services and software industries.

COLUMBIA QUALITY, INC.

PO Box 506
Orefield, PA 18069, USA
Tel: 610-391-0270; Fax: 610-391-9497
Contact: J P Russell, President
Services: Columbia Quality, Inc. provides pre-certification
audits and consulting by certified or registered

auditors. CQI offers training programs and services for
implementing ISO 9000.
In Business: 7 years
Clients: Allied-Signal; American Cyanamid; Internal
Revenue Service; Owens/Corning Fiberglass; John
Deere, Inc.; Cargill, Inc.; Calumet Lubricants Co.;
AEG Transportation Systems; Tecumseh Products
Company.
Qualifications/Certifications: CQI's staff consists of RBA
(IQA) registered assessors and ASQC certified quality
auditors.

COMPLIANCE QUALITY *INTERNATIONAL*

#5 Hidden Trail
Lancaster, NY 14086-9685, USA
Tel: 716-685-0048; Fax: Same
Contact: Allen R Bailey, President
4883 Hawaiian Terrace
Cincinnati, OH 45223, USA
Tel: 513-542-2086
Contact: George Reed, Partner
Services: Compliance Quality International provides
customized training on documentation, internal and
customer auditing, implementation, team building
and laboratory certification. Their trained profession-
als can tailor the training to any level of an organiza-
tion. Compliance Quality International also provides
assistance for a company's compliance needs for both
ISO 9000 certification and product certification.
In Business: 2 years
Clients: Compliance Quality International specializes in
small-to-medium-size medical devices and electronic
companies.
Qualifications/Certifications: Compliance Quality
International's staff consists of National Registration
Scheme trained assessors, and subject matter experts
from a wide range of technical backgrounds and
market sectors who are all quality professionals.

CONSULTANT IN QUALITY

319 Friendship Street
Iowa City, IA 52245, USA
Tel: 319-337-8283; Fax: 319-338-3320
Contact: Richard B Stump, Principal Consultant
Services: Services are offered in all aspects of total quality
for manufacturing, service and government organiza-
tions. Specialties include the following:
- Executive awareness and overview of ISO 9000 and
Total Quality Management concepts
- Internal quality audit training and assistance in
performing audits
- Third-party assessment and preparation for ISO
9000 registration

- Internal or national competition using the Malcolm Baldrige National Quality Award criteria. Dick Stump emphasizes quantitative problem-solving techniques and measures of achievement. Consultant in Quality has network associations with a wide range of other expert consultants to meet client needs.

In Business: 8 years

Clients: Motorola, Inc.; Dana Corp.; Intel Corp.; CSX Corp. (Commercial Services); Baxter Healthcare; US Department of Education and a variety of smaller businesses, working in such areas as electronics, plastics, hoists, construction, forgings, electric ballasts and construction engineering.

Qualifications/Certifications: Dick Stump is an ASQC Certified Quality Engineer, an ASQC Quality Auditor, a Certified Quality Action Team Facilitator and a BSi trained Lead Auditor for ISO 9000 programs. Mr. Stump is experienced in software quality assurance related to data processing and service industry needs. He is a technical expert for the NVLAP Fasteners and Metals program sponsored by NIST.

DELAWARE COUNTY COMMUNITY COLLEGE
Center for Quality and Productivity
901 S Media Line Road
Media, PA 19063-1094, USA
Tel: 215-359-5288; Fax: 215-359-7384
Contact: Paul L McQuay, Executive Director
Tel: 215-359-7344; Fax: 215-359-7393
Contact: Donald K Entner, Director
Tel: 215-359-5035; Fax: 215-359-7393
Contact: Angela R. Kitson, Marketing Manager
Services: Delaware County Community College provides knowledge and direction to companies who are seeking ISO certification. DCCC's consulting services will prepare organizations for compliance with ISO 9000 standards. Services include the following:

- Pre-assessment audits
- ISO workshops
- Internal audit systems
- Quality manual review
- Preparation for registration
- Total Quality Management training/consulting.

In Business: 25 years

Clients: Defense Personnel Support Center; Life Sciences International; Mars Electronics International; Matheson Gas Products; North American Drager; Tecot Electric Supply Company, Inc.; Teleflex, Inc.; US Coast Guard; US Steel - Fairless Plant; Speakman Company.

Qualifications/Certifications: Delaware County Community College provides training and consulting services to organizations implementing Total Quality Management and to companies seeking ISO 9000 certification. The College has received the approval of the Federal Quality Institute to provide assistance to federal agencies implementing TQM and considering the implications of ISO certification in their procurement process. The College's ISO trainers and consultants are certified lead auditors who have worked with manufacturing, service and government agencies.

DILLINGHAM QUALITY CONSULTING, INC.
37264 Thinbark Road
Wayne, MI 48184, USA
Tel: 313-721-5606; Fax: 313-721-8271
Contact: David R Dillingham, President
Services: Dillingham Quality Consulting provides consulting in ISO 9000 introduction, preparation, quality auditing, quality manuals and procedures, development and quality systems leading to TQM. Dillingham Quality Consulting utilizes consulting and training to help start the business or build on what has already been developed.

In Business: 5 years, plus 40 years working on quality systems.

Clients: Automotive suppliers, general manufacturing, basic metals, metal fabricating, machine tool, plastic molding. Examples include: Truesdell Enterprises, Budd Corp., Hydro Aluminum-Bohn, ITT Teves, Beaver Industries, Select Tool & Gage and Koppy Corporation.

Qualifications/Certifications: David Dillingham was employed at General Motors for 37 years. He had a number of management positions in purchasing, reliability and quality control. He is a past chairman of the Greater Detroit Section of ASQC. He is a Certified ASQC Reliability Engineer, Quality Engineer, Quality Auditor and a Certified RAB Quality Systems Lead Auditor. Mr. Dillingham has a network of eight former GM executives, managers and engineers who are active in the quality systems field. All consultants bring hands-on experience to each client and task. Mr. Dillingham has established a teaching and working relationship with Washtenaw Community College, Macomb Community College and Schoolcraft College. These facilities could be utilized for training, if required.

DONALD W. MARQUARDT AND ASSOCIATES

1415 Athens Road
Wilmington, DE 19803, USA
Tel: 302-478-6695; Fax: 302-478-9329
Contact: Donald W Marquardt, President
Services: Donald W. Marquardt and Associates provides
  consulting and training in all phases of preparing for
  ISO 9000 certification including strategic quality
  planning. Consulting and training services are
  provided in designing and analyzing experiments, and
  Statistical Process Control using the Twin Metric
  improvement of Shewhart and CUSUM methods.
In Business: 2 years
Clients: Industrial companies and trade associations.
Qualifications/Certifications: Mr. Marquardt was with the
  Du Pont Company for 39 years. His assignments
  included management of engineering services and
  consulting services. He organized and managed the
  Du Pont Quality Management and Technology
  Center. Mr. Marquardt is Chairman of the US
  Technical Advisory Group and leader of the US
  delegation to the ISO/TC176 committee, which
  developed the ISO 9000 series standards. He was chair
  of the ISO/TC176 international task force that
  prepared the Vision 2000 report establishing the
  strategic intent for implementing and revising the ISO
  9000 series in the 1990s. He is a former president of
  the American Statistical Association, a Shewhart
  Medalist of the American Society for Quality Control,
  and has been a Senior Examiner for the Malcolm
  Baldrige National Quality Award. He has an IQA-
  approved Lead Assessor training certificate. He is a
  member of the Board of Directors of the Registrar
  Accreditation Board.

DUPONT ISO 9000 SERVICES

1007 Market Street
Brandywine Building, Room 11209
Wilmington, DE 19898, USA
Tel: 800-441-8040; Fax: 302-774-2135
Services: DuPont ISO 9000 Services offers seminars and
  consulting services to companies that desire to
  implement an effective quality system that meets ISO
  9000 standards. DuPont can help companies increase
  their competitive advantage through measurable and
  sustainable performance improvement and/or reduced
  costs of operations.
In Business: 4 years
Clients: Aluminum Company of America, AT&T
  Technology Systems, Atomic Energy of Canada
  Limited, The Bendix Corporation, Bethlehem Steel
  Corporation, Citgo Petroleum Corporation, The
  Clorox Company, Control Data, Adolph Coors Co.,

Corning Glass Works, R.J. Reynolds Tobacco Co.
Qualifications/Certifications: DuPont consultants have
  helped DuPont achieve over 200 ISO 9000 registrations worldwide. Their business perspective, hands-on
  experience and skills work effectively with all levels of
  an organization.

EASTERN MICHIGAN UNIVERSITY
Center for Quality

34 N Washington
Ypsilanti, MI 48197, USA
Tel: 800-932-8689/313-487-2259; Fax: 313-481-0509
Contact: Terry Carew, Accounts Manager
  Kathy A Trent, Program Coordinator
Services: Eastern Michigan University Center for Quality
  (formerly Corporate Services) provides training,
  consulting and assistance to some of the world's largest
  corporations. The Center for Quality offers many
  programs on-site including the following:
  - Total Quality Management
  - Applied statistical process control
  - SPC implementation
  - Quality operating systems implementation
  - Benchmarking
  - Statistical Process Control I and II
  - Design of Experiments I and II
  - ISO quality systems standards
  - ISO 9000 auditing.
  All Center for Quality programs can be customized to
  meet and exceed the specific needs of an organization.
In Business: 10 years
Clients: Allegro Microsystems, Allied Signal, American
  Yazaki, Ervin Industries, Ford Motor Company,
  General Motors Corporation, GNB Incorporated,
  Harman Electronics, Imperial Oil, Johnson Controls,
  Mazda, Motorola, Philips Display, Raychem, Rouge
  Steel, Tilden Mines, TRW, W.R. Grace.
Qualifications/Certifications: The Center for Quality's
  instructors are seasoned trainers with extensive
  industrial experience. Over 20,000 individuals from
  over 4,000 companies have participated in EMU
  sponsored training programs.

EXCEL PARTNERSHIP, INC.

75 Glen Road
Sandy Hook, CT 06482, USA
Tel: 203-426-3281; Fax: 203-426-7811
Contact: David N Middleton, Vice President
Services: EXCEL Partnership, Inc., is an international
  quality management consultancy and training
  organization with offices in both the United Kingdom
  and the United States EXCEL Partnership can
  integrate a "quality philosophy" by developing quality
  management systems to ISO 9000 in the manufactur-

ing, process and service industries. EXCEL offers a variety of "tailor-made" ISO 9000 courses and regular training courses that cover all aspects of quality management. Consulting support is designed to complement the training courses with emphasis placed on a pragmatic "hands-on" approach.

In Business: 5 years

Clients: Over 300 companies in the United States including: Compaq Computer Corporation; BP Chemicals, Inc.; GE Medical Systems; Corning Incorporated; Chevron Chemical Co.; Hewlett-Packard.

Qualifications/Certifications: The EXCEL Partnership includes staff who have worked at the forefront of ISO 9000 and quality auditor training in the United Kingdom for over a decade. Their courses are accredited by both the RAB in the United States and the IQA in the United Kingdom.

FED-PRO, INC.

5615 Jensen Drive
Rockford, IL 61111, USA
Tel: 800-833-3776; Fax: 815-282-4304
Contact: Serge E Gaudry, Senior Consultant
Services: FED-PRO provides ISO 9000 training and offers computer software to assist in the preparation of an ISO 9001, 9002 or 9003 quality assurance manual. Services have included providing specialized on-site training on the US Department of Defense's MIL-Q-9858A and MIL-I-45208A specifications. To obtain timely information on the ISO standards, FED-PRO now has a representative based in London. The latest video training program offered by FED-PRO is a 30-minute overview on the revisions made to the ISO standards in ISO /DIS 9000-1, ISO/DIS 9001, 9002, 9003 and ISO/DIS 9004-1.

In Business: 11 years

Clients: Eli Lilly & Co., James River Corp., E.I. duPont, GAF Building Materials, Allied Signal, TRW, Raytheon Corp., Fairchild Aircraft Corp., AT&T, General Electric, Olin Chemicals, North American Salt Co., Hoke Rubber Products Co., Eastman Kodak, Martin Marietta.

Qualifications/Certifications: FED-PRO, Inc. has been providing quality assurance training services to the US defense industry for the past ten years. FED-PRO consultants have written quality assurance manuals for firms ranging from twenty-person machine shops to Fortune 500 companies. FED-PRO has also been involved in quality-related projects with the US Navy nuclear program. During the past three years, they have taken an active role in assisting defense clients in adapting their quality program to the ISO 9000

standards. In 1991, FED-PRO published a video training program on ISO 9000 as well as a software program to assist its clients to prepare an ISO 9001, 9002 or 9003 quality assurance manual.

GILBERT EUROPE

US Operations
PO Box 1498
Reading, PA 19603, USA
Tel: 215-775-2600; Fax: 215-775-9736
Contact: Gil Dutton, TickIT Project Manager
    Tom Heist, Manager Quality Services
Gilbert Europe (UK)
Fraser House, 15 London Road
Twickenham, TW1 3ST, England
Tel: 081-891-4383; Fax: 081-891-5885
Contact: K H Millard, Managing Director
Services: Gilbert Europe was formed in 1981 to act as a focal point to provide international management consulting services and to provide auditing, training and consulting in support of ISO 9000 quality management systems development and implementation. Gilbert Europe provides a full range of quality management system services and has extensive experience in implementing quality systems based on ISO 9000 and similar standards. Services include the following:

- Quality systems planning
- Training in quality management
- Development and implementation of business process assessments/re-engineering in support of continuous quality improvement.

Gilbert Europe also provides TickIT software segment training, consulting and auditing services.

In Business: 13 years

Clients: ARCO Chemical Company, Phillips Petroleum, EG&G, E.I. duPont, Westinghouse, Department of Energy (US), Department of Health (UK), ASQC, Hewlett-Packard, AT&T, British Rail, Bellcore, Allied Signal, Alcon, YAUSA-Exide, E. Penn Manufacturing.

Qualifications/Certifications: Gilbert Europe (UK) is registered under ISO 9001 by BSI to provide quality management consulting, training, auditing and business process assessments. The Gilbert Europe Lead Auditor Training Program was accepted by the IQA as the model for lead auditor training programs. Gilbert Europe developed the registered TickIT Assessors' Training Course for the department for Enterprise (DTI) in the United Kingdom.

INDEPENDENT QUALITY CONSULTANTS

7480 W Colorado Drive
Lakewood, CO 80232-6970, USA
Tel: 303-989-1210; Fax: 303-989-0157
Contact: G (Jay) H Jones, Sr.
Services: Independent Quality Consultants' services include the following:
- ISO/TQM/SPC/MBNQA assessment
- Program development, training, & implementation.

In Business: 9 years
Clients: Coleman Outdoor Products; Coors Industries; Lear Siegler; Unocal 76 Corporation; Molycorp, Inc.; SAS Circuits; Defense Contract Management Command; Ohmeda Medical.
Qualifications/Certifications: Principal consultant, Jay Jones, is a graduate of California State University - Long Beach, a past Chairman of the Denver Section of the ASQC, and a senior member of the ASQC. He is a certified quality auditor, quality engineer, reliability engineer, and mechanical inspector.

INTEGRATED QUALITY SYSTEMS, INC. (IQS)

20525 Center Ridge Road, Suite 400
Cleveland, OH 44116, USA
Tel: 800-635-5901/216-333-1344; Fax: 216-333-3752
Contact: John M Cachat, President
Craig L Young, Vice President
Services: IQS provides consulting and training services, supported by a line of software products. IQS has implementation-focused services and provides software tools to make it happen.

In Business: 7 years
Clients: Amoco Laser Company; Birmingham Metal Products; Gables Engineering; Honeywell, Inc.; Kaiser Aluminum; Litton Industries Automotive; Parker Hannifin - Control; Rockwell - Rocketdyne Division; Union Carbide; C&P Company, Inc.; Westinghouse Electric.
Qualifications/Certifications: IQS has years of hands-on experience, backed by extensive academic credentials. IQS has helped several organizations prepare for and pass ISO 9000 assessments. IQS' software product also helps clients with ISO 9000 certification.

INTERNATIONAL SYSTEMS REGISTRARS, LTD.

15005 W San Mateo Drive
New Berlin, WI 53151-4350, USA
Tel: 414-785-1867; Fax: 414-785-1867
Contact: Dennis L Gorectke, President
Services: International Systems Registrars Ltd. is a private consulting, auditing, training and registration referral service firm for companies seeking ISO 9000 series quality systems registration. Made up of quality professionals with many years of experience, ISRg.

Ltd. helps companies with a wide variety of quality needs. ISRg. Ltd. provides complete ISO 9000 registration services including the following:
- Executive overview
- Survey audit and project estimate
- Develop action plan with ISO team
- Internal auditor training referral
- Documentation assistance (quality manual and quality systems procedures)
- Interim audits as documentation is developed
- Referral application to a competent registrar
- In-depth pre-assessment audit
- Follow-up with third party audits to maintain registration.

In addition ISRg. Ltd. provides a self-assessment package for registration that includes the following:
- ISO 9001 self audit matrix
- 2 ISO 9001 registrar approved manuals
- 2 Checklists, one for survey audit, the other for in-depth pre-assessment audits based on the ISO 9000-2 guidance standard.

In Business: International Systems Registrars Ltd. has been incorporated since July 21, 1992
Clients: La Belle Industries, Quality Calibration Services, Eaton Corporation - Cutler Hammer Products Division, Spacesaver Corporation, Plexus Corporation - Electronics Assembly Division, Nelson Container Corporation, Monopanel Technologies, Johnson Controls - Battery Division, Northwestern Industrial Distributors.
Qualifications/Certifications: Dennis Gorectke is president of International Systems Registrars Ltd. He is a Certified Quality Auditor by the ASQC, a Certified Quality Engineer and a Certified Quality Technician. Mr. Gorectke has more than 20 years of quality engineering and quality auditing experience in many industries including industrial and electromechanical controls, motorcycles, transformers, robotics and others. In addition, he has consulted with more than 20 Wisconsin area corporations, helping three achieve ISO 9000 registration.

INTERTEK TECHNICAL SERVICES

9900 Main Street
Fairfax, VA 22031, USA
Tel: 703-ISO-9000 ext. 3116; Fax: 703-273-4124
Contact: Frederick J Becker, Director, Training and Consulting
Services: INTERTEK TECHNICAL SERVICES provides consulting services in preparation of quality management system certification as well as ISO 9000 training courses including: 5-Day Lead Assessor and 2-, 3- and 4-Day Introduction and Practical Auditing to the ISO

9000 Series of Standards. INTERTEK's 36-hour Lead Assessor course satisfies additional criteria by being recognized by both the IQA and the RAB. This requirement is mandatory for any student who wishes to become a registered assessor/lead assessor. INTERTEK TECHNICAL SERVICES also provides quality contract services that include management services, consulting, training, systems development, audits, surveys and inspections as well as key supplier services. INTERTEK'S sister company, Intertek Services Corp., is accredited to perform quality management system certification and registration. INTERTEK's corporate headquarters is located in Fairfax, Virginia with its west coast office located in the Los Angeles area. INTERTEK has ten domestic regional offices strategically located throughout North America and nine international offices to support and satisfy its customers' requirements.

In Business: 20 years

Clients: Fortune 500 companies as well as smaller companies in the aerospace, aircraft, automotive, computer, communications, electronics, medical, chemical, utilities, and many other industries.

Qualifications/Certifications: INTERTEK TECHNICAL SERVICES' quality management system is certified to ISO 9002 by an independent registrar with accreditation traceability to the NACCB and the RAB. This made INTERTEK the first US-based contract labor organization certified to ISO 9000. The scope of certification is as follows: "Provider of technical specialists for quality assurance applications; provider of program management services, quality system training courses and quality system consulting and preparation services." INTERTEK'S consulting services have been evaluated and registered to the same ISO 9000 series standards that it prepares its clients for. INTERTEK's trained consultants have a proven track record of preparing clients for a successful registration assessment. Also within the scope of certification are INTERTEK's ISO 9000 training courses. From student registration to certificate issuance, the entire process of delivering training courses has been certified to the same series of standards as those being taught.

J-E-T-S, INC.

2843 Edwin Jones Drive
Charlotte, NC 28269, USA
Tel: 800-944-1994; Fax: 704-547-9178
Contact: John H Johnson, President
Services: J-E-T-S training services are customized for client needs. Training programs include the following:

- Performance-Based Auditing/Assessment

- Advanced Assessment Training
- Improving Observation Techniques
- Performance-Based Assessment (for DOE contractors)
- Effective Communications
- Regulatory and Code Training (site or company specific)
- TQM and ISO 9000 Training.

J-E-T-S consulting services are directed toward real, measurable improvement in operations efficiency, reliability and safety. From a simple review to a major reengineering, J-E-T-S consultants work in partnerships with clients to enable organizations to optimize their operations. J-E-T-S consulting service programs include the following:

- ReEngineering Advantages Program (REAP)
- Operations effectiveness reviews
- Independent assessments
- Level III inspection
- Methods and procedures analysis and development
- QA program development and review.

In Business: 9 years

Clients: J-E-T-S specialty is working with highly regulated environments, including nuclear power plants, insurance, government, government contractors and banking. A partial list of clients includes: US Department of Energy, Commonwealth Edison Company, Pacific Gas & Electric, Apex Environmental Consultants, Duke Power, Florida Power and Light, EG&G, Brookhaven National Laboratories, Rockwell International, Northeast Utilities Group.

Qualifications/Certifications: J-E-T-S consultants are qualified personnel providing a variety of needs, including administrative, operations, advanced manufacturing, processing and customer service environments. Personnel are available with almost any certification that may be required, including Level III per NQA-1, lead auditor, certified quality auditor or engineer, professional engineer and others. J-E-T-S also has personnel with a variety of security and access clearances, including nuclear power plant and DOE "Q" clearances.

JOHN A. KEANE & ASSOCIATES

575 Ewing Street
Princeton, NJ 08540, USA
Tel: 609-924-7904; Fax: 609-924-1078
Contact: Michael E Kane, Marketing Director
Leonard F Newton, Senior Associate
Seymour Altucher, Senior Associate
Services: John A. Keane and Associates, Inc. offers
specialized services to help clients plan, design, select,
implement and operate computer-based ISO 9000
execution solutions. With a detailed knowledge of ISO
9000 quality requirements and the latest computer
technology, JKA helps bridge the gap between the
quality group and the information technology group
within the modern corporation. Services include the
following:

- Consulting: On strategic planning of integrated
  ISO 9000 solutions, including interrelations with
  other manufacturing applications (e.g. MRPII,
  CAD, Data Collection, etc.)
- Methodology: To establish needs, weight features,
  compare alternatives and select optimum solutions
- Training: To implement solutions selected and to
  operate the QMS system.

In Business: 25 years
Clients: American National Can, BASF Japan Ltd.,
Caterpillar Tractor Company, Digital Equipment
Corporation, E.I. Dupont de Nemours & Company,
General Electric, Hoffman La Roche, IBM Corporation, Lockheed Electronics, Monsanto Company.
Qualifications/Certifications: John A. Keane and Associates, Inc. has been a leader in computer-based,
integrated quality information systems for more than
25 years. The Company has helped over 100 mid- and
large-sized manufacturers plan, design, select,
implement and operate "industrial strength" computer
execution solutions for ISO 9000, MIL-Q-9858A,
FDA-GMP/GLP and other regulated/audited
environments.

JOSEPH TIRATTO AND ASSOCIATES, INC.

5 N Longview Road
Howell, NJ 07731-1701, USA
Tel: 908-367-0837; Fax: 908-367-8898
Contact: Joseph Tiratto, President
Services: Joseph Tiratto and Associates, Inc. services include
the following:

- Quality systems consulting
- Audits for ISO 9000 series standards
- Auditor training
- Lectures/seminars on ISO 9000 series
- Registration and accreditation systems.

In Business: 2 years

Clients: Machinery manufacturers, electrical manufacturers,
electronic manufacturers, steel mills, forge plants,
chemical manufacturers, service industries, shipping
and shipbuilding, in the United States and abroad.
Qualifications/Certifications: Joseph Tiratto has more than
35 years of engineering and quality management
service. He has BS degrees in naval architecture and
marine engineering and mechanical engineering. He
has an MS degree in quality management. His
qualifications also include Professional Engineer's
license, Marine Engineer's license, Registered
European Engineer (EC and EFTA Countries),
Chartered Engineer (England), Registered Lead
Assessor (IQA), Registered Lead Assessor Instructor,
Member of Board of Directors of Registrar Accreditation Board (RAB), Member of ASQC Z-1 Committee
on QA, and Member of TAG to ISO 176 Committee
on QA.

KEVIN DRAYTON ASSOCIATES

190 Fox Road
Dalton, MA 01226, USA
Tel: 800-538-3338; Fax: 413-684-4648
Contact: Kevin G Drayton, Senior Consultant
Services: Kevin Drayton Associates provide services in the
area of third-party certification and validation of
suppliers through education, training, implementation
and manpower in the following areas:

- Total quality performance
- ISO 9000
- Project management
- Cost-of-quality systems
- Custom-designed training programs
- Configuration management
- Contract compliance
- Organizational development for quality improvement.

In Business: 4 years
Clients: Albany International; GE; CIBA Vision; Atwood
& Morril; Insulated Materials, Inc.; Lau Technologies;
Raytheon; Mobil Oil Corp.; GTE; Boston Edison.
Qualifications/Certifications: Kevin Drayton is a graduate
of BSI's Lead Assessor course for ISO-9000 and is
certified through Rochester Institute of Technology.

KOLKA & ASSOCIATES

2193 Spear Point Drive
Marietta, GA 30062, USA
Tel: 404-977-4049; Fax: 404-651-9185
Contact: Dr. James W Kolka, President
Services: Kolka & Associates services include the following:

- International legal consulting in product, services,
  environmental liability, product safety and EC
  directives

- Global Liability preventive law programs integrated with ISO 9000 quality assurance programs designed to reduce liability exposure in US and EC markets
- Certification for EC New Approach Directives, including Medical Device Directives and new FDA ISO 9000 GMPs.

Kolka & Associates provide product certification programs, preventive law seminars, training workshops, strategic planning for manufacturers, engineering firms, services companies, law firms and insurance companies.

In Business: 25 years

Clients: Georgia Tech Research Institute, Kaiser Aluminum & Chemical Corporation, Society for Automotive Engineers, International, Popham, Haik, Schnobrich & Kaufman, Ltd., National Electrical Manufacturers Association/Diagnostic Imaging Division, American Petroleum Institute, Quality Systems Update, Ministry of Education-Spain, Ministry of the Presidency-Costa Rica, Johnson & Johnson.

Qualifications/Certifications: Dr. Kolka has a Ph.D. in Political Science & International Affairs from the University of Kansas, a JD in Product Liability, Environmental Law from the University of Wisconsin-Madison and a BS in Political Science (Economics/Chemistry) from the University of Wisconsin-Eau Claire. He is a member of the Wisconsin Bar Association, American Bar Association, and a Fellow at the American Council on Education, Ford Foundation. He served as full professor, published numerous articles, served as Vice President at Drake University and in the University system of Georgia. Dr. Kolka has held Senior Management positions in the University of Wisconsin system and developed Wisconsin's statewide Adult Extended Degree Program. He was instrumental in creating the Center for International Standards and Quality at Georgia Tech and has conducted seminars, workshops and programs throughout the United States, Europe and Latin America.

KPMG PEAT MARWICK
ISO 9000 Quality Services
150 John F. Kennedy Parkway
Short Hills, NJ 07078, USA
Tel: 201-912-6623; Fax: 201-912-6158
Contact: James J Tuchi, Partner
Services: Through its global network, KPMG Peat Marwick's ISO 9000 Quality Services Practice can provide certified lead assessors to assist companies in every aspect of preparing for registration in any area of the world. Its ability to rely on resources based in the United States and across the world facilitates the process of implementing ISO 900 in multi-site organizations and can reduce the overall cost. Services include the following:
- Readiness assessments
- Training and education
- Implementation planning
- Business process analyses
- Communications
- Quality systems audits.

In Business: Over 80 years

Clients: References will be provided upon request.

Qualifications/Certifications: KPMG Peat Marwick has been in the consulting field for more than 200 years. Its ISO 9000 consulting and training methodology has been used successfully in assisting more than 400 companies in achieving ISO 9000 registration.

L. MARVIN JOHNSON AND ASSOCIATES, INC.
822 Montezuma Way
West Covina, CA 91791, USA
Tel: 818-919-1728; Fax: 818-919-7128
Contact: L. Marvin Johnson, CEO
Services: L. Marvin Johnson and Associates, Inc., consulting for quality management, performs management quality assurance and software system audits. They train quality and evaluation auditors as well as ISO 9000 auditors. L. Marvin Johnson and Associates, Inc. provides ISO 9000 lead auditor certification courses and internal auditor certification courses. Courses are approved, certified and registered with IQA/RBA of the United Kingdom.

In Business: 24 years

Clients: Partial listing of sponsors and attendees to L. Marvin Johnson and Associates' audit seminars include the following: AT&T, BF Goodrich, General Electric, General Motors, Boeing, Hughes, Boston Edison, US Army, US Department of Energy, NASA, US Navy, and the French, Italian, Swedish and British governments.

Qualifications/Certifications: CEO L. Marvin Johnson graduated from the University of Southern California in 1949 with a degree in industrial engineering. He is a Registered Professional Industrial Engineer and Professional Quality Engineer. He has 43 years of experience in quality assurance and related fields. His industrial experience with Firestone Tire and Rubber, Rheem and Whitaker companies and the Polaris Missile Program is where he developed and implemented his comprehensive evaluation techniques. Mr. Johnson lectures and conducts quality audit courses for industrial contractors, government agencies, NASA centers, utilities, DOE, United Kingdom (CEGB,

IQA), Italian (CNEN), Mexican (CFE) and British Ministry of Defense. He is author of "Quality Assurance Program Evaluation" and "Quality Assurance Evaluator's Workbook," which are the first in the world for performing intensive quality assessments and audits. He is a member of American Nuclear Society, a senior member of the ASQC and a member of ASQC's Audit Division. He is certified by the IQA/RBA of the United Kingdom as a quality system Lead Assessor.

MALLOY & ASSOCIATES, INC.

321 Regatta Way
Seal Beach, CA 90740, USA
Tel: 310-493-1672; Fax: 310-493-5272
Contact: John J Malloy, President
Tel: 310-493-0073; Fax: 310-493-5272
Contact: Marianne A Malloy, Seminar Coordinator
Services: Malloy & Associates, Inc. is a professional consulting and training firm specializing in ISO 9000 and US Food and Drug Administration (FDA) standards. Malloy & Associates, Inc. can help a company meet FDA requirements as well as establish criteria and quality review systems for ISO 9000 certification. Services include the following:

- ISO 9000 strategic planning and gap assessment
- Implementation of ISO 9000 standards and quality manual(s)
- ISO 9000 quality system audit and training
- ISO 9000 registration readiness reviews
- International device submissions
- Good Manufacturing Practices (GMP)
- Preproduction Quality Assurance (PQA) audits and training.

In Business: 15 years
Clients: 3M Divisions, Abbott Labs. Division, Adv. Cardiovascular Sys., Adv. Technology Labs., Alcon Surgical, Allergan Division, American Red Cross, AT&T Network Sys., Baxter Divisions, Beckman Inst., Becton Dickinson Divs., Bio-Rad Labs., Bio-Tek Instruments, Birtcher Medical Sys., Boehringer Mannheim, California Dept. of Health Services.
Qualifications/Certifications: Malloy & Associates, Inc. has consulted for and trained representatives from over 400 international medical device manufacturers as well as the US FDA and state regulatory agencies. Mr. Malloy, president and founder of Malloy & Associates, Inc., is a registered ISO lead assessor. He has over 25 years of experience within the medical industry, having served as an FDA Investigator and having held industry management positions in manufacturing, regulatory, quality and marketing. Mr. Malloy has broad product line and process experience. He is the author of articles appearing in journals such as MDDI, Bio-Medical Science & Technology and Medical Equipment Designer. Mr. Malloy received his MBA degree from the University of Evansville.

MCDERMOTT ASSOCIATES

12212 N Paradise Village Parkway S, Suite 209C
Phoenix, AZ 85032, USA
Tel: 602-494-9500; Fax: 602-494-9500
Contact: Patrick J McDermott, President
Services: McDermott Associates is an international management consulting and training firm devoted to operations improvement for manufacturing and service organizations. It employs associates who are skilled in industrial engineering, quality assurance and material management. McDermott Associates offers clients a variety of services that include analysis, development and implementation of quality systems, preparation and review of documentation, second- and third-party auditing and comprehensive training courses. These services are available for clients working to ISO 9000, TQM, MIL-Q-9858A, MIL-I-45208 and other recognized quality system standards. These include: Education and Training courses, Internal and External Quality Audit Workshops, ISO Quality Management System Design and Implementation Assistance, Registration Guidance (including assistance in the selection of an accredited registrar) and Registration Readiness Reviews.
In Business: 2 years
Clients: McDermott Associates specializes in small and medium businesses.
Qualifications/Certifications: Patrick McDermott, President of McDermott Associates is the developer of a Cost-Effective 9000 process for ISO 9000 preparation for companies seeking ISO 9000 registration. He is a trained IQA Lead Auditor to ISO 9000. Patrick has more than 20 years experience working with both service and manufacturing companies in the United States, Europe and the Pacific Rim countries. He and his associates have helped small and large companies apply operations improvements, quality principles and practices in all areas of their business. Patrick holds an MBA degree in management and a BA degree in business/statistics; post-graduate work in industrial engineering at the University of Northern Illinois. He is a board member of IIE Chapter (Institute of Industrial Engineers), board member of ASQC Societies, and a guest lecturer at Governors State University on quality assurance.

MOORHILL INTERNATIONAL GROUP, INC.

2015 N Dobson Road, Suite #4-B56
Chandler, AZ 85224, USA
Tel: 602-491-2007; Fax: 602-732-9089

Contact: Erik V Myhrberg, Director, CEO
Robert Paetschow, Director, CFO

Services: Moorhill International Group, Inc. provides certified training courses (pending final RBA and RAB approval) in the area of ISO 9000. TickIT training courses will be offered in mid-1994. Moorhill also works in the areas of international marketing, global sourcing, worldwide matchmaking and cross-cultural training.

In Business: Began operations as Myhrberg & Associates in January 1992, incorporated as Moorhill International Group, Inc. in July 1993.

Clients: Arizona Department of Commerce; Japan External Trade Organization; Shubi International, Inc.; Creative Investments, Inc.; IBM (Phoenix and Tuscon, AZ); Innova, Inc.

Qualifications/Certifications: Moorhill International Group, Inc. will receive ISO 9000 training certification in late 1993 and TickIT training certification in mid-1994. All directors have completed a recognized lead assessor training course and have passed the written examination. All trainers will be recognized as certified lead assessors (including training time and assessments). The company will also be implementing courses in several languages and cultural content. Each director holds higher education degrees, including: MIM, MSE, MBA, JD, BS. Memberships include the ASQC and the World Trade Center.

MOYE COMPANY LIMITED

59 Breadner Drive, Suite 102
Toronto, Ontario M9R 3M5, Canada
Tel: 416-248-9187; Fax: Same

Contact: Bohdan Dyczkowsky, Principal Engineer, Director

Services: Moye Company offers unique programs on quality management to companies in all stages of development. Moye's eight-step program helps companies assess their needs in obtaining ISO 9000 quality system registration including the following:

- Documentation
- Awareness
- Quality training
- Implementation teams
- Quality system development
- Preregistration assessment
- Registration audit
- Compliance audit.

In Business: 3 years

Clients: Honeywell Canada (Residential and Building Controls Division), Centennial College, Ontario Provincial Government (Ontario Skills Development).

Qualifications/Certifications: Bohdan Dyczkowsky, Director of MOYE Company Limited, is a native of Toronto, Ontario. He graduated from the University of Toronto with a BASc in mechanical engineering. He has broad manufacturing experience in construction, steel fabricating, nuclear piping and electronics. Major career accomplishments include being the Secretary of the Canadian Delegation to the ISO Technical Committee 176 during the development of the ISO 9000 series. Mr. Dyczkowsky is a registered Professional Engineer, a Registered Auditor with the IQA in England and the RAB in the United States, and an active member of the ASQC.

N.C. KIST & ASSOCIATES, INC.

900 E Porter Avenue
Naperville, IL 60540, USA
Tel: 708-357-1180; Fax: 708-357-3349

Contact: Nicolaas C Kist, President

Services: N.C. Kist & Associates, Inc. offers a complete line of consulting services in ISO 9000 including the following:

- Preparation of quality manuals and quality systems procedures
- Quality systems auditor/lead auditor training
- Training in ISO 9000 requirements
- Implementation assistance
- Pre-registrar assessment audits
- Assistance during registrar assessment
- Periodic quality systems evaluation.

In Business: 21 years

Clients: Aoki Industries Co., Ltd.; Bakrie Pipe Industries; Crane Kemlite; FRESA; International Computers, Ltd.; Rhinelander Paper; Sonoco Fibre Drum; Vallinox; Milwaukee Gear; Milwaukee Drive; Stainless Foundry & Engineering; Hoechst Celanese; AEC Engineering; Stepan.

Qualifications/Certifications: N.C. Kist & Associates, Inc. specializes in developing cost-effective quality systems based on national and international standards. Since 1972, it has assisted more than 250 clients worldwide. In 1987, N.C. Kist & Associates began to offer ISO 9000 consulting with 36 ISO 9000 customers in the United States, Europe and the Pacific Rim. N.C. Kist also has an IQA Lead Auditor and an RAB Lead Auditor on staff.

OMNI TECH INTERNATIONAL, LTD.
2715 Ashman Street, Suite 100
Midland, MI 48640, USA
Tel: 517-631-3377; Fax: 517-631-7360
Contact: Douglas B Todd, Vice President, Business Services
Services: Omni Tech International, Ltd.'s services include interpretation and implementation of manuals and procedures, diagnostic audits and principles of auditing and ISO 9000 training. Omni Tech conducts ISO pre-certification assessments. Once a client has determined that registration under an ISO standard is needed, Omni Tech will assess the client's quality manual (if one exists) and quality systems to determine how well they comply with the criteria of the specific ISO standard. If these audits indicate that the client's manual and/or systems are not in compliance, Omni Tech will work with the client to develop the quality manual and to implement the quality systems required.
In Business: 7 years
Clients: Akzo Chemicals, BASF, Ferro Corporation, Franklin International, Hewlett-Packard, Monsanto, Occidental Chemical, Rhone-Poulenc, Texaco, Union Carbide, Chevron Chemical, SC Johnson, Kerr-McGee, Pioneer Chlor Alkali, A.P. Parts, Johnson Controls.
Qualifications/Certifications: Omni Tech's qualifications include provisional RAB Auditor, provisional IQA Assessor, IQA Lead Auditor, RAB Lead Auditor, member of ASQC-CQA Chemical Interest Committee.

OXFORD TECHNOLOGIES, INC.
1414 South Friendswood Drive
Friendswood, TX 77546, USA
Tel: 713-992-2229; Fax: 713-482-8088
Contact: Alan H Taylor, President
Rusty Heft
Services: Oxford Technologies, Inc. offers a complete package of services designed to guide companies through documentation and implementation in support of a specific ISO 9000 series quality management standard. This multi-phased process is intended to assist companies in achieving ISO certification. Services include the following:
- Client-specific awareness and requirements training
- Baseline assessment of existing practices to the applicable ISO standard
- Documentation development and training
- Internal auditor training
- System assessment prior to certification.
In Business: 2 years
Clients: GE Supply, Coastal Corporation, Cook Manley, a Division of Dover Corporation, HWC Distribution

Corporation, Allied Metals and other companies.
Qualifications/Certifications: The staff at Oxford are qualified lead assessors with extensive background in disciplines ranging from engineering, distribution and sales, to manufacturing.

P-E HANDLEY-WALKER, INC.
17371 Irvine Boulevard, Suite 200
Tustin, CA 92680, USA
Tel: 714-730-0122; Fax: 714-730-0439
Contact: Michael V Mathews, Executive Vice President
6000 Freedom Square Drive, Suite 140
Independence, OH 44131, USA
Tel: 216-524-2200; Fax: 216-524-1488
Contact: John Palazzo, Director
Services: P-E Handley-Walker, a P-E International company, provides general consulting and training in 50 different disciplines as a full service international management consulting firm. Since 1979, P-E Handley-Walker has offered training and consulting assistance for ISO 9000 and BS 5750 quality standards certification worldwide. ISO 9000 offered services include the following:
- Management overview
- Initial adequacy audit
- Documentation review and assistance
- Implementation assistance
- Pre-registration compliance audit
- Guide to ISO 9000
- Implementation training
- Documentation training
- Auditor training
- Lead Assessor training (registered).
In Business: P-E Handley-Walker, Inc.: 27 years, P-E International: 60 years.
Clients: Baxter Healthcare Corp., Apple Computer, Bausch & Lomb, Honeywell, Pennzoil, Du Pont, Georgia Pacific, Western Digital, Shell Oil Company, Morton International.
Qualifications/Certifications: P-E Handley Walker, Inc. is part of the largest ISO 9000 consulting and training company in the world and has assisted over 1,600 clients through certification. P-E Handley-Walker operates in the following countries: United Kingdom, Ireland, Netherlands, France, Hungary, Hong Kong, Malaysia, India, Indonesia, Taiwan, Singapore, Australia, Curacao N.A., Mexico, the United States and Canada. Several divisions of P-E International are ISO 9000 certified and many others are in the process with a certification target of early 1994.

PERRY JOHNSON, INC.
3000 Town Center, Suite 2960
Southfield, MI 48075, USA
Tel: 313-356-4410; Fax: 313-356-4230
Contact: Bob Hammill, ISO Services Manager
Services: Perry Johnson, Inc. (PJI) is a full-service TQM
and ISO 9000 consulting, training and implementa-
tion firm. In addition to providing training courses,
PJI provides proprietary TQM and ISO 9000 training
support products, including programmed instruction
workbooks, overhead transparency presentation
packages, videotape presentations and computer
software packages.
In Business: 10 years
Clients: 85% of the Fortune 500, including Johnson Wax,
Mobil, Riverwood International, Northrop, US Navy,
Graham Packaging, Heinz Pet Products, Ford Motor
Company, Nabisco, Litton.
Qualifications/Certifications: Since 1983, PJI has trained
employees of more than 1,200 organizations throughout North America and Europe, implemented TQM
in more than 500 facilities, presented seminars to
more than 600,000 people and trained more than
1,300,000 others via its product catalog. PJI holds a
contract awarded by the US Office of Personnel
Management to provide TQM services and products
to agencies of the Federal government (OPM-89-
2870). PJI is also a training contractor to the US
General Services Administration (GS-02F-7576A).

PLANTE & MORAN
27400 Northwestern Highway
PO Box 307
Southfield, MI 48037-0307, USA
Tel: 313-352-2500; Fax: 313-352-0018
Contact: Jeffrey R Jenkins, Manager
Craig M Fitzgerald
Timothy J Erdmann
Services: Plante & Moran provides an array of comprehen-
sive consulting and training services. Services include
system assessments and audits, quality planning
support, implementation support and quality award/
certification preparation activities. Primary areas of
professional management consulting services include:
- Total Quality Management
- ISO 9000
- Continuous process improvement
- Planning and operations
- Management information services
- Organizational development and training
- Human resources
- Individual and employment assessment and testing
- Executive search

- Telecommunications.
In Business: 69 years
Clients: Small and medium-size, closely-held companies.
Medium and large-size public companies. Primary
industries include manufacturing, health care, service
companies, municipalities, not-for-profit and
education.
Qualifications/Certifications: In addition to numerous
technical and academic degrees, certifications of
professional staff include the following:
- The successful completion of the IQA recognized
Lead Assessor examination. (Application for Lead
Assessor certification has been submitted)
- Certified Management Consultant (CMC)
- Certified Public Accountant (CPA)
- Certified Management Accountant (CMA)
- Certified Production and Inventory Manager
(CPIM)
- Certified Information Systems Auditor (CISA)
- Certified Systems Professional (CSP).
Affiliated with Moores Rowland International.

PROCESS MANAGEMENT INTERNATIONAL
7801 E Bush Lake Road, Suite 360
Minneapolis, MN 55439-3115, USA
Tel: 800-258-0313; Fax: 612-893-0502
Contact: Peter M Malkovich
Services: Process Management International (PMI),
provides consultation, education and training of Total
Quality Management and offers a full range of ISO
9000 consulting and training services. PMI has
teamed its TQM expertise with the ISO 9000
consulting experience of Optimum Systems for
Quality (OSQ), based in Lancashire, England.
Together, PMI and OSQ have developed systems that
make ISO 9000 consulting and training more effective
and more efficient. Based on more than five years of
practice and research, these services assist companies
with ISO 9000 registration and provide an effective
means to enhance quality management within a
company.
In Business: 10 years
Clients: Alusuisse Flexible Packaging, Inc.; BHP Engineering and Construction Company; DATALINK; E-C
Apparatus Corporation; Fleischmann Kurth Malting;
Hopeman Brothers; IMED Corporation; Leeds
Precision Instruments, Inc.; Liquid Carbonic
Corporation; Monsanto Company; StarTex Corpora-
tion; Weather-Rite, Inc.; Whale Scientific, Inc.; Zytec
Corporation.
Qualifications/Certifications: PMI's teaming with OSQ
has resulted in the following:
- A proven ISO 9000 model, based on over 5 years
of practice and research

- More than 100 organizations have achieved registration on their first attempt
- A network of experienced quality consultants nationwide who are able to integrate TQM methods with ISO 9000 quality standards
- Certified Lead Auditor training by consultants who know first-hand how internal auditing fits with the ISO 9000 effort and who have successfully worked with organizations for the past 8 years in improving the quality of their products and services.

PRODUCTIVITY IMPROVEMENT CENTRE (PIC)

Durham College
PO Box 385, 2000 Simcoe Street N
Oshawa, Ontario L1H 7L7, USA
Tel: 416-721-3317; Fax: 416-721-3339
Contact: Jacqui Sharpe, Marketing Manager
Alan Duffy, Director
Sandra Kazmirchuk, Program Manager
Services: The Productivity Improvement Centre (PIC) of Durham College is a non-profit entrepreneurial training and consulting group. PIC offers ISO 9000 training and consulting services across North America including:
- Needs assessments/pre-assessment audits
- Public seminars
- Customized in-house training
- Systems development
- ISO 9000 Introduction
- ISO 9000 Internal Auditor
- ISO 9000 Quality System Documentation for Manufacturing (QMI course)
- ISO 9000 Quality System Documentation for Service Industries (QMI course)
- ISO 9000 Lead Auditor (QMI course)
- ISO 9000 Software
- ISO 9000 Train-the-Trainer.

In June 1993, PIC partnered with QMI, a division of the Canadian Standards Association, to deliver their training programs in ISO 9000 Documentation and Lead Auditor.
In Business: 8 years
Clients: All sizes of manufacturing and service businesses. A comprehensive list available on request.
Qualifications/Certifications: PIC has been proactive to the needs of manufacturing and service companies in the field of quality assurance training, and has assisted many companies to meet international, automotive, aerospace and government standards as required. Its comprehensive evening studies programs in Quality Assurance, Total Quality Management and Quality Auditing have been adopted by other training institutions.

PROUDFOOT CROSBY

3260 University Boulevard
PO Box 6006
Winter Park, FL 32793-6006, USA
Tel: 800-722-1474/407-677-3084; Fax: 407-677-3055
Contact: Joan Buchanan, Client Services
Corporate 500 Centre
520 Lake Cook Road, Suite 550
Deerfield, IL 60015, USA
Tel: 800-722-1474
Contact: Joan Buchanan, Client Services
1735 Technology Drive, Suite 850
San Jose, CA 95110, USA
Tel: 800-722-1474
Contact: Joan Buchanan, Client Services
Services: Proudfoot Crosby offers consultancy support, education and workshops to all organizations aiming to achieve ISO 9000 certification and other related quality standards. The Crosby approach establishes management determination then provides education leading to implementation. Support is available at all stages during a company's process to achieve certification. Other services include the following:
- Business reviews
- Quality management education and implementation
- Communication and team building skills
- Process re-engineering
- Sales training.

In Business: 15 years
Clients: AMOCO Petroleum Additives Company; Bristol Aerospace; Chevron, Inc.; DSI Transports; Heinz Europe; Kone Elevators; Marconi Communications, Inc.; McDermott International; Perle Systems Ltd.; Rheem Australia; Riverwood International; Sicartsa Mexico; Trustee Savings Bank; Western Atlas; Wilkerson Corporation; Zimmer.
Qualifications/Certifications: Proudfoot Crosby has helped over 1,500 companies (many Fortune 500) reach their quality goals in the last 15 years and has also helped many businesses register and achieve ISO 9000 certification.

Q.A. SYSTEMS, INC.

PO Box 3090
Kearny, NJ 07032, USA
Tel: 201-998-2627; Fax: 201-998-4292
Contact: Denis McNamee, President
Deborah Worthington
Services: ISO 9000 training, education and consulting as needed to assist clients achieve registration, including:
- Pre-assessment audits
- Documentation preparation and training
- Internal auditor training

- Management and employee ISO 9000 awareness training
- Programmed ISO 9000 instruction for in-house training
- TQM training, implementation and consulting
- SQC/SPC training and implementation
- MBNQA assessment and preparation.

In Business: 5 years

Clients: ABB Turbocharger, The New York Times, Croda International and numerous small and medium-size companies in most industries.

Qualifications/Certifications: Staff qualifications include IQA Lead Assessor, ASQC CQA and CQE.

QUALIFIED SPECIALISTS, INC. (QSI)

13231 Champion Forest Drive, Suite 104
Houston, TX 77069, USA
Tel: 713-444-5366; Fax: 713-444-6127

Contact: R.T. "Bud" Weightman, President
Denise Weightman, Director of Operations

Services: Consulting, staff augmentation, How To Select a Registrar (SM) software, ISO pre-assessment, GAP analysis, quality system development, ISO/EC and specialized training programs. QSI will build from your current business practices to create a strong ISO 9000 foundation for your TQM or Malcolm Baldrige efforts. QSI uses a non-traditional, creative approach to implementing ISO 9000 as well as other quality systems.Some of QSI's training programs include:

- Executive overview of ISO 9000
- Recognized lead assessor training
- ISO 10011 internal auditor training
- ISO 9001/2 quality systems implementation.

In Business: 4 years

Clients: National Oilwell, Shell Oil, Society of Automotive Engineers, JM Huber, BJ Services, Lafarge, Eastman Christensen, Mobil, Baker Companies, Applied Hydraulics, American Petroleum Institute, Decibel Products, Chevron, Dresser Rand, Setpoint, API, O'Brien Powder Products.

Qualifications/Certifications: Bud Weightman has been in quality for 20 years, and is involved in every QSI project. Mr. Weightman is an IQA (UK) Lead Assessor, RAB Lead Auditor, ASQC-CQA and has been selected as an examiner for the Texas Quality Award 1993. He is a member of the ASQC's Committee ISO/TC176 (US Technical Advisory Group on Quality Assurance and Quality Management). He has chaired and served in key positions in various ASQC and API committees and moderates industry quality symposia. He has given numerous presentations internationally on ISO and has authored serveral published articles. QSI's staff members are quality consultants, engineers, professional auditors and business experts with strong academic accreditations and experience.

QUALITAS USA, INC.

3040 Charlevoix Drive SE, Suite 101
Grand Rapids, MI 49546, USA
Tel: 616-285-4010; Fax: 616-949-2812

Contact: James T Wilkinson

Services: Qualitas USA, Inc. provides ISO 9000 consulting and training services including the following :

- ISO 9000 implementation consulting
- Baseline and final audit
- ISO 9000 interpretation and application
- ISO 9000 documentation
- Internal auditing
- Lead assessor training.

In Business: 5 years

Clients: Steelcase, Inc., North America's largest office furniture manufacturer; Sicartsa, Mexico's major steel producer; Chee Cheung Hing Co., a Hong Kong building contractor; RMD Fire Control, a UK company designing, manufacturing and installing automatic sprinkler systems; Teignbridge District Council, a UK local authority whose activities include architectural, civil and building design and maintenance.

Qualifications/Certifications: Qualitas is a member of the British Quality Foundation and the Enterprise Initiative. Its worldwide staff has the following various credentials: Registered IQA Lead Assessors, member AQMC, member ASQC, member CIPS, fellow IQA, fellow AQMC, MIMechE, MIEngDesigners, United Nations ILO Quality Assurance Expert for South America, approved API supplier, Aramo Approved Inspector of Pressure Retaining Parts, senior ASQC, and CQE.

QUALITY ALERT INSTITUTE
In-House Training and Consulting Services

257 Park Avenue S, 12th Floor
New York, NY 10010-7304, USA
Tel: 800-221-2114/212-353-4425; Fax: 212-353-4526

Contact: Chris B Greg, Corporate Director

5208 Fox Hills Drive
Fort Collins, CO 80526, USA
Tel: 303-229-1402

Contact: Michael Demma, Senior ISO 9000 Quality Specialist

830 Shoreline Drive
Columbus, IN 47201, USA
Tel: 812-342-9389

Contact: John O Brown, Senior ISO 9000 Quality Specialist

Services: Quality Alert Institute's ISO 9000 Group provides a complete series of proven comprehensive ISO 9000/Q90 training, auditing and consulting services for small, mid-size and large organizations. It assists organizations through the entire registration preparation process. Services include the following:
- Auditing
  - Pre-assessment
  - Registration readiness review
- Training
  - Implementation for manufacturing, service, software, medical device and automotive suppliers
  - Documentation for writing and controlling procedures
  - Internal auditing
- Consulting
  - Strategic planning
  - Periodic implementation assistance.

Over 100 specialized TQM/SPC services are also available upon request.

In Business: 12 years

Clients: Abbott Diagnostics, Coca-Cola U.S.A., Ohmeda/BOC Healthcare Group, Eastman Kodak, General Cable, Xerox, IBM Corporation, Seagate Technology, PPG Industries, Bell Canada, BP Oil, Becton Dickinson, Hubbell Wiring Device, Fisher Controls.

Qualifications/Certifications: For more than 12 years, Quality Alert Institute has provided manufacturing, service, health care and government organizations with the systems training, consulting and implementation services they need to improve and control the quality of their products and services under a Total Quality Management philosophy. The Quality Alert Institute's ISO 9000 Group started 3 years ago. The group is made up of individuals who are prior executives with Fortune 500 companies. All 24 staff members have practical hands-on experience in all phases of the ISO 9000 registration preparation process. Quality Alert Institute has taken its staff members' personal experiences with planning, implementing and managing successful ISO 9000 registrations and has added their current experiences assisting Quality Alert ISO 9000 clients to formulate the ISO 9000 Group's Fourteen-Step implementation system.

QUALITY MANAGEMENT CONSULTING SERVICES

62 Murray Drive
Oceanside, NY 11572-5722, USA
Tel: 516-536-1859; Fax: 516-536-1859
Contact: Dan Epstein
Services: Quality Management Consulting Services' ISO

9000 services include the following:
- Needs and pre-audit assessment
- Customized quality manuals and procedures
- Motivational and awareness training
- Quality management system implementation.

For other quality related areas, services include the following:
- Motivational training
- TQM and SPC initiatives
- Military quality systems implementation
- Quality improvement tools
- Seminars/workshops
- Problem-solving tools.

In Business: 2.5 years

Clients: Koehler Instrument Company; Davis Vision Systems; Technology Systems Corporation; ADEMCO; J. LeBoyer and Company; Renco Electronics, Inc.; Stony Point Electronics; AIL Systems, Inc.

Qualifications/Certifications: Qualifications include more than 39 years experience in standards, reliability, quality control, safety and motivational training. Prior to his present consultancy, Mr. Epstein had 16 years' experience as a Senior Vice President of a major east coast electronics manufacturer. While there, he had domestic and international responsibilities for product assurance, as well as responsibilities for overall manufacturing in Japan and Taiwan. Mr. Epstein is an author and lecturer, has provided testimony to Congress, was an Examiner for the Malcolm Baldrige National Quality Award, is currently an Examiner for the New York State Excelsior Award, and has been certified as an ISO 9000 lead assessor/auditor by QMI Ltd. (UK).

QUALITY MANAGEMENT SERVICES

PO Box 51
503 4th Avenue
Fayetteville, TN 37334, USA
Tel: 615-433-6834; Fax: Same
Contact: James T Rutledge, System Implementor
Services: Quality Management Services provides the following services:
- Quality system evaluation
- Strategic planning for ISO
- ISO training
- Technical writing
- Calibration system coordination
- Management representative seminars.

In Business: 1 year

Clients: National Scale; Disc Manufacturing, Inc.; Continental Conveyor.

Qualifications/Certifications: Qualifications include:

- Quality engineer during implementation and certification to 9001 for a nationally known appliance manufacturer
- 15 years quality related experience in the chemical industry, metal forming, and OEM
- IQA Lead Assessor Training.

QUALITY MANAGEMENT SOLUTIONS

PO Box 349
Uncasville, CT 06382, USA
Tel: 203-442-9393; Fax: 203-442-3393
Contact: Craig R Mesler, President
James B Malone, Vice President
Laurie Newman, Client Relations
Services: Quality Management Solutions provides the following services:
- ISO 9000 training, implementation, and consulting
- ISO 9000 gap assessments and registration readiness reviews
- ISO 9000 implementation for:
  - medical device manufacturers (GMPs)
  - automotive suppliers
  - software developers (ISO 9000-3)
  - service industry (ISO 9004-2)
  - environmental management
- Quality system implementation training
- Internal quality auditor training
- Documentation preparation training
- Statistical process control training and programs
- Authorized distributor for ISO 9000 Forum and ISO 9000 News.

In Business: 4 years
Clients: Creative Industries, Thermo Electron, Reflectone, UNC Manufacturing Technology, QualityAlert Institute, US Steel, F.L. Fuller Company, J.M. Ney, Ensign Bickford, Gerber Scientific, Seagate Technology, Ingres Software, IBM, Silicon Graphics, Exacta Technology, Artisan Industries, General Cable Corporation, Enthone-OMI.
Qualifications/Certifications: Quality Management Solutions staff include ISO 9000 auditors, Certified Quality Auditors (CQA), Certified Quality Engineers (CQE), Certified Quality Systems Auditors (RAB and IQA), Certified Quality Systems Lead Auditors (RAB and IQA).

QUALITY PRACTITIONERS U.S., INC.

401 2nd Street E, Suite 231
Indian Rocks Beach, FL 34635, USA
Tel: 813-596-2296; Fax: 813-595-4054
Contact: Charles McRobert, President
3100 Ridgeway Drive, Unit 2
Mississauga, Ontario L5L 5M5, Canada
Tel: 905-569-6431; Fax: 905-569-7651

Contact: Charles McRobert, President
Services: Quality Practitioners Inc. provides consulting and training services based on the ISO 9000 and ISO 10011 quality standards. They specialize in the use of these standards and are not involved with the application of other quality philosophies. They provide in-house training; registration audits (on a contract basis); implementation training for system orientation and internal audits; confidential pre-assessment audits; and they act as liaison with the registrar.
In Business: 5 years
Clients: Russelsteel; Standard Machine; Prairie Machine; Doepker Industries; Amoco Chemical Company; Amoco Performance Products, Inc.; Iron Ore of Canada; Petro-Canada; Lubplex; Novacor Chemicals, Ltd.; Polysar Rubber Corporation.
Qualifications/Certifications: Staff is experienced in using the ISO 9000 standards and has assisted companies to achieve ISO registration. Staff members are accredited auditors.

QUALITY SCIENCES CONSULTANTS, INC. (QSCI)

22531 SE 42nd Court
Issaquah, WA 98027-7241, USA
Tel: 206-392-4006; Fax: 206-392-2621
Contact: Frank Caplan, President
Services: QSCI conducts Train-the-Trainer workshops in ISO 9000 implementation, internal auditing, and documentation (typically for instructors from community and junior colleges) each of which involves follow-on meetings, updates, and unlimited duplication of student workbooks for one fixed fee. The Company also trains manufacturing and service organizations in the above subjects, plus supplier assessment and improvement, statistical process control and TQM. QSCI conducts assessments and audits against ISO 9000, Malcolm Baldrige, Q101 and other criteria (or combinations thereof). It also helps companies become ISO registered with a 100 percent success rate at the first audit.
In Business: QSCI was incorporated in 1989 as a successor corporation to Quality Services Inc. Altogether, the business has been in existence since July 1983.
Clients: For ISO training: Bellevue Community College, Rock Valley Community College, St. Louis Community College, South Seattle Community College. For ISO consulting: AT&T Microelectronics: Hi Performance IC's, AT&T Microelectronics: Lightwave, AT&T Microelectronics: MOS, AT&T Microelectronics: Submarine Systems.
Qualifications/Certifications: QSCI is staffed by five

professionals. Two of them are registered lead assessors. The remaining three are provisional lead assessors and are in the process of building their audit bases for complete registration. Among them are a PE in quality and a fellow of ASQC. Together they hold the following ASQC certifications: 3 CQE's, a CQA and a CQT. The president of the company has been awarded the Eugene L. Grant Award of ASQC for lifelong efforts and achievements in the educational field vis-a-vis quality.

QUALITYWORKS, INC.

19 Old Town Square, Suite 238
Fort Collins, CO 80524, USA
Tel: 303-224-2887; Fax: 303-482-0251
Contact: Warren E Castro, President
Tami Romero, Registrar
Services: QualityWorks specializes in assisting clients with the development and implementation of quality management systems using the ISO 9000 series of standards as a model. Services include the following:
- ISO 9000 strategic planning consulting
- ISO 9000 implementation consulting
- Quality system audits
- Auditor training
- Documentation preparation and evaluation
- Training courses.
In Business: 3 years
Clients: Coors Ceramics Co., Eaton Corporation, Hewlett-Packard Co., Hitachi Computer Products, Moore-Norman Vocational-Technical Center, NCR Corporation, Seiscor Division of Raytheon, Sundstrand Fluid Handling, Teledyne WaterPik, Texas A&M University Engineering Extension Service, Western Sugar Co.
Qualifications/Certifications: QualityWorks consultants all have strong backgrounds in quality management and audit, and are all trained or registered lead assessors.

QUEST USA, INC.

27941 Harper
St. Clair Shores, MI 48081, USA
Tel: 800-878-1669/313-774-9480; Fax: 313-774-2709
Contact: Deborah Griffiths, National Sales Manager
Gerry Utych, US Representative
Services: Quest USA, Inc., is a full-service consulting and training organization specializing in ISO 9000 Quality Systems. Quest's European-based consultants have years of practical knowledge implementing ISO 9000 and coordinated training in a wide variety of industries. Services include the following:
- ISO 9000 strategic planning and consulting
- Quality system audits and auditor training (internal audits and pre-assessments)

- Quality manual evaluation
- Public and on-site training seminars.
In Business: Quest International Associates Ltd., England: May 1990; Quest USA, Inc.: May 1992
Clients: A.J. Oster; Basic Vegetable Products; Champion International, Inc.; Cincinnati Milacron; Freudenberg Nonwovens; Laser Mike, Inc.; Motorola; Plastipak Packaging, Inc.; The Rexroth Corporation; Snyder General; Sumitomo Electric.
Qualifications/Certifications: Quest USA, Inc. is registered to ISO 9001: 1987 Quality Systems with SGS ICS. Quest has guided US companies to successful registration of their quality system to ISO-9001 and ISO-9002, utilizing the guidelines described in the ISO 9000-3 TickIT scheme.

r. bowen international, inc.

149 W Market Street
York, PA 17401-1314, USA
Tel: 717-843-4880; Fax: 717-854-8591
Contact: Robert D Bowen, President
Randy T Byrnes, Principal
Services: r. bowen international provides project planning, education, training, audits, on-site resources, documentation services and supplier services.
In Business: 2 years
Clients: AT&T Microelectronics, Storage Technology, Hershey Foods, Carbide Graphite, Donsco Incorporated, Dentsply International. r. bowen international, inc. also serves clients in the following industries: electronics, food processing, computer manufacturers, micrographics and metallurgy.
Qualifications/Certifications: Robert D. Bowen is ASQC certified as a Quality Engineer and Quality Auditor with 16 years experience.

R.P. COONEY & ASSOCIATES

240 S Monaco Parkway, Suite 707
Denver, CO 80224, USA
Tel: 303-320-4210; Fax: 303-320-4210 (call first)
Contact: Ray P Cooney, President
Services: R.P. Cooney & Associates help clients develop ISO 9000-conforming quality management systems. Services include the following:
- Assistance in integrating ISO 9000 into existing TQM and continuous improvement efforts
- Management and staff training in the ISO 9000 standards
- Assessment of quality systems against ISO 9001, 9002 or 9003
- Gap analysis and corrective action assistance
- Facilitating ISO 9000 implementation planning and cost estimation

- Registrar selection and interface
- Pre-registration audit preparation.

In Business: Providing ISO 9000 services since January 1993.

Clients: Not available at time of publication.

Qualifications/Certifications: Raymond P. Cooney has had extensive experience successfully implementing continuous improvement while holding a variety of technical and managerial positions during 14 years with Exxon Chemical Company. Prior to joining Exxon, he worked for Amoco, US Gypsum Co., and the Gillette Co. He received his Doctorate in Chemistry from the University of Florida. In 1991, Mr. Cooney received the Intermediates President's Award for leading Exxon Chemical's first ISO 9000 registration in North America. He also served in an advisory capacity for Exxon Chemical's second North American ISO 9000 registration. His implementation efforts give him experience in applying ISO 9000 in discrete and continuous manufacturing and service situations. He has helped design and implement ISO 9000 conforming auditing, corrective action, document control systems, and quality manuals. Mr. Cooney currently serves on the Accreditation Council of the American Association for Laboratory Accreditation (A2LA). This Committee reviews and approves A2LA's registration of reference materials suppliers' quality systems to ISO 9001 and ISO 9002. Mr. Cooney helped develop Exxon Chemical's Quality Principles Course and Baldrige Award Management Self-Assessment Module. He is co-author of SQC software and has helped design and implement a company-wide internal quality benchmarking network. He has started and led self-managed quality improvement teams and championed employee recognition and suggestion systems. Mr. Cooney has taken the 5-day BSI Lead Auditor and ASQC Quality Auditing courses. He is a member of ASQC, Organization Development Network, and the American Chemical Society, and he has presented papers at national ASTM and worldwide Exxon TQM Conferences.

ROBERT PEACH AND ASSOCIATES, INC.

200 W Cornwall Road, #126
Cary, NC 27511-3802, USA
Tel: 919-319-1982; Fax: 919-319-1984

Contact: Robert W Peach, Principal

Services: Robert Peach and Associates, Inc. evaluates quality management practices, conducts comprehensive quality fitness reviews, and makes in-depth analyses of quality systems. Assessments based on ISO 9000 and Baldrige Award criteria are used to develop quality manuals and documentation to meet customer requirements.

In Business: 13 years

Clients: North American Philips; Inland Steel Company; Motorola, Inc.; Corning, Inc.; Sematech; Institute of Industrial Launderers; ASQC (As Administrator of Malcolm Baldrige Consortium); Management Association of Illinois; Georgia Institute of Technology; University of Wisconsin.

Qualifications/Certifications: Mr. Peach chairs the Registration Accreditation Board and the Standards Council of the ASQC. He is a delegate to the ISO TC176 Committee, where he chairs the Working Group that developed and updates ISO 9004-1, Quality management and quality system elements—Guidelines. He established and managed the quality assurance activity at Sears, Roebuck and Company for over 25 years. Mr. Peach served as project manager of the Malcolm Baldrige National Quality Award Consortium and later as technical advisor to the award administrator. He is an ASQC Fellow, recipient of their Edwards Medal, a Certified Quality Engineer and Registered Professional Engineer in Quality Engineering.

ROCHESTER INSTITUTE OF TECHNOLOGY
Center for Quality and Applied Statistics (CQAS)

Hugh L. Carey Building
98 Lomb Memorial Drive
Rochester, NY 14623-5604, USA
Tel: 716-475-6990; Fax: 716-475-5959

Contact: Donald D Baker, Associate Director

Services: The Center for Quality and Applied Statistics (CQAS), provides quality and productivity seminars, custom training programs and consultative expertise. Instructors combine theory and practical experience to provide comprehensive programs relevant to client needs. CQAS provides seminars including the following:

- The ISO 9000 Seminar
- Internal Auditing to ISO 9000
- BSI Lead Auditor Course
- Developing ISO 9000 Documentation
- Implementing ISO 9000 Compliant Software Quality Systems
- Impact of the Revised ISO 9000 Standards
- ISO 9000: Small Manufacturers Focus Group.

In Business: 10 years

Clients: During the past decade, CQAS has conducted statistical quality/process control and quality technologies courses and programs at RIT or on site for more than 200 industry, business, government and service agencies and for thousands of individuals. A growing client base includes small and medium-sized companies.

Qualifications/Certifications: The staff at CQAS are consultants, real-world problem solvers, respected speakers, prominent authors, and active members of professional societies. They have industrial or business experience and have completed the BSI Lead Assessor program. Staff serve in several capacities including the RAB and Technical Committee 176.

SAFETY AND COMPLIANCE ENGINEERING, INC.

PO Box 44
Dana Point, CA 92629-9998, USA
Tel: 714-363-1402; Fax: 714-240-7218
Contact: Gilbert C Walter, President
Daniel Pitkin, V.P. of Development/ISO 9000
Tel: 916-268-0917
Contact: Bill Lapham, V.P., EMI/RFI/ESD
Services: Safety and Compliance Engineering, Inc. services include the following:

- Product safety tests and assessments
- EMI/RFI tests and seminars
- Quality engineer and technical specification
- Photography (technical)
- Engineering consulting
- Component engineering and spec writing
- Conformance to the federal NISTIR4721 directive
- New product development and marketing
- ISO 9000 implementation.

In Business: 10 years
Clients: Everex, Eltech, Momentum, APEX, AST Research, Unisys, ICOT Corp., ALPHA Micro, ASEMTEC, IAC Industries, Wilden Pump and Engr., and other engineering/manufacturing companies.
Qualifications/Certifications: Safety and Compliance Engineering, Inc. (SCE) is a team of 25 senior engineering consultants. SCE has five trained ISO 9000 auditors. The founder of SCE is a state- and internationally-certified professional in product safety certification, a quality control engineer, a California-certified professional engineer, a California-licensed electrical inspector, a member of IEEE, a member of the American Society of Safety Engineers, and is certified as an international product safety manager.

SANDERS & ASSOCIATES

820 Gessner, Suite 940
Houston, TX 77024, USA
Tel: 800-856-8772/713-465-8772; Fax: 713-465-9742
Contact: Dr. Judith A Sanders, Director
Annette F Harrington, Quality Coordinator
Jose L Jimenez, V.P. Latin-American Services
Services: Sanders & Associates provides training and consulting in Continuous Quality Improvement

(CQI) and ISO 9000. In addition to a comprehensive two-day course on the implementation of ISO 9000 standards, Sanders offers courses that integrate SPC skills and the "people side" of quality, as well as ISO 9000 and CQI. Other training is available in Leadership for Quality and Performance Enhancement.

In Business: 12 years
Clients: VISTA Chemical; General Dynamics; Quanex Tube Group; Groth Corporation; Hollywood Marine; Mayer Electric; Industrial Distribution Association; Ethyl Corporation; Lyondell; PDVSA Services; Inc.; PDVSA Services; BV; Bariven; SA; Industrial Distribution Group.
Qualifications/Certifications: Authors of the AMA Book/ Course ISO 9000: How to Qualify for ISO 9000. Sanders associates hold Ph.D.s in statistics and instructional design and are certified in lead auditor training. Sanders ssociates received their original lead auditor training via British Standards Institute and Stat-A-Matrix approved courses.

SCOTT TECHNICAL SERVICES

34 Channing Street, Suite 400
Newton, MA 02158, USA
Tel: 617-527-7032; Fax: 617-527-0618
Contact: Stephen Keneally, President
Otis Russell, Senior Consultant
Services: Scott Technical Services provides the following services:

- Documentation, training and implementation of quality management systems per ISO 9000 guidelines
- Operations management consulting that fosters rapid organizational improvement leading to ISO 9000 certification.

In Business: 8 years
Clients: Abiomed, Inc.; Allied-Signal Aerospace Corporation (Bendix Communications Division); Cobra Industries, Inc.; ELBIT Computer Ltd.; GTE-Government Systems; Inductotherm Corp.; Lavolin Corporation; LEPEL Corp.; MBTA-Mass. Bay Transportation Authority; Pacesetter Systems; Polymer Technology Corporation; Schwartzkopf Technologies Corporation; Thermatool Corp.
Qualifications/Certifications: Qualifications include more than 100 years of combined experience in all phases of quality assurance and operations management. Initially focused on the aerospace and defense industries, STS services now include the computer, telecommunications, medical devices, electronics, capital equipment, transportation and service industries.

SERVICE PROCESS CONSULTING, INC.

76 George Avenue
Edison, NJ 08820, USA
Tel: 908-321-0045; Fax: 908-549-9117
Contact: Ian Durand, President
April Cormaci, Executive Vice President
Services: Service Process Consulting, Inc. delivers customized consulting and training to service organizations and manufacturing companies to support their implementation of effective quality management systems. The firm also leads public workshops on behalf of trade and business organizations. The principals have particular expertise and experience in the ISO 9000 series of quality standards and in TQM. Service Process Consulting recently created a comprehensive video seminar package on ISO 9000.
In Business: 4 years
Clients: AT&T; Dorman-Roth Foods, Inc.; Hexcel Corp.; New Zealand Milk Products; Pittman; W.R. Grace; Delaware County Community College; Northeast Wisconsin Technical College.
Qualifications/Certifications: The president and principal consultant has been actively involved for more than 7 years in ISO 9000 series efforts. Mr. Durand has served as a senior examiner for the Malcolm Baldrige National Quality Award, and has studied and practiced in the areas of individual and group dynamics. Mr. Durand also has more than 30 years of experience in technical and management positions with AT&T Bell Laboratories, including developing a process quality and management methodology that is standard across the corporation. Other staff members have diverse experience in training, group dynamics, interpersonal skills, and process management.

SOFTWARE QUALITY ASSOCIATES

2725 Coliseum Street
Los Angeles, CA 90018, USA
Tel: 213-292-5288
Contact: Edward L Jordan, President
Services: ISO 9000 and ISO 9000-3 services encompass pre- and post-registration and include initial planning/organizing; adequacy/compliant audits; QMS development, training and registrar selection/evaluation; and QMS maintenance. Other services include integration of ISO QMS with DoD, FAA, FDA, DOE, NASA, NATO, and European Space Agency requirements as well as seminars development (ISO, DoD, Software Engineering Institute, etc.).
In Business: 11 years
Clients: Alenia S.p.a., McDonnell Douglas, General Research, Contel, Air Force, Navy, Army.
Qualifications/Certifications: Edward Jordan, an international consultant and a TickIT Auditor, has more than 30 years' experience in software engineering. He specializes in software quality management, quality assurance, and software process evaluation (SEI). He has assisted firms in business and industry, including aerospace, computers, software, medical devices, telecommunications, etc. He is knowledgeable of standards and schemes, including ISO 9000/9000-3, DoD-STD-2167A/2168, DO-178A/B, NATO, FDA, ESA, IEEE, NASA & TickIT. Mr. Jordan received both his BA in business administration (1975) and MBA in management (1977) from Pepperdine University. He is also a graduate of IQA-approved TickIT Auditor Course, Gilbert, Oxford, England, 1993.

STAT-A-MATRIX GROUP

2124 Oak Tree Road
Edison, NJ 08820, USA
Tel: 908-548-0600; Fax: 908-548-0409
Contact: Alan S Marash, Vice President, Operations
2711 Jefferson Davis Highway, Suite 200
Arlington, VA 22202, USA
Tel: 703-415-2591; Fax: 703-415-1684
Contact: Ira Epstein, Vice President, Government Services
43000 W Nine Mile Road, Suite 210
Novi, MI 48375, USA
Tel: 313-344-9596; Fax: 313-380-3798
Contact: Paul Berman, Director of Support Services
Services: The STAT-A-MATRIX Group has been helping companies since 1968 develop quality systems and train personnel to meet the requirements of regulatory and consensus standards. Hence, their ISO 9000 activities are a direct outgrowth of prior successes in meeting TQM implementation and in meeting nuclear, defense, FDA, and other quality requirements. They offer ISO 9000 and GMP consulting services, including the following:
- Initial baseline evaluation
- Top management orientation
- Action planning
- Quality system documentation and implementation
- All levels of employee training
- Formal pre-assessment
- Support during third-party assessment
- Follow-on services after registration.
In addition, STAT-A-MATRIX offers public seminars in ISO 9000 implementation and documentation, lead assessor certification; internal auditor training; and other specialized areas such as software, FDA, DoD and the auto industry.
In Business: 25 years
Clients: Fortune 500 companies, middle-market compa-

nies, government agencies and small firms. Industries served include medical and pharmaceutical, manufacturing, services, software, aerospace/defense, automotive, chemicals, fibers, graphics, telecommunications and others.

Qualifications/Certifications: STAT-A-MATRIX's worldwide staff of more than 75 includes approximately 40 ISO 9000 management consultants, certified assessors and certified lead assessors. The average staff member has over 25 years of industry experience, plus an advanced degree and/or professional credentials, such as PE, CQA, CQE, IQA and/or RAB certification. STAT-A-MATRIX Group staff includes TC 176 members, ASQC fellows, and Baldrige Award examiners. They were the first US-based organization registered by the IQA to provide lead assessor certification training and the first to receive RAB accreditation for lead auditor training. This program is also recognized by SEQUAL in France. Members of their US, UK, Belgian, Japanese and Brazilian offices have assisted hundreds of companies in attaining ISO 9000 registration.

THORNHILL USA

PO Box 3643
Wilmington, DE 19807, USA
Tel: 215-444-3998; Fax: 215-444-1365
Contact: Ralph D. Schmidt, Director
Services: Thornhill USA's services include the following:
- ISO 9001-2
- Malcolm Baldrige
- Auto, aircraft, military standards
- Supplier and contractor audits
- Training in quality TOOLS
- Design of quality systems, procedures and manuals
- Contacting third-party auditors
- Resourcing leadership on strategy and business plans.

In Business: 2 years
Clients: Thornhill USA's clients are primarily in the following industries:Service providers, automotive suppliers, plastic resin compounders, major chemical and petroleum companies in North and South America
Qualifications/Certifications: Each consultant has lead assessor training and over five years of "hands-on" quality system experience with Fortune 500 companies prior to joining the firm. Members include RAB Certified Lead Auditors and Auditors as well as IQA Certified Members. Thornhill USA is affiliated with Alberto Levy & Company of Buenos Aires.

TOTAL QUALITY MANAGEMENT ASSOCIATES, INC.

11500 Olive Boulevard, Suite 240
St. Louis, MO 63141
Tel: 314-994-0092; Fax: 314-994-0035
Contact: Norman G Siefert, Vice President
Jack Finney, Vice President
Services: Total Quality Management Associates, Inc. (TQMA) products and services include the following:

ISO 9000 Implementation
- Executive overviews
- Organizational awareness programs
- Gap analysis
- Certification guidance
- Steering committee coaching
- Internal auditor training
- Documentation writing.

Supplier Certifications Systems
- Customized supplier certification development
- Supplier compliance audits.

General Quality System Evaluation
- Strength and weakness assessments
- Corrective action planning.

English/Spanish bilingual services available.

In Business: 3 years
Clients: ABB, Boise Cascade, Emerson Electric, Glaxo. In addition to these larger clients, TQMA has assisted numerous small-to-medium-sized companies achieve quality improvement and ISO 9000 registration. The client base has business scopes including hard goods, service, contract engineering and electronics.
Qualifications/Certifications: TQMA is a group of highly qualified quality system specialists led by Norm Siefert. ISO 9000 deliverables are a key specialty, but not the only service. Norm is a graduate of Washington University in St. Louis, MO. He has over 25 years of industrial and service hands-on experience as a quality professional, Plant Manager and Marketing Services Director. His ISO 9000 experience began in 1986. He is a member of the ISO Technical Committee 176 and an RAB Certified Lead Auditor. Additionally, Norm has done in-house and public seminars on ISO 9000 implementation and internal auditor training.

VERITY CONSULTING GROUP, INC., THE

12021 Wilshire Boulevard, Suite 825
Los Angeles, CA 90025, USA
Tel: 213-389-9700; Fax: 213-389-9701
Contact: Jeff Rumburg, Vice President
Services: Verity Consulting specializes in competitive

analysis and competitive benchmarking. Its services include the following:

- Proprietary studies (benchmarking, strategic-level competitive analysis, and industry attractiveness studies)
- Seminars and workshops (hands-on benchmarking techniques, implementing benchmarking in your organization, competitive data acquisition and analysis, and integrating competitive analysis into strategic plans)
- On-site assistance (building the benchmarking team, competitive data acquisition and analysis, implementing benchmarking results, and strategy facilitation).

In Business: 11 years

Clients: IBM, AT&T, Du Pont, Exxon, General Motors, United Airlines, Proctor & Gamble, Rockwell International, Pacific Gas and Electric Company, American National Standards Institute (ANSI).

Qualifications/Certifications: The directors of Verity Consulting have completed hundreds of proprietary benchmarking projects in a variety of different industries, including the following: Chemicals, automotive, pharmaceuticals, gas and electric utilities, banking, computers, consumer products, airlines, telecommunications, and forest and paper products. Equally broad is its range of functional experience. Verity has completed proprietary benchmarking studies in virtually every functional area, including the following: Manufacturing, information systems, engineering, human resources, sales, research and development, product development, marketing, strategic planning, finance, training, and purchasing.

VICTORIA GROUP INCORPORATED, THE

10529 Braddock Road
Fairfax, VA 22030, USA
Tel: 800-845-0567/703-250-4990;
Fax: 800-845-0767/703-250-5523
Contact: Connie Johnson, Business Manager
Lynne Plante, Operations Manager
Services: The Victoria Group Incorporated provides a full range of services management and ISO 9000 related services including the following:

- Implementation planning and facilitation
- Executive orientation
- Staff and associate training in quality concepts
- ISO 9000 and Total Quality Management disciplines.

The Victoria Group operates a lead auditor training program that is recognized by the Governing Board of the Assessor Registration Scheme in the United Kingdom.

In Business: 3 years
Clients: The L.S. Starrett Company (Scotland) Ltd., Eastman Kodak, Hewlett-Packard, York International, Siemens Industrial Automation, Millipore Waters, Eli Lilly, GTE, Coors, AT&T.
Qualifications/Certifications: The Victoria Group has experience in implementing quality systems based on ISO 9000 or similar standards; its principals and associates can claim well over 100 successful registrations. Most staff are registered assessors or registered lead assessors within the British government recognized scheme. All have been functionally responsible for the successful implementation and management of ISO 9001 or ISO 9002 based quality systems. They have extensive experience with many other industry and national standards, including MIL-Q-9858A, AQAP-1, Ford Q1, IBM and others.

WICKHAM INTERNATIONAL MANAGEMENT SERVICES LTD.

63 Sherwood Way
West Wickham, Kent BR4 9PB, England
Tel: 44 81 777 9137; Fax: 44 81 776 2489
Contact: Bill Ferguson, Director and Principal Consultant
1 Covill Close, Belton Lane
Great Gonerby
Grantham Lincolnshire, NG31 8PP, England
Tel: 44 476 593 727; Fax: Same
Contact: David W.B. Ferguson, Consultant
PO Box 86
Sugar Land, TX 77487, USA
Tel: 800-486-4138; Fax: 713-242-6462
Contact: Jim Dunn, Consultant
Services: Wickham International Management Services provides consulting services including the following:

- Quality assurance consulting
- Pre-assessment audits
- Sub-contractor and internal auditing
- Benchmarking exercises
- Technical writing
- Auditor training.

In Business: 8 years
Clients: Wickham International Management Services has assisted a number of companies, large and small, to achieve accreditation to the UK equivalent of the ISO series of standards. Recent assignments have involved work in the following fields: packaging, chemicals, printing, textiles and bar code production. Recently Bill has been actively engaged in the United States, providing consultancy advice to a number of multinational companies, all of whom have received registration.
Qualifications/Certifications: Bill Ferguson, C.Eng.,

F.inst.E., F.I.Q.A., has been employed in quality assurance for 20 years. During this time he has been involved with defining the quality requirements for chemicals, papers and textiles used by the UK Ministry of Defence. He has also worked in evaluating the quality system of suppliers and potential suppliers of these materials and for the subsequent approval and monitoring of their performance. Bill is a fellow of the Institute for Quality Assurance (IQA) and a Lead Assessor registered by the UK Registration Board for Assessors (RBA). In this capacity he is engaged by a number of assessing bodies. David W.B. Ferguson has the following credentials: C.Eng., M.I.Mech.E.; he has recently completed a lead assessor training course. He has extensive experience in technical and procedures writing. Jim Dunn is an assessor registered by the UK Registration Board of Assessors (RBA) and an ASQC Certified Quality Auditor.

WILMINGTON QUALITY ASSOCIATES

303 Water Street, Box 9205
Wrightsville Beach, NC 28480, USA
Tel: 910-256-8149; Fax: Same
Contact: Thomas Hudgin, President
Services: Wilmington Quality Associates helps companies compete effectively by realizing their full potential in meeting customer demands. The firm accomplishes this by providing education and training in ISO 9000 quality standards and Total Quality Management through lectures, workshops and on-site training using client's data. The firm offers evaluation and implementation services in the following disciplines:
- ISO quality standards
- Total Quality Management
- Supplier/vendor audits and certification
- Team training
- Customer satisfaction surveys
- Continuous improvement measurements
- Project management.

In Business: 3 years
Clients: Information on clients in the United States and Europe available upon request.
Qualifications/Certifications: Thomas Hudgin has been employed in the chemical and pharmaceutical industries for 27 years with Warren-Teed, Hoechst-Roussel, Adria (Montedison/Farmitalia), Glaxo and Applied Analytical Industries. During this period, he managed the disciplines of quality assurance, Total Quality Management, regulatory affairs, project management, document control, production planning, new business development in manufacturing and services industries. He has a BS in chemistry and an MBA. He is an active member of ASQC and the Regulatory Affairs Professional Society.

WRIGHT QUALITY/RELIABILITY PLANNING

6 Susan Road
Marlborough, MA 01752-1535, USA
Tel: 508-481-2631; Fax: 508-481-2631
Contact: Donald Wright, Quality/Reliability Engineer
Services:
- Conduct preliminary ISO 9000 audit to determine current compliance to requirements
- Develop ISO 9000 quality manuals for compliance to requirements
- Flow chart the manufacturing process for compliance to ISO 9000 requirements
- Meet customer performance expectations through Quality Function Deployment (QFD)
- Plan and establish controls for a Total Quality Management (TQM) program to ISO 9004
- Educate and prepare company for meeting the requirements of ISO 9000 certification
- Statistical Process Control (SPC) and Taguchi ANOVA methods for controlling customer quality expectations at optimum costs.

In Business: 3.5 years
Clients: Not available at time of publication.
Qualifications/Certifications: Donald Wright's qualifications include: auditor for ISO 9000, ASQC Reliability Engineer certification, RCA Institutes in Electronics (audio/video). Mr. Wright has a BGS degree from Rollins College and a MS in systems management from Florida Institute of Technology. Mr. Wright has more than 30 years experience as an engineer with training in design, all phases of reliability (physics and mathematical modeling), Statistical Process Control (SPC), quality (management, planning and measures), writing software and teaching reliability and quality methods.

Appendix D

ISO 9000 REGISTRARS

This section contains a list of registrars that offer third-party auditing services and registration to the ISO 9000 series standards.

Editor's Note: *This listing, which is neither official nor guaranteed to be complete, is provided for information purposes only. CEEM Information Services does not endorse any of the registrars by including them in this Handbook.*

A.G.A. QUALITY, A Service of International Approval Services (A.G.A)
8501 E Pleasant Valley Road
Cleveland, OH 44131
Tel: 216-524-4990; Fax: 216-642-3463

ABS Quality Evaluations, Inc. (ABS QE)
16855 Northchase Drive
Houston, TX 77060
Tel: 713-873-9400; Fax: 713-874-9564

AIB-Vincotte (AV Qualité)
2900 Wilcrest
Suite 300
Houston, TX 77042
Tel: 713-465-2850; Fax: 713-465-1182

American Association For Laboratory Accreditation (A2LA)
656 Quince Orchard Road, #620
Gaithersburg, MD 20878-1409
Tel: 301-670-1377; Fax: 301-869-1495

American European Services Incorporated (AES)
1054 31st Street NW
Suite 120
Washington, DC 20007
Tel: 202-337-3214; Fax: 202-337-3709

American Quality Assessors (AQA)
1201 Main Street, Suite 2010
Columbia, SC 29202
Tel: 803-254-1164; Fax: 803-252-0056

American Society of Mechanical Engineers, The (ASME)
United Engineering Center
345 E 47th Street
New York, NY 10017
Tel: 212-605-4796; Fax: 212-605-8713

Asociacion Española de Normalizacion y Certificacion (AENOR)
Fernandez de la Hoz, 52
Madrid, 28010, Spain
Tel: 34-1-410-4851; Fax: 34-1-410-4976

Associated Offices Quality Certification (AOQC)
650 N Sam Houston Parkway East, Suite 228
Houston, TX 77060
Tel: 713-591-7882; Fax: 713-448-1401

AT&T Quality Registrar (AT&T QR)
650 Liberty Avenue
Union, NJ 07083
Tel: 908-851-3058; Fax: 908-851-3158

Bellcore Quality Registration (BQR)
6 Corporate Place
Room 1A230
Piscataway, NJ 08854
Tel: 908-699-3739; Fax: 908-336-2244

British Standards Institution (BSI QA)
PO Box 375
Milton Keynes, MK14 6LL, United Kingdom
Tel: 44-90-822-0908; Fax: 44-90-822-0671

Bureau Veritas Quality International (North America), Inc. (BVQI)
North American Central Offices
509 N Main Street
Jamestown, NY 14701
Tel: 716-484-9002; Fax: 716-484-9003

Canadian General Standards Board (CGSB)
222 Queen Street
Suite 1402
Ottawa, Ontario K1A 1G6, Canada
Tel: 613-941-8657; Fax: 613-941-8706

Ceramic Industry Certification Scheme, Ltd. (CICS)
Queens Road
Penkhull
Stoke-On-Trent, ST4 7LQ, United Kingdom
Tel: 44-782-411-008; Fax: 44-782-412-331

CGA Approvals — Canadian Operations of International Approval Services (CGA)
55 Scarsdale Road
Toronto, Ontario M3B 2R3, Canada
Tel: 416-447-6468; Fax: 416-447-7067

Det Norske Veritas Industry, Inc. (DNV)
16340 Park Ten Place, Suite 100
Houston, TX 77084
Tel: 713-579-9003; Fax: 713-579-1360

DLS Quality Technology Associates, Inc. (DLS)
108 Hallmore Drive
Camillus, NY 13031
Tel: 315-468-5811; Fax: 315-699-6332

Electronic Industries Quality Registry (EQR)
2001 Pennsylvania Avenue NW
Washington, DC 20006-1813
Tel: 202-457-4970; Fax: 202-457-4985

Entela, Inc., Quality System Registration Division (ENTELA)
3033 Madison Avenue SE
Grand Rapids, MI 49548
Tel: 616-247-0515, 800-888-3787; Fax: 616-247-7527

Factory Mutual Research Corporation (FMRC)
1151 Boston-Providence Turnpike
PO Box 9102
Norwood, MA 02062
Tel: 617-255-4883; Fax: 617-762-9375

GBJD Registrars Limited (GBJD)
32 Clarissa Drive, Suite 822
Richmond Hill, Ontario L4C 9R6, CANADA
Tel: 905-508-9417; Fax: 905-471-0822

German Association for the Certification of Quality Management Systems (DQS)
August-Schanz
Str. 21
Frankfurt/Main, D-60433, GERMANY
Tel: 49-69-954213-0; Fax: 49-69-954213-11

Intertek Services Corporation (INTERTEK)
9900 Main Street, Suite 500
Fairfax, VA 22031
Tel: 703-ISO-9000 ext. 3011; Fax: 703-273-2895 or 4124

KEMA Registered Quality, Inc. (KEMA)
4379 County Line Road
Chalfont, PA 18914
Tel: 215-822-4258; Fax: 215-822-4285

KPMG Quality Registrar (KPMG)
150 John F Kennedy Parkway
Short Hills, NJ 07078
Tel: 800-716-5595; Fax: 201-912-6050

Litton Systems Canada Limited Quality System Registrars (LSL QSR)
25 City View Drive
Etobicoke, Ontario M9W 5A7, CANADA
Tel: 416-249-1231 x2308 or 800-267-0861
Fax: 416-246-2049

Lloyd's Register Quality Assurance Limited (LRQA)
33-41 Newark Street, Riverview Historical Plaza II
Hoboken, NJ 07030
Tel: 201-963-1111; Fax: 201-963-3299

Loss Prevention Certification Board, Ltd., The (LPCB)
Melrose Avenue
Borehamwood, Hertfordshire WD6 2BJ, United Kingdom
Tel: 44-081-207-2345; Fax: 44-081-207-6305

MET Laboratories, Inc. (MET)
914 W Patapsco Avenue
Baltimore, MD 21230-3432
Tel: 410-354-3300; Fax: 410-354-3313

National Quality Assurance, Ltd. (NQA)
1146 Massachusetts Avenue
Boxborough, MA 01719
Tel: 508-635-9256; Fax: 508-266-1073

National Standards Authority of Ireland (NSAI)
Worldwide Certification Services
5 Medallion Center (Greeley Street)
Merrimack, NH 03054
Tel: 603-424-7070; Fax: 603-429-1427

NSF International (NSF)
3475 Plymouth Road, PO Box 130140
Ann Arbor, MI 48113-0140
Tel: 313-769-6728; Fax: 313-769-0109

OTS Quality Registrars, Inc. (OTSQR)
10700 Northwest Freeway, Suite 455
Houston, TX 77092
Tel: 713-688-9494; Fax: 713-688-9590

Quality Assurance Association of France (AFAQ)
Woodfield Executive Center
1101 Perimeter Drive, Suite 450
Schaumburg, IL 60173, USA
Tel: 708-330-0606; Fax: 708-330-0707

Quality Certification Bureau, Inc. (QCB)
#208, Advanced Technology Centre, 9650 - 20th Avenue
Edmonton, Alberta T6N 1G1, Canada
Tel: 800-268-7321; Fax: 403-496-2464

Quality Management Institute (QMI)
Suite 800, Mississauga Executive Center
Two Robert Speck Parkway
Mississauga, Ontario L4Z 1H8 , Canada
Tel: 905-272-3920; Fax: 905-272-3942

Quality Systems Registrars, Inc. (QSR)
13873 Park Center Road
Suite 217
Herndon, VA 22071-3279
Tel: 703-478-0241; Fax: 703-478-0645

Quebec Quality Certification Group (GQCQ)
70, rue Dalhousie, Bureau 220
Quebec, Quebec G1K 4B2, Canada
Tel: 418-643-5813; Fax: 418-646-3315

Scott Quality Systems Registrars, Inc. (SQSR)
8 Grove Street, Suite 200
Wellesley, MA 02181
Tel: 617-239-1110; Fax: 617-239-0433

SGS International Certification Services, Inc. (SGS ICS)
1415 Park Avenue
Hoboken, NJ 07030
Tel: 800-777-8378; Fax: 201-792-2558

SGS International Certification Services Canada, Inc. (SGS ICS Canada)
90 Gough Road, Unit 4
Markham, Ontario L3R 5V5, Canada
Tel: 905-479-1160; Fax: 905-479-9452

Sira Certification Service/Sira Test and Certification, Ltd. (SCS)
Saighton Lane
Saighton, Chester CH36EG, United Kingdom
Tel: 44-024-433-2200; Fax: 44-024-433-2112

Smithers Quality Assessments, Inc. (SQA)
425 W Market Street
Akron, OH 44303-2099
Tel: 216-762-4231; Fax: 216-762-7447

Steel Related Industries Quality System Registrars (SRI)
SRI Quality System Registrar
2000 Corporate Drive, Suite 450
Wexford, PA 15090
Tel: 412-935-2844; Fax: 412-935-6825

TRA Certification, A Division of T.R. Arnold & Associates, Inc. (TRA-CD)
700 E Beardsley Avenue
PO Box 1081
Elkhart, IN 46515
Tel: 219-264-0745; Fax: 219-264-0740

Tri-Tech Services, Inc., Auditors/Registrar Division (TRI TECH)
4700 Clairton Boulevard
Pittsburgh, PA 15236
Tel: 412-884-2290; Fax: 412-884-2268

TUV America (TUV AMERICA)
TUV America, Inc. and TUV Product Service, Inc. (Headquarters)
5 Cherry Hill Drive
Danvers, MA 01923
Tel: 508-777-7999; Fax: 508-777-8441

TÜV ESSEN (TUV ESSEN)
6 Brighton Road
Clifton, NJ 07012
Tel: 201-773-8880; Fax: 201-773-8834

TUV Rheinland of North America, Inc. (TUVRHEINLAND)
North American Headquarters
12 Commerce Road
Newtown, CT 06470
Tel: 203-426-0888; Fax: 203-270-8883

Underwriters Laboratories Inc. (UL)
1285 Walt Whitman Road
Melville, NY 11747-3081
Tel: 516-271-6200; Fax: 516-271-6242

Underwriters Laboratories of Canada (UL Canada)
7 Crouse Road
Scarborough, Ontario M1R 3A9, Canada
Tel: 416-757-3611; Fax: 416-757-1781

Warnock Hersey Professional Services, Ltd. (WH)
8810 Elmslie Street
LaSalle, Quebec H8R 1V8, Canada
Tel: 514-366-3100; Fax: 514-366-5350

Appendix E

ADDITIONAL RESOURCES

This appendix contains additional ISO 9000 and European Community resources, including the following:
- Economic Development Centers
  - MTCs
  - TAACs
- Hotlines
- Networks and support groups
- On-line databases
- Publications
  - Accreditation/Certification
  - European Community
  - International Trade
  - ISO 9000
  - Standards and Directives
- Software
- Tapes
  - Audio
  - Video.

Editor's Note: *This partial listing is provided for information purposes only. CEEM Information Services does not endorse any of the products or services by including them in this Handbook. CEEM Information Services has made every effort to verify the accuracy of the information contained in this section. Please notify CEEM of any errors.*

ECONOMIC DEVELOPMENT CENTERS

Economic development centers offer help to companies struggling to maintain their status in a technology-driven world. Included are the National Institute for Standards and Technology's Manufacturing Technology Centers (MTCs) and the US Department of Commerce's Trade Adjustment Assistance Centers (TAACs).

The MTCs, designed to bridge the "technology gap" between sources of improved manufacturing technology and the companies that need it, offer assistance in helping smaller companies institute new high-technology practices

and encourage the establishment of continuous improvement programs.

The TAACs offer financial assistance to companies that require consulting services, including costs related to ISO 9000 certification. Companies that have experienced recent declines in sales and employment, due at least in part to increasing imports of competitive products, are eligible for the program. The government pays up to 75 percent of the cost of consulting services.

MTCs

California MTC
Contact: John Chernesky
Location: 13430 Hawthorne Boulevard, Hawthorne, CA 90250
Tel: 310-355-3060
Description: Serves California.

Great Lakes MTC
Contact: Dennis Rosa
Location: 2415 Woodland Avenue, Cleveland, OH 44115
Tel: 216-987-3204
Description: Serves Ohio, Western New York, Western Pennsylvania and West Virginia.

Mid-America MTC
Contact: Alan Lund
Location: 10561 Barkley, Suite 602, Overland Park, KS 66212
Tel: 913-649-4333
Description: Serves Colorado, Kansas and Missouri. Also offers a network which serves ISO 9000 needs.

Midwest MTC
Contact: Janet Mitchell, Quality Expert
Location: PO Box 1485, 2901 Hubbard Road, Ann Arbor, MI 48106
Tel: 313-769-4377
Description: Serves Illinois, Indiana, Michigan, Ohio and Wisconsin. Also provides quality networking through continuous improvement user groups.

Northeast MTC
Contact: Mike Levy
Location: 385 Jordan Road, Troy, NY 12180
Tel: 518-283-1112
Description: Serves New York, northern Pennsylvania and all of New England. Also offers quality networks in the form of ISO 9000 seminar series.

Southeast MTC
Contact: Jim Bishop, Director
Location: PO Box 1149, Columbia, SC 29202
Tel: 803-252-6976
Description: Serves Florida, Georgia, North Carolina, South Carolina and Tennessee.

Upper Midwest MTC
Contact: John Connelly
Location: 111 Third Avenue S, Suite 400, Minneapolis, MN 55401
Tel: 612-338-7722
Description: Serves Minnesota. Also provides quality networks.

TAACs

Great Lakes TAAC
Contact: Margaret Creger, Director
Location: University of Michigan, School of Business Administration, 506 E Liberty Street, 3rd Floor, Ann Arbor, MI 48104-2210
Tel: 313-998-6213
Description: Serves Indiana, Michigan and Ohio.

Mid-America TAAC
Contact: Paul Schmid, Director
Location: University of Missouri at Columbia, University Place, Suite 1700, Columbia, MO 65211
Tel: 314-882-6162
Description: Serves Arkansas, Kansas and Missouri.

Mid-Atlantic TAAC
Contact: William Gates, Director
Location: 486 Norristown Road, Suite 130, Blue Bell, PA 19422
Tel: 215-825-7819
Description: Serves Delaware; Maryland; Pennsylvania; Virginia; Washington, DC; and West Virginia.

Mid-West TAAC
Contact: Howard Yefsky, Director
Location: Applied Strategies International, 150 N Wacker
    Drive, Suite 2240, Chicago, IL 60606
Tel: 312-368-4600
Description: Serves Illinois, Iowa, Minnesota and Wisconsin.

New England TAAC
Contact: Richard McLaughlin, Executive Director
Location: 120 Boylston Street, Boston, MA 02116
Tel: 617-542-2395
Description: Serves Connecticut, Maine, Massachusetts,
    New Hampshire, Rhode Island and Vermont.

New Jersey TAAC
Contact: John Walsh, Director
Location: 200 South Warren Street, CN 990 Capital Place
    One, Trenton, NJ 08625
Tel: 609-292-0360
Description: Serves New Jersey.

New York TAAC
Contact: John Lacey, Director
Location: 117 Hawley Street, Binghamton, NY 13901
Tel: 607-771-0875
Description: Serves New York.

Northwest TAAC
Contact: Ronald Horst, Director
Location: Bank of California Center, 900 4th Avenue, Suite
    2430, Seattle, WA 98164
Tel: 206-622-2730
Description: Alaska, Idaho, Montana, Oregon and
    Washington.

Rocky Mountain TAAC
Contact: Robert Stansbury, Director
Location: 5353 Manhattan Circle, Suite 200, Boulder, CO
    80303
Tel: 303-499-8222
Description: Serves Colorado, Nebraska, New Mexico,
    North Dakota, South Dakota, Utah and Wyoming.

Southeast TAAC
Contact: Charles Estes, Director
Location: Georgia Institute of Technology, Economic
    Development Institute, 151 6th Street, O'Keefe Bldg,
    Room 224, Atlanta, GA 30332
Tel: 404-894-6106
Description: Serves Alabama, Florida, Georgia, Kentucky,
    Mississippi, North Carolina, South Carolina and
    Tennessee.

Southwest TAAC
Contact: Robert Velasquez, Director
Location: 301 S Frio Street, Suite 227, San Antonio, TX
    78207-4414
Tel: 210-220-1240
Description: Serves Louisiana, Oklahoma and Texas.

Western TAAC
Contact: Daniel Jiminez, Director
Location: 3716 S Hope Street, Room 200, Los Angeles, CA
    90007
Tel: 213-743-8427
Description: Serves Arizona, California, Hawaii and
    Nevada.

HOTLINES

EU Hotline
Description: This hotline reports on draft standards of
    CEN, CENELEC and ETSI. It also provides
    information on selected EU directives. The recorded
    message is updated weekly and gives the product,
    document number and closing date for comments.
Tel: 301-921-4164
Price Information: No hotline user fee

The Export Hotline
Description: Supported by the US Chamber of Commerce,
    this privately-sponsored FAX retrieval system can
    provide reports on country markets, trade fairs, trade
    and investment issues, key contacts, shipping

requirements and news/risks/advisories.
Tel: 800-872-9767
Price Information: Free initial call and information kit

GATT Hotline
Description: This hotline provides current information
    received from the GATT Secretariat in Geneva,
    Switzerland, on proposed foreign regulations that may
    significantly affect trade. The recorded message is
    updated weekly and gives the product, country,
    closing date for comments (if any), and the Technical
    Barriers to Trade (TBT) notification number.
Tel: 301-975-4041
Price Information: No hotline user fee

The Trade Information Center
Description: Operated by the Department of Commerce, this is a focal point for information on federal export assistance programs available from the 19 member agencies of the Trade Promotion Coordinating Committee (TPCC). Specialists advise on how to locate and use federal export programs.
Tel: 800-872-8723
Price Information: No user fee

NETWORKS: THE ASQC MODEL FOR LEVERAGE

by Dave Ling

Please refer to the chart "ASQC Model for Leverage."

Need

Individuals at all levels of a company should understand the business impact of ISO 9000 and its role in product regulations and environmental issues. These individuals have diverse needs, however, and are at different stages of understanding. Despite these different stages, everyone is looking for the following:

- Accurate and useful information regarding ISO 9000 and related issues

- Sharing experiences with other companies
- Guidance from experts in the field
- Networking opportunities to form alliances and partnerships.

ASQC Model for Leverage

Individuals who need ISO 9000 information can participate in a number of ISO 9000 formal and informal user-groups. Usually, individuals can only obtain value from these groups if they attend the

(continued on next page)

Model For Leverage

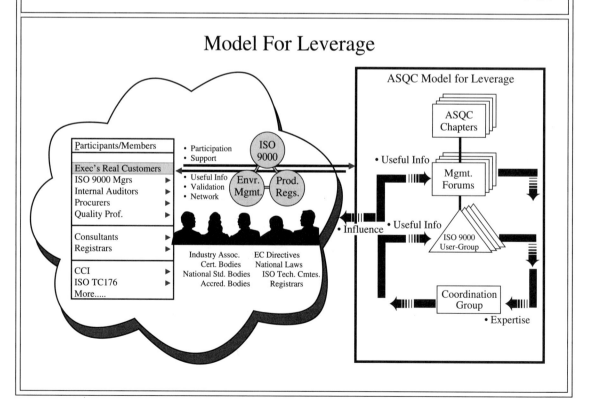

The ASQC Model for Leverage

(continued from previous page)

meetings, for the information generated in meetings is not fully documented for those unable to attend.

The ASQC Santa Clara Chapter is providing a Model for Leverage, where a formalized structure is in place to capture the knowledge generated in these user-groups and to provide useful information to attendees and non-attendees alike. This model consists of four main types of groups with specific purposes:

1. ASQC Chapters: This non-profit organization provides the established services and networks for sponsoring the Model for Leverage.

2. Management Forum: This is an ISO 9000 user-group that shares non-proprietary information related to implementing and sustaining ISO 9000 registered quality systems. It addresses the management issues of an ISO 9000 program.

3. ISO 9000 User-group: This ISO 9000 user-group shares general knowledge of ISO 9000 issues, including implementation and registration guidance.

4. Coordination Group: Sponsored by an ASQC chapter, this group collects the expertise and shared best practices from the Management Forum and ISO 9000 User Group. The Coordination Group will then compile this information into an ISO 9000 Management Kit, update it monthly, and make it available to all participants.

The long-term goal of the Model for Leverage is to capture the knowledge, expertise and best practices from a majority of formal and informal ISO 9000 groups across the country in the ISO 9000 Management Kit.

The Model for Leverage can become a powerful method to learn more about ISO 9000. Furthermore, the model will link individuals and companies across the country to discuss the issues and share ideas. Thus, this Model for Leverage is also a method to influence those who set the future direction of ISO 9000 (e.g.. ISO TC 176, national accreditation bodies and registrars, etc.).

Next Steps

At this time, the Model for Leverage is being implemented in the Silicon Valley/San Francisco Bay Area. When the model is determined to be successful, it will be promoted to help establish the model in other ASQC chapters.

Contact the following people for more information.

Dave Ling
Model for Leverage
Management Forum (Santa Clara) Coordination Group
Phone: 415-857-5057

Stan Salot
ISO 9000 User Group (Santa Clara)
Phone: 510-713-0292

NETWORKS AND SUPPORT GROUPS

In addition to the networks listed below, several MTCs offer network services. Please refer to the Economic Development Centers section for their listings (they have also been listed below for your convenience).

Cleveland Consortium

Description: This is a group of nine manufacturing companies that have joined forces in a consortium effort to achieve ISO 9000 registration. They are sharing experiences and costs. This effort is being managed by the Cleveland Advanced Manufacturing Program (CAMP) and the Work in Northeast Ohio Council (WINOC).
Contact: Ray DePuy
Tel: 216-432-5300; Fax: 216-361-2900

Mid-America MTC

Description: Serves Colorado, Kansas and Missouri. Also offers a network which serves ISO 9000 needs.
Contact: Alan Lund
Tel: 913-649-4333

Midwest MTC

Description: Serves Illinois, Indiana, Michigan, Ohio and Wisconsin. Also provides quality networking through continuous improvement user groups.
Contact: Janet Mitchell, Quality Expert
Tel: 313-769-4377

Minnesota Technology Inc.

Description: Minnesota Technology, working through its Upper Midwest Manufacturing Technology Center, assists Minnesota companies, both one-on-one and in consortia, in working toward ISO 9000 registration. Minnesota Technology partners with state technical colleges, community colleges and private resources to assist and mentor small/medium-sized manufacturers in learning about, implementing, documenting and attaining ISO 9000 registration.
Tel: 612-338-7722; Fax: 612-339-5214

The National ISO 9000 Support Group

Description: This group's services are directed at the professionals interested in guiding their companies to compliance with ISO 9000. They include: fax and modem access to ISO 9000 experts; quick summary reports on all aspects of registration and implementation; a monthly newsletter filled with how-to articles on conforming to ISO 9000; a computer bulletin-board service featuring information, advice, open forums and technical support from IQA-trained lead assessors; audio tapes with an overview of the registration process; and up-to-the-minute news on ISO developments. $150/year.
Contact: Rick Clements
Tel: 616-891-9114; Fax: 616-891-9114

Northeast MTC

Description: Serves New York, northern Pennsylvania and all of New England. Also offers quality networks in the form of ISO 9000 seminar series.
Contact: Mike Levy
Tel: 518-283-1112

Portland ISO 9000 Users Group

Description: Organized in April 1992, the Portland ISO 9000 Users Group is a volunteer organization dedicated to furthering the implementation efforts and education of companies and individuals interested in ISO 9000. The monthly meetings are free and membership is not required.
Contact: Diane Hunt
Tel: 503-238-9835; Fax: 503-235-4668

Upper Midwest MTC

Description: Serves Minnesota. Also provides quality networks.
Contact: John Connelly
Tel: 612-338-7722

Washington ISO 9000 Initiative (WAISO)

Description: WAISO is an open membership, non-profit corporation comprised of representatives from manufacturing, services, education and government. WAISO is dedicated to improving the competitiveness of Washington's business and its economy. It acts as a clearinghouse and coordinates ISO 9000-related information, seminars, training programs, business-to-business networking and assessment/certification services. It offers a resource center and directory, an annual conference, monthly informational meetings and a quarterly newsletter.
Contact: K.C. Ayers
Tel: 206-392-7610; Fax: 206-392-7630

ON-LINE DATABASES

INFO 92
Parent Company: EUROBASES/Commission of the
European Communities
Description: INFO 92 is a database focusing on the
progress of the EU toward a single market and
includes summaries of EU legislation, adopted and in
preparation. The database is broken down into three
areas: removal of physical barriers, removal of
technical barriers and removal of fiscal barriers. INFO
92 also covers the incorporation of EC legislation into
the Member States' own national law and the Social
Charter program.
Tel: 32-2-295-00-01, 32-2-295-00-03

RAPID
Parent Company: EUROBASES/Commission of the
European Communities
Description: The RAPID service includes press releases and
information issued by the Spokesman Service of the
European Commission and press releases issued by the
Council of Ministers. It contains the full text of all
documents issued including memos, speeches and
other key documents.
Tel: 32-2-295-00-01, 32-2-295-00-03

SCAD
Parent Company: EUROBASES/Commission of the
European Communities
Description: SCAD provides EU proposals and acts, official
publications and documents published by various
institutions, in addition to articles, statements and opinions
from industry about the European Union.
Tel: 32-2-295-00-01, 32-2-295-00-03

SESAME
Parent Company: EUROBASES/Commission of the
European Communities
Description: SESAME is a database that monitors research
and development and demonstration and technology
projects associated with the European Community.
Tel: 32-2-295-00-01, 32-2-295-00-03

Standards Council of Canada On-line Database
Parent Company: Standards Council of Canada
Description: This database, located in Ottawa, allows access
to bibliographic information on a variety of standards
including Canadian standards, standards referenced in
Canadian federal legislation, ISO standards and draft
standards, and Draft European Standards and GATT
notifications. In addition, the database includes
information on Canadian and US laboratories offering
calibration and testing services in a wide range of fields.
Tel: 613-238-3222
Price Information: $60/hour

PUBLICATIONS

This section includes books, catalogs, directories, magazines, newsletters, reports and workbooks available from a
variety of sources listed according to subject.

Accreditation/Certification

The ABC's of Standards-Related Activities in the United States (NBSIR 87-3576)
Author: NIST
Description: This report is an introduction to voluntary
standardization, product certification and laboratory
accreditation.
Publisher: National Technical Information Service (NTIS)
Tel: 301-975-2000
ISBN or Reference Number: PB 87-224309

The ABC's of Certification Activities in the United States (NBSIR 88-3821)
Author: NIST
Description: This report, a sequel to NBSIR 87-3576, The
ABC's of Standards-Related Activities in the United
States, provides an introduction to certification. It
provides the reader with information necessary to
make informed purchases and serves as background for
using available documents and services.
Publisher: National Technical Information Service (NTIS)
Tel: 301-975-2000
ISBN or Reference Number: PB 88-239793

Achieving Laboratory Accreditation...A How-To Guide

Author: CEEM Information Services

Description: This guide provides a step-by-step process for accreditation and helps a company prepare and document a quality system. The guide includes essential elements required for accreditation, the concept of quality and how it relates to the laboratory, how to prepare documentation, standard operating procedures, how to complete the application, the assessment procedure and requirements for proficiency testing.

Publisher: CEEM Information Services

Tel: 800-745-5565

Price Information: $95

Directory of Federal Government Certification Programs (NBS SP 739)

Author: NIST

Description: This directory presents information on government certification programs for products and services. Entries describe the scope and nature of each certification program, testing and inspection practices, standards used, methods of identification and enforcement, reciprocal recognition or acceptance of certification, and other relevant details.

Publisher: National Technical Information Service (NTIS)

Tel: 301-975-2000

ISBN or Reference Number: PB 88-201512

Directory of Federal Government Laboratory Accreditation/Designation Programs (NIST SP 808)

Author: NIST

Description: This directory provides updated information on 31 federal government laboratory accreditation and similar type programs conducted by the federal government. These programs, which include some type of assessment regarding laboratory capability, designate sets of laboratories or other entities to conduct testing to assist federal agencies in carrying out their responsibilities. The directory also lists 13 other federal agency programs of possible interest, including programs involving very limited laboratory assessment and programs still under development.

Publisher: National Technical Information Service (NTIS)

Tel: 301-975-2000

ISBN or Reference Number: PB 91-167379

Directory of International and Regional Organizations Conducting Standards-Related Activities (NIST SP 767)

Author: NIST

Description: This directory contains information on 338 international and regional organizations that conduct standardization, certification, laboratory accreditation, or other standards-related activities. It describes their work in these areas, the scope of each organization, national affiliations of members, US participants, restrictions on membership, and the availability of any standards in English.

Publisher: National Technical Information Service (NTIS)

Tel: 301-975-2000

ISBN or Reference Number: PB 89-221147

Directory of Private Sector Product Certification Programs (NIST SP 774)

Author: NIST

Description: This directory presents information from 132 private sector organizations in the United States that engage in product certification activities. Entries describe the type and purpose of each organization, the nature of the activity, the product certified, standards used, certification requirements, the availability and cost of services, and other relevant details.

Publisher: National Technical Information Service (NTIS)

Tel: 301-975-2000

ISBN or Reference Number: PB 90-161712

Directory of State and Local Government Laboratory Accreditation/ Designation Programs (NIST SP 815)

Author: NIST

Description: This directory provides updated information on 21 state and 11 local government laboratory accreditation and similar programs. These programs, which include some type of assessment regarding laboratory capability, designate private sector laboratories or other entities to conduct testing to assist state and local government agencies in carrying out their responsibilities. Entries describe the scope and nature of each program, laboratory assessment criteria and the procedures used in the program, products and fields of testing covered, program authority, and other relevant details.

Publisher: National Technical Information Service (NTIS)

Tel: 301-975-2000

ISBN or Reference Number: PB 92-108968

ISO/IEC Compendium of Conformity Assessment Documents

Author: ISO and IEC

Description: The 160-page volume contains 19 guides on requirements, methods, model rules, statements of policy and recommendations for efficient product certification, as well as reference documents and a set of definitions of relevant terms. These guides make due reference where appropriate to the ISO 9000

series of quality assurance standards issued in a companion publication (ISO 9000 International Standards for Quality Management).
Publisher: ANSI
Tel: 212-642-4900
Price Information: $85

Laboratory Accreditation in the United States (NISTIR 4576)

Author: NIST
Description: This report, a sequel to NBSIR 87-3576, The ABC'S of Standards-Related Activities in the United States and NBSIR 88-3821, The ABC's of Certification Activities in the United States, is designed to provide information on laboratory accreditation to readers who are new to this field. It discusses some of the more significant facets of this topic, provides information necessary to make informed decisions on the selection and use of laboratories, and serves as background for using other available documents and services.
Publisher: National Technical Information Service (NTIS)
Tel: 301-975-2000
ISBN or Reference Number: PB 91-194495

European Union (EU)

1992 Single Market Communications Review

Author: Kline Publishing
Description: This magazine is published quarterly.
Publisher: Kline Publishing
Tel: 44-81-675-6460 (England)

Compulsory Technical Regulations

Author: EFTA
Description: This guide lists the competent national authorities in each EFTA country. It is only published in English.
Publisher: EFTA Press and Information Service
Tel: 41-22-749-1111 (Switzerland)

EC and Environmental Policy & Regulations (4/1/92)

Author: Single Internal Market Information Service
Publisher: US Department of Commerce
Tel: 202-482-5823
Price Information: Free

EC Brief

Author: European Community office of Ernst & Young
Description: This bimonthly newsletter provides up-to-date information on EC happenings.
Publisher: European Community office of Ernst & Young
Tel: 32-2-648-7666 (Belgium)

The EC Builds an Integrated, Modern Transportation System (10/1/91)

Author: Single Internal Market Information Service
Publisher: US Department of Commerce
Tel: 202-482-5823
Price Information: Free

EC Bulletin

Author: Price Waterhouse - EC Services
Description: This bimonthly bulletin provides up-to-date information on EC happenings.
Publisher: Price Waterhouse - EC Services
Tel: 32-2-773-4911 (Belgium)

EC Labor Policy and Workplace Safety - An Integral Part of 1992 (10/1/91)

Author: Single Internal Market Information Service
Publisher: US Department of Commerce
Tel: 202-482-5823
Price Information: Free

The EC Liberalizes Transportation Rules and Upgrades Its Infrastructure (6/1/93)

Author: Single Internal Market Information Service
Publisher: US Department of Commerce
Tel: 202-482-5823
Price Information: Free

EC's Policy and Regulations on Food and Beverages (8/1/93)

Author: Single Internal Market Information Service
Publisher: US Department of Commerce
Tel: 202-482-5823
Price Information: Free

EC Single Market Law Affecting Exporting and Distribution: Agents, Distributors, Franchises (12/1/91)

Author: Single Internal Market Information Service
Publisher: US Department of Commerce
Tel: 202-482-5823
Price Information: Free

EC Telecommunications (10/1/91)

Author: Single Internal Market Information Service
Publisher: US Department of Commerce
Tel: 202-482-5823
Price Information: Free

EC Testing and Certification Procedures Under the Internal Market Program (11/1/91)

Author: Single Internal Market Information Service
Publisher: US Department of Commerce
Tel: 202-482-5823
Price Information: Free

EC-US Business Report
Description: This report is published monthly.
Publisher: C&M International Ltd.
Tel: 202-624-2895
Price Information: $200/year

Effective Lobbying in the European Community
Author: James Gardner
Description: This how-to manual provides a full-scale
    analysis of the techniques of European lobbying from
    the practical perspective of the professional legislative
    advocate.
Publisher: Kluwer Publishing
Tel: 617-354-0140
Price Information: $45

EFTA Bulletin
Author: EFTA Press and Information Service
Description: This newsletter is published quarterly in
    English, French, German, and Swedish/Norwegian
    editions.
Publisher: EFTA Press and Information Service
Tel: 41-22-749-1111 (Switzerland)

EFTA Fact Sheets
Author: EFTA Press and Information Service
Description: This report presents facts and figures about the
    EFTA including its history, trade, activities and
    organization. It includes an overview of the negotia-
    tions with the European Community and is published
    in English, French and German.
Publisher: EFTA Press and Information Service
Tel: 41-22-749-1111 (Switzerland)

The EFTA Industrial Development Fund for Portugal
Author: EFTA Press and Information Service
Description: This report includes general information about
    the fund and its statutes. It is published in English.
Publisher: EFTA Press and Information Service
Tel: 41-22-749-1111 (Switzerland)

EFTA News
Author: EFTA
Description: This free newsletter is published in English,
    French and German.
Publisher: EFTA Press and Information Service
Tel: 41-22-749-1111 (Switzerland)

EFTA: What It Is, What It Does
Author: EFTA
Description: This guide offers general information on the
    history and purpose of the EFTA.
Publisher: EFTA Press and Information Service
Tel: 41-22-749-1111 (Switzerland)

Eurecom
Description: This newsletter is published ten times a year.
Publisher: New York Delegation of the Commission of the
    European Communities
Tel: 212-371-3804
Price Information: Free

Europe
Author: Commission of the European Communities
Description: This newsletter is published ten times a year.
Publisher: Commission of the European Communities
Tel: 800-627-7961
Price Information: $19.95 (US) or $29.95 (International)

Europe Now
Author: US DOC - ITA
Description: This newsletter is published quarterly.
Publisher: US DOC - ITA
Tel: 202-482-5279
Price Information: Free

The European Free Trade Association
Author: EFTA Press and Information Service
Description: This guide provides an in-depth history of the
    EFTA. It is published in French, German and
    Norwegian.
Publisher: EFTA Press and Information Service
Tel: 41-22-749-1111 (Switzerland)

Eurowatch: Economics Policy and Law in the New Europe
Description: This newsletter is published bimonthly.
Publisher: Buraff Publications
Tel: 202-862-0900
Price Information: $797/year

The Free Trade Agreements of the EFTA Countries With the European Communities
Author: EFTA Press and Information Service
Description: This report is published in English, French
    and German.
Publisher: EFTA Press and Information Service
Tel: 41-22-749-1111 (Switzerland)

Handbook on EFTA Markets for Yugoslav Products
Author: EFTA
Description: This is a guide to the markets of five EFTA
    countries. It is published in English.
Publisher: EFTA Press and Information Service
Tel: 41-22-749-1111 (Switzerland)

The OECD Observer

Author: OECD Publications Service

Description: This newsletter is published bimonthly in English and French.

Publisher: OECD Publications Service

Tel: 33-1-45-24-82-00 (France)

Price Information: Single copy: $4.50, annual subscription: $22.00

Single Market for Intellectual Property Protection (8/1/93)

Author: Single Internal Market Information Service

Publisher: US Department of Commerce

Tel: 202-482-5823

Price Information: Free

The Stockholm Convention

Author: EFTA Press and Information Service

Description: This report is published in an English/French bilingual edition.

Publisher: EFTA Press and Information Service

Tel: 41-22-749-1111 (Switzerland)

A Summary of the New European Community Approach to Standards Development (NBSIR 88-3793-1)

Author: NIST

Description: Summary of the European Community's plans to aggressively pursue the goal of achieving an "internal market" by 1992. It also discusses the standards-related implications of such programs on US exporters.

Publisher: National Technical Information Service (NTIS)

Tel: 301-975-2000

ISBN or Reference Number: PB 88-229489/AS

International Trade

Barriers Encountered by US Exporters of Telecommunications Equipment (NBSIR 87-3641)

Author: NIST

Description: This report addresses the perceived institution of unreasonable technical trade barriers by major European trading partners to the export of telecommunications products and systems by US companies.

Publisher: National Technical Information Service (NTIS)

Tel: 301-975-2000

ISBN or Reference Number: PB 88-153630

Business America

Author: US Department of Commerce

Description: This magazine is published biweekly and reports regularly on current developments affecting international trade and US exports.

Publisher: US Department of Commerce

Tel: 202-783-3238

Price Information: $53.00 US, $66.25 International

EuroMarketing A Strategic Planner for Selling into the New Europe

Author: Rick Arons

Description: This publication shows marketing executives of any size company how to market and sell products successfully in today's Europe. (May be available for a reduced rate for educational use, according to specific qualifications.)

Publisher: Probus Publishing Company

Tel: 312-868-1100

Price Information: $32.50

Euronotes

Author: LeBoeuf, Lamb, Leiby & MacRae

Description: This report addresses European law developments affecting international business.

Publisher: LeBoeuf, Lamb, Leiby & MacRae

Tel: 32-2-514-5650 (Belgium)

The Export Yellow Pages

Author: Venture Publishing, in cooperation with the International Trade Administration of the US Department of Commerce)

Description: Over 12,000 companies are listed by industry sector in this annual directory. Included are manufacturers and companies that provide service to exporters. The directory is useful for US companies seeking export services and for foreign buyers seeking sources of US goods and services. US companies interested in listing their name in the directory (free of charge) should contact the ITA district office of the Department of Commerce in their area.

Publisher: Venture Publishing

Tel: 202-482-2000

Price Information: Free

Faulkner & Gray's European Business Directory

Author: Faulkner & Gray

Description: This comprehensive resource guide for US companies doing business in Europe provides names, addresses, phone numbers and economic profiles of the twelve European Community and six Eastern European nations. The directory also has information on a wide variety of European service companies with expertise in banking, law, insurance, and accounting.

Publisher: Faulkner & Gray

Tel: 800-535-8403

Price Information: $295

Technical Barriers to Trade

Author: NIST

Description: This booklet explains the basic rules of the international agreement on technical barriers to trade negotiated during the Tokyo Round of the Multilateral Trade Negotiations (MTN). It describes Title IV of the US Trade Agreements Act of 1979 that implements the United States' obligations under the Agreement. The booklet also describes the functions of the Departments of Commerce and Agriculture, the Office of the US Trade Representative, and the State Department on carrying out US responsibilities.

Publisher: Standards Code & Information Program (SCI)

Tel: 301-975-4029

Trade Implications of Processes and Production Methods (PPMs) (NISTIR 90-4265)

Author: NIST

Description: This report discusses processes and production methods and their relationship to trade, the GATT Agreement on Technical Barriers to Trade, and traditional product standards used in international commerce. The report provides background information on PPMs, a suggested definition, and the possible extension of their application from the agricultural sector to industrial products.

Publisher: National Technical Information Service (NTIS)

Tel: 301-975-2000

ISBN or Reference Number: PB 90-205485

ISO 9000

Documenting Quality for ISO 9000 and Other Industry Standards

Author: Gary E. MacLean

Description: A basic, but very specific "how-to" guide targeted for small- to medium-sized companies that teaches them to document their administrative procedures from start to finish. It is a fully detailed, step-by-step guide to documenting quality systems.

Publisher: ASQC Quality Press

Tel: 800-248-1946

Price Information: List Price: $24.95, Member Price: $21.95

ISBN or Reference Number: ISBN: 0-87389-212-7, Item H0761

A Guidebook to ISO 9000 and ANSI/ASQC Q90

Author: Ronald J. Cottman

Description: This book provides a brief, general, question/answer overview of the ISO 9000 and the ANSI/ASQC Q90 standards. It features the ANSI/ASQC

Q90 standards in their entirety.

Publisher: ASQC Quality Press

Tel: 800-248-1946

Price Information: List Price: $53.95, Member Price: $45.95

ISBN or Reference Number: ISBN: 0-87389-194-5, Item H0737

How to Qualify for ISO 9000

Author: Sanders & Associates

Description: This self-study course takes you step-by-step through the ISO 9000 registration process, from the initial implementation of a quality assurance program and documentation of procedures, to the registration visit and audit. The inclusion of numerous examples, diagrams, charts and checklists simplifies the learning process. This course also includes one multiple-choice test and one case study.

Publisher: Sanders & Associates

Tel: 800-538-4761

Price Information: $130, AMA Member Price: $117

ISBN or Reference Number: Stock # 95003GF1

ISO 9000: A Comprehensive Guide to Registration, Audit Guidelines, and Successful Certification

Author: Greg Hutchins

Description: This book is a comprehensive, yet user-friendly, guide to ISO 9000 that fully explains ISO 9000, quality audits, compliance standards and the registration process. It clearly details the challenges, pitfalls, opportunities and benefits of ISO 9000 registration. In addition, it helps companies determine whether or not ISO 9000 registration is required.

Publisher: Oliver Wright

Tel: 800-343-0625

Price Information: $37.50

ISBN or Reference Number: ISBN 0-939246-29-5, Item # 5095

The ISO 9000 Book: A Global Competitor's Guide to Compliance & Certification

Author: John T. Rabbitt and Peter A. Bergh

Description: This practical guide takes a company through every step of the certification process, from preparation to the final audit. It takes the mystery out of ISO 9000 by showing companies how to: interpret the standard, determine the cost and length of time needed to invest in the certification process and focus on the areas of quality assurance that are subject to a rigorous audit during certification.

Publisher: Quality Resources

Tel: 800-247-8519

Price Information: $26.95

ISBN or Reference Number: ISBN 0-527-91721-4, Order # 6600-917214

ISO Bulletin

Author: ISO Central Secretariat

Description: This newsletter is published monthly in English and in French. It contains updates and articles as well as lists of published standards available.

Publisher: ISO Central Secretariat

Tel: 212-642-4900

Price Information: Price varies according to current exchange rate.

ISO 9000 Certification • Total Quality Management

Author: Subhash C. Puri

Description: This book discusses Total Quality Management and ISO 9000 certification. Subjects include: developing a TQM model, TQM model via ISO 9004, service quality model, software quality model, quality system accreditation, quality system standards, quality manuals, quality system auditing, and quality system guidelines and checklists.

Publisher: Standards-Quality Management Group

Tel: 613-820-2445

Price Information: $40

ISO 9000 Compendium: International Standards for Quality Management

Author: ISO Central Secretariat

Description: Includes the entire ISO 9000 (1987) series, 10011 and 10012 series standards, 8402 vocabulary standards, draft standards, guideline documents and Vision 2000, A Strategy for International Standards Implementation in the Quality Arena during the 1990's... In addition, it explains what quality management is, how to run a quality assurance system, what sort of quality operations are appropriate for you and the coming trends in quality standardization.

Publisher: ISO Central Secretariat

Tel: 212-642-4900

Price Information: $235

ISBN or Reference Number: ISBN 92-67-101 72-2

ISO 9000 Documentation: A 20-Section Quality Manual

Author: Jack Kanholm

Description: This book contains the first two levels of a quality system documentation: a quality manual and 26 operating procedures. It was designed to represent a generic model of a quality system that is simple, natural and free from excessive paperwork. Also available on computer disk.

Publisher: AQA Company

Tel: 213-222-3600

Price Information: $88

ISO 9000 Explained: An Interpretation Guide

Author: Jack Kanholm

Description: This guide systematically interprets the ISO 9001, 9002 and 9003 standards. It explains the purpose, importance, scope and application of every requirement and offers illustrative examples of practical ways to achieve compliance. It also contains a comprehensive list of procedures and records needed to document an ISO 9000 system.

Publisher: AQA Company

Tel: 213-222-3600

Price Information: $57

ISO 9000 Forum

Author: ISO Central Secretariat

Description: This newsletter on quality management standards is published six times each year in English and in French. It features up-to-date information about the ISO 9000 series standards, their development and probable future revisions, information sources on training programs for quality managers and quality systems auditors, upcoming and newsworthy events, and more. The newsletter is part of an "ISO Forum 9000" global package. Call for more information.

Publisher: ISO Central Secretariat

Tel: 212-642-4995

Price Information: 400 Swiss francs

ISO 9000: Handbook of Quality Standards and Compliance

Author: Bureau of Business Practice

Description: This book answers questions pertaining to ISO 9000 and its implications in four sections: the development of ISO 9000 and its proliferation, third-party registration, ISO 9000 & TQM, and US companies' advice for ISO 9000 success. It includes the complete ANSI/ASQC Q90 series of standards.

Publisher: Bureau of Business Practice

Tel: 800-248-1946

Price Information: List Price: $69.95, Member Price: $59.95

ISBN or Reference Number: ISBN 0-87622-186-X, Item P474

An ISO 9000 Implementation Plan...and the Documents to Take You There

Author: dK Press

Description: This book includes all of the procedures and records required by the ISO 9000 series. It can be used without modification or can be formatted for your company's specific needs. In addition, a floppy disk containing the contents of the book is available.

Publisher: The dK Press

Tel: 714-502-6649

Price Information: $59

ISO 9000 In Your Company: Self-Study Course for Personnel

Author: Jack Kanholm

Description: This workbook explains what the ISO 9000 standards and their requirements are, how a quality system works, what the role is of an individual employee in maintaining and improving a quality system and how employees should prepare for the certification audit.

Publisher: AQA Company

Tel: 213-222-3600

Price Information: $28

ISO 9000: Meeting the New International Standards

Author: Perry Johnson

Description: This book describes the three basic parts of the ISO 9000 standards: design, manufacturing and final inspection and test procedures. It targets the 20 most important sections of the standards, including contract review, purchasing, process control and training. In addition, it outlines the most cost-effective approach to certification.

Publisher: McGraw-Hill, Inc.

Tel: 800-262-4729

Price Information: $40

ISBN or Reference Number: ISBN 0-07-032691-6

ISO 9000: Preparing for Registration

Author: James L. Lamprecht

Description: This book is a complete guide to ISO 9000, offering efficient ways to initiate an ISO 9000-based system, from documentation through registration. It supplies thorough reviews of the five ISO 9000 standards, including a paragraph-by-paragraph explanation of the ISO 9001 standard.

Publisher: Marcel Dekker, Inc.

Tel: 800-248-1946

Price Information: List Price: $45.00, ASQC Member Price: $40.50

ISBN or Reference Number: 0-8247-8741-2, Item # H0776

ISO 9000 Registered Company Directory

Author: CEEM Information Services

Description: This directory lists US and Canadian company sites registered to the ISO 9000 series standard and is updated quarterly to bring a subscriber the most up-to-date information available. In addition, it includes the history of the ISO and an overview of the requirements for a quality system, key questions to consider when seeking ISO 9000 registration, and how to select a registrar. Subscribers also have access to a toll-free research service that can provide personalized searches.

Publisher: CEEM Information Services

Tel: 800-745-5565

More Questions and Answers: the ISO 9000 Standard Series and Related Issues

Author: NIST

Description: This report attempts to answer additional questions on ISO 9000 related issues that NIST has received since the publication of NISTIR 4721. It also identifies sources for further help in this area.

Publisher: US Department of Commerce

Tel: 703-487-4650

Price Information: Free

ISBN or Reference Number: PB-93-140689

Quality Systems Update (QSU)

Author: CEEM Information Services

Description: The *QSU* is an information service on all aspects of ISO 9000 and related issues. The Executive Service includes the monthly newsletter, special bulletins on specific topics, the ISO 9000 Registered Company Directory and access to a research service. Subscribers also receive discounts on related publications.

Publisher: CEEM Information Services

Tel: 800-745-5565, 703-250-5900

Price Information: Executive Service subscription: $495/ $520 outside US; Associate Service (newsletter only): $345/$370 outside US; ISO 9000 Registered Company Directory only: $195/$220 outside US

Questions and Answers on Quality, the ISO 9000 Standard Series, Quality System Registration, and Related Issues

Author: NIST

Description: This report provides information on the ISO 9000 series standards and related issues to readers unfamiliar with some of the developments in this area.

Publisher: US Department of Commerce

Tel: 703-487-4650

Price Information: Free

QP: A Fully Correlated Quality Manual

Author: Edward P. Link

Description: QP is a fully correlated quality system workbook that provides policies, procedures and forms supporting ISO 9001 documentation. Beginning with Corporate Policy and taking a company step-by-step through Quality Policy, Quality Procedures, Quality Instructions, Quality Records and Quality Forms, this book guides a company to successfully reduce variation and implement a cost-effective quality system necessary for certification. It includes one 3.5" or 5.25" diskette.

Publisher: TQN Publishing

Tel: 800-836-3174

Price Information: $389

Software Quality & ISO 9000

Author: Systems & Software (A division of Integratise Inc.)

Description: Software Quality & ISO 9000 is a monthly newsletter devoted to global software quality and its relation to ISO 9000.

Publisher: Systems & Software

Tel: 908-946-0005

Price Information: $75/year; $140/2 years

An Update of US Participation in International Standards Activities (NISTIR 89-4124)

Author: NIST

Description: This report presents updated information on the current level of US participation in ISO and IEC (reference: NBSIR 88-3698).

Publisher: National Technical Information Service (NTIS)

Tel: 301-975-2000

ISBN or Reference Number: PB 89-228282/AS

Standards and Directives

ANSI Standards Action

Author: ANSI

Description: Published biweekly by ANSI, this newsletter lists proposed and recently approved American National Standards, ISO and IEC standards, CEN/ CENELEC standards activity, a registration of organization names in the United States, and proposed foreign government regulations. Standards Action is sold jointly with ANSI's monthly newsletter, The ANSI Reporter, which reports on current activities of ANSI and the US voluntary standards community.

Publisher: ANSI

Tel: 212-642-9000

Price Information: Free for members, $200/year for non-members

ANSI Global Standardization Reports - Volumes 1-8

Author: ANSI

Description: These reports are issued by ANSI's Brussels office for the period of July 1989 through January 1993. They contain information on the results of a series of private sector meetings between delegations under ANSI's auspices, and CEN, CENELEC, the European Organization for Testing and Certification, the Commission of the European Communities and the European Telecommunications Standards Institute.

Publisher: ANSI

Tel: 212-642-4900

Price Information: Prices vary between $24 and $75 for each report

BSI News

Author: BSI

Description: This is a monthly publication detailing happenings in the British Standards Institution.

Publisher: BSI

Tel: 071-629-9000

CEN Catalogue

Author: CEN

Description: This catalog contains lists of European standards, harmonization documents and other publications such as European prestandards and reports.

Publisher: ANSI

Tel: 212-642-4900

CEN General Technical Report for 1993

Author: CEN

Description: This report lists projects and stages of items in progress, by committee.

Publisher: ANSI

Tel: 212-642-4900

CEN N525 - National Implementation of Approved Documents - 1992

Author: ANSI

Description: This publication lists the European Standards, Harmonization Documents, European Prestandards and Reports that have been adopted and published by CEN together with a reference of the national standards needed to implement these documents at the national level.

Publisher: ANSI

Tel: 212-642-4900

CEN The Technical Programme - Standards for Europe - 1992

Author: CEN

Description: This publication includes a series of separate modules: a general introduction; a module dealing with subjects such as quality assurance, certification, conformity assessment, public procurement logistics that relate to all areas of the technical work and a module that groups together the various sectors of engineering standards work, etc.

Publisher: ANSI

Tel: 212-642-4900

CENELEC Catalogue

Author: CENELEC

Description: This catalog contains a complete list of harmonization documents, European standards and other information.

Publisher: ANSI

Tel: 212-642-4900

CENELEC Technical Report

Author: CENELEC

Description: This report lists projects and stages of items in progress, by committee.

Publisher: ANSI

Tel: 212-642-4900

Chemicals and European Community Directives (10/1/91)

Author: Single Internal Market Information Service

Publisher: US Department of Commerce

Tel: 202-482-5823

Price Information: Free

Directory of European Regional Standards-Related Organizations (NIST SP 795)

Author: NIST

Description: This directory identifies more than 150 European regional organizations— both government and private— that engage in standards development, certification, laboratory accreditation and other standards-related activities, such as quality assurance. Entries describe the type and purpose of each organization, acronyms, national affiliations of members, the nature of the standards-related activity, and other related information.

Publisher: National Technical Information Service (NTIS)

Tel: 800-336-4700

ISBN or Reference Number: PB 91-107599

Consensus

Author: National Standards System

Description: A quarterly publication, Consensus includes news and features on Canadian and international standards. Available in English and in French.

Publisher: Standards Council of Canada

Tel: 613-238-3222

Price Information: $12/year (Canada), $20/year (outside Canada)

EC Product Liability and Safety Directives Report

Author: CEEM Information Services

Description: This report thoroughly explains the legal implications of the current and pending EC directives. It discusses the Product Liability, Product Safety, Machinery Safety and proposed Services Liability directives, along with the scope and legal implications of each. In addition, it explains key product liability issues and a section on how to develop an effective product liability prevention program within an organization.

Publisher: CEEM Information Services

Tel: 800-745-5565

Price Information: $35

EC Product Standards Under the Internal Market Program (12/1/91)

Author: Single Internal Market Information Service

Publisher: US Department of Commerce

Tel: 202-482-5823

Price Information: Free

GATT Standards Code Activities

Author: NIST

Description: This brochure gives a brief description of NISTs activities in support of the Standards Code. These activities include operating the US GATT inquiry point for information on standards and certification systems, notifying the GATT Secretariat of proposed US regulations, assisting US industry with trade-related standards problems, responding to inquiries on foreign and US proposed regulations, and preparing reports on the Standard Code.

Publisher: Standards Code & Information Program (SCI)

Tel: 301-975-4029

GATT Standards Code Activities of the National Institute of Standards and Technology

Author: NIST

Description: This annual report describes the GATT Standards Code activities conducted by the Standards Code and Information Program for each calendar year. NIST responsibilities include operating the GATT inquiry point, notifying the GATT Secretariat of proposed US federal government regulations that may affect trade, assisting US industry with standards-related trade problems, and responding to inquiries about proposed foreign and US regulations.

Publisher: Standards Code & Information Program (SCI)

Tel: 301-975-4029

Medical Devices (8/15/93)

Author: Single Internal Market Information Service

Description: This report includes information on standards relating to medical devices.

Publisher: US Department of Commerce

Tel: 202-482-5823

Price Information: Free

A Review of US Participation in International Standards Activities (NBSIR 88-3698)

Author: NIST

Description: This report describes the role of international standards, their increasingly significant importance in world trade, and the extent of past and current US participation in the two major international standardization bodies—ISO and IEC. The degree of participation covers the 20 year period, 1966 through 1986.

Publisher: National Technical Information Service (NTIS)

Tel: 301-975-2000

ISBN or Reference Number: PB 88-164165

Standards Activities of Organizations in the United States (NIST SP 806)

Author: NIST

Description: The directory identifies and describes activities of over 750 US public and private sector organizations that develop, publish, and revise standards; participate in this process; or identify standards and make them available through information centers or distribution channels. NIST SP 806, a revision of NBS SP 681, covers activities related to both mandatory and voluntary standards. SP 806 also contains a subject index and related listings that cover acronyms and initials, defunct bodies and organizations with name changes.

Publisher: National Technical Information Service (NTIS)

Tel: 301-975-2000

ISBN or Reference Number: PB 91-177774

tbt News

Author: NIST

Description: This newsletter provides information on government programs and available services established in support of the GATT agreement on technical barriers to trade. It reports on the latest notifications of proposed foreign regulations, bilateral consultations with major US trade partners, programs of interest to US exporters, and availability of standards and certification information.

Publisher: Standards Code & Information Program (SCI)

Tel: 301-975-4029

Price Information: Subscription is free upon request.

Trade Winds

Author: Standards Council of Canada

Description: This is a monthly newsletter including information on standardization that effects global trade.

Publisher: Standards Council of Canada

Tel: 613-238-3222

Price Information: $75 (Canada), $85 (outside Canada)

US Voluntary Standardization System: Meeting the Global Challenge

Author: ANSI

Description: This report provides an overview of the role and participation of the US in the global standardization arena, highlighting the many US technical and non-technical activities that constitute the strength of the US system.

Publisher: ANSI

Tel: 212-642-4900

SOFTWARE

The ACCELERATOR

Description: The ACCELERATOR is a quick and easy software program for the systematic implementation of ISO 9000/Q90. It includes an internal auditing module that systematically selects which questions should be asked of whom, in which department, and how. Each question comes with complete instructions on the appropriate method of collecting and documenting data. In addition, the software can print a worksheet for each audit question. According to the results, the ACCELERATOR can also generate a step-by-step corrective action plan.

Publisher: ISO Software Solutions

Tel: 800-476-2378

Price Information: $299

IQS, Inc. Software

Description: This software includes: Customer Management, System Documentation, Product Documentation, Process Documentation, Preventive Maintenance, Calibration Management, Employee Involvement, Corrective Action and Supplier Management. Future releases include Data Collection, SPC, Nonconformance Management and Quality Costs. Leasing Program available.

Publisher: IQS, Inc.

Tel: 800-635-5901

ISO 9000 Assessment, Documentation and Certification Software

Description: This software package is designed to walk a company through the ISO 9000 standards and to conduct a pre-assessment of its operation. It can be used to double-check procedural documentation, to improve a company's in-house quality manual or to provide a framework for developing one. It also includes a management improvement system which allows a company to set performance benchmarks in the certification process. The software package comes with a complete user's guide, a demonstration diskette, a copy of an ISO 9000 book and 90 days of free customer support.

Publisher: Oliver Wright

Tel: 800-343-0625

Price Information: $995

Reference Number: #5202

ISO 9000 Checklists

Description: This program provides the auditor with a systematic and comprehensive method of conducting an audit. An auditor can use the provided hard-copy workbook as is, or modify it to reflect the company's own requirements. The package contains one hard-copy workbook and a diskette containing three workbooks in WordPerfect format for ISO 9001, 9002 and 9003, respectively.

Publisher: G.R. Technologies Ltd.

Tel: 416-886-1307

Price Information: $105.00, plus $7.50 shipping and handling

ISO 9000/MIL-Q-9858A Quality Assurance Manual Software

Description: This software has been created to provide clients with a generic quality assurance manual that covers all the basic requirements stated in ISO 9001, 9002, 9003, 9004 and MIL-Q-9858A. For relatively simple operations, the manual can be used as written with little or no editing. In more complex situations, the word processing capabilities of the program enable a company to modify the content to meet its needs. Having such a generic, basic manual on disk will save a company time and money as opposed to writing a manual from scratch.

Publisher: FED-PRO

Tel: 800-833-3776

Price Information: $345

ISO 9001 Quality Assurance Manual Software

Description: This software has been created to provide clients with a generic quality assurance manual that covers all the basic requirements stated in ISO 9001. For relatively simple operations, the manual can be used as written with little or no editing. In more complex situations, the word processing capabilities of the program will enable you to edit, add to, delete and/or modify the content to meet the needs of your company. Having such a generic, basic manual on disk will save you a considerable amount of time and money versus attempting to write such a manual from scratch.

Publisher: FED-PRO

Tel: 800-833-3776

Price Information: $275

ISO Q.A. Writer II

Description: With ISO Q.A. Writer II, a company can use a PC to write its own quality assurance manual in compliance with ISO 9000-3. The software is completely menu-driven and contains all policies and procedures of ISO 9000-3/9001. Companies can use it as-is or edit the text to meet their specific needs. ISO Q.A. Writer II can save time and money.

Publisher: FED-PRO
Tel: 800-833-3776
Price Information: $395

ISOxPERT

Description: ISOxPERT software processes all the information required for Q90 and ISO 9000 registration. It provides a solid, user-flexible framework for the ISO quality plan, systematizes the measurements and automates 18 quality analysis reports to identify improvement areas. ISOxPERT software assures immediate participation of an organization by clearly communicating ISO quality system performance expectations. With ISOxPERT, quality problems are readily identified and tracked so that continuous improvement of quality processes can occur. Available for DOS, Windows and Macintosh.

Publisher: Management Software International, Inc.
Tel: 800-476-3279
Price Information: Pricing dependent upon platform

Ki-QMS

Description: Ki-QMS, Knowledge-integrated Quality Management System, is a software product that helps organizations establish quality systems in accordance with ISO 9000 standards and maintain documentation pertaining to these systems. It consists of a Quality Systems Audit Module, a Quality Systems Documentation Module and a Deviations Module which, together, can significantly reduce lead time and cost involved in acquiring ISO 9000 registration, provide continuous evaluation and maintenance of quality systems, and produce an automated quality systems manual.

Publisher: Sundram Information Systems
Tel: 91-44-844350 (India)

Q9000™ Manufacturing Quality Assurance System

Description: Q9000™ is an integrated application environment with a fully integrated, relational database that is easy to use. It addresses Customer and Supplier Information, Sales and Marketing, Purchasing and RFQs, Shipping and Invoicing, Accounting, Reporting, Quality Assurance, Product Data and Inventory Management, and Manufacturing and Production. It is the only fully- integrated PC-based MIS system that supports ISO 9000, ANSI/ASQC Q90 and CSA/CAN Q9000. This software package includes free upgrades for two years.

Publisher: Synapse Software Systems, Inc.
Tel: 403-269-2754, 800-331-0160

QMS Programs® ISO 9000 Compliance Group

Description: QMS executes ISO 9001-2-3 procedures, computations, analyses, records and reports, eliminating some 80 percent of the daily effort needed to comply with ISO 9000, and has been tested in over 100 locations. It uses modules and a framework which easily adapt to your plants' needs, supporting these ISO requirements: Management, Quality System Manual, Design Control, Document Control, Purchasing, Purchasers/Suppliers, Product ID/ Traceability, Process Control, Inspect/Test, Inspect/ Measure/Test Eq, Inspect/Test Status, Nonconformance Control, Corrective Action, Product Storage, Quality Records, Internal Audits, Training, Servicing, and Statistical Techniques.

Publisher: John A. Keane & Associates, Inc.
Contact: Michael Kane
Tel: 609-924-7904, Fax: 609-924-1078
Price Information: $4,500 up
Reference Number: 4.01-4.20

QRecords-9000

Description: QRecords-9000 is a software product that helps a company manage the quality records pertaining to ISO 9000. It is organized as three modules: Application Definition Workbench, Workflow Management Workbench and Report Generation Workbench, which let a company define the form and attributes of the quality records, manage the actual instances of the quality records, and generate reports of the data contained in the quality records. These modules allow for rapid implementation of changes to the quality record management process, security of information and the ability to handle large volumes of information.

Publisher: Sundram Information Systems
Tel: 91-44-844350 (India)

ScoreBoard™

Description: ScoreBoard™ is a PC-based software product designed to assist in the critical self assessment/audit process for ISO 9000. This software automates the evaluation process by prompting a company with a list of questions that parallel the sections of the ISO 9000 standards. A company can choose the most appropriate score for each question from a list. ScoreBoard™ automatically captures the entries and uses them to calculate an overall score for comparison. The data is then used to benchmark company performance using graphical scoreboards. A variety of benchmark comparisons are available.
Publisher: American Information Systems, Inc.
Tel: 717-724-1588

TQS-9000

Description: TQS-9000 is a windows-based software system for easy implementation of a quality system based on ISO 9001 and 9002 standards. The system features seven modules including an introduction, situation analysis, standards interpretation, a sample quality manual, forms and documents, audit checklists and cost and benefit tracking. The system is designed to help a company reach its goal of developing an ISO-based quality system.
Publisher: Advance Design Systems, Inc.
Tel: 313-271-1520
Price Information: $990

TAPES

Audio

ISO 9000: Opportunity Within Confusion

Description: This tape covers the basics of getting your quality system and documentation in place, selecting a registrar and getting certified. 90 minutes.
Author: Richard B. Clements
Tel: 800-248-1946
Price Information: $19.95
ISBN or Reference Number: Item # PA112

ISO 9000: Tips and Techniques

Description: This tape examines the elements of the ISO 9000 standard and how to conform, how to implement and how to take corrective actions. All 20 elements of ISO 9001 are addressed with helpful tips and techniques of implementation. 90 minutes.
Author: Richard B. Clements
Tel: 800-248-1946
Price Information: $19.95
ISBN or Reference Number: Item # PA113

Video

BSI ISO 9000 Video Training Seminar

Description: This video seminar provides an easy-to-understand explanation of the ISO 9000 standard and its profitable applications. In addition, it explains the steps involved in certification—what is needed and the purpose of a documented quality assurance management system, how to apply the principles of the Standard in a wide range of businesses, and much more. The package includes two 43-minute videos, a complete audio cassette recording and a workbook that includes program highlights for easy reference.
Author: BSI/CEEM Information Services, Inc.
Tel: 800-745-5565
Price Information: $295

Building Quality Excellence with ISO 9000

Description: This is a video-based guide to becoming a certified supplier of quality. Two units, approximately 45 minutes each, cover the history and global importance of the ISO 9000 standards and the implementation and certification process. Package includes reference guide and ISO 9000 book.
Author: Videolearning Resource Group
Tel: 800-648-4336
Price Information: $745 (can be previewed for $45)

Implementing ISO 9000 or ANSI/ASQC Q90 Standards

Description: This in-house video training program consists of three video tapes that provide an understanding of the global perspective of quality, knowledge on how to implement elements of the ISO series standards, tips on how to select an appropriate standard, samples of documentation, and more.
Author: Statistical Quality Control & Circle Institute
Tel: 414-922-7938
Price Information: $199 each, or $525 for all three

Introduction to ISO 9000

Description: This 22-minute video, geared toward manufacturing and service companies, provides an introduction to ISO 9000 in addition to training for managers, employees and vendors.
Author: The Media Group, Inc.
Tel: 800-678-1003
Price Information: $129 US, $165 Canada
ISBN or Reference Number: Order #1000BM

ISO 9000

Description: This seminar is designed to provide a broad initial appreciation for management—at all levels and in all functions—of the nature, purpose and principles of ISO 9000. It describes an approach to TQM and outlines the quality assurance standards and procedures.
Author: Videolearning Resource Group
Tel: 800-648-4336
Price Information: $295 (can be previewed for $45)

ISO 9000: Executive Briefing

Description: This briefing communicates to executive management the importance of ISO 9000 in a global economy. What are the ISO 9000 standards and why are they capturing so much management attention? Includes one VHS videotape (25 minutes) and an audio cassette of the program. 1993. Narrated by Ian Durand.
Author: International Quality Systems
Tel: 407-546-5191
Price Information: $195

ISO 9000 Operations Training Program

Description: A video-based program with interactive workbook designed to teach what ISO 9000 is and how its requirements help ensure quality in process information. It consists of six segments, including production, marketing, purchasing, documentation, statistical methods and audits. (45 minutes)
Author: Videolearning Resource Group
Tel: 800-648-4336
Price Information: $1,350 (can be rented for $250)

ISO 9000: The First Step to the Future

Description: This seminar consists of two modules relating to ISO 9000. Module 1 provides an overview of the subject, dispelling misconceptions and addressing management's role. Module 2 provides information about the requirements, registration process, costs and benefits of ISO 9000 qualification. (37 minutes)
Author: Videolearning Resource Group
Tel: 800-648-4336
Price Information: $495 (can be rented for $150)

ISO 9000 Video Seminar

Description: This series is an informative video program offering authoritative information that will help provide an understanding of the ISO 9000 quality standards. Includes two tapes (45 minutes each), a workbook and a complete set of the ISO 9000 standards. Narrated by Ian Durand.
Author: International Quality Systems
Tel: 800-247-8519
Price Information: $595
ISBN or Reference Number: ISBN 0-52791727-3, Order # 1080-917273

ISO 9000 Video Training Program

Description: This presentation provides a 30-minute executive briefing and a 60-minute detailed explanation of the compliance and certification requirements. The training program consists of the video presentation, an extensive reference and training manual, and a copy of the ISO 9000-9004 series of standards.
Author: FED-PRO, Inc.
Tel: 800-833-3776
Price Information: $245

What Is ISO 9000, and Why Do I Care?

Description: This video shows how two companies become ISO certified. It shows what the ISO standards are, what the certification process is all about, where to start, and why implementing ISO 9000 can lead a company to greater profitability and improved control. (33 minutes)
Author: Videolearning Resource Group
Tel: 800-648-4336
Price Information: $450 (can be rented for $95)

Appendix F

ACRONYMS & GLOSSARY

ACRONYMS

A2LA .... American Association for Laboratory Accreditation

AAMI .... Association for the Advancement of Medical Instrumentation

ABCB .... Association of British Certification Bodies

ABS QE .... ABS Quality Evaluations, Inc.

AENOR .... Asociación Española de Normalización y Certificación (Spanish Association for Normalization and Certification)

AES ....American European Services, Incorporated

AFAQ .... Association Française pour l'Assurance de la Qualité (French accreditation body and quality system registrar)

AFNOR......... Association française de normalisation (French standards association)

A.G.A .... A.G.A. Quality, a service of International Approval Services

AIAG .... Automotive Industry Action Group

ANSI .... American National Standards Institute

AQAP-1 .... Allied Quality Assurance Publication 1

ASC .... Accredited Standards Committee

ASQC........... American Society for Quality Control

AT&T QR .... AT&T Quality Registrar

AV Qualité .... AIB-Vincotte

BEC .... British Electrotechnical Committee

BQR .... Bellcore Quality Registration

BSI .... British Standards Institution

BSI QA .... British Standards Institution Quality Assurance

BVQI .... Bureau Veritas Quality International North America, Inc.

CASE .... Conformity Assessment Systems Evaluation, now NVCASE (See separate listing.)

CD .... Committee Draft

CDRH .... Center for Devices and Radiological Health, FDA

CE Mark .... Conformité Européene (official French name for the EC mark)

CEB/BEC ..... Comité électrotechnique Belge/Belgisch Elektrotechnisch Comité (Belgian Electrotechnical Committee)

CEI .... Comitato Elettrotecnico Italiano (Italian Electrotechnical Committee)

CEN .... Comité Européen de Normalisation (European Committee for Standardization)

CENELEC .... Comité Européen de Normalisation Électrotechnique (European Committee for Electrotechnical Standardization)

CGA .... Canadian Gas Association

CGSB .... Canadian General Standards Board

CICS .... Ceramic Industry Certification Scheme, Ltd.

CMA .... Canadian Manufacturer's Association

CQA.............. Certified Quality Auditor

DEK .... Dansk Elektroteknisk Komité (Danish Electrotechnical Committee)

DESC .... Defense Electronics Supply Center, DoD

DFARS .... DoD Federal Acquisition Regulation Supplement

DHHS .... US Department of Health and Human Services

DIN .... Deutsches Institut für Normung (German Standards Institute)

DIS............... Draft International Standard

DITI .... UK's Department of Trade and Industry

DKE .... Deutsche Elektrotechnische Kommission im DIN und VDE (German Electrotechnical Commission)

DNV .... Det Norske Veritas Industry, Inc.

DOC .... US Department of Commerce

DoD .... US Department of Defense

DOE .... US Department of Energy

DOT .... US Department of Transportation

DS .... Dansk Standardiseringsrad (Danish standards body)

EAC .... European Accreditation of Certification

EC .... European Community

EEA .... European Economic Area

EFTA .... European Free Trade Association

ELOT	Hellenic Organization for Standardization
EN	European Norm
ENTELA	Entela, Inc., QSRD
ENV	European Prestandards
EOQ	European Organization for Quality
EOTA	European Organization for Technical Approvals
EOTC	European Organization for Testing and Certification
EQNET	European Network for Quality System Assessment and Certification
EQS	European Committee for Quality System Assessment and Certification
ETCI	Electro-Technical Council of Ireland
ETSI	European Telecommunications Standards Institute
EU	European Union
FAA	Federal Aviation Administration, DOT
FAR	Federal Acquisition Regulation
FDA	US Food and Drug Administration, DHHS
GATT	General Agreements on Tariffs & Trade
GMP	Good Manufacturing Practices (US Food and Drug Administration)
GQCQ	Quebec Quality Certification Group
GSA	General Services Administration
HD	Harmonization Documents
HIMA	Health Industry Manufacturers Association
IBN/BIN	Institut belge de normalisation/Belgisch Instituut voor Normalisatie (Belgian Institute for Standardization)
IEC	International Electrotechnical Commission
INTERTEK ..	Intertek Services Corporation
IPQ	Instituto Português da Qualidade (Portuguese Quality Institute)
IQA	Institute for Quality Assurance
ISO	International Organization for Standardization
ITA	US International Trade Administration
ITM	Inspection du travail et des mines (Luxembourg inspecting body)
ITQS	Recognition Arrangement for Assessment and Certification of Quality Systems in the Information Technology Sector
JAS-ANZ	Australia/New Zealand Accreditation Body for Quality System Registrars
KEMA	KEMA Registered Quality, Inc.
LPCB	The Loss Prevention Certification Board Limited
LRQA	Lloyd's Register Quality Assurance
MBNQA	Malcolm Baldrige National Quality Award
MET	MET Laboratories, Inc.
MOU	Memorandum of Understanding
MRA	Mutual Recognition Agreement
MTC	Manufacturing Technology Center
NAC-QS	Comité National pour L'Accreditation Des Organismes de Certification (Belgian Organization responsible for the accreditation of quality system registrars)
NACCB	National Accreditation Council for Certification Bodies (UK)
NACE	Nomenclature Générale des Activités Économique dans les Communautés Européennes
NATO	North Atlantic Treaty Organization
NCCLS	National Committee for Clinical Laboratory Standards
NCSCI	National Center for Standards and Certification Information, NIST
NEC	Nederlands Elektrotechnisch Comité (Dutch Electrotechnical Committee)
NEMA	National Electrical Manufacturers Association
NIST	National Institute of Standards and Technology, DOC
NNI	Nederlands Normalisatie Instituut (Dutch Normalization Institute)
NQA	National Quality Assurance, Ltd.
NRC	Nuclear Regulatory Commission
NSAI	National Standards Authority of Ireland
NSF	NSF International
NTIS	National Technical Information Service
NVCASE	National Voluntary Conformity Assessment System Evaluation, formerly the CASE Program
NVLAP	National Voluntary Laboratory Accreditation Program, NIST
OEM	Original Equipment Manufacturers
OTSQR	OTS Quality Registrars, Inc.
prEN	Proposed European Norm
QA	Quality Assurance
QA-A	Quality Systems Auditor
QA-LA	Quality Systems Lead Auditor
QA-PA	Quality Systems Provisional Auditor
QM	Quality Manual
QMI	Quality Management Institute
QS	Quality System
QSR	Quality Systems Registrars, Inc.
RAB	Registrar Accreditation Board
RvC	Raad voor de Certificatie (Dutch Council for Certification)
SC	Subcommittee
SCC	Standards Council of Canada
SCI	Standards Code and Information Program
SCS	Sira Certification Service/Sira Test & Certification Ltd.
SIC	Standard Industrial Classification code

SPC .... Statistical Process Control
Sub-TAG ...... Subgroup of a TAG
TAAC .... Trade Adjustment Assistance Centers
TAG .... Technical Advisory Group
TC .... Technical Committee, as in TC 176
TickIT .... UK Quality System Registration Scheme
                  for Software Companies

TQM .... Total Quality Management
UNI .... Ente Nazionale italiano di unificazione
                  (Italian national association for standardiza-
                  tion)
UTE .... Union technique de l'électricité (French
                  electrotechnical union)
WD .... Working Draft
WG .... Working Group

GLOSSARY

Accreditation .... Procedure by which an authoritative body formally recognizes that a body or person is competent to carry out specific tasks. (ISO/IEC Guide 2)

Accreditation Mark .. An insignia that indicates accreditation. Only accredited certification bodies and the companies they certify are allowed to use an accreditation mark. Non-accredited certification bodies and the companies they certify may not.

ANSI .... American National Standards Institute. (Adopts but does not write American standards.) Assures that member organizations that do write standards follow rules of consensus and broad participation by interested parties. ANSI is the US member of ISO.

ASQC .... American Society for Quality Control. A technical society of over 70,000 quality professionals. Individual members from throughout the world, but primarily from the United States. Publishes quality-related American national standards.

Assessment .... An estimate or determination of the significance, importance or value of something. (ASQC Quality Auditing Technical Committee)

Assessment Body ... Third party that assesses products and registers the quality systems of suppliers.

Assessment System .. Procedural and managerial rules for conducting an assessment leading to issue of a registration document and its maintenance.

Audit .... A planned, independent and documented assessment to determine whether agreed-upon requirements are being met. (ASQC Quality Auditing Technical Committee)

Audit Program ...... The organizational structure, commitment and documented methods used to plan and perform audits. (ASQC Quality Auditing Technical Committee)

Auditee .... An organization being audited. (ISO 8402, Clause 4.12)

Auditor (quality) ... A person who has the qualification to perform audits. (ISO 10011-1, Clause 3.2)

BSI .... British Standards Institution. This is the UK's standards-writing body.

BSI QA .... BSI Quality Assurance. One of 15 accredited certification bodies (registrars) in the UK. Assesses suppliers for conformance to the appropriate ISO 9000 series standard; registers those that meet the requirements. Organizationally separate from BSI.

CE Mark .... Conformité Européenne. The mark of approval used by the European Union. This mark signifies that the equipment complies with all applicable directives and product standards.

CEN .... European Committee for Standardization. Publishes regional standards (for EU and EFTA) covering nonelectrical, nonelectronic subject fields. (See also CENELEC.)

CENELEC .... European Committee for Electrotechnical Standardization. Publishes regional standards (for EU and EFTA) covering electrical/electronic subject fields. (See also CEN.)

Certification .... Procedure by which a third party gives written assurance that a product, process or service conforms to specified requirements. (ISO/IEC Guide 2)

Certified .... The quality system of a company, location or plant is certified for compliance to ISO 9000 after it has demonstrated such compliance through the audit process. When used to indicate quality system certification, it means the same thing as registration.

Company .... Term used primarily to refer to a business first party, the purpose of which is to supply a product or service. (DIS 9004-3, Clause 3.2)

Compliance .... An affirmative indication or judgment that the supplier of a product or service has met the requirements of the relevant specifications, contract or regulation; also the state of meeting the requirements. (ANSI/ASQC A3) (See also conformance.)

Conformance .... An affirmative indication or judgement that a product or service has met the requirements of the relevant specifica-tions, contract or regulation; also the state of meeting the requirements. (ANSI/ASQC A3) (See also compli-ance.)

Conformity Assessment .... Conformity assessment includes all activities that are intended to assure the conformity of products to a set of standards. This can include testing, inspection, certification, quality system assessment and other activities.

Contractor .... The organization that provides a product to the customer in a contrac-tual situation. (ISO 8402, Clause 1.12)

Convention .... A customary practice, rule or method. (ASQC Quality Auditing Technical Committee)

Corrective Action .. An action taken to eliminate the causes of an existing nonconformity, defect or other undesirable situation in order to prevent recurrence. (ISO 8402, Clause 4.14)

Customer .... Ultimate consumer, user, client, beneficiary, or second party. (DIS 9004-3, Clause 3.4)

Design Review ...... A formal, documented, comprehensive and systematic examination of a design to evaluate the design requirements and the capability of the design to meet these requirements and to identify problems and propose solutions. (ISO 8402, Clause 3.13)

EEC .... The European Economic Community. This comprises the EU and EFTA countries.

EFQM .... European Federation for Quality Management. An organization of upper-level managers concerned with quality.

EFTA .... European Free Trade Association. A group of nations whose goal is to remove import duties, quotas and other obstacles to trade and to uphold nondiscriminatory practices in world trade. Current members are Austria, Finland, Iceland, Norway, Sweden and Switzerland.

EN 45000 .... A series of standards set up by the EU to regulate and harmonize certifica-tion, accreditation and testing activities. National accreditation structures and inspection body standards are still being developed.

EOQ .... European Organization for Quality, formerly EOQC (European Organiza-tion for Quality Control.) An independent organization whose mission is to improve quality and reliability of goods and services primarily through publications, conferences and seminars. Members are quality-related organizations from countries throughout Europe, including Eastern-bloc countries. ASQC is an affiliate society member.

EOTC .... European Organization for Testing and Certification. Set up by the EU and EFTA to focus on conformity assessment issues in the nonregulated spheres.

EQS ...... European Committee for Quality System Assessment and Certification. The function of EQS is to harmonize rules for quality system assessment and certification (registration), facilitate mutual recognition of registrations, and provide advice and counsel to other committees in the EOTC framework on matters related to quality system assessment and certification.

EU ...... European Union. The EU is a framework within which member states have agreed to integrate their economies and eventually form a political union. Current members are Belgium, Denmark, France, Germany, Greece, Ireland, Italy, Luxembourg, Netherlands, Portugal, Spain and the United Kingdom.

Finding ...... A conclusion of importance based on observation(s). (ASQC Quality Auditing Technical Committee)

Follow-up Audit .... An audit whose purpose and scope are limited to verifying that corrective action has been accomplished as scheduled and to determining that the action effectively prevented recurrence. (ASQC Quality Auditing Technical Committee)

Grade ...... A category or rank given to entities, having the same functional use but different requirements for quality. (ISO 8402, Clause 2.2)

IEC ...... International Electrotechnical Commission. A worldwide organization that produces standards in the electrical and electronic fields. Members are the national committees, composed of representatives of the various organizations which deal with electrical/electronic standardization in each country. Formed in 1906.

Inspection ...... Activities such as measuring, examining, testing, gauging one or more characteristics of a product or service and comparing these with specified requirements to determine conformity. (ISO 8402, Clause 3.14)

IQA ...... Institute for Quality Assurance. A British organization of quality professionals; operates a widely-recognized system of certification of auditors for quality systems.

ISO ...... International Organization for Standardization. A worldwide federation of national standards bodies (92 at present). ISO produces standards in all fields, except electrical and electronic (which are covered by IEC). Formed in 1947.

Modules ...... The EU has devised a conformity assessment system, consisting of modules, to handle the diversity of testing, inspection, and certification activities. Modules in the "modular approach" range from manufacturer declaration—through a variety of routes involving design and type approval—to full third-party certification.

MOU ...... Memorandum of understanding; a written agreement among a number of organizations covering specific activities of common interest. There are a number of MOUs covering mutual recognition of quality system registrations in which one of the signatories is a non-European registrar.

MRA ...... Mutual Recognition Agreement. A company holds the title of a certificate issued by a signer of an MRA. The other signer recognizes the certification performed, and an attestation of equivalence signed by both certification bodies will be delivered to the company upon request.

NACCB ...... National Accreditation Council for Certification Bodies. This is the British authority for recognizing the competence and reliability of organizations that perform third-party certification of products and registration of quality systems. Formed in 1984, it is the world's second such organization.

Nonconformity ..... The nonfulfillment of a specified requirement. (ISO 8402, Clause 3.20)

Notified Body .... A notified body is a testing organization that has been selected to perform assessment activities for (a) particular directive(s). It is approved by the competent authority of its member state and notified to the European Commission and all other member states.

Organization .... A company, corporation, firm, enterprise or association, or part thereof, whether incorporated or not, public or private, that has its own functions and administration. (ISO 8402:1994)

Organizational Structure .... The responsibilities, authorities and relationships, arranged in a pattern, through which an organization performs its functions. (ISO 8402:1994)

Procedure .... A specified way to perform an activity. (ISO 8402:1994)

Process .... A set of interrelated resources and activities which transform inputs into outputs. (ISO 8402:1994)

Process Quality Audit .... An analysis of elements of a process and appraisal of completeness, correctness of conditions and probable effectiveness. (ANSI/ASQC A3)

Product .... The result of activities or processes. (ISO 8402:1994)

Product Quality Audit .... A quantitative assessment of conformance to required product characteristics. (ANSI/ASQC A3)

Protocol Agreement . An agreement signed between two organizations that operate in different but complementary fields of activity and that commit themselves to take into account their respective assessment results accordingly to conditions specified in advance.

Purchaser .... The customer in a contractual situation (ISO 8402:1994)

Qualification Process .... The process of demonstrating whether an entity is capable of fulfilling specified requirements. (ISO 8402:1994)

Quality .... The totality of features and characteristics of an entity that bear on its ability to satisfy stated or implied needs. (ISO 8402:1994)

Quality Assurance . All the planned and systematic activities implemented within the quality system and demonstrated as needed, to provide adequate confidence that an entity will fulfill requirements for quality. (ISO 8402:1994)

Quality Audit .... A systematic and independent examination to determine whether quality activities and related results comply with planned arrangements and whether these arrangements are implemented effectively and are suitable to achieve objectives. (ISO 10011-1, 3.1)

Quality Control .... The operational techniques and activities that are used to fulfill requirements for quality. (ISO 8402:1994)

Quality Management .... All activities of the overall management function that determine the quality policy, objectives and responsibilities, and implement them by means such as quality planning, quality control, quality assurance and quality improvement within the quality system. (ISO 8402:1994)

Quality Manual ..... A document stating the quality policy and describing the quality system of an organization. (ISO 8402:1994)

Quality Plan .... A document setting out the specific quality practices, resources and sequence of activities relevant to a particular product, project or contract. (ISO 8402:1994)

Quality Planning ... The activities that establish the objectives and requirements for quality and for the application of quality system elements. (ISO 8402:1994)

Quality Policy .... The overall quality intentions and direction of an organization with regard to quality, as formally expressed by top management. (ISO 8402:1994)

Quality Surveillance .... The continuing monitoring and verification of the status of procedures, methods, conditions, products, processes and services and the analysis of records in relation to stated references to ensure that requirements for quality are being met. (ANSI/ASQC A3)

Quality System ...... The organizational structure, procedures, processes and resources needed to implement quality management. (ISO 8402:1994)

Quality System Audit .... A documented activity to verify, by examination and evaluation of objective evidence, that applicable elements of the quality system are suitable and have been developed, documented and effectively implemented in accordance with specified requirements. (ANSI/ASQC A3)

Quality System Review .... A formal evaluation by management of the status and adequacy of the quality system in relation to quality policy and/or new objectives resulting from changing circumstances. (ANSI/ASQC A3)

RAB .... Registrar Accreditation Board. A US organization whose mission is to recognize the competence and reliability of registrars of quality systems, and to achieve international recognition of registrations issued by accredited registrars.

Registered .... A procedure by which a body indicates the relevant characteristics of a product, process or service, or the particulars of a body or person, in a published list. ISO 9000 registration is the evaluation of a company's quality system against the requirements of ISO 9001, 9002 or 9003.

Registration .... Procedure by which a body indicates relevant characteristics of a product, process or service, or particulars of a body or person, and then includes or registers the product, process or service in an appropriate publicly available list. (ISO/IEC Guide 2)

Registration Document .... Documentation that a supplier's quality system conforms to specified standards. Issued by an assessment body.

Requirements of Society .... Requirements including laws, statutes, rules and regulations, codes, environmental considerations, health and safety factors, and conservation of energy and materials. (DIS 9004-3, Clause 3.3)

Root Cause .... A fundamental deficiency that results in a nonconformance and must be corrected to prevent recurrence of the same or similar nonconformance. (ASQC Quality Auditing Technical Committee)

RvC .... Raad voor de Certificatie (Dutch Council for Certification). The Dutch authority for recognizing the competence and reliability of organizations that perform third-party certification of products, accreditation of laboratories and registration of quality systems. The first such organization, formed in 1980.

Service .... The result generated, by activities at the interface between the supplier and the customer and by supplier internal activities to meet the customer needs. (ISO 8402:1994)

Service Delivery ..... Those supplier activities necessary to provide the service. (ISO 8402:1994)

Software .... An intellectual creation consisting of information, instructions, concepts, transactions or procedures. (ISO 9000-1, Clause 3.3)

Software Product .. Complete set of computer programs, procedures and associated documentation and data designated for delivery to a user. (ISO 9000-3, Clause 3.2)

Specification .... The document that prescribes the requirements with which the product or service must conform. (ANSI/ASQC A3)

Subcontractor .... An organization that provides a product to the supplier. (ISO 8402:1994)

Supplier .... An organization that provides a product to the customer. (ISO 8402:1994)

Survey .... An examination for some specific purpose; to inspect or consider carefully; to review in detail. (ASQC Quality Auditing Technical Committee)

TAG .... Technical advisory group. A term used specifically in the United States for groups that are responsible for input on international standards within their respective scopes; other countries may use other terms.

Testing .... A means of determining an item's capability to meet specified requirements by subjecting them to a set of physical, chemical, environmental, or operating actions and conditions. (ANSI/ASQC A3)

Total Quality Management .... A management approach of an organization, centered on quality, based on the participation of all its members and aiming at long term success through customer satisfaction, and benefits to the members of the organization and to society. (ISO 8402:1994)

Traceability .... The ability to trace the history, application or location of an entity, by means of recorded identifications. (ISO 8402:1994)

Validation (for software) .... The process of evaluating software to ensure compliance with specified requirements. (ISO 9000-3, Clause 3.7)

Verification .... The act of reviewing, inspecting, testing, checking, auditing or otherwise establishing and documenting whether items, processes, services or documents conform to specified requirements. (ANSI/ASQC A3)

Appendix G

ANSI/ASQC Q9000 SERIES STANDARDS

American National Standard

ANSI/ASQC Q9000-1-1994

QUALITY MANAGEMENT AND QUALITY ASSURANCE STANDARDS— GUIDELINES FOR SELECTION AND USE

Prepared by
American Society for Quality Control
Standards Committee
for
American National Standards Committee
Z-1 on Quality Assurance

Descriptors: Quality management, quality assurance, quality audit, quality systems, selection, use, general conditions.

American National Standards: An American National Standard implies a consensus of those substantially concerned with its scope and provisions. An American National Standard is intended as a guide to aid the manufacturer, the consumer, and the general public. The existence of an American National Standard does not in any respect preclude anyone, whether he or she has approved the standard or not, from manufacturing, purchasing, or using products, processes, or procedures not conforming to the standard. American National Standards are subject to periodic review and users are cautioned to obtain the latest edition.

Caution Notice: This American National Standard may be revised or withdrawn at any time. The procedures of the American National Standards Institute require that action be taken to reaffirm, revise, or withdraw this standard no later than five years from the date of publication. Purchasers of American National Standards may receive current information on all standards by calling or writing the American National Standards Institute.

© 1994 by ASQC

ASQC Mission: To facilitate continuous improvement and increase customer satisfaction by identifying, communicating, and promoting the use of quality principles, concepts, and technologies; and thereby be recognized throughout the world as the leading authority on, and champion for, quality.

10 9 8 7 6 5 4 3 2 1

Printed in the United States of America

Printed on acid-free recycled paper

Published by:
ASQC
611 East Wisconsin Avenue
Milwaukee, Wisconsin 53202

CONTENTS

1   Scope
2   Normative reference
3   Definitions
4   Principal concepts
4.1 Key objectives and responsibilities for quality
4.2 Stakeholders and their expectations
4.3 Distinguishing between quality-system requirements and product requirements
4.4 Generic product categories
4.5 Facets of quality
4.6 Concept of a process
4.7 Network of processes in an organization
4.8 Quality system in relation to the network of processes
4.9 Evaluating quality systems
5   Roles of documentation
5.1 The value of documentation
5.2 Documentation and evaluation of quality systems
5.3 Documentation as a support for quality improvement
5.4 Documentation and training
6   Quality-system situations
7   Selection and use of International Standards and American National Standards on quality
7.1 General
7.2 Selection and use
7.3 Application guidelines
7.4 Software
7.5 Dependability

7.6 Quality assurance: design, development, production, installation, and servicing
7.7 Quality assurance: production, installation, and servicing
7.8 Quality assurance: final inspection
7.9 Quality management
7.10 Services
7.11 Processed materials
7.12 Quality improvement
7.13 Audits
7.14 Auditors
7.15 Managing audits
7.16 Quality assurance for measurement
8   Selection and use of International Standards and American National Standards for external quality assurance
8.1 General guidance
8.2 Selection of model
8.3 Demonstration of conformance to the selected model
8.4 Additional considerations in contractual situations

Annexes
A   Terms and definitions taken from ISO 8402
B   Product and process factors
B.1 Purpose
B.2 Factors
C   Proliferation of standards
D   Cross-reference list of clause numbers for corresponding topics
E   Bibliography

FOREWORD

(This Foreword is not a part of American National Standard *Quality Management and Quality Assurance Standards—Guidelines for Selection and Use.*)

This American National Standard corresponds to the International Standard ISO 9000-1:1994. This standard is the road map document for use of all other International Standards in the entire ISO 9000 family; that is, all the standards published by ISO Technical Committee 176, Quality Management and Quality Assurance. The initial five ISO 9000 series standards, ISO 9000, ISO 9001, ISO 9002, ISO 9003, and ISO 9004, when published in the United States as American National Standards in 1987, were designated as ANSI/ASQC Q90 through ANSI/ASQC Q94 respectively. The five 1987 standards in their 1994 international revisions are now designated ISO 9000-1, ISO 9001, ISO 9002, ISO 9003, and ISO 9004-1 respectively. Their publication as American National Standards are now designated ANSI/ASQC Q9000-1-1994, ANSI/ASQC Q9001-1994, ANSI/ASQC Q9002-1994, ANSI/ASQC Q9003-1994, and ANSI/ASQC Q9004-1-1994 respectively. This new numbering system is intended to emphasize the word-for-word correspondence of the International and American National Standards.

ISO (the International Organization for Standardization) is a worldwide federation of national standards bodies (ISO member bodies). The work of preparing International Standards is normally carried out through ISO technical committees. Each member body interested in a subject for which a technical committee has been established has the right to be represented on that committee. International organizations, governmental and nongovernmental, in liaison with ISO, also take part in the work. ISO collaborates closely with the International Electrotechnical Commission (IEC) on all matters of electrotechnical standardization. The American National Standards Institute (ANSI) is the U.S. member body of ISO. ASQC is the U.S. member of ANSI responsible for quality management and related standards.

This standard provides guidelines for selection and use of all standards in the ISO 9000 family. At this writing not all of the ISO 9000 family standards have been adopted as American National Standards, but this standard provides guidelines for the entire family as currently published internationally. See clause 7 in the standard for detailed discussion of the designations for all standards in the ISO 9000 family.

Users should note that all ANSI/ASQC standards undergo revision from time to time. In the case of International Standards adopted as American National Standards, the revision timing is influenced by the international revision timing. Reference herein to any other standard implies the latest American National Standard revision unless otherwise stated.

Comments concerning this standard are welcome. They should be sent to the sponsor of the standard, American Society for Quality COntrol, 611 East Wisconsin Avenue, P.O. Box 3005, Milwaukee, WI 53201-3005, c/o Standards Administrator.

INTRODUCTION

Organizations—industrial, commercial, or governmental—supply products intended to satisfy customers' needs and/or requirements. Increased global competition has led to increasingly more stringent customer expectations with regard to quality. To be competitive and to maintain good economic performance, organizations/suppliers need to employ increasingly effective and efficient systems. Such systems should result in continual improvements in quality and increased satisfaction of the organization's customers and other stakeholders (employees, owners, subsuppliers, society).

Customer requirements often are incorporated in "specifications." However, specifications may not in themselves guarantee that a customer's requirements will be met consistently, if there are any deficiencies in the organizational system to supply and support the product. Consequently, these concerns have led to the development of quality-system standards and guidelines that complement relevant product requirements given in the technical specifications. The International Standards in the ISO 9000 family are intended to provide a generic core of quality-system standards applicable to a broad range of industry and economic sectors (clause 7).

The management system of an organization is influenced by the objectives of the organization, by its products, and by the practices specific to the organization and, therefore, quality systems also vary from one organization to another. A major purpose of quality management is to improve the systems and processes so that continual improvement of quality can be achieved.

ANSI/ASQC Q9000-1-1994, which has the role of road map for the ISO 9000 family, has been expanded substantially. In particular, it contains guidance concepts not included in the 1987 version. These additional concepts

— are needed for effective understanding and current application of the ISO 9000 family, and

— are planned for complete integration into the architecture and content of future revisions of the ISO 9000 family.

In revision of the ISO 9000 family, there are no major changes in the architectures of ANSI/ASQC Q9001-1994, ANSI/ASQC Q9002-1994, ANSI/ASQC Q9003-1994, and ANSI/ASQC Q9004-1-1994. (However, ANSI/ASQC Q9003-1994 does contain additional clauses compared to the 1987 version.) Each of these American National Standards has had small-scale changes. These changes move toward future revisions to meet better the needs of users.

ANSI/ASQC Q9000-1-1994 and all International Standards in the ISO 9000 family are independent of any specific industry or economic sector. Collectively they provide guidance for quality management and general requirements for quality assurance.

The International Standards in the ISO 9000 family describe what elements quality systems should encompass but not how a specific organization implements these elements. It is not the purpose of these International Standards to enforce uniformity of quality systems. Needs of organizations vary. The design and implementation of a quality system must necessarily be influenced by the particular objectives, products and processes, and specific practices of the organization.

ANSI/ASQC Q9000-1-1994 clarifies the principal quality-related concepts contained within the quality management and quality assurance International Standards generated by ISO/TC 176 and provides guidance on their selection and use.

Quality Management and Quality Assurance Standards— Guidelines for Selection and Use

1 SCOPE

ANSI/ASQC Q9000-1-1994

a) clarifies principal quality-related concepts and the distinctions and interrelationships among them;

b) provides guidance for the selection and use of the ISO 9000 family of International Standards and the ANSI/ASQC Q9000 series of American National Standards on quality management and quality assurance.

2 NORMATIVE REFERENCE

The following standard contains provisions which, through reference in this text, constitute provisions of this part of ISO 9000. At the time of publication, the edition indicated was valid. All standards are subject to revision, and parties to agreements based on ANSI/ASQC Q9000-1-1994 are encouraged to investigate the possibility of applying the most recent edition of the standard indicated below. Members of IEC and ISO maintain registers of currently valid International Standards.

ANSI/ASQC Q9000-1-1994	Subsupplier →	supplier or organization →	customer
ANSI/ASQC Q9001-1994 ANSI/ASQC Q9002-1994 ANSI/ASQC Q9003-1994	Subcontractor →	supplier →	customer
ANSI/ASQC Q9004-1-1994	Subcontractor →	organization →	customer

Table 1. Relationships of organizations in the supply chain.

ISO 8402:1994, *Quality management and quality assurance—Vocabulary*

3 DEFINITIONS

This revision of ANSI/ASQC Q9000-1-1994, ANSI/ASQC Q9001-1994, ANSI/ASQC Q9002-1994, ANSI/ASQC Q9003-1994, and ANSI/ASQC Q9004-1994 has improved the harmonization of terminology for organizations in the supply chain. Table 1 shows the supply-chain terminology used in these American National Standards.

The usage of all of these terms conforms with their formal definitions in ISO 8402. The remaining differences in terminology in Table 1 reflect, in part, a desire to maintain historical continuity with usage in the 1987 edition of these American National Standards.

NOTES

1   In all these American National Standards, the grammatical format of the guidance or requirements text is addressed to the organization in its role as a supplier of products (the third column of Table 1).

2   In the ANSI/ASQC Q9000-1-1994 row of Table 1, the use of "subsupplier" emphasizes the supply-chain relationship of the three organizational units, using the self-defining term in relation to "supplier." Where appropriate, especially in discussing quality-management situations, the term "organization" is used rather than "supplier."

3   In the ANSI/ASQC Q9001-1994, ANSI/ASQC Q9002-1994, and ANSI/ASQC Q9003-1994 rows of Table 1, the use of "subcontractor" reflects the fact that, in an external quality-assurance context, the relevant relationship often is (explicitly or implicitly) contractual.

4   In the ANSI/ASQC Q9004-1-1994 row of Table 1, the use of "organization" reflects the fact that quality-management guidance is applicable to any organizational unit, irrespective of the categories of products it may supply, or whether it is a free-standing unit or part of a larger organization.

For the purposes of ANSI/ASQC Q9000-1-1994, the definitions given in ISO 8402, together with the following definitions, apply.

NOTE 5   For the convenience of users of ANSI/ASQC Q9000-1-1994, some relevant definitions from ISO 8402 are contained in annex A.

3.1 Hardware

Tangible, discrete product with distinctive form

NOTE 6   Hardware normally consists of manufactured, constructed, or fabricated pieces, parts, and/or assemblies.

3.2 Software

An intellectual creation consisting of information expressed through supporting medium.

NOTES

7   Software can be in the form of concepts, transactions, or procedures.

8   A computer program is a specific example of software.

3.3 Processed material

Tangible product generated by transforming raw material into a desired state.

NOTES

9   The state of processed material can be liquid, gas, particulate material, ingot, filament, or sheet.

10   Processed material is typically delivered in drums, bags, tanks, cylinders, cans, pipelines, or rolls.

3.4 Industry/economic sector

A grouping of suppliers whose offerings meet similar customer needs and/or whose customers are closely interrelated in the marketplace.

NOTES

11   Dual use of "industry sector" and "economic sector" recognizes that each term is used for the intended meaning in specific countries or languages.

12   Industry/economic sectors include administration, aerospace, banking, chemicals, construction, education, food, health care, leisure, insurance, mining, retailing, telecommunica-

tions, textiles, tourism, and so forth.

13   Industry/economic sectors apply to the global economy or a national economy.

3.5 Stakeholder

An individual or group of individuals with a common interest in the performance of the supplier organization and the environment in which it operates.

3.6 ISO 9000 family

All those International Standards produced by the technical committee ISO/TC 176.

NOTE 14   At present, the family comprises

a)   all the International Standards numbered ISO 9000 through to ISO 9004, including all parts of ISO 9000 and ISO 9004;

b)   all the International Standards numbered ISO 10001 through 10020, including all parts; and

c)   ISO 8402.

4 PRINCIPAL CONCEPTS

4.1 Key objectives and responsibilities for quality

An organization should:

a)   achieve, maintain, and seek to improve continuously the quality of its products in relationship to the requirements for quality;

b)   improve the quality of its own operations, so as to meet continually all customers' and other stakeholders' stated and implied needs;

c)   provide confidence to its internal management and other employees that the requirements for quality are being fulfilled and maintained, and that quality improvement is taking place;

d)   provide confidence to the customers and other stakeholders that the requirements for quality are being, or will be, achieved in the delivered product;

e)   provide confidence that quality-system requirements are fulfilled.

4.2 Stakeholders and their expectations

Every organization as a supplier has five principal groups of stakeholders: its customers, its employees,

its owners, its subsuppliers, and society.

The supplier should address the expectations and needs of all its stakeholders.

Supplier's stakeholders	Typical expectations/ needs
Customers	Product quality
Employees	Career/work
Owners	Investment performance
Subsuppliers	Continuing business opportunity
Society	Responsible stewardship

The International Standards in the ISO 9000 family focus their guidance and requirements on satisfying the customer.

The requirements of society, as one of the five stakeholders, are becoming more stringent worldwide. In addition, expectations and needs are becoming more explicit for considerations such as: workplace health and safety; protection of the environment (including conservation of energy and natural resources); and security. Recognizing that the ISO 9000 family of International Standards provides a widely used approach for management systems that can meet requirements for quality, these management principles can be useful for other concerns of society. Compatibility of the management-system approach in these several areas can enhance the effectiveness of an organization. In the same manner that product and process technical specifications are separate from management-systems requirements, the technical specifications in these other areas should be separately developed.

4.3 Distinguishing between quality-system requirements and product requirements

The ISO 9000 family of International Standards makes a distinction between quality-system requirements and product requirements. By means of this distinction, the ISO 9000 family applies to organizations providing products of all generic product categories, and to all product quality characteristics. The quality-system requirements are complementary to the technical requirements of the product. The applicable technical specifications of the product (e.g., as set out in product standards) and technical specifications of the process are separate and distinct from the applicable ISO 9000 family requirements or guidance.

International Standards in the ISO 9000 family, both guidance and requirements, are written in terms of the quality-system objectives to be satisfied. These International Standards do not prescribe how to achieve the objectives but leave that choice to the management of the organization.

4.4 Generic product categories

It is useful to identify four generic product categories (see clause 3 and annex A), as follows:

a) hardware;

b) software;

c) processed materials;

d) services.

These four generic product categories encompass all the kinds of product supplied by organizations. International Standards in the ISO 9000 family are applicable to all four generic product categories. The quality-system requirements are essentially the same for all generic product categories, but the terminology and management-system details and emphases may differ.

Two or more of the generic product categories usually are present in the marketplace offerings of any organization, whatever the industry/economic sector (see clause 3) in which the organization operates. For example, most organizations that supply hardware, software, or processed materials have a service component to their offering. Customers (and other stakeholders) will look for value in each generic product category that is present in the offering.

Analytical instruments are examples where hardware (i.e., the instrument), software (for computing tasks within the instrument), processed materials (such as titrating solutions or reference standard materials), and services (such as training or maintenance servicing) might all be important features of the offering. A service organization such as a restaurant will have hardware, software, and processed materials as well as service components.

4.5 Facets of quality

Four facets that are key contributors to product quality may be identified as follows.

a) Quality due to definition of needs for the product

The first facet is quality due to defining and updating the product, to meet marketplace requirements and opportunities.

b) Quality due to product design

The second facet is quality due to designing into the product the characteristics that enable it to meet marketplace requirements and opportunities, and to provide value to customers and other stakeholders. More precisely, quality due to product design is the product design features that influence intended performance within a given grade, plus product design features that influence the robustness of product performance under variable conditions of production and use.

c) Quality due to conformance to product design

The third facet is quality due to maintaining day-to-day consistency in conforming to product design and in providing the designed characteristics and values for customers and other stakeholders.

d) Quality due to product support

The fourth facet is quality due to furnishing support throughout the product life-cycle, as needed, to provide the designed characteristics and values for customers and other stakeholders.

For some products, the important quality characteristics include dependability characteristics. Dependability (i.e., reliability, maintainability, and availability) may be influenced by all four facets of product quality.

A goal of the guidance and requirements of the International Standards in the ISO 9000 family is to meet the needs for all four facets of product quality. Some facets of quality may be specifically important, for example, in contractual situations, but, in general, all facets contribute to the quality of the product. The ISO 9000 family explicitly provides generic quality-management guidance and external quality-assurance requirements on facets a, b, c, and d.

When considering the complete product offering, the customer will bear in mind additional factors. These include the following.

— The supplier's market status and strategy: if the supplier has an established and reputable marketplace status and/or a strategy that is achieving a satisfactory market share, the customer is likely to place higher value on the supplier's offering.

— The supplier's financial status and strategy: if the supplier has an established and reputable financial status and/or a strategy that is improving financial performance, the customer is likely to place higher value on the supplier's offering.

— The supplier's human resources status and strategy: if the supplier has an established and reputable human resources status and/or a strategy that is developing improved skills, diversity, and commitment in its human resources, the customer is likely to place higher value on the supplier's offering.

These additional factors are of vital importance in managing a supplier organization as a total enterprise.

NOTE 15 Product value involves both quality and price and, as such, price is not a facet of quality.

4.6 Concept of a process

The International Standards in the ISO 9000 family are founded upon the understanding that all work is accomplished by a process (see Figure 1). Every process has inputs. The outputs are the results of the process. The outputs are products, tangible or intangible. The process itself is (or should be) a transformation that adds value. Every process involves people and/or other resources in some way. An output may be, for example, an invoice, computing software, liquid fuel, a clinical device, a banking

service, or a final or intermediate product of any generic category. There are opportunities to make measurements on the inputs, at various places in the process, as well as on the outputs. As shown in Figure 2, inputs and outputs are of several types.

Type	Examples
Product-related (solid lines in Fig. 2)	Raw materials Intermediate product Final Product Sampled product
Information-related (dashed lines in Fig. 2)	Product requirements Product characteristics and status information Support-function communications Feedback on product performance needs Measurement data from sampled product

Figure 2 shows the supplier in a supply-chain relationship to a subsupplier and a customer. In this supply-chain structure, the various inputs and outputs need to flow in different directions, as illustrated in Figure 2. It is emphasized that in this context "product" includes all four generic product categories.

Quality management is accomplished by managing the processes in the organization. It is necessary to manage a process in two senses:

— the structure and operation of the process itself within which the product or information flows; and

— the quality of the product or information flowing within the structure.

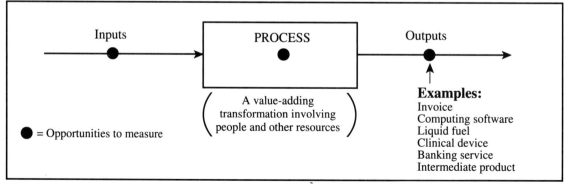

Figure 1. All work is accomplished by a process.

4.7 Network of processes in an organization

Every organization exists to accomplish value-adding work. The work is accomplished through a network of processes. The structure of the network is not usually a simple sequential structure, but typically is quite complex.

In an organization there are many functions to be performed. They include production, product design, technology management, marketing, training, human resources management, strategic planning, delivery, invoicing, and maintenance. Given the complexity of most organizations, it is important to highlight the main processes and to simplify and prioritize processes for quality-management purposes.

An organization needs to identify, organize, and manage its network of processes and interfaces. The organization creates, improves, and provides consistent quality in its offerings through the network of processes. This is a fundamental conceptual basis for the ISO 9000 family. Processes and their interfaces should be subject to analysis and continuous improvement.

Problems tend to arise where people have to manage several processes and their interrelationships, particularly for large processes that may span several functions. To clarify interfaces, responsibilities, and authorities, a process should have an owner as the person responsible. The quality of executive management's own processes, such as strategic planning, is especially important.

4.8 Quality system in relation to the network of processes

It is conventional to speak of a quality system as consisting of a number of elements. The quality system is carried out by means of processes, which exist both within and across functions. For a quality system to be effective, these processes and the associated responsibilities, authorities, procedures, and resources should be defined and deployed in a consistent manner. A system is more than a sum of processes. To be effective, the quality system needs coordination and compatibility of its component processes, and definition of their interfaces.

4.9 Evaluating quality systems

4.9.1 General

When evaluating quality systems, there are three essential questions that have to be asked in relation to every process being evaluated, as follows.

a) Are the processes defined and their procedures appropriately documented?

b) Are the processes fully deployed and implemented as documented?

c) Are the processes effective in providing the expected results?

The collective answers to these questions relating respectively to the approach, deployment, and results, will determine the outcome of the evaluation. An evaluation of a quality system may vary in scope, and encompass a wide range of activities, some of which are discussed in 4.9.2 and 4.9.3.

4.9.2   Management review

One of the important activities that executive management of the supplier organization needs to carry out systematically is an evaluation of the status

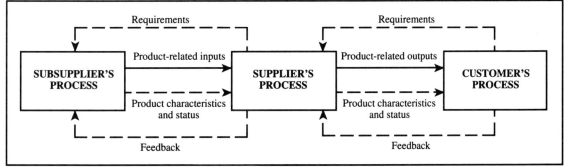

Figure 2. Supply-chain relationship of processes, with product-related and information-related flow.

and adequacy of the quality system, including the quality policy, in relation to the expectations of the stakeholders. Management reviews usually take into account many additional factors beyond the requirements found in ANSI/ASQC Q9001-1994, ANSI/ASQC Q9002-1994, and ANSI/ASQC Q9003-1994. The results of internal audits and external audits are an important source of information. It is important that the outcome of the management review should lead to increased effectiveness and efficiency of the quality system.

4.9.3 Quality-system audits

In evaluating the effectiveness of a quality system, audits are an important element. Audits may be conducted by, or on behalf of, the organization itself (first party), its customers (second parties), or independent bodies (third parties). The second- or third-party audit may provide an enhanced degree of objectivity from the customer's perspective.

First-party internal quality audits may be conducted by members of the organization or by other persons on behalf of the organization. These provide information for effective management review and corrective, preventive, or improvement action.

Second-party quality audits may be conducted by customers of the organization, or by other persons on behalf of the customer where there is a contract or a series of contracts under consideration. These provide confidence in the supplier.

Third-party quality audits may be carried out by competent certification bodies to gain certification/registration, thereby providing confidence to a range of potential customers.

The basic requirements for quality systems are contained in ANSI/ASQC Q9001-1994, ANSI/ASQC Q9002-1994, and ANSI/ASQC Q9003-1994. ANSI/ASQC Q10011-1-1994, ANSI/ASQC Q10011-2-1994, and ANSI/ASQC Q10011-3-1994 give guidance on auditing.

NOTE 16 A first-party audit is often called an "internal" audit, whereas second-party and third-party quality audits are often called "external" quality audits.

5 ROLES OF DOCUMENTATION

5.1 The value of documentation

In the context of the ISO 9000 family, the preparation and use of documentation is intended to be a dynamic high-value-adding activity. Appropriate documentation is essential for several critical roles:

— achieving required (product) quality;

— evaluating quality systems;

— quality improvement;

— maintaining the improvements.

5.2 Documentation and evaluation of quality systems

For auditing purposes, documentation of procedures is objective evidence that

— a process has been defined,

— the procedures are approved, and

— the procedures are under change control.

Only under these circumstances can internal or external audits provide a meaningful evaluation of the adequacy of both deployment and implementation.

5.3 Documentation as a support for quality improvement

Documentation is important for quality improvement. When procedures are documented, deployed, and implemented, it is possible to determine with confidence how things are done currently and to measure current performance. Then reliable measurement of the effect of a change is enhanced. Moreover, documented standard operating procedures are essential for maintaining the gains from quality-improvement activities.

5.4 Documentation and training

Maintaining consistency of the procedures that are deployed and implemented results from a combination of the documentation and the skills and training of personnel. In each situation an appropriate balance between the extent of documentation and the extent of skills and training should be sought, so as to keep documentation to a reasonable level that can be maintained at appropriate intervals. Quality-system audits should be performed with this necessary balancing in mind.

6 QUALITY-SYSTEM SITUATIONS

The ISO 9000 family is intended to be used in four situations:

a) guidance for quality management;

b) contractual, between first and second parties;

c) second-party approval or registration; and

d) third-party certification/registration.

The supplier's organization should install and maintain a quality system designed to cover all the situations (among those listed under a, b, c, and d) that the organization meets.

For situation a, this system will strengthen its own competitiveness to fulfill the requirements for product quality in a cost-effective way.

In situation b, the customer may be interested in certain elements of the supplier's quality system which affect the supplier's ability consistently to produce product to requirements, and the associated risks. The customer, therefore, contractually requires that certain quality-system elements and processes, as appropriate, be part of the supplier's quality system, by specifying a particular quality-assurance model.

In situation c, the supplier's quality system is assessed by the customer. The supplier may be given formal recognition of conformance with the standard.

In situation d, the supplier's quality system is evaluated by the certification body, and the supplier agrees to maintain the quality system for all customers unless otherwise specified in an individual contract. This type of quality-system certification or registration often reduces the number and/or extent of quality-system assessments by customers.

A single supplier often will be involved in situations of all types. The supplier may purchase some materials or components from standard inventory without contractual quality-system requirements, and purchase others with contractual quality-system requirements. The same supplier may sell some products in noncontractual situations, with or without customers expecting quality-system certification, and may sell other products in contractual situations.

A supplier can elect to use the ISO 9000 family in either of two ways, which may be called "management motivated" and "stakeholder motivated," respectively. In either case, the supplier should initially consult ANSI/ASQC Q9000-1-1994, the road map for the ISO 9000 family, to understand basic concepts and the types of standards available in the family.

The stakeholder-motivated approach is the predominant practice in many nations and industry/economic sectors. The increasing use of quality-system certification/registration is a factor in the spread of this approach.

In the stakeholder-motivated approach, the supplier initially implements a quality system in response to immediate demands by customers or other stakeholders. The selected quality system conforms to the requirements of ANSI/ASQC Q9001-1994, ANSI/ASQC Q9002-1994, or ANSI/ASQC Q9003-1994, as applicable. The supplier's management must play a significant leadership role in this approach, but the effort is driven by external stakeholders. Typically, the supplier finds that significant improvements in product quality, costs, and internal operating results are obtained. At the same time, or later, the supplier may initiate a quality-management effort to gain further improvements, building a more comprehensive quality system from the selected quality-assurance model as a core building block.

In the management-motivated approach, the supplier's own management initiates the effort in anticipation of emerging marketplace needs and trends. In this route, ANSI/ASQC Q9004-1-1994 (and other applicable parts of ISO 9004) are used first, to guide a quality-management approach to installing a quality system that will enhance the supplier's quality achievement. Subsequently, the supplier can use the applicable requirement standard, ANSI/ASQC Q9001-1994, ANSI/ASQC Q9002-1994, or ANSI/ASQC Q9003-1994, as the quality-assurance model for demonstrating quality-system adequacy, possibly seeking certification/registration in advance of any customer requirement as a preparatory measure.

The quality system implemented in this management-motivated approach will normally be more comprehensive and fruitful than the model used for demonstrating quality-system adequacy.

7 SELECTION AND USE OF INTERNATIONAL STANDARDS AND AMERICAN NATIONAL STANDARDS ON QUALITY

7.1 General

For quality-management purposes, organizations should use the ISO 9000 family of International Standards in order to develop, implement and improve their quality system in both the management-motivated and stakeholder-motivated situations.

The ISO 9000 family contains two types of guidance standards. Application guidance for quality-assurance purposes is provided by several parts of ISO 9000. Specialized application guidance for quality-management purposes is provided by the parts of ISO 9004. These parts of ISO 9004 are not intended to be used to interpret the requirements of the quality-assurance standards, however, they can provide useful references. Likewise, International Standards with numbers in the 10000 sequence may be used for reference.

Throughout the ISO 9000 family, emphasis is placed on the satisfaction of customers' needs, the establishment of functional responsibilities, and the importance of assessing (as far as possible) the potential risk and benefits. All these aspects should be considered in establishing and maintaining an effective quality system, and its continuous improvement.

Special attention should be paid to ANSI/ASQC Q9004-1-1994 which deals with quality management of any product (see 7.9) and applies to all generic product categories and all industry/economic sectors.

Using ANSI/ASQC Q9004-1-1994, the supplier should determine according to a specific situation the extent to which each quality-system element is applicable and which specific methods and technologies are to be applied; appropriate parts of the ISO 9000 family give further guidance.

Subclauses 7.2 to 7.16 give guidance to enable organizations to select appropriate International Standards from the ISO 9000 family and American National Standards from the ANSI/ASQC Q9000 series or Q10011 series that would provide useful information for implementing and operating quality systems.

7.2 Selection and use

ANSI/ASQC Q9000-1-1994, *Quality Management and Quality Assurance Standards—Guidelines for Selection and Use*

Reference should be made to ANSI/ASQC Q9000-1-1994 by any organization which is contemplating the development and implementation of a quality system.

Increased global competition has led to increasingly more stringent customer expectations with regard to quality. To be competitive and sustain good economic performance, organizations/suppliers need to employ increasingly effective and efficient systems.

ANSI/ASQC Q9000-1-1994 clarifies the principal quality-related concepts and provides guidance for the selection and use of the ISO 9000 family for this purpose.

7.3 Application guidelines

ISO 9000-2:1993, *Quality management and quality assurance standards—Part 2: Generic guidelines for the application of ISO 9001, ISO 9002 and ISO 9003*

ISO 9000-2 should be selected when assistance is needed in the implementation and application of ANSI/ASQC Q9001-1994, ANSI/ASQC Q9002-1994, and ANSI/ASQC Q9003-1994 (see clause 8).

It provides guidance on the implementation of the clauses in the quality assurance standards and is particularly useful during the initial implementation.

7.4 Software

ISO 9000-3:1991, *Quality management and quality assurance standards—Part 3: Guidelines for the application of ISO 9001 to the development, supply and maintenance of software*

(ISO 9000-3 deals exclusively with computer software.)

Reference should be made to ISO 9000-3 by supplier organizations implementing a quality system in accordance with ANSI/ASQC Q9001-1994 for a software product or a product which includes a software element.

The process of development, supply, and maintenance of software is different from that of most other types of industrial products in that there is no distinct manufacturing phase. Software does not "wear out" and, consequently, quality activities during the design phase are of paramount importance to the final quality of the product.

ISO 9000-3 sets out guidelines to facilitate the application of ISO 9001 in organizations developing, supplying, and maintaining software, by suggesting appropriate controls and methods for this purpose.

7.5 Dependability

ISO 9000-4:1993, *Quality management and quality assurance standards—Part 4: Guide to dependability programme management*

ISO 9000-4 should be selected when the supplier needs to provide assurance of the dependability (i.e., reliability, maintainability, and availability) characteristics of a product.

Society's increasing reliance upon services such as transportation, electricity, telecommunications, and information services leads to higher customer requirements and expectations with regard to quality of service. The dependability of products used for such services is a major contributing factor to their quality of service.

ISO 9000-4 provides guidance on dependability-program management. It covers the essential features of a comprehensive dependability programme for the planning, organization, direction, and control of resources to produce products that will be reliable and maintainable.

7.6 Quality assurance: design, development, production, installation, and servicing

ANSI/ASQC Q9001-1994, *Quality Systems—Model for Quality Assurance in Design, Development, Production, Installation, and Servicing*

ANSI/ASQC Q9001-1994 should be selected and used when the need is to demonstrate the supplier's capability to control the processes for design as well as production of conforming product. The requirements specified are aimed primarily at achieving customer satisfaction by preventing nonconformity at all stages from design through to servicing. ANSI/ASQC Q9001-1994 specifies a quality-assurance model for this purpose.

7.7 Quality assurance: production, installation, and servicing

ANSI/ASQC Q9002-1994, *Quality systems—Model for Quality Assurance in Production, Installation, and Servicing*

ANSI/ASQC Q9002-1994 should be selected and used when the need is to demonstrate the supplier's capability to control the processes for production of conforming product. ANSI/ASQC Q9002-1994 specifies a quality-assurance model for this purpose.

7.8 Quality assurance: final inspection

ANSI/ASQC Q9003-1994, *Quality systems—Model for Quality Assurance in Final Inspection and Test*

ANSI/ASQC Q9003-1994 should be selected and used when conformance to specified requirements is to be assured by the supplier solely at final inspection and test. ANSI/ASQC Q9003-1994 specifies a quality-assurance model for this purpose.

7.9 Quality management

ANSI/ASQC Q9004-1-1994, *Quality Management and Quality System Elements—Guidelines*

Reference should be made to ANSI/ASQC Q9004-1-1994 by any organization intending to develop and implement a quality system.

In order to meet its objectives, the organization should ensure that the technical, administrative, and human factors affecting the quality of its products will be under control, whether hardware, software, processed materials, or services.

ANSI/ASQC Q9004-1-1994 describes an extensive list of quality-system elements pertinent to all phases and activities in the life-cycle of a product to assist an organization to select and apply elements appropriate to its needs.

7.10 Services

ISO 9004-2:1991, *Quality management and quality system elements—Part 2: Guidelines for services*

Reference should be made to ISO 9004-2 by organizations that provide services or whose products include a service component.

The characteristics of a service can differ from those of other products and can include such aspects as personnel, waiting time, delivery time, hygiene, credibility, and communication delivered directly to the final customer. Customer assessment, often very subjective, is the ultimate measure of the quality of a service.

ISO 9004-2 supplements the guidance of ANSI/ASQC Q9004-1-1994 with respect to products in the services category. It describes the concepts, principles, and quality-system elements which are applicable to all forms of service offerings.

7.11 Processed materials

ISO 9004-3:1993, *Quality management and quality system elements—Part 3: Guidelines for processed materials*

Reference should be made to ISO 9004-3 by organizations whose products (final or intermediate) are prepared by transformations, and which consist of solids, liquids, gases, or combinations thereof (including particulate materials, ingots, filaments, or sheet structures). Such products are typically delivered in bulk systems such as pipelines, drums, bags, tanks, cans, or rolls.

By their nature, processed (bulk) materials present unique difficulties with regard to the verification of the product at important points in the production process. This increases the importance of the use of statistical sampling and evaluation procedures and their application to in-process controls and final product specifications.

ISO 9004-3 supplements the guidance of ANSI/ASQC Q9004-1-1994 with respect to products in the processed-materials category.

7.12 Quality improvement

ISO 9004-4:1993, *Quality management and quality system elements—Part 4: Guidelines for quality improvement*

Reference should be made to ISO 9004-4 by any organization wishing to improve its effectiveness (whether or not it has implemented a formal quality system).

A constant goal of management of all functions and at all levels of an organization should be to strive for customer satisfaction and continuous quality improvement.

ISO 9004-4 describes fundamental concepts and principles, management guidelines, and methodology (tools and techniques) for quality improvements.

7.13 Audits

ANSI/ASQC Q10011-1-1994, *Guidelines for Auditing Quality Systems—Auditing*

ANSI/ASQC Q10011-1-1994 should be selected when establishing, planning, carrying out, and documenting audits of quality systems. It provides guidelines for verifying the existence and implementation of elements of a quality system, and for verifying the system's ability to achieve defined quality objectives.

7.14 Auditors

ANSI/ASQC Q10011-2-1994, *Guidelines for Auditing Quality Systems—Qualification Criteria for Quality Systems Auditors*

ANSI/ASQC Q10011-2-1994 should be selected when staff selection and training for quality-systems auditors is needed.

It provides guidance on the qualification criteria for quality-systems auditors. It contains guidance on the education, training, experience, personal attributes, and management capabilities needed to carry out an audit.

7.15 Managing audits

ANSI/ASQC Q10011-3-1994, *Guidelines for Auditing Quality Systems—Management of Audit Programs*

ANSI/ASQC Q10011-3-1994 should be selected when planning the management of an audit program. It provides basic guidelines for managing quality-systems audit programs. It is consistent with ANSI/ASQC Q10011-1-1994 and ANSI/ASQC Q10011-2-1994.

7.16 Quality assurance for measurement

ISO 10012-1:1992, *Quality assurance requirements for measuring equipment—Part 1: Metrological confirmation system for measuring equipment*

ISO 10012-1 should be selected when the product or process quality depends heavily on the ability to measure accurately. It specifies the main features of the confirmation system to be used for a supplier's measuring equipment. It contains the quality-assurance requirements for a supplier's measurement equipment to ensure that measurements are made with the intended accuracy and consistency. It contains more detailed requirements than those found in ANSI/ASQC Q9001-1994, ANSI/ASQC Q9002-1994, and ANSI/ASQC Q9003-1994, and is presented with guidance for implementation.

8 SELECTION AND USE OF INTERNATIONAL STANDARDS AND AMERICAN NATIONAL STANDARDS FOR EXTERNAL QUALITY ASSURANCE

8.1 General guidance

In second-party approval or registration (situations b and c in clause 6), the supplier and the other party should agree on which International Standard or American National Standard will be used as the basis for approval. The selection and application of a model for quality assurance appropriate to a given situation should provide benefits to both customer and supplier.

Examining the benefits, risks, and costs for both parties will determine the extent and nature of reciprocal information and the measures each party should take to provide adequate confidence that the intended quality will be achieved. The supplier has the responsibility to select the model for subcontracts unless otherwise agreed with the customer.

In third-party certification/registration, the supplier and the certification body should agree on which International Standard or American National Standard will be used as the basis for certification/registration. The selected model should be adequate and not misleading from the point of view of the supplier's customers. For example, the role and character of design activities, if any, is especially important in selecting between ANSI/ASQC Q9001-1994 and ANSI/ASQC Q9002-1994. The selection and application of a model for quality assurance appropriate to a given situation should also support the supplier's objectives. Examining the scope of the supplier's activities which will be encompassed by the certificate will determine the extent and nature of reciprocal information and the measures each party should take to provide confidence that the certification/registration is maintained in accordance with the requirements of the selected model.

8.2 Selection of model

8.2.1 Three models for quality assurance

As indicated in 7.6 to 7.8, in the three relevant American National Standards, certain quality-system elements have been grouped to form three distinct models suitable for the purpose of suppliers demonstrating their capabilities and for assessment of such supplier capability by external parties.

a)   ANSI/ASQC Q9001-1994: for use when conformance to specified requirements is to be assured by the supplier during design, development, production, installation, and servicing.

b)   ANSI/ASQC Q9002-1994: for use when conformance to specified requirements is to be assured by the supplier during production, installation, and servicing.

NOTE 17   ANSI/ASQC Q9002-1994 is identical to ANSI/ASQC Q9001-1994 except for the deletion of all quality-system requirements for design control.

c)   ANSI/ASQC Q9003-1994: for use when conformance to specified requirements is to be assured by the supplier at final inspection and test.

In 4.6 to 4.8 and elsewhere, a process perspective is emphasized. The goal of the quality system is to fulfill the requirements for quality in the results from the supplier's processes. But the quality-system requirements are directed toward the procedures for these processes. Therefore, specific quality-system requirements in ANSI/ASQC Q9001-1994, ANSI/ASQC Q9002-1994, and ANSI/ASQC Q9003-1994 usually are phrased: "The supplier shall establish and maintain documented procedures..."

8.2.2 Selection

The scopes of the American National Standards as summarized in 8.2.1 indicate how the choice should be made among ANSI/ASQC Q9001-1994, ANSI/ASQC Q9002-1994, or ANSI/ASQC Q9003-1994 consistent with the situations a, b, c, and d in clause 6.

8.3 Demonstration of conformance to the selected model

The quality-system elements should be documented and demonstrable in a manner consistent with the requirements of the selected model.

Demonstration of the quality-system elements and

their associated processes provides confidence on:

a) adequacy of the quality system;

b) capability to achieve product conformity with the specified requirements.

The responsibility for demonstrating the adequacy and effectiveness of the quality system lies with the supplier. However, the supplier may need to consider the expectations for demonstration of the relevant interested parties as described in clause 6 b, c, and d. These considerations may determine the means adopted to demonstrate conformance to the selected model. Methods may include:

— supplier's declaration of conformity;

— providing basic documented evidence;

— providing evidence of approvals or registrations by other customers;

— audit by the customer;

— audit by a third party;

— providing evidence of competent third-party certificates.

Any of these means or a combination of them may apply in situations b and c of clause 6. In the 6d situation, the last two means are applicable.

The nature and degree of demonstration may vary from one situation to another in accordance with such criteria as:

a) the economics, uses, and conditions of use of the product;

b) the complexity and innovation required to design the product;

c) the complexity and difficulty of producing the product;

d) the ability to judge product quality on the basis of final inspection and test alone;

e) the requirements of society regarding the product;

f) the past performance of the supplier;

g) the degree of partnership in the relationship with the customer.

8.4 Additional considerations in contractual situations

8.4.1 Tailoring and contractual elements

Experience has shown that with a small fixed number of International Standards and American National Standards available, it is possible in almost every given contractual situation to select one that will meet needs adequately. However, on occasions, certain quality-system elements or subelements called for in the selected International Standard or American National Standard may be deleted and, on other occasions, elements or subelements may be added. Tailoring may also concern the degree of demonstration of quality-system elements. If tailoring should prove necessary, it should be agreed between the customer and the supplier, and should be specified in the contract.

8.4.2 Review of contractual quality-system elements

Both parties should review the proposed contract to be sure that they understand the quality-system requirements and that the requirements are mutually acceptable considering the economics and risks in their respective situations.

8.4.3 Supplementary quality-assurance requirements

There may be a need to specify supplementary requirements in the contract, such as statistical process control or systems requirements for safety-critical items.

8.4.4 Precontract assessment

Assessments of a supplier's quality system according to ANSI/ASQC Q9001-1994, ANSI/ASQC Q9002-1994, or ANSI/ASQC Q9003-1994 and, when appropriate, supplementary requirements often are utilized prior to a contract to determine the supplier's ability to satisfy the requirements. In many cases, assessments are performed directly by the customer.

8.4.5 Audits after award of the contract

Continuing demonstration of the supplier's quality system after award of the contract may be achieved by a series of quality audits conducted by the customer, the customer's agent, or an agreed third party.

ANNEX A (NORMATIVE)

Terms and Definitions
Taken from ISO 8402

A.1 Quality

Totality of characteristics of an entity that bear on its ability to satisfy stated and implied needs.

NOTES

18 In a contractual environment, or in a regulated environment, such as the nuclear safety field, needs are specified, whereas in other environments, implied needs should be identified and defined.

19 In many instances, needs can change with time; this implies periodic review of requirements for quality.

20 Needs are usually translated into characteristics with specified criteria. Needs may include, for example, aspects of performance, usability, dependability (availability, reliability, maintainability), safety, environment, economics, and aesthetics.

21 The term "quality" is not used as a single term to express a degree of excellence in a comparative sense nor is it used in a quantitative sense for technical evaluations. To express these meanings, a qualifying adjective should be used. For example, use can be made of the following terms:

   a) "relative quality" where entities are ranked on a relative basis in the "degree of excellence" or "comparative" sense (not to be confused with "grade");

   b) "quality level" in a "quantitative" sense (as used in acceptance sampling) and "quality measure" where precise technical evaluations are carried out.

22 The achievement of satisfactory quality involves all stages of the quality loop as a whole. The contributions to quality of these various stages are sometimes identified separately for emphasis, for example, quality due to definition of needs, quality due to product design, quality due to conformance, quality due to product support throughout its lifetime.

23 In some references, quality is referred to as "fitness for use" or "fitness for purpose" or "customer satisfaction" or "conformance to the requirements." These represent only certain facets of qual*ity, as defined above.*

A.2 Quality policy

Overall intentions and direction of an organization with regard to quality, as formally expressed by top management.

NOTE 24 The quality policy forms one element of the corporate policy and is authorized by top management.

A.3 Quality management

All activities of the overall management function that determine the quality policy, objectives and responsibilities, and implement them by means such as quality planning, quality control, quality assurance and quality improvement within the quality system.

NOTES

25 Quality management is the responsibility of all levels of management but must be led by top management. Its implementation involves all members of the organization.

26 In quality management, consideration is given to economic aspects.

A.4 Quality system

Organizational structure, procedures, processes and resources needed to implement quality management.

NOTES

27 The quality system should only be as comprehensive as needed to meet the quality objectives.

28 The quality system of an organization is designed primarily to meet the internal managerial needs of the organization. It is broader than the requirements of a particular customer, who evaluates only the relevant part of the quality system.

29 For contractual or mandatory quality assessment purposes, demonstration of the implementation of the identified quality system elements may be required.

A.5 Quality control

Operational techniques and activities that are used to fulfill the requirements for quality.

NOTES

30 Quality control involves operational techniques and activities aimed both at monitoring a process and at eliminating causes of unsatisfactory performance at all stages of the quality loop in order to result in economic effectiveness.

31 Some quality control and quality assurance actions are interrelated.

A.6 Quality assurance

All the planned and systematic activities implemented within the quality system, and demonstrated as needed, to provide adequate confidence that an entity will fulfill requirements for quality.

NOTES

32 There are both internal and external purposes for quality assurance:

a) internal quality assurance: within an organization quality assurance provides confidence to the management;

b) external quality assurance: in contractual or other situations, quality assurance provides confidence to the customers or others.

33 Some quality control and quality assurance actions are interrelated.

34 Unless requirements for quality fully reflect the needs of the user, quality assurance may not provide adequate confidence.

A.7 Quality improvement

Actions taken throughout the organization, to increase the effectiveness and efficiency of activities and processes to provide added benefits to both the organization and its customers.

A.8 Product

Result of activities or processes.

NOTES

35 A product may include service, hardware, processed materials, software, or a combination thereof.

36 A product can be tangible (e.g., assemblies or processed materials) or intangible (e.g., knowledge or concepts), or a combination thereof.

37 Product can be intended (e.g., offering to customers) or unintended (e.g., pollutant or unwanted effects).

A.9 Service

Result generated by activities at the interface between the supplier and the customer and by supplier internal activities, to meet customer needs.

NOTES

38 The supplier or the customer may be represented at the interface by personnel or equipment.

39 Customer activities at the interface with the supplier may be essential to the service delivery.

40 Delivery or use of tangible products may form part of the service delivery.

41 A service may be linked with the manufacture and supply of tangible product.

A.10 Customer

Recipient of a product provided by the supplier.

NOTES

42 In a contractual situation, the customer is called the "purchaser."[1]

43 The customer may be, for example, the ultimate consumer, user, beneficiary, or purchaser.

44 The customer can be either external or internal to the organization.

A.11 Supplier

Organization that provides a product to the customer.

NOTES

45 In a contractual situation, the supplier may be called the "contractor."

46 The supplier may be, for example, the producer, distributor, importer, assembler, or service organization.

47 The supplier can be either external or internal to the organization.

A.12 Process

Set of interrelated resources and activities which transform inputs into outputs.

NOTE 48 Resources may include personnel, finance, facilities, equipment, techniques, and methods.

ANNEX B (INFORMATIVE)

Product and process factors

B.1 Purpose

Product and process characteristics are important in the application of the ISO 9000 family. This annex highlights a number of product and process factors that should be considered, for example:

a) by a supplier's management for quality-management purposes, when planning the approach and extent of implementing a quality-system element (see 7.1);

b) by auditors, when planning first-, second-, or third-party audits (see 4.9.3);

c) by supplier and customer jointly when selecting and/or tailoring quality-system requirements for a two-party contract (see 8.4).

NOTE 49 In ANSI/ASQC Q90-1987, these factors were given as guidance only for purposec.

B.2 Factors

a) Complexity of designing

This factor deals with difficulty of designing the product and designing the production and support processes if they have to be designed, or if the design needs periodic change.

b) Maturity and stability of product designs

This factor deals with the extent to which the total product design is known and proven, either by performance testing or field experience.

c) Production process complexity

This factor deals with:

1) the availability of proven production processes;

2) the need for development of new processes;

3) the number and variety of processes required;

4) the impact of the process(es) on the performance of the product;

5) the need for process control.

d) Product characteristics

This factor deals with the complexity of the product, the number of interrelated characteristics, and whether each characteristic is critical to the performance.

e) Product safety

This factor deals with the risk of the occurrence of failure and the consequences of such failure.

f) Economics

This factor deals with the economic costs, to both supplier and customer, of the preceding factors weighed against the risk of costs due to nonconformities in the product.

ANNEX C (INFORMATIVE)

Proliferation of Standards

This ISO 9000 family—in particular, the International Standards for contractual, assessment, or certification/registration use (ISO 9001, ISO 9002 and ISO 9003)—are being employed worldwide in many industry/economic sectors for products in all four generic product categories. Various schemes have been developed specific to particular industry/economic sectors.

It is important to distinguish schemes which implement, without change, the ISO 9000 family, from schemes which involve localized versions of these International Standards. If the ISO 9000 family were to become only the nucleus of a proliferation of localized standards derived from, but varying in content and architecture from, the ISO 9000 family, then there would be little worldwide standardization.

Once again, there could be worldwide restraint of trade because of the proliferation of standards and inconsistent requirements.

Fortunately, current global marketplace trends are driving many standards users toward strategic recognition that they need and should conform to International Standards. The International Standards in the ISO 9000 family, and the plans for continuing revision, are intended to provide the needed scope, content, and flexibility to meet current and emerging marketplace needs in a timely way.

Figure C.1 shows in matrix form which standards-implementation activities are recommended in each of four implementation domains, within the quality management and quality assurance arena. Any third-party assessment and certification scheme should operate under procedures that conform fully to all the International Standards, guides, and practices as required for mutual international recognition of quality-system certification.

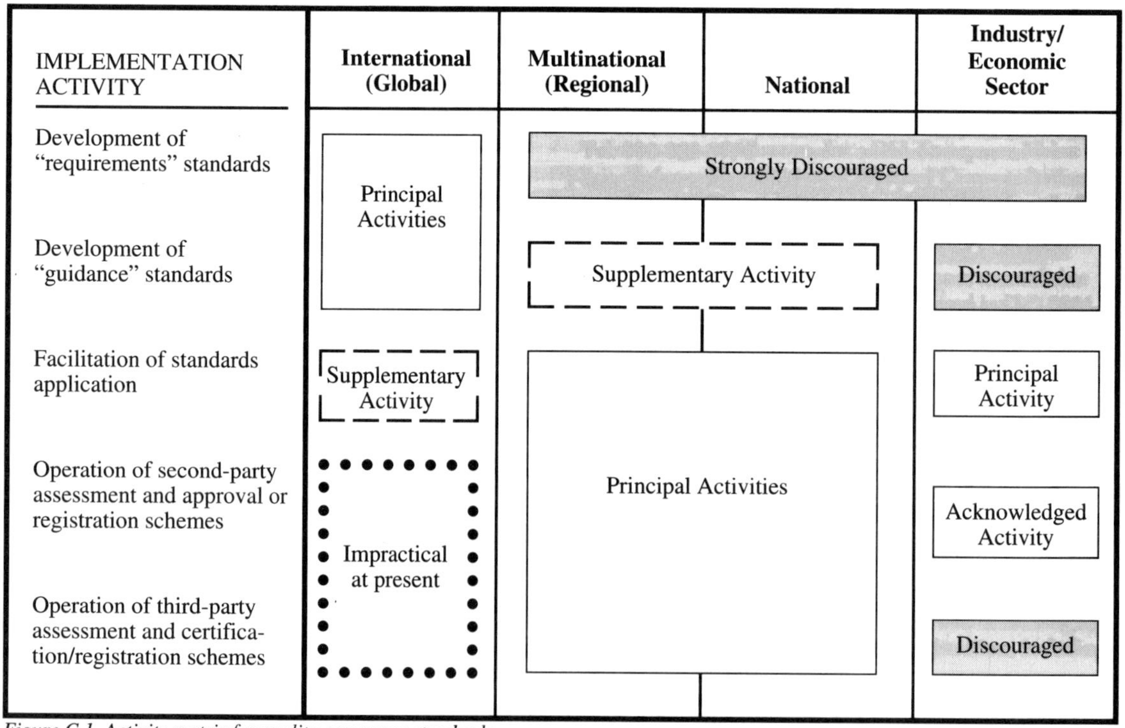

IMPLEMENTATION ACTIVITY	International (Global)	Multinational (Regional)	National	Industry/ Economic Sector
Development of "requirements" standards	Principal Activities	Strongly Discouraged		
Development of "guidance" standards		Supplementary Activity		Discouraged
Facilitation of standards application	Supplementary Activity	Principal Activities		Principal Activity
Operation of second-party assessment and approval or registration schemes	Impractical at present			Acknowledged Activity
Operation of third-party assessment and certification/registration schemes				Discouraged

Figure C.1. Activity matrix for quality-assurance standards.

ANNEX D (INFORMATIVE)

External Quality Assurance					QM Guidance	Road Map
Requirements			Application Guide ISO 9000-2	Clause Title in ANSI/ASQC Q9001-1994	ANSI/ASQC Q9004-1 1994	QNSI/ASQC Q9000-1 1994
ANSI/ASQC Q9001-1994	ANSI/ASQC Q9002-1994	ANSI/ASQC Q9003-1994				
4.1 •	•	ø	4.1	Management responsibility	4	4.1; 4.2; 4.3
4.2 •	•	ø	4.2	Quality system	5	4.4; 4.5; 4.8
4.3 •	•	•	4.3	Contract review	§	8
4.4 •	§	§	4.4	Design control	8	
4.5 •	•	•	4.5	Document and data control	5.3; 11.5	
4.6 •	•	§	4.6	Purchasing	9	
4.7 •	•	•	4.7	Customer-supplied product	§	
4.8 •	•	ø	4.8	Product identification and traceability	11.2	5
4.9 •	•	§	4.9	Process control	10; 11	4.6; 4.7
4.10 •	•	ø	4.10	Inspection and testing	12	
4.11 •	•	•	4.11	Control of inspection, measuring, and test equipment	13	
4.12 •	•	•	4.12	Inspection and test status	11.7	
4.13 •	•	ø	4.13	Control of nonconforming product	14	
4.14 •	•	ø	4.14	Corrective and preventive action	15	
4.15 •	•	•	4.15	Handling, storage, packaging, preservation, and delivery	10.4; 16.1; 16.2	
4.16 •	•	ø	4.16	Control of quality records	5.3; 17.2; 17.3	
4.17 •	•	ø	4.17	Internal quality audits	5.4	4.9
4.18 •	•	ø	4.18	Training	18.1	5.4
4.19 •	•	§	4.19	Servicing	16.4	
4.20 •	•	ø	4.20	Statistical techniques	20	
				Quality economics	6	
				Product safety	19	
				Marketing	7	

Key:
• = Comprehensive requirement
ø = Less-comprehensive requirement than ANSI/ASQC Q9001-1994 and ANSI/ASQC Q9002-1994
§ = Element not present

Table D.1. Cross-reference list of clause numbers for corresponding topics.

ANNEX E (INFORMATIVE)

Bibliography

[1] ANSI/ASQC Q9001-1994, *Quality Systems— Model for Quality Assurance in Design, Development, Production, Installation, and Servicing.*

[2] ANSI/ASQC Q9002-1994, *Quality Systems— Model for Quality Assurance in Production, Installation, and Servicing.*

[3] ANSI/ASQC Q9003-1994, *Quality Systems— Model for Quality Assurance in Final Inspection and Test.*

[4] ANSI/ASQC Q9004-1-1994, *Quality Management and Quality Systems—Guidelines.*

[5] ANSI/ASQC Q10011-1-1994, *Guidelines for Auditing Quality Systems—Auditing.*

[6] ANSI/ASQC Q10011-2-1994, *Guidelines for Auditing Quality Systems—Qualification Criteria for Quality Systems Auditors.*

[7] ANSI/ASQC Q10011-3-1994, *Guidelines for Auditing Quality Systems—Management of Audit Programs.*

[8] ISO 9000-2:1993, *Quality management and quality assurance standards—Part 2: Generic guidelines for the application of ISO 9001, ISO 9002 and ISO 9003.*

[9] ISO 9000-3:1991, *Quality management and quality assurance standards—Part 3: Guidelines for the application of ISO 9001 to the development, supply and maintenance of software.*

[10] ISO 9000-4:1993, *Quality management and quality assurance standards—Part 4: Guide to dependability programme management.*

[11] ISO 9004-2:1991, *Quality management and quality system elements—Part 2: Guidelines for services.*

[12] ISO 9004-3:1993, *Quality management and quality system elements—Part 3: Guidelines for processed materials.*

[13] ISO 9004-4:1993, *Quality management and quality system elements—Part 4: Guidelines for quality improvement.*

[14] ISO 10012-1:1992, *Quality assurance requirements for measuring equipment—Part 1: Metrological confirmation system for measuring equipment.*

[15] ISO 10013:—[2] *Guidelines for developing quality manuals.*

[16] ISO Handbook 3:1989, *Statistical methods.*

ENDNOTES:

[1] The recommended harmonized term is "customer" as shown in Table 1 of ANSI/ASQC Q9000-1-1994. The term "purchaser" was used in ANSI/ASQC Q91-1987, ANSI/ASQC Q92-1987, and ANSI/ASQC Q93-1987.

[2] To be published.

American National Standard

ANSI/ASQC Q9001-1994

QUALITY SYSTEMS—MODEL FOR QUALITY ASSURANCE IN DESIGN, DEVELOPMENT, PRODUCTION, INSTALLATION, AND SERVICING

[Revision of first edition (ANSI/ASQC Q91-1987)]

Prepared by
American Society for Quality Control
Standards Committee
for
American National Standards Committee
Z-1 on Quality Assurance

Descriptors: Quality assurance, quality assurance program, quality systems, design, development (work), production, installation, after-sales services, reference models.

American National Standards: An American National Standard implies a consensus of those substantially concerned with its scope and provisions. An American National Standard is intended as a guide to aid the manufacturer, the consumer, and the general public. The existence of an American National Standard does not in any respect preclude anyone, whether he or she has approved the standard or not, from manufacturing, purchasing, or using products, processes, or procedures not conforming to the standard. American National Standards are subject to periodic review and users are cautioned to obtain the latest edition.

Caution Notice: This American National Standard may be revised or withdrawn at any time. The procedures of the American National Standards Institute require that action be taken to reaffirm, revise, or withdraw this standard no later than five years from the date of publication. Purchasers of American National Standards may receive current information on all standards by calling or writing the American National Standards Institute.

ASQC Mission: To facilitate continuous improvement and increase customer satisfaction by identifying, communicating, and promoting the use of quality principles, concepts, and technologies; and thereby be recognized throughout the world as the leading authority on, and champion for, quality.

10 9 8 7 6 5 4 3 2 1

Printed in the United States of America

Printed on acid-free recycled paper

Published by:
ASQC
611 East Wisconsin Avenue
Milwaukee, Wisconsin 53202

CONTENTS

1   Scope

2   Normative reference

3   Definitions

4   Quality-system requirements

4.1   Management responsibility

4.2   Quality system

4.3   Contract review

4.4   Design control

4.5   Document and data control

4.6   Purchasing

4.7   Control of customer-supplied product

4.8   Product identification and traceability

4.9   Process control

4.10 Inspection and testing

4.11 Control of inspection, measuring, and test
      equipment

4.12 Inspection and test status

4.13 Control of nonconforming product

4.14 Corrective and preventive action

4.15 Handling, storage, packaging, preservation,
      and delivery

4.16 Control of quality records

4.17 Internal quality audits

4.18 Training

4.19 Servicing

4.20 Statistical techniques

Annex

A   Bibliography

FOREWORD

(This Foreword is not a part of American National Standard *Quality Systems—Model for Quality Assurance in Design, Development, Production, Installation, and Servicing.*)

This American National Standard corresponds to the International Standard ISO 9001:1994. The initial five ISO 9000 series standards, ISO 9000, ISO 9001, ISO 9002, ISO 9003, and ISO 9004, when published in the United States as American National Standards in 1987, were designated as ANSI/ASQC Q90 through ANSI/ASQC Q94 respectively. The five 1987 standards in their 1994 international revisions are now designated ISO 9000-1, ISO 9001, ISO 9002, ISO 9003, and ISO 9004-1 respectively. Their publication as American National Standards are now designated ANSI/ASQC Q9000-1-1994, ANSI/ASQC Q9001-1994, ANSI/ASQC Q9002-1994, ANSI/ASQC Q9003-1994, and ANSI/ASQC Q9004-1-1994 respectively. This new numbering system is intended to emphasize the word-for-word correspondence of the International and American National Standards.

ISO (the International Organization for Standardization) is a worldwide federation of national standards bodies (ISO member bodies). The work of preparing International Standards is normally carried out through ISO technical committees. Each member body interested in a subject for which a technical committee has been established has the right to be represented on that committee. International organizations, governmental and nongovernmental, in liaison with ISO, also take part in the work. ISO collaborates closely with the International Electrotechnical Commission (IEC) on all matters of electrotechnical standardization. The American National Standards Institute (ANSI) is the U.S. member body of ISO. ASQC is the U.S. member of ANSI responsible for quality management and related standards.

Users should note that all ANSI/ASQC standards undergo revision from time to time. In the case of International Standards adopted as American National Standards, the revision timing is influences by the international revision timing. Reference herein to any other standard implies the latest American National Standard revision unless otherwise stated.

Comments concerning this standard are welcome. They should be sent to the sponsor of the standard, American Society for Quality COntrol, 611 East Wisconsin Avenue, P.O. Box 3005, Milwaukee, WI 53201-3005, c/o Standards Administrator.

INTRODUCTION

This American National Standard is one of three American National Standards dealing with quality-system requirements that can be used for external quality-assurance purposes. The quality-assurance models, set out in the three American National Standards listed below, represent three distinct forms of quality-system requirements suitable for the purpose of a supplier demonstrating its capability, and for the assessment of the capability of a supplier by external parties.

a)   ANSI/ASQC Q9001-1994, *Quality Systems— Model for Quality Assurance in Design, Develop-ment, Production, Installation, and Servicing*

— for use when conformance to specified requirements is to be assured by the supplier during design, development, production, installation, and servicing.

b)   ANSI/ASQC Q9002-1994, *Quality Systems— Model for Quality Assurance in Production, Installation, and Servicing*

— for use when conformance to specified requirements is to be assured by the supplier during production, installation, and servicing.

c)   ANSI/ASQC Q9003-1994, *Quality Systems— Model for Quality Assurance in Final Inspection and Test*

— for use when conformance to specified requirements is to be assured by the supplier solely at final inspection and test.

It is emphasized that the quality-system requirements specified in this American National Standard, ANSI/ASQC Q9002-1994, and ANSI/ASQC Q9003-1994 are complementary (not alternative) to the technical (product) specified requirements. They specify

requirements which determine what elements quality systems have to encompass, but it is not the purpose of these American National Standards to enforce uniformity of quality systems. They are generic and independent of any specific industry or economic sector. The design and implementation of a quality system will be influenced by the varying needs of an organization, its particular objectives, the products and services supplied, and the processes and specific practices employed.

It is intended that these American National Standards will be adopted in their present form, but on occasions they may need to be tailored by adding or deleting certain quality-system requirements for specific contractual situations. ANSI/ASQC Q9000-1-1994 provides guidance on such tailoring as well as on selection of the appropriate quality-assurance model, *viz.* ANSI/ASQC Q9001-1994, ANSI/ASQC Q9002-1994, or ANSI/ASQC Q9003-1994.

Quality Systems—Model for Quality Assurance in Design, Development, Production, Installation, and Servicing

1 SCOPE

This American National Standard specifies quality-system requirements for use where a supplier's capability to design and supply conforming product needs to be demonstrated.

The requirements specified are aimed primarily at achieving customer satisfaction by preventing nonconformity at all stages from design through to servicing.

This American National Standard is applicable in situations when:

a)   design is required and the product requirements are stated principally in performance terms, or they need to be established, and

b)   confidence in product conformance can be attained by adequate demonstration of a supplier's capabilities in design, development, production, installation, and servicing.

NOTE 1   For informative references, see annex A.

2 NORMATIVE REFERENCE

The following standard contains provisions which, through reference in this text, constitute provisions of this American National Standard. At the time of publication, the edition indicated was valid. All standards are subject to revision, and parties to agreements based on this American National Standard are encouraged to investigate the possibility of applying the most recent edition of the standard indicated below. The American National Standards Institute and members of IEC and ISO maintain registers of currently valid American National Standards and International Standards.

ISO 8402:1994, *Quality management and quality assurance—Vocabulary.*

3 DEFINITIONS

For the purposes of this American National Standard, the definitions given in ISO 8402 and the following definitions apply.

3.1 Product

Result of activities or processes.

> **NOTES**
>
> 2 *A product may include service, hardware, processed materials, software, or a combination thereof.*
>
> 3 *A product can be tangible (e.g., assemblies or processed materials) or intangible (e.g., knowledge or concepts), or a combination thereof.*
>
> 4 *For the purposes of this American National Standard, the term "product" applies to the intended product offering only and not to unintended "by-products" affecting the environment. This differs from the definition given in ISO 8402.*

3.2 Tender

Offer made by a supplier in response to an invitation to satisfy a contract award to provide product.

3.3 Contract; accepted order

Agreed requirements between a supplier and customer transmitted by any means.

4 QUALITY-SYSTEM REQUIREMENTS

4.1 Management responsibility

4.1.1 Quality policy

The supplier's management with executive responsibility shall define and document its policy for quality, including objectives for quality and its commitment to quality. The quality policy shall be relevant to the supplier's organizational goals and the expectations and needs of its customers. The supplier shall ensure that this policy is understood, implemented, and maintained at all levels of the organization.

4.1.2 Organization

4.1.2.1 Responsibility and authority

The responsibility, authority, and the interrelation of personnel who manage, perform, and verify work affecting quality shall be defined and documented, particularly for personnel who need the organizational freedom and authority to:

a) initiate action to prevent the occurrence of any nonconformities relating to product, process, and quality system;

b) identify and record any problems relating to the product, process, and quality system;

c) initiate, recommend, or provide solutions through designated channels;

d) verify the implementation of solutions;

e) control further processing, delivery, or installation of nonconforming product until the deficiency or unsatisfactory condition has been corrected.

4.1.2.2 Resources

The supplier shall identify resource requirements and provide adequate resources, including the assignment of trained personnel (see 4.18), for management, performance of work, and verification activities including internal quality audits.

4.1.2.3 Management representative

The supplier's management with executive responsibility shall appoint a member of the supplier's own management who, irrespective of other responsibilities, shall have defined authority for

a) ensuring that a quality system is established, implemented, and maintained in accordance with this American National Standard, and

b) reporting on the performance of the quality system to the supplier's management for review and as a basis for improvement of the quality system.

NOTE 5 The responsibility of a management representative may also include liaison with external parties on matters relating to the supplier's quality system.

4.1.3 Management review

The supplier's management with executive responsibility shall review the quality system at defined intervals sufficient to ensure its continuing suitability and effectiveness in satisfying the requirements of this American National Standard and the supplier's stated quality policy and objectives (see 4.1.1). Records of such reviews shall be maintained (see 4.16).

4.2 Quality system

4.2.1 General

The supplier shall establish, document, and maintain a quality system as a means of ensuring that product conforms to specified requirements. The supplier shall prepare a quality manual covering the requirements of this American National Standard. The quality manual shall include or make reference to the quality-system procedures and outline the structure of the documentation used in the quality system.

NOTE 6 Guidance on quality manuals is given in ISO 10013.

4.2.2 Quality-system procedures

The supplier shall

a) prepare documented procedures consistent with the requirements of this American National Standard and the supplier's stated quality policy, and

b) effectively implement the quality system and its documented procedures.

For the purposes of this American National Standard, the range and detail of the procedures that form part of the quality system depend on the complexity of the work, the methods used, and the skills and training needed by personnel involved in carrying out the activity.

NOTE 7 Documented procedures may make reference to work instructions that define how an activity is performed.

4.2.3 Quality planning

The supplier shall define and document how the requirements for quality will be met. Quality planning shall be consistent with all other requirements of a supplier's quality system and shall be documented in a format to suit the supplier's method of operation. The supplier shall give consideration to the following activities, as appropriate, in meeting the specified requirements for products, projects, or contracts:

a) the preparation of quality plans;

b) the identification and acquisition of any controls, processes, equipment (including inspection and test equipment), fixtures, resources, and skills that may be needed to achieve the required quality;

c) ensuring the compatibility of the design, the production process, installation, servicing, inspection, and test procedures, and the applicable documentation;

d) the updating, as necessary, of quality control, inspection, and testing techniques, including the development of new instrumentation;

e) the identification of any measurement requirement involving capability that exceeds the known state of the art, in sufficient time for the needed capability to be developed;

f) the identification of suitable verification at appropriate stages in the realization of product;

g) the clarification of standards of acceptability for all features and requirements, including those which contain a subjective element;

h) the identification and preparation of quality records (see 4.16).

NOTE 8 The quality plans referred to (see 4.2.3a) may be in the form of a reference to the appropriate documented procedures that form an integral part of the supplier's quality system.

4.3 Contract review

4.3.1 General

The supplier shall establish and maintain documented procedures for contract review and for the coordination of these activities.

4.3.2 Review

Before submission of a tender, or at the acceptance of a contract or order (statement of requirement), the tender, contract, or order shall be reviewed by the supplier to ensure that:

a) the requirements are adequately defined and documented; where no written statement of requirement is available for an order received by verbal means, the supplier shall ensure that the order requirements are agreed before their acceptance;

b) any differences between the contract or accepted order requirements and those in the tender are resolved;

c) the supplier has the capability to meet the contract or accepted order requirements.

4.3.3 Amendment to contract

The supplier shall identify how an amendment to a contract is made and correctly transferred to the functions concerned within the supplier's organization.

4.3.4 Records

Records of contract reviews shall be maintained (see 4.16).

NOTE 9 Channels for communication and interfaces with the customer's organization in these contract matters should be established.

4.4 Design control

4.4.1 General

The supplier shall establish and maintain documented procedures to control and verify the design of the product in order to ensure that the specified requirements are met.

4.4.2 Design and development planning

The supplier shall prepare plans for each design and development activity. The plans shall describe or reference these activities, and define responsibility for their implementation. The design and development activities shall be assigned to qualified personnel equipped with adequate resources. The plans shall be updated, as the design evolves.

4.4.3 Organizational and technical interfaces

Organizational and technical interfaces between different groups which input into the design process shall be defined and the necessary information documented, transmitted, and regularly reviewed.

4.4.4 Design input

Design-input requirements relating to the product, including applicable statutory and regulatory requirements, shall be identified, documented, and their selection reviewed by the supplier for adequacy. Incomplete, ambiguous, or conflicting requirements shall be resolved with those responsible for imposing these requirements.

Design input shall take into consideration the results of any contract-review activities.

4.4.5 Design output

Design output shall be documented and expressed in terms that can be verified against design-input requirements and validated (see 4.4.8).

Design output shall:

a) meet the design-input requirements;

b) contain or make reference to acceptance criteria;

c) identify those characteristics of the design that are crucial to the safe and proper functioning of the product (e.g., operating, storage, handling, maintenance, and disposal requirements).

Design-output documents shall be reviewed before release.

4.4.6 Design review

At appropriate stages of design, formal documented reviews of the design results shall be planned and conducted. Participants at each design review shall include representatives of all functions concerned with the design stage being reviewed, as well as other specialist personnel, as required. Records of such reviews shall be maintained (see 4.16).

4.4.7 Design verification

At appropriate stages of design, design verification shall be performed to ensure that the design-stage output meets the design-stage input requirements. The design-verification measures shall be recorded (see 4.16).

NOTE 10 In addition to conducting design reviews (see 4.4.6), design verification may include activities such as

— performing alternative calculations,

— comparing the new design with a similar proven design, if available,

— undertaking tests and demonstrations, and

— reviewing the design-stage documents before release.

4.4.8 Design validation

Design validation shall be performed to ensure that product conforms to defined user needs and/or requirements.

NOTES

11 Design validation follows successful design verification (see 4.4.7).

12 Validation is normally performed under defined operating conditions.

13 Validation is normally performed on the final product, but may be necessary in earlier stages prior to product completion.

14 Multiple validations may be performed if there are different intended uses.

4.4.9 Design changes

All design changes and modifications shall be identified, documented, reviewed, and approved by authorized personnel before their implementation.

4.5 Document and data control

4.5.1 General

The supplier shall establish and maintain documented procedures to control all documents and data that relate to the requirements of this American National Standard including, to the extent applicable, documents of external origin such as standards and customer drawings.

NOTE 15 Documents and data can be in the form of any type of media, such as hard copy or electronic media.

4.5.2 Document and data approval and issue

The documents and data shall be reviewed and approved for adequacy by authorized personnel prior to issue. A master list or equivalent document-control procedure identifying the current revision status of documents shall be established and be readily available to preclude the use of invalid and/or obsolete documents.

This control shall ensure that:

a) the pertinent issues of appropriate documents are available at all locations where operations essential to the effective functioning of the quality system are performed;

b) invalid and/or obsolete documents are promptly removed from all points of issue or use, or otherwise assured against unintended use;

c) any obsolete documents retained for legal and/or knowledge-preservation purposes are suitably identified.

4.5.3 Document and data changes

Changes to documents and data shall be reviewed and approved by the same functions/organizations that performed the original review and approval, unless specifically designated otherwise. The designated functions/organizations shall have access to pertinent background information upon which to base their review and approval.

Where practicable, the nature of the change shall be identified in the document or the appropriate attachments.

4.6 Purchasing

4.6.1 General

The supplier shall establish and maintain documented procedures to ensure that purchased product (see 3.1) conforms to specified requirements.

4.6.2 Evaluation of subcontractors

The supplier shall:

a) evaluate and select subcontractors on the basis of their ability to meet subcontract requirements including the quality system and any specific quality-assurance requirements;

b) define the type and extent of control exercised by the supplier over subcontractors. This shall be dependent upon the type of product, the impact of subcontracted product on the quality of final product, and, where applicable, on the quality audit reports and/or quality records of the previously demonstrated capability and performance of subcontractors;

c) establish and maintain quality records of acceptable subcontractors (see 4.16).

4.6.3 Purchasing data

Purchasing documents shall contain data clearly describing the product ordered, including where applicable:

a) the type, class, grade, or other precise identification;

b) the title or other positive identification, and applicable issues of specifications, drawings, process requirements, inspection instructions, and other relevant technical data, including requirements for approval or qualification of product, procedures, process equipment, and personnel;

c) the title, number, and issue of the quality-system standard to be applied.

The supplier shall review and approve purchasing documents for adequacy of the specified requirements prior to release.

4.6.4 Verification of purchased product

4.6.4.1 Supplier verification at subcontractor's premises

Where the supplier proposes to verify purchased product at the subcontractor's premises, the supplier shall specify verification arrangements and the method of product release in the purchasing documents.

4.6.4.2 Customer verification of subcontracted product

Where specified in the contract, the supplier's customer or the customer's representative shall be afforded the right to verify at the subcontractor's premises and the supplier's premises that subcontracted product conforms to specified requirements. Such verification shall not be used by the supplier as evidence of effective control of quality by the subcontractor.

Verification by the customer shall not absolve the supplier of the responsibility to provide acceptable product, nor shall it preclude subsequent rejection by the customer.

4.7 Control of customer-supplied product

The supplier shall establish and maintain documented procedures for the control of verification, storage, and maintenance of customer-supplied product provided for incorporation into the supplies or for related activities. Any such product that is lost, damaged, or is otherwise unsuitable for use shall be recorded and reported to the customer (see 4.16).

Verification by the supplier does not absolve the customer of the responsibility to provide acceptable product.

4.8 Product identification and traceability

Where appropriate, the supplier shall establish and maintain documented procedures for identifying the product by suitable means from receipt and during all stages of production, delivery, and installation.

Where and to the extent that traceability is a specified requirement, the supplier shall establish and maintain documented procedures for unique identification of individual product or batches. This identification shall be recorded (see 4.16).

4.9 Process control

The supplier shall identify and plan the production, installation, and servicing processes which directly affect quality and shall ensure that these processes are carried out under controlled conditions. Controlled conditions shall include the following:

a) documented procedures defining the manner of production, installation, and servicing, where the absence of such procedures could adversely affect quality;

b) use of suitable production, installation, and servicing equipment, and a suitable working environment;

c) compliance with reference standards/codes, quality plans, and/or documented procedures;

d) monitoring and control of suitable process parameters and product characteristics;

e) the approval of processes and equipment, as appropriate;

f) criteria for workmanship, which shall be stipulated in the clearest practical manner (e.g., written standards, representative samples, or illustrations);

g) suitable maintenance of equipment to ensure continuing process capability.

Where the results of processes cannot be fully verified by subsequent inspection and testing of the product and where, for example, processing deficiencies may become apparent only after the product is in use, the processes shall be carried out by qualified operators and/or shall require continuous monitoring and control of process parameters to ensure that the specified requirements are met.

The requirements for any qualification of process operations, including associated equipment and personnel (see 4.18), shall be specified.

NOTE 16 Such processes requiring prequalification of their process capability are frequently referred to as special processes.

Records shall be maintained for qualified processes, equipment, and personnel, as appropriate (see 4.16).

4.10 Inspection and testing

4.10.1 General

The supplier shall establish and maintain documented procedures for inspection and testing activities in order to verify that the specified requirements for the product are met. The required inspection and testing, and the records to be established, shall be detailed in the quality plan or documented procedures.

4.10.2 Receiving inspection and testing

4.10.2.1 The supplier shall ensure that incoming product is not used or processed (except in the circumstances described in 4.10.2.3) until it has been inspected or otherwise verified as conforming to specified requirements. Verification of the specified

requirements shall be in accordance with the quality plan and/or documented procedures.

4.10.2.2 In determining the amount and nature of receiving inspection, consideration shall be given to the amount of control exercised at the subcontractor's premises and the recorded evidence of conformance provided.

4.10.2.3 Where incoming product is released for urgent production purposes prior to verification, it shall be positively identified and recorded (see 4.16) in order to permit immediate recall and replacement in the event of nonconformity to specified requirements.

4.10.3 In-process inspection and testing

The supplier shall:

a) inspect and test the product as required by the quality plan and/or documented procedures;

b) hold product until the required inspection and tests have been completed or necessary reports have been received and verified, except when product is released under positive-recall procedures (see 4.10.2.3). Release under positive-recall procedures shall not preclude the activities outlined in 4.10.3a.

4.10.4 Final inspection and testing

The supplier shall carry out all final inspection and testing in accordance with the quality plan and/or documented procedures to complete the evidence of conformance of the finished product to the specified requirements.

The quality plan and/or documented procedures for final inspection and testing shall require that all specified inspection and tests, including those specified either on receipt of product or in-process, have been carried out and that the results meet specified requirements.

No product shall be dispatched until all the activities specified in the quality plan and/or documented procedures have been satisfactorily completed and the associated data and documentation are available and authorized.

4.10.5 Inspection and test records

The supplier shall establish and maintain records

which provide evidence that the product has been inspected and/or tested. These records shall show clearly whether the product has passed or failed the inspections and/or tests according to defined acceptance criteria. Where the product fails to pass any inspection and/or test, the procedures for control of nonconforming product shall apply (see 4.13).

Records shall identify the inspection authority responsible for the release of product (see 4.16).

4.11 Control of inspection, measuring, and test equipment

4.11.1 General

The supplier shall establish and maintain documented procedures to control, calibrate, and maintain inspection, measuring, and test equipment (including test software) used by the supplier to demonstrate the conformance of product to the specified requirements. Inspection, measuring, and test equipment shall be used in a manner which ensures that the measurement uncertainty is known and is consistent with the required measurement capability.

Where test software or comparative references such as test hardware are used as suitable forms of inspection, they shall be checked to prove that they are capable of verifying the acceptability of product, prior to release for use during production, installation, or servicing, and shall be rechecked at prescribed intervals. The supplier shall establish the extent and frequency of such checks and shall maintain records as evidence of control (see 4.16).

Where the availability of technical data pertaining to the measurement equipment is a specified requirement, such data shall be made available, when required by the customer or customer's representative, for verification that the measuring equipment is functionally adequate.

NOTE 17 For the purposes of this American National Standard, the term "measuring equipment" includes measurement devices.

4.11.2 Control procedure

The supplier shall:

a) determine the measurements to be made and the accuracy required, and select the appropriate inspection, measuring, and test equipment that is capable of the necessary accuracy and precision;

b) identify all inspection, measuring, and test equipment that can affect product quality, and calibrate and adjust them at prescribed intervals, or prior to use, against certified equipment having a known valid relationship to internationally or nationally recognized standards. Where no such standards exist, the basis used for calibration shall be documented;

c) define the process employed for the calibration of inspection, measuring, and test equipment, including details of equipment type, unique identification, location, frequency of checks, check method, acceptance criteria, and the action to be taken when results are unsatisfactory;

d) identify inspection, measuring, and test equipment with a suitable indicator or approved identification record to show the calibration status;

e) maintain calibration records for inspection, measuring, and test equipment (see 4.16);

f) assess and document the validity of previous inspection and test results when inspection, measuring, and test equipment is found to be out of calibration;

g) ensure that the environmental conditions are suitable for the calibrations, inspections, measurements, and tests being carried out;

h) ensure that the handling, preservation, and storage of inspection, measuring, and test equipment is such that the accuracy and fitness for use are maintained;

i) safeguard inspection, measuring, and test facilities, including both test hardware and test software, from adjustments which would invalidate the calibration setting.

NOTE 18 The metrological confirmation system for measuring equipment given in ISO 10012 may be used for guidance.

4.12 Inspection and test status

The inspection and test status of product shall be identified by suitable means, which indicate the conformance or nonconformance of product with regard to inspection and tests performed. The identification of inspection and test status shall be maintained, as defined in the quality plan and/or documented procedures, throughout production, installation, and servicing of the product to ensure that only product that has passed the required inspections and tests [or released under an authorized concession (see 4.13.2)] is dispatched, used, or installed.

4.13 Control of nonconforming product

4.13.1 General

The supplier shall establish and maintain documented procedures to ensure that product that does not conform to specified requirements is prevented from unintended use or installation. This control shall provide for identification, documentation, evaluation, segregation (when practical), disposition of nonconforming product, and for notification to the functions concerned.

4.13.2 Review and disposition of nonconforming product

The responsibility for review and authority for the disposition of nonconforming product shall be defined.

Nonconforming product shall be reviewed in accordance with documented procedures. It may be

a) reworked to meet the specified requirements,

b) accepted with or without repair by concession,

c) regraded for alternative applications, or

d) rejected or scrapped.

Where required by the contract, the proposed use or repair of product (see 4.13.2b) which does not conform to specified requirements shall be reported for concession to the customer or customer's representative. The description of the nonconformity that has been accepted, and of repairs, shall be recorded to denote the actual condition (see 4.16).

Repaired and/or reworked product shall be reinspected in accordance with the quality plan and/or documented procedures.

4.14 Corrective and preventive action

4.14.1 General

The supplier shall establish and maintain documented procedures for implementing corrective and preventive action.

Any corrective or preventive action taken to eliminate the causes of actual or potential nonconformities shall be to a degree appropriate to the magnitude of problems and commensurate with the risks encountered.

The supplier shall implement and record any changes to the documented procedures resulting from corrective and preventive action.

4.14.2 Corrective action

The procedures for corrective action shall include:

a) the effective handling of customer complaints and reports of product nonconformities;

b) investigation of the cause of nonconformities relating to product, process, and quality system, and recording the results of the investigation (see 4.16);

c) determination of the corrective action needed to eliminate the cause of nonconformities;

d) application of controls to ensure that corrective action is taken and that it is effective.

4.14.3 Preventive action

The procedures for preventive action shall include:

a) the use of appropriate sources of information such as processes and work operations which affect product quality, concessions, audit results, quality records, service reports, and customer complaints to detect, analyze, and eliminate potential causes of nonconformities;

b) determination of the steps needed to deal with any problems requiring preventive action;

c) initiation of preventive action and application of controls to ensure that it is effective;

d) confirmation that relevant information on actions taken is submitted for management review (see 4.1.3).

4.15 Handling, storage, packaging, preservation, and delivery

4.15.1 General

The supplier shall establish and maintain documented procedures for handling, storage, packaging, preservation, and delivery of product.

4.15.2 Handling

The supplier shall provide methods of handling product that prevent damage or deterioration.

4.15.3 Storage

The supplier shall use designated storage areas or stock rooms to prevent damage or deterioration of product, pending use or delivery. Appropriate methods for authorizing receipt to and dispatch from such areas shall be stipulated.

In order to detect deterioration, the condition of product in stock shall be assessed at appropriate intervals.

4.15.4 Packaging

The supplier shall control packing, packaging, and marking processes (including materials used) to the extent necessary to ensure conformance to specified requirements.

4.15.5 Preservation

The supplier shall apply appropriate methods for preservation and segregation of product when the product is under the supplier's control.

4.15.6 Delivery

The supplier shall arrange for the protection of the quality of product after final inspection and test. Where contractually specified, this protection shall be extended to include delivery to destination.

4.16 Control of quality records

The supplier shall establish and maintain documented procedures for identification, collection, indexing, access, filing, storage, maintenance, and disposition of quality records.

Quality records shall be maintained to demonstrate conformance to specified requirements and the effective operation of the quality system. Pertinent quality records from the subcontractor shall be an element of these data.

All quality records shall be legible and shall be stored and retained in such a way that they are readily retrievable in facilities that provide a suitable environment to prevent damage or deterioration and to prevent loss. Retention times of quality records shall be established and recorded. Where agreed contractu-

ally, quality records shall be made available for evaluation by the customer or the customer's representative for an agreed period.

NOTE 19 Records may be in the form of any type of media, such as hard copy or electronic media.

4.17 Internal quality audits

The supplier shall establish and maintain documented procedures for planning and implementing internal quality audits to verify whether quality activities and related results comply with planned arrangements and to determine the effectiveness of the quality system.

Internal quality audits shall be scheduled on the basis of the status and importance of the activity to be audited and shall be carried out by personnel independent of those having direct responsibility for the activity being audited.

The results of the audits shall be recorded (see 4.16) and brought to the attention of the personnel having responsibility in the area audited. The management personnel responsible for the area shall take timely corrective action on deficiencies found during the audit.

Follow-up audit activities shall verify and record the implementation and effectiveness of the corrective action taken (see 4.16).

NOTES

20 The results of internal quality audits form an integral part of the input to management review activities (see 4.1.3).

21 Guidance on quality-system audits is given in ANSI/ASQC Q10011-1-1994, ANSI/ASQC Q10011-2-1994, and ANSI/ASQC Q10011-3-1994.

4.18 Training

The supplier shall establish and maintain documented procedures for identifying training needs and provide for the training of all personnel performing activities affecting quality. Personnel performing specific assigned tasks shall be qualified on the basis of appropriate education, training, and/or experience, as required. Appropriate records of training shall be maintained (see 4.16).

4.19 Servicing

Where servicing is a specified requirement, the supplier shall establish and maintain documented procedures for performing, verifying, and reporting that the servicing meets the specified requirements.

4.20 Statistical techniques

4.20.1 Identification of need

The supplier shall identify the need for statistical techniques required for establishing, controlling, and verifying process capability and product characteristics.

4.20.2 Procedures

The supplier shall establish and maintain documented procedures to implement and control the application of the statistical techniques identified in 4.20.1.

ANNEX A (INFORMATIVE)

Bibliography

[1] ANSI/ASQC Q9000-1-1994, *Quality Management and Quality Assurance Standards—Guidelines for Selection and Use.*

[2] ANSI/ASQC Q9002-1994, *Quality Systems—Model for Quality Assurance in Production, Installation, and Servicing.*

[3] ANSI/ASQC Q9003-1994, *Quality Systems—Model for Quality Assurance in Final Inspection and Test.*

[4] ANSI/ASQC Q10011-1-1994, *Guidelines for Auditing Quality Systems—Auditing.*

[5] ANSI/ASQC Q10011-2-1994, *Guidelines for Auditing Quality Systems—Qualification Criteria for Quality Systems Auditors.*

[6] ANSI/ASQC Q10011-3-1994, *Guidelines for Auditing Quality Systems—Management of Audit Programs.*

[7] ISO 9000-2:1993, *Quality management and quality assurance standards—Part 2: Generic guidelines for the application of ISO 9001, ISO 9002 and ISO 9003.*

[8] ISO 9000-3:1991, *Quality management and quality assurance standards—Part 3: Guidelines for the application of ISO 9001 to the development, supply and maintenance of software.*

[9] ISO 10012-1:1992, *Quality assurance requirements for measuring equipment—Part 1: Metrological confirmation system for measuring equipment.*

[10] ISO 10013:—[1]), *Guidelines for developing quality manuals.*

ENDNOTE:

[1] To be published.

American National Standard

ANSI/ASQC Q9002-1994

QUALITY SYSTEMS—MODEL FOR QUALITY ASSURANCE IN PRODUCTION, INSTALLATION, AND SERVICING

[Revision of first edition (ANSI/ASQC Q92-1987)]

Prepared by

American Society for Quality Control
Standards Committee

for

American National Standards Committee
Z-1 on Quality Assurance

Descriptors: Quality assurance, quality assurance program, quality systems, production, installation, after-sale services, reference models.

American National Standards: An American National Standard implies a consensus of those substantially concerned with its scope and provisions. An American National Standard is intended as a guide to aid the manufacturer, the consumer, and the general public. The existence of an American National Standard does not in any respect preclude anyone, whether he or she has approved the standard or not, from manufacturing, purchasing, or using products, processes, or procedures not conforming to the standard. American National Standards are subject to periodic review and users are cautioned to obtain the latest edition.

Caution Notice: This American National Standard may be revised or withdrawn at any time. The procedures of the American National Standards

Institute require that action be taken to reaffirm, revise, or withdraw this standard no later than five years from the date of publication. Purchasers of American National Standards may receive current information on all standards by calling or writing the American National Standards Institute.

©1994 by ASQC

ASQC Mission: To facilitate continuous improvement and increase customer satisfaction by identifying, communicating, and promoting the use of quality principles, concepts, and technologies; and thereby be recognized throughout the world as the leading authority on, and champion for, quality.

10 9 8 7 6 5 4 3 2 1

Printed in the United States of America

Printed on acid-free recycled paper

Published by:
ASQC
611 East Wisconsin Avenue
Milwaukee, Wisconsin 53202

Contents

1   Scope

2   Normative reference

3   Definitions

4   Quality-system requirements

4.1   Management responsibility

4.2   Quality system

4.3   Contract review

4.4   Design control

4.5   Document and data control

4.6   Purchasing

4.7   Control of customer-supplied product

4.8   Product identification and traceability

4.9   Process control

4.10   Inspection and testing

4.11   Control of inspection, measuring, and test equipment

4.12   Inspection and test status

4.13   Control of nonconforming product

4.14   Corrective and preventive action

4.15   Handling, storage, packaging, preservation, and delivery

4.16   Control of quality records

4.17   Internal quality audits

4.18   Training

4.19   Servicing

4.20   Statistical techniques

Annex

A   Bibliography

FOREWORD

(This Foreword is not a part of American National Standard *Quality Systems—Model for Quality Assurance in Production, Installation, and Servicing.*)

This American National Standard corresponds to the International Standard ISO 9002:1994. The initial five ISO 9000 series standards, ISO 9000, ISO 9001, ISO 9002, ISO 9003, and ISO 9004, when published in the United States as American National Standards in 1987, were designated as ANSI/ASQC Q90 through ANSI/ASQC Q94 respectively. The five 1987 standards in their 1994 international revisions are now designated ISO 9000-1, ISO 9001, ISO 9002, ISO 9003, and ISO 9004-1 respectively. Their publication as American National Standards are now designated ANSI/ASQC Q9000-1-1994, ANSI/ASQC Q9001-1994, ANSI/ASQC Q9002-1994, ANSI/ASQC Q9003-1994, and ANSI/ASQC Q9004-1-1994 respectively. This new numbering system is intended to emphasize the word-for-word correspondence of the International and American National Standards.

ISO (the International Organization for Standardization) is a worldwide federation of national standards bodies (ISO member bodies). The work of preparing International Standards is normally carried out through ISO technical committees. Each member body interested in a subject for which a technical committee has been established has the right to be represented on that committee. International organizations, governmental and nongovernmental, in liaison with ISO, also take part in the work. ISO collaborates closely with the International Electrotechnical Commission (IEC) on all matters of electrotechnical standardization. The American National Standards Institute (ANSI) is the U.S. member body of ISO. ASQC is the U.S. member of ANSI responsible for quality management and related standards.

Users should note that all ANSI/ASQC standards undergo revision from time to time. In the case of International Standards adopted as American National Standards, the revision timing is influences by the international revision timing. Reference herein to any other standard implies the latest American National Standard revision unless otherwise stated.

Comments concerning this standard are welcome.

They should be sent to the sponsor of the standard, American Society for Quality COntrol, 611 East Wisconsin Avenue, P.O. Box 3005, Milwaukee, WI 53201-3005, c/o Standards Administrator.

INTRODUCTION

This American National Standard is one of three American National Standards dealing with quality-system requirements that can be used for external quality-assurance purposes. The quality-assurance models, set out in the three American National Standards listed below, represent three distinct forms of quality-system requirements suitable for the purpose of a supplier demonstrating its capability, and for the assessment of the capability of a supplier by external parties.

a) ANSI/ASQC Q9001-1994, *Quality systems—Model for Quality Assurance in Design, Develop-ment, Production, Installation, and Servicing*

   — for use when conformance to specified requirements is to be assured by the supplier during design, development, production, installation, and servicing.

b) ANSI/ASQC Q9002-1994, *Quality Systems—Model for Quality Assurance in Production, Installation, and Servicing*

   — for use when conformance to specified requirements is to be assured by the supplier during production, installation, and servicing.

c) ANSI/ASQC Q9003-1994, *Quality Systems—Model for Quality Assurance in Final Inspection and Test*

   — for use when conformance to specified requirements is to be assured by the supplier solely at final inspection and test.

It is emphasized that the quality-system requirements specified in this American National Standard, ANSI/ASQC Q9001-1994 and ANSI/ASQC Q9003-1994 are complementary (not alternative) to the technical (product) specified requirements. They specify requirements which determine what elements quality systems have to encompass, but it is not the purpose of these American National Standards to enforce

uniformity of quality systems. They are generic and independent of any specific industry or economic sector. The design and implementation of a quality system will be influenced by the varying needs of an organization, its particular objectives, the products and services supplied, and the processes and specific practices employed.

It is intended that these American National Standards will be adopted in their present form, but on occasions they may need to be tailored by adding or deleting certain quality-system requirements for specific contractual situations. ANSI/ASQC Q9000-1-1994 provides guidance on such tailoring as well as on selection of the appropriate quality-assurance model, viz. ANSI/ASQC Q9001-1994, ANSI/ASQC Q9002-1994, or ANSI/ASQC Q9003-1994.

Quality Systems—Model for Quality Assurance in Production, Installation, and Servicing

1 SCOPE

This American National Standard specifies quality-system requirements for use where a supplier's capability to supply conforming product to an established design needs to be demonstrated.

The requirements specified are aimed primarily at achieving customer satisfaction by preventing nonconformity at all stages from production through to servicing.

This American National Standard is applicable in situations when

a) the specified requirements for product are stated in terms of an established design or specification, and

b) confidence in product conformance can be attained by adequate demonstration of a supplier's capabilities in production, installation, and servicing.

NOTE 1 For informative references, see annex A.

2 NORMATIVE REFERENCE

The following standard contains provisions which, through reference in this text, constitute provisions of this American National Standard. At the time of publication, the edition indicated was valid. All standards are subject to revision, and parties to agreements based on this American National Standard are encouraged to investigate the possibility of applying the most recent edition of the standard indicated below. The American National Standards Institute and members of IEC and ISO maintain registers of currently valid American National Standards and International Standards.

ISO 8402:1994, *Quality management and quality assurance—Vocabulary*

3 DEFINITIONS

For the purposes of this American National Standard, the definitions given in ISO 8402 and the following definitions apply.

3.1 Product

Result of activities or processes.

NOTES

2   A product may include service, hardware, processed materials, software, or a combination thereof.

3   A product can be tangible (e.g., assemblies or processed materials) or intangible (e.g., knowledge or concepts), or a combination thereof.

4   For the purposes of this American National Standard, the term "product" applies to the intended product offering only and not to unintended "by-products" affecting the environment. This differs from the definition given in ISO 8402.

3.2 Tender

Offer made by a supplier in response to an invitation to satisfy a contract award to provide product.

3.3 Contract; accepted order

Agreed requirements between a supplier and customer transmitted by any means.

4 Quality-system requirements

4.1 Management responsibility

4.1.1 Quality policy

The supplier's management with executive responsibility shall define and document its policy for quality, including objectives for quality and its commitment to quality. The quality policy shall be relevant to the supplier's organizational goals and the expectations and needs of its customers. The supplier shall ensure that this policy is understood, implemented, and maintained at all levels of the organization.

4.1.2 Organization

4.1.2.1 Responsibility and authority

The responsibility, authority, and the interrelation of personnel who manage, perform, and verify work affecting quality shall be defined and documented, particularly for personnel who need the organizational freedom and authority to:

a)   initiate action to prevent the occurrence of any nonconformities relating to product, process, and quality system;

b)   identify and record any problems relating to the product, process, and quality system;

c)   initiate, recommend, or provide solutions through designated channels;

d)   verify the implementation of solutions;

e)   control further processing, delivery, or installation of nonconforming product until the deficiency or unsatisfactory condition has been corrected.

4.1.2.2 Resources

The supplier shall identify resource requirements and provide adequate resources, including the assignment of trained personnel (see 4.18), for management, performance of work, and verification activities including internal quality audits.

4.1.2.3 Management representative

The supplier's management with executive responsibility shall appoint a member of the supplier's own management who, irrespective of other responsibilities, shall have defined authority for

a)   ensuring that a quality system is established, implemented, and maintained in accordance with this American National Standard, and

b)   reporting on the performance of the quality system to the supplier's management for review and as a basis for improvement of the quality system.

NOTE 5 The responsibility of a management representative may also include liaison with external parties on matters relating to the supplier's quality system.

4.1.3 Management review

The supplier's management with executive responsibility shall review the quality system at defined intervals sufficient to ensure its continuing suitability and effectiveness in satisfying the requirements of this American National Standard and the supplier's stated quality policy and objectives (see 4.1.1). Records of such reviews shall be maintained (see 4.16).

4.2 Quality system

4.2.1 General

The supplier shall establish, document, and maintain a quality system as a means of ensuring that product conforms to specified requirements. The supplier shall prepare a quality manual covering the requirements of this American National Standard. The quality manual shall include or make reference to the quality-system procedures and outline the structure of the documentation used in the quality system.

NOTE 6 Guidance on quality manuals is given in ISO 10013.

4.2.2 Quality-system procedures

The supplier shall

a) prepare documented procedures consistent with the requirements of this American National Standard and the supplier's stated quality policy, and

b) effectively implement the quality system and its documented procedures.

For the purposes of this American National Standard, the range and detail of the procedures that form part of the quality system depend on the complexity of the work, the methods used, and the skills and training needed by personnel involved in carrying out the activity.

NOTE 7 Documented procedures may make reference to work instructions that define how an activity is performed.

4.2.3 Quality planning

The supplier shall define and document how the requirements for quality will be met. Quality planning shall be consistent with all other requirements of a supplier's quality system and shall be documented in a format to suit the supplier's method of operation. The supplier shall give consideration to the following activities, as appropriate, in meeting the specified requirements for products, projects or contracts:

a) the preparation of quality plans;

b) the identification and acquisition of any controls, processes, equipment (including inspection and test equipment), fixtures, resources, and skills that may be needed to achieve the required quality;

c) ensuring the compatibility of the production process, installation, servicing, inspection, and test procedures and the applicable documentation;

d) the updating, as necessary, of quality control, inspection, and testing techniques, including the development of new instrumentation;

e) the identification of any measurement requirement involving capability that exceeds the known state of the art, in sufficient time for the needed capability to be developed;

f) the identification of suitable verification at appropriate stages in the realization of product;

g) the clarification of standards of acceptability for all features and requirements, including those which contain a subjective element;

h) the identification and preparation of quality records (see 4.16).

NOTE 8 The quality plans referred to (see 4.2.3a) may be in the form of a reference to the appropriate documented procedures that form an integral part of the supplier's quality system.

4.3 Contract review

4.3.1 General

The supplier shall establish and maintain documented procedures for contract review and for the coordination of these activities.

4.3.2 Review

Before submission of a tender, or the acceptance of a

contract or order (statement of requirement), the tender, contract, or order shall be reviewed by the supplier to ensure that:

a)   the requirements are adequately defined and documented; where no written statement of requirement is available for an order received by verbal means, the supplier shall ensure that the order requirements are agreed before their acceptance;

b)   any differences between the contract or accepted order requirements and those in the tender are resolved;

c)   the supplier has the capability to meet the contract or accepted order requirements.

4.3.3 Amendment to a contract

The supplier shall identify how an amendment to a contract is made and correctly transferred to the functions concerned within the supplier's organization.

4.3.4 Records

Records of contract reviews shall be maintained (see 4.16).

NOTE 9 Channels for communication and interfaces with the customer's organization in these contract matters should be established.

4.4 Design control

The scope of this American National Standard does not include quality-system requirements for design control. This subclause is included to align the clause numbering with ANSI/ASQC Q9001-1994.

4.5 Document and data control

4.5.1 General

The supplier shall establish and maintain documented procedures to control all documents and data that relate to the requirements of this American National Standard including, to the extent applicable, documents of external origin such as standards and customer drawings.

NOTE 10 Documents and data can be in the form of any type of media, such as hard copy or electronic media.

4.5.2 Document and data approval and issue

The documents and data shall be reviewed and approved for adequacy by authorized personnel prior to issue. A master list or equivalent document-control procedure identifying the current revision status of documents shall be established and be readily available to preclude the use of invalid and/or obsolete documents.

This control shall ensure that:

a)   the pertinent issues of appropriate documents are available at all locations where operations essential to the effective functioning of the quality system are performed;

b)   invalid and/or obsolete documents are promptly removed from all points of issue or use, or otherwise assured against unintended use;

c)   any obsolete documents retained for legal and/or knowledge-preservation purposes are suitable identified.

4.5.3 Document and data changes

Changes to documents and data shall be reviewed and approved by the same functions/organizations that performed the original review and approval, unless specifically designated otherwise. The designated functions/organizations shall have access to pertinent background information upon which to base their review and approval.

Where practicable, the nature of the change shall be identified in the document or the appropriate attachments.

4.6 Purchasing

4.6.1 General

The supplier shall establish and maintain documented procedures to ensure that purchased product (see 3.1) conforms to specified requirements.

4.6.2 Evaluation of subcontractors

The supplier shall:

a)   evaluate and select subcontractors on the basis of their ability to meet subcontract requirements including the quality system and any specific quality-assurance requirements;

b)   define the type and extent of control exercised by the supplier over subcontractors. This shall be dependent upon the type of product, the impact of subcontracted product on the quality of final product, and, where applicable, on the quality audit reports and/or quality records of the previously demonstrated capability and performance of subcontractors;

c) establish and maintain quality records of acceptable subcontractors (see 4.16).

4.6.3 Purchasing data

Purchasing documents shall contain data clearly describing the product ordered, including where applicable:

a) the type, class, grade, or other precise identification;

b) the title or other positive identification, and applicable issues of specifications, drawings, process requirements, inspection instructions, and other relevant technical data, including requirements for approval or qualification of product, procedures, process equipment, and personnel;

c) the title, number, and issue of the quality-system standard to be applied.

The supplier shall review and approve purchasing documents for adequacy of the specified requirements prior to release.

4.6.4 Verification of purchased product

4.6.4.1 Supplier verification at subcontractor's premises

Where the supplier proposes to verify purchased product at the subcontractor's premises, the supplier shall specify verification arrangements and the method of product release in the purchasing documents.

4.6.4.2 Customer verification of subcontracted product

Where specified in the contract, the supplier's customer or the customer's representative shall be afforded the right to verify at the subcontractor's premises and the supplier's premises that subcontracted product conforms to specified requirements. Such verification shall not be used by the supplier as evidence of effective control of quality by the subcontractor.

Verification by the customer shall not absolve the supplier of the responsibility to provide acceptable product, nor shall it preclude subsequent rejection by the customer.

4.7 Control of customer-supplied product

The supplier shall establish and maintain documented procedures for the control of verification, storage, and maintenance of customer-supplied product provided for incorporation into the supplies or for related activities. Any such product that is lost, damaged, or is otherwise unsuitable for use shall be recorded and reported to the customer (see 4.16).

Verification by the supplier does not absolve the customer of the responsibility to provide acceptable product.

4.8 Product identification and traceability

Where appropriate, the supplier shall establish and maintain documented procedures for identifying the product by suitable means from receipt and during all stages of production, delivery, and installation.

Where and to the extent that traceability is a specified requirement, the supplier shall establish and maintain documented procedures for unique identification of individual product or batches. This identification shall be recorded (see 4.16).

4.9 Process control

The supplier shall identify and plan the production, installation, and servicing processes which directly affect quality and shall ensure that these processes are carried out under controlled conditions. Controlled conditions shall include the following:

a) documented procedures defining the manner of production, installation, and servicing, where the absence of such procedures could adversely affect quality;

b) use of suitable production, installation, and servicing equipment, and a suitable working environment;

c) compliance with reference standards/codes, quality plans, and/or documented procedures;

d) monitoring and control of suitable process parameters and product characteristics;

e) the approval of processes and equipment, as appropriate;

f) criteria for workmanship, which shall be stipulated in the clearest practical manner (e.g., written standards, representatives samples, or illustrations);

g) suitable maintenance of equipment to ensure continuing process capability.

Where the results of processes cannot be fully verified by subsequent inspection and testing of the product and where, for example, processing deficiencies may become apparent only after the product is in use, the processes shall be carried out by qualified operators and/or shall require continuous monitoring and control of process parameters to ensure that the specified requirements are met.

The requirements for any qualification of process operations, including associated equipment and personnel (see 4.18), shall be specified.

NOTE 11 Such processes requiring prequalification of their process capability are frequently referred to as special processes.

Records shall be maintained for qualified processes, equipment, and personnel, as appropriate (see 4.16).

4.10 Inspection and testing

4.10.1 General

The supplier shall establish and maintain documented procedures for inspection and testing activities in order to verify that the specified requirements for product are met. The required inspection and testing, and the records to be established, shall be detailed in the quality plan or documented procedures.

4.10.2 Receiving inspection and testing

4.10.2.1 The supplier shall ensure that incoming product is not used or processed (except in the circumstances described in 4.10.2.3) until it has been inspected or otherwise verified as conforming to specified requirements. Verification of the specified requirements shall be in accordance with the quality plan and/or documented procedures.

4.10.2.2 In determining the amount and nature of receiving inspection, consideration shall be given to

the amount of control exercised at the subcontractor's premises and the recorded evidence of conformance provided.

4.10.2.3 Where incoming product is released for urgent production purposes prior to verification, it shall be positively identified and recorded (see 4.16) in order to permit immediate recall and replacement in the event of nonconformity to specified requirements.

4.10.3 In-process inspection and testing

The supplier shall:

a) inspect and test the product as required by the quality plan and/or documented procedures;

b) hold product until the required inspection and tests have been completed or necessary reports have been received and verified, except when product is released under positive-recall procedures (see 4.10.2.3). Release under positive-recall procedures shall not preclude the activities outlined in 4.10.3a.

4.10.4 Final inspection and testing

The supplier shall carry out all final inspection and testing in accordance with the quality plan and/or documented procedures to complete the evidence of conformance of the finished product to the specified requirements.

The quality plan and/or documented procedures for final inspection and testing shall require that all specified inspection and tests, including those specified either on receipt of product or in-process, have been carried out, and that the results meet specified requirements.

No product shall be dispatched until all the activities specified in the quality plan and/or documented procedures have been satisfactorily completed and the associated data and documentation are available and authorized.

4.10.5 Inspection and test records

The supplier shall establish and maintain records which provide evidence that the product has been inspected and/or tested. These records shall show clearly whether the product has passed or failed the inspections and/or tests according to defined acceptance criteria. Where the product fails to pass any inspection and/or test, the procedures for control of nonconforming product shall apply (see 4.13).

Records shall identify the inspection authority responsible for the release of product (see 4.16).

4.11 Control of inspection, measuring, and test equipment

4.11.1 General

The supplier shall establish and maintain documented procedures to control, calibrate, and maintain inspection, measuring, and test equipment (including test software) used by the supplier to demonstrate the conformance of product to the specified requirements. Inspection, measuring, and test equipment shall be used in a manner which ensures that the measurement uncertainty is known and is consistent with the required measurement capability.

Where test software or comparative references such as test hardware are used as suitable forms of inspection, they shall be checked to prove that they are capable of verifying the acceptability of product, prior to release for use during production, installation, or servicing, and shall be rechecked at prescribed intervals. The supplier shall establish the extent and frequency of such checks and shall maintain records as evidence of control (see 4.16).

Where the availability of technical data pertaining to the measurement equipment is a specified requirement, such data shall be made available, when required by the customer or customer's representative, for verification that the measuring equipment is functionally adequate.

NOTE 12 For the purposes of this American National Standard, the term "measuring equipment" includes measurement devices.

4.11.2 Control procedure

The supplier shall:

a) determine the measurements to be made and the accuracy required, and select the appropriate inspection, measuring and test equipment that is capable of the necessary accuracy and precision;

b) identify all inspection, measuring, and test equipment that can affect product quality, and calibrate and adjust them at prescribed intervals,

or prior to use, against certified equipment having a known valid relationship to internationally or nationally recognized standards. Where no such standards exist, the basis used for calibration shall be documented;

c) define the process employed for the calibration of inspection, measuring, and test equipment, including details of equipment type, unique identification, location, frequency of checks, check method, acceptance criteria, and the action to be taken when results are unsatisfactory;

d) identify inspection, measuring, and test equipment with a suitable indicator or approved identification record to show the calibration status;

e) maintain calibration records for inspection, measuring, and test equipment (see 4.16);

f) assess and document the validity of previous inspection and test results when inspection, measuring, or test equipment is found to be out of calibration;

g) ensure that the environmental conditions are suitable for the calibration, inspections, measurements, and tests being carried out;

h) ensure that the handling, preservation, and storage of inspection, measuring, and test equipment is such that the accuracy and fitness for use are maintained;

i) safeguard inspection, measuring, and test facilities, including both test hardware and test software, from adjustments which would invalidate the calibration setting.

NOTE 13 The metrological confirmation system for measuring equipment given in ISO 10012 may be used for guidance.

4.12 Inspection and test status

The inspection and test status of product shall be identified by suitable means, which indicate the conformance or nonconformance of product with regard to inspection and tests performed. The identification of inspection and test status shall be maintained, as defined in the quality plan and/or documented procedures, throughout production, installation, and servicing of the product to ensure that only product that has passed the required inspections and tests [or released under an authorized concession (see 4.13.2)] is dispatched, used, or installed.

4.13 Control of nonconforming product

4.13.1 General

The supplier shall establish and maintain documented procedures to ensure that product that does not conform to specified requirements is prevented from unintended use or installation. This control shall provide for identification, documentation, evaluation, segregation (when practical), disposition of nonconforming product, and for notification to the functions concerned.

4.13.2 Review and disposition of nonconforming product

The responsibility for review and authority for the disposition of nonconforming product shall be defined.

Nonconforming product shall be reviewed in accordance with documented procedures. It may be

a)   reworked to meet the specified requirements,

b)   accepted with or without repair by concession,

c)   regraded for alternative applications, or

d)   rejected or scrapped.

Where required by the contract, the proposed use or repair of product (see 4.13.2b) which does not conform to specified requirements shall be reported for concession to the customer or customer's representative. The description of the nonconformity that has been accepted, and of repairs, shall be recorded to denote the actual condition (see 4.16).

Repaired and/or reworked product shall be reinspected in accordance with the quality plan and/or documented procedures.

4.14 Corrective and preventive action

4.14.1 General

The supplier shall establish and maintain documented procedures for implementing corrective and preventive action.

Any corrective or preventive action taken to eliminate the causes of actual or potential nonconformities shall

be to a degree appropriate to the magnitude of problems and commensurate with the risks encountered.

The supplier shall implement and record any changes to the documented procedures resulting from corrective and preventive action.

4.14.2 Corrective action

The procedures for corrective action shall include:

a)   the effective handling of customer complaints and reports of product nonconformities;

b)   investigation of the cause of nonconformities relating to product, process, and quality system, and recording the results of the investigation (see 4.16);

c)   determination of the corrective action needed to eliminate the cause of nonconformities;

d)   application of controls to ensure that corrective action is taken and that it is effective.

4.14.3 Preventive action

The procedures for preventive action shall include:

a)   the use of appropriate sources of information such as processes and work operations which affect product quality, concessions, audit results, quality records, service reports, and customer complaints to detect, analyze, and eliminate potential causes of nonconformities;

b)   determination of the steps needed to deal with any problems requiring preventive action;

c)   initiation of preventive action and application of controls to ensure that it is effective;

d)   confirmation that relevant information on actions taken is submitted for management review (see 4.1.3).

4.15 Handling, storage, packaging, preservation, and delivery

4.15.1 General

The supplier shall establish and maintain documented procedures for handling, storage, packaging, preservation, and delivery of product.

4.15.2 Handling

The supplier shall provide methods of handling

product that prevent damage or deterioration.

4.15.3 Storage

The supplier shall use designated storage areas or stock rooms to prevent damage or deterioration of product, pending use or delivery. Appropriate methods of authorizing receipt to and dispatch from such areas shall be stipulated.

In order to detect deterioration, the condition of product in stock shall be assessed at appropriate intervals.

4.15.4 Packaging

The supplier shall control packing, packaging, and marking processes (including materials used) to the extent necessary to ensure conformance to specified requirements.

4.15.5 Preservation

The supplier shall apply appropriate methods for preservation and segregation of product when the product is under the supplier's control.

4.15.6 Delivery

The supplier shall arrange for the protection of the quality of product after final inspection and test. Where contractually specified, this protection shall be extended to include delivery to destination.

4.16 CONTROL OF QUALITY RECORDS

The supplier shall establish and maintain documented procedures for identification, collection, indexing, access, filing, storage, maintenance, and disposition of quality records.

Quality records shall be maintained to demonstrate conformance to specified requirements and the effective operation of the quality system. Pertinent quality records from the subcontractor shall be an element of these data.

All quality records shall be legible and shall be stored and retained in such a way that they are readily retrievable in facilities that provide a suitable environment to prevent damage or deterioration and to prevent loss. Retention times of quality records shall be established and recorded. Where agreed contractually, quality records shall be made available for evaluation by the customer or the customer's representative for an agreed period.

NOTE 14 Records may be in the form of any type of media, such as hard copy or electronic media.

4.17 Internal quality audits

The supplier shall establish and maintain documented procedures for planning and implementing internal quality audits to verify whether quality activities and related results comply with planned arrangements and to determine the effectiveness of the quality system.

Internal quality audits shall be scheduled on the basis of the status and importance of the activity to be audited and shall be carried out by personnel independent of those having direct responsibility for the activity being audited.

The results of the audits shall be recorded (see 4.16) and brought to the attention of the personnel having responsibility in the area audited. The management personnel responsible for the area shall take timely corrective action on deficiencies found during the audit.

Follow-up audit activities shall verify and record the implementation and effectiveness of the corrective action taken (see 4.16).

NOTES

15 The results of internal quality audits form an integral part of the input to management review activities (see 4.1.3).

16 Guidance on quality-system audits is given in ANSI/ASQC Q10011-1-1994, ANSI/ASQC Q10011-2-1994, and ANSI/ASQC Q10011-3-1994.

4.18 Training

The supplier shall establish and maintain documented procedures for identifying training needs and provide for the training of all personnel performing activities affecting quality. Personnel performing specific assigned tasks shall be qualified on the basis of appropriate education, training, and/or experience, as required. Appropriate records of training shall be maintained (see 4.16).

4.19 Servicing

Where servicing is a specified requirement, the supplier shall establish and maintain documented procedures for performing, verifying, and reporting that the servicing meets the specified requirements.

4.20 Statistical techniques

4.20.1 Identification of need

The supplier shall identify the need for statistical techniques required for establishing, controlling, and verifying process capability and product characteristics.

4.20.2 Procedures

The supplier shall establish and maintain documented procedures to implement and control the application of the statistical techniques identified in 4.20.1.

ANNEX A (INFORMATIVE)

Bibliography

[1] ANSI/ASQC Q9000-1-1994, *Quality Management and Quality Assurance Standards—Guidelines for Selection and Use.*

[2] ANSI/ASQC Q9001-1994, *Quality Systems— Model for Quality Assurance in Design, Development, Production, Installation, and Servicing.*

[3] ANSI/ASQC Q9003-1994, *Quality Systems— Model for Quality Assurance in Final Inspection and Test.*

[4] ANSI/ASQC Q10011-1-1994, *Guidelines for Auditing Quality Systems—Auditing.*

[5] ANSI/ASQC Q10011-2-1994, *Guidelines for Auditing Quality Systems—Qualification Criteria for Quality Systems Auditors.*

[6] ANSI/ASQC Q10011-3-1994, *Guidelines for Auditing Quality Systems—Management of Audit Programs.*

[7] ISO 9000-2:1993, *Quality management and quality assurance standards—Part 2: Generic guidelines for the application of ISO 9001, ISO 9002 and ISO 9003.*

[8] ISO 9000-3:1991, *Quality management and quality assurance standards—Part 3: Guidelines for the application of ISO 9001 to the development, supply and maintenance of software.*

[9] ISO 10012-1:1992, *Quality assurance requirements for measuring equipment—Part 1: Metrological confirmation system for measuring equipment.*

[10] ISO 10013:—1), *Guidelines for developing quality manuals.*

ENDNOTE:

1 To be published.

American National Standard

ANSI/ASQC Q9003-1994

QUALITY SYSTEMS—MODEL FOR QUALITY ASSURANCE IN FINAL INSPECTION AND TEST

[Revision of first edition (ANSI/ASQC Q93-1987)]

Prepared by

American Society for Quality Control
Standards Committee

for

American National Standards Committee
Z-1 on Quality Assurance

Descriptors: Quality assurance, quality assurance program, quality systems, tests, inspection, reference models.

American National Standards: An American National Standard implies a consensus of those substantially concerned with its scope and provisions. An American National Standard is intended as a guide to aid the manufacturer, the consumer, and the general public. The existence of an American National Standard does not in any respect preclude anyone, whether he or she has approved the standard or not, from manufacturing, purchasing, or using products, processes, or procedures not conforming to the standard. American National Standards are subject to periodic review and users are cautioned to obtain the latest edition.

Caution Notice: This American National Standard may be revised or withdrawn at any time. The procedures of the American National Standards Institute require that action be taken to reaffirm, revise, or withdraw this standard no later than five years from the date of publication. Purchasers of American National Standards may receive current information on all standards by calling or writing the American National Standards Institute.

ASQC Mission: To facilitate continuous improvement and increase customer satisfaction by identifying, communicating, and promoting the use of quality principles, concepts, and technologies; and thereby be recognized throughout the world as the leading authority on, and champion for, quality.

10 9 8 7 6 5 4 3 2 1

Printed in the United States of America

Printed on acid-free recycled paper

Published by:
ASQC
611 East Wisconsin Avenue
Milwaukee, Wisconsin 53202

CONTENTS

1   Scope

2   Normative reference

3   Definitions

4   Quality-system requirements

4.1   Management responsibility

4.2   Quality system

4.3   Contract review

4.4   Design control

4.5   Document and data control

4.6   Purchasing

4.7   Control of customer-supplied product

4.8   Product identification and traceability

4.9   Process control

4.10 Inspection and testing

4.11 Control of inspection, measuring, and test equipment

4.12 Inspection and test status

4.13 Control of nonconforming product

4.14 Corrective action

4.15 Handling, storage, packaging, preservation, and delivery

4.16 Control of quality records

4.17 Internal quality audits

4.18 Training

4.19 Servicing

4.20 Statistical techniques

Annex

A   Bibliography

FOREWORD

(This Foreword is not a part of American National Standard *Quality Systems—Model for Quality Assurance in Final Inspection and Test.*)

This American National Standard corresponds to the International Standard ISO 9003:1994. The initial five ISO 9000 series standards, ISO 9000, ISO 9001, ISO 9002, ISO 9003, and ISO 9004, when published in the United States as American National Standards in 1987, were designated as ANSI/ASQC Q90 through ANSI/ASQC Q94 respectively. The five 1987 standards in their 1994 international revisions are now designated ISO 9000-1, ISO 9001, ISO 9002, ISO 9003, and ISO 9004-1 respectively. Their publication as American National Standards are now designated ANSI/ASQC Q9000-1-1994, ANSI/ASQC Q9001-1994, ANSI/ASQC Q9002-1994, ANSI/ASQC Q9003-1994, and ANSI/ASQC Q9004-1-1994 respectively. This new numbering system is intended to emphasize the word-for-word correspondence of the International and American National Standards.

ISO (the International Organization for Standardization) is a worldwide federation of national standards bodies (ISO member bodies). The work of preparing International Standards is normally carried out through ISO technical committees. Each member body interested in a subject for which a technical committee has been established has the right to be represented on that committee. International organizations, governmental and nongovernmental, in liaison with ISO, also take part in the work. ISO collaborates closely with the International Electrotechnical Commission (IEC) on all matters of electrotechnical standardization. The American National Standards Institute (ANSI) is the U.S. member body of ISO. ASQC is the U.S. member of ANSI responsible for quality management and related standards.

Users should note that all ANSI/ASQC standards undergo revision from time to time. In the case of International Standards adopted as American National Standards, the revision timing is influences by the international revision timing. Reference herein to any other standard implies the latest American National Standard revision unless otherwise stated.

Comments concerning this standard are welcome. They should be sent to the sponsor of the standard, American Society for Quality Control, 611 East Wisconsin Avenue, P.O. Box 3005, Milwaukee, WI 53201-3005, c/o Standards Administrator.

INTRODUCTION

This American National Standard is one of three American National Standards dealing with quality-system requirements that can be used for external quality-assurance purposes. The quality-assurance models, set out in the three American National Standards listed below, represent three distinct forms of quality-system requirements suitable for the purpose of a supplier demonstrating its capability, and for the assessment of the capability of a supplier by external parties.

a) ANSI/ASQC Q9001-1994, Quality Systems—Model for Quality Assurance in Design, Development, Production, Installation, and Servicing

   — for use when conformance to specified requirements is to be assured by the supplier during design, development, production, installation, and servicing.

b) ANSI/ASQC 9002-1994, Quality Systems—Model for Quality Assurance in Production, Installation, and Servicing

   — for use when conformance to specified requirements is to be assured by the supplier during production, installation, and servicing.

c) ANSI/ASQC Q9003-1994, Quality Systems—Model for Quality Assurance in Final Inspection and Test

   — for use when conformance to specified requirements is to be assured by the supplier solely at final inspection and test.

It is emphasized that the quality-system requirements specified in this American National Standard, ANSI/ASQC Q9001-1994, and ANSI/ASQC Q9002-1994 are complementary (not alternative) to the technical (product) specified requirements. They specify requirements which determine what elements quality systems have to encompass, but it is not the purpose of these American National Standards to enforce uniformity of quality systems. They are generic and independent of any specific industry or economic sector. The design and implementation of a quality system will be influenced by the varying needs of an organization, its particular objectives, the products and services supplied, and the processes and specific practices employed.

It is intended that these American National Standards will be adopted in their present form, but on occasions they may need to be tailored by adding or deleting certain quality-system requirements for specific contractual situations. ANSI/ASQC Q9000-1-1994 provides guidance on such tailoring as well as on selection of the appropriate quality-assurance model, viz. ANSI/ASQC Q9001-1994, ANSI/ASQC Q9002-1994, or ANSI/ASQC Q9003-1994.

Quality Systems—Model for Quality Assurance in Final Inspection and Test

1 SCOPE

This American National Standard specifies quality-system requirements for use where a supplier's capability to detect and control the disposition of any product nonconformity during final inspection and test needs to be demonstrated.

It is applicable in situations when the conformance of product to specified requirements can be shown with adequate confidence providing that certain suppliers' capabilities for inspection and tests conducted on finished product can be satisfactorily demonstrated.

NOTE 1   For informative references, see annex A.

2 NORMATIVE REFERENCE

The following standard contains provisions which, through reference in this text, constitute provisions of this American National Standard. At the time of publication, the edition indicated was valid. All standards are subject to revision, and parties to agreements based on this American National Standard are encouraged to investigate the possibility of applying the most recent edition of the standard indicated below. The American National Standards Institute and members of IEC and ISO maintain registers of currently valid American National Standards and International Standards.

ISO 8402:1994, *Quality management and quality assurance—Vocabulary*

3 Definitions

For the purposes of this American National Standard, the definitions given in ISO 8402 and the following definitions apply.

3.1 Product

Result of activities or processes.

NOTES

2   A product may include service, hardware, processed materials, software, or a combination thereof.

3   A product can be tangible (e.g., assemblies or processed materials) or intangible (e.g., knowledge or concepts), or a combination thereof.

4   For the purposes of this American National Standard, the term "product" applies to the intended product offering only and not to unintended "by-products" affecting the environment. This differs from the definition given in ISO 8402.

3.2 Tender

Offer made by a supplier in response to an invitation to satisfy a contract award to provide product.

3.3 Contract; accepted order

Agreed requirements between a supplier and customer transmitted by any means.

4 QUALITY-SYSTEM REQUIREMENTS

4.1 Management responsibility

4.1.1 Quality policy

The supplier's management with executive responsibility shall define and document its policy for quality, including objectives for quality and its commitment to quality. The quality policy shall be relevant to the supplier's organizational goals and the expectations and needs of its customers. The supplier shall ensure that this policy is understood, implemented, and maintained at all levels of the organization.

4.1.2 Organization

4.1.2.1 Responsibility and authority

The responsibility, authority, and the interrelation of personnel who manage, perform, and verify work that is subject to the requirements of this American National Standard shall be defined and documented, particularly for personnel who need the organizational freedom and authority to

a)   conduct final inspection and tests, and

b)   ensure that finished product that does not conform to specified requirements is prevented from being used or delivered.

4.1.2.2 Resources

The supplier shall identify resource requirements and provide adequate resources, including the assignment of trained personnel (see 4.18), for management, performance of work, and verification activities including internal quality audits.

4.1.2.3 Management representative

The supplier's management with executive responsibility shall appoint a member of the supplier's own management who, irrespective of other responsibilities, shall have defined authority for

a)   ensuring that a quality system is established, implemented, and maintained in accordance with this American National Standard, and

b)   reporting on the performance of the quality system to the supplier's management for review and as a basis for improvement of the quality system.

NOTE 5   The responsibility of a management representative may also include liaison with external parties on matters relating to the supplier's quality system.

4.1.3 Management review

The supplier's management with executive responsibility shall review the quality system at defined intervals sufficient to ensure its continuing suitability and effectiveness in satisfying the requirements of this American National Standard and the supplier's stated quality policy and objectives (see 4.1.1). Records of such reviews shall be maintained (see 4.16).

4.2 Quality system

4.2.1 General

The supplier shall establish, document, and maintain a quality system as a means of ensuring that product on completion conforms to specified requirements. The supplier shall prepare a quality manual covering the requirements of this American National Standard. The quality manual shall include or make reference to the quality-system procedures and outline the structure of the documentation used in the quality system.

NOTE 6 Guidance on quality manuals is given in ISO 10013.

4.2.2 Quality-system procedures

The supplier shall

a) prepare documented procedures consistent with the requirements of this American National Standard and the supplier's stated quality policy, and

b) effectively implement the quality system and its documented procedures.

For the purposes of this American National Standard, the range and detail of the procedures that form part of the quality system depend on the complexity of the work, the methods used, and the skills and training needed by personnel involved in carrying out the activity.

NOTE 7 Documented procedures may make reference to work instructions that define how an activity is performed.

4.2.3 Quality planning

The supplier shall define and document how the requirements for quality of the finished product will be met. Quality planning shall be consistent with all other requirements of a supplier's quality system and shall be documented in a format to suit the supplier's method of operation. The supplier shall give consideration to the following activities, as appropriate:

a) the preparation of a quality plan for final inspection and tests;

b) the identification and acquisition of any final inspection and test equipment, resources, and skills that may be needed to achieve the required quality;

c) the updating, as necessary, of final inspection and testing techniques;

d) the identification of any final inspection and test measurement requirement involving capability that exceeds the known state of the art in sufficient time for the needed capability to be developed;

e) the identification of suitable verification at the finished product state;

f) the clarification of standards of acceptability for all features and requirements, including those which contain a subjective element;

g) the identification and preparation of quality records (see 4.16).

NOTE 8 The quality plan referred to (see 4.2.3a) may be in the form of a reference to the appropriate documented procedures that form an integral part of the supplier's quality system.

4.3 Contract review

4.3.1 General

The supplier shall establish and maintain documented procedures for contract review and for the coordination of these activities.

4.3.2 Review

Before submission of a tender, or the acceptance of a contract or order (statement of requirement), the tender, contract, or order shall be reviewed by the supplier to ensure that:

a) the requirements are adequately defined and documented; where no written statement of requirement is available for an order received by verbal means, the supplier shall ensure that the order requirements are agreed before their acceptance;

b) any difference between the contract or accepted order requirements and those in the tender are resolved;

c) the supplier has the capability to meet the contract or accepted order requirements for finished product.

4.3.3 Amendment to a contract

The supplier shall identify how an amendment to a

contract is made and correctly transferred to the functions concerned within the supplier's organization.

4.3.4 Records

Records of contract reviews shall be maintained (see 4.16).

NOTE 9   Channels for communication and interfaces with the customer's organization in these contract matters should be established.

4.4 Design control

The scope of this American National Standard does not include quality-system requirements for design control. This subclause is included to align the clause numbering with ANSI/ASQC Q9001-1994.

4.5 Document and data control

4.5.1 General

The supplier shall establish and maintain documented procedures to control all documents and data that relate to the requirements of this American National Standard including, to the extent applicable, documents of external origin such as standards and customer drawings.

NOTE 10   Documents and data may be in the form of any type of media, such as hard copy or electronic media.

4.5.2 Document and data approval and issue

The documents and data shall be reviewed and approved for adequacy by authorized personnel prior to issue. A master list or equivalent document-control procedure identifying the current revision status of documents shall be established and be readily available to preclude the use of invalid and/or obsolete documents.

This control shall ensure that:

a)   the pertinent issues of appropriate documents are available at all locations where operations essential to the effective functioning of the quality system are performed;

b)   invalid and/or obsolete documents are promptly removed from all points of issue or use, or otherwise assured against unintended use;

c)   any obsolete documents retained for legal and/or knowledge-preservation purposes are suitably identified.

4.5.3 Document and data changes

Changes to documents and data shall be reviewed and approved by the same functions/organizations that performed the original review and approval, unless specifically designated otherwise. The designated functions/organizations shall have access to pertinent background information upon which to base their review and approval.

Where practicable, the nature of the change shall be identified in the document or the appropriate attachments.

4.6 Purchasing

The scope of this American National Standard does not include quality-system requirements for purchasing. This subclause is included to align the clause numbering with ANSI/ASQC Q9001-1994.

4.7 Control of customer-supplied product

The supplier shall establish and maintain documented procedures for the control of verification, storage, and maintenance of customer-supplied product provided for incorporation into the finished product or for related activities. Any such product that is lost, damaged, or is otherwise unsuitable for use shall be recorded and reported to the customer (see 4.16).

Verification by the supplier does not absolve the customer of the responsibility to provide acceptable product.

4.8 Product identification and traceability

Where and to the extent that traceability is a specified requirement, the supplier shall establish and maintain documented procedures for unique identification of individual product or batches. This identification shall be recorded (see 4.16).

4.9 Process control

The scope of this American National Standard does not include quality-system requirements for process control. This subclause is included to align the clause numbering with ANSI/ASQC Q9001-1994.

4.10 Inspection and testing

4.10.1 General

The supplier shall establish and maintain documented procedures for final inspection and testing activities in order to verify that the specified requirements for finished product are met. The required final inspection and testing, and the records to be established, shall be detailed in the quality plan or documented procedures.

4.10.2 Final inspection and testing

The supplier shall carry out all final inspection and testing in accordance with the quality plan and/or documented procedures and maintain appropriate records to complete the evidence of conformance of product to the specified requirements. When the specified requirements cannot be fully verified on the finished product, then a verification of acceptable results of other necessary inspection and tests performed previously shall be included for the purpose of verifying product requirements at final inspection and test.

Records shall identify the inspection authority responsible for the release of conforming product (see 4.16).

4.11 Control of inspection, measuring, and test equipment

4.11.1 General

The supplier shall establish and maintain documented procedures to control, calibrate, and maintain final inspection, measuring, and test equipment (including test software) used by the supplier to demonstrate the conformance of product to the specified requirements. Inspection, measuring, and test equipment shall be used in a manner which ensures that the measurement uncertainty is known and is consistent with the required measurement capability.

Where test software or comparative references such as test hardware are used as suitable forms of inspection, they shall be checked to prove that they are capable of verifying the acceptability of product, prior to release for use during final inspection and testing, and shall be rechecked at prescribed intervals. The supplier shall establish the extent and frequency of such checks and shall maintain records as evidence of control (see 4.16).

Where the availability of technical data pertaining to the measurement equipment is a specified requirement, such data shall be made available, when required by the customer or customer's representative, for verification that the measuring equipment is functionally adequate.

NOTE 11 For the purposes of this American National Standard, the term "measuring equipment" includes measurement devices.

4.11.2 Control procedure

The supplier shall:

a) determine the measurements to be made and the accuracy required, and select the appropriate inspection, measuring, and test equipment that is capable of the necessary accuracy and precision;

b) identify all inspection, measuring, and test equipment that can affect product quality, and calibrate and adjust them at prescribed intervals, or prior to use, against certified equipment having a known valid relationship to internationally or nationally recognized standards. Where no such standards exist, the basis used for calibration shall be documented;

c) define the process employed for the calibration of inspection, measuring, and test equipment, including details of equipment type, unique identification, location, frequency of checks, check method, acceptance criteria, and the action to be taken when results are unsatisfactory;

d) identify inspection, measuring, and test equipment with a suitable indicator or approved identification record to show the calibration status;

e) maintain calibration records for inspection, measuring, and test equipment (see 4.16);

f) assess and document the validity of previous inspection and test results when inspection, measuring, or test equipment is found to be out of calibration;

g) ensure that the environmental conditions are suitable for the calibrations, inspections, measurements, and tests being carried out;

h)   ensure that the handling, preservation, and storage of inspection, measuring, and test equipment is such that the accuracy and fitness for use are maintained;

i)   safeguard inspection, measuring, and test facilities, including both test hardware and test software, from adjustments which would invalidate the calibration setting.

NOTE 12 The metrological confirmation system for measuring equipment given in ISO 10012 may be used for guidance.

4.12 Inspection and test status

The inspection and test status of product shall be identified by suitable means, which indicate the conformance or nonconformance of product with regard to inspection and tests performed. The identification of inspection and test status shall be maintained, as defined in the quality plan and/or documented procedures, to ensure that only product that has passed the required final inspection and test [or released under an authorized concession (see 4.13)] is dispatched.

4.13 CONTROL OF NONCONFORMING PRODUCT

The supplier shall establish and maintain control of product that does not conform to specified requirements to ensure that unintended use or delivery is avoided.

Control shall provide for identification, documentation, evaluation, segregation (when practical), disposition of nonconforming product, and for notification to the functions concerned.

The description of repairs, and of any nonconformity that has been accepted under authorized concession, shall be recorded to denote the actual condition (see 4.16).

Repaired and/or reworked product shall be reinspected in accordance with the quality plan and/or documented procedures.

4.14 Corrective action

The supplier shall:

a)   investigate nonconformities that have been

identified from the analysis of final inspection and test reports and customer complaints of product;

b)   determine and implement appropriate corrective action on the nonconformities;

c)   ensure that relevant information on the actions taken is submitted for management review (see 4.1.3).

4.15 Handling, storage, packaging, preservation, and delivery

4.15.1 General

The supplier shall establish and maintain documented procedures for handling, storage, packaging, preservation, and delivery of completed product after final inspection and test.

4.15.2 Handling

The supplier shall provide methods of handling product that prevent damage or deterioration.

4.15.3 Storage

The supplier shall use designated storage areas or stock rooms to prevent damage or deterioration of product, pending delivery. Appropriate methods for authorizing receipt to and dispatch from such areas shall be stipulated.

In order to detect deterioration, the condition of product in stock shall be assessed at appropriate intervals.

4.15.4 Packaging

The supplier shall control packing, packaging, and marking processes (including materials used) to the extent necessary to ensure conformance to specified requirements.

4.15.5 Preservation

The supplier shall apply appropriate methods for preservation and segregation of product when the product is under the supplier's control.

4.15.6 Delivery

The supplier shall arrange for the protection of the quality of product after final inspection and test. Where contractually specified, this protection shall be extended to include delivery to destination.

4.16 Control of quality records

The supplier shall establish and maintain control of appropriate quality records to demonstrate conformance of the finished product to specified requirements and the effective operation of the quality system.

Quality records shall be legible and identifiable to the product involved. Quality records that substantiate conformance of the finished product with the specified requirements and the effective operation of the quality system shall be retained for an agreed period and made available on request.

NOTE 13 Records may be in the form of any type of media, such as hard copy or electronic media.

4.17 Internal quality audits

The supplier shall carry out internal quality audits to verify whether quality activities and related results comply with planned arrangements covering the requirements of this American National Standard and to determine the effectiveness of the quality system.

Internal quality audits shall be scheduled on the basis of the status and importance of the activity to be audited and shall be carried out by personnel independent of those having direct responsibility for the activity being audited.

The results of the audits shall be recorded (see 4.16) and brought to the attention of the personnel having responsibility in the area audited. The management personnel responsible for the area shall take timely corrective action on deficiencies found during the audit.

Follow-up audit activities shall verify and record the implementation and effectiveness of the corrective action taken (see 4.16).

NOTES

14 The results of internal quality audits form an integral part of the input to management review activities (see 4.1.3).

15 Guidance on quality-system audits is given in ANSI/ASQC Q10011-1-1994, ANSI/ASQC Q10011-2-1994, and ANSI/ASQC Q10011-3-1994.

4.18 Training

Personnel performing final inspection and test activities covering the requirements of this American National Standard shall have appropriate experience and/or training, including any necessary qualification for specific assigned tasks. Appropriate records of training shall be maintained (see 4.16).

4.19 Servicing

The scope of this American National Standard does not include quality-system requirements for servicing. This subclause is included to align the clause numbering with ANSI/ASQC Q9001-1994.

4.20 Statistical techniques

The supplier shall:

a) identify the need for statistical techniques required for the acceptability of product characteristics;

b) implement and control the application of the statistical techniques.

ANNEX A (INFORMATIVE)

Bibliography

[1] ANSI/ASQC Q9000-1-1994, *Quality Management and Quality Assurance Standards—Guidelines for Selection and Use.*

[2] ANSI/ASQC Q9001-1994, *Quality Systems—Model for Quality Assurance in Design, Development, Production, Installation, and Servicing.*

[3] ANSI/ASQC Q9002-1994, *Quality Systems—Model for Quality Assurance in Production, Installation, and Servicing.*

[4] ANSI/ASQC Q10011-1-1994, *Guidelines for Auditing Quality Systems—Auditing.*

[5] ANSI/ASQC Q10011-2-1994, *Guidelines for Auditing Quality Systems—Qualification Criteria for Quality Systems Auditors.*

[6] ANSI/ASQC Q10011-3-1994, *Guidelines for Auditing Quality Systems—Management of Audit Programs.*

[7] ISO 9000-2:1993, *Quality management and quality assurance standards—Part 2: Generic guidelines for the application of ISO 9001, ISO 9002 and ISO 9003.*

[8] ISO 9000-3:1991, *Quality management and quality assurance standards—Part 3: Guidelines for the application of ISO 9001 to the development, supply and maintenance of software.*

[9] ISO 10012-1:1992, *Quality assurance requirements for measuring equipment—Part 1: Metrological confirmation system for measuring equipment.*

[10] ISO 10013:—¹), *Guidelines for developing quality manuals.*

ENDNOTE:

¹ To be published.

American National Standard

ANSI/ASQC Q9004-1-1994

QUALITY MANAGEMENT AND QUALITY SYSTEM ELEMENTS—GUIDELINES

Prepared by
American Society for Quality Control
Standards Committee

for

American National Standards Committee
Z-1 on Quality Assurance

Descriptors: Quality management, quality systems, components, general conditions.

American National Standards: An American National Standard implies a consensus of those substantially concerned with its scope and provisions. An American National Standard is intended as a guide to aid the manufacturer, the consumer, and the general public. The existence of an American National Standard does not in any respect preclude anyone, whether he or she has approved the standard or not, from manufacturing, purchasing, or using products, processes, or procedures not conforming to the standard. American National Standards are subject to periodic review and users are cautioned to obtain the latest edition.

Caution Notice: This American National Standard may be revised or withdrawn at any time. The procedures of the American National Standards Institute require that action be taken to reaffirm, revise, or withdraw this standard no later than five years from the date of publication. Purchasers of American National Standards may receive current information on all standards by calling or writing the American National Standards Institute.

ASQC Mission: To facilitate continuous improvement and increase customer satisfaction by identifying, communicating, and promoting the use of quality principles, concepts, and technologies; and thereby be recognized throughout the world as the leading authority on, and champion for, quality.

10 9 8 7 6 5 4 3 2 1

Printed in the United States of America

Printed on acid-free recycled paper

Published by:
ASQC
611 East Wisconsin Avenue
Milwaukee, Wisconsin 53202

CONTENTS

1   Scope

2   Normative references

3   Definitions

4   Management responsibility

5   Quality-system elements

6   Financial considerations of quality systems

7   Quality in marketing

8   Quality in specification and design

9   Quality in purchasing

10 Quality of processes

11 Control of processes

12 Product verification

13 Control of inspection, measuring, and test equipment

14 Control of nonconforming product

15 Corrective action

16 Postproduction activities

17 Quality records

18 Personnel

19 Product safety

20 Use of statistical methods

Annex

A   Bibliography

FOREWORD

(This Foreword is not a part of American National Standard *Quality Management and Quality System Elements—Guidelines.*)

This American National Standard corresponds to the International Standard ISO 9004-1:1994. The initial five ISO 9000 series standards, ISO 9000, ISO 9001, ISO 9002, ISO 9003, and ISO 9004, when published in the United States as American National Standards in 1987, were designated as ANSI/ASQC Q90 through ANSI/ASQC Q94 respectively. The five 1987 standards in their 1994 international revisions are now designated ISO 9000-1, ISO 9001, ISO 9002, ISO 9003, and ISO 9004-1 respectively. Their publication as American National Standards are now designated ANSI/ASQC Q9000-1-1994, ANSI/ASQC Q9001-1994, ANSI/ASQC Q9002-1994, ANSI/ASQC Q9003-1994, and ANSI/ASQC Q9004-1-1994 respectively. This new numbering system is intended to emphasize the word-for-word correspondence of the International and American National Standards.

ISO (the International Organization for Standardization) is a worldwide federation of national standards bodies (ISO member bodies). The work of preparing International Standards is normally carried out through ISO technical committees. Each member body interested in a subject for which a technical committee has been established has the right to be represented on that committee. International organizations, governmental and nongovernmental, in liaison with ISO, also take part in the work. ISO collaborates closely with the International Electrotechnical Commission (IEC) on all matters of electrotechnical standardization. The American National Standards Institute (ANSI) is the U.S. member body of ISO. ASQC is the U.S. member of ANSI responsible for quality management and related standards.

Users should note that all ANSI/ASQC standards undergo revision from time to time. In the case of International Standards adopted as American National Standards, the revision timing is influenced by the international revision timing. Reference herein to any other standard implies the latest American National Standard revision unless otherwise stated.

Comments concerning this standard are welcome. They should be sent to the sponsor of the standard, American Society for Quality Control, 611 East Wisconsin Avenue, P.O. Box 3005, Milwaukee, WI 53201-3005, c/o Standards Administrator.

INTRODUCTION

0.1 General

ANSI/ASQC Q9004-1-1994 and all the International Standards in the ISO 9000 family are generic and independent of any specific industry or economic sector. Collectively they provide guidance for quality management and models for quality assurance.

The International Standards in the ISO 9000 family describe what elements quality systems should encompass, but not how a specific organization should implement these elements. Because the needs of organizations vary, it is not the purpose of these International Standards or the corresponding American National Standards to enforce uniformity of quality systems. The design and implementation of a quality system will be influenced by the particular objectives, products, processes, and individual practices of the organization.

A primary concern of any organization should be the quality of its products. (See 3.5 for the definition of "product" which includes service.)

In order to be successful, an organization should offer products that:

a) meet a well-defined need, use, or purpose;

b) satisfy customers' expectations;

c) comply with applicable standards and specifications;

d) comply with requirements of society (see 3.3);

e) reflect environmental needs;

f) are made available at competitive prices;

g) are provided economically.

0.2 Organizational goals

In order to meet its objectives, the organization should ensure that the technical, administrative, and human factors affecting the quality of its products will be under control, whether hardware, software, processed materials, or services. All such control should be oriented towards the reduction, elimination, and, most importantly, prevention of quality nonconformities.

A quality system should be developed and implemented for the purpose of accomplishing the objectives set out in the organization's quality policy.

Each element (or requirement) in a quality system varies in importance from one type of activity to another and from one product to another.

In order to achieve maximum effectiveness and to satisfy customer expectations, it is essential that the quality system be appropriate to the type of activity and to the product being offered.

0.3 Meeting customer/organization needs and expectations

A quality system has two interrelated aspects, as follows.

a) **The customer's needs and expectations**

   For the customer, there is a need for confidence in the ability of the organization to deliver the desired quality as well as the consistent maintenance of that quality.

b) **The organization's needs and interests**

   For the organization, there is a business need to attain and to maintain the desired quality at an optimum cost; the fulfillment of this aspect is related to the planned and efficient utilization of the technological, human, and material resources available to the organization.

Each of the above aspects of a quality system requires objective evidence in the form of information and data concerning the quality of the system and the quality of the organization's products.

0.4 Benefits, costs, and risks

Benefit, cost, and risk considerations have great importance for both the organization and customer. These considerations are inherent aspects of most products. The possible effects and ramifications of these considerations are given in a to c.

a) **Benefit considerations**

   For the customer, consideration has to be given to reduced costs, improved fitness for use, increased satisfaction, and growth in confidence.

   For the organization, consideration has to be given to increased profitability and market share.

b)   **Cost considerations**

For the customer, consideration has to be given to safety, acquisition cost, operating, maintenance, downtime and repair costs, and possible disposal costs.

For the organization, consideration has to be given to costs due to marketing and design deficiencies, including unsatisfactory product, rework, repair, replacement, reprocessing, loss of production, warranties, and field repair.

c)   **Risk considerations**

For the customer, consideration has to be given to risks such as those pertaining to the health and safety of people, dissatisfaction with product, availability, marketing claims, and loss of confidence.

For the organization, consideration has to be given to risks related to deficient products which lead to loss of image or reputation, loss of market, complaints, claims, liability, and waste of human and financial resources.

0.5 Conclusions

An effective quality system should be designed to satisfy customer needs and expectations while serving to protect the organization's interests. A well-structured quality system is a valuable management resource in the optimization and control of quality in relation to benefit, cost, and risk considerations.

Quality Management and Quality System Elements—Guidelines

1 SCOPE

ANSI/ASQC Q9004-1-1994 provides guidance on quality management and quality-system elements.

The quality-system elements are suitable for use in the development and implementation of a comprehensive and effective in-house quality system, with a view to ensuring customer satisfaction.

ANSI/ASQC Q9004-1-1994 is not intended for contractual, regulatory, or certification use. Consequently, it is not a guideline for the implementing of ANSI/ASQC Q9001, ANSI/ASQC Q9002-1994,

and ANSI/ASQC Q9003-1994. ISO 9000-2 should be used for that purpose.

The selection of appropriate elements contained in this part of ANSI/ASQC Q9004-1-1994 and the extent to which these elements are adopted and applied by an organization depends upon factors such as the market being served, nature of the product, production processes, and customer and consumer needs.

References in ANSI/ASQC Q9004-1-1994 to a "product" should be interpreted as applicable to the generic product categories of hardware, software, processed materials or service (in accordance with the definition of "product" in ISO 8402).

NOTES

1   For further guidance, see ISO 9004-2 and ISO 9004-3.

2   For informative references, see annex A.

2 NORMATIVE REFERENCES

The following standards contain provisions which, through reference in this text, constitute provisions of ANSI/ASQC Q9004-1-1994. At the time of publication, the editions indicated were valid. All standards are subject to revision, and parties to agreements based on ANSI/ASQC Q9004-1-1994 are encouraged to investigate the possibility of applying the most recent editions of the standards indicated below. Members of IEC and ISO maintain registers of currently valid International Standards.

ANSI/ASQC Q9000-1-1994, Quality Management and Quality Assurance Standards—Guidelines for Selection and Use.

ISO 8402:1994, *Quality management and quality assurance—Vocabulary.*

3 DEFINITIONS

This revision of ANSI/ASQC Q94-1987 has improved the harmonization of terminology with other American National Standards in the ANSI/ASQC Q9000 series and with other International Standards in the ISO 9000 family. Table 1 shows the supply-chain terminology used in these American National Standards.

Thus, the term "subcontractor" is used rather than

ANSI/ASQC Q9000-1-1994	Subsupplier	➜	supplier or organization	➜	customer
ANSI/ASQC Q9001-1994 ANSI/ASQC Q9002-1994 ANSI/ASQC Q9003-1994	Subcontractor	➜	supplier	➜	customer
ANSI/ASQC Q9004-1-1994	Subcontractor	➜	organization	➜	customer

Table 1. Relationships of organizations in the supply chain.

the term "supplier" in ANSI/ASQC Q9004-1-1994 to avoid confusion with the meaning of the term "supplier" in ANSI/ASQC Q9000-1-1994 and ANSI/ASQC Q9001-1994. See ANSI/ASQC Q9000-1-1994 for a fuller explanation of the basis for usage of these terms.

For the purposes of ANSI/ASQC Q9004-1-1994, the definitions given in ISO 8402 apply.

For the convenience of users of ANSI/ASQC Q9004-1-1994, the following definitions are quoted from ISO 8402.

3.1 Organization

Company, corporation, firm, enterprise, or institution, or part thereof, whether incorporated or not, public or private, that has its own functions and administration.

3.2 Customer

Recipient of a product provided by the supplier.

NOTES

3   In a contractual situation, the customer is called the "purchaser."[1]

4   The customer may be, for example, the ultimate consumer, user, beneficiary, or purchaser.

5   The customer can be either external or internal to the organization.

3.3 Requirements of society

Obligations resulting from laws, regulations, rules, codes, statutes, and other considerations.

NOTES

6   "Other considerations" include protection of the environment, health, safety, security, and conservation of energy and natural resources.

7   All requirements of society should be taken into account when defining the requirements for quality.

8   Requirements of society include jurisdictional and regulatory requirements. These may vary from one jurisdiction to another.

3.4 Quality plan

Document setting out the specific quality practices, resources, and sequence of activities relevant to a particular product, project, or contract.

NOTES

9   A quality plan usually makes reference to the parts of the quality manual applicable to the specific case.

10   Depending on the scope of the plan, a qualifier may be used, for example, quality assurance plan, quality management plan.

3.5 product

Result of activities or processes.

NOTES

11   A product may include service, hardware, processed materials, software, or a combination thereof.

12   A product can be tangible (e.g., assemblies or processed materials) or intangible (e.g., knowledge or concepts), or a combination thereof.

13   A product can be intended (e.g., offering to customers) or unintended (e.g., pollutant or unwanted effects).

3.6 Service

Result generated by activities at the interface between the supplier and the customer and by supplier internal activities to meet the customer needs.

NOTES

14   The supplier or the customer may be represented at the interface by personnel or equipment.

15   Customer activities at the interface with the supplier may be essential to the service delivery.

16   Delivery or use of tangible products may form part of the service delivery.

17   A service may be linked with the manufacture and supply of tangible product.

4 MANAGEMENT RESPONSIBILITY

4.1 General

The responsibility for and commitment to a quality policy belongs to the highest level of management. Quality management encompasses all activities of the overall management function that determine the quality policy, objectives, and responsibilities, and implement them by means such as quality planning, quality control, quality assurance, and quality improvement within the quality system.

4.2 Quality policy

The management of an organization should define and document its quality policy. This policy should be consistent with other policies within the organization. Management should take all necessary measures to ensure that its quality policy is understood, implemented, and reviewed at all levels of the organization.

4.3 Quality objectives

4.3.1 Management should document objectives and commitments pertaining to key elements of quality, such as fitness for use, performance, safety, and dependability.

4.3.2 The calculation and evaluation of costs associated with all quality elements and objectives should always be an important consideration, with the objective of minimizing quality losses.

4.3.3 Appropriate levels of management should document specific quality objectives consistent with

quality policy as well as other objectives of the organization.

4.4 Quality system

4.4.1 A quality system is the organizational structure, procedures, processes, and resources needed to implement quality management.

4.4.2 The organization's management should develop, establish, and implement a quality system to accomplish the stated policies and objectives.

4.4.3 The quality system should be structured and adapted to the organization's particular type of business and should take into account the appropriate elements outlined in ANSI/ASQC Q9004-1-1994.

4.4.4 The quality system should function in such a manner as to provide confidence that:

a)   the system is understood, implemented, maintained, and effective;

b)   the products actually do satisfy customer needs and expectations;

c)   the needs of both society and the environment have been addressed;

d)   emphasis is placed on problem prevention rather than dependence on detection after occurrence.

5 QUALITY-SYSTEM ELEMENTS

5.1 Extent of application

5.1.1 The quality system typically applies to, and interacts with, all activities pertinent to the quality of a product. It will involve all phases in the life-cycle of a product and processes, from initial identification of market needs to final satisfaction of requirements. Typical phases are:

a)   marketing and market research;

b)   product design and development;

c)   process planning and development;

d)   purchasing;

e)   production, or provision of services;

f)   verification;

g)   packaging and storage;

h)   sales and distribution;

i) installation and commissioning;

j) technical assistance and servicing;

k) after sales;

l) disposal or recycling at the end of useful life.

NOTE 18 Figure 1 gives a schematic representation of the typical life-cycle phases of a product.

5.1.2 In the context of interacting activities within an organization, marketing and design should be emphasized as especially important for

— determining and defining customer needs, expectations, and other product requirements, and

— providing the concepts (including supporting data) for producing a product to documented specifications at optimum cost.

5.2 Structure of the quality system

5.2.1 General

Input from the market should be used to improve new and existing products and to improve the quality system.

Management is ultimately responsible for establishing the quality policy and for decisions concerning the initiation, development, implementation, and maintenance of the quality system.

5.2.2 Responsibility and authority

Activities contributing to quality, whether directly or indirectly, should be defined and documented, and the following actions taken.

a) General and specific quality-related responsibilities should be explicitly defined.

b) Responsibility and authority delegated to each activity contributing to quality should be clearly established. Responsibility, organizational freedom, and authority to act should be sufficient to attain the assigned quality objectives with the desired efficiency.

c) Interface control and coordination measures between different activities should be defined.

d) In organizing a well-structured and effective quality system, emphasis should be placed on the identification of potential or actual quality

problems and the implementation of preventive or corrective action (see clauses 14 and 15).

5.2.3 Organizational structure

Functions related to the quality system should be clearly established within the overall organizational structure. The lines of authority and communication should be defined.

5.2.4 Resources and personnel

Management should identify resource requirements, and provide sufficient and appropriate resources essential to the implementation of the quality policy and the achievement of quality objectives. For example, these resources can include:

a) human resources and specialized skills;

b) design and development equipment;

c) manufacturing equipment;

d) inspection, test, and examination equipment;

e) instrumentation and computer software.

Management should determine the level of competence, experience, and training necessary to ensure the capability of personnel (see clause 18).

Management should identify quality-related factors affecting market position and objectives relative to products, processes, or associated services, in order to allocate organization resources on a planned and timely basis.

Programs and schedules covering these resources and skills should be consistent with the organization's overall objectives.

5.2.5 Operational procedures

The quality system should be organized in such a way that adequate and continuous control is exercised over all activities affecting quality.

The quality system should emphasize preventive actions that avoid occurrence of problems, while maintaining the ability to respond to and correct failures, should they occur.

Documented operational procedures coordinating different activities with respect to an effective quality system should be developed, issued, and maintained to implement the quality policy and objectives. These documented procedures should specify the objectives and performance of the various activities having an impact on quality (see Figure 1).

All documented procedures should be stated simply, unambiguously, and understandably, and should indicate methods to be used and criteria to be satisfied.

5.2.6 Configuration management

The quality system should include documented procedures for configuration management to the extent appropriate. This discipline is initiated early in the design phase and continues through the whole life-cycle of a product. It assists in the operation and control of design, development, production, and use of a product, and gives management visibility of the state of documentation and product during its lifetime.

Configuration management can include: configuration identification, configuration control, configuration status accounting, and configuration audit. It relates to several of the activities described in ANSI/ASQC Q9004-1-1994.

5.3 Documentation of the quality system

5.3.1 Quality policies and procedures

All the elements, requirements, and provisions adopted by an organization for its quality system should be documented in a systematic, orderly, and understandable manner in the form of policies and procedures. However, care should be taken to limit documentation to the extent pertinent to the application.

The quality system should include adequate provision for the proper identification, distribution, collection, and maintenance of all quality documents.

5.3.2 Quality-system documentation

5.3.2.1 The typical form of the main document used to demonstrate or describe a documented quality system is a "quality manual." For further guidance, see ISO 10013.

5.3.2.2 The primary purpose of a quality manual is to define an outline structure of the quality system while serving as a permanent reference in the implementation and maintenance of that system.

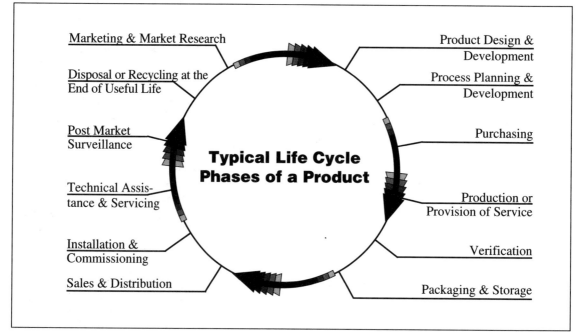

Figure 1. Main activities having an impact on quality.

5.3.2.3 Documented procedures should be established for making changes, modifications, revisions, or additions to the contents of a quality manual.

5.3.2.4 Supporting the quality manual are documented quality-system procedures (e.g., design, purchasing, and process work instructions). These documented procedures can take various forms, depending on

— the size of the organization,

— the specific nature of the activity, and

— the intended scope and structure of the quality manual.

Documented procedures may apply to one or more parts of the organization.

5.3.3 Quality plans

For any product or process, management should ensure that documented quality plans are prepared and maintained. These should be consistent with all other requirements of the organization's quality system, and should ensure that specified requirements for a product, project, or contract are met. A quality plan may be a part of a larger overall plan. A quality plan is particularly necessary for a new product or process, or when there is significant change to an existing product or process.

Quality plans should define:

a) the quality objectives to be attained (e.g., characteristics or specifications, uniformity, effectiveness, aesthetics, cycle time, cost, natural resources, utilization, yield, and dependability);

b) the steps in the processes that constitute the operating practice of the organization (a flowchart or similar diagram can be used to demonstrate the elements of the process);

c) the specific allocation of responsibilities, authority, and resources during the different phases of the project;

d) the specific documented procedures and instructions to be applied;

e) suitable testing, inspection, examination, and audit programs at appropriate stages (e.g., design and development);

f) a documented procedure for changes and modifications in a quality plan as projects proceed;

g) a method for measuring the achievement of the quality objectives;

h) other actions necessary to meet the objectives.

Quality plans may be included or referenced in the quality manual, as appropriate.

To facilitate achievement of the objectives of a quality plan, documented operational control as described in ANSI/ASQC Q9004-1-1994 should be used.

5.3.4 Quality records

Quality records, including charts pertaining to design, inspection, testing, survey, audit, review, or related results, should be maintained as important evidence to demonstrate conformance to specified requirements and the effective operation of the quality system (see clause 17).

5.4 Auditing the quality system

5.4.1 General

Audits should be planned and carried out to determine if the activities and related results of the organization's quality system comply with planned arrangements, and to determine the effectiveness of the quality system. All elements should be internally audited and evaluated on a regular basis, considering the status and importance of the activity to be audited. For this purpose, an appropriate audit program should be established and implemented by the organization's management.

5.4.2 Audit program

The audit program should cover:

a) planning and scheduling the specific activities and areas to be audited;

b) assignment of personnel with appropriate qualifications to conduct audits;

c) documented procedures for carrying out audits, including recording and reporting the results of the quality audit and reaching agreement on timely corrective actions on the deficiencies found during the audit.

Apart from planned and systematic audits, other factors necessitating audits can be organizational changes, market feedback, nonconformity reports, and surveys.

5.4.3 Extent of audits

Objective evaluations of quality-system activities by competent personnel should include the following activities or areas:

a) organizational structures;

b) administrative, operational, and quality-system procedures;

c) personnel, equipment, and material resources;

d) work areas, operations, and processes;

e) products being produced (to establish the degree of conformance to standards and specifications);

f) documentation, reports, and record keeping.

Personnel conducting audits of quality-system elements should be independent of those having direct responsibilities for the specific activities or areas being audited. An audit plan should be prepared and documented to include the items listed in a to f.

5.4.4 Audit reporting

Audit observations, conclusions, and agreements on timely corrective action should be recorded and submitted for appropriate action by the management responsible for the area audited, and communicated for the information of management with executive responsibility for quality.

The following items should be covered in the audit report:

a) all examples of nonconformities or deficiencies;

b) appropriate and timely corrective action.

5.4.5 Follow-up action

Implementation and effectiveness of corrective actions resulting from previous audits should be assessed and documented.

NOTE 19 For further guidance on quality auditing, qualifications of auditors and management of audit programs, see ANSI/ASQC Q10011-1-1994, ANSI/ASQC Q10011-2-1994, and ANSI/ASQC Q10011-3-1994.

5.5 Review and evaluation of the quality system

The organization's management should provide for independent review and evaluation of the quality system at defined intervals. The reviews of the quality policy and objectives should be carried out by top management, and the review of supporting activities should be carried out by management with executive responsibilities for quality and other appropriate members of management, utilizing competent independent personnel as decided on by the management.

Reviews should consist of well-structured and comprehensive evaluations which include:

a) results from internal audits centred on various elements of the quality system (see 5.4.3);

b) the overall effectiveness in satisfying the guidance of ANSI/ASQC Q9004-1-1994 and the organization's stated quality policy and objectives;

c) considerations for updating the quality system in relation to changes brought about by new technologies, quality concepts, market strategies, and social or environmental conditions.

Observations, conclusions, and recommendations reached as a result of review and evaluation should be documented for necessary action.

5.6 Quality improvement

When implementing a quality system, the management of an organization should ensure that the system will facilitate and promote continuous quality improvement.

Quality improvement refers to the actions taken throughout the organization to increase the effectiveness and efficiency of activities and processes to provide added benefits to both the organization and its customers.

In creating an environment for quality improvement, consideration should be given to:

a) encouraging and sustaining a supportive style of management;

b) promoting values, attitudes, and behavior that foster improvement;

c) setting clear quality-improvement goals;

d) encouraging effective communication and teamwork;

e) recognizing successes and achievements;

f) training and educating for improvement.

NOTE 20 Further guidance is given in ISO 9004-4.

6 FINANCIAL CONSIDERATIONS OF QUALITY SYSTEMS

6.1 General

It is important that the effectiveness of a quality system be measured in financial terms. The impact of an effective quality system upon the organization's profit and loss statement can be highly significant, particularly by improvement of operations, resulting in reduced losses due to error and by making a contribution to customer satisfaction.

Such measurement and reporting can provide a means for identifying inefficient activities, and initiating internal improvement activities.

By reporting quality-system activities and effectiveness in financial terms, management will receive the results in a common business language from all departments.

6.2 Approaches to financial reporting of quality-system activities

6.2.1 General

Some organizations find it useful to report the financial benefits using systematic quality financial reporting procedures.

The approach(es) to financial reporting selected and used by particular organizations will be dependent upon their individual structures, their activities, and the maturity of their quality systems.

6.2.2 Approaches

There are various approaches to gathering, presenting, and analyzing the elements of financial data. The approaches given in a to c have been found to be useful, but do not exclude others, or adaptations or combinations of them.

a) Quality-costing approach

This approach addresses quality-related costs, which are broadly divided into those arising from internal operations and external activities.

Cost elements for internal operations are analyzed according to the PAF (prevention, appraisal, failure) costing model.

Prevention and appraisal costs are considered as investments, while failure costs are considered as losses. The components of the costs are:

1) prevention: efforts to prevent failures;

2) appraisal: testing, inspection, and examination to assess whether requirements for quality   are being fulfilled;

3) internal failure: costs resulting from a product failing to meet the quality requirements prior to delivery (e.g., re-performing a service, reprocessing, rework, retest, scrap);

4) external failure: costs resulting from a product failing to meet the quality requirements after delivery (e.g., product maintenance and repair, warranty and returns, direct costs and allowances, product recall costs, liability costs).

b) **Process-cost approach**

This approach analyzes the costs of conformity and the costs of nonconformity for any process, both of which can be the source of savings. These are defined as:

1) cost of conformity: cost to fulfill all of the stated and implied needs of customers in the absence of failure of the existing process;

2) cost of nonconformity: cost incurred due to failure of the existing process.

c) **Quality-loss approach**

This approach focuses on internal and external losses due to poor quality and identifies tangible and intangible loss types. Typical external intangible losses are loss of future sales due to customer dissatisfaction. Typical internal intangible losses arise from lower work efficiency due to rework, poor ergonomics, missed opportunities, etc. Tangible losses are internal and external failure costs.

6.3 Reporting

The financial reporting of quality activities should be regularly provided to and monitored by management, and be related to other business measures such as "sales," "turnover," or "added value" in order to provide for a realistic, entrepreneurial

— evaluation of the adequacy and effectiveness of the quality system,

— identification of additional areas requiring attention and improvement, and

— establishment of quality and cost objectives for the following period.

The elements of financial quality reports are in many cases already available in the organization, but in other forms. Their reporting as a financial quality report can require regrouping of individual elements from other reports.

7 QUALITY IN MARKETING

7.1 Marketing requirements

The marketing function should establish adequately defined and documented requirements for the quality of the product. Particularly at this early stage in the product life-cycle, it is important to consider the requirements for all the elements of the total product, whether hardware, software, processed materials, or services. In fact, all products involve some element of service, and many products involve several generic product categories. The marketing function should:

a) determine the need for a product;

b) define the market demand and sector, so that product grade, quantity, price, and timing can be determined;

c) determine specific customer requirements, or review general market needs; actions include assessment of any unstated expectations or biases held by customers;

d) communicate all customer requirements within the organization;

e) ensure that all relevant organizational functions agree that they have the capability to meet customer requirements.

7.2 Defining product specification

The marketing function should provide the organization with a formal statement or outline of product requirements. Specific customer and general market requirements and expectations should be translated into a preliminary set of specifications as the basis for subsequent design work. Among the elements that may be included are the following requirements:

a) performance characteristics (e.g., environmental and usage conditions and dependability);

b) sensory characteristics (e.g., style, color, taste, smell);

c) installation, arrangement layout or fit;

d) applicable standards and statutory regulations;

e) packaging;

f) quality verification and/or assurance.

7.3 Customer feedback information

The marketing function should establish an information-monitoring and feedback system on a continuous basis. All information pertinent to the customers' use of and satisfaction with the quality of a product should be analyzed, collated, interpreted, verified, and reported in accordance with documented procedures. Such information will help to determine the nature and extent of product problems in relation to customer experience and expectations. In addition, the feedback information can lead to management action resulting in product improvement or to new product offerings (see also 8.8, 8.9, clause 15, and 16.6).

8 QUALITY IN SPECIFICATION AND DESIGN

8.1 Contribution of specification and design to quality

The specification and design function should provide for the translation of customer needs into technical specifications for materials, products, and processes. This should result in a product that provides customer satisfaction at an acceptable price that gives a satisfactory financial return for the organization. The specification and design should be such that the product is producible, verifiable, and controllable under the proposed production, installation, commissioning, or operational conditions.

8.2 Design planning and objectives (defining the project)

8.2.1 Management should prepare plans that define the responsibility for each design and development activity inside and/or outside the organization, and ensure that all those who contribute to design are aware of their responsibilities in relation to the full scope of the project.

8.2.2 In its delegation of responsibilities and authority for quality, management should ensure that design functions provide clear and definitive technical data for procurement, the execution of work, and verification of conformance of products and processes to specification requirements.

8.2.3 Management should establish time-phased design programs with holdpoints appropriate to the nature of the product and process. The extent of each phase, and the position of the holdpoints at which evaluations of the product or the process will take place, can depend upon several elements, such as

— the product's application,

— its design complexity,

— the extent of innovation and technology being introduced, and

— the degree of standardization and similarity with past proven designs.

8.2.4 In addition to customer needs, consideration should be given to the requirements relating to safety, environmental, and other regulations, including items in the organization's quality policy which may go beyond existing statutory requirements (see also 3.3).

8.2.5 The design should unambiguously and adequately define characteristics important to quality, such as the acceptance criteria. Both fitness for purpose and safeguards against misuse should be considered. Product definition can also include dependability and serviceability through a reasonable life expectancy, including benign failure and safe disposability, as appropriate.

8.3 Product testing and measurement

The methods of measurement and test, and the acceptance criteria applied to evaluate the product and processes during both the design and production

phases, should be specified. These should include the following:

a) performance target values, tolerances, and attribute features;

b) acceptance criteria;

c) test and measurement methods, equipment, and computer software (see clause 13).

8.4 Design review

8.4.1 General

At the conclusion of each phase of design development, a formal, documented, systematic, and critical review of the design results should be planned and conducted. This should be distinguished from a project progress meeting. Participants at each design review should include representatives of all functions affecting quality, as appropriate to the phase being reviewed. The design review should identify and anticipate problem areas and inadequacies, and initiate corrective actions to ensure that the final design and supporting data meet customer requirements.

8.4.2 Elements of design reviews

As appropriate to the design phase and product, the elements outlined in a to c should be considered.

a) **Items pertaining to customer needs and satisfaction**

1) comparison of customer needs expressed in the product specification with technical specifications for materials, products, and processes;

2) validation of the design through prototype tests;

3) ability to perform under expected conditions of use and environment;

4) unintended uses and misuses;

5) safety and environmental compatibility;

6) compliance with regulatory requirements, national and International Standards, and organization practices;

7) comparisons with competitive designs;

8) comparison with similar designs, especially analysis of the history of internal and

external problems to avoid repeating problems.

b) **Items pertaining to product specification**

   1) dependability and serviceability requirements;

   2) permissible tolerances and comparison with process capabilities;

   3) product acceptance criteria;

   4) installability, ease of assembly, storage needs, shelf-life, and disposability;

   5) benign failure and fail-safe characteristics;

   6) aesthetic specifications and acceptance criteria;

   7) failure mode and effect analysis, and fault tree analysis;

   8) ability to diagnose and correct problems;

   9) labeling, warnings, identification, traceability requirements, and user instructions;

   10) review and use of standard parts.

c) **Items pertaining to process specification**

   1) ability to produce product conforming to the design, including special process needs, mechanization, automation, assembly, and installation of components;

   2) capability to inspect and test the design, including special inspection and test requirements;

   3) specification of materials, components, and subassemblies, including approved supplies and subcontractors as well as availability;

   4) packaging, handling, storage, and shelf-life requirements, especially safety factors relating to incoming and outgoing items.

8.4.3 Design verification

All designs should be verified to ensure that product specifications are fulfilled (see 7.2). In addition to design review, design verification should include one or more of the following methods:

a) performing alternative calculations, made to verify the correctness of the original calculations and analyses;

b) testing and demonstrations (e.g., by model or prototype tests); if this method is adopted, the test programs should be clearly defined and the results documented;

c) independent verification, to verify the correctness of the original calculations and/or other design activities.

8.5 Design qualification and validation

The design process should provide periodic evaluation of the design at significant stages. Such evaluation can take the form of analytical methods, such as FMEA (failure mode and effect analysis), fault tree analysis, or risk assessment, as well as inspection and test of prototype models and/or actual production samples. The amount and degree of testing (see 8.3) should be related to the identified risks. Independent evaluation can be used, as appropriate, to verify original calculations, provide alternative calculations, or perform tests. A number of samples should be examined by tests and/or inspection to provide adequate statistical confidence in the results. The tests should include the following activities:

a) evaluation of performance, durability, safety, reliability, and maintainability under expected storage and operational conditions;

b) inspections to verify that all design features conform to defined user needs and that all authorized design changes have been accomplished and recorded;

c) validation of computer systems and software.

The results of all tests and evaluations should be documented regularly throughout the qualification test-cycle. Review of test results should include nonconformity and failure analysis.

8.6 Final design review and production release

The final design should be reviewed and the results appropriately documented in specifications and drawings, which then form the design baseline. Where appropriate, this should include a description of initial test units and any modifications made to correct deficiencies identified during the qualification test programmes. The total document package that defines the design baseline (output) should require approval at appropriate levels of management affected by or contributing to the product. This approval constitutes the production release and signifies that the design can be realized.

8.7 Market-readiness review

A determination should be made as to whether the organization has the capability to deliver the new or redesigned product. Depending upon the type of product, the review can cover the following points:

a) availability and adequacy of installation, operation, maintenance, and repair manuals;

b) existence of adequate distribution and customer after-sales service;

c) training of field personnel;

d) availability of spare parts;

e) field trials;

f) satisfactory completion of qualification tests;

g) physical inspection of early production units and their packaging and labeling;

h) evidence of process capability to meet specification on production equipment.

8.8 Design-change control

The quality system should include documented procedures for controlling the release, change, and use of documents that define the design input and the design baseline (output), and for authorizing the necessary work to be performed to implement changes and modifications that can affect product during its entire life-cycle, including changes in software and service instructions. The procedures should provide for various necessary approvals, specified points and times for implementing changes, removing obsolete drawings and specifications from work areas, and verification that changes are made at the appointed times and places. These procedures should handle emergency changes necessary to prevent production or delivery of nonconforming product. Consideration should be given to instituting formal design reviews and validation testing when the magnitude, complexity, or risk associated with the change warrant such actions.

8.9 Design requalification

Periodic evaluation of product should be performed in order to ensure that the design is still valid. This should include a review of customer needs and technical specifications in the light of field experiences, field performance surveys, or new technology and techniques. The evaluation should also consider process modifications. The quality system should ensure that any production and field experience indicating the need for design change is fed back for analysis. Care should be taken that design changes do not cause degradation of product quality for example, and that proposed changes are evaluated for their impact on all product characteristics in the original product specification.

8.10 Configuration management in design

This discipline may be initiated once the requirements have been defined, but is most useful during the design phase. It continues through the whole life-cycle of a product (see 5.2.6).

9 QUALITY IN PURCHASING

9.1 General

Purchases become part of the organization's product and directly affect the quality of its product. All purchasing activities should be planned and controlled by documented procedures. Purchased services such as testing, calibration, and subcontracted processing should also be included. A close working relationship and feedback system should be established with each subcontractor. In this way, continual quality improvements can be maintained and disputes avoided or settled quickly. This close working relationship and feedback system will benefit both parties.

The quality system for purchasing should include the following elements as a minimum:

a) The applicable issue of specifications, drawings, purchase documents and other technical data (see 9.2);

b) selection of qualified subcontractors (see 9.3);

c) agreement on quality assurance (see 9.4);

d) agreement on verification methods (see 9.5);

e) provisions for settlement of disputes (see 9.6);

f) receiving inspection procedures (see 9.7);

g) receiving controls (see 9.7);

h)   receiving quality records (see 9.8).

9.2 Requirements for specifications, drawings, and purchase documents

The successful purchase of supplies begins with a clear definition of the requirements. Usually these requirements are contained in contract specifications, drawings, and purchase documents which are provided to the subcontractor.

The purchasing activity should develop documented procedures to ensure that the requirements for the supplies are clearly defined, communicated, and, most importantly, are completely understood by the subcontractor. These methods may include documented procedures for the preparation of specifications, drawings, and purchase documents, meetings with subcontractors prior to the release of the purchase document, and other activities appropriate for the supplies being procured.

Purchasing documents should contain data clearly describing the product ordered. Typical elements are as follows:

a)   precise identification of type, class, and grade;

b)   inspection instructions and applicable issue of specifications;

c)   quality-system standard to be applied.

Purchasing documents should be reviewed and approved for accuracy and completeness prior to release.

9.3 Selection of acceptable subcontractors

Each subcontractor should have a demonstrated capability to furnish product which meets all the requirements of the specifications, drawings, and purchase documents.

The methods of establishing this capability can include, but are not limited to, any combination of the following:

a)   on-site evaluation of subcontractor's capability and/or quality system;

b)   evaluation of product samples;

c)   past history with similar products;

d)   test results of similar products;

e)   published experience of other users.

9.4 Agreement on quality assurance

The organization should develop a clear agreement with subcontractors for the assurance of product supplied. This can be achieved by one or more of the following:

a)   reliance on subcontractor's quality system;

b)   submission of specified inspection/test data and process-control records with shipments;

c)   100% inspection/testing by the subcontractor;

d)   lot acceptance inspection/testing by sampling by the subcontractor;

e)   implementation of a formal quality system by the subcontractor as specified by the organization; in certain cases, a formal quality-assurance model may be involved (see ANSI/ASQC Q9001-1994, ANSI/ASQC Q9002-1994, and ANSI/ASQC Q9003-1994 for further information);

f)   periodic evaluation of subcontractor quality practices by the organization or by a third party;

g)   in-house receiving inspection or sorting.

9.5 Agreement on verification methods

A clear agreement should be developed with the subcontractor on the methods by which conformance to requirements will be verified. Such agreements may also include the exchange of inspection and test data with the aim of furthering quality improvements. Reaching agreement can minimize difficulties in the interpretation of requirements as well as inspection, test, or sampling methods.

9.6 Provisions for settlement of disputes

Systems and procedures should be established by which settlement of disputes regarding quality can be reached with subcontractors. Provisions should exist for dealing with routine and nonroutine matters.

A very important aspect of these systems and procedures is the provision of improved communication channels between the organization and the subcontractor on matters affecting quality.

9.7 Receiving inspection planning and control

Appropriate measures should be established to ensure that received materials are properly controlled. These procedures should include quarantine areas or other appropriate methods to prevent unintended use or installation of nonconforming materials (see 14.3).

The extent to which receiving inspection will be performed should be carefully planned. The characteristics to be inspected should be based on the cruciality of the product. The capability of the subcontractor should also be considered, taking into account the factors listed in 9.3. The level of inspection should be selected so as to balance the costs of inspection against the consequences of inadequate inspection.

It is also necessary to ensure, before the incoming product arrives, that all the necessary tools, gauges, meters, instruments, and equipment are available and properly calibrated. Personnel should be adequately trained.

9.8 Quality records related to purchasing

Appropriate quality records related to product received should be maintained. This will ensure the availability of historical data to assess subcontractor performance and quality trends.

In addition, it may be useful, and in certain instances essential, to maintain records of lot identification for the purposes of traceability.

10 QUALITY OF PROCESSES

10.1 Planning for process control

10.1.1 Planning of processes should ensure that these proceed under controlled conditions in the specified manner and sequence. Controlled conditions include appropriate controls for materials, approved production, installation, and servicing equipment, documented procedures or quality plans, computer software, reference standards/codes, suitable approval of processes and personnel, as well as associated supplies, utilities, and environments.

The operation of processes should be specified to the necessary extent by documented work instructions.

Process-capability studies should be conducted to determine the potential effectiveness of a process (see 10.2).

Common practices that can be beneficially applied throughout the organization should be documented and referenced in all appropriate procedures and instructions. These should describe the criteria for determining satisfactory work completion and conformity to specification and standards of good workmanship. Workmanship criteria should be stipulated in the clearest practical manner by written standards, photographs, illustrations, and/or representative samples.

10.1.2 Verification of the quality status of a hardware product, process, software, processed material, service, or environment should be considered at important points in the production sequence to minimize effects of errors and to maximize yields. The use of control charts and statistical sampling procedures and plans are examples of techniques employed to facilitate process control (see also 12.2).

10.1.3 Monitoring and control of processes should relate directly to finished product specifications or to an internal requirement, as appropriate. If verification of the process variables through some measurement procedure is not physically or economically practical or feasible, then verification will have to depend primarily on verification of final product characteristics. In all cases, relationships between in-process controls, their specifications, and final product specifications should be developed, communicated to the personnel concerned, and then documented.

10.1.4 All in-process and final verifications should be planned and specified. Documented test and inspection procedures should be maintained for each quality characteristic to be checked. These should include the specific equipment to perform such checks and tests, and the specified requirements and workmanship criteria.

10.1.5 The appropriate methods of cleaning and preserving, and the details of packing, including moisture elimination, cushioning, blocking, and crating, should be established and maintained in documented procedures.

10.1.6 Efforts to develop new methods for improving process quality should be encouraged.

10.2 Process capability

Processes should be verified as being capable of producing product in accordance with specifications. Operations associated with product or process characteristics that can have a significant effect on product quality should be identified. Appropriate control should be established to ensure that these characteristics remain within the specification, or that appropriate modifications or changes are made.

Verification of processes should include material, equipment, computer system and software, procedures, and personnel.

10.3 Supplies, utilities and environment

Where important to product quality characteristics, auxiliary materials and utilities, such as water, compressed air, electrical power, and chemicals used for processing, should be controlled and verified periodically to ensure uniformity of effect on the process. Where environmental conditions, such as temperature, humidity and cleanliness, are important to product quality, appropriate limits should be specified, controlled, and verified.

10.4 Handling

The handling of product requires proper planning, control, and a documented system for incoming, in-process, and final product; this applies not only during delivery but up to the time of being put into use.

The methods of handling of product should provide for the correct selection and use of suitable pallets, containers, conveyors, and vehicles to prevent damage or deterioration due to vibration, shock abrasion, corrosion, temperature, or any other conditions occurring during the production or delivery processes.

11 CONTROL OF PROCESSES

11.1 General

Product quality should be addressed in each phase of the life-cycle (see 5.1.1).

11.2 Material control, traceability, and identification

11.2.1 Material control

All materials and parts should conform to specified requirements before being introduced into a process. However, in determining the amount and nature of receiving inspection necessary, consideration should be given to cost impact and the effect that substandard material quality will have on production flow.

In-process product, including that in in-process inventory stockrooms, should be appropriately stored, segregated, handled, and preserved to maintain its suitability. Special consideration should be given to shelf-life and deterioration control, including assessment of product in stock at appropriate intervals. (For final product storage, see 16.1.)

11.2.2 Traceability

Where traceability of product is important, appropriate identification should be maintained throughout the process, from receipt and during all stages of production, delivery, and installation, to ensure traceability to original material identification and verification status (see 11.7 and 14.2).

11.2.3 Identification

The marking and labeling of materials should be legible, durable and in accordance with specifications. Materials should be uniquely identified from the time of initial receipt, to delivery and installation at the final destination. The identification should be in accordance with documented procedures, and should be recorded. This should enable a particular product to be identified in the event that a recall or special inspection becomes necessary.

11.3 Equipment control and maintenance

All equipment, including fixed machinery, jigs, fixtures, tooling, templates, patterns, and gauges, should be proved for accuracy prior to use. Special attention should be paid to computers used in controlling processes, and especially the maintenance of the related software (see 13.1).

Equipment should be appropriately stored and adequately protected between use, and verified or recalibrated at appropriate intervals to ensure that the requirements concerning accuracy (trueness and precision) are fulfilled.

A program of preventive maintenance should be established to ensure continued process capability. Special attention should be given to equipment characteristics that contribute to product quality.

11.4 Process-control management

Processes which are important to product quality should be planned, approved, monitored, and controlled. Particular consideration should be given to product characteristics which cannot be easily or economically measured, and those requiring special skills.

Process variables should be monitored, controlled, and verified at appropriate frequencies to assure:

a) the accuracy and variability of equipment used;

b) the skill, capability, and knowledge of operators;

c) the accuracy of measurement results and data used to control the process;

d) process environment and other factors affecting quality, such as time, temperature, and pressure;

e) appropriate documentation of process variables, equipment, and personnel.

In some cases, for example where process deficiencies may become apparent only after the product is in use, the results of processes cannot be directly verified by subsequent inspection or test of the product itself. Such processes require prequalification (validation) to ensure process capability and control of all critical variables during process operation.

11.5 Documentation

Documentation should be controlled as specified by the quality system (see 5.3 and 17.3).

11.6 Process-change control

Those responsible for authorization of process changes should be clearly designated and, where necessary, customer approval should be sought. As with design changes, all changes to production tooling or equipment, materials, or processes should be documented. The implementation should be covered by defined procedures.

A product should be evaluated after any change to verify that the change instituted had the desired effect upon product quality. Any changes in the relationship between process and product characteristics resulting from the change should be documented and appropriately communicated.

11.7 Control of verification status

Verification status of product output should be identified. Such identification should be suitable means, such as stamps, tags, notations, or inspection records that accompany the product, or by computer entries or physical location. The identification should distinguish among unverified, conforming, or nonconforming product. It should also identify the organizational unit responsible for verification.

11.8 Control of nonconforming product

Provision should be made for the identification and control of all nonconforming products and materials (see clause 14).

12 PRODUCT VERIFICATION

12.1 Incoming materials and parts

The method used to ensure quality of purchased materials, component parts and assemblies that are received into the production facility will depend on the importance of the item to quality, the state of control and information available from the subcontractor, and impact on costs (see clause 9, in particular 9.7 and 9.8).

12.2 In-process verification

Verification, typically by inspections or tests, should be considered at appropriate points in the process to verify conformity. Location and frequency will depend on the importance of the characteristics and ease of verification during processing. In general, verification should be made as close as possible to the point of realization of the characteristic.

Verifications for hardware products may include the following:

a) set-up and first-piece inspection;

b) inspections or tests by machine operator;

c) automatic inspection or test;

d) fixed inspection stations at intervals throughout the process;

e) monitoring specific operations by patrolling inspectors.

Product should not be released for further use until it has been verified in accordance with the quality plan, except under positive recall procedures.

12.3 Finished product verification

To augment inspections and tests made during processing, two forms of verification of finished product are available. Either or both of the following may be used, as appropriate.

a) Acceptance inspections or tests may be used to ensure that finished product conforms to the specified requirements. Reference may be made to the purchase order to verify that the product to be shipped agrees in type and quantity. Examples include 100% inspection of items, lot sampling, and continuous sampling.

b) Product-quality auditing of sample units selected as representative of completed lots may be either continuous or periodic.

Acceptance inspection and product-quality auditing may be used to provide rapid feedback for corrective action of product, process, or the quality system. Nonconforming product should be reported and reviewed, removed, or segregated, and repaired, accepted with or without concession, reworked, regraded, or scrapped (see clause 14). Repaired and/or reworked products should be reinspected or retested.

No product should be dispatched until all the activities specified in the quality plan or documented procedures have been satisfactorily completed and the associated data and documentation are available and authorized.

13 CONTROL OF INSPECTION, MEASURING, AND TEST EQUIPMENT

13.1 Measurement control

Control should be maintained over all measuring systems used in the development, production, installation, and servicing of product to provide confidence in decisions or actions based on measurement data. Control should be exercised over gauges, instruments, sensors, special test equipment, and related test software. In addition, manufacturing jigs, fixtures such as test hardware, comparative references, and process instrumentation that can affect the specified characteristics of a product or process should be suitably controlled (see 11.3).

Documented procedures should be established to monitor and maintain the measurement process itself in a state of statistical control, including equipment, procedures, and operator skills. Inspection, measuring, and test equipment, including test software, should be used in conjunction with documented procedures to ensure that measurement uncertainty is known and is consistent with the required measurement capability. Appropriate action should be taken when accuracy is not adequate to measure properly the process and product.

13.2 Elements of control

The procedures for control of inspection, measuring, and test equipment and test methods should include, as appropriate:

a) suitable specification and selection, including range, accuracy, and robustness, under specified environmental conditions;

b) initial calibration prior to first use in order to validate the required accuracy (accuracy and precision); the software and procedures controlling automatic test equipment should also be tested;

c) periodic recall for adjustment, repair, and recalibration, considering the manufacturer's specification, the results of prior calibration, and the method and extent of use, to maintain the required accuracy in use;

d) documentary evidence covering unique identification of instruments, frequency of recalibration, calibration status, and procedures for recall, handling, preservation, and storage, adjustment, repair, calibration, installation, and use;

e) traceability to reference standards of known accuracy and stability, preferably to nationally or internationally recognized standards; where such standards do not exist, the basis used for calibration should be documented.

13.3 Subcontractor measurement controls

The control of measuring and test equipment and test methods may be extended to all subcontractors.

13.4 Corrective action

Where measuring processes are found to be out of control, or where inspection, measuring, and test equipment are found to be out of calibration, appropriate action is necessary. Evaluation should be made to determine the effects on completed work and to what extent reprocessing, retesting, recalibration, or complete rejection may be necessary. In addition, investigation of cause is important in order to avoid recurrence. This can include review of calibration methods and frequency, training, and adequacy of test equipment.

13.5 Outside testing

The facilities of outside organizations may be used for inspection, measurement, testing, or calibration to avoid costly duplication or additional investment, provided that the conditions given in 13.2 and 13.4 are satisfied. (For further information, see ISO 10012-1.)

14 CONTROL OF NONCONFORMING PRODUCT

14.1 General

The steps for dealing with nonconforming product should be established and maintained in documented procedures. The objectives of procedures for nonconformity control are to prevent the customer from inadvertently receiving nonconforming product and to avoid the unnecessary costs of further processing nonconforming product. The steps outlined in 14.2 to 14.7 should be taken as soon as indications occur that materials, components, or completed product do not, or may not, conform to the specified requirements.

14.2 Identification

Suspected nonconforming items or lots should be immediately identified and the occurrence(s) recorded.

Provision should be made as necessary to examine or reexamine previous lots.

14.3 Segregation

The nonconforming items should be segregated, when practical, from the conforming items and adequately identified to prevent further unintended use of them until the appropriate disposition is decided.

14.4 Review

Nonconforming product should be subjected to review by designated persons to determine whether it can be accepted with or without repair by concession, repaired, reworked, regraded, or scrapped. Persons carrying out the review should be competent to evaluate the effects of the decision on interchangeability, further processing, performance, dependability, safety, and aesthetics (see 9.7 and 11.8).

14.5 Disposition

Disposition of nonconforming product should be taken as soon as practicable. A decision to accept such product should be documented, together with the reason for doing so, in authorized waivers, with appropriate precautions.

14.6 Action

Action should be taken as soon as possible to prevent unintended use or installation of nonconforming product. This action can include review of other product designed or processed following the same procedures as the product found to be nonconforming, and/or previous lots of the same product.

For work in progress, corrective action should be instituted as soon as practical in order to limit the costs of repair, reworking, or scrapping. Repaired, reworked, and/or modified product should be reinspected or retested to verify conformance with specified requirements.

In addition, it may be necessary to recall completed product, whether in a finished product warehouse, in transit to distributors, in their stores, or already in use (see 11.2). Recall decisions are affected by considerations of safety, product liability, and customer satisfaction.

14.7 Avoidance of recurrence

Appropriate steps should be taken to avoid the recurrence of nonconformity (see 15.5 and 15.6).

15 CORRECTIVE ACTION

15.1 General

The implementation of corrective action begins with the detection of a quality-related problem and involves taking measures to eliminate or minimize the recurrence of the problem. Corrective action also presupposes the repair, reworking, recall, or scrapping of unsatisfactory product. The need for action to eliminate the cause of nonconformities can originate from sources such as:

a) audits (internal and/or external);

b) process-nonconformity reports;

c) management reviews;

d) market feedback;

e)   customer complaints.

Specific actions to eliminate the causes of either an existing nonconformity or a potential nonconformity are given in steps 15.2 to 15.8.

15.2 Assignment of responsibility

The responsibility and authority for instituting corrective action should be defined as part of the quality system. The coordination, recording, and monitoring of corrective action related to all aspects of the quality system should be assigned within the organization. The analysis and implementation may involve a variety of functions, such as design, purchasing, engineering, processing, and quality control.

15.3 Evaluation of importance

The significance of a problem affecting quality should be evaluated in terms of its potential impact on such aspects as processing costs, quality-related costs, performance, dependability, safety, and customer satisfaction.

15.4 Investigation of possible causes

Important variables affecting the capability of the process to meet specified requirements should be identified. The relationship of cause and effect should be determined, with all potential causes considered. The results of the investigation should be recorded.

15.5 Analysis of problem

In the analysis of a quality-related problem, the root cause or causes should be determined before corrective action is planned. Often the root cause is not obvious, thus requiring careful analysis of the product specifications and of all related processes, operations, quality records, servicing reports, and customer complaints. Statistical methods can be useful in problem analysis (see clause 20).

Consideration should be given to establishing a file listing nonconformities to help identify those problems having a common source, contrasted with those that are unique occurrences.

15.6 Elimination of causes

Appropriate steps should be taken to eliminate causes of actual or potential nonconformities. Identification of the cause or potential causes may result in changes to production, packing, service, transit or storage

processes, a product specification, and/or revision of the quality system. Action should be initiated to a degree appropriate to the magnitude of the problem and to avoid the recurrence of nonconformities.

15.7 Process controls

Sufficient controls of processes and procedures should be implemented to avoid recurrence of the problem. When the corrective action is implemented, its effect should be monitored in order to ensure that desired goals are met.

15.8 Permanent changes

Permanent changes resulting from corrective action should be recorded in work instructions, production-process documentation, product specifications, and/or the quality-system documentation. It may also be necessary to revise the procedures used to detect and eliminate potential problems.

16 POSTPRODUCTION ACTIVITIES

16.1 Storage

Appropriate storage methods should be specified to ensure shelf-life and to avoid deterioration. Storage conditions and the condition of product in stock should be checked at appropriate intervals for compliance with specified requirements and to detect any loss, damage, or deterioration of product (see also 10.1.5 and 10.4).

16.2 Delivery

Provision for protection of the quality of product is important during all phases of delivery. All product, in particular product with limited shelf-life or requiring special protection during transport or storage, should be identified and procedures established, documented, and maintained to ensure that deteriorated product is not shipped and put into use.

16.3 Installation

Installation procedures, including warning notices, should contribute to proper installations and should be documented. They should include provisions which preclude improper installation or factors degrading the quality, reliability, safety, and performance of any product or material.

16.4 Servicing

16.4.1 Special-purpose tools or equipment for

handling and servicing products during or after installation should have their design and function validated, as for any new product (see 8.5).

16.4.2 Inspection, measuring, and test equipment used in the field should be controlled (see clause 13).

16.4.3 Documented procedures and associated instructions for field assembly and installation, commissioning, operation, administration of spares or parts lists, and servicing of any product should be comprehensive and be established and supplied in a timely manner. The suitability of instructions for the intended reader should be verified.

16.4.4 Adequate logistic back-up, to include technical advice, spares or parts supply, and competent servicing, should be assured. Responsibility should be clearly assigned and agreed among subcontractors, distributors, and customers.

16.5 After sales

Consideration should be given to the establishment of an early warning system for reporting instances of product failure of shortcomings, to ensure rapid corrective action.

Information on complaints, the occurrence and modes of failure, or any problem encountered in use should be made available for review and corrective action in the design, processing, and/or use of the product.

16.6 Market feedback

A feedback system regarding performance in use should exist to monitor the quality characteristics of products throughout the life-cycle. This system can permit the analysis, on a continuing basis, of the degree to which the product satisfies customer requirements or expectations on quality, including safety and dependability.

17 QUALITY RECORDS

17.1 General

The organization should establish and maintain documented procedures as a means for identification, collection, indexing, access, filing, storage, maintenance, retrieval, and disposition of pertinent quality records. Policies should be established concerning availability and access of records to customers and subcontractors. Policies concerning documented

procedures should also be established for changes and modifications in various types of documents.

17.2 Quality records

The quality system should require that sufficient records be maintained to demonstrate conformance to specified requirements and verify effective operation of the quality system. Analysis of quality records provides an important input for corrective action and improvement. The following are examples of the types of quality records, including charts, requiring control:

— inspection reports,

— test data,

— qualification reports,

— validation reports,

— survey and audit reports,

— material review reports,

— calibration data, and

— quality-related cost reports.

Quality records should be retained for a specified time, in such a manner as to be readily retrievable for analysis, in order to identify trends in quality measures and the need for, and the effectiveness of, corrective action.

While in storage, quality records should be protected in suitable facilities from damage, loss and deterioration (e.g., due to environmental conditions).

17.3 Quality-records control

The quality system should require that sufficient documentation be available to follow and demonstrate conformance to specified requirements and the effective operation of the quality system. Pertinent subcontractor documentation should be included. All documentation should be legible, dated (including revision dates), clean, readily identifiable, retrievable, and maintained in facilities that provide a suitable environment to minimize deterioration or damage and to prevent loss. Records may be in the form of any type of media such as hard copy, electronic media, etc.

In addition, the quality system should provide a method for defining retention times, removing and/

or disposing of documentation when that documentation has become outdated.

The following are examples of the types of documents requiring control:

— drawings,

— specifications,

— inspection procedures and instructions,

— test procedures,

— work instructions,

— operation sheets,

— quality manual (see 5.3.2),

— quality plans,

— operational procedures, and

— quality-system procedures.

18 PERSONNEL

18.1 Training

18.1.1 General

The need for training of personnel should be identified, and documented procedures for providing that training should be established and maintained. Appropriate training should be provided to all levels of personnel within the organization performing activities affecting quality. Particular attention should be given to the qualifications, selection, and training of newly recruited personnel and personnel transferred to new assignments. Appropriate records of training should be maintained.

18.1.2 Executive and management personnel

Training should be given which will provide executive management with an understanding of the quality system, together with the tools and techniques needed for full executive management participation in the operation of the system. Executive management should also be aware of the criteria available to evaluate the effectiveness of the system.

18.1.3 Technical personnel

Training should be given to the technical personnel to enhance their contribution to the success of the quality system. Training should not be restricted to personnel with primary quality assignments, but

should include assignments such as marketing, purchasing, and process and product engineering. Particular attention should be given to training in statistical techniques, such as those listed in 20.2.

18.1.4 Process supervisors and operating personnel

All process supervisors and operating personnel should be trained in the procedures and skills required to perform their tasks, i.e.

— the proper operation of instruments, tools and machinery they have to use,

— reading and understanding the documentation provided,

— the relationship of their duties to quality, and

— safety in the workplace.

As appropriate, personnel should be certified in their skills, such as welding. Training in basic statistical techniques should also be considered.

18.2 Qualification

The need to require and document qualifications of personnel performing certain specialized operations, processes, tests, or inspections should be evaluated and implemented where necessary, in particular for safety-related work. The need to assess periodically and/or require demonstrations of skills and/or capability should be addressed. Considerations should also be given to appropriate education, training, and experience.

18.3 Motivation

18.3.1 General

Motivation of personnel begins with their understanding of the tasks they are expected to perform and how those tasks support the overall activities. Personnel should be made aware of the advantages of proper job performance at all levels, and of the effects of poor job performance on other people, customer satisfaction, operating costs, and the economic well-being of the organization.

18.3.2 Applicability

Efforts to encourage personnel toward quality of performance should be directed not only at production workers, but also at personnel in marketing, design, documentation, purchasing, inspection, test, packing and shipping, and servicing. Management, professional, and staff personnel should be included.

18.3.3 Quality awareness

The need for quality should be emphasized through an awareness program which can include introduction and elementary programs for new personnel, periodic refresher programs for long-standing personnel, provision for personnel to initiate preventive and corrective actions, and other procedures.

18.3.4 Measuring quality

Where appropriate, objective and accurate means of measuring quality achievements should be developed. These may be publicized to let personnel see for themselves what they, as a group or as individuals, are achieving. This can encourage them to improve quality. Recognition of performance should be provided.

19 PRODUCT SAFETY

Consideration should be given to identifying safety aspects of products and processes with the aim of enhancing safety. Steps can include:

a) identifying relevant safety standards in order to make the formulation of product specifications more effective;

b) carrying out design evaluation tests and prototype (or model) testing for safety and documenting the test results;

c) analyzing instructions and warnings to the user, maintenance manuals, and labeling and promotional material in order to minimize misinterpretation, particularly regarding intended use and known hazards;

d) developing a means of traceability to facilitate product recall (see 11.2, 14.2 and 14.6);

e) considering development of an emergency plan in case recall of a product becomes necessary.

20 USE OF STATISTICAL METHODS

20.1 Applications

Identification and correct application of modern statistical methods are important elements to control every phase of the organization's processes. Documented procedures should be established and maintained for selecting and applying statistical methods to:

a) market analysis;

b) product design;

c) dependability specification, longevity, and durability prediction;

d) process-control and process-capability studies;

e) determination of quality levels in sampling plans;

f) data analysis, performance assessment, and nonconformity analysis;

g) process improvement;

h) safety evaluation and risk analysis.

20.2 Statistical techniques

Specific statistical methods for establishing, controlling, and verifying activities include, but are not limited to, the following:

a) design of experiments and factorial analysis;

b) analysis of variance and regression analysis;

c) tests of significance;

d) quality-control charts and cusum techniques;

e) statistical sampling.

NOTE 21 Guidance on the International Standards to be used for the statistical techniques that are identified may be found in ISO/TR 13425 and ISO Handbook 3. For guidance on dependability applications, reference should be made to ISO 9000-4 and to IEC publications.

ANNEX A (INFORMATIVE)

Bibliography

[1] ANSI/ASQC Q9000-1-1994, *Quality Management and Quality Assurance Standards—Guidelines for Selection and Use.*

[2] ANSI/ASQC Q9001-1994, *Quality Systems—Model for Quality Assurance in Design, Development, Production, Installation, and Servicing.*

[3] ANSI/ASQC Q9002-1994, *Quality Systems—Model for Quality Assurance in Production, Installation, and Servicing.*

[4] ANSI/ASQC Q9003-1994, *Quality Systems—Model for Quality Assurance in Final Inspection and Test.*

[5] ANSI/ASQC Q10011-1-1994, *Guidelines for Auditing Quality Systems—Auditing.*

[6] ANSI/ASQC Q10011-2-1994, *Guidelines for Auditing Quality Systems—Qualification Criteria for Quality Systems Auditors.*

[7] ANSI/ASQC Q10011-3-1994, *Guidelines for Auditing Quality Systems—Management of Audit Programs.*

[8] ISO 9000-2:1993, *Quality management and quality assurance standards—Part 2: Generic guidelines for the application of ISO 9001, ISO 9002 and ISO 9003.*

[9] ISO 9000-3:1991, *Quality management and quality assurance standards—Part 3: Guidelines for the application of ISO 9001 to the development, supply and maintenance of software.*

[10] ISO 9000-4:1993, *Quality management and quality assurance standards—Part 4: Guide to dependability programme management.*

[11] ISO 9004-2:1991, *Quality management and quality system elements—Part 2: Guidelines for services.*

[12] ISO 9004-3:1993, *Quality management and quality system elements—Part 3: Guidelines for processed materials.*

[13] ISO 9004-4:1993, *Quality management and quality system elements—Part 4: Guidelines for quality improvement.*

[14] ISO 10012-1:1992, *Quality assurance requirements for measuring equipment—Part 1: Metrological confirmation system for measuring equipment.*

[15] ISO 10013:—2), *Guidelines for developing quality manuals.*

[16] ISO Handbook 3:1989, *Statistical methods.*

ENDNOTES:

1 The recommended harmonized term is "customer" as shown in Table 1 of ANSI/ASQC Q9004-1-1994. The term "purchaser" was used in ANSI/ASQC Q91-1987, ANSI/ASQC Q92-1987, and ANSI/ASQC Q93-1987.

2 To be published.

INDEX

A

Accreditation 6, 315, 442, 490
   Auditor Certification 396-399
   in Canada 387
   in Europe 382-383
   in the United States 384-387
   International Acceptance of Certificates
      420-421
   Mutual Recognition 375-376
   of Registrars 133, 382-387
   RAB Registrar Criteria 384
   Recognition of Registration Certificates 391-
      396
   Registrar Criteria 388
Accreditation Body 133, 404
   in Europe 382
   in Japan 426
Achieving customer satisfaction by preventing
   nonconformance 41
Acronyms 522
AIAG 474, 477
Amendment to contract 54
American Iron and Steel Institute 485
American National Standards Institute (See ANSI)
American Petroleum Institute 378
American Society for Quality Control (See ASQC)
Annex IV Machinery 332
ANSI 339
ANSI/ASQC Q9000 series 3
Arter, Dennis 503
Asian Countries
   ISO 9000 Developments in 425-427
ASQC 266, 339, 384

ASQC Code of Ethics 418
Assessment 138, 143
Association of British Certification Bodies (ABCB)
   143
Audit 150, 286 (See also Internal Audit)
   Appoint Escorts for the Audit Team 200
   Auditee Stress 164
   Auditor Facilities 200
   Body Language 166
   Checklist 155, 156
   Communication Skills 164-168
   Conflicts/Difficult Situations 166-167
   Cooperation 201
   Corrective Action 201
   Ethics 167, 168
   Inform Employees 199
   Interview Questions 199
   Interview Techniques 165
   Introductory and Closing Meeting 143
   Listening Skills 165
   Objectivity 167
   Process 197
   Questions 157
   Scope 189
Audit Report 161
Auditing 36
Auditor
   Certification Programs 396-399
   Qualifications 139
Australian Standard
   Software Quality Management System 271
Authoritative body 133
Auto Industry 474-483
   Case Study 483

Future Developments 479
ISO 9000 Requirements 478
Joint Quality Initiatives 474-476
Resistance to Change 474
Automotive Industry Action Group (See AIAG)
AW Chesterton 204

B

Baldrige (See MBNQA)
Barriers to Trade 359, 4, 11, 359, 366
Belfit, Bob 448, 501
Benchmarking 347, 350, 352
Benefits of Registration 183
Betz Laboratories, Inc. 463
Big Three (See Auto Industry)
Bowen, Robert 504
British Computer Society 265
BS 7750 337-338

C

Cachat, John 504
Calibration 453, 456-457
    Problems 192-194
CAN-P-10 387, 425
Canada
    ISO 9000 Developments in 425
Canadian Manufacturer's Association (CMA) 424
Canadian Standards Association (CSA) 422
Capability evaluation 270
CASCO 392, 404, 420
CASE 386, 431
Case Studies
    Auto Industry 474-483
    Chemical Industry 463-469
    Computer Industry 470-473
    Small Companies 495, 497
    Steel Industry 484-488
    Surveillance Audits 204-205
    TickIT 273-275
Casis de Dijon 4, 360
Caveat emptor 329
CE Mark 364
CE Mark Directive 365

Center for Devices and Radiological Health
    (CDRH) 433
Central Secretariat 407
Certification 6, 390 (See also Registration)
Certification and Testing Bodies (See Conformity
    Assessment)
Certified bodies 133
Certified Quality Auditor (CQA) 399
Checklist 258 (See also Registration)
Chemical Industry 340, 448-469
    Case Study 463-469
    Contract Review 449, 453
    Customer-Supplied Product 454
    Design Control 449, 453
    Document and Data Control 449, 454
    Handling, Packaging and Delivering Chemicals
        450, 458
    Inspection and Testing 450, 456-457
    Inspection, Measuring and Test Equipment 456
    Nonconformances and Corrective Action 450
    Nonconforming Product 457
    Process Control 449, 455
    Product Identification and Traceability 455
    Purchasing 449, 454
    Quality Plans 452
    Servicing 458
    Statistical Techniques 458
    Supplier Questionnaire 451
    Training 458
Chemical Manufacturers Association (CMA)
    340, 451
Chiaramonte, Joseph 504
China 427
Chove, Jacques 302, 504
Chrysler 474, 475
Chrysler, Ford, General Motors Quality System
    Stand 475
Clause 4, Quality System Requirements 42
Close out 163
CMA Criteria for Continuous Improvement 451
Code of Conduct 407, 416-417
Code of Ethics 418
Comité Ténico Nacional de Normalización de
    Sistemas 420

Committee for European Electrotechnical Standard-
    ization (CENELEC) 367, 368, 369
Committee for European Standardization (CEN)
    367, 368
Committee of Permanent Representatives 5
Company policy 171
Competent authority 363
Computer Industry 470-473
    Case Study 470-473
Conditional approval 144
Configuration Management 28, 300
Conflict of Interest 387, 391, 407, 414-415,
    416, 442
Conformance Standards 21, 33
Conformite Europeene 364
Conformity Assessment 5, 8
    ANSI Activities 379
    Certification and Testing Bodies 7
    Certification and Testing bodies 374
    Consistent Procedures 369, 374
    Definition 358
    Degree of Complexity 373
    Major Components 359, 374
    Modular Approach (See Modular Approach)
    Procedures 6
    Quality Systems Registration 7
    US and EC 376
    versus Industry Standards 377
Conformity Assessment Systems Evaluation (See
    CASE)
Consultant 185, 442
    Qualifications 186, 188
    References 186
Consulting versus Registration 134, 136
Continuous Improvement 183, 191, 342
Continuous manufacture 455
Continuous quality improvement 25, 29
Contract 141
Contract Review 53, 196, 288
Contractor 18
Contractual situation 17, 25
Contractual versus Noncontractual 311
Controlled Documents (See Document and Data
    Control)

Cooney, Raymond 504
Corrective Action 31, 162, 196, 144, 184,
    201, 202
Corrective action loop 197
Corrective action requests (CARs) 159
Corrective and Preventive Action 286
Cost of Registration (see ISO 9000)
Costs (See Registration)
Council Committee on Conformity Assessment
    (See CASCO)
Council of Ministers 5, 360
Countries of the EC 4
Cox, William 505
Credibility (See Registration)
Crosby, Philip 13, 182
Customer 18
Customer-supplied product 289

D

Data Control (See Document and Data Control)
Daughtrey, Taz 259, 502
de Arriortua, Jose Ignacio Lopez 475
DeCarlo, Joseph 504
Defective Product 327
Deficiency 158
Definition of Terms 17
Definitions 17-21 (See Vocabulary)
Degree of prescriptiveness 353
Deibler, William 505
Deming, W. E. 346, 425
Deming's 14 points 347
Department of Commerce (DOC) 386, 430
Department of Defense (DoD) 340, 432
Department of Education (DOEd) 432
Department of Energy (DOE) 340, 432
Department of Health and Human Services (DHHS)
    433
Department of Industry, Science and Technology
    424
Department of Interior (DOI) 434
Department of Labor (DOL) 434
Department of National Defense 424
Department of State 435
Department of Trade and Industry (DTI) 264

Dependability program management 35
Descriptive requirements 22
Design 29, 179
Design and Development Planning 56
Design Changes 59
Design Control 288
Design Input 57
Design Output 57
Design Process 174
Design Review 58
Design Validation 59
Design Verification 58
Developing Countries 420
Development Committee (DEVCO) 420
Directives 5, 329, 359-360, 366
    Machinery Safety 332
    Product Liability 329-330
    Product Safety 330-331
    Proposed Services Liability 332
Discrepancy 158
Distribution 220
Document and Data Approval and Issue 66
Document and Data Change 67
Document Control 288
    Problems 191-192
Document Review 142
Documentation 24, 28, 172, 182, 188, 227,
    228, 286, 296, 333, 352, 442, 446, 453
    as a Paper Trail 326
    Benefits 210
    Implementation 216
    Levels 215, 216
    Quality Manual 216
    Records 216
    Review 217
    What to Document 210
    Work Instructions 216
Documenting Personnel Qualifications 123
Drayton, Kevin 504
Dual registration 423
Durand, Ian 277, 292, 500
Dutch Council for Certification (RvC) 382
Duty of care 322
Dyczkowsky, Bohdan 499

E

E4 339, 340
E4, Quality Systems Requirements for Environ-
    mental (See E4)
EC 92 4, 304, 361
EC Commission 4, 342, 366
EC Council 369
Eco Audit 339
Eco-labeling 342
Eco-Verifier 339
Eggebrecht, Kirk 504
Ehlers, Norman 475
Electronic Control of Documents 116
Electronic versus Hard Copy 232
Empowerment 172, 184, 188, 224, 229, 448
EN 29001 265
EN 45000 series 7, 315, 364, 374, 376, 387,
    389, 391
EN 45012 133, 388, 400, 402, 425
Environment
    Need/Benefits of One Standard 337
    Policital Awareness 336
    Reasons for an EMS 336
    Various EMS Initiatives 337
Environmental Commission 339
Environmental Management Systems (EMS) (See
    Environment)
Environmental Protection Agency (EPA) 340
Epstein, Dan 503
Epstein, Ira 504
EU 357-380
    EU Countries 4
    EU Regulatory Hierarchy 5
    EU Regulatory Process 5
European Accreditation of Certification (EAC)
    135, 143, 390, 395
European Commission 5, 396
European Committee for Information Technology
    Testing and Certification (ECITC) 396
European Committee for Quality System Assess-
    ment 394
European Community (see EC)
European Council 5

European Court of Justice 5
European Free Trade Association (EFTA)
    362, 367
European Network for Quality System Assessment
    388, 394
European Organization for Technical Approvals
    (EOTA) 367
European Organization for Testing and Certification
    7, 374, 379, 395-396
European Parliament 5
European Telecommunications Standardization
    Institu 369
European Telecommunications Standards Institute
    (ETSI) 367, 369
European Union (See EU)
Evaluation of Subcontractors 73

F

Federal Agencies (See Government Agencies)
Federal Trade Commission (FTC) 435
Ferguson, Bill 452
Ferguson, William 502
Final Inspection and Testing 93
Financial Considerations 29
Finlay, Joel 501
Finley, Foster 503
Five Quality Failures 191
Flow chart 186, 224
Follow-up 162
Ford 474, 475
Ford of Europe 483
Fundamental Statistical Process Control 475

G

Gap analysis 188
Gaudry, Serge 505
General Motors 474, 475
General Services Administration (GSA) 435
Generic Product Categories 306-307, 309,
    310-311, 312-314, 406
Global Competition 303, 312
Good Manufacturing Practice (GMP) 433
Goult, Rod 169, 219, 229, 502

Gousie, Stephen 505
Government Agencies 3, 8, 329, 340, 377, 436
Guidance Standards 21
Guide 40 48, 133, 388, 404
Guides 2-56 393

H

Hammil, Robert 504
Hardware 18, 306
Harmonized Standards 5, 359, 366-369
Harral, William 502
Heaps, Terry 505
Hedman, Stephen 505
Hierarchy 220
Highlands, James 504
Hinds, John 13
Hold point 203
Hong Kong Quality Assurance 427
Hooper, J.H. 407

I

Identification (See Product Identification and
    Traceability)
IEEE Software Engineering Standards 268
In-Process Inspection and Testing 92
Independent Association of Accredited Registrars
    (IAAR) 386-387
Industry Standards 377
Information technology 264, 397
Information Technology Sector (ITQS) 265, 397
Inspection and test records 93
Inspection and test status 288
Inspection, Measuring and Test Equipment 31,
    289
Institute for Quality Assurance (IQA) 398
Institute of Certification of Information Technology
    265
Instituto Colombiano de Normas Técnicas
    (ICONTEC) 420
Instituto Nacional de Normalización (INN) 420
Internal Audit
    Audit Report 161
    Auditing the Internal Audit System 163

Closing Meeting 159
Collecting Information 156
Corrective Action 162-163
Information Sources 155
Introductory Meeting 156
Nonconformities 158
Objective and Scope 154
Planning 155
Selecting the Team 154
Verifying Observations 158
Internal audit system 151
Internal auditing 28, 286
Internal Quality Audit 150
International Accreditation Forum (IAF)
    135, 392, 394
International Electrotechnical Commission (IEC)
    3, 367, 426
International Organization for Standardization (See
    ISO)
ISO 3, 292, 367
ISO 9000 Series (See also Registration)
    as a National Standard 3
    Asking the Right Questions 176
    Barriers 190
    Benefits 10, 183
    Choosing a Standard 178, 181, 405
    Compared to MBNQA 347
    Compared to TQM 350
    Concerns about registration 11-13
    Generic Standard 2
    Goals 308
    in Canada 425
    in Mexico 420, 421
    in South America 420
    in the Pacific Rim 425, 427
    Inadequacies 305
    Overview 346
    Preparing for Registration 183, 190
    Problems/Failures 191
    Reasons to Register 11, 133-134
    Recommendations 314
    Revisions Time Line 313

ISO 9000
    ISO 9000-1 22, 25, 281, 294
    ISO 9000-2 35
    ISO 9000-3 35, 261, 265
    ISO 9000-4 35
ISO 9001 33
    4.1 Management Responsibility 42
    4.2 Quality System 49
    4.3 Contract Review 53
    4.4 Design Control 55
    4.5 Document and Data Control 65
    4.6 Purchasing 73
    4.7 Control of Customer-Supplied Product 80
    4.8 Product Identification and Traceability 81
    4.9 Process Control 82
    4.10 Inspection and Testing 90
    4.11 Control of Inspection, Measuring and Test
        Equipment 97
    4.12 Inspection and Test Status 104
    4.13 Control of Nonconforming Product 105
    4.14 Corrective and Preventive Action 107
    4.15 Handling, Storage, Packaging, Preserva-
        tion 110
    4.16 Control of Quality Records 114
    4.17 Internal Quality Audits 117
    4.18 Training 121
    Key Points 41
    Standard 39
    versus 9002 178, 181
ISO 9002 33
ISO 9003 33
ISO 9004
    ISO 9004-1 25, 299, 322, 326
        Legal Questions 324
        Liability 322
        Product Safety 323
    ISO 9004-2 35, 282
    ISO 9004-3 35, 459, 462
    ISO 9004-4 36
ISO 90011 36, 198, 315, 396, 425
ISO 90012 36
    ISO 10012-1 206
ISO/IEC Guides 393

J

Japan
    ISO 9000 Developments in 425-427
    Quality Management and Assurance (QMA)
        System 426
Japanese Industrial Standards Committee (JISC)
    426
Jensen, K.E. 302, 504
JIS Z 9900-9904 426
Juran, Joseph 183, 425

K

Keneally, Stephen 505
KISS principle 228
Klock, Joseph 504
Kolka, Jim, 500
Korea 427

L

Labeling 343
Laboratory Accreditation Program (NVLAP) 430
Lake, Peter 484, 501
Lamprecht, James 503
Leadership and Improvement 286
Level Playing Field 12
Liability 9 (See also Product Liability and Safety)
Life-cycle phases 301
    of a Product 20
Line Organizations 288
Ling, Dave 503
Lofgren, George 407

M

Machinery Safety Directive 332
Malaysia 427
Malcolm Baldrige (See MBNQA)
Malkovich, Peter 504
Management Commitment 183
Management Representative 45
Management Responsibility 27, 42
Management Review 23, 48-49, 162, 172,
    196, 286

Map of countries adopting ISO 9000 2
Marketing department quality 29
Marquardt, Don 1, 292, 302, 500
MBNQA 451, 485, 490
    Compared to ISO 9000 347
    Compared to TQM 350
    Overview 346
McRobert, Charles 503
McSweeney, Michael 424, 504
Measurement 36
Measurement Systems Analysis 475
Measuring Equipment (See also Inspection,
    Measuring and Test Equipment)
Medical devices 362
Memorandum of Understanding (MOU) 133, 427
Metrological confirmation system 206
Mexican National Laboratory of Industrial Promo-
    tion 420
Mexico
    ISO 9000 Developments in 420, 421
Middleton, David 499
Modifications to the ISO 9000 Series (See Revi-
    sions)
Modular Approach 7, 369, 395
    Conformity to Type 371
    Full Quality Assurance 373
    Internal Control of Production 371
    Product Quality Assurance 373
    Product Verification 373
    Production Quality Assurance 373
    Type-Examination 371
    Unit-Verification 373
Monsanto Chemical Company 467, 469
MOU 385
MRA 386
Muldoon, Ronald 505
Multiple Assessments 10
Mutual Recognition 4, 6, 266, 361, 375-376,
    421
Mutual Recognition Agreement (MRA) 361, 376

N

NACCB 375
National Accreditation Council for Certification
    Bodies 179, 382 (See also NACCB)
National Aeronautics and Space Administration
    (NASA) 436
National Institute for Occupational Safety and
    Health 433
National Institute of Standards and Technology
    (See NIST)
National Quality Institute 424
Network for Total Quality 424
New-Approach Directives 360
    Components 361-362
Nicholas, Stephen 505
NIST 386
Non-Annex IV Machinery 332
Non-Regulated Products 5, 360, 383, 395
Nonconformance 158, 198, 201, 202, 203
Nonconforming Product 31, 289
Nonconformity report 159, 162
Noncontractual situation 16
Notified Bodies 363-364, 374, 375, 376, 386
Nuclear Regulatory Commission (NRC) 436

O

Objective evidence 156, 198, 200
Office of Management and Budget (OMB) 437
Official Journal 362
Old-Approach Directives 360, 365, 395
O'Neil, James 504
Operating procedures 216, 221
Ordering Information 507
    EU Hotline 519
    EU Standards 516
    European Community Directives 508
    GATT Hotline 519
    Single Market Information 519
Organization 17, 44
Organizational chart 220
Original equipment manufacturers (OEMs)
    477, 484
Other Useful Standards in the ISO 9000 Family 35

P

Pacific Rim Countries
    ISO 9000 Developments in 425-427
Peach, Bob 292, 407
Peer Review 391
Personnel 32
Personnel Qualifications (See Training)
Petrick, Klaus 302, 504
Policy Statement 220
Potential Failure Mode and Effects Analysis 475
Potts, Elizabeth 141, 500
Pratt, Roger 164, 505
Pre-Assessment 142
Prescriptive requirements 21
Presumption of Conformity 361
Prevention (See Product Liability and Safety)
Prevention 323
Preventive Action 184, 196, 201 (See also
    Corrective and Preventive Action)
Principle of Mutual Recognition (See Mutual
    Recognition)
Procedure Index 218, 221, 237
Procedures 188, 216, 222
    Administration and Control 227, 233
    Amendment and Revision 231-232
    Benefits 222
    Check List 225
    Computerized Versions versus Hard Copies
        232
    Current Practice 223
    Definitions 226
    Distribution 231
    Documentation 227
    Format 223
    Need 222
    Numbering System 231
    Planning and Development 222, 225
    Preparation 223
    Purpose 226
    References 226
    Samples 239, 240
    Scope 223, 226
    Structure and Format 225, 227

Templates 227
Time Line 223
Process 23, 283
Process Characteristics 311
Process Control 281-282, 288, 353
Process-cost approach 29
Processed Material 18, 35, 306
Processes
    Control 30
    Quality 30
Product 18, 307, 405
    Characteristics 311
    Hardware 18
    Processed Material 18
    Services 18
    Software 18
Product Certification 6, 342, 364 (see also
    European Community)
Product identification and traceability 288
Product Liability and Safety 9, 25, 322, 334
    9004-1 322, 326
    Answering Tough Questions 324-326
    Limiting Exposure 328
    Prevention 333-334
    Product Objectives 323
    Registration Concerns 326-328
    US Laws and EC Directives 329
Product Liability Directive 326, 329-330
Product Safety 32
Product Safety Directive 330, 331
Product type 371
Production Part Approval Process 475
Purchaser 18
Purchaser-Supplied Product (See Customer-
    Supplied Product)
Purchasing 30, 288
Purchasing Data 74
Pyle, James 292, 302, 504

Q

QSU/Deloitte & Touche Survey
    by Company Size 489-494
    by Industry 445-447
    Overview Article 441, 444
Quality 19
Quality Assurance 20 (see also European Commu-
    nity)
Quality Concepts 21
Quality cost approaches 25
Quality economics 25
Quality Expo International 424
Quality Improvement 29, 300
Quality in Marketing 29
Quality loop 301
Quality loss approach 29
Quality Management 20
Quality Manual 142, 216, 218-219, 221, 325
Quality plan 28, 217, 325
Quality Planning 50
Quality Policy 43, 218, 219-220, 286
Quality Records 28
Quality System 19, 49
Quality-costing approach 29

R

Raad voor de Certificatie (RvC) 423
RAB 266, 375, 384-385
    Auditor Certification 398, 399
    Code of Conduct 416-417
    MOU 385
    Policy Principles and Implementation Regard-
        ing Confirmation 414-416
    White Paper—Defining the Scope of the
        Certification 408, 413
Receiving Inspection and Testing 91
Recognition body 404
Records 32, 54, 216, 288, 325
Reengineering 183, 186
Registrar Accreditation Board (see RAB)
Registrars
    Accreditation 133 (See also Accreditation)
    Background Checks 137

Consulting versus Registration 136, 391
Financial Stability 137
Legal Issues 326, 327
Selecting One 442, 490
Technical Competency of Auditors 390
Registrars 404
Registration 6, 143 (See also ISO 9000)
Application 141
Approval 143
Assessment 143
Barriers 190, 442, 446, 491
Benefits 304, 305, 443
Checklist 258
Code of Conduct 407
Compliance with US Laws and EC Directives 329
Conditional Approval 144
Costs 12, 146, 443, 446, 492
Credibility Issues 404, 418
Document Review 142
Pre-assessment 143
Product Liability and Safety Concerns 326, 328
Reasons to Register 441, 445, 489
Savings 444, 447, 493
Scope 177, 405-407, 408-413
Surveillance 144
Time 12, 146
Time Line 176, 185
Worldwide Acceptance 420-421
Registration Accreditation Subcommittee (RASC) 387
Registration Process (see ISO 9000 Series)
Registrtation
Disapproval 144
Regulated Products 6, 360, 383
Relationship of Quality Concepts 21
Release for Urgent Production Purposes 91
Resources 44
Resources Ordering Information 507
Responsibility 172, 184, 220, 229, 448
Responsibility and Authority 44
Responsible Care® 340-342, 450, 452
Review, Management 162

Review and disposition of nonconforming product 106
Revisions 292, 299
Benefits 301
Purpose 292
to All Standards 293
to ISO 9000-1 294-296
to ISO 9001, 9002 and 9003 297-299
to ISO 9004-1 299-301
Risk-benefit analysis 326
Roberts, Jim 266

S

Safety of Products (See Product Liability and Safety)
Sample Procedure 239, 240
Sample Quality Manual 234
Schedule of conformity 189
Schmidt, Ralph 504
Scope
Audit 189
Procedures 226
Registration 177, 180, 405, 406, 407, 408, 413
Scott, Greg 500
Scott, Peter 504
Second-Party Registration 17
SEI Capability Maturity Model 270
Self-certification 329
Service 18, 307
Service Industry
Applicable ISO 9001 Clauses 289
Benefits 285
Definitions 279
Process Control 281-282
Proposed EU Directive 332
Service versus Servicing 280
Special Characteristics 280
Subjective/Qualitative Characteristics 281
Use of ISO 9000 278-282
Services Liability Directive 332
Singapore 427
Singapore Institute of Standards and Industrial Research 427

Single European Act 4
Single Internal Market 4, 359
    Objectives 359
Single Market Information 519
SISAP 485, 486
    and ISO 9000 485-486
    Benefits 485
    Purpose 485
Small Companies 489-497
    Case Study 495-497
Society of Automotive Engineers 378
Software 18, 232, 260, 272, 306
    Additional Arrangements 265
    Auditor Qualifications 267
    Australian Software Quality Management
        System 271
    Definitions 261
    Development Process 262
    IEEE Software Engineering Standards 268
    ISO 9004-2 282
    Mapping ISO 9001 to 9000-3 261-263
    SEI Capability Maturity Model 270
    Sensitivity Issues 267
    Software-Certified Auditors 266
    TickIT 264
    Use of ISO 9001 261
Software Capability Evaluation 270
Software Process Assessment 270
Software Quality Systems Registration (SQSR)
    266
South America
    ISO 9000 Developments in 420, 421
Stakeholders 23
Stallkamp, Thomas 475, 476
Stamatis, Dean 503
Standard Industrial Classification (SIC) codes 445
Standards
    Development Implications 313
    Proliferation of 305, 310-312, 314
Standards Council of Canada (SCC) 387, 423
Statistical Methods 32
Statistical Process Control (SPC) 194, 455
Statistical Techniques 288
Stebbing, Lionel 191

Steel Industry 484-488
    Case Study 486-488
    Overview 484
Steel Industry Supplier Audit Process (See SISAP)
Strahle, Donald 302, 503
Strategic Action Group on the Environment
    (SAGE) 343
Structure of ISO 9000 22
Subcontracting 375
Subcontractors 10, 18, 454
Subsuppliers 18
Supplier 18
    of Services 332
Supplier Quality Requirements Task Force 475
Supplier-Chain Terminology 17, 293
Supply and Service Canada 424
Supply Chain 406
Surveillance 144
Surveillance Audit 202, 203
    Case Study 204
Survey (See also QSU/Deloitte & Touche Survey)
    Barriers 442, 446, 491
    Benefits 443
    Costs 443, 446, 492
    Marketing Registration 444
    Reasons to Register 441, 445, 489
    Savings 444, 447, 493
    Selecting Registrars and Consultants 442, 490
    Supplier Involvement 441
Systems Outline 218, 221, 236

T

Taiwan 427
Taylor-Wharton Cylinders 486-488
TC 176 8, 292, 302, 303, 308, 315, 404,
    422, 426
TC 207 343
Team Training 185
Techni-Test 495-497
Technical Advisory Groups (TAGs) 3
Technical Barriers 6 (See also Trade Barriers and
    Barriers to Trade)
Technical Committee 3, 176 (See also TC 176)
Technical requirements 361

Technical Standards 6, 362
Tehnical Committee 20 (See also TC 207)
Templates 227
Terminal Data Corporation 273
Terms 17, 21
Test Equipment (See Inspection, Measuring and
    Test Equipment)
Test Status (See Inspection and Test Status)
Testing and Certification Bodies (See Conformity
    Assessment)
Thailand 427
Third-Party Registration 17
TickIT 264-265
Time and Costs of Registration 146
Time Line
    Registration 176, 185
Time to Register (See Registration)
Tiratto, Joe 501
Toll manufacturing 454
Total Quality Council 451
Total Quality Management (See TQM)
TQM 478, 485
    Compared to ISO 9000 350
    Compared to MBNQA 350
    Overview 347
Traceability (See Product Identification and
    Traceability)
Trade Barriers 11
Training 289
    Records 194-195
Transition period 362
Treaty of Rome 4
Truck Advisory Group 477
Truth-in-advertising 146
Tuthill, Jeffrey 504
Type examination 362
Types of standards in the ISO 9000 Series 21

U

Unisys 470, 473
US International Trade Commission (USITC) 435
US Postal Service 437
Uses of the Standards 16

V

Validation 175, 453
Verification 31, 175, 453
Verification of Purchased Product 74
Victoria Group 505
Vision 2000 302, 312-316
Vocabulary 17
Voluntary Standards 361

W

Weightman, Bud 132, 163, 499
Weights and Measures Program 431
Work instructions 216

Y

Young, Ollie 209, 501

Z

Z299 422, 423, 425

NOTES

NOTES

NOTES

NOTES

NOTES

NOTES